Arctic Ocean

NORWAY
SWEDEN
FINLAND
ESTONIA
LATVIA
LITHUANIA
DENMARK
Spy Neander Valley BELARUS
Heidelberg (Mauer) POLAND
NETH. GERMANY
BEL. CZECH REP. UKRAINE
LUX. SLOVAKIA
Krapina HUNG. MOLDOVA
SWITZERLAND ROMANIA
Arago ITALY BULGARIA GEORGIA
Ceprano Petralona TURKEY ARMENIA AZERBAIJAN
Tighenif TUNISIA GREECE SYRIA IRAQ IRAN
Amud LEBANON Shanidar
Skhūl/Tabūn ISRAEL JORDAN KUWAIT
JORDAN AFGHANISTAN

RUSSIA

KAZAKHSTAN

Sungir

Dmanisi
Teshik Tash UZBEKISTAN
TURKMENISTAN KYRGYZSTAN
TAJIKISTAN

MONGOLIA

Jinniushan
Zhoukoudian NORTH KOREA JAPAN
Lantian Dali SOUTH KOREA
Hexian
CHINA
Maba

ALGERIA LIBYA EGYPT SAUDI ARABIA BAHRAIN QATAR U.A.E. PAKISTAN NEPAL BHUTAN

NIGER CHAD SUDAN ERITREA YEMEN OMAN

Toros-Menalla

INDIA BANGLADESH MYANMAR (BURMA) LAOS TAIWAN HONG KONG MACAU

Pacific Ocean

TROPIC OF CANCER

NIGERIA CENTRAL AFRICAN REP. ETHIOPIA
Hadar DJIBOUTI THAILAND VIETNAM PHILIPPINES NORTHERN MARIANA ISLANDS (U.S.)
Bodo Middle Awash (Aramis, Bouri, Herto) CAMBODIA
Omo SOMALIA SRI LANKA REPUBLIC OF THE MARSHALL ISLANDS
CAMEROON UGANDA East and West Turkana MALDIVES
Tugen Hills KENYA BRUNEI
SÃO TOMÉ GABON CONGO RWANDA Kanapoi MALAYSIA SINGAPORE
PRÍNCIPE DEMOCRATIC BURUNDI Olduvai/Laetoli FEDERATED STATES OF MICRONESIA
CABINDA REPUBLIC OF THE CONGO TANZANIA Sumatra Borneo
(Angola) SEYCHELLES INDONESIA PAPUA NEW GUINEA
Sangiran Ngandong SOLOMON ISLANDS
Trinil Flores

EQUATOR

ANGOLA MALAWI
ZAMBIA COMOROS IS.
Broken Hill ZIMBABWE MADAGASCAR
NAMIBIA BOTSWANA MOZAMBIQUE MAURITIUS

Indian Ocean

TUVALU

FIJI
VANUATU
NEW CALEDONIA (Fr.)

WALVIS BAY (Status to be determined)
Taung Sterkfontein/Swartkrans/Drimolen
Florisbad SWAZILAND LESOTHO
SOUTH AFRICA Border Cave
Klasies River Mouth

AUSTRALIA

TROPIC OF CAPRICORN

Lake Mungo
Kow Swamp NEW ZEALAND

1. SLOVENIA
2. CROATIA
3. BOSNIA AND HERZEGOVINA
4. ALBANIA
5. MACEDONIA
6. SERBIA AND MONTENEGRO

ANTARCTICA

ANTARCTIC CIRCLE

www.wadsworth.com

www.wadsworth.com is the World Wide Web site for Wadsworth and is your direct source to dozens of online resources.

At www.wadsworth.com you can find out about supplements, demonstration software, and student resources. You can also send email to many of our authors and preview new publications and exciting new technologies.

www.wadsworth.com
Changing the way the world learns®

Essentials of
Physical Anthropology

SIXTH EDITION

Robert Jurmain
Professor Emeritus, San Jose State University

Lynn Kilgore
Colorado State University

Wenda Trevathan
New Mexico State University

THOMSON
━━━━━✦━━━━━ ™
WADSWORTH

Australia • Canada • Mexico • Singapore • Spain
United Kingdom • United States

Senior Acquisitions Editor: *Lin Marshall*
Development Editor: *Julie Sakaue*
Assistant Editor: *Nicole Root*
Editorial Assistant: *Kelly McMahon*
Technology Project Manager: *Dee Dee Zobian*
Marketing Manager: *Lori Grebe Cook*
Marketing Assistant: *Teresa Jessen*
Marketing Communications Manager: *Linda Yip*
Project Manager, Editorial Production: *Catherine Morris*
Art Director: *Maria Epes*
Print Buyer: *Judy Inouye*
Permissions Editor: *Joohee Lee*

Production Service: *Patti Zeman, Hespenheide Design*
Compositor: *Hespenheide Design*
Text Designer: *Ellen Pettengell Design*
Photo Researcher: *Hespenheide Design*
Copy Editor: *Janet Greenblatt*
Illustrator: *Alexander Productions, DLF Group, Hespenheide Design, Randy Miyake, Paragon 3, Sue Sellars, Cyndie Wooley*
Cover Designer: *Cheryl Carrington*
Cover Image: *Tetsuro Matsuzawa*
Cover Printer: *Phoenix Color Corp*
Printer: *R.R. Donnelley/Willard*

For more information about our products, contact us at:
Thomson Learning Academic Resource Center
1-800-423-0563

For permission to use material from this text or product, submit a request online at
http://www.thomsonrights.com.

Any additional questions about permissions can be submitted by email to thomsonrights@thomson.com.

Library of Congress Control Number: 2004117747

Student Edition: ISBN 0-495-03061-9
Instructor's Edition: ISBN 0-495-00389-1

Thomson Higher Education
10 Davis Drive
Belmont, CA 94002-3098
USA

Asia (including India)
Thomson Learning
5 Shenton Way
#01-01 UIC Building
Singapore 068808

Australia/New Zealand
Thomson Learning Australia
102 Dodds Street
Southbank, Victoria 3006
Australia

Canada
ThomsonNelson
1120 Birchmount Road
Toronto, Ontario M1K 5G4
Canada

Europe/Middle East/Africa
Thomson Learning
High Holborn House
50/51 Bedford Row
London WC1R 4LR
United Kingdom

Latin America
Thomson Learning
Seneca, 53
Colonia Polanco
11560 Mexico
D.F. Mexico

Spain (including Portugal)
Thomson Paraninfo
Calle Magallanes, 25
28015 Madrid, Spain

Brief Contents

Contents

Robert Jurmain

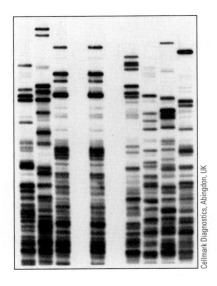

Cellmark Diagnostics, Abingdon, UK

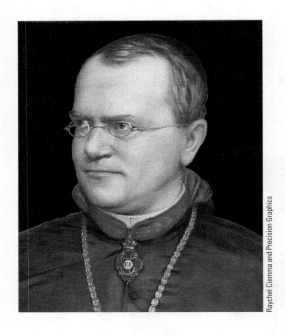

Raychel Ciemma and Precision Graphics

Courtesy, Fred Jacobs

Lynn Kilgore

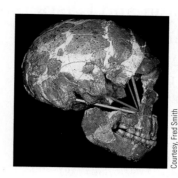

Courtesy, Fred Smith

Courtesy, David Lordkipanidze

Norman Lightfoot/Photo Researchers

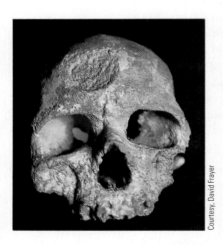

Courtesy, David Frayer

Lynn Kilgore

Preface

This sixth edition of *Essentials of Physical Anthropology* obviously follows a series of prior editions. You could reasonably ask, "Why now write a new edition?" All academic fields change, of course, and new finds and perspectives often lead to a need for revising textbooks.

The biological sciences have changed especially quickly in recent years, and it is important to recognize that physical anthropology is a part of human biology; in fact, the field is often called "biological anthropology." Stimulated by remarkable advances in molecular biology, physical anthropology (and all aspects of biology) has been revolutionized. For example, in 2004, anthropologists working with other biologists completed the first stage of the genetic mapping of chimpanzee DNA, and a full map is expected within months. So, very soon, with the ability to make much more precise genetic comparisons with our closest relative, evolutionary biologists can understand more fully the vast genetic similarities, as well as the relatively few differences, we have with chimpanzees. Such information will contribute tremendously to understanding what it is to be "human."

Moreover, new finds of human fossils are announced regularly, and sometimes they are quite surprising. Perhaps no such find has ever been quite as startling as the discovery in 2003 of 3-foot-tall, small-brained humans on an island in Indonesia. These 18,000-year-old "little people" are very different from modern humans and, consequently they belong to a different species from us. How they compare with us, what they were like, and how they evolved in such an unusual way are all intriguing questions—and ones that require an understanding of evolutionary biology to answer.

The immediate rationale for this current revision is to include such important new findings. But, at a more basic level, the key goal of all our textbooks is to present to students the biological principles of evolution in an understandable way. In this edition we use both new molecular and fossil evidence to not just tell the tale of human evolution, but also to illuminate how evolution itself works.

What's New in the Sixth Edition?

Readers familiar with earlier editions will notice one major organizational change in the order of chapters. Chapter 5 (Macroevolution: Processes of Vertebrate and Mammalian Evolution) has been moved forward (formerly Chapter 7). We believe this organization will work better, since the broad evolutionary processes influencing vertebrates and, more specifically, mammals, are now discussed prior to the materials on primates (in Chapters 6 and 7). A further organizational change involves moving the coverage of early primate fossils to Chapter 8 (where the question of human origins is first discussed).

As mentioned, we have also updated materials throughout and expanded certain sections to reflect contemporary research. Updates include those discussed earlier relating to molecular biology and new fossil finds from Indonesia. Other significant new fossil/molecular research is also represented, including the discovery of the earliest modern human fossils from Ethiopia and the first DNA sequencing of early modern humans found in Europe (involving fossils from France, Belgium, Italy, and Russia). Finally, we have updated our coverage of the evolution of human disease, including expanded materials on both AIDS and SARS.

We have also worked to improve the pedagogical aids for students, especially to make them more visually accessible. You will find in every chapter concise

"Quick Review" boxes that very briefly summarize complex and/or controversial material. Further, at the end of each chapter, along with the written summary, there is now also a Visual Summary. Again, our pedagogical goal is to provide an accessible visual learning aid.

Since a central goal of our text is to stimulate critical thinking, the Critical Thinking Questions at the end of each chapter have been thoroughly revised to emphasize a more critical and intellectually creative approach to incorporating *and* applying knowledge. These components, as well as other new ones and those retained from earlier editions, are listed below.

IN-CHAPTER LEARNING AIDS

- **Chapter outlines** at the beginning of each chapter list all major topics covered.

- **Focus Questions,** a new feature that appears at the beginning of each chapter, highlight the central topic of that chapter.

- A **"Click" Icon** at the beginning of each chapter directs students to the appropriate CD-ROM covering materials pertinent to that chapter. One or more of the three supplemental CD-ROMs will be listed: *Virtual Laboratories for Physical Anthropology CD-ROM, Third Edition, Basic Genetics for Anthropology CD-ROM: Principles and Applications,* and *Hominid Fossils CD-ROM: An Interactive Atlas.*

- A **running glossary** in the margins provides definitions of terms immediately adjacent to the text where the term is first introduced. A **full glossary** is provided in the back of the book.

- **Quick Reviews,** a new feature for the Sixth Edition, briefly summarize complex or controversial material in a visually simple fashion.

- **Figures,** including numerous photographs, line drawings, maps, most in full color, are carefully selected to clarify text materials and are placed to directly support discussion in the text.

- **Visual Summaries,** a new feature found with the written summary at the end of each chapter, provide a simple and visually appealing aid for students as they review the chapter.

- **Critical Thinking Questions** at the end of each chapter have been completely revised to reinforce key concepts and encourage students to think critically about what they have read.

- **Readings of Interest,** also found at the end of each chapter, are fully updated and are carefully selected to direct interested students toward recent accessible and interesting sources for further reading.

- **Full bibliographical citations** throughout the entire book provide sources from which the materials are drawn. This type of documentation guides students to published source materials and illustrates for students the proper use of referencing; all cited sources are listed in the comprehensive bibliography at the back of the book.

- **Media Resources** is a learning aid found at the end of each chapter.

- Students are directed to the Companion Web site for this text as well as the three different CD-ROMs developed to supplement materials in each chapter.

Acknowledgments

Over the years many friends and colleagues have assisted us with our books. For this edition we are especially grateful to the reviewers who so carefully commented on the manuscript and made such helpful suggestions: Barrett Brenton, St. John's University; Phyllisa Eisentraut, Shasta College; David Himmelgreen, University of South Florida; Joan Miller, San Diego State University; Dwight Read, University of California, Los Angeles; James Sewastynowicz, Jacksonville State University; and Mark Taylor, Northern Arizona University.

We also wish to thank at Wadsworth Publishing Lin Marshall, Senior Acquisitions Editor; Nicole Root, Assistant Editor; Kelly McMahon, Editorial Assistant; Julie Sakaue, Developmental Editor; Dee Dee Zobian, Technology Product Manager; Lori Grebe Cook, Marketing Manager; Catherine Morris, Project Editor; Eve Howard, Editor-in-Chief; Sean Wakely, President, Thomson Higher Education, Humanities and Behavioral and Social Sciences; and Susan Badger, CEO of Thomson Higher Education. Moreover, for their unflagging expertise and patience we are grateful to our copy editor, Janet Greenblatt, our production coordinator, Gary Hespenheide and his skilled staff at Hespenheide Design: Patti Zeman, project coordinator and Bridget Neumayr, proofreader/editor.

To the many friends and colleagues who have generously provided photographs we are greatly appreciative: C. K. Brain, Günter Bräuer, Desmond Clark, Ron Clarke, Raymond Dart, Jean deRousseau, Denis Etler, Diane France, David Frayer, Kathleen Galvin, David Haring, Ellen Ingmanson, Fred Jacobs, Peter Jones, Leslie Knapp, Arlene Kruse, Richard Leakey, Carol Lofton, Margaret Maples, Lorna Moore, John Oates, Bonnie Pedersen, Lorna Pierce, David Pilbeam, Willaim Pratt, Judith Regensteiner, Sastrohamijoyo Sartono, Eugenie Scott, Rose Sevick, Elwyn Simons, Meredith Small, Fred Smith, Judy Suchey, Heather Thew, Li Tianyuan, Philip Tobias, Alan Walker, Milford Wolpoff, and Xinzhi Wu.

Robert Jurmain
Lynn Kilgore
Wenda Trevathan

Supplements

SUPPLEMENTS FOR THE INSTRUCTOR

Instructor's Manual with Test Bank By Wesley A. Niewoehner of California State University, San Bernardino. This comprehensive manual includes chapter outlines, learning objectives, key terms and concepts, lecture suggestions, and enrichment topics, as well as 40–60 test questions per chapter. It also includes a Resource Integration Guide that shows how and where to use various supplements to the text including multimedia, videos, and enrichment material. Concise user guides for InfoTrac and WebTutor are included as appendices.

ExamView® **Computerized Testing** Create, deliver, and customize tests and study guides (both print and online) in minutes with this easy-to-use assessment and tutorial system. *ExamView* offers both a Quick Test Wizard and an Online Test Wizard that guide you step-by-step through the process of creating tests, while its "what you see is what you get" interface allows you to see the test you are creating on the screen exactly as it will print or display online. You can build tests of up to 250 questions using up to 12 question types. Using *ExamView*'s complete word processing capabilities, you can enter an unlimited number of new questions or edit existing questions.

CLASSROOM PRESENTATION TOOLS FOR INSTRUCTORS

JoinIn™ *on TurningPoint*® Transform your lecture into an interactive student experience with *JoinIn*. Combined with your choice of keypad systems, *JoinIn* turns your PowerPoint® application into audience response software. With a click on a hand-held device, students can respond to multiple-choice questions, short polls, and interactive exercises. You can also take attendance, check student comprehension of concepts, collect student demographics to better assess student needs, and even administer quizzes. In addition, there are interactive text-specific slide sets that you can modify and merge with any of your own PowerPoint lecture slides. This tool is available to qualified adopters. http://turningpoint.thomson learningconnections.com

CNN Today Physical Anthropology **Video Series, Volumes IV–VI** The *CNN Today Physical Anthropology* Video Series is an exclusive series jointly created by Wadsworth and CNN for the physical anthropology course. Each video in the series consists of approximately 45 minutes of footage originally broadcast on CNN within the last several years. The videos are broken into short two- to seven-minute segments, which are perfect for classroom use as lecture launchers, or to illustrate key anthropological concepts. An annotated table of contents accompanies each video with descriptions of the segments and suggestions for their possible use within the course.

Visual Anthropology Video From Documentary Educational Resources and Wadsworth Publishing, this 60-minute video features clips from over 30 new and classic anthropological films. An engaging and effective lecture launcher. To accompany this valuable resource, Wadsworth also offers you a Visual Guide to Anthropology.

Transparency Acetates for Physical Anthropology 2006 This set of four-color acetates features images from Wadsworth's Physical Anthropology texts to help prepare lecture presentations.

Multimedia Manager Instructor Resource CD-ROM for Anthropology 2006: A Microsoft® PowerPoint® Tool This 2006 CD-ROM contains digital media and Microsoft PowerPoint lecture slides for all of Wadsworth's 2006 introductory anthropology texts, placing images, lectures, and video clips at instructors' fingertips. Start with Wadsworth's pre-assembled PowerPoint slides, which include chapter outlines and key terms, then easily add video clips and images from Wadsworth's anthropology texts. Instructors can also add their own lecture notes and images to create a custom-made lecture presentation. The Multimedia Manager also includes documents from the Instructor's Manual in Microsoft Word, the book's Test Bank, and links to many of Wadsworth's important anthropology resources. All of your media teaching resources in one place!

SUPPLEMENTS FOR STUDENTS

Study Guide By Andrew Kramer, University of Tennessee. Correlated chapter by chapter with the text! Features learning objectives, chapter outlines, key terms, concept applications, and practice tests consisting of multiple-choice and true/false questions with page references, in addition to several short-answer and essay questions.

Basic Genetics for Anthropology CD-ROM: Principles and Applications This new student CD-ROM expands on the genetic/evolutionary concepts covered in the book, focusing on basic processes of cell division, structure and function of DNA, patterns of inheritance, fundamental aspects of evolution (emphasizing genetic drift and natural selection), and principles and applications of population genetics. Animations and simulations utilize human examples of genetic and evolutionary processes that will bring these concepts to life and help make them more relevant for students. Also available are comprehensive multiple-choice questions. This CD can be bundled free to your students.

Virtual Laboratories for Physical Anthropology CD-ROM, Third Edition By John Kappelman, University of Texas at Austin. The new edition of this interactive CD-ROM provides students with a hands-on computer component for doing lab assignments at school or at home. It encourages students to participate actively in their physical anthropology lab or course through the taking of measurements and the plotting of data, as well as giving them a format for testing their knowledge of important concepts. Contains full-color images, video clips, 3-D animations, sounds, and more. The CD-ROM also includes a special quizzing section where students can take online tutorial quizzes based on the 12 laboratories and have their answers scored and emailed to their instructor! Also available are new instructor resources, such as a test bank, an instructor's manual, suggested class and homework activities, PowerPoint slides, computerized testing, and more. Ask your Wadsworth sales rep for the new Instructor Edition.

Hominid Fossils CD-ROM: An Interactive Atlas This interactive atlas CD-ROM includes over 75 key fossils important for a clear understanding of human evolution. The QuickTime Virtual Reality (QTVR) format for each fossil will enable students to have a near-authentic experience of working with these important finds by allowing them to rotate the fossil 360 degrees. Unlike some VR media, QTVR objects are made using actual photographs of the real objects, thus better preserving details of color and texture. The fossils used are high-quality research casts and real fossils. The organization of the atlas enables students to see how the fossil fits into the map of human evolution in terms of geography, time, and evolution. The CD-ROM's Compare section presents the specimen side by side and points students to significant features to look for in their comparisons. Also, compelling and highly visual Tutorials help students gain perspective and a better understanding of why the study of the fossil record is important to anthropology. The CD-ROM offers students an inviting, authentic, learning environment, one that also contains a dynamic quizzing feature that will allow students to test their knowledge of fossil and species identification, as well as provide more detailed information about the fossil record.

Researching Anthropology on the Internet Online, Third Edition Written by David Carlson, this online guide is designed to assist anthropology students in all of their needs when doing research on the Internet. Part One contains general information necessary to get started, and answers questions about security, the type of anthropology material available on the Internet, the information that is reliable and the sites that are not, and the best links to take students where they want to go. Part Two looks at each main subfield in anthropology and refers students to sites where the most enlightening research can be obtained. Available online only.

InfoTrac® College Edition with InfoMarks™ Available as a free option with newly purchased texts, InfoTrac College Edition gives instructors and students four months of free access to an extensive online database of reliable, full-length articles (not just abstracts) from thousands of scholarly and popular publications going back as far as 22 years. Among the journals available 24/7 are *Time, Newsweek, Science, Forbes,* and *USA Today.* InfoTrac College Edition now also comes with InfoMark, a tool that allows you to save your search parameters, as well as save links to specific articles. (Available to North American college and university students only; journals are subject to change.)

InfoTrac College Edition Student Guide for Anthropology This brief booklet offers information on how to get the most out of InfoTrac College Edition and includes user instructions, troubleshooting tips, and frequently asked questions. In addition, key word search terms are provided for students to find articles related to the following topics: cultural anthropology, linguistic anthropology, biological anthropology, paleoanthropology/archaeology, and primatology.

WEB RESOURCES AND SUPPLEMENTS FOR INSTRUCTORS AND STUDENTS

Anthropology Online: Wadsworth's Anthropology Resource Center at

http://anthropology.wadsworth.com
Combine this text with Anthropology Online's exciting range of Web resources, and you will have truly integrated technology into your learning system. Anthropology Online provides instructors and students with a wealth of FREE information and resources, such as the Wadsworth exclusive Earthwatch Journal; Applying Anthropology Online, which includes career, internship, and graduate school information; The Latest Dirt, an interactive resource that presents important recent finds including those in Chad, Georgia, and South Africa; links to relevant online articles, and more!

The Companion Website for *Essentials of Physical Anthropology,* Sixth Edition

http://anthropology.wadsworth.com/jurmain6e_ess
The book's companion site includes a rich array of teaching and learning resources. Students can supplement their review of each chapter with the site's online practice quizzes, use the flash cards to master key terms, and learn about important discoveries by checking the "Latest Dirt" feature authored by Robert Jurmain. This outstanding site also includes Internet exercises, **InfoTrac® College Edition** exercises, crossword puzzles, and web links. The instructor's password-protected section of the site includes learning objectives, chapter outlines and summaries, the Instructor's Manual with Test Bank, and Microsoft® PowerPoint® lecture slides.

WebTutor Advantage on WebCT and Blackboard for Essentials of Physical Anthropology, Sixth Edition This Web-based software for students and instructors takes a course beyond the classroom to an anywhere, anytime environment. Students gain access to a full array of study tools, including chapter outlines, chapter-specific quizzing material, interactive games and maps, and videos. With WebTutor Advantage, instructors can provide virtual office hours, post syllabi, track student progress with the quizzing material, and even customize the content to suit their needs.

Molecular Anthropology Module Written by Leslie Knapp, this module explores how molecular genetic methods are used to understand the organization and expression of genetic information in humans and nonhuman primates. Students will learn about the common laboratory methods used to study genetic variation and evolution in molecular anthropology. Examples will be drawn from up-to-date research on human evolutionary origins and comparative primate genomics to demonstrate that scientific research is an ongoing process with theories frequently being questioned and re-evaluated.

Primate Evolution Module When we look at primate evolution, we are looking at our own evolution as well. With this central theme in mind, this module, written by Robert Jurmain, explores the fossil history of primates over the last 60 million years. Using what they currently know about primate anatomy (teeth, limbs, etc.) and social behavior, students will learn to "flesh out" the bones and teeth that make up the evolutionary record of primate origins. In this way, the ecological adaptations and evolutionary relationships of these fossil forms to each other (and to contemporary primates) will become more meaningful.

Forensics Anthropology Module: A Brief Review Written by Diane France, this module provides an introduction to forensic anthropology. It explores the myths and realities of the search for human remains in crime scenes, what should be expected from a forensic anthropology expert in the courtroom, some of the special challenges in mass fatality incident responses (such as plane crashes and terrorist acts), and what a student should consider if they want to pursue a career in forensic anthropology.

1 | Introduction

Focus Questions

What is physical anthropology, and why do you think it's an important subject to study?

What are some of its contributions to society?

Introduction

Hominidae The taxonomic family to which humans belong; also includes other, now extinct, bipedal relatives.

hominids Colloquial term for members of the family Hominidae, which includes all bipedal hominoids back to the divergence from African great apes.

bipedally On two feet. Walking habitually on two legs is the single most distinctive feature of the family Hominidae.

One day, perhaps at the beginning of the rainy season some 3.7 million years ago, two or three animals walked across a grassland in East Africa. These individuals were early members of the taxonomic family **Hominidae,** the family that also includes ourselves, modern *Homo sapiens.* Fortunately for us, a record of their passage on that long-forgotten day remains in the form of fossilized footprints, preserved in hardened volcanic deposits.

As chance would have it, shortly after heels and toes were pressed into dampened soil, a nearby volcano erupted. The ensuing ash fall blanketed everything on the ground, including the hominid footprints. In time, the ash layer hardened into a deposit that preserved them for almost 4 million years (Fig. 1-1). These now famous prints indicate that two **hominids,** one smaller than the other, perhaps walked side by side, leaving parallel sets of tracks. But since the tracks of the larger individual are partly blurred, possibly by those of a third, it's unclear exactly how many individuals made that journey so long ago. However, we do know that the prints were left by an animal that habitually walked **bipedally** (on two feet), and that tells us that those ancient travelers were hominids.

FIGURE 1-1 Early hominid footprints at Laetoli, Tanzania. The tracks to the left were made by one individual, while those to the right appear to have been formed by two individuals, the second stepping in the tracks of the first.

Courtesy, Peter Jones

In addition to the footprints, scientists at this site, called Laetoli, and at other locations have discovered numerous fossilized parts of skeletons of an animal we call *Australopithecus afarensis*. After analyzing these remains, we know that these hominids were anatomically similar to ourselves, although their brains were only about one-third the size of ours. And even though they may have used stones and sticks as simple tools, there isn't any evidence to suggest that they actually made stone tools. In short, they were very much at the mercy of nature's whims. They certainly couldn't outrun most predators, and since their canine teeth were small they were pretty much defenseless.

Chimpanzees often serve as living models for our early ancestors, and there are several good reasons for this. But the earliest hominids occupied a different habitat and probably had more to fear from predators than do chimpanzees. So, however much we may be tempted to compare early forms to living ones, we need to remind ourselves that there is no living animal that perfectly represents them. Just like every other living thing, extinct **species** were unique.

We could ask hundreds of questions about the Laetoli hominids, but we will never be able to answer them all. They walked down a path into what became their future, and their immediate journey ended long ago. So it remains for us to learn as much as we can about the species they represent. In this sense, then, their greater journey continues.

On July 20, 1969, a television audience numbering in the hundreds of millions watched as two human beings stepped out of a spacecraft and onto the surface of the moon. To anyone born after that date, this event is taken for granted. But the significance of that first moonwalk can't be overstated, because it represents humanity's presumed mastery over the natural forces that govern our presence on earth. For the first time ever, people actually walked upon the surface of a celestial body that has never given birth to biological life.

As the astronauts gathered rock samples and frolicked in near weightlessness, they left traces of their adventure in the form of footprints in the lunar dust (Fig. 1-2). On the surface of the moon, where no rain falls and no wind blows, the footprints remain undisturbed to this day. They survive as mute testament to a brief visit by a medium-sized, big-brained creature who dared to challenge the very forces that created it.

You may be wondering why anyone would care about early hominid footprints and how they can possibly be relevant to your life. And even though you know that a moon landing occurred in the late 1960s, you may not have spent much time actually thinking about it. Furthermore, why would a textbook about physical anthropology begin with a discussion of two such seemingly unrelated phenomena?

Physical, or biological, anthropology is a scientific discipline concerned with the biological and behavioral characteristics of human beings; our closest relatives, the nonhuman **primates** (apes, monkeys, and prosimians); and their ancestors. This kind of research helps us explain what it means to be human. While this may be an ambitious and not fully attainable goal, it's certainly worth pursuing. We are the only species to ponder our own existence and wonder how we fit into the spectrum of life on earth. Many people are curious about the similarities we share with other species. Maybe, as a child, you wondered how your dog's front legs might correspond to your arms. Perhaps during a visit to the zoo, you recognized the similarities between a chimpanzee's

Go to the following CD-ROMs for interactive activities and exercises on topics covered in this chapter:

 Virtual Laboratories for Physical Anthropology CD-ROM, Third Edition

 Basic Genetics for Anthropology CD-ROM: Principles and Applications

 Hominid Fossils CD-ROM: An Interactive Atlas

species A group of organisms that can interbreed to produce fertile offspring. Members of one species are reproductively isolated from members of all other species (i.e., they can't mate with them to produce fertile offspring).

FIGURE 1-2 Human footprint left on the lunar surface during the *Apollo* mission.

primates Members of the order of mammals Primates (pronounced "pry-may´-tees"), which includes prosimians, monkeys, apes, and humans.

savanna (also spelled savannah) A large flat grassland with scattered trees and shrubs. Savannas are found in many regions of the world with warm (or hot) and dry climates.

evolution A change in the genetic structure of a population. The term is also frequently used to refer to the appearance of a new species.

adaptation Functional response of organisms or populations to the environment. Adaptation results from evolutionary change (specifically, as a result of natural selection).

microevolution Small genetic changes that occur within a species.

macroevolution Changes that occur only after many generations, such as the appearance of a new species (speciation).

culture All aspects of human adaptation, including technology, traditions, language, religion, marriage patterns, and social roles. Culture is a set of *learned* behaviors; it is transmitted from one generation to the next through learning and not by biological or genetic means.

world view General cultural orientation or perspective shared by members of a society.

behavior Anything organisms do that involves action in response to internal or external stimuli; the response of an individual, group, or species to its environment. Such responses may or may not be deliberate, and they aren't necessarily the result of conscious decision making.

predisposition The capacity or inclination to do something. A situation whereby an organism is susceptible to behavioral or anatomical modification because of preexisting traits.

hands or facial expressions and your own. Did you think that maybe they also shared our thoughts and feelings? If you've ever had thoughts like these, then you've indeed been curious about humankind's place in nature.

In 1978, biological anthropologists and archaeologists uncovered the Laetoli footprints, and they continue to raise questions about the animal that made them. Perhaps one day, creatures as yet unimagined will ponder the essence of the creature that made the lunar footprints. What do you suppose they will think?

We humans can barely comprehend a century, let alone grasp at the enormity of 3.7 million years. We want to know more about those creatures who traveled that day across the **savanna.** We want to know how an insignificant but clever bipedal primate such as *Australopithecus afarensis,* or perhaps a close relative, gave rise to a species that would eventually walk on the surface of a moon some 230,000 miles from earth.

How did *Homo sapiens,* a result of the same evolutionary forces that produced all other life on this planet, gain the power to control the flow of rivers and alter the earth's weather patterns? We are tropical animals; so how were we able to leave the tropics and eventually occupy most of the earth's land surfaces? How did we adjust to different local environmental conditions as we dispersed? How could our species, which numbered fewer than 1 billion individuals until the mid-nineteenth century, come to number more than 6 billion worldwide today and, as we now do, add another billion people every 11 years?

These are some of the many questions that physical anthropologists want to answer through the detailed study of human **evolution,** variation, and **adaptation.** These issues, and many others, are the topics covered directly or indirectly in this textbook, because physical anthropology is, in part, human biology seen from an evolutionary perspective.

On hearing the term *evolution,* most people think of the appearance of new species. New species formation is one important consequence of evolution, but biologists see evolution as an ongoing biological process with a precise genetic meaning. Quite simply, evolution is a change in the genetic makeup of a population from one generation to the next, and the accumulation of such changes, over considerable periods of time, can result in the appearance of a new species. Therefore, evolution can be defined and studied at two different levels. At one level, there are genetic alterations *within* populations. Although this type of change may not lead to the development of new species, it often results in variation between populations regarding the frequency of certain traits. Evolution at this level is referred to as **microevolution.** At the other level, there is sufficient genetic change to result in the appearance of a new species, a process termed **macroevolution** or speciation. Evolution as it occurs at both these levels is addressed in this book.

But biological anthropologists don't just study physiological and biological systems. When these topics are considered within the context of human evolution, another factor must also be considered, and that factor is **culture.** Culture is a vitally important concept, not only as it relates to modern human beings, but also because of its role in human evolution. Quite simply, and in the very broadest terms, culture can be said to be the strategy by which humans adapt to the natural environment. In this sense, culture includes technologies that range from stone tools to computers; subsistence patterns ranging from hunting and gathering to agribusiness on a global scale; housing types, from thatched huts to skyscrapers; and clothing, from animal skins to

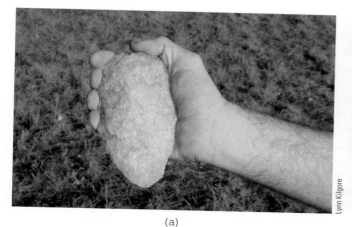
(a)

Lynn Kilgore
(b)

Lynn Kilgore
(c)

Robert Jurmain
(d)

high-tech synthetic fibers (Fig. 1-3). Because religion, values, social organization, language, kinship, marriage rules, gender roles, inheritance of property, and so on, are all aspects of culture, each culture shapes people's perceptions of the external environment, or **world view,** in ways that distinguish that culture from all others.

One fundamental point to remember is that culture isn't genetically passed from one generation to the next. Culture is *learned,* and the process of learning one's culture begins at birth. All humans are products of the culture they are raised in, and since most human **behavior** is learned, it follows that most behaviors, perceptions, and reactions are shaped by culture. But even though culture isn't genetically determined, the human **predisposition** to assimilate culture is *influenced* by genetic factors. Most nonhuman animals, especially primates, depend to some extent on learned behavior. And many nonhuman primates (chimpanzees in particular) exhibit numerous aspects of culture. The predisposition for culture is perhaps the most critical component of human evolutionary history, and it was inherited from early hominid or prehominid ancestors. Indeed, it probably already existed in the common ancestor we

FIGURE 1-3 (a) An early stone tool from East Africa. This artifact represents one of the oldest types of stone tools found anywhere. (b) Assortment of implements available today in a modern hardware store. (c) A Samburu woman building a simple, traditional dwelling of stems, plant fibers, and mud. (d) A modern high-rise apartment complex, typical of industrialized cities.

share with chimpanzees. But during the course of human evolution, the role of culture increasingly assumed an added importance. Over time, culture and biology interacted in such a way that humans are said to be the result of **biocultural evolution.** In this respect, humans are unique among biological organisms.

biocultural evolution The mutual, interactive evolution of human biology and culture; the concept that biology makes culture possible and that developing culture further influences the direction of biological evolution; a basic concept in understanding the unique components of human evolution.

Many major anatomical and behavioral changes (increased brain size, reorganization of brain structures, smaller teeth, and the development of language) all came about through biocultural interactions during the course of human evolution. Today, biocultural interactions are still critically important, and they even continue to influence changes in disease patterns. For example, in the last 200 years, rapid culture change in Africa (driven by several centuries of contact with western cultures and technological change) has profoundly altered traditional lifeways.

So how does biological anthropology differ from human biology? In many ways it doesn't, because human biologists also study human physiology, genetics, and adaptation. But human biology as a discipline doesn't focus on nonhuman primates or human evolution. So when biological research also considers these topics as well as how cultural factors have shaped our species, it's placed within the discipline of anthropology.

What Is Anthropology?

anthropology The field of inquiry that studies human culture and evolutionary aspects of human biology; includes cultural anthropology, archaeology, linguistics, and physical, or biological, anthropology.

Stated ambitiously but simply, **anthropology** is the study of humankind. (The term *anthropology* is derived from the Greek words *anthropos,* meaning "human," and *logos,* meaning "word" or "study of.") The goals of anthropology are shared by other disciplines within the social, behavioral, and biological sciences. The main difference between anthropology and related fields is that anthropology integrates the findings of many disciplines, including sociology, economics, history, psychology, and biology.

In the United States, anthropology includes three main subfields: cultural, or social, anthropology; archaeology; and physical, or biological, anthropology. Some universities also include linguistic anthropology as a fourth area. Each of these subdisciplines, in turn, is divided into several specialized areas of interest. Following is a brief discussion of the main subdisciplines of anthropology.

Cultural Anthropology

Cultural anthropology is the study of all aspects of human behavior. The beginnings of cultural anthropology are found in the nineteenth century, when Europeans became increasingly aware of what they called "primitive" societies in Africa and Asia. And, in the New World, some scholars were interested in the vanishing cultures of Native Americans.

ethnographies Detailed descriptive studies of human societies. In cultural anthropology, an ethnography is traditionally the study of a non-Western society.

The interest in traditional societies led numerous early anthropologists to study and record lifeways that unfortunately are now mostly extinct. These studies produced many descriptive **ethnographies** that covered a range of topics, including religion, ritual, myth, use of symbols, subsistence strategies, technology, gender roles, child-rearing practices, dietary preferences, taboos, medical practices, and so on.

Ethnographic accounts, in turn, formed the basis for comparative studies of cultures. By examining the similarities and differences between cultures, anthropologists have been able to formulate many theories about fundamental aspects of human behavior.

The focus of cultural anthropology shifted over the course of the twentieth century. In recent decades, for example, ethnographic techniques have been used to study diverse subcultures and their interactions with one another in contemporary metropolitan areas. The subfield of cultural anthropology that deals with issues of inner cities is appropriately called *urban anthropology.* Another relevant area for cultural anthropologists today is in the resettlement of refugees in many parts of the world. To develop plans that properly accommodate the needs of displaced peoples, governments may find the special talents of cultural anthropologists of considerable benefit.

Medical anthropology is the subfield of cultural anthropology that explores the relationship between various cultural attributes and health and disease. One area of interest is how different groups view disease processes and how these views affect treatment or the willingness to accept treatment. When a medical anthropologist focuses on the social dimensions of disease, physicians and physical anthropologists may also collaborate. In fact, many medical anthropologists also have a background in physical anthropology.

Like medical anthropology, numerous other subfields of cultural anthropology have practical applications and are pursued by anthropologists working outside the university setting. This approach is called *applied anthropology,* and all anthropological disciplines have wide practical applications. Indeed, the various fields of anthropology, as practiced in the United States, overlap to a considerable degree, which, after all, was why they were combined under the umbrella of anthropology in the first place.

Archaeology

Archaeology is the study of earlier cultures and lifeways by anthropologists who specialize in the scientific recovery, analysis, and interpretation of the material remains of human groups who lived in the past. Although archaeology often deals with cultures that existed before the invention of writing (the period commonly known as *prehistory*), *historic archaeologists* examine the evidence of later, complex civilizations that produced written records.

Archaeologists are concerned with culture, but they differ from cultural anthropologists in that they don't study living people but rather the **artifacts** that earlier people and societies left behind. Obviously, no one has ever excavated such aspects of culture as religious belief, spoken language, or a political system. However, the surviving evidence of human occupation has something to tell us about these important but less tangible features of the culture that created them. In other words, the material remains of a given ancient society may inform us about the nature of that society.

Today, the main goal of archaeology is to answer specific questions pertaining to human behavior. Sites aren't excavated just because they exist or for the artifacts they may contain. Rather, they're excavated to gain information about human behavior. Patterns of behavior are reflected in the dispersal of human settlements across a landscape and in the distribution of cultural remains within them. Through the identification of these patterns,

artifacts Objects or materials made or modified for use by hominids (extinct forms and modern humans). The earliest artifacts tend to be tools made of stone or, occasionally, bone.

archaeologists can identify the commonalities shared by many or all populations as well as those features that differ between groups.

In the United States, the greatest expansion in archaeology in the past 30 years or so has been in the important area of *cultural resource management (CRM)*. This applied approach arose from environmental legislation requiring archaeological evaluation and sometimes excavation of sites that may be threatened by development. Many contract archaeologists (so called because their services are contracted out to developers or contractors) are affiliated with private consulting firms, state or federal agencies, or educational institutions. In fact, an estimated 40 percent of all archaeologists in the United States now fill such positions.

Archaeological techniques are used to identify and excavate not only remains of human cities and settlements, but also paleontological sites containing remains of extinct species, including everything from dinosaurs to early hominids. Together, prehistoric archaeology and physical anthropology form the core of a joint science called *paleoanthropology*, described below.

Linguistic Anthropology

Linguistic anthropology is the study of human speech and language, including the origins of language in general as well as specific languages. By examining similarities among contemporary languages, linguists have been able to identify many language families and some past relationships between human populations. Linguistic anthropologists are also interested in the relationship between language and culture. For example, they may want to know how language reflects the way members of a society perceive phenomena and how the use of language shapes perceptions in different cultures.

Linguistic anthropologists also study language acquisition in infants, partly because the spontaneous acquisition and use of language is a uniquely human characteristic. Since a better understanding of this process provides insights into the development of language skills in children, it also can shed light on language development in human evolution. For these reasons, language studies are also important to physical anthropologists.

Physical Anthropology

As we already said, *physical anthropology* is the study of human biology within the framework of evolution and with an emphasis on the interaction between biology and culture. This subdiscipline is also referred to as *biological anthropology*, and you will find the terms used interchangeably. *Physical anthropology* is the original term, and it reflects the initial interests of anthropologists in describing human physical variation. The American Association of Physical Anthropologists, its journal, many college courses, and numerous publications retain this term. The designation *biological anthropology* reflects the shift in emphasis to more biologically oriented topics, such as genetics, evolutionary biology, nutrition, physiological adaptation, and growth and development. This shift occurred largely as a result of advances in the field of genetics since the late 1950s. Although we have continued to use the traditional term in the title of this textbook, you will find that all the major topics pertain to biological issues.

FIGURE 1-4 Paleoanthropologists excavating at an early
hominid site in South Africa.

The origins of physical anthropology are found in two main areas of interest among nineteenth-century scholars. First, there was increasing concern among many scientists (at the time called *natural historians*) regarding the mechanisms by which modern species had come to be. In other words, they were beginning to doubt the literal, biblical interpretation of creation. Although most scientists weren't actually prepared to believe that humans had evolved from earlier forms, discoveries of several Neandertal fossils in the 1800s had raised questions about the origins and antiquity of the human species.

The sparks of interest in biological change over time were fueled into flames by the publication of Charles Darwin's *On the Origin of Species* in 1859. Today, **paleoanthropology,** or the study of human evolution, particularly as revealed in the fossil record, is one of the major subfields of physical anthropology (Fig. 1-4). There are now thousands of specimens of human ancestors housed in research collections. Taken together, these fossils cover a span of at least 4 million years of human prehistory, and although incomplete, they provide us with significantly more knowledge than was available just 10 years ago. The ultimate goal of paleoanthropological research is to identify the various early hominid species, establish a chronological sequence of relationships among them, and gain insights into their adaptation and behavior. Only then will we have a clear picture of how and when humankind came into being.

Observable physical variation was a second nineteenth-century interest that had direct relevance to anthropology. Enormous effort was aimed at describing and explaining the biological differences among human populations. Although some endeavors were misguided and even racist, they gave birth to literally thousands of body measurements that could be used to compare people. Physical anthropologists use many of the techniques of **anthropometry** today, not only to study living groups, but also to study skeletal remains from archaeological sites (Fig. 1-5). Moreover, anthropometric techniques have

paleoanthropology The interdisciplinary approach to the study of earlier hominids—their chronology, physical structure, archaeological remains, habitats, etc.

anthropometry Measurement of human body parts. When osteologists measure skeletal elements, the term *osteometry* is often used.

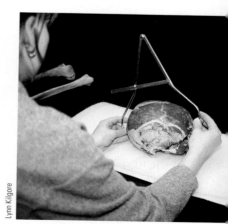

FIGURE 1-5 This anthropology student is measuring the length of a human cranium with spreading calipers.

considerable application in the design of everything from airplane cockpits to office furniture.

Today, anthropologists are concerned with human variation because of its *adaptive significance* and also because they want to identify the evolutionary factors that have produced variability. In other words, some traits evolved as biological adaptations to local environmental conditions, including infectious disease. Others may simply be the results of geographical isolation or the descent of populations from small founding groups.

Some physical anthropologists examine other aspects of human variation, including how various groups respond physiologically to different kinds of environmentally induced stress (Fig. 1-6). Examples of such stresses include high altitude, cold, and heat. Others conduct nutritional studies, investigating the relationships between various dietary components, cultural practices, physiology, and certain aspects of health and disease (Fig. 1-7). Investigations of human fertility, growth, and development are closely related to the topic of nutrition and are fundamental to studies of adaptation in modern human populations.

It would be impossible to study evolutionary processes without knowledge of genetic principles. For this reason and others, **genetics** is a crucial field for physical anthropologists. Modern physical anthropology wouldn't exist as an evolutionary science if not for rapidly developing advances in the understanding of genetic mechanisms.

Molecular anthropologists use cutting-edge technologies to investigate evolutionary relationships between human populations and also between humans and nonhuman primates. To do this, they examine similarities and differences in DNA sequences among individuals, populations, and species. In addition, by extracting DNA from certain fossils, they've contributed to our understanding of relationships between extinct and living species. As genetic technologies continue to improve, molecular anthropologists will play a key role in

FIGURE 1-6 Researcher using a treadmill test to assess a subject's heart rate, blood pressure, and oxygen consumption.

Courtesy, Judith Regensteiner

genetics The study of gene structure and action and the patterns of inheritance of traits from parent to offspring. Genetic mechanisms are the underlying foundation for evolutionary change.

FIGURE 1-7 Dr. Kathleen Galvin measures upper arm circumference in a young Maasai boy in Tanzania. Data derived from various body measurements, including height and weight, were used in a health and nutrition study of groups of Maasai cattle herders.

Courtesy, Kathleen Galvin

Robert Jurmain

FIGURE 1-8 Cloning and sequencing methods are frequently used to identify genes in humans and nonhuman primates. This graduate student identifies a genetically modified bacterial clone.

primatology The study of the biology and behavior of nonhuman primates (prosimians, monkeys, and apes).

osteology The study of skeletal material. Human osteology focuses on the interpretation of the skeletal remains of past groups. Some of the same techniques are used in paleoanthropology to study early hominids.

explaining human evolution, adaptation, and our biological relationships with other species (Fig. 1-8).

Primatology, the study of nonhuman primates, has become increasingly important since the late 1950s (Fig. 1-9). Behavioral studies, especially conducted in the wild, have implications for numerous scientific disciplines. Because nonhuman primates are our closest living relatives, the identification of underlying factors related to social behavior, communication, infant care, reproductive behavior, and so on, helps us develop a better understanding of the natural forces that have shaped so many aspects of modern human behavior.

But an even more important reason to study nonhuman primates is that most species are threatened or seriously endangered. Only through research will scientists be able to recommend policies that can better ensure the survival of many nonhuman primates and thousands of other species as well.

Primate paleontology, the study of the primate fossil record, has implications not only for nonhuman primates but also for hominids. Virtually every year, fossil-bearing beds in North America, Africa, Asia, and Europe yield important new discoveries. In fact, in late 2004, just as this edition of this book was being written, the discovery of a new hominid species on an island near Java, stunned physical anthropologists around the world. This fossil is discussed on p. 292. By studying fossil primates and comparing them with anatomically similar living species, primate paleontologists can learn a great deal about such things as diet or locomotion in earlier forms. They can also make assumptions about social behavior in some extinct primates and attempt to clarify what we know about evolutionary relationships between extinct and living species, including ourselves.

Osteology, the study of the skeleton, is central to physical anthropology. In fact, it's so important that when many people think of biological anthropology, the first thing that comes to mind is bones. The emphasis on osteology exists partly because of the importance of fossil analysis, which requires a thorough knowledge of the structure and function of the skeleton.

Courtesy, Bonnie Pedersen/Arlene Kruse

FIGURE 1-9 Yahaya Alamasi, a member of the senior field staff at Gombe National Park, Tanzania. Alamasi is recording behaviors in free-ranging chimpanzees.

FIGURE 1-10 (a) A partially healed fracture of the femur (thigh bone) from a child's skeleton (estimated age at death is 6 years). Cause of death was probably an infection resulting from this injury. (b) Very severe congenital scoliosis in an adult male from Nubia. The curves are due to several developmental defects that affect individual vertebrae (this is not the most common form of scoliosis).

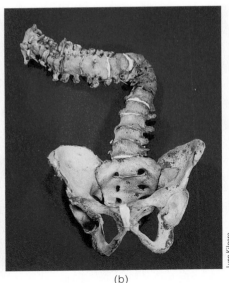

(a)   (b)

Lynn Kilgore   Lynn Kilgore

paleopathology The branch of osteology that studies evidence of disease and injury in human skeletal or, occasionally, mummified remains from archaeological sites.

forensic anthropology An applied anthropological approach dealing with legal matters. Physical anthropologists work with coroners and others in the identification and analysis of human remains.

FIGURE 1-11 Physical anthropologists Lorna Pierce (left) and Judy Suchey (center) working as forensic consultants. The dog has just located a concealed human cranium during a training session.

Courtesy, Lorna Pierce/Judy Suchey

Bone biology and physiology are of major importance to many other aspects of physical anthropology. Many osteologists specialize in studies that emphasize various measurements of skeletal elements. This type of research is essential, for example, to the identification of stature and growth patterns in archaeological populations.

One subdiscipline of osteology is the study of disease and trauma in skeletons from archaeological sites. **Paleopathology** is a prominent subfield that investigates the prevalence of trauma, certain infectious diseases (such as syphilis and tuberculosis), nutritional deficiencies, and many other conditions that may leave evidence in bone (Fig. 1-10). This research tells us a great deal about the lives of individuals and populations from the past. Paleopathology also provides information pertaining to the history of certain disease processes, making it of interest to scientists in biomedical fields.

Forensic anthropology is directly related to osteology and paleopathology. Technically, this approach is the application of anthropological (usually osteological and sometimes archaeological) techniques to legal issues (Fig. 1-11). Forensic anthropologists are routinely called on to help identify skeletal remains in cases of mass disaster or other situations where a human body has been found.

Forensic anthropologists have been involved in numerous cases having important legal, historical, and human consequences. They were prominent in the identification of the skeletons of most of the Russian imperial family, executed in 1918. They also participated in the identification of missing American sol-

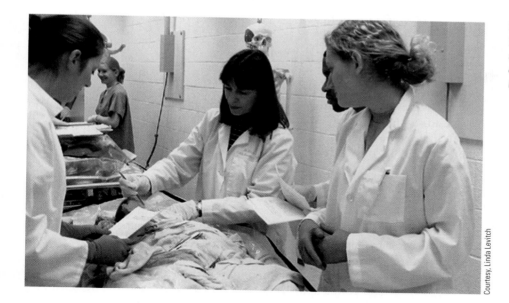

Courtesy, Linda Levitch

diers in Southeast Asia. And more recently, many forensic anthropologists participated in the overwhelming task of trying to identify human remains in the aftermath of the September 11, 2001, terrorist attacks in the United States.

Anatomical studies are another area of interest for physical anthropologists. In living organisms, bones and teeth are intimately linked to the muscles and other tissues that surround and act on them. Consequently, a thorough knowledge of soft tissue anatomy is essential to the understanding of biomechanical relationships involved in movement. Knowledge of such relationships is fundamental to the accurate interpretation of the structure and function of limbs and other structures in extinct animals now represented only by fossilized remains. For such reasons, many physical anthropologists specialize in anatomical studies. In fact, several physical anthropologists hold professorships in anatomy departments at universities and medical schools (Fig.1-12).

Applied anthropology As we mentioned in our discussions of medical and forensic anthropology, applied approaches in biological anthropology are numerous. And while applied anthropology is aimed at the practical application of anthropological theories and methods outside the academic setting, applied and academic anthropology aren't mutually exclusive approaches. Applied anthropology relies on the research and theories of academic anthropologists and at the same time has much to contribute to theory and techniques. Probably the majority of applied anthropologists are trained as cultural anthropologists, but the best example is that of archaeologists working in cultural resource management.

The practical application of the techniques of physical anthropology isn't new. During World War II, for example, physical anthropologists were extensively involved in the design of gun turrets and airplane cockpits. Since that time, physical anthropologists have pursued careers in genetic and biomedical research, public health, evolutionary medicine, medical anthropology, and the conservation of nonhuman primates, and many work in museums and zoos. In fact, a background in physical anthropology is excellent preparation for almost any career in the medical and biological fields.

Physical Anthropology and the Scientific Method

science A body of knowledge gained through observation and experimentation; from the Latin *scientia,* meaning "knowledge."

empirical Relying on experiment or observation; from the Latin *empiricus,* meaning "experienced."

scientific method A research method whereby a problem is identified, a hypothesis (or hypothetical explanation) is stated, and that hypothesis is tested through the collection and analysis of data. If the hypothesis is verified, it becomes a theory.

hypothesis (*pl.,* hypotheses) A provisional explanation of a phenomenon. Hypotheses require verification or falsification through testing.

data (*sing.,* datum) Facts from which conclusions can be drawn; scientific information.

quantitatively In a manner involving measurements of quantity and including such properties as size, number, and capacity. When data are quantified, they are expressed numerically and are capable of being tested statistically.

scientific testing The precise repetition of an experiment or expansion of observed data to provide verification; the procedure by which hypotheses and theories are verified, modified, or discarded.

theory A broad statement of scientific relationships or underlying principles that has been at least partially verified through rigorous testing.

Science is a process of explaining and understanding phenomena through observation and experimentation. That is, it involves an **empirical** approach to acquiring information. Because biological anthropologists do scientific research, they must adhere to the principles of the **scientific method,** whereby they ask a question or identify a problem and then try to come up with an answer or solution.

First, they develop a **hypothesis,** a provisional explanation of a given phenomenon or set of circumstances. But before a hypothesis can be accepted, it must be tested. This involves setting up a research design that is appropriate for testing the hypothesis in question with the possibility of proving it false (i.e., falsifying it). This is the very basis of the scientific method.

Hypothesis testing is accomplished by means of **data** collection and analysis. Data collection is simply the gathering of information, and when scientists use a rigorously controlled approach (established by the research design), they are able to precisely describe their methods and results so that they can be compared with the work of others. For example, when scientists collect data on tooth size in hominid fossils, they specify which teeth are measured, how they are measured, and what the results of the measurements are (expressed numerically or **quantitatively**). Using standard statistical techniques, they then draw conclusions as to the meaning and significance of their measurements. This body of information then becomes the basis of future studies, perhaps by other researchers, who can compare their own results with those from the earlier studies.

Scientific testing of hypotheses may take several years and may even include researchers who weren't involved with the original work. In subsequent studies, other investigators may attempt to obtain the original results, but that may not happen. For example, repeated failures to duplicate the results of highly publicized cold fusion experiments led most scientists to question and ultimately reject the claims made in the original research.

If a hypothesis can't be falsified, it's accepted as a **theory.** There's a popular misconception that theories are just hunches or unfounded beliefs. But in scientific terms, a theory is much more than that because it's a hypothesis that's been repeatedly tested, and scientists haven't been able to disprove it. As such, theories not only help organize current knowledge, but also predict how new facts may fit into an established pattern.

Use of the scientific method not only allows for the development and testing of hypotheses, but also permits various types of *bias* to be controlled. It's important to realize that bias occurs in all studies. Sources of bias include how the investigator was trained and by whom; what particular questions researchers are interested in; what earlier results (if any) have been obtained and by whom (e.g., the researcher, close colleagues, or those with rival approaches or even rival personalities); and what sources of data are available (e.g., accessible countries or museums) and thus what samples can be collected.

The goal of science isn't to establish "truth" in any absolute sense, but rather to generate ever more accurate and consistent explanations of phenomena in our universe. At its very heart, scientific methodology is an exercise in rational thought and critical thinking.

The development of critical thinking skills is an important and lasting benefit of a college education. Such skills enable people to evaluate, compare, analyze, critique, and synthesize information so they won't accept everything they hear at face value. Perhaps the most glaring need for critical thinking is in how we evaluate advertising claims. For example, people spend billions of dollars every year on "natural" dietary supplements based on marketing claims that in fact may not have been tested. So when a salesperson tells you that, for example, echinacea helps prevent colds you should ask if that statement has been scientifically tested, how it was tested, when, and by whom. Similarly, when politicians make claims in 30-second sound bites, check those claims before you accept them as truth. Be skeptical. And if you do check on the validity of advertising and political statements, you'll find that they're frequently misleading or just plain wrong.

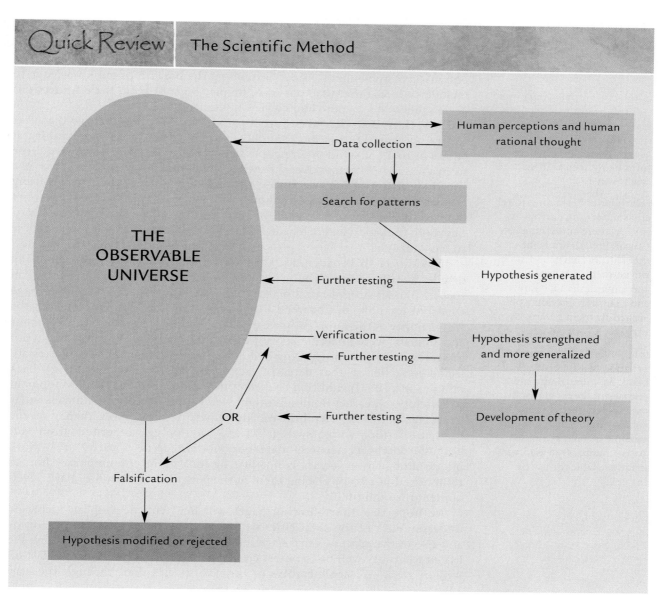

Quick Review   The Scientific Method

Human perceptions and human rational thought

Data collection

Search for patterns

THE OBSERVABLE UNIVERSE

Hypothesis generated

Further testing

Verification

Hypothesis strengthened and more generalized

Further testing

Further testing

Development of theory

OR

Falsification

Hypothesis modified or rejected

The Anthropological Perspective

Perhaps the most important benefit you will receive from this textbook (and this course) is a wider appreciation of the human experience. To understand human beings and how our species came to be, we need to broaden our viewpoint, both through time and over space. All branches of anthropology fundamentally seek to do this in what we call the *anthropological perspective.*

Physical anthropologists, for example, are interested in how humans differ from, and are similar to, other animals, especially nonhuman primates. For example, we have defined *hominids* as bipedal primates, but what are the major components of bipedal locomotion, and how do they differ from, say, those in a quadrupedal ape? To answer these questions, anthropologists have for years meticulously studied human locomotion and compared it with the locomotion seen in various nonhuman primates.

Through a broadened perspective, we can begin to understand the diversity of the human experience within the context of biological and behavioral continuity with other species. In this way, we may better understand the limits and potentials of humankind. And by extending the breadth of our knowledge to include cultures other than our own, we may hope to avoid the **ethnocentric** pitfalls inherent in a more limited view of humanity.

This **relativistic** view of culture is perhaps more important now than ever before, because in our increasingly interdependent global community, it allows us to understand other people's concerns and to view our own culture from a less narrow perspective. Likewise, by examining our species as part of a broad spectrum of life, we realize that we can't judge other species using human criteria. Each species is unique, with needs and a behavioral repertoire not exactly like that of any other. By recognizing that we share many similarities (both biological and behavioral) with other animals, perhaps we may come to recognize that they have a place in nature just as surely as we ourselves do.

In addition to broadening perspectives over space (i.e., encompassing diverse human cultures and ecological circumstances as well as nonhuman species), an anthropological perspective also extends our horizons *through time.* For example, in Chapter 13 we discuss human nutrition. However, the vast majority of the foods people eat today (coming from domesticated plants and animals) were unavailable prior to 10,000 years ago. But human physiological mechanisms for chewing and digesting foods were already well established long before that date. In fact, these adaptive complexes go back millions of years. In addition to dietary differences prior to the development of agriculture), earlier hominids might well have differed from humans today in average body size, **metabolism,** and activity patterns. How, then, does the basic evolutionary "equipment" (i.e., physiology) inherited from our hominid forebears accommodate our modern diets? Clearly, the way to understand such processes is not just by looking at contemporary human responses, but also by placing them in the perspective of evolutionary development through time.

We hope that the following pages will help you develop an increased understanding of the similarities we share with other biological organisms and also of the processes that have shaped the traits that make us unique. We live in what may well be the most crucial period for our planet in the last 65 million years. We are members of the one species that, through the very

ethnocentric Viewing other cultures from the inherently biased perspective of one's own culture. Ethnocentrism usually results in other cultures being seen as inferior to one's own.

relativistic Pertaining to relativism; viewing entities as they relate to something else. Cultural relativism is the view that cultures have merits within their own historical and environmental contexts and that they shouldn't be judged through comparison with one's own culture.

metabolism The chemical processes within cells that break down nutrients and release energy for the body to use. (When nutrients are broken down into their component parts, such as amino acids, energy is released and made available for use by the cell.)

agency of culture, has wrought such devastating changes in ecological systems that we must now alter our technologies or face potentially disastrous consequences. In such a time, it's vital that we attempt to gain the best possible understanding of what it means to be human. We believe that the study of physical anthropology is one endeavor that aids in this attempt, and that is indeed the goal of this text.

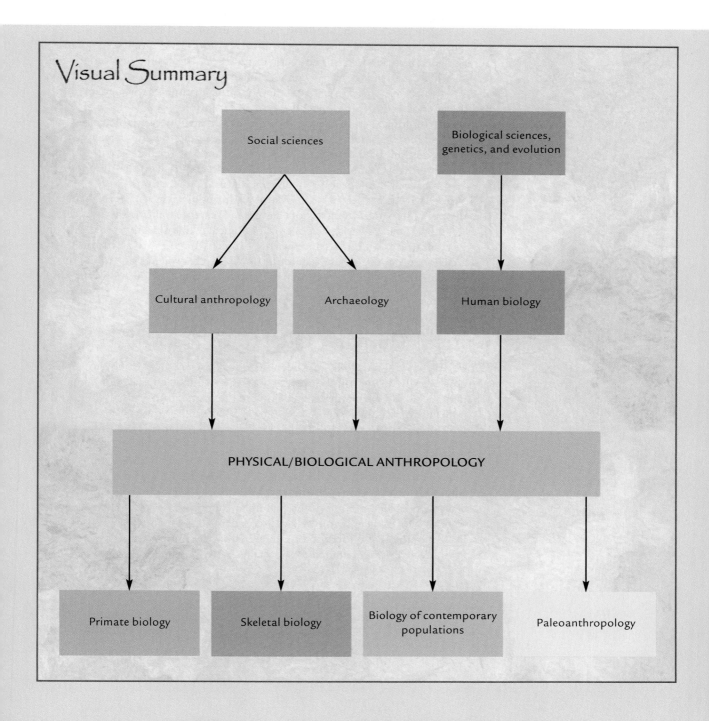

Summary

In this chapter, we have introduced you to the field of physical, or biological, anthropology, placing it within the overall context of anthropological studies. As a major academic discipline within the social sciences, anthropology also includes archaeology, cultural anthropology, and linguistic anthropology as its other major subfields.

Physical anthropology is the study of many aspects of human biology, including genetics, genetic variation, adaptations to environmental factors, nutrition, and anatomy. These topics are discussed within an evolutionary framework because all human characteristics are either directly or indirectly the results of biological evolution, which in turn is driven by genetic change. Hence, biological anthropologists also study our closest relatives, the nonhuman primates, primate evolution, and the genetic and fossil evidence for human evolution.

Because biological anthropology is a scientific discipline, the role of the scientific method in research was also discussed. We presented the importance of objectivity, observation, data collection and analysis, and the formation and testing of hypotheses to explain natural phenomena. We also emphasized that this approach is an empirical one and doesn't rely on supernatural explanations.

Since evolution is the core of physical anthropology, in the next chapter we present a brief historical overview of changes in Western scientific thought that led to the discovery of the basic principles of biological evolution. As you are probably aware, evolution is a highly controversial subject (much more so in the United States than in other countries). Therefore, we'll briefly explain some of the reasons for this controversy as well as discuss the evidence for evolution as the single thread that unites all the biological sciences.

Critical Thinking Questions

1. Given that you have only just been introduced to the field of physical anthropology, why do you think subjects such as anatomy, genetics, nonhuman primate behavior, and human evolution are integrated into a discussion of what it means to be human?

2. Is it important to you, personally, to know about human evolution? Why or why not?

3. Do you see a connection between hominid footprints that are almost 4 million years old and human footprints left on the moon in 1969? If so, do you think this relationship is important? What does the fact that there are human footprints on the moon say about human adaptation? (You may wish to refer to both biological and cultural adaptation.)

4. Do you think that understanding the scientific method and developing critical thinking skills can benefit you personally? Why?

Media Resources

The Companion Website for *Essentials of Physical Anthropology*, Sixth Edition
http://anthropology.wadsworth.com/jurmain6e_ess

Supplement your review of this chapter by going to this text's companion website to take one of the practice quizzes, use the flash cards to master key terms, and check out the many other resources and study aids. Also visit the website to learn about important new discoveries in paleoanthropology by checking the "Latest Dirt" feature authored by Robert Jurmain.

CD-ROMs in Physical Anthropology

Wadsworth Publishing has also developed three CD-ROMs to accompany this text and enhance learning in physical anthropology (for further descriptions of these CD-ROMs, see p. xix):

Virtual Laboratories for Physical Anthropology CD-ROM, Third Edition

Basic Genetics for Anthropology CD-ROM: Principles and Applications

Hominid Fossils CD-ROM: An Interactive Atlas

For this chapter, quickly review all three CD-ROMs to see many aspects of physical anthropology.

Readings of Interest

Angeloni, Elvio (ed.). 2003. Annual Editions: Physical Anthropology. Guildford, CT: Dushkin Publishing Group (a division of McGraw-Hill).

Boaz, Noel and Linda D. Wolfe. 1995. *Biological Anthropology: The State of the Science*. Bend, OR: International Institute for Human Evolution.

Strum, S., D. G. Lundburg, and D. Hamburg. 1999. *The New Physical Anthropology: Science, Humanism, and Cultural Reflection*. Upper Saddle River, NJ: Prentice Hall.

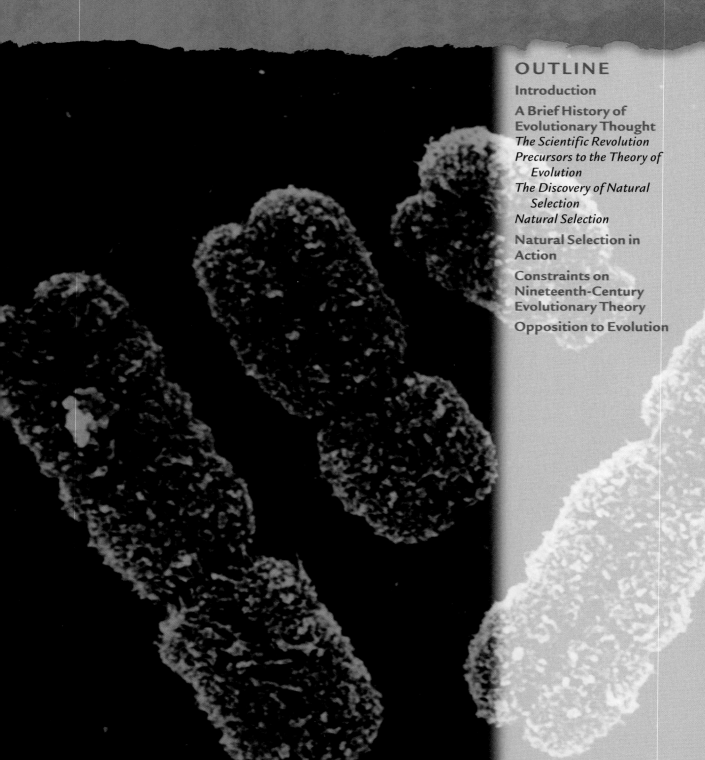

2 | The Development of Evolutionary Theory

Focus Questions

What are the basic premises of natural selection?
What are some examples you may know of that aren't mentioned in this chapter?

Introduction

Has anyone ever asked you, "If humans evolved from monkeys, then why do we still have monkeys?" Or maybe you've heard this one: "If evolution happens, then why don't we ever see new species?" These are the kinds of questions asked by people who have no understanding of evolutionary processes and who may not even believe they exist. The fact that anyone today, given the overwhelming evidence for biological evolution, would ask such questions is a depressing reflection of the poor quality of education. Evolution is one of the most fundamental of biological processes and also one of the most misunderstood. This is partly because the topic is commonly avoided in primary and secondary schools and students are simply not exposed to it. And at colleges and universities evolution is covered only in classes that directly relate to it. Indeed, if you're not an anthropology or biology major and you're taking a class in biological anthropology mainly to fill a science requirement, you'll probably never study evolution again.

By the end of this course, you'll know the answers to the two questions that opened the previous paragraph. Briefly, no one who studies evolution would ever say that humans evolved from monkeys, because they didn't. They didn't evolve from chimpanzees either. The earliest human ancestors evolved from a species that lived some 5 to 8 million years ago (m.y.a.). That ancestral species, the last *common ancestor* we share with the African apes, also gave rise to the lineage now represented by chimpanzees and gorillas. In turn, the lineage that led to the apes and ourselves separated from a monkey-like ancestor some 20 m.y.a., and monkeys are still around because as lineages diverged from a common ancestor, each group went its separate way. Over time, some of these groups became extinct and others evolved into the species that exist today. Each species is the current product of processes that go back millions of years. Because evolution takes time, and lots of it, we rarely witness the appearance of new species (although microorganisms are a different matter). But we do see *microevolutionary* changes in living species.

The subject of evolution is controversial, particularly in the United States, because some religious views hold that evolutionary statements run counter to biblical teachings. Indeed, as you are probably aware, there continues to be strong opposition to the teaching of evolution in public schools.

People who deny that evolution happens often comment that "evolution is only a theory," implying that evolution is mere supposition. Actually, referring to a concept as "theory" supports it. As we discussed in Chapter 1, theories are hypotheses that have been tested and subjected to verification through accumulated evidence. Evolution is a theory, one that has increasingly been supported by a mounting body of genetic evidence. It's a theory that has stood the test of time, and today it stands as the most fundamental unifying force in biological science.

Click

Go to the following CD-ROM for interactive activities and exercises on topics covered in this chapter:

Basic Genetics for Anthropology CD-ROM: Principles and Applications

Because physical anthropology is concerned with all aspects of how humans came to be and how we adapt physiologically to the external environment, understanding the details of the evolutionary process is crucial. Therefore, it's beneficial to know how the mechanics of the process came to be discovered. Also, if we want to appreciate the nature of the controversy that still surrounds the issue, we need to see how social and political events influenced the discovery of evolutionary principles.

A Brief History of Evolutionary Thought

The discovery of evolutionary principles first took place in western Europe and was made possible by advances in scientific thinking that date back to the sixteenth century. Having said this, we must recognize that Western science borrowed many of its ideas from other cultures, especially the Arabs, Indians, and Chinese. Intellectuals in these cultures and in ancient Greece had notions of biological evolution (Teresi, 2002), but they never formulated them into a cohesive theory.

Charles Darwin was the first person to explain the basic mechanics of the evolutionary process. But while he was developing his theory of **natural selection,** a Scottish naturalist named Alfred Russel Wallace independently reached the same conclusion. That natural selection, the single most important force of evolutionary change, should be proposed at more or less the same time by two British men in the mid-nineteenth century may seem like a strange coincidence. But in fact, if Darwin and Wallace hadn't made their simultaneous discoveries, someone else soon would have, and that someone would probably have been British or French. That's because the groundwork had already been laid in Britain and France, and many scientists there were prepared to accept explanations of biological change that would have been unacceptable even 25 years before.

Like other human endeavors, scientific knowledge is usually gained through a series of small steps rather than giant leaps, and just as technological change is based on past achievements, scientific knowledge builds on previously developed theories. For this reason, it's informative to examine the development of ideas that led Darwin and Wallace to independently develop the theory of evolution by natural selection.

Throughout the Middle Ages, one predominant feature of the European world view was that all aspects of nature, including all forms of life and their relationships to one another, never changed. This view was partly shaped by a feudal society that was itself a hierarchical, rigid class system that hadn't changed much for centuries. It was also influenced by an extremely powerful religious system where the teachings of Christianity were taken literally. Consequently, it was generally accepted that all life on earth had been created by God exactly as it existed in the present, and the belief that life forms couldn't change came to be known as **fixity of species.**

The plan of the entire universe was viewed as God's design. In what is called the "argument from design," anatomical structures were planned to meet the purpose for which they were required. Wings, arms, eyes, and so on,

natural selection The mechanism of evolutionary change first articulated by Charles Darwin; refers to genetic change or changes in the frequencies of certain traits in populations due to differential reproductive success between individuals.

fixity of species The notion that species, once created, can never change; an idea diametrically opposed to theories of biological evolution.

fit the functions they performed, and nature was a deliberate plan of the Grand Designer. Also, pretty much everybody believed that the Grand Designer had completed his works fairly recently. An Irish archbishop named James Ussher (1581–1656) analyzed the "begat" chapter of Genesis and determined that the earth was created in 4004 B.C. Archbishop Ussher wasn't the first person to suggest a recent origin of the earth, but he was the first to propose a precise date for it. And this date was so important to people that, for decades, book printers put it in bibles, in the margin next to the Genesis account of the creation.

The prevailing notion of the earth's brief existence, together with fixity of species, provided a huge obstacle to the development of evolutionary theory because evolution requires time, and the idea of immense geological time, which today we take for granted, simply didn't exist. In fact, until the concepts of fixity and time were fundamentally altered, it was impossible to conceive of biological evolution.

THE SCIENTIFIC REVOLUTION

So, what transformed centuries-old beliefs in a rigid, static universe to a view of worlds in continuous motion? How did the earth's brief history become an immense expanse of incomprehensible time? How did the scientific method as we know it today develop? These are important questions, but it would be equally appropriate to ask why it took so long for Europe to break from the constraints of traditional belief systems when Arab and Indian scholars had developed concepts of planetary motion centuries earlier.

For Europeans, the discovery of the New World and circumnavigation of the globe in the fifteenth century overturned some very basic ideas about the planet. For one thing, the earth could no longer be thought of as flat. Also, as Europeans began to explore the New World, their awareness of biological diversity was greatly expanded as they saw plants and animals previously unknown to them.

There were other attacks on traditional beliefs. In 1514, a Polish mathematician named Copernicus challenged Aristotle's long-believed notion that the earth, circled by the sun, moon, and stars, was the center of the universe. In fact, in India, scholars had figured this out long before Copernicus, but Copernicus is generally credited with removing the earth as the center of all things by proposing a sun-centered solar system.

Copernicus' theory didn't attract much attention at the time, but in the early 1600s, it was restated by an Italian mathematics professor named Galileo Galilei. Galileo came into direct confrontation with the Catholic Church over his publications, to the extent that he spent the last nine years of his life under house arrest. Even so, in intellectual circles, the universe had changed from an earth-centered to a solar-centered one, and from one of fixity to one of motion.

European scholars of the sixteenth and seventeenth centuries developed methods and theories that revolutionized scientific thought. Their technological advances permitted investigations of natural phenomena and opened up entire new worlds for discoveries such as never before had been imagined. But, even with these advances, the idea that, over time, living forms could change simply didn't occur to people.

binomial nomenclature
(*binomial*, meaning "two names") In taxonomy, the convention established by Carolus Linnaeus whereby genus and species names are used to refer to species. For example, *Homo sapiens* refers to human beings.

taxonomy The branch of science concerned with the rules of classifying organisms on the basis of evolutionary relationships.

FIGURE 2-1 Linnaeus developed a classification system for plants and animals.

FIGURE 2-2 Buffon recognized the influence of the environment on life forms.

PRECURSORS TO THE THEORY OF EVOLUTION

Before early naturalists could begin to understand the many forms of organic life, it was necessary to list and describe them. And as research progressed, scholars were increasingly impressed with the amount of biological diversity they saw.

John Ray It wasn't until the seventeenth century that John Ray (1627–1705), a minister educated at Cambridge University, developed the concept of species. He was the first to recognize that groups of plants and animals could be distinguished from other groups by their ability to mate with one another and produce offspring. He placed such groups of reproductively isolated organisms into a single category, which he called the *species* (*pl.,* species). Thus, by the late 1600s, the biological criterion of reproduction was used to define species, much as it is today (Young, 1992).

Ray also recognized that species frequently shared similarities with other species, and he grouped these together in a second level of classification he called the *genus* (*pl.,* genera). He was the first to use the labels *genus* and *species* in this way, and they're the terms we still use today. But he also strongly believed in the fixity of species, and he wrote his 1691 publication, *The Wisdom of God Manifested in the Works of Creation,* to show how nature reflected God's plan.

Carolus Linnaeus Swedish naturalist Carolus Linnaeus (1707–1778) is best known for developing a classification of plants and animals, the *Systema Naturae* (Systems of Nature), first published in 1735 (Fig. 2-1). In this publication, he standardized Ray's use of genus and species terminology and established the system of **binomial nomenclature.** He also added two more categories: class and order. Linnaeus' four-level system became the basis for **taxonomy,** the system of classification we continue to use.

Another of Linnaeus' innovations was to include humans in his classification of animals, placing them in the genus *Homo* and species *sapiens.* Including humans in this scheme was controversial because it defied contemporary thought that humans, made in God's image, should be considered unique and not part of the animal kingdom.

Linnaeus also believed in fixity of species, although in later years, faced with mounting evidence to the contrary, he came to question it. Indeed, fixity was being challenged on many fronts, especially in France, where voices were being raised in favor of a universe based on change and, more to the point, in favor of a biological relationship between similar species based on descent from a common ancestor.

Count George-Louis Leclerc de Buffon Buffon (1707–1788) was Keeper of the King's Gardens in Paris (Fig. 2-2). Unlike others, he recognized the dynamic relationship between the external environment and living forms. In his *Natural History,* first published in 1749, he repeatedly stressed the importance of change in the universe and in the changing nature of species.

Buffon believed that when groups of organisms migrated to new areas, they would gradually be altered as a result of adaptation to a somewhat different environment. Buffon's recognition of the external environment as an agent of change in species was an important innovation. However, he rejected the idea that one species could give rise to another.

Erasmus Darwin Today, Erasmus Darwin (1731–1802) is best known as Charles Darwin's grandfather (Fig. 2-3). This is somewhat unfortunate, because he was also a physician, inventor, naturalist, philosopher, poet, and leading member of a well-known intellectual community in Lichfield, England. Living in the English midlands, the birthplace of the industrial revolution, then in full swing, Darwin counted among his friends some of the leading figures of this time of rapid technological and social change.

During his lifetime, Darwin achieved considerable fame as a poet. His most famous work was *Zoonomia*, a medical book of over 500,000 words written entirely in verse. In this book (which, admittedly, few of us would read today), he publicly expressed his views that life had originated in the seas and that all species had descended from a common ancestor. Thus, he introduced many of the ideas that would be proposed 56 years later by his grandson. These concepts include vast expanses of time for life to evolve, competition for resources, and the importance of the environment in evolutionary processes. From letters and other sources, we know that Charles Darwin read his grandfather's writings. But the degree to which his theories were influenced by him isn't known.

Jean-Baptiste Lamarck Neither Buffon nor Erasmus Darwin attempted to *explain* the evolutionary process. The first scientist to do this was Jean-Baptiste Pierre Antoine de Monet Chevalier de Lamarck (1744–1829) of France. (Thankfully, most references to Lamarck use only his surname.)

Lamarck (Fig. 2-4) expanded beyond the views of Buffon by trying to explain *how* species could change. He suggested a dynamic relationship between species and the environment such that if the external environment changed, an animal's activity patterns would also change to accommodate the new circumstances. This would result in the increased or decreased use of certain body parts, and consequently, body parts would be modified. According to Lamarck, these physical changes would occur in response to bodily "needs" so that if a particular part of the body felt a certain need, "fluids and forces" would be directed to that point and the structure would be modified. Because the alteration would make the animal better suited to its habitat, the new trait would be passed on to offspring. This theory is known as the *inheritance of acquired characteristics,* or the *use-disuse* theory.

One of the most frequently given hypothetical examples of Lamarck's theory is the giraffe, who, having stripped all the leaves from the lower branches of a tree (environmental change), tries to reach leaves on upper branches. As "vital forces" move to tissues of the neck, it becomes slightly longer, and the giraffe can reach higher. The longer neck is subsequently transmitted to offspring, with the eventual result that all giraffes have longer necks than their predecessors had (Fig. 2-5a). Thus, according to this theory, *a trait acquired by an animal during its lifetime can be passed on to offspring.* Today we know that this explanation is incorrect, since only those traits coded for by genetic information contained within sex cells (eggs and sperm) can be inherited (see Chapter 3).

Because Lamarck's explanation of species change isn't genetically correct, it's sometimes made fun of and dismissed. But actually, Lamarck deserves a lot of credit because he was the first person to emphasize the importance of interactions between organisms and the external environment in the evolutionary process. He also coined the term "biology" to refer to studies of living organisms.

FIGURE 2-3 Erasmus Darwin, grandfather of Charles Darwin, believed in species change.

FIGURE 2-4 Lamarck believed that species change was influenced by environmental change. He is best known for his theory of the inheritance of acquired characteristics.

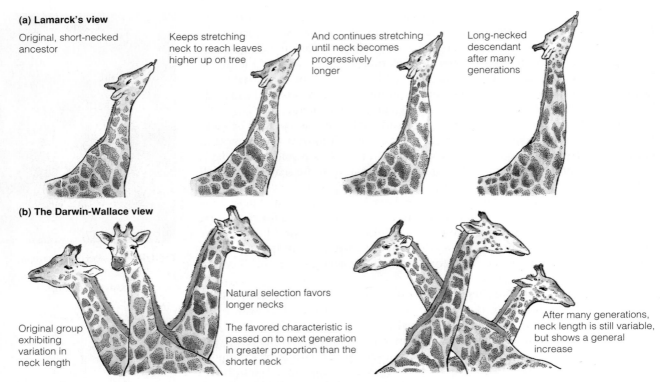

(a) Lamarck's view

Original, short-necked ancestor

Keeps stretching neck to reach leaves higher up on tree

And continues stretching until neck becomes progressively longer

Long-necked descendant after many generations

(b) The Darwin-Wallace view

Original group exhibiting variation in neck length

Natural selection favors longer necks

The favored characteristic is passed on to next generation in greater proportion than the shorter neck

After many generations, neck length is still variable, but shows a general increase

FIGURE 2-5 Contrasting ideas about the mechanism of evolution. (a) According to Lamarck's theory, acquired characteristics can be passed to subsequent generations. Thus, short-necked giraffes stretched their necks to reach higher into trees for food, and, according to Lamarck, this acquired trait was passed on to offspring, who were born with longer necks. (b) According to the Darwin-Wallace theory of natural selection, among giraffes there is variation in neck length. If having a longer neck provides an advantage for feeding, this trait will be passed on to a greater number of offspring, leading to an overall increase in the length of giraffe necks over many generations.

catastrophism The view that the earth's geological landscape is the result of violent cataclysmic events. This view was promoted by Cuvier, especially in opposition to Lamarck.

FIGURE 2-6 Cuvier explained the fossil record as the result of a succession of catastrophes followed by new creation events.

Courtesy, Dept. of Library Services, American Museum of Natural History

Georges Cuvier Georges Cuvier (1769–1832), the most vehement opponent of Lamarck, was a French vertebrate paleontologist who introduced the concept of extinction to explain the disappearance of animals represented by fossils (Fig. 2-6). Although a brilliant anatomist, Cuvier never grasped the dynamic concept of nature, and he insisted on the fixity of species. So, rather than assume that similarities between certain fossil forms and living species indicated evolutionary relationships, he suggested a variation of a theory known as **catastrophism.**

Catastrophism was the belief that the earth's geological features were the results of sudden, worldwide cataclysmic events like the Noah flood. Cuvier's version of catastrophism suggested that a series of regional disasters had destroyed most or all of the plant and animal life in various places. These areas were then restocked with new, similar species that migrated in from unaffected regions. But he needed to be consistent with emerging fossil evidence that indicated that organisms had become more complex over time. So he proposed that after each disaster, incoming migrants had a more modern appearance because they were the results of more recent creation events.

(The last of these creations was the one depicted in Genesis.) Thus, Cuvier's explanation of increased complexity over time avoided any notion of evolution while still being able to account for the evidence for change preserved in the fossil record.

Thomas Malthus In 1798, Thomas Malthus (1766–1834), an English clergyman and economist, wrote *An Essay on the Principle of Population*, which inspired both Charles Darwin and Alfred Wallace in their separate discoveries of natural selection (Fig. 2-7). In his essay, Malthus said that human populations could double in size every 25 years if they weren't kept in check by limited food supplies. That is, population size increases exponentially while food supplies remain relatively stable.

Malthus, who was arguing for limits to population growth, focused on humans because we can increase food supplies artificially and therefore reduce constraints on population size. However, the same logic could be applied to nonhuman organisms. In nature, the tendency for populations to increase is always checked by resource availability, so there is constant competition for food and other resources. In time, both Darwin and Wallace would extend Malthus' principles to all organisms, not just humans.

FIGURE 2-7 Thomas Malthus' *Essay on the Principle of Population* led both Darwin and Wallace to the principle of natural selection.

Charles Lyell Charles Lyell (1797–1875), the son of Scottish landowners, is considered the founder of modern geology (Fig. 2-8). He was a barrister, a geologist, and for many years Charles Darwin's friend and mentor. Before he met Darwin in 1836, Lyell had earned acceptance in Europe's most prestigious scientific circles, thanks to his highly praised *Principles of Geology*, first published during the years 1830–1833.

In this immensely important work, Lyell argued that the geological processes observed in the present are the same as those that occurred in the past. This theory, called **uniformitarianism**, didn't originate entirely with Lyell, having been proposed by James Hutton in the late 1700s. Nevertheless, it was Lyell who demonstrated that such forces as wind, water erosion, local flooding, frost, the decomposition of vegetable matter, volcanoes, earthquakes, and glacial movements had all contributed in the past to produce the geological landscape that exists in the present. Moreover, the fact that these processes could still be seen in operation indicated that geological change continued to occur and that the forces that drove such change were consistent, or *uniform*, over time. In other words, while various aspects of the earth's surface (e.g., climate, plants, animals, and land surfaces) are variable through time, the *underlying processes* that influence them are constant.

The theory of uniformitarianism flew in the face of Cuvier's catastrophism. Additionally, Lyell emphasized the obvious: namely, that for such slow-acting forces to produce momentous change, the earth would have to be far older than anyone had ever suspected.

By providing an immense time scale and thereby altering perceptions of earth's history from a few thousand to many millions of years, Lyell changed the framework within which scientists viewed the geological past. Thus, the concept of "deep time" (Gould, 1987) remains one of Lyell's most significant contributions to the discovery of evolutionary principles. The immensity of geological time permitted the necessary time depth for the inherently slow process of evolutionary change.

FIGURE 2-8 Lyell, the father of geology, stated the theory of uniformitarianism in his *Principles of Geology*.

uniformitarianism The theory that the earth's features are the result of long-term processes that continue to operate in the present as they did in the past. Elaborated on by Lyell, this theory opposed catastrophism and contributed strongly to the concept of immense geological time.

The Natural History Museum, London

FIGURE 2-9 Portrait of Mary Anning

Mary Anning In the late eighteenth and early nineteenth centuries, when the fields of geology and paleontology were emerging, amateurs and scientists alike were obsessed with collecting fossils. Previously, no one had recognzed fossils for what they were, but by the mid-1700s, many people believed they were the remains of creatures killed in the biblical flood. Because of this interest, a girl named Mary Anning (1799–1847), who lived in a town on the south coast of England, became an important but largely unknown contributor to the developing scientific discipline of paleontology (Fig. 2-9).

Anning's father died when she was 11, leaving the family destitute. But before his death, he had taught her to recognize fossils embedded in nearby cliffs along the shore. So, to support her family, Mary began to collect and sell fossils. After her discovery of the first complete fossilized skeleton of an *Ichthyosaurus,* a large, fishlike marine reptile, the Anning home was visited by most of the leading scientists in England. Over the years, Anning supplied researchers, museums, and wealthy private collectors with hundreds of fossils. Her discoveries formed the basis of some of the earliest research collections in Britain and she became known as one of the world's leading "fossilists." However, because she was a woman in humble circumstances, she was never acknowledged in scientific publications. Fortunately, she has now achieved recognition, and her portrait hangs prominently in the British Museum (Natural History) in London near one of her famous *Ichthyosaurus* fossils.

THE DISCOVERY OF NATURAL SELECTION

Charles Darwin Having already been introduced to Erasmus Darwin, you shouldn't be surprised that his grandson Charles grew up in an educated family with ties to intellectual circles. Charles Darwin (1809–1882) was one of six children of Dr. Robert and Susanna Darwin (Fig. 2-10). Being the grandson not only of Erasmus Darwin, but also of the wealthy Josiah Wedgwood (of Wedgewood china fame), Charles grew up enjoying the comfortable lifestyle of the landed gentry in rural England.

As a boy, he had a keen interest in nature and spent his days fishing and collecting shells, birds' eggs, and rocks. However, this interest in natural history didn't dispel the generally held view of family and friends that he was in no way remarkable. In fact, his performance at school was no more than ordinary.

After the death of his mother when he was eight, Darwin's upbringing was guided by his father and his older sisters. Because he showed little interest in, or aptitude for, anything except hunting, shooting, and perhaps science, his father sent him to Edinburgh University to study medicine. It was there that Darwin first became acquainted with the evolutionary theories of Lamarck and others.

During this time (the 1820s), notions of evolution were becoming feared in England and elsewhere. Anything identifiable with postrevolutionary France was viewed with suspicion by the established order in England. Lamarck was especially vilified by British professors, the majority of whom were also members of the Anglican clergy.

This was also a time of growing political unrest in Britain. The Reform Movement, which sought to undo many of the wrongs of the class system, was under way, and like most social movements, this one had a radical faction. Because many of the radicals were atheists and socialists who also supported Lamarck's ideas, many people came to associate evolution with atheism and

transmutation The change of one species to another. The term evolution did not assume its current meaning until the late nineteenth century.

political subversion. Such was the growing fear of evolutionary ideas that many believed that if they were generally accepted, "the Church would crash, the moral fabric of society would be torn apart, and civilized man would return to savagery" (Desmond and Moore, 1991, p. 34). It's unfortunate that some of the most outspoken early proponents of **transmutation** were so vehemently anti-Christian, because their rhetoric helped establish the entrenched suspicion and misunderstanding of evolutionary theory that persists today.

While at Edinburgh, young Darwin studied with professors who were outspoken supporters of Lamarck. Darwin's second year in Edinburgh saw him examining museum collections and attending natural history lectures. Therefore, although he hated medicine and left Edinburgh after two years, his experience there was a formative period in his intellectual development.

Even though Darwin was fairly indifferent to religion, he next went to Christ's College, Cambridge, to study theology. It was during his Cambridge years that he seriously cultivated his interests in natural science, immersing himself in botany and geology. It's no wonder that following his graduation in 1831 at age 22, he was invited to accompany a scientific expedition that would circle the globe. And so it was that Darwin set sail aboard the HMS *Beagle* on December 17, 1831 (Fig. 2-11). The famous voyage of the *Beagle* was to last for almost five years and would forever change not only the course of Darwin's life, but also the history of biological science.

Darwin went aboard the *Beagle* believing in fixity of species. But during the voyage, he privately began to have doubts. For example, he came across fossils

FIGURE 2-10 Charles Darwin, photographed five years before the publication of *Origin of Species*.

FIGURE 2-11 The route of the HMS *Beagle*.

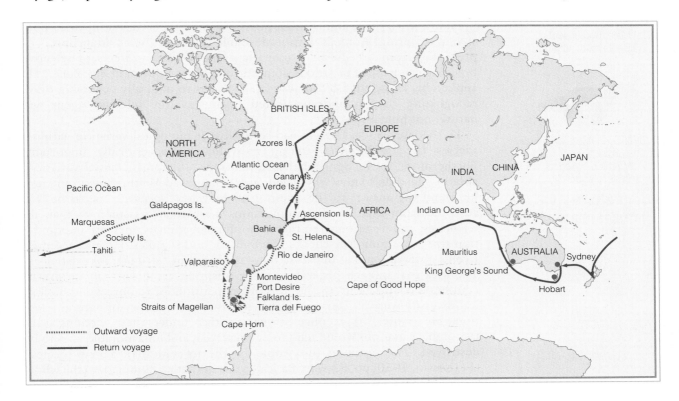

(a) Ground finch
Main food: seeds
Beak: heavy

(b) Tree finch
Main food: leaves, buds,
blossoms, fruits
Beak: thick, short

(c) Tree finch (called
woodpecker finch)
Main food: insects
Beak: stout, straight

(d) Ground finch (known as
warbler finch)
Main food: insects
Beak: slender

FIGURE 2-12 Beak variation
in Darwin's Galápagos finches.

of ancient giant animals that, except for size, looked very much like species that still lived in the same vicinity, so he wondered if the fossils represented ancestors of those living forms.

During the famous stopover at the Galápagos Islands (see Fig. 2-11), Darwin noted that the vegetation and animals (especially birds) shared many similarities with those on the mainland of South America. But they weren't identical to them. Moreover, the birds of one island were somewhat different from those living on another. Darwin collected 13 different varieties of Galápagos finches and it was clear that they represented a closely affiliated group, but they differed with regard to certain physical traits, particularly the shape and size of their beaks (Fig. 2-12). He also collected finches from the mainland, and these appeared to represent only one group, or species.

The insight that Darwin gained from the finches is legendary. He recognized that the various Galápagos finches had all descended from a common, mainland ancestor and had been modified over time in response to different island habitats and dietary preferences. But actually, it wasn't until *after* he returned to England that Darwin recognized the significance of the variation in beak structure. In fact, during the voyage, he had paid little attention to the finches. It was only later that he considered the factors that could lead to the modification of 1 species into 13 (Gould, 1985; Desmond and Moore, 1991).

Darwin arrived back in England in October 1836 and was immediately accepted into the most prestigious scientific circles. He married his cousin Emma Wedgwood and moved to the village of Down, near London, where he spent the rest of his life writing on topics ranging from fossils to orchids. But the question of species change was his overriding passion.

At Down, Darwin began to develop his views on what he called *natural selection*. This concept was borrowed from animal breeders, who "select" as breeding stock those animals that possess certain traits they want to emphasize in offspring. Animals with undesirable traits are "selected against," or prevented from breeding. A dramatic example of the effects of selective breeding can be seen in various domestic dog breeds shown in Fig. 2-13.) He applied his knowledge of domesticated species to naturally occurring ones, recognizing that in undomesticated organisms, the selective agent was nature, not humans.

By the late 1830s, Darwin had realized that biological variation within a species (i.e., differences among individuals) was critically important. Furthermore, he recognized that sexual reproduction increased variation, although he didn't know why. Then, in 1838, he read Malthus' essay, and in it he found the answer to the question of how new species came to be. He accepted from Malthus that populations increase at a faster rate than do resources, and he recognized that in nonhuman animals, increase in population size is continuously checked by limited food supplies. He also accepted Lyell's observation that in nature there is a constant "struggle for existence." The idea that in each generation more offspring are born than survive to adulthood coupled with the notions of competition for resources and biological diversity were all Darwin needed to develop his theory of natural selection. He wrote: "It at once struck me that under these circumstances favourable variations would tend to be preserved, and unfavourable ones to be destroyed. The result of this would be the formation of a new species" (F. Darwin, 1950, pp. 53–54). Basically, this quotation summarizes the whole of natural selection theory.

By 1844, Darwin had written a short summary of his views on natural selection but he didn't think he had enough data to support his hypothesis, so he continued his research without publishing. He also had other reasons for not publishing what he knew would be, to say the least, a highly controversial work. He was deeply troubled by the fact that his wife Emma saw his ideas as running counter to her strong religious convictions (Keynes, 2002). Also, as a member of the established order, he knew that many of his friends and associates were concerned with threats to the status quo, and evolutionary theory was viewed as a very serious threat. So he waited.

Alfred Russel Wallace Unlike Darwin, Alfred Russel Wallace (1823–1913) was born into a family of modest means (Fig. 2-14). He went to work at the age of 14, and with little formal education, he moved from one job to the next. He became interested in collecting plants and animals, and in 1848 he joined an expedition to the Amazon, where he acquired firsthand knowledge of many natural phenomena. Then, in 1854, he sailed for Southeast Asia and the Malay Peninsula to collect bird and insect specimens.

In 1855, Wallace published a paper suggesting that species were descended from other species and that the appearance of new species was influenced by environmental factors. The Wallace paper caused Lyell and others to urge Darwin to publish, but still he hesitated.

Then, in 1858, Wallace sent Darwin another paper titled "On the Tendency of Varieties to Depart Indefinitely from the Original Type." In it, Wallace described evolution as a process driven by competition and natural selection. When he received Wallace's paper, Darwin feared that Wallace might get credit for a theory (natural selection) that he himself had developed. He quickly

FIGURE 2-13 All domestic dog breeds share a common ancestor, the wolf. The extreme variation that dog breeds exhibit today has been achieved in a relatively short period of time through artificial selection. In this situation, humans allow only certain dogs to breed because they possess specific characteristics that humans want to emphasize. (We should note that not all traits deemed desirable by human breeders are advantageous to the dogs themselves.)

Courtesy of Down House and The Royal College of Surgeons of England

FIGURE 2-14 Alfred Russel Wallace independently discovered the key to the evolutionary process.

wrote a paper presenting his ideas, and the papers of both men were read before the Linnean Society of London. Neither author was present. Wallace was out of the country, and Darwin was mourning the recent death of his young son.

The papers received little notice at the time, but when Darwin completed and published his greatest work, *On the Origin of Species,** in December 1859, the storm broke, and it still hasn't abated. While public opinion was negative there was much scholarly praise for the book and scientific opinion gradually came to Darwin's support. The riddle of species was now explained: Species were mutable, not fixed; and they evolved from other species through the mechanism of natural selection.

NATURAL SELECTION

Early in his research, Darwin had realized that selection was the key to evolution. With the help of Malthus' ideas, he saw *how* selection in nature could be explained. In the struggle for existence, those *individuals* with favorable variations would survive and reproduce, but those with unfavorable variations wouldn't. For Darwin, the explanation of evolution was simple. The basic processes, as he understood them, are as follows:

1. All species are capable of producing offspring at a faster rate than food supplies increase.
2. There is biological variation within all species. (Today we know that except for identical twins, no two individuals are genetically the same.)
3. Since, in each generation more offspring are produced than can survive, and owing to limited resources, there is competition between individuals. (*Note:* This statement doesn't mean that there is constant fierce fighting.)
4. Individuals who possess favorable variations or traits (e.g., speed, resistance to disease, protective coloration) have an advantage over those who don't have them. In other words, the favorable trait increases the likelihood of survival and reproduction.
5. The environmental context determines whether or not a trait is beneficial. What is favorable in one setting may be a liability in another. In this way, which traits become most advantageous is the result of a natural process.
6. Traits are inherited and passed on to the next generation. Because individuals who possess favorable traits contribute more offspring to the next generation than others, over time, such characteristics become more common in the population; less favorable ones aren't passed on as frequently, and they become less common, or they are "weeded out." Individuals who produce more offspring, compared to others, are said to have greater **reproductive success.**

reproductive success The number of offspring an individual produces and rears to reproductive age; an individual's genetic contribution to the next generation.

---

* The full title is *On the Origin of Species by Means of Natural Selection, or the Preservation of Favoured Races in the Struggle for Life.*

7. Over long periods of geological time, successful variations accumulate in a population, so that later generations may be distinct from ancestral ones. Thus, in time, a new species may appear.
8. Geographical isolation also contributes to the formation of new species. As populations of a species become geographically isolated from one another, for whatever reasons, they begin to adapt to different environments. Over time, as populations continue to respond to different **selective pressures** (i.e., different ecological circumstances), they may become distinct species. The 13 species of Galápagos finches are presumably all descended from a common ancestor on the South American mainland, and they provide an example of the role of geographical isolation.

Before Darwin, individual members of species weren't considered important, so they weren't studied. But as we've seen, Darwin recognized the uniqueness of individuals and realized that variation among them could explain how selection occurred. Favorable variations were selected for survival by nature; unfavorable ones were eliminated. *Natural selection operates on individuals,* favorably or unfavorably, but *it's the population that evolves.* The unit of natural selection is the individual; the unit of evolution is the population (because individuals don't change, but over time, populations do).

selective pressures Forces in the environment that influence reproductive success in individuals.

Natural Selection in Action

The most frequently cited example of natural selection documents changes in the coloration of "peppered" moths around Manchester, England. In recent years, the moth story has come under some criticism, but since the basic premise remains valid, we use it to illustrate how natural selection works.

Before the nineteenth century, the most common variety of the peppered moth was a mottled gray color. During the day, as moths rested on lichen-covered tree trunks, their coloration provided camouflage (Fig. 2-15). There was also a dark gray variety of the same species, but since the dark moths were uncamouflaged, they fell prey to birds more frequently and consequently they were less common. (In this example, the birds are the *selective agent,* and they apply *selective pressures* on the moths.) Therefore, the dark moths produced fewer offspring than the camouflaged moths. Yet, by the end of the nineteenth century, the common gray form had been almost completely replaced by the darker variety.

(a)

(b)

FIGURE 2-15 Variation in the peppered moth. (a) The dark form is more visible on the light, lichen-covered tree. (b) On trees darkened by pollution, the lighter form is more visible.

Michael Tweedie/Photo Researchers

Breck P. Kent/Animals Animals

The cause of this change was the changing environment of industrialized nineteenth-century England. Coal dust from factories and fireplaces settled on trees, turning them dark gray and killing the lichen. The moths continued to rest on the trees, but the light gray ones became more conspicuous as the trees became darker, and they were increasingly targeted by birds. Since fewer of the light gray moths were living long enough to reproduce, they contributed fewer genes to the next generation than the darker moths, and the proportion of lighter moths decreased while the dark moths became more common. A similar color shift had also occurred in North America. But as clean air acts in both Britain and the United States reduced the amount of air pollution (at least from coal), the predominant color of the peppered moth once again became the light mottled gray. This kind of evolutionary shift in response to environmental change is called *adaptation*.

Another example of natural selection is provided by the medium ground finch of the Galápagos Islands. In 1977, drought killed many of the plants that produced the smaller, softer seeds favored by these birds. This forced a population of finches on one of the islands to feed on larger, harder seeds. Even before 1977, some birds had smaller, less thick beaks than others (i.e., there was variation), and during the drought, because they were less able to process the larger seeds, more smaller-beaked birds died than larger-beaked birds. Therefore, although population size declined, average beak thickness in the survivors and their offspring increased, simply because thicker-beaked individuals were surviving in greater numbers and producing more offspring. In other words, they had greater reproductive success. But during heavy rains in 1982–1983, smaller seeds became more plentiful again and the pattern in beak size reversed itself, demonstrating how reproductive success is related to environmental conditions (Grant, 1975, 1986; Ridley, 1993).

The best illustration of natural selection, however, and certainly one with potentially grave consequences for humans, is the recent increase in resistant strains of disease-causing microorganisms. When antibiotics were first introduced in the 1940s, they were haled as the end of bacterial disease. But that optimistic view didn't take into account the fact that bacteria, like other organisms, possess genetic variability. Consequently, while exposure to an antibiotic will kill most bacteria in an infected person, any bacterium with an inherited resistance to that particular therapy will survive. Subsequently, the survivors reproduce and pass their drug resistance to future generations so that eventually, the population is mostly made up of bacteria that don't respond to treatment. Moreover, because bacteria produce new generations every few hours, antibiotic-resistant strains are continuously being produced. As a result, many types of infection no longer respond to treatment. For example, tuberculosis was once thought to be well controlled, but it's seen a resurgence in recent years because the bacterium that causes it is now resistant to many antibiotics.

These examples provide the following insights into the fundamentals of evolutionary change produced by natural selection:

1. *A trait must be inherited if natural selection is to act on it*. A characteristic that isn't hereditary (such as a temporary change in hair color produced by the hairdresser) won't be passed on to succeeding generations. In finches, for example, beak size is a hereditary trait.

2. *Natural selection can't occur without population variation in inherited characteristics.* If, for example, all the peppered moths had initially been gray (you will recall that some dark forms were always present) and the trees had become darker, the survival and reproduction of all moths could have been so low that the population might have become extinct. *Selection can only work with variation that already exists.*

3. **Fitness** *is a relative measure that changes as the environment changes.* Fitness is simply *differential reproductive success.* In the initial stage, the lighter moths were the more fit because they produced more offspring. But as the environment changed, the dark gray moths became more fit, and a further change reversed the adaptive pattern. Likewise, the majority of medium ground finches have larger or smaller beaks, depending on external conditions. So it should be obvious that statements regarding the "most fit" mean nothing without reference to specific environments.

4. *Natural selection can only act on traits that affect reproduction.* If a characteristic isn't expressed until later in life, after organisms have reproduced, then natural selection can't influence it. This is because the inherited components of the trait have already been passed on to offspring. Many forms of cancer and cardiovascular disease are influenced by hereditary factors, but because these diseases usually affect people after they've had children, natural selection can't act against them. By the same token, if a condition usually kills or compromises the individual before he or she reproduces, natural selection acts against it because the trait won't be passed on.

fitness Pertaining to natural selection, a measure of *relative* reproductive success of individuals. Fitness can be measured by an individual's genetic contribution to the next generation compared to that of other individuals. The terms *genetic fitness, reproductive fitness,* and *differential reproductive success* are also used.

So far, our examples have shown how different death rates influence natural selection (e.g., moths or finches that die early leave fewer offspring). But mortality isn't the entire picture. Another important aspect of natural selection is fertility, since an animal that gives birth to more young passes its genes on at a faster rate than one that bears fewer offspring. However, fertility isn't the whole story either, because the crucial element is the number of young raised successfully to the point at which they themselves reproduce. We call this *differential net reproductive success.* The way this mechanism works can be demonstrated through another example.

In swifts (small birds that resemble swallows), data show that producing more offspring doesn't necessarily guarantee that more young will be successfully raised. The number of eggs hatched in a breeding season is a measure of fertility. The number of birds that mature and are eventually able to leave the nest is a measure of net reproductive success, or offspring successfully raised. The following table shows the correlation between the number of eggs hatched (fertility) and the number of young that leave the nest (reproductive success) averaged over four breeding seasons (Lack, 1966):

Number of eggs hatched (fertility)	**2 eggs**	**3 eggs**	**4 eggs**
Average number of young raised (reproductive success)	1.92	2.54	1.76
Sample size (number of nests)	72	20	16

As you can see, the most efficient number of eggs is three, since that number yields the highest reproductive success. Raising two is less beneficial to the parents, since the end result isn't as successful as with three eggs. Trying to raise more than three is actually detrimental, since the parents may not be able

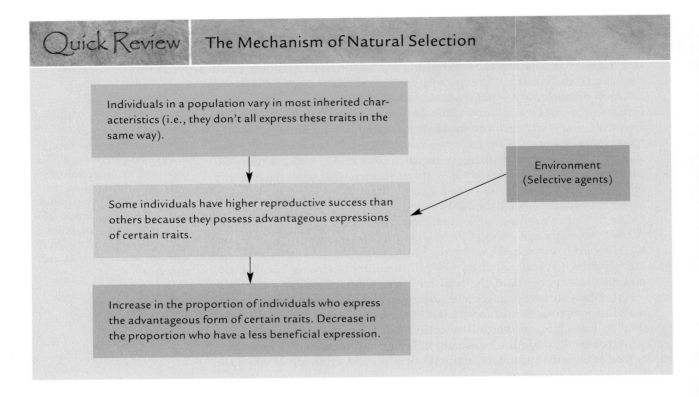

Quick Review — The Mechanism of Natural Selection

Individuals in a population vary in most inherited characteristics (i.e., they don't all express these traits in the same way).

Some individuals have higher reproductive success than others because they possess advantageous expressions of certain traits.

Increase in the proportion of individuals who express the advantageous form of certain traits. Decrease in the proportion who have a less beneficial expression.

Environment (Selective agents)

to provide enough nourishment for any of the offspring. Offspring that die before reaching reproductive age are, in evolutionary terms, equivalent to never being born. Actually, death of young can be a minus to the parents, because before it dies, the offspring drains parental resources. It may even inhibit their ability to raise other offspring, thereby reducing their reproductive success even further. Selection favors those genetic traits that yield the maximum net reproductive success. If the number of eggs laid is a genetic trait in birds (and it seems to be), natural selection in swifts should act to favor the laying of three eggs as opposed to two or four.

Constraints on Nineteenth-Century Evolutionary Theory

Darwin argued for the concept of evolution in general and the role of natural selection in particular, but he didn't entirely comprehend the exact mechanisms of evolutionary change. As we have seen, natural selection acts on variation within species. But neither Darwin nor anyone else in the nineteenth century understood the actual source of variation. Also, no one understood how parents pass traits to offspring. Almost without exception, nineteenth-century scholars believed that inheritance was a *blending* process in which parental characteristics were mixed together to produce intermediate expressions in offspring. Given this notion, we can see why the true nature of genes was unimaginable, and with no alternate explanations, Darwin accepted it. As it turns out, a contemporary of Darwin's had actually worked out the rules of heredity. However, the work of this Augustinian monk named Gregor Mendel (whom you will meet in Chapter 4) wasn't recognized until the beginning of the twentieth century.

The first three decades of the twentieth century saw the merger of Mendel's discoveries and natural selection. This was a crucial development because until then, scientists thought they were unrelated. Then, in 1953, the structure of **deoxyribonucleic acid (DNA)** was discovered. This landmark achievement has been followed by even more amazing advances in the field of genetics, including the sequencing of the human **genome.** We may finally be on the threshold of revealing the remaining secrets of the evolutionary process. If only Darwin could know!

Deoxyribonucleic acid (DNA) The double-stranded molecule that contains the genetic code.

genome The entire genetic makeup of an individual or species.

Opposition to Evolution

Almost 150 years later, the debate over evolution is far from over. For the vast majority of scientists today, evolution is indisputable. The genetic evidence for it is solid and accumulates daily. Anyone who appreciates and understands genetic mechanisms can't avoid the conclusion that populations and species evolve. Moreover, the majority of Christians don't believe that biblical depictions should be taken literally. But at the same time, some surveys show that about half of all Americans don't believe that evolution occurs. There are a number of reasons for this.

The mechanisms of evolution are complex and don't lend themselves to simple explanations. Understanding them requires some familiarity with genetics and biology, a familiarity that most people don't have. Moreover, many people who haven't been exposed to scientific training want definitive and clear-cut answers to complex questions. But as you learned in Chapter 1, scientific research doesn't always provide definitive answers to questions, and it's not capable of establishing absolute truths. Another thing to consider is that regardless of their culture, most people are raised in belief systems that don't emphasize **biological continuity** between species.

The relationship between science and religion has never been easy (remember Galileo). While both serve, in their own ways, to explain phenomena, scientific explanations are based in data analysis, hypothesis testing, and interpretation. Religion, meanwhile, is a system of beliefs based in faith, and it isn't amenable to scientific testing. Religion and science concern different aspects of the human experience; nevertheless, we should remember that although they use different approaches in areas where they overlap, they aren't inherently mutually exclusive. Moreover, not all religions or even all forms of Christianity are opposed to evolutionary theories. Some years ago, the Vatican hosted an international conference on human evolution, and in 1996, Pope John Paul II issued a statement acknowledging that "fresh knowledge leads to recognition of the theory of evolution as more than just a hypothesis." Today, the official position of the Catholic Church is that evolutionary processes do occur but that the human soul is of divine creation and not subject to evolutionary processes. Likewise, mainstream Protestants don't generally see a conflict. Unfortunately, those who believe absolutely in a literal interpretation of the Bible (called fundamentalists) accept no form of compromise.

In 1925, a law banning the teaching of evolution in public schools was passed in Tennessee. To test the validity of the law, the American Civil

biological continuity Refers to a *biological continuum*, the fact that organisms are related through common ancestry and that behaviors and physical traits present in one species are also seen to varying degrees in others. When expressions of a phenomenon continuously grade into one another so that there are no discrete categories, they exist on a continuum. Color is one such phenomenon, and life forms are another.

Liberties Union persuaded a high school teacher named John Scopes to allow himself to be arrested and tried for teaching evolution. The subsequent trial (called the Scopes Monkey Trial) was a 1920s equivalent of current celebrity trials, and in the end, Scopes was convicted and fined $100. In the more than 80 years since the trial, religious fundamentalists have relentlessly tried to remove evolution from public school curricula. Known as creationists because they explain the existence of the universe as a result of a sudden creation, they are determined either to eliminate the teaching of evolution or to introduce antievolutionary material into public school classes. In the past 20 years, creationists have insisted that "creation science" is just as valid a scientific endeavor as is the study of evolution. They argue that in the interest of fairness, a balanced view should be offered: If evolution is taught as science, then creationism should also be taught as science. Sounds fair, doesn't it? But "creation science" isn't science at all for the simple reason that creationists insist that their view is absolute and infallible. Consequently, creationism isn't a hypothesis that can be tested, nor is it amenable to falsification. Since hypothesis testing is the basis of all science, creationism, by its very nature, cannot be considered science. It is religion.

Nevertheless, creationists remain active in state legislatures, promoting laws that mandate the teaching of creationism in public schools. In 1981, the Arkansas state legislature passed one such law that was overturned in 1982. In his ruling against the state, the judge justifiably stated that "a theory that is by its own terms dogmatic, absolutist and never subject to revision is not a scientific theory." And he added: "Since creation is not science, the conclusion is inescapable that the only real effect of [this law] is the advancement of religion." In 1987, the United States Supreme Court struck down a similar law in Louisiana.

So far, these and similar laws have been overturned because they violate the principle of separation of church and state provided in the First Amendment to the Constitution. But this hasn't stopped the creationists, who encourage teachers to claim "academic freedom" to teach creationism. They've also dropped the word *creationism* in favor of less religious sounding terms, such as *intelligent design theory*. Moreover, antievolution feeling remains extremely strong among politicians. In 1999, one very prominent U.S. congressman went so far as to say that the teaching of evolution is one of the factors behind violence in America today! (Now that's a stretch!)

Visual Summary

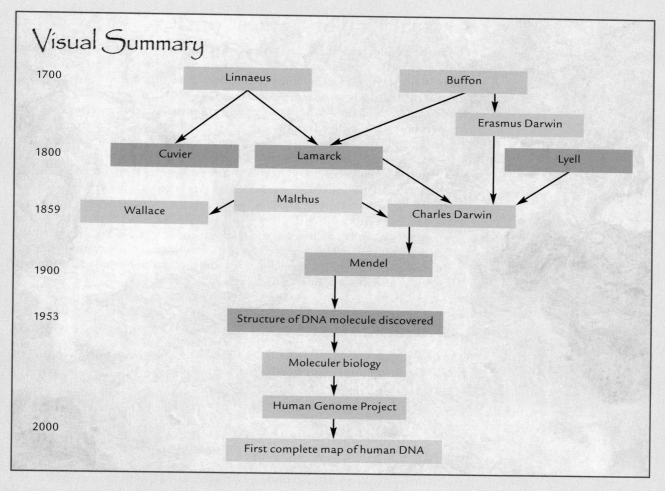

1700	Linnaeus — Buffon
1800	Cuvier — Lamarck — Erasmus Darwin — Lyell
1859	Wallace — Malthus — Charles Darwin
1900	Mendel
1953	Structure of DNA molecule discovered
	Moleculer biology
	Human Genome Project
2000	First complete map of human DNA

Summary

Our current understanding of evolutionary processes is directly traceable to developments in intellectual thought in western Europe over the last 300 years. Many people contributed to this shift in perspective, and we've named only a few. Linnaeus placed humans in the same taxonomic scheme as all other animals. Importantly, Lamarck and Buffon both recognized that species could change in response to environmental circumstances, but Lamarck also attempted to explain *how* the changes occurred. He proposed the idea of *inheritance of acquired characteristics,* which was later discredited. Lyell, in his theory of uniformitarianism, provided the necessary expanse of time for evolution to occur, and Malthus discussed how population size is kept in check by the availability of resources. Darwin and Wallace, influenced by their predecessors, independently recognized that because of competition for resources, individuals with favorable characteristics would tend to survive and pass those traits on to offspring. Those lacking beneficial traits would produce fewer offspring, if they survived to reproductive age at all. That is, they would have lower reproductive success and reduced fitness. Thus, over time, advantageous characteristics accumulate in a population (i.e., they are selected for) while disadvantageous ones are eliminated (selected against). This, in a nutshell, is the theory of evolution by means of natural selection.

Critical Thinking Questions

1. After having read this chapter, how would you respond to the following questions?
   • Why are there monkeys if humans evolved from monkeys?
   • Why don't we ever see the appearance of new species?
2. Do you, personally, object to the idea that humans are closely related to chimpanzees? (By closely related, we mean that the two species are extremely similar genetically and that they share a recent common ancestor.) Explain your answer.
3. What are selective agents? Can you think of some examples we didn't discuss? Why did Darwin look at domesticated species as models for natural selection, and what is the selective agent in artificial selection? List some examples of artificial selection.
4. Given what you've read about the scientific method, how would you explain the differences between science and religion as methods of explaining natural phenomena? Do you personally see a conflict between evolutionary and religious explanations of how species came to be?

Media Resources

The Companion Website for *Essentials of Physical Anthropology*, Sixth Edition
http://anthropology.wadsworth.com/jurmain6e_ess

Supplement your review of this chapter by going to this text's companion website to take one of the practice quizzes, use the flash cards to master key terms, and check out the many other resources and study aids.

CD-ROMs in Physical Anthropology

Wadsworth Publishing has also developed three CD-ROMs to accompany this text and enhance learning in physical anthropology (for further descriptions of these CD-ROMs, see p. xix):

Virtual Laboratories for Physical Anthropology CD-ROM, Third Edition

Basic Genetics for Anthropology CD-ROM: Principles and Applications

Hominid Fossils CD-ROM: An Interactive Atlas

For this chapter, see especially the Basic Genetics for Anthropology CD-ROM: Principles and Applications.

Readings of Interest

Cadbury, D. 2001. *Terrible Lizard: The First Dinosaur Hunters and the Birth of a New Science*. New York: Holt.

Desmond, Adrian, and James Moore. 1991. *Darwin*. New York: Warner Books.

Gould, Stephen Jay. 1987. *Time's Arrow, Time's Cycle*. Cambridge, MA: Harvard University Press.

Grant, P. R. 1991. "Natural Selection in Darwin's finches." *Scientific American* 265(4): 82–87.

Keynes, Randal. 2002. *Darwin, His Daughter, and Human Evolution*. New York: Riverhead Books.

Mayr, Ernst. 2000. "Darwin's Influence on Modern Thought." *Scientific American* 283(1): 78–83.

Scott, Eugenie C. 1997. "Antievolutionism and Creationism in the United States." *Annual Review of Anthropology* 2: 263–289.

3 | The Biological Basis of Life

Introduction

Envision yourself, tired after a rotten day, watching the evening news on TV. The first story, following an endless string of commercials, is about genetically modified foods, a newly cloned species, or the controversy over human cloning. What do you do? Change the channel? Leave the room? Go to sleep? Or do you follow the story? And if you do follow it, do you understand it? Do you think it's important or relevant to you personally? Well, the fact is, you live in an age when genetic discoveries and genetically based technologies are advancing daily, and they will have a profound effect on your life.

At some point, you or someone you love will probably need lifesaving medical treatment, perhaps for cancer, and this treatment will very likely be made possible by genetic research. Like it or not, you already eat genetically modified foods, and, sadly, you may soon see genetically altered bacteria and viruses used to make biological weapons. Fortunately, you will also see many of the secrets of evolution revealed through genetic research. So even if you haven't been particularly interested in genetic issues, you should be aware that they affect your life on a daily basis.

As you already know, this book is about human evolution and adaptation, both of which are intimately linked to life processes that involve cells, the replication and decoding of genetic information, and the transmission of this information between generations. So, to present human evolution and adaptation in the broad sense, we need to examine the fundamental principles of genetics. Genetics is the study of how traits are transmitted from one generation to the next, and even though many physical anthropologists don't actually specialize in this field, it's genetics that ultimately links the various subdisciplines of biological anthropology.

Click ▲

Go to the following CD-ROMs for interactive activities and exercises on topics covered in this chapter:

💿 **Virtual Laboratories for Physical Anthropology CD-ROM, Third Edition**

💿 **Basic Genetics for Anthropology CD-ROM: Principles and Applications**

The Cell

To discuss genetic and evolutionary principles, we need to start with a fundamental understanding of cell function. Cells are the basic units of life in all living organisms. In some forms, such as bacteria, a single cell constitutes the entire organism. However, more complex *multicellular* forms, such as plants, insects, birds, and mammals, are composed of billions of cells. Indeed, an adult human is made up of perhaps as many as 1,000 billion (1,000,000,000,000) cells, all functioning in complex ways that ultimately promote the survival of the individual.

Life on earth began at least 3.7 billion years ago in the form of *prokaryotic* cells. Prokaryotes are single-celled organisms, represented today by bacteria and blue-green algae. More complex *eukaryotic* cells appeared approximately 1.2 billion years ago, and since they're the kind of cell multicellular organisms are made of, the remainder of this discussion focuses on them. In spite of the

FIGURE 3-1 Structure of a generalized eukaryotic cell, illustrating the cell's three-dimensional nature. Although various organelles are shown, for the sake of simplicity only those we discuss are labeled.

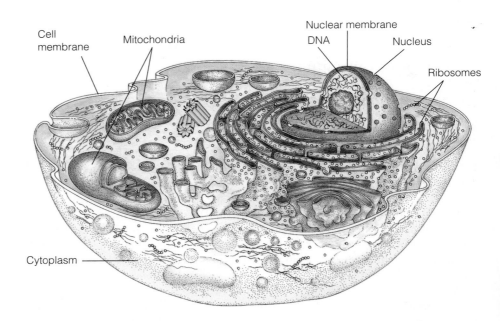

organelles Structures contained within cells, surrounded by a membrane. There are many different types, and each performs specific functions.

nucleus A structure (organelle) found in all eukaryotic cells. The nucleus contains chromosomes (nuclear DNA).

molecules Structures made up of two or more atoms. Molecules can combine with other molecules to form more complex structures.

deoxyribonucleic acid (DNA) The double-stranded molecule that contains the genetic code. DNA is a main component of chromosomes.

ribonucleic acid (RNA) A molecule that is similar in structure to DNA. There are several kinds of RNA, and many are single-stranded. Three forms of single-stranded RNA are essential to protein synthesis. They are messenger RNA (mRNA), transfer RNA (tRNA), and ribosomal RNA (rRNA).

cytoplasm The portion of the cell contained within the cell membrane, excluding the nucleus. The cytoplasm consists of a semifluid material and contains numerous structures involved with cell function.

proteins Three-dimensional molecules that serve a wide variety of functions through their ability to bind to other molecules.

differences between various life forms, the cells of all living organisms share many similarities as a result of their common evolutionary past.

In general, a eukaryotic cell is a three-dimensional structure composed of *carbohydrates, lipids (fats), nucleic acids,* and *proteins.* It contains a variety of structures called **organelles** within the *cell membrane* (Fig. 3-1). One of these organelles is the **nucleus** (*pl.,* nuclei), a discrete unit surrounded by a thin membrane (the nuclear membrane). Within it there are two nucleic acids that contain the genetic information that controls the cell's functions. These two critically important **molecules** are deoxyribonucleic acid (DNA) and **ribonucleic acid (RNA).** (In prokaryotic cells, genetic information isn't contained within an enclosed nucleus.) The nucleus is surrounded by a gel-like substance called the **cytoplasm,** which contains numerous other types of organelles involved in various activities, such as metabolism, eliminating waste, and manufacturing **proteins (protein synthesis).**

Two of these organelles, **mitochondria** and **ribosomes,** require further mention. The mitochondria (*sing.,* mitochondrion) are responsible for producing energy in the cell and they can loosely be thought of as the cell's "engines." Mitochondria are oval structures enclosed within a folded membrane, and they contain their own distinct DNA, called **mitochondrial DNA (mtDNA),** which directs mitochondrial activities. Mitochondrial DNA has the same molecular structure and function as nuclear DNA (i.e., DNA found in the nucleus), but it's organized somewhat differently. In recent years, mtDNA has attracted a lot of attention because of particular traits that it influences and because it has significance for studies of certain evolutionary processes. For these reasons, mitochondrial inheritance will be discussed in more detail in Chapters 4 and 11. Ribosomes are roughly spherical in shape and are the most common type of cytoplasmic organelle. They are made up partly of RNA and are essential to the synthesis of proteins (see p. 49).

There are basically two types of cells: **somatic cells** and **gametes.** Somatic cells are the cellular components of tissues, such as muscle, bone, skin, nerve, heart, and brain. Gametes, or sex cells, are specifically involved in reproduction and aren't important as structural components of the body. In animals, there are two types of gametes: egg cells, produced in female ovaries, and *sperm* cells, which develop in male testes. The sole function of a sex cell is to unite with a gamete from another individual to form a **zygote,** which has the potential of developing into a new individual. In this way, gametes transmit genetic information from parent to offspring.

DNA Structure

Because it directs all cellular functions, DNA is the very basis of life. The exact physical and chemical properties of DNA were unknown until 1953 when, in Cambridge, England, an American researcher named James Watson and three British scientists, Francis Crick, Maurice Wilkins, and Rosalind Franklin, developed a structural and functional model (Fig. 3-2) of DNA (Watson and Crick, 1953a, 1953b). It would be difficult to overstate the importance of their achievement because it completely revolutionized the fields of biology and medicine and forever altered our understanding of biological and evolutionary mechanisms.

The DNA molecule is composed of two chains of even smaller molecules called **nucleotides.** A nucleotide, in turn, is made up of three components: a sugar molecule (deoxyribose), a phosphate unit, and one of four nitrogenous bases (Fig. 3-3). In DNA, nucleotides are stacked on top of one another to form a chain that is bonded along its bases to another nucleotide chain. Together the two twist to form a spiral, or helical, shape. The resulting DNA molecule, then, is two-stranded and is described as forming a *double helix* that resembles a twisted ladder. If we follow the twisted ladder analogy, the sugars and phosphates represent the two sides, while the bases and the bonds between them form the rungs.

protein synthesis The assembly of chains of amino acids into functional protein molecules. DNA directs the process.

mitochondria (*sing.*, mitochondrion) Structures contained within the cytoplasm of eukaryotic cells that convert energy, derived from nutrients, into a form that is used by the cell.

ribosomes Structures composed of a form of RNA called ribosomal RNA (rRNA) and protein. Ribosomes are found in the cell's cytoplasm and are essential to the manufacture of proteins.

mitochondrial DNA (**mtDNA**) DNA found in the mitochondria. Mitochondrial DNA is inherited only from the mother.

somatic cells Basically, all the cells in the body except those involved with reproduction.

gametes Reproductive cells (eggs and sperm in animals) developed from precursor cells in ovaries and testes.

zygote A cell formed by the union of an egg and a sperm cell. It contains the full complement of chromosomes (in humans, 46) and has the potential of developing into an entire organism.

nucleotides Basic units of the DNA molecule, composed of a sugar, a phosphate, and one of four DNA bases.

A. Barrington Brown / Photo Researchers, Inc.

FIGURE 3-2 James Watson (left) and Francis Crick in 1953 with their model of the structure of the DNA molecule.

FIGURE 3-3 Part of a DNA molecule. The illustration shows the two DNA strands with the sugar and phosphate backbone and the bases extending toward the center.

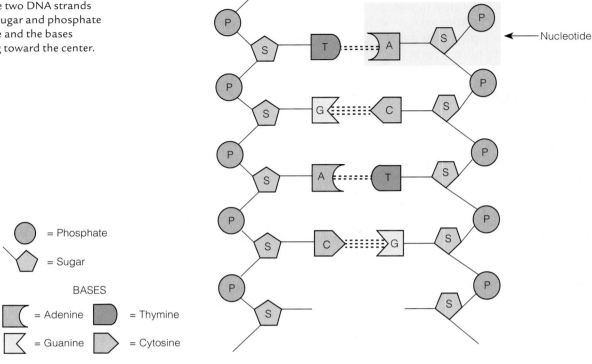

The secret of how DNA functions lies within the four bases. These bases are *adenine, guanine, thymine,* and *cytosine,* and they're usually referred to by their initial letters, A, G, T, and C. In the formation of the double helix, it's possible for one type of base to pair, or bond, with only one other type. Base pairs can form *only* between adenine and thymine and between guanine and cytosine (see Fig. 3-3). This specificity is essential to the DNA molecule's ability to **replicate,** or make an exact copy of itself.

replicate To duplicate. The DNA molecule is able to make copies of itself.

DNA Replication

Cells multiply by dividing, which in turn makes it possible for organisms to reproduce as well as to grow and repair tissues. In the simpler type of cell division, cells divide in a way that ensures that each new cell receives a full set of genetic material. This is important because a cell can't function properly without the correct amount of DNA, but for this to happen, the DNA must first replicate.

enzymes Specialized proteins that initiate and direct chemical reactions in the body.

Before a cell divides, **enzymes** break the bonds between bases at many locations in the DNA molecule. This leaves the two previously joined strands of nucleotides with their bases exposed (Fig. 3-4). These bases then attract unattached DNA nucleotides, which are present in the cell nucleus. Because a base can only pair with one other (e.g., A with T), the attraction between them occurs in a **complementary** fashion. Thus, the two previously joined parental nucleotide chains serve as models for the formation of new strands of nucleotides. As each new strand is formed, its bases are joined to the bases of an original strand. When the process is completed, there are two double-

complementary Referring to the fact that DNA bases form base pairs in a precise manner. For example, adenine can bond only to thymine. These two bases are said to be *complementary* because one requires the other to form a complete DNA base pair.

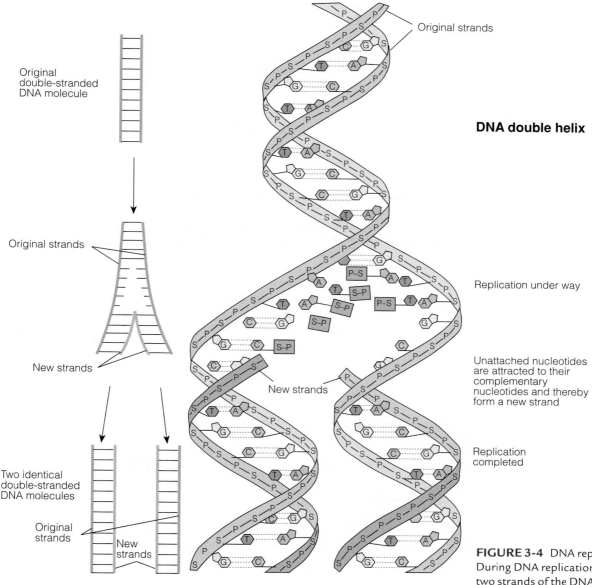

DNA double helix

Original strands

Replication under way

Unattached nucleotides
are attracted to their
complementary
nucleotides and thereby
form a new strand

Replication
completed

Original
double-stranded
DNA molecule

Original strands

New strands

New strands

Two identical
double-stranded
DNA molecules

Original
strands

New
strands

FIGURE 3-4 DNA replication.
During DNA replication, the
two strands of the DNA molecule are separated, and each
strand serves as a template for
the formation of a new strand.
When replication is complete,
there are two DNA molecules.
Each molecule consists of one
new and one original DNA
strand.

stranded DNA molecules exactly like the original one, and each newly formed
molecule consists of one original nucleotide chain joined to a newly formed
chain (see Fig. 3-4).

Protein Synthesis

One of the most important activities of DNA is to direct protein synthesis
within the cell. Proteins are complex, three-dimensional molecules that function through their ability to bind to other molecules. For example, the protein
hemoglobin, found in red blood cells, binds to oxygen and carries it to cells
throughout the body.

hemoglobin A protein molecule that occurs in red blood
cells and binds to oxygen
molecules.

Proteins function in countless ways. Some bind directly to DNA to regulate gene activity. Others, like collagen, are structural components of tissues. Collagen, is the most common protein in the body, and is a major component of all connective tissues. Enzymes are also proteins, and they regulate chemical reactions. For instance, a digestive enzyme called lactase breaks down milk sugar (lactose) into two simpler sugars. Another class of proteins includes many types of **hormones.** Specialized cells produce and release hormones into the bloodstream to circulate to other areas of the body, where they produce various effects in tissues and organs. Insulin is a hormone that's produced by cells in the pancreas and it causes liver cells to absorb energy-producing glucose (sugar) from the blood. (Hormones will be discussed in more detail in Chapter 13.)

As you can see, proteins make us what we are. They are major components of all tissues, and they direct and perform physiological and cellular functions. Therefore, protein synthesis has to occur accurately, because if it doesn't, physiological development and cellular activities can be disrupted or even prevented.

Proteins are composed of chains of smaller molecules called **amino acids.** In all, there are 20 amino acids, 8 of which must be obtained from foods (see Chapter 13). The remaining 12 are produced in cells. These 20 amino acids are combined in different amounts and sequences to produce at least 90,000 different proteins. What makes proteins different from one another is the number and sequence of their amino acids.

In part, DNA is a recipe for making a protein, since it's the sequence of DNA bases that ultimately determines the order of amino acids in a protein molecule. In the DNA instructions, a *triplet,* or group of three bases, specifies a particular amino acid. For example, if a triplet consists of the base sequence

hormones Substances (usually proteins) that are produced by specialized cells and that travel to other parts of the body, where they influence chemical reactions and regulate various cellular functions.

amino acids Small molecules that are the components of proteins.

TABLE 3-1 | The Genetic Code

Amino Acid Symbol	Amino Acid	mRNA Codon	DNA Triplet
Ala	Alanine	GCU, GCC, GCA, GCG	CGA, CGG, CGT, CGC
Arg	Arginine	CGU, CGC, CGA, CGG, AGA, AGG	GCA, GCG, GCT, GCC, TCT, TCC
Asn	Asparagine	AAU, AAC	TTA, TTG
Asp	Aspartic acid	GAU, GAC	CTA, CTG
Cys	Cysteine	UGU, UGC	ACA, ACG
Gln	Glutamine	CAA, CAG	GTT, GTC
Glu	Glutamic acid	GAA, GAG	CTT, CTC
Gly	Glycine	GGU, GGC, GGA, GGG	CCA, CCG, CCT, CCC
His	Histidine	CAU, CAC	GTA, GTG
Ile	Isoleucine	AUU, AUC, AUA	TAA, TAG, TAT
Leu	Leucine	UUA, UUG, CUU, CUC, CUA, CUG	AAT, AAC, GAA, GAG, GAT, GAC
Lys	Lysine	AAA, AAG	TTT, TTC
Met	Methionine	AUG	TAC
Phe	Phenylalanine	UUU, UUC	AAA, AAG
Pro	Proline	CCU, CCC, CCA, CCG	GGA, GGG, GGT, GGC
Ser	Serine	UCU, UCC, UCA, UCG, AGU, AGC	AGA, AGG, AGT, AGC, TCA, TCG
Thr	Threonine	ACU, ACC, ACA, ACG	TGA, TGG, TGT, TGC
Trp	Tryptophan	UGG	ACC
Tyr	Tyrosine	UAU, UAC	ATA, ATG
Val	Valine	GUU, GUC, GUA, GUG	CAA, CAG, CAT, CAC
Terminating triplets		UAA, UAG, UGA	ATT, ATC, ACT

CGA, it specifies the amino acid *alanine* (see Table 3-1). Therefore, a DNA recipe might look like this (except there would be no spaces between the triplets as shown here): AGA CGA ACA ACC TAC TTT TTC CTT AAG GTC, and so on.

Protein synthesis actually takes place outside the nucleus at structures in the cytoplasm called *ribosomes* (see p. 44). But the DNA molecule can't leave the cell's nucleus. So the first step in protein synthesis is to copy the DNA message into a form of RNA called **messenger RNA (mRNA),** which can pass through the nuclear membrane into the cytoplasm. RNA is a molecule similar to DNA, but it differs in three important ways:

1. It's usually single-stranded. (This is true of the forms we discuss, but it's not true for all.)
2. It contains a different type of sugar.
3. It contains the base uracil as a substitute for the DNA base thymine. (Uracil is attracted to adenine, just as thymine is.)

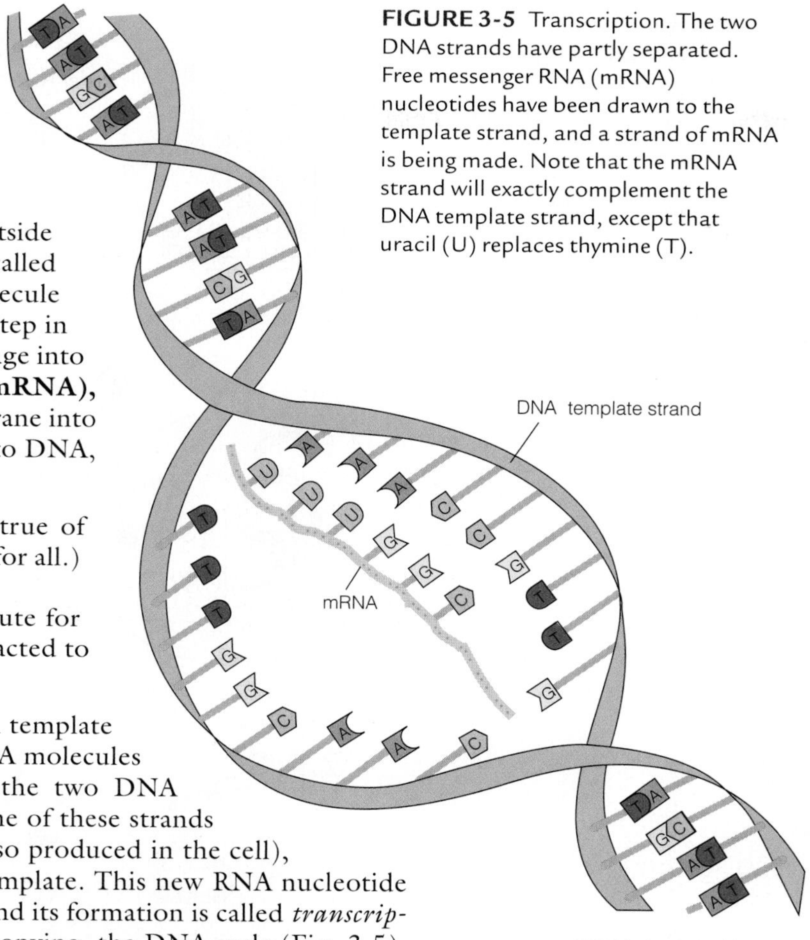

The RNA molecule forms on the DNA template in pretty much the same way that new DNA molecules are assembled. As in DNA replication, the two DNA strands separate, but only partially, and one of these strands attracts free-floating RNA nucleotides (also produced in the cell), which are joined together on the DNA template. This new RNA nucleotide chain is called messenger RNA (mRNA), and its formation is called *transcription* because, in fact, it's transcribing, or copying, the DNA code (Fig. 3-5). Once the appropriate segment has been copied, the mRNA strand peels away from the DNA model, and a portion of it travels through the nuclear membrane to a ribosome. Meanwhile, the bonds between the DNA bases rejoin, and the DNA molecule is once more intact.

As the mRNA strand arrives at the ribosome, the message it contains is translated. (This stage is called *translation* because at this point, the genetic instructions are actually being decoded and implemented.) Just as each DNA triplet specifies one amino acid, so do mRNA triplets, called **codons.** Therefore, the mRNA strand is "read" in codons, or groups of three bases taken together (see Table 3-1).

A third kind of RNA, **transfer RNA (tRNA),** is essential to the actual assembly of a protein. Each tRNA molecule can bind to one specific amino acid, and during protein synthesis, a tRNA molecule takes an amino acid that matches the codon being translated to the ribosome (Fig. 3-6). The ribosome then joins that amino acid to another one in the order dictated by the sequence of mRNA codons. In this way, amino acids are linked together to form a structure that will eventually be a protein or part of a protein. Importantly, if a DNA base, or the sequence of bases, is changed through **mutation,** the manufacture of some proteins may not occur. In this case, cells won't function properly, if at all.

FIGURE 3-5 Transcription. The two DNA strands have partly separated. Free messenger RNA (mRNA) nucleotides have been drawn to the template strand, and a strand of mRNA is being made. Note that the mRNA strand will exactly complement the DNA template strand, except that uracil (U) replaces thymine (T).

DNA template strand

mRNA

messenger RNA (mRNA) A form of RNA that is assembled on a sequence of DNA bases. It carries the DNA code to the ribosome during protein synthesis.

codons Triplets of messenger RNA bases that code for specific amino acids during protein synthesis.

transfer RNA (tRNA) The type of RNA that binds to specific amino acids and transports them to the ribosome during protein synthesis.

mutation A change in DNA; can refer to changes in DNA bases (specifically called *point mutations*) and also to changes in chromosome number or structure.

FIGURE 3-6 Assembly of an amino acid chain in protein synthesis.

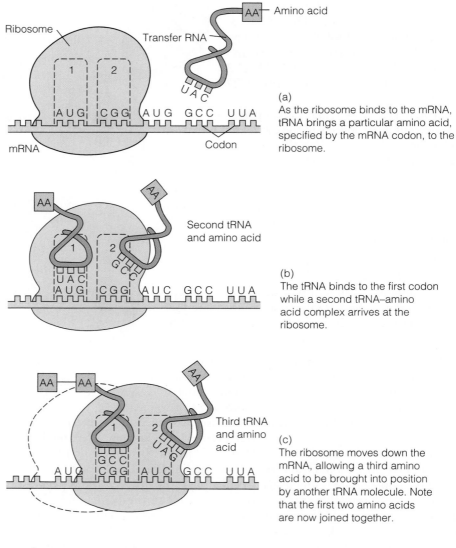

(a)
As the ribosome binds to the mRNA, tRNA brings a particular amino acid, specified by the mRNA codon, to the ribosome.

(b)
The tRNA binds to the first codon while a second tRNA–amino acid complex arrives at the ribosome.

(c)
The ribosome moves down the mRNA, allowing a third amino acid to be brought into position by another tRNA molecule. Note that the first two amino acids are now joined together.

What Is a Gene?

gene A sequence of DNA bases that specifies the order of amino acids in an entire protein, a portion of a protein, or any functional product. A gene may be made up of hundreds or thousands of DNA bases organized into coding and noncoding segments. (Coding sequences produce proteins; noncoding sequences don't.)

For decades, biologists have defined a **gene** as the entire series of DNA bases responsible for the synthesis of a protein or, in some cases, part of a protein. Or, put another way, a gene is a segment of DNA that specifies the sequence of amino acids in a particular protein. This definition, based on the concept of a one gene-one protein relationship, has been a core principle in biology for almost 50 years but it's been qualified partly in recognition of the fact that DNA also codes for RNA and DNA nucleotides. We also now know that some forms of RNA can also influence DNA function. Therefore, one new and more inclusive definition simply states that a gene is "a complete DNA segment responsible for making a functional product" (Snyder and Gerstein, 2003).

It's important to understand that gene action is incredibly complex and still only partly understood. For example, the DNA segments that are ultimately translated into specific amino acids are called *exons*. But most of the DNA in a gene isn't expressed during protein synthesis! In fact, some sequences, called *introns*, are initially transcribed (i.e., mRNA copies are manufactured) but subsequently deleted (Figure 3-7). But even though introns aren't instrumental in protein synthesis, they are part of the DNA molecule and many have other functions. So, it's the combination of introns and exons, interspersed along a strand of DNA, that makes up the unit we call a gene.

REGULATORY GENES

Some genes act solely to control the expression of other genes. Basically, these *regulatory genes* make products that switch other DNA segments on and off. Consequently, their functions are critical to individual organisms, and they play an important role in evolution.

All somatic cells contain the same genetic information, but in any given cell, only a fraction of the DNA contained within exons is actually involved in protein synthesis. For example, bone and stomach cells both have genes that code for the production of digestive enzymes. But bone cells don't produce digestive enzymes. Instead, they make collagen, the major organic component of bone. This is because cells become specialized during embryonic development to

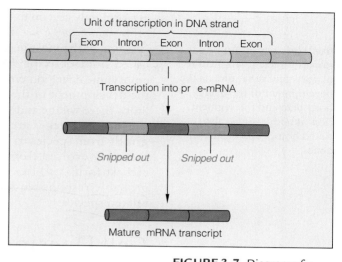

FIGURE 3-7 Diagram of a DNA sequence being transcribed. The introns are deleted from the pre-mRNA before it leaves the cell nucleus. The remaining mature mRNA contains only exons.

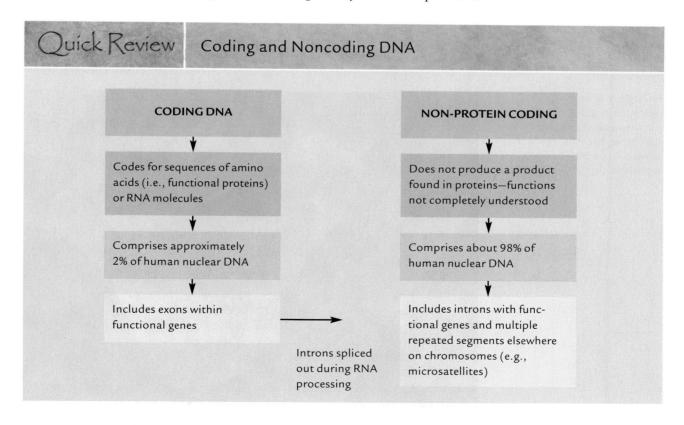

Quick Review — Coding and Noncoding DNA

CODING DNA	NON-PROTEIN CODING
Codes for sequences of amino acids (i.e., functional proteins) or RNA molecules	Does not produce a product found in proteins—functions not completely understood
Comprises approximately 2% of human nuclear DNA	Comprises about 98% of human nuclear DNA
Includes exons within functional genes	Includes introns with functional genes and multiple repeated segments elsewhere on chromosomes (e.g., microsatellites)

Introns spliced out during RNA processing

perform only certain functions, and most of their DNA is permanently switched off by *regulatory genes.* In other words, they become specific types of cells.

Some of the most important regulatory genes are the **homeotic genes** (also called homeobox or *Hox* genes.) These genes are expressed only during embryonic development, and they interact with other genes and cells to direct the development of the body plan (i.e., front to back, head to tail; how many limbs there will be and where they will develop; how many vertebrae; etc.)

Homeotic genes are present in all insects and vertebrates and don't vary greatly from species to species. This means that they're vitally important and that they evolved from genes that ultimately were present in some of the earliest forms of life. Also, changes in the behavior of homeotic genes are probably responsible for some of the physical differences between closely related species.

Cell Division: Mitosis and Meiosis

Throughout much of a cell's life, its DNA exists as an uncoiled, threadlike substance. (Incredibly, there are about 6 feet of DNA in the nucleus of every one of your somatic cells!) But at various times in the life of most cells, normal functions are interrupted and the cell divides. During cell division, which produces new cells, the DNA becomes tightly coiled and is visible under a microscope as a set of structures called **chromosomes** (Fig. 3-8). A chromosome is composed of a DNA molecule and proteins (Fig. 3-9). During normal cell function, if chromosomes were visible, they would be single-stranded. However, during the early stages of cell division, they have two strands, or two DNA molecules joined together at a constricted area called the **centromere.** The reason there are two strands is simple: The DNA molecules have *replicated,* and one strand is an exact copy of the other.

homeotic genes An evolutionarily ancient family of regulatory genes that directs the development of the overall body plan and the segmentation of body tissues; also called homeobox or *Hox* genes.

chromosomes Discrete structures composed of DNA and protein found only in the nuclei of cells. Chromosomes are only visible under magnification during certain phases of cell division.

centromere The constricted portion of a chromosome. After replication, the two strands of a double-stranded chromosome are joined at the centromere.

FIGURE 3-8 Scanning electron micrograph of human chromosomes during cell division. Note that these chromosomes are composed of two strands, or two DNA molecules.

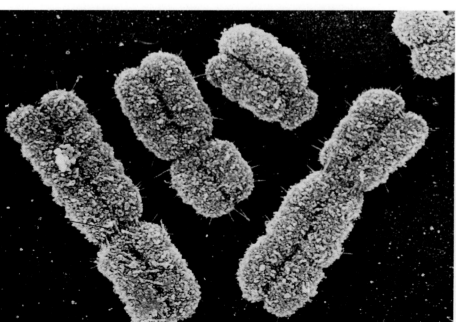

Centromere

© Biophoto Associates/Science Source/Photo Researchers

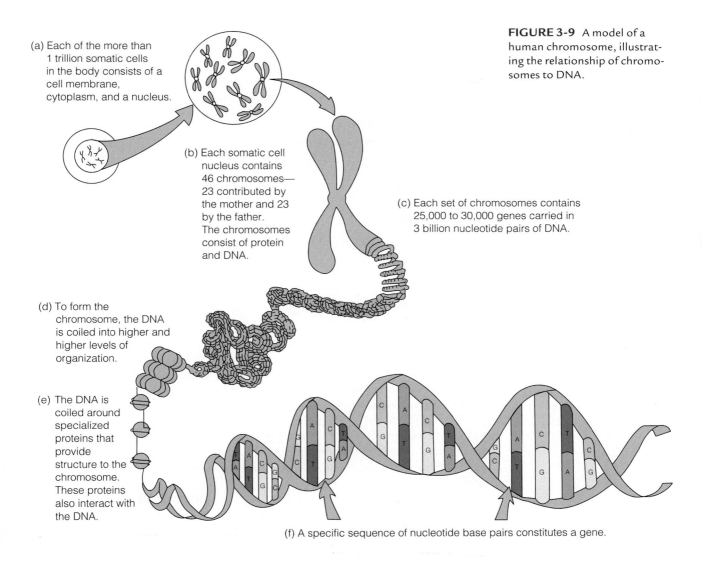

(a) Each of the more than 1 trillion somatic cells in the body consists of a cell membrane, cytoplasm, and a nucleus.

(b) Each somatic cell nucleus contains 46 chromosomes—23 contributed by the mother and 23 by the father. The chromosomes consist of protein and DNA.

(c) Each set of chromosomes contains 25,000 to 30,000 genes carried in 3 billion nucleotide pairs of DNA.

(d) To form the chromosome, the DNA is coiled into higher and higher levels of organization.

(e) The DNA is coiled around specialized proteins that provide structure to the chromosome. These proteins also interact with the DNA.

FIGURE 3-9 A model of a human chromosome, illustrating the relationship of chromosomes to DNA.

(f) A specific sequence of nucleotide base pairs constitutes a gene.

Every species has a specific number of chromosomes (Table 3-2). In humans, there are 46. Chimpanzees and gorillas have 48. This difference doesn't mean that humans have less DNA than chimpanzees and gorillas. The DNA is simply packaged differently in the three species.

Chromosomes occur in pairs, so human somatic cells contain 23 pairs. One member of each pair is inherited from the father (paternal), while the other member is inherited from the mother (maternal). Members of chromosomal pairs are said to be **homologous** because they are alike in size and position of the centromere and they carry genetic information that governs the same *traits*. This doesn't mean that homologous chromosomes are genetically identical; they simply influence the same characteristics.

There are two basic types of chromosomes: **autosomes** and **sex chromosomes.** Autosomes carry genetic information that governs all physical characteristics except primary sex determination. The two sex chromosomes are the X and Y chromosomes. In mammals, the Y chromosome is directly involved with determining maleness. Although the X chromosome is called a "sex

homologous Referring to members of chromosome pairs. Homologous chromosomes carry genes that govern the same traits, and they are alike with regard to size and position of the centromere. During meiosis, homologous chromosomes pair and exchange segments of DNA.

autosomes All chromosomes except the sex chromosomes.

sex chromosomes In mammals, the X and Y chromosomes.

TABLE 3-2	Standard Chromosomal Complement in Various Organisms		
Organism	Chromosome Number in Somatic Cells	Chromosome Number in Gametes
Human (*Homo sapiens*)	46	23
Chimpanzee (*Pan troglodytes*)	48	24
Gorilla (*Gorilla gorilla*)	48	24
Dog (*Canis familiaris*)	78	39
Chicken (*Gallus domesticus*)	78	39
Frog (*Rana pipiens*)	26	13
Housefly (*Musca domestica*)	12	6
Onion (*Allium cepa*)	16	8
Corn (*Zea mays*)	20	10
Tobacco (*Nicotiana tabacum*)	48	24

Source: Cummings, 1991, p. 16.

chromosome," it acts more like an autosome because it isn't really involved in primary sex determination. But it does influence a number of other traits.

Among mammals, all genetically normal females have two X chromosomes (XX), and they're female only because there is no Y chromosome. (In other words, female is the default setting.) All genetically normal males have one X and one Y chromosome (XY). In other classes of animals, such as birds or insects, primary sex determination is governed by other chromosomal mechanisms.

It's important to remember that *all* autosomes occur in pairs. Normal human somatic cells have 22 pairs of autosomes and one pair of sex chromosomes. Abnormal numbers of autosomes, with few exceptions, are fatal, usually soon after conception. Although abnormal numbers of sex chromosomes aren't usually fatal, they may cause sterility and frequently they also have other consequences. Therefore, to function normally, human cells must contain both members of each chromosomal pair, or a total of 46 chromosomes.

MITOSIS

mitosis Simple cell division; the process by which somatic cells divide to produce two identical daughter cells.

Cell division in somatic cells is called **mitosis,** and it's the way these cells reproduce. Mitosis occurs during growth and development, and it also repairs injured tissues and replaces older cells with newer ones.

In the early stages of mitosis, a human somatic cell has 46 double-stranded chromosomes. As the cell begins to divide, its chromosomes line up along its center and split apart at their centromeres so that the strands separate (Fig. 3-10). The strands pull away from each other and move to opposite ends of the dividing cell and, at this point, each one is a distinct chromosome, composed of one DNA molecule. The cell membrane then pinches in and seals, so that two new cells are formed, each with a full complement of DNA, or 46 chromosomes.

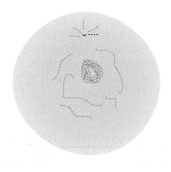

(a) The cell is involved in metabolic activities. DNA replication occurs, but chromosomes are not visible.

(b) The nuclear membrane disappears, and double-stranded chromosomes are visible.

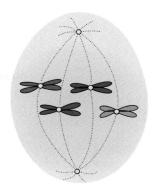

(c) The chromosomes align themselves at the center of the cell.

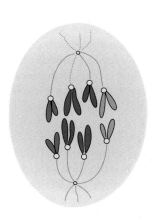

(d) The chromosomes split at the centromere, and the strands separate and move to opposite ends of the dividing cell.

(e) The cell membrane pinches in as the cell continues to divide. The chromosomes begin to uncoil (not shown here).

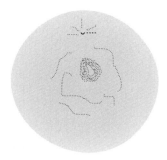

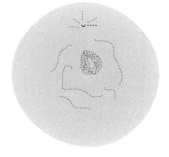

(f) After mitosis is complete, there are two identical daughter cells. The nuclear membrane is present, and chromosomes are no longer visible.

FIGURE 3-10 Mitosis.

Mitosis is referred to as "simple cell division" because a somatic cell divides one time to produce two daughter cells that are genetically identical to each other and to the original cell. In mitosis, the original cell contains 46 chromosomes, and each new daughter cell inherits an exact copy of each one. This is possible because of the DNA molecule's ability to replicate. Therefore, replication ensures that the amount of genetic material remains constant from one generation of cells to the next.

We should mention that not all somatic cells undergo mitosis. Red blood cells are continuously produced by bone marrow cells, but they can't divide and they don't have DNA. Also, once the brain and nervous system are fully developed, brain and nerve cells (neurons) don't typically divide, although there's some debate about this. Liver cells also don't divide after growth has stopped unless this vital organ is damaged through injury or disease. However, with these three exceptions (red blood cells, mature neurons, and liver cells), somatic cells are regularly duplicated through the process of mitosis.

MEIOSIS

meiosis Cell division in specialized cells in ovaries and testes. Meiosis involves two divisions and results in four daughter cells, each containing only half the original number of chromosomes. These cells can develop into gametes.

While mitosis produces new cells, **meiosis** can lead to the development of an entire new organism, since it produces reproductive cells, or gametes. Although meiosis is similar to mitosis, it's a more complicated process. In meiosis, there are two divisions instead of one. Also, meiosis produces four daughter cells, not two, and each of these contains only half the original number of chromosomes.

During meiosis, cells in male testes and female ovaries divide and eventually develop into sperm and egg cells. Initially, these cells contain the full complement of chromosomes. But during meiosis, the number of chromosomes is cut in half (to 23 in humans). This reduction is crucial because a resulting gamete may unite with another gamete that also carries 23 chromosomes. The product of this union (fertilization) is called a zygote, and it has the original number of chromosomes (46). In other words, the zygote inherits the full amount of DNA it needs (half from each parent) to develop and function normally. If it weren't for *reduction division* (the first division) in meiosis, it wouldn't be possible to maintain the correct number of chromosomes from one generation to the next.

During the first division, partner chromosomes come together to form pairs of double-stranded chromosomes that line up along the cell's center (Fig. 3-11). Pairing of homologous chromosomes is extremely important, because while they're together, members of pairs exchange genetic information in a process called **recombination,** or crossing over. Pairing is also important because it ensures that each new daughter cell receives only one member of each pair.

recombination The exchange of genetic material between homologous chromosomes during meiosis.

As the cell begins to divide, the chromosomes themselves remain intact (i.e., double-stranded), but *members of pairs* pull apart and move to opposite ends of the cell. After the first division, there are two new daughter cells. But they aren't identical to each other or to the parent cell because they contain only one member of each chromosome pair, each of which still has two strands (Figures 3-11 and 3-12). Moreover, because of recombination, each chromosome now contains combinations of genes it didn't have before.

The second division happens pretty much the same way as in mitosis. In the two newly formed cells, the 23 double-stranded chromosomes align themselves at the cell's center, and as in mitosis, the strands of each chromosome separate and move apart. Once this second division is completed, there are four daughter cells, each with 23 single-stranded chromosomes, or 23 DNA molecules.

The Evolutionary Significance of Meiosis Meiosis occurs in all sexually reproducing organisms, and because it increases genetic variation, it's an extremely important evolutionary innovation. As a result of meiosis, members of sexually reproducing species aren't genetically identical clones of other individuals since they inherit a combination of genes from two parents. The genetic

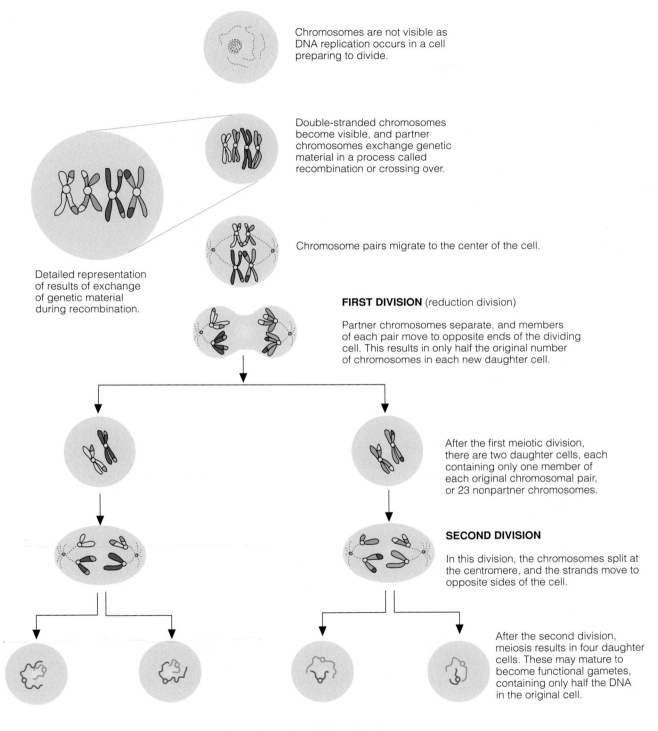

Chromosomes are not visible as DNA replication occurs in a cell preparing to divide.

Double-stranded chromosomes become visible, and partner chromosomes exchange genetic material in a process called recombination or crossing over.

Detailed representation of results of exchange of genetic material during recombination.

Chromosome pairs migrate to the center of the cell.

FIRST DIVISION (reduction division)

Partner chromosomes separate, and members of each pair move to opposite ends of the dividing cell. This results in only half the original number of chromosomes in each new daughter cell.

After the first meiotic division, there are two daughter cells, each containing only one member of each original chromosomal pair, or 23 nonpartner chromosomes.

SECOND DIVISION

In this division, the chromosomes split at the centromere, and the strands move to opposite sides of the cell.

After the second division, meiosis results in four daughter cells. These may mature to become functional gametes, containing only half the DNA in the original cell.

FIGURE 3-11 Meiosis.

uniqueness of each individual is also enhanced by recombination between homologous chromosomes. Furthermore, recombination produces new *arrangements* of genetic information, and these rearrangements potentially provide additional material for natural selection. As you've already learned,

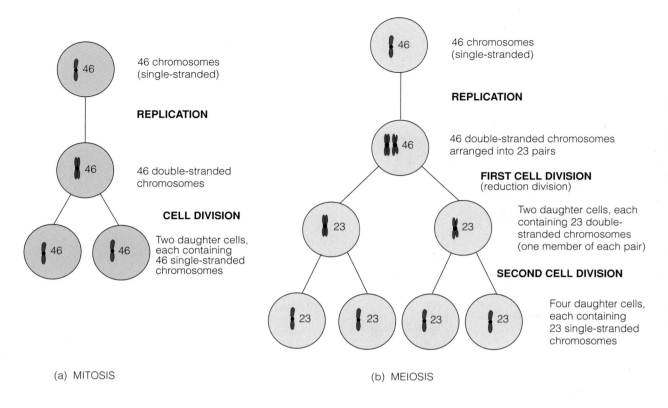

(a) MITOSIS

46 chromosomes
(single-stranded)

REPLICATION

46 double-stranded
chromosomes

CELL DIVISION

Two daughter cells,
each containing
46 single-stranded
chromosomes

(b) MEIOSIS

46 chromosomes
(single-stranded)

REPLICATION

46 double-stranded chromosomes
arranged into 23 pairs

FIRST CELL DIVISION
(reduction division)

Two daughter cells, each
containing 23 double-
stranded chromosomes
(one member of each pair)

SECOND CELL DIVISION

Four daughter cells,
each containing
23 single-stranded
chromosomes

FIGURE 3-12 Mitosis and meiosis compared. In mitosis, one division produces two daughter cells, each of which contains 46 chromosomes. Meiosis is characterized by two divisions. After the first, there are two cells, each containing only 23 chromosomes (one member of each original chromosome pair). Each daughter cell divides again, so that the final result is four cells, each with only half the original number of chromosomes.

nondisjunction The failure of homologous chromosomes or chromosome strands to separate during cell division.

polymerase chain reaction (PCR) A method of producing millions of copies of a DNA segment using the enzyme DNA polymerase.

genetic variation is essential if species are to adapt to changing selective pressures. So, you can see that meiosis is important to the evolutionary process because it increases variation in populations.

Problems with Meiosis For meiosis to provide an opportunity for normal fetal development, the process needs to be exact. The two divisions must produce a viable gamete with only one member of each chromosome pair. If chromosomes or chromosome strands don't separate during either division, serious problems can develop. This failure to separate is called **nondisjunction**. The result of nondisjunction is that one of the daughter cells receives two copies of the affected chromosome, while the other daughter cell receives none. If such an affected gamete unites with a normal gamete containing 23 chromosomes, the resulting zygote will have either 45 or 47 chromosomes.

You can appreciate the potential effects of an abnormal number of chromosomes if you remember that the zygote reproduces itself through mitosis. Consequently, every cell in the developing body will also have the abnormal chromosome number. Most situations of this type that involve autosomes are lethal, and the embryo is usually spontaneously aborted very early in the pregnancy.

One example of an abnormal number of autosomes is trisomy 21, formerly called Down syndrome, where there are three copies of the twenty-first chromosome. This is the only example of an abnormal number of autosomes being compatible with life beyond the first few years after birth. Trisomy 21, which occurs in approximately 1 out of every 1,000 live births, is associated with a number of developmental and health problems. These problems include congenital heart defects (seen in about 40 percent of affected newborns), increased susceptibility to respiratory infections, and leukemia. However, the most widely recognized effect is mental impairment, which is variably expressed and ranges from mild to severe.

Nondisjunction also occurs in sex chromosomes. Although this usually doesn't cause death, it frequently results in sterility and other problems. Clearly, normal development relies on the presence of the correct number of chromosomes.

New Frontiers

Since the discovery of DNA structure and function in the 1950s, the field of genetics has revolutionized biological science and reshaped our understanding of inheritance, genetic disease, and evolutionary processes. For example, a technique developed in 1986 called **polymerase chain reaction (PCR)** enables scientists to make thousands of copies of small DNA samples which can then be analyzed. This is important, since there may not be enough DNA from crime scenes or fossils, for example, for reliable analysis of nucleotide sequences. Using PCR, scientists have been able to examine nucleotide sequences in, for example, Neandertal fossils and Egyptian mummies. As you can imagine, PCR has limitless potential for many disciplines, including forensic science, medicine, and evolutionary biology.

By examining multiplied DNA samples provided by PCR, scientists can identify *DNA fingerprints,* so called because they appear as patterns of repeated DNA sequences that are unique to each individual. For example, one person might have a segment of six bases such as ATTCTA repeated 3 times, and another might have the same sequence repeated 10 times. DNA fingerprinting is perhaps the most powerful tool available for human identification (Fig. 3-13). Scientists have used it to identify scores of unidentified remains, including members of the Russian royal family murdered in 1918 and victims of the September 11, 2001, terrorist attacks. The technique has also been used to exonerate innocent people wrongly convicted of crimes and imprisoned for years.

Over the last two decades, scientists using the techniques of **recombinant DNA technology** have been able to transfer genes from the cells of one species into those of another. The most common method has been to insert human genes that direct the production of various proteins into bacterial cells. The altered bacteria can then produce human gene products such as insulin. Until the early 1980s, diabetic patients relied on insulin derived from nonhuman animals. However, this insulin wasn't plentiful, and some patients developed allergies to it. But since 1982, abundant supplies of human insulin, produced by bacteria, have been available, and bacteria-derived insulin doesn't cause allergic reactions.

recombinant DNA technology A process in which genes from the cell of one species are transferred to somatic cells or gametes of another species.

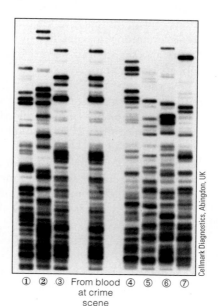

① ② ③ From blood at crime scene ④ ⑤ ⑥ ⑦

Cellmark Diagnostics, Abingdon, UK

FIGURE 3-13 Eight DNA fingerprints, one of which is from a blood sample left at an actual crime scene. The other seven are from suspects. By comparing the banding patterns, it's easy to identify the guilty person.

In recent years, genetic manipulation has become increasingly controversial owing to questions related to product safety, environmental concerns, and animal welfare. For example, the insertion of bacterial DNA into certain crops has made them toxic to leaf-eating insects, thus reducing the need for pesticide use. And cattle and pigs are commonly treated with antibiotics and genetically engineered growth hormone to increase growth rates. There is no current evidence that humans are harmed by the insect-repelling bacterial DNA or by consuming meat from animals treated with growth hormone. But, there are concerns over the unknown effects of long-term exposure. In fact, opposition to genetically modified foods has resulted in greatly increased demand for organically grown produce and hormone-free meats, especially in Europe and Africa.

Regardless of how contentious these new techniques may be, nothing has generated as much controversy as cloning. The controversy escalated in 1997 with the birth of Dolly, a **clone** of a female sheep (Wilmut et al., 1997). Actually, cloning isn't as new as you might think. Anyone who has ever taken a cutting from a plant and rooted it to grow a new one has produced a clone. The list of cloned mammals now includes mice, rats, rabbits, cats, sheep, cattle, a horse, and recently a mule (Woods et al., 2003). How successful or common cloning will be hasn't been determined. Dolly, who had developed health problems, was euthanized in February 2003 at the age of 6 years (Giles and Knight, 2003). Long-term studies have yet to show whether cloned animals live out their normal life span, but some evidence in mice suggests that they don't. Also, only about 3 percent of cloning attempts actually result in a live birth (Giles and Knight, 2003).

Probably the single most important advance in genetics has come from the **Human Genome Project**. The goal of this international effort, begun in 1990, was to sequence the entire human **genome,** which consists of some 3 billion bases comprising approximately 25,000 to 30,000 genes. This goal was achieved in 2003, but scientists are still several years away from identifying the functions of many of the proteins produced by these genes. It's one thing to know a gene's chemical makeup, but quite another to know what it does. Nevertheless, the magnitude and importance of the achievement can't be overstated, because it will ultimately transform biomedical and pharmaceutical research and will change forever how many human diseases are diagnosed and treated.

At the same time scientists were sequencing human genes, the genomes of other organisms were also being studied. As of September 2000, the genomes of over 600 species (mostly microorganisms) had been at least partially identified. In December 2002, the mouse genome had been completely sequenced (Waterstone et al., 2002). Then, in December 2003, a rough draft of the chimpanzee genome was announced. Already scientists have begun to compare human, chimpanzee, and mouse DNA for evidence as to how our lineage became distinct from that of chimpanzees (Clark et al., 2003). This research has enormous implications for studies of evolutionary relationships among species. Eventually, comparative genome analysis should provide a thorough assessment of genetic similarities and differences, and thus the evolutionary relationships, between humans and other primates. Indeed, it wouldn't be an exaggeration to say that this is the most exciting time in the history of evolutionary biology since Darwin published *On the Origin of Species.*

clone An organism that is genetically identical to another organism. The term may also be used to refer to genetically identical DNA segments, molecules, and cells.

Human Genome Project An international effort aimed at sequencing and mapping the entire human genome.

genome The entire genetic makeup of an individual or species. In humans, it is estimated that each individual possesses approximately 3 billion DNA nucleotides.

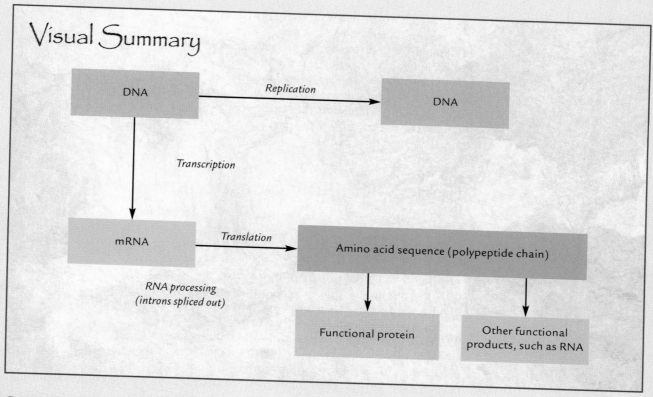

Summary

The topics covered in this chapter relate almost entirely to discoveries made after Darwin and Wallace described the fundamentals of natural selection. But all the issues presented here are basic to an understanding of biological evolution, adaptation, and human variation.

Cells are the fundamental units of life, and in multicellular organisms there are basically two types. Somatic cells make up body tissues, while gametes (eggs and sperm) are reproductive cells that transmit genetic information from parents to offspring.

Genetic information is contained in the DNA molecule, found in the nuclei of cells. The DNA molecule is capable of replication, or making copies of itself. Replication makes it possible for daughter cells to receive a full complement of DNA (contained in chromosomes).

DNA also controls protein synthesis by directing the cell to arrange amino acids in the proper sequence for each particular type of protein. A similar molecule called RNA is also involved. Many genes regulate the function of other genes. These are called regulatory genes, and they switch other genes on and off. Homeotic genes are regulatory genes that are expressed only in embryonic development, and they direct the development of the body plan.

There are also many segments of DNA that don't code for protein production, and much of their function is unknown. These are called introns and they're initially transcribed into mRNA but they're deleted before the mRNA leaves the cell nucleus.

Cells multiply by dividing, and during cell division, DNA is visible under a microscope in the form of chromosomes. In humans, there are 46 chromosomes

(23 pairs). If they aren't precisely distributed to succeeding generations of cells, severe consequences may follow.

Somatic cells divide during growth or tissue repair or to replace old or damaged cells. Somatic cell division is called mitosis. A cell divides one time to produce two daughter cells, each possessing a complete and identical set of chromosomes.

Sex cells are produced when specialized cells in the ovaries and testes divide during meiosis. In meiosis there are two divisions that produce four nonidentical daughter cells, each of which contains only half the amount of DNA (23 chromosomes) carried by the original cell.

Critical Thinking Questions

1. We only briefly touched on the topic of recombinant DNA technologies. From what we said and from things you have heard elsewhere, what is your view on this important topic? Are you generally in favor of most of the goals of recombinant DNA research? What are your objections?

2. Before you read this chapter, were you aware that the DNA in your body is structurally the same as in all other organisms? How do you see this fact as having potential to clarify some of the many questions we still have regarding biological evolution?

3. How would you describe genes and their functions?

4. What are proteins, and why are they important? Although we didn't discuss it in this chapter, do you think proteins are exactly the same in all species? If not, how would you guess they might vary structurally? Why would such differences be of interest to an evolutionary anthropologist?

🌐 Media Resources

The Companion Website for *Essentials of Physical Anthropology,* Sixth Edition
http://anthropology.wadsworth.com/jurmain6e_ess

Supplement your review of this chapter by going to this text's companion website to take one of the practice quizzes, use the flash cards to master key terms, and check out the many other resources and study aids.

CD-ROMs IN PHYSICAL ANTHROPOLOGY

Wadsworth Publishing has also developed three CD-ROMs to accompany this text and enhance learning in physical anthropology (for further descriptions of these CD-ROMs, see p. xix):

Virtual Laboratories for Physical Anthropology CD-ROM, Third Edition

Basic Genetics for Anthropology CD-ROM: Principles and Applications

Hominid Fossils CD-ROM: An Interactive Atlas

For this chapter, see especially the Virtual Laboratories for Physical Anthropology CD-ROM, Third Edition, and the Basic Genetics for Anthropology CD-ROM: Principles and Applications.

Focus Question

Why is it important to know the basic mechanisms of inheritance to understand the processes of evolution?

Introduction

Have you ever had a cat with five, six, or even seven toes? Even if you haven't, you may have seen one, because it's fairly common in cats. Maybe you've known someone with an extra finger or toe, because it's not unheard of in people. Anne Boleyn, mother of England's Queen Elizabeth I and the first of Henry VIII's wives to lose her head, apparently had an extra little finger. (Of course, this had nothing to do with her early demise—that's another story.)

Having extra digits is called polydactyly, and it's fairly certain that one of Anne Boleyn's parents was also polydactylous. It's also likely that any polydactylous cat has a parent with extra toes. But how do we know this? Actually, it's fairly simple. We know this because polydactyly is a Mendelian characteristic, meaning that its pattern of inheritance works like those discovered almost 150 years ago by a monk named Gregor Mendel (Fig. 4-1).

For at least 10,000 years, beginning with the domestication of plants and animals, people have tried to explain how offspring inherit characteristics from their parents. And even though their explanations were wrong, farmers still knew that they could enhance the frequency and expression of desirable traits through selective breeding. But they didn't know why.

Since the ancient Greek philosophers considered the problem until well into the nineteenth century, one common belief was that characteristics of offspring resulted from the *blending* of parental traits. Blending supposedly occurred because of certain particles found in every part of the body. These particles contained miniatures of the body part (limbs, organs, etc.) they came from, and they traveled through the blood to the reproductive organs and ultimately blended with particles of another individual during reproduction. There were variations on this theme, and numerous scholars, including Charles Darwin, adhered to some aspects of the theory.

The Genetic Principles Discovered by Mendel

It wasn't until Gregor Mendel (1822–1884) addressed the question of heredity that it began to be resolved. Mendel was living in an abbey at Brno in what is now the Czech Republic. At the time he began his research, he had already studied botany, physics, and mathematics at the University of Vienna, and he had performed various experiments in the monastery gardens. These experiments led him to explore the ways that physical traits, such as color or height, could be expressed in plant **hybrids.**

Click

Go to the following CD-ROMs for interactive activities and exercises on topics covered in this chapter:

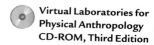
Virtual Laboratories for Physical Anthropology CD-ROM, Third Edition

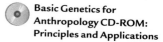
Basic Genetics for Anthropology CD-ROM: Principles and Applications

Raychel Ciemma and Precision Graphics

FIGURE 4-1 Portrait of Gregor Mendel.

hybrids Offspring of individuls that differ with regard to certain traits or certain aspects of genetic makeup; heterozygotes.

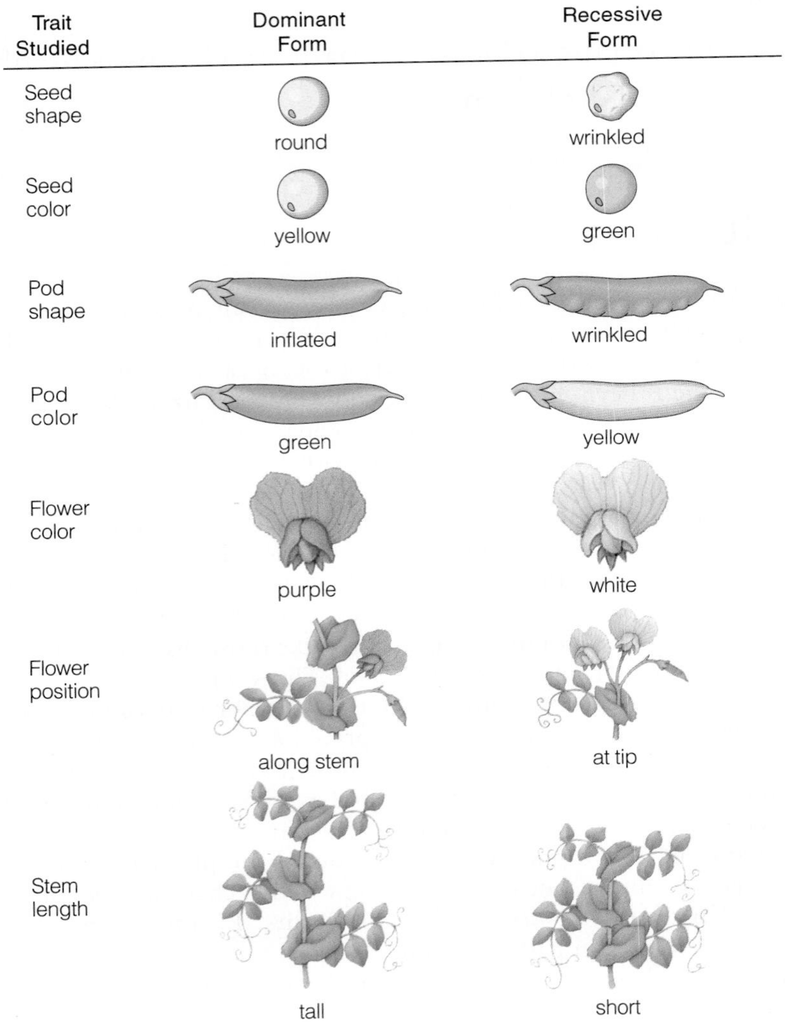

FIGURE 4-2 The traits Mendel studied in peas.

Trait Studied	Dominant Form	Recessive Form
Seed shape	round	wrinkled
Seed color	yellow	green
Pod shape	inflated	wrinkled
Pod color	green	yellow
Flower color	purple	white
Flower position	along stem	at tip
Stem length	tall	short

Mendel worked with garden peas, concentrating on seven different traits, each of which could be expressed two ways (Fig. 4-2). We want to emphasize that we discuss Mendel's pea experiments only to illustrate the basic rules of inheritance. The principles Mendel discovered apply to all biological organisms, including humans.

SEGREGATION

Mendel called the plants he used in the first cross the P (parental) generation, and in the first stage of the experiment, he crossed tall plants with short ones. But the hybrid offspring of the P generation, the F_1 generation, weren't intermediate in height, as blending theories of inheritance would have predicted. To the contrary, they were all tall (Fig. 4-3).

Next, he allowed the F_1 plants to self-fertilize and produce a second generation (the F_2 generation). But this time, only approximately ¾ of the offspring were tall, and the remaining ¼ were short. One expression of the

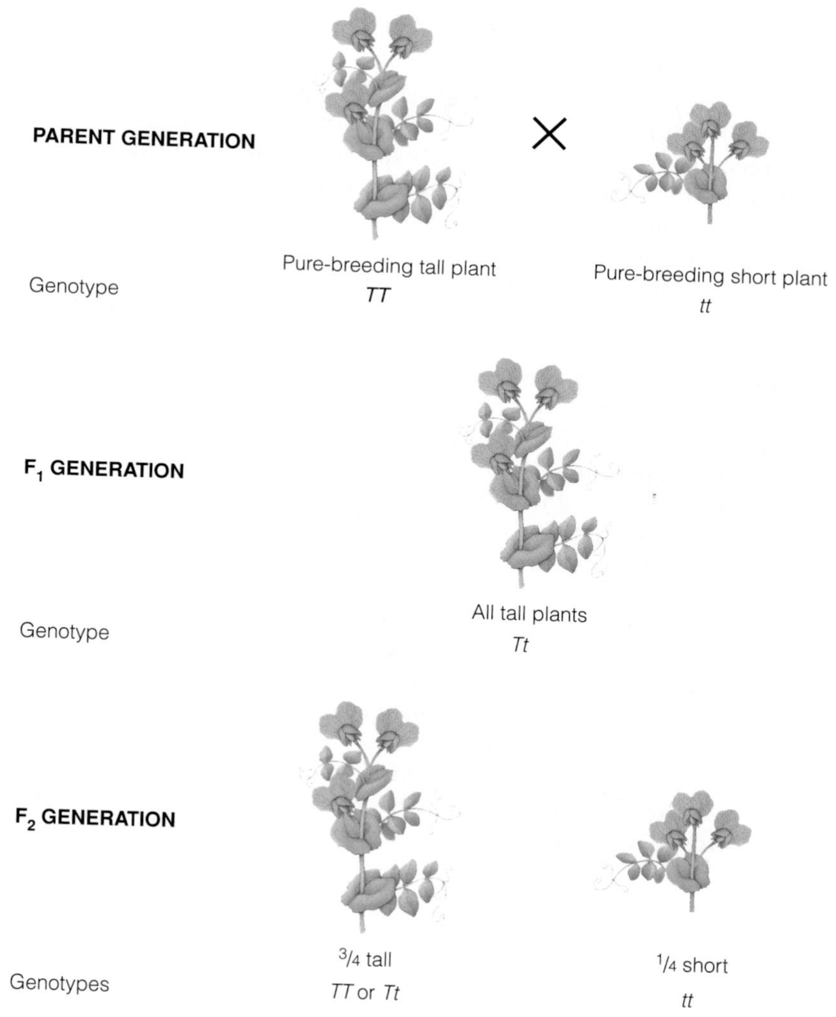

FIGURE 4-3 Results of crosses when only one trait at a time is considered.

PARENT GENERATION

Genotype

Pure-breeding tall plant
TT

Pure-breeding short plant
tt

F₁ GENERATION

Genotype

All tall plants
Tt

F₂ GENERATION

Genotypes

³/₄ tall
TT or *Tt*

¹/₄ short
tt

trait had completely disappeared in the F_1 generation and then reappeared in the F_2 generation. Moreover, the expression that was present in all the F_1 plants was more common in the F_2 plants, occurring in a ratio of approximately 3:1.

These results suggested that different expressions of a trait were controlled by discrete *units* (we would call them genes), which occurred in pairs, and that offspring inherited one unit from each parent. Mendel realized that the members of a pair of units controlling a trait somehow separated into different sex cells and were again united with another member during fertilization of the egg. This is Mendel's *first principle of inheritance*, known as the **principle of segregation.**

Today we know that meiosis explains Mendel's principle of segregation. You will remember that during meiosis, paired chromosomes, and the genes they carry, separate from each other and are distributed to different gametes. However, in the zygote, the full complement of chromosomes is restored, and both members of each chromosome pair are present in the offspring.

principle of segregation Genes (alleles) occur in pairs (because chromosomes occur in pairs). During gamete production, the members of each gene pair separate, so that each gamete contains one member of each pair. During fertilization, the full number of chromosomes is restored, and members of gene or allele pairs are reunited.

DOMINANCE AND RECESSIVENESS

Mendel also realized that the expression that was absent in the F₁ plants hadn't actually disappeared at all. It had remained present, but somehow was masked and couldn't be expressed. Mendel described the trait that seemed to be lost as **"recessive,"** and he called the expressed trait **"dominant."** Thus, the important principles of *dominance* and *recessiveness* were developed, and today they are still important concepts in the field of genetics.

As you already know, *gene* can be defined as a segment of DNA that directs the production of a specific protein, part of a protein, or any functional product. Furthermore, the location of a gene on a chromosome is its **locus** (*pl.,* loci). At many genetic loci, however, there may be more than one form of the gene, and such variations of genes at specific loci are called **alleles** (Fig. 4-4). Put simply, alleles are different versions of a gene, each of which can direct the cell to produce a slightly modified form of the same protein and, ultimately, a different expression of the trait.

As it turns out, plant height in garden peas is controlled by two different alleles at one genetic locus. The allele that determines tall is dominant to the allele for short. (It's worth mentioning that height isn't controlled this way in all plants.) In Mendel's experiments, all the parent (P) plants had two copies of the same allele, either dominant or recessive, depending on whether they were tall or short. When two copies of the same allele are present, the individual is said to be **homozygous.** Thus, all the tall P plants were homozygous for the dominant allele, and all the short P plants were homozygous for the recessive allele. (This explains why tall plants crossed with tall plants produced only tall offspring, and short plants crossed with short plants produced all short offspring; that is, they lacked genetic variation at this locus.) However, all the F₁ plants (hybrids) had inherited one allele from each parent plant; therefore,

recessive Describing a trait that is not expressed in heterozygotes; also refers to the allele that governs the trait. For a recessive allele to be expressed, there must be two copies of the allele (i.e., the individual must be homozygous).

dominant Describing a trait governed by an allele that can be expressed in the presence of another, different allele (i.e., in heterozygotes). Dominant alleles prevent the expression of recessive alleles in heterozygotes. (This is the definition of *complete* dominance.)

locus (*pl.,* loci) (lo´-kus, lo-sigh´) The position on a chromosome where a given gene occurs. The term is sometimes used interchangeably with *gene,* but this usage is technically incorrect.

alleles Alternate forms of a gene. Alleles occur at the same locus on homologous chromosomes and thus govern the same trait. However, because they are slightly different, their action may result in different expressions of that trait. The term is sometimes used synonymously with *gene.*

homozygous Having the same allele at the same locus on both members of a chromosome pair.

FIGURE 4-4 As this diagram illustrates, alleles are located at the same locus on paired chromosomes, but they aren't always identical. For the sake of simplicity, they are shown here as single-stranded chromosomes.

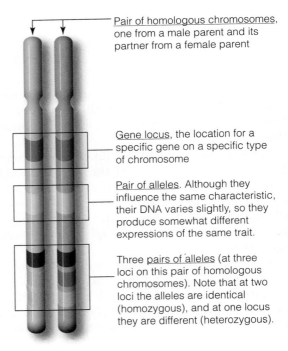

Pair of homologous chromosomes, one from a male parent and its partner from a female parent

Gene locus, the location for a specific gene on a specific type of chromosome

Pair of alleles. Although they influence the same characteristic, their DNA varies slightly, so they produce somewhat different expressions of the same trait.

Three pairs of alleles (at three loci on this pair of homologous chromosomes). Note that at two loci the alleles are identical (homozygous), and at one locus they are different (heterozygous).

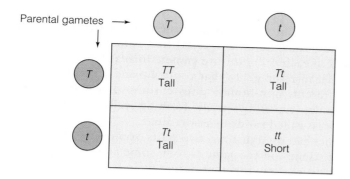

Parental gametes →

FIGURE 4-5 Punnett square representing possible genotypes and phenotypes and their proportions in the F$_2$ generation. The circles across the top and at the left of the Punnett square represent the gametes of the F$_1$ parents. The four squares illustrate that ¼ of the F$_2$ plants can be expected to be homozygous tall (*TT*); another ½ also can be expected to be tall but will be heterozygous (*Tt*); and the remaining ¼ can be expected to be short (*tt*). Thus, ¾ can be expected to be tall and ¼ to be short.

they all possessed two different alleles at this locus. Individuals that possess two different alleles at a locus are **heterozygous.**

Figure 4-3 illustrates the crosses that Mendel initially performed. Uppercase letters refer to dominant alleles (or dominant traits), and lowercase letters refer to recessive alleles (or recessive traits). Therefore,

T = the allele for tallness
t = the allele for shortness

The same symbols are combined to describe an individual's actual genetic makeup, or **genotype.** The term *genotype* can be used to refer to an organism's entire genetic makeup or to the alleles at a specific genetic locus. Thus, the genotypes of the plants in Mendel's experiments were

TT = homozygous tall plants
Tt = heterozygous tall plants
tt = homozygous short plants

Figure 4-5 is a *Punnett square*. It represents the different ways the alleles can be combined when the F$_1$ plants are self-fertilized to produce an F$_2$ generation. In this way, the figure shows all the *genotypes* that are possible in the F$_2$ generation, and it also demonstrates that approximately ¼ of the F$_2$ plants are homozygous dominant (*TT*); ½ are heterozygous (*Tt*); and the remaining ¼ are homozygous recessive (*tt*).

The Punnett square also shows the proportions of F$_2$ **phenotypes,** or the observed physical manifestations of genes. And it illustrates why Mendel saw approximately three tall plants for every short plant in the F$_2$ generation. By examining the Punnett square, you can see that ¼ of the F$_2$ plants are tall because they have the *TT* genotype. Furthermore, an additional ½, which are heterozygous (*Tt*), will also be tall because *T* is dominant to *t* and will therefore be expressed in the phenotype. The remaining ¼ are homozygous recessive (*tt*), and they will be short because no dominant allele is present. It's important to note that the *only* way a recessive allele can be expressed is if it occurs with another recessive allele, that is, if the individual is homozygous recessive at the particular locus in question.

heterozygous Having different alleles at the same locus on members of a chromosome pair.

genotype The genetic makeup of an individual. Genotype can refer to an organism's entire genetic makeup or to the alleles at a particular locus.

phenotypes The observable or detectable physical characteristics of an organism; the detectable expressions of genotypes.

INDEPENDENT ASSORTMENT

Mendel also determined that traits aren't necessarily inherited together. He did this by showing that plant height and seed color are independent of each

principle of independent assortment The distribution of one pair of alleles into gametes doesn't influence the distribution of another pair. The genes controlling different traits are inherited independently of one another.

random assortment The chance distribution of chromosomes to daughter cells during meiosis. There is nothing to dictate which member of a chromosome pair moves to which end of a dividing cell. Along with recombination, a source of variation resulting from meiosis.

other. That is any tall pea plant had a 50-50 chance of producing either yellow or green peas. This relationship, called the **principle of independent assortment,** says that the units (genes) that code for different traits assort independently of each other during gamete formation. Today we know that this happens because the genes that control plant height and seed color are located on different, non-homologous chromosomes, and during meiosis, the chromosomes travel to newly forming cells independently of one another, a process called **random assortment.**

But if Mendel had used just *any* two traits, some of his results would have been different. Genes on the same chromosome aren't independent of each other and they usually stay together during meiosis. Therefore, the traits they influence don't conform to the ratios predicted by independent assortment. While Mendel didn't know about chromosomes, he was certainly aware that all characteristics weren't independent of one another in the F_2 generation. He therefore reported only on those traits that did in fact illustrate independent assortment.

In 1866, Mendel's results were published, but the methodology and statistical nature of the research were beyond the thinking of the time, and their significance was overlooked and unappreciated. However, by the end of the nineteenth century, several investigators had made important contributions to the understanding of chromosomes and cell division. These discoveries paved the way for the acceptance of Mendel's work in 1900, when three different groups of scientists came across his paper. Regrettably, Mendel had died 16 years earlier and never saw his work vindicated.

Mendelian Inheritance in Humans

Mendelian traits Characteristics that are influenced by alleles at only one genetic locus. Examples include many blood types, such as ABO. Many genetic disorders, including sickle-cell anemia and Tay-Sachs disease, are also Mendelian traits.

Mendelian traits, also called *discrete traits,* are characteristics controlled by alleles at only one genetic locus (or, in some cases, two or more very closely linked loci). The most comprehensive listing of Mendelian traits in humans is V. A. McKusick's (1998) *Mendelian Inheritance in Man,* first published in 1965 and now in its twelfth edition. This volume, as well as its continuously updated Internet version, *Online Mendelian Inheritance in Man* (www.ncbi.nlm.nih.gov/omim/), currently lists over 15,000 human characteristics inherited according to Mendelian principles.

Although there are some Mendelian characteristics that have readily visible phenotypic expressions (e.g., polydactyly), most don't. Most Mendelian traits are biochemical in nature, and many genetic disorders (some of which do produce visible phenotypic abnormalities) result from harmful alleles inherited in Mendelian fashion (Table 4-1). So if it seems like textbooks overly emphasize genetic disease in discussions of Mendelian traits, it's because many of the known Mendelian characteristics are the results of harmful alleles.

antigens Large molecules found on the surface of cells. Several different loci govern various antigens on red and white blood cells.

The blood groups, like the ABO system, provide some of the best examples of Mendelian traits in humans. The ABO system is governed by three alleles, *A, B,* and *O,* found at the ABO locus on the ninth chromosome.* These alleles determine which blood type an individual has by coding for the production of molecules called **antigens** on the surface of red blood cells. If only antigen A

---

* Human chromosomes are numbered in order of size of the autosomes (1 through 22) plus X and Y.

TABLE 4-1 | Some Mendelian Traits in Humans

Dominant Traits		Recessive Traits	
Condition	**Manifestations**	**Condition**	**Manifestations**
Achondroplasia	Dwarfism due to growth defects involving the long bones of the arms and legs; trunk and head size usually normal.	Cystic fibrosis	Among the most common genetic (Mendelian) disorders among European Americans; abnormal secretions of the exocrine glands, with pronounced involvement of the pancreas; most patients develop obstructive lung disease. Until the recent development of new treatments, only about half of all patients survived to early adulthood.
Brachydactyly	Shortened fingers and toes.		
Familial hyper-cholesterolemia	Elevated cholesterol levels and cholesterol plaque deposition; a leading cause of heart disease, with death frequently occurring by middle age.		
Neurofibromatosis	Symptoms range from the appearance of abnormal skin pigmentation to large tumors resulting in gross deformities; can, in extreme cases, lead to paralysis, blindness, and death.	Tay-Sachs disease	Most common among Ashkenazi Jews; degeneration of the nervous system beginning at about 6 months of age; lethal by age 2 or 3 years.
Marfan syndrome	The eyes and cardiovascular and skeletal systems are affected; symptoms include greater than average height, long arms and legs, eye problems, and enlargement of the aorta; death due to rupture of the aorta is common. (Abraham Lincoln may have had Marfan syndrome.)	Phenylketonuria (PKU)	Inability to metabolize the amino acid phenylalanine; results in mental retardation if left untreated during childhood; treatment involves strict dietary management and some supplementation.
Huntington disease	Progressive degeneration of the nervous system accompanied by dementia and seizures; age of onset variable but commonly between 30 and 40 years.	Albinism	Inability to produce normal amounts of the pigment melanin; results in very fair, untannable skin, light blond hair, and light eyes; may also be associated with vision problems. (There is more than one form of albinism.)
Camptodactyly	Malformation of the hands whereby the fingers, usually the little finger, is permanently contracted.	Sickle-cell anemia	Caused by an abnormal form of hemoglobin (HbS) that results in collapsed red blood cells, blockage of capillaries, reduced blood flow to organs, and, without treatment, death.
Hypodontia of upper lateral incisors	Upper lateral incisors are absent or only partially formed (peg-shaped). Pegged incisors are a partial expression of the allele.		
Cleft chin	Dimple or depression in the middle of the chin; less prominent in females than males.	Thalassemia	A group of disorders characterized by reduced or absent alpha or beta chains in the hemoglobin molecule; results in severe anemia and, in some forms, death.
PTC tasting	The ability to taste the bitter substance phenylthiocarbamide (PTC). Tasting thresholds vary, suggesting that alleles at another locus may also exert an influence.	Absence of permanent dentition	Failure of the permanent dentition to erupt. The primary dentition isn't affected.

TABLE 4-2	ABO Genotypes and Associated Phenotypes		
Genotype		**Antigens on Red Blood Cells**	**ABO Blood Type (Phenotype)**
AA, AO		A	A
BB, BO		B	B
AB		A and B	AB
OO		None	O

is present, the blood type (phenotype) is A; if only B is present, the blood type is B; if both are present, the blood type is AB; and when neither is present, the blood type is O (Table 4-2).

Dominance and recessiveness are clearly illustrated by the ABO system. The *O* allele is recessive to both *A* and *B;* therefore, if a person has type O blood, he or she must be homozygous (*OO*) for the *O* allele. However, since both *A* and *B* are dominant to *O*, an individual with blood type A can actually have one of two genotypes: *AA* or *AO*. The same is true of type B, which results from the genotypes *BB* and *BO* (see Table 4-2). However, type AB presents a slightly different situation and is an example of **codominance.**

Codominance is seen when two different alleles occur in heterozygous condition, but instead of one having the ability to mask the expression of the other, the products of *both* are expressed in the phenotype. Therefore, when both *A* and *B* alleles are present, both A and B antigens can be detected on the surface of red blood cells.

A number of genetic disorders are caused by dominant alleles (see Table 4-1). This means that if a person inherits only one copy of a harmful dominant allele, the condition it causes will be present, regardless of the existence of a different, recessive allele on the corresponding chromosome.

Recessive conditions are commonly associated with the lack of a substance, usually an enzyme (see Table 4-1). For a person actually to have a recessive disorder, he or she must have two copies of the recessive allele that causes it. Heterozygotes who have only one copy of a harmful recessive allele are unaffected, but they're frequently called *carriers*. Although carriers don't actually have the recessive condition, they can pass the allele that causes it to their children. (Remember, half their gametes will carry the recessive allele.) If their mate is also a carrier, then it's possible for them to have a child who will be homozygous for the allele, and that child will be affected. In fact, in a mating between two carriers, the risk of having an affected child is 25 percent (refer back to Fig. 4-5).

MISCONCEPTIONS REGARDING DOMINANCE AND RECESSIVENESS

Traditional methods of teaching genetics have led to some misunderstanding of dominance and recessiveness. Consequently, most people have the impression that dominance and recessiveness are all-or-nothing situations. This misconception especially pertains to recessive alleles, and the general view is that

codominance The expression of two alleles in heterozygotes. In this situation, neither allele is dominant or recessive; thus, both influence the phenotype.

when these alleles occur in carriers, they have absolutely no effect on the phenotype. That is, they are completely inactivated by the presence of another (dominant) allele, or at least that's how it appeared to Gregor Mendel.

However, various biochemical techniques available today show that many recessive alleles *do* influence the phenotype, although these effects aren't usually detectable through simple observation. In fact, many recessive alleles only reduce the amount of whatever gene product they influence, but they don't always eliminate it entirely. Indeed, it's clear that our perception of recessive alleles greatly depends on whether we examine them at the directly observable phenotypic level or the biochemical level.

There are also a number of misconceptions about dominant alleles. The majority of people see dominant alleles as somehow "stronger" or "better," and there is always the mistaken notion that dominant alleles are more common in populations because natural selection favors them. These misconceptions undoubtedly stem partly from the label "dominant" and the connotations that the term carries. But in genetic usage, those connotations can be misleading. Just think about it. If dominant alleles were always more common, then a majority of people would have conditions such as achondroplasia and Marfan syndrome (see Table 4-1).

As you can see, the relationships between recessive and dominant alleles are more complicated than they first appear to be. Previously held views of dominance and recessiveness were guided by available technologies; as genetic technologies continue to change, new theories emerge, and our perceptions will be further altered. In fact, it's possible that one day the concepts of dominance and recessiveness, as traditionally taught, will be obsolete.

Polygenic Inheritance

Mendelian traits are said to be *discrete,* or *discontinuous,* because their phenotypic expressions don't overlap; instead, they fall into clearly defined categories (Fig. 4-6a). For example, Mendel's pea plants were either short or tall, but none was intermediate in height. In the ABO system, the four phenotypes are completely distinct from one another; that is, there is no intermediate form between type A and type B. In other words, Mendelian traits don't show *continuous* variation.

However, many traits do have a wide range of phenotypic expressions that form a graded series (Fig. 4-6b). These are called **polygenic,** or *continuous,* traits. While Mendelian traits are governed by only one genetic locus, polygenic characteristics are influenced by alleles at two or more loci, and each locus makes a contribution to the phenotype. For example, one of the most frequently cited examples of polygenic inheritance in humans is skin color. The single most important factor influencing skin color is the amount of the pigment melanin present.

Melanin production is believed to be influenced by between three and six genetic loci, with each locus having at least two alleles, neither of which is dominant. As there are perhaps six loci and at least 12 alleles, there are numerous ways in which these alleles can combine in individuals. If a person inherits 11 alleles coding for maximum pigmentation and only one for reduced melanin production, his or her skin will be very dark. A person who inherits a higher proportion of reduced pigmentation alleles will have lighter skin. This

polygenic Referring to traits that are influenced by genes at two or more loci. Examples of such traits are stature, skin color, and eye color. Many polygenic traits are also influenced by environmental factors.

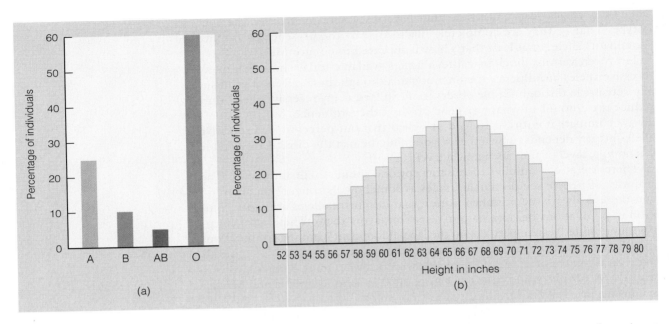

FIGURE 4-6 (a) This histogram shows the discontinuous distribution of a Mendelian trait (ABO blood type) in a hypothetical population. The expression of the trait is described in terms of frequencies. (b) This histogram represents the continuous expression of a polygenic trait (height) in a large group of people. Note that the percentage of extremely short or tall individuals is low; the majority of people are closer to the mean (or average) height, represented by the vertical line at the center of the distribution.

is because in this system, as in some other polygenic systems, there is an *additive effect*. This means that each allele that codes for melanin production makes a contribution to increased melanin (although for some characteristics the contributions of the alleles aren't all equal). Likewise, each allele coding for reduced melanin production contributes to reduced pigmentation. Therefore, the effect of multiple alleles at several loci, each making a contribution to individual phenotypes, is to produce continuous variation from very dark to very fair skin within the species. (Skin color is also discussed in Chapter 12.)

Polygenic traits actually account for most of the readily observable phenotypic variation seen in humans, and they have traditionally served as a basis for racial classification (see Chapter 12). In addition to skin color, polygenic inheritance in humans is seen in hair color, weight, stature, eye color (Fig. 4-7), shape of face, shape of nose, and fingerprint pattern. Because they exhibit continuous variation, most polygenic traits can be measured on a scale composed of equal increments. For example, height (stature) is measured in feet and inches (or meters and centimeters). If one were to measure height in a large number of individuals, the distribution of measurements would continue uninterrupted from the shortest extreme to the tallest. That's what is meant by *continuous traits*.

Because polygenic traits usually lend themselves to metric analysis, physical anthropologists treat them statistically. The use of simple summary statistics, such as the *mean* (average) or *standard deviation* (a measure of variation within a group), permits basic descriptions of, and comparisons between, populations. For example, one might be interested in average height in two different populations and whether or not differences between the two are significant, and if so, why. (Incidentally, you should also note that *all* physical traits measured and statistically treated in fossils are polygenic in nature.)

These particular statistical manipulations aren't possible with Mendelian traits simply because those traits can't be measured in the same way. But Mendelian characteristics can be described in terms of frequency within popu-

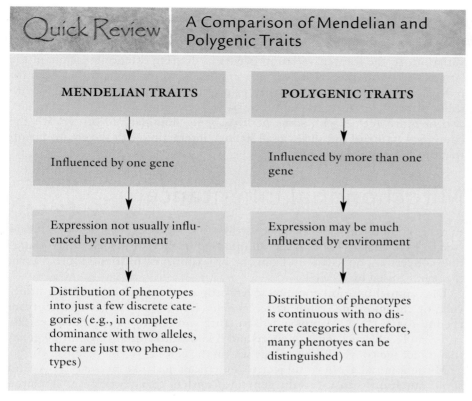

Quick Review   **A Comparison of Mendelian and Polygenic Traits**

MENDELIAN TRAITS	POLYGENIC TRAITS
Influenced by one gene	Influenced by more than one gene
Expression not usually influenced by environment	Expression may be much influenced by environment
Distribution of phenotypes into just a few discrete categories (e.g., in complete dominance with two alleles, there are just two phenotypes)	Distribution of phenotypes is continuous with no discrete categories (therefore, many phenotyes can be distinguished)

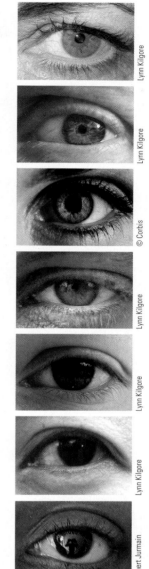

FIGURE 4-7 Examples of the continuous variation seen in human eye color.

lations, and then we can compare groups for differences in prevalence. Also, Mendelian traits can be analyzed for mode of inheritance (dominant or recessive). Finally, for many Mendelian traits, the approximate or exact positions of genetic loci are known, and this makes it possible to examine the mechanisms and patterns of inheritance at these loci. This type of study isn't yet possible for polygenic traits because they're influenced by several genes and they can't yet be traced to specific loci.

Genetic and Environmental Factors

You may have the impression that the phenotype is completely the expression of the genotype, but that's not true. (Here the terms *genotype* and *phenotype* are used in a broader sense to refer to an individual's *entire* genetic makeup and *all* observable or detectable characteristics.) The genotype sets limits and potentials for development, but it also interacts with the environment, and many aspects of the phenotype are influenced by this genetic-environmental interaction. Adult stature is a good example of a trait that's influenced by both genes and the environment because even though maximum height is genetically determined, nutrition during childhood is also very important. However, for most traits, it's not possible to identify the *specific* environmental components that influence the phenotype.

Mendelian traits are less likely to be influenced by environmental factors. For example, ABO blood type is determined at fertilization and remains fixed throughout the individual's lifetime, regardless of diet, exposure to ultraviolet radiation, temperature, and so on.

Mendelian and polygenic inheritance show different patterns of phenotypic variation. In the former, variation occurs in discrete categories, while in the latter, it's continuous. However, it's important to understand that even for polygenic characteristics, Mendelian principles still apply at individual loci. In other words, if a trait is influenced by six loci, each one of those loci may have two or more alleles, with some perhaps being dominant to others. It's the combined action of the alleles at all six loci, interacting with the environment, that produces the phenotype.

Mitochondrial Inheritance

Another component of inheritance involves the organelles called *mitochondria* (see p. 44). All cells contain several hundred of these oval-shaped structures that convert energy (derived from the breakdown of nutrients) into a form that can be used by the cell.

Each mitochondrion contains several copies of a ring-shaped DNA molecule, or chromosome. While *mitochondrial DNA (mtDNA)* is distinct from chromosomal DNA, its molecular structure and functions are the same. The entire molecule has been sequenced and is known to contain around 40 genes that direct the conversion of energy within the cell.

Mitochondrial DNA is subject to mutations just like nuclear DNA, and some mutations cause certain genetic disorders that result from impaired energy conversion. Importantly, animals of both sexes inherit all their mtDNA, and thus all mitochondrial traits, from their mothers. This is so because mitochondria occur in cellular cytoplasm, and while egg cells retain their cytoplasm, sperm cells lose theirs prior to fertilization. Because mtDNA is inherited from only one parent, meiosis and recombination don't occur. This means that all the variation in mtDNA among individuals is caused by mutation, which makes it extremely useful for studying genetic change over time. So far, geneticists have used rates of mutation in mtDNA to investigate evolutionary relationships between species; to trace ancestral relationships within the human lineage; and to study genetic variability among individuals and/or populations. While these techniques are still being refined, it's clear that we have a lot to learn from mtDNA.

Modern Evolutionary Theory

By the beginning of the twentieth century, the foundations for evolutionary theory had already been developed. Darwin and Wallace had described natural selection 40 years earlier, and the rediscovery of Mendelian genetics in 1900 contributed the other major component—a mechanism for inheritance. We might expect that these two basic contributions would have been combined into a consistent theory of evolution, but they weren't. For the first 30 years of the twentieth century, some scientists argued that mutation was the main factor in evolution, while others emphasized natural selection. What they really needed was a merger of both views (not an either-or situation), but this didn't happen until the mid-1930s.

The Modern Synthesis

Biologists working on mathematical models of evolutionary change in the late 1920s and early 1930s realized that mutation and natural selection weren't opposing processes and that both actually contributed to biological evolution. The two major foundations of the biological sciences had thus been brought together in what is called the Modern Synthesis. From such a "modern" (i.e., the middle of the twentieth century onward) perspective, we define evolution as a two-stage process. These two stages are:

1. The production and redistribution of **variation** (inherited differences among organisms)
2. *Natural selection* acting on this variation, whereby inherited differences, or variation, among individuals differentially affect their ability to successfully reproduce.

variation (genetic) Inherited differences among individuals; the basis of all evolutionary change.

A Current Definition of Evolution

As we discussed in Chapter 2, Darwin saw evolution as the gradual unfolding of new varieties of life from previous forms over long periods of time. And this is indeed one result of the evolutionary process. But these long-term effects can come about only by the accumulation of many small genetic changes occurring over the generations. Today, we're able to demonstrate how evolution works by looking at some of the small genetic changes that occur between generations. From such a modern genetic perspective, we define **evolution** as *a change in allele frequency from one generation to the next.*

Allele frequencies are indicators of the genetic makeup of an interbreeding group of individuals known as a **population.** To show how allele frequencies change, we'll use a simplified example of an inherited characteristic, again the ABO blood groups (see p. 70). (*Note:* There are several blood type systems controlled by different loci that determine other genetically transmitted properties of the red blood cells.)

Let's assume that the students in your anthropology class represent a population, an interbreeding group of individuals, and that we've determined the ABO blood type of each member. (To be considered a population, individuals must choose mates more often from *within* the group than from outside it. Obviously, your class won't meet this requirement, but we'll overlook this point for now.) The proportions of the *A, B,* and *O* alleles are the allele frequencies for this trait. If 50 percent of all the ABO alleles in your class are *A*, 40 percent are *B*, and 10 percent are *O*, then the frequencies of these alleles are *A* = .50, *B* = .40, and *O* = .10.

Since the frequencies for these alleles represent only proportions of a total, it's obvious that allele frequencies can refer only to groups of individuals—that is, populations. Individuals don't have allele frequencies; they have either *A, B,* or *O* in any combination of two. Therefore, only a population can evolve over time; individuals can't.

Assume that 25 years from now, we calculate the frequencies of the ABO alleles for the children (offspring) of our classroom population and find the following: *A* = .30, *B* = .40, and *O* = .30. We can see that the relative proportions have changed: *A* has decreased, *O* has increased, and *B* has remained the same. This wouldn't really be a big deal, but in a biological sense, these kinds of apparently minor change constitute evolution. Over the short span of just a

evolution (modern genetic definition) A change in the frequency of alleles from one generation to the next.

allele frequency In a population, the percentage of all the alleles at a locus accounted for by one specific allele.

population Within a species, a community of individuals where mates are usually found.

microevolution Small changes occurring within species, such as a change in allele frequencies.

macroevolution Changes produced only after many generations, such as the appearance of a new species.

few generations, such changes in inherited traits may be very small; but if they continue to happen, and particularly if they go in one direction as a result of natural selection, they can produce new adaptation and even new species.

Whether we are talking about the short-term effects (as in our classroom population) from one generation to the next, which is sometimes called **microevolution,** or the long-term effects through time, called speciation or **macroevolution,** the basic evolutionary mechanisms are similar. But how do allele frequencies change? Or, to put it another way, what causes evolution? As we've already said, evolution is a two-stage process. Genetic variation must first be produced by mutation, and then it can be acted on by natural selection.

Factors That Produce and Redistribute Variation

MUTATION

You've already learned that a change in DNA is one type of mutation. A gene may exist in one of several alternative forms, which we've defined as alleles (*A, B,* or *O,* for example). If one allele changes to another (i.e., if the gene itself is altered), a mutation has occurred. In fact, alleles are the results of mutation. Even the substitution of one single DNA base for another, called a *point mutation,* can cause the allele to change. But point mutations have to occur in sex cells if they're going to be important to the evolutionary process. This is because evolution is a change in allele frequencies *between* generations. If a mutation doesn't occur in a gamete, the individual will have it but won't transmit it to offspring. If, however, a genetic change occurs in the sperm or egg of one of the students in our classroom (*A* mutates to *B,* for instance), the offspring's blood type will be different from that of the parent, causing a minute shift in the allele frequencies of the next generation.

Actually, it would be rare to see evolution occurring by mutation alone, except in microorganisms. Mutation rates for any given trait are usually low, so we wouldn't really expect to see a mutation at the ABO locus in so small a population as your class. In larger populations, mutations might be observed in, say, 1 individual out of 10,000, but by themselves they would have little impact on allele frequencies. However, when mutation is combined with natural selection, evolutionary changes not only can occur, but can occur more rapidly.

It's important to remember that mutation is the basic creative force in evolution, since it's the *only* way to produce *new* genes (i.e., variation). Its role in the production of variation is key to the first stage of the evolutionary process.

GENE FLOW

gene flow Exchange of genes between populations.

Gene flow is the exchange of genes between populations. The term *migration* is also frequently used; but strictly speaking, migration means movement of people, whereas gene flow refers to the exchange of *genes* between groups, and this can only happen if the migrants interbreed. Also, even if individuals move temporarily and mate in the new population (thus leaving a genetic contribution), they don't necessarily remain in the population. For example, the offspring of U.S. soldiers and Vietnamese women represent gene flow, even though the fathers returned to their native population.

Population movements (particularly in the last 500 years) have reached enormous proportions, and few breeding isolates remain. However, significant population movements also happened in the past. Migration between populations has been a consistent feature of hominid evolution since the first dispersal of our genus, and gene flow between populations (even though sometimes limited) helps explain why, in the last million years, speciation has been rare. Of course, migration patterns are a manifestation of human cultural behavior, and this emphasizes the essential biocultural nature of human evolution.

An interesting example of how gene flow influences microevolutionary changes in modern human populations is seen in African Americans. African Americans in the United States are largely of West African descent, but there has also been considerable genetic admixture with European Americans. By measuring allele frequencies for specific genetic loci, we can estimate the amount of migration of European alleles into the African American gene pool. Data from northern and western U.S. cities (including New York, Detroit, and Oakland) have shown the migration rate (i.e., the proportion of *non*-African genes in the African American gene pool) at 20 to 25 percent (Cummings, 2000). However, more restricted data from the southern United States (Charleston and rural Georgia) have suggested a lower degree of gene flow (4 to 11 percent).

Gene flow doesn't require large-scale movements of entire groups. In fact, significant changes in allele frequencies can come about through long-term patterns of mate selection whereby members of a group obtain mates from one or more other groups. If mate exchange consistently moves in one direction over a long period of time, allele frequencies will eventually be altered.

GENETIC DRIFT AND FOUNDER EFFECT

Genetic drift is the random factor in evolution, and it's directly related to population size. Genetic drift occurs when, because of small population size, some individuals contribute a disproportionate share of genes to succeeding generations. This can be a function of social status in some small societies where, for example, high-ranking males have numerous mates while others don't. This effect may also be seen in nonhuman species in which low-ranking individuals may have fewer mating opportunities. In such a situation, one individual who carries a rare allele may pass it on to a high proportion of his or her descendants, and the frequency of the allele consequently increases in succeeding generations. Drift may also occur solely because the population is small; just by chance, alleles with low frequencies may simply not be passed on to offspring, so they eventually disappear from the population.

The results of the particular kind of genetic drift called **founder effect** are seen in many modern populations. Founder effect can occur when a small migrant band of "founders" colonizes a new region away from its parent group. Over time, a new population will be established, and as long as mates are chosen only from within this population, all of its members will be descended from the founders. In effect, all the genes in the expanding group will have come from the original colonists. In such a case, an allele that was rare in the founders' parent population but is carried by even one of the founders can eventually become common.

Colonization isn't the only way founder effect can happen. Small founding groups may simply be a few survivors of a large group ravaged by famine, war, disease, or other disasters. The small founder population (the survivors)

genetic drift Evolutionary changes—that is, changes in allele frequencies—produced by random factors. Genetic drift is a result of small population size.

founder effect A type of genetic drift in which allele frequencies are altered in small populations that are taken from, or are remnants of, larger populations.

gene pool The total complement of genes shared by the reproductive members of a population.

possesses only a sample of all the alleles that were present in the original group. Just by chance alone, some alleles may be completely removed from the **gene pool;** other alleles may become the only allele at a locus that previously had two or more. Whatever the cause, the outcome is a reduction of genetic diversity, and the allele frequencies of succeeding generations may be substantially different from those of the original large population. The loss of genetic diversity in this type of situation is called a *genetic bottleneck,* and the effects can be very detrimental to a species.

There are many known examples (both human and nonhuman) of species or populations that have passed through genetic bottlenecks. Genetically, cheetahs are an extremely uniform species, and it's believed that at some point in the past, these magnificent cats suffered a catastrophic decline in numbers. For reasons we don't know but that are related to the species-wide loss of numerous alleles, male cheetahs produce a high percentage of defective sperm compared to other cat species. Decreased reproductive potential, greatly reduced genetic diversity, and other factors (including human hunting) have combined to jeopardize the continued existence of this species. Other examples include California elephant seals, sea otters, and condors. Indeed, our own species is genetically uniform, compared to chimpanzees, and it appears that all modern human populations are the descendants of a few small groups (see Chapter 11).

Many examples of founder effect in human populations have been documented in small, usually isolated populations (e.g., island groups or small agricultural villages in New Guinea or South America). Even larger populations that are descended from fairly small groups of founders can show the effects of genetic drift many generations later. For example, French Canadians in Quebec, who currently number close to 6 million, are all descended from about 8,500 founders who left France during the sixteenth and seventeenth centuries. Because the genes carried by the initial founders represented only a sample of the gene pool from which they were derived, just by chance a number of alleles now occur in different frequencies from those of the current population of France. These differences include an increased presence of several harmful alleles, including those that cause some of the diseases listed in Table 4-1, such as cystic fibrosis, a variety of Tay-Sachs, thalassemia, and PKU (Scriver, 2001).

In small populations, drift plays a major evolutionary role because fairly sudden fluctuations in allele frequency occur solely because of small population size. Throughout much of human evolution (at least the last 4 to 5 million years), hominids probably lived in small groups, and drift would have had significant impact.

While drift has caused evolutionary change in certain circumstances, the effects have been irregular and nondirectional. (Remember, drift is *random* in nature.) Certainly, the pace of evolutionary change could have been accelerated if many small populations were isolated and thus subject to drift. By modifying such populations, drift can provide significantly greater opportunities for natural selection, the only truly directional force in evolution.

As we've seen, both gene flow and genetic drift can produce some evolutionary changes by themselves. However, these changes are usually *microevolutionary* ones; that is, they produce changes within species over the short term. To have the kind of evolutionary changes that ultimately result in entire new groups (e.g., the diversification of the first primates or the appearance of the hominids), natural selection would be necessary. But natural selection can't operate independently of the other evolutionary factors—mutation, gene flow, and genetic drift.

RECOMBINATION

As we saw in Chapter 3, in sexually reproducing species both parents contribute genes to offspring. Thus, the genetic information is reshuffled every generation. By itself, recombination doesn't change allele frequencies (i.e., cause evolution). However, it does produce different combinations of genes that natural selection may be able to act on. In fact, the reshuffling of chromosomes during meiosis can produce literally trillions of gene combinations, making every human being genetically unique.

Natural Selection Acts on Variation

The evolutionary factors just discussed—mutation, gene flow, genetic drift, and recombination—interact to produce variation and to distribute genes within and between populations. But there is no long-term *direction* to any of these factors. So how do populations adapt? The answer is natural selection. Natural selection provides directional change in allele frequency relative to *specific environmental factors*. As you've already seen, if the environment changes, then the selection pressures also change. Such a functional shift in allele frequencies is what we mean by *adaptation*. If there are long-term environmental changes in a consistent direction, then allele frequencies should also shift gradually each generation.

In Chapter 2, we discussed the general principles underlying natural selection and gave some nonhuman examples. The best documented example of natural selection in humans involves hemoglobin S an abnormal form of hemoglobin that results from a point mutation in the gene that produces part of the hemoglobin molecule. The allele for hemoglobin S, Hb^S, is recessive to the allele for normal hemoglobin, Hb^A. People who are homozygous for the Hb^A allele produce normal hemoglobin. Heterozygotes (whose genotype is Hb^A/Hb^S) have a condition called sickle-cell trait. Although some of their hemoglobin is abnormal, enough of it is normal to enable them to function normally under most circumstances. But people who inherit the recessive allele from both parents i.e., they are homozygous (Hb^S/Hb^S), have sickle-cell anemia.

There are many manifestations of sickle-cell anemia, but basically, the abnormal hemoglobin reduces the ability of red blood cells to transport oxygen. When the body has an increased demand for oxygen (as during exercise or at high altitude), the red blood cells collapse and form a shape similar to a sickle (Fig.4-8). As a result, they can't carry normal amounts of oxygen, and they also clump together and block small capillaries, depriving vital organs of oxygen. Even with treatment, life expectancy in the United States today is less than 45 years for patients with sickle-cell anemia. Worldwide, sickle-cell anemia causes an estimated 100,000 deaths each year, and in the United States, approximately 40,000 to 50,000 individuals, mostly of African descent, suffer from this disease.

Hb^S is a mutation that occurs occasionally in all human populations, but it's usually rare. In some populations, however, it's more common, and this is

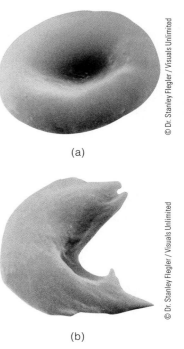

(a)

(b)

FIGURE 4-8 (a) Scanning electron micrograph of a normal, fully oxygenated red blood cell. (b) Scanning electron micrograph of a collapsed, sickle-shaped red blood cell that contains Hb^S.

© Dr. Stanley Flegler / Visuals Unlimited

FIGURE 4-9 A frequency map of the sickle-cell distribution in the Old World.

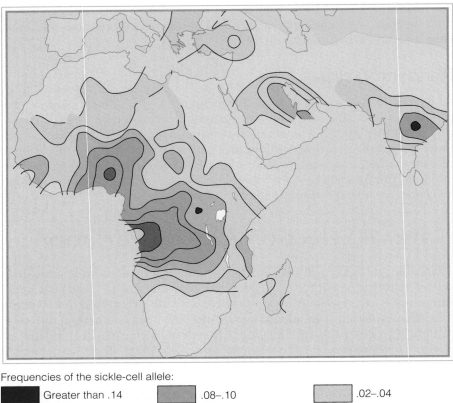

Frequencies of the sickle-cell allele:

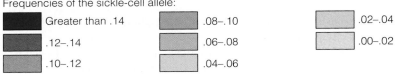

Greater than .14		.08–.10		.02–.04	
.12–.14		.06–.08		.00–.02	
.10–.12		.04–.06			

especially true in western and central Africa, where its frequency approaches 20 percent. The frequency of the allele is also moderately high in parts of Greece and India (Fig. 4-9). Given the devastating effects of Hb^S in homozygotes, how do we explain its higher prevalence in some populations? The answer to this question is malaria, an infectious disease that currently kills an estimated 1 to 3 million people a year worldwide.

Malaria is caused by a single-celled organism that is transmitted to humans by mosquitoes. Very briefly, after an infected mosquito bite, these parasites invade red blood cells, where they get the oxygen they need for reproduction. The consequences of this infection to the human host include fever, chills, headache, nausea, vomiting, and, frequently, death. In parts of western and central Africa, where malaria is always present, the burden of the disease is borne by children, with as many as 50 to 75 percent of 2- to 9-year-olds being afflicted.

The geographical correlation between malaria and the distribution of the sickle-cell allele is indirect evidence of a biological relationship (Figs. 4-9 and 4-10). Today, we know that individuals with one Hb^S allele (i.e., those with sickle-cell trait), and thus some hemoglobin S have greater resistance to malaria than homozygous "normals." Heterozygotes resist infection because their red blood cells don't provide a suitable environment for the parasite to reproduce. Thus, in areas where malaria is always present, individuals with sickle-cell trait have higher reproductive success than those with normal hemoglobin. Those with sickle-cell anemia, of course, have the lowest reproductive success, since without treatment, most die before reaching adulthood.

The relationship between malaria and Hb^S provides one of the best examples we have of natural selection in contemporary humans. In this case, natural selection has favored the heterozygous phenotype, thus increasing the frequency of Hb^S, an allele that in homozygotes causes severe disease and early death.

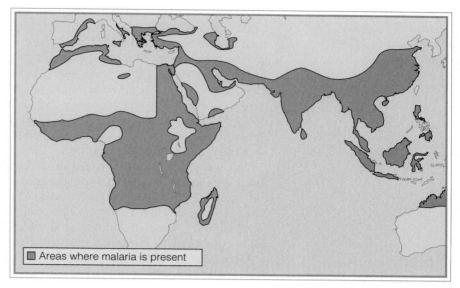

Areas where malaria is present

FIGURE 4-10 Malaria distribution in the Old World.

Review of Genetics and Evolutionary Factors

In this chapter, we discussed how genetic information is passed from individuals in one generation to those in the next. We also reviewed evolutionary theory and its current applications, emphasizing the crucial role of natural selection. These different levels (molecular, cellular, individual, and populational) are different components of the evolutionary process, and they're related to each other in a way that can eventually produce evolutionary change. A step-by-step example will make this clear.

We begin with a situation in which everyone in the population has the same hemoglobin type; therefore, initially no variation for this trait exists, and without some source of new variation, evolution isn't possible. How does this gene change? We have seen that a substitution of a single base in the DNA sequence can alter the code enough to change the protein product and ultimately the phenotype of the individual. Consider that in each generation such an incident occurs in one or a few individuals. For a mutated allele to be passed on to succeeding offspring, the gametes must carry the alteration. Any new mutation, therefore, must be transmitted during sex cell formation.

Once a mutation has occurred, it will be packaged into chromosomes, and these chromosomes in turn will assort during meiosis to be passed to offspring. We can see the results of this process by looking at phenotypes (traits) in individuals, and the mode of inheritance is described simply by Mendel's principle of segregation. In other words, if our initial individual has a mutation in only one paired allele on a set of homologous chromosomes, there will be a 50 percent chance of passing this chromosome (with the new mutation) to an offspring.

But what does all this have to do with *evolution*? To repeat an earlier definition, evolution is a change in allele frequency in a *population* from one generation to the next. The key point here is that we are considering populations, and it's the populations that may change over time.

We know whether allele frequencies have changed in a population where sickle-cell hemoglobin is found by determining the percentage of individuals with the sickling allele (Hb^S) versus those with the normal allele (Hb^A). If the relative proportions of these alleles change with time, evolution has occurred. But it's also important to know why. There are several possible explanations. First, the only way the new allele Hb^S could have arisen is by mutation, and we have shown how this can happen in a single individual. But this isn't an evolutionary change, since in a relatively large population, the alteration of one individual's genes won't alter allele frequencies of the entire population. Somehow, this new allele must *spread* in the population.

One way this can happen is in a small population, where mutations in one or just a few individuals and their offspring may indeed alter the overall frequency quite quickly. This would be genetic drift. As discussed, drift acts in small populations, where random factors may cause significant changes in allele frequency. Consequently, some alleles may be completely removed from the population, while others may end up being the only allele at that particular locus.

In the course of human evolution, drift has probably played a significant role, and it's important to remember that at this microevolutionary level, drift and/or gene flow can (and will) produce evolutionary change, even in the absence of natural selection. However, directional evolutionary trends could only have been sustained by *natural selection*. The way this has worked in the past and still operates today (as in sickle-cell) is through differential reproduction. That is, individuals who carry a particular allele or combination of alleles produce more offspring than other individuals with different alleles. Hence, the frequency of a new allele in the population increases slowly from generation to generation. When this process is compounded over hundreds of generations for numerous loci, the result is significant evolutionary change. The levels of organization in the evolutionary process are summarized in Table 4-3.

TABLE 4-3 | Levels of Organization in the Evolutionary Process

Evolutionary Factor	Level	Evolutionary Process	Technique of Study
Mutation	DNA	Storage of genetic information; ability to replicate; influences phenotype by production of proteins	Biochemistry, electron microscope, recombinant DNA
Mutation	Chromosomes	A vehicle for packaging and transmitting genetic material (DNA)	Light or electron microscope
Recombination (sex cells only)	Cell	The basic unit of life that contains the chromosomes and divides for growth and for production of sex cells	Light or electron microscope
Natural selection	Organism	The unit, composed of cells, that reproduces and which we observe for phenotypic traits	Visual study, biochemistry
Drift, gene flow	Population	A group of interbreeding organisms; changes in allele frequencies between generations; it's the population that evolves	Statistical analysis

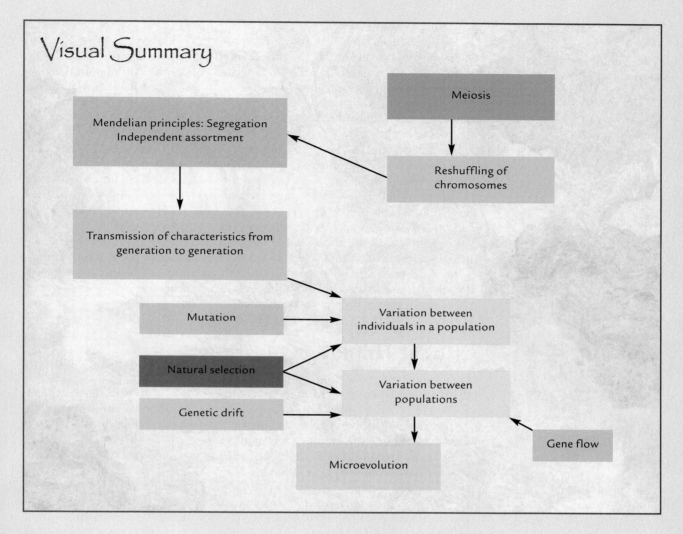

Visual Summary

Meiosis

Mendelian principles: Segregation
Independent assortment

Reshuffling of
chromosomes

Transmission of characteristics from
generation to generation

Mutation

Variation between
individuals in a population

Natural selection

Variation between
populations

Genetic drift

Gene flow

Microevolution

Summary

We've seen how Gregor Mendel discovered the principles of segregation, independent assortment, and dominance and recessiveness by doing experiments with pea plants. Although the field of genetics progressed dramatically during the twentieth century, the concepts first put forth by Gregor Mendel remain as the basis of our current knowledge of how traits are inherited.

Basic Mendelian principles are applied to the study of the various modes of inheritance we are familiar with today. The most important factor in all the Mendelian modes of inheritance is the role of segregation of chromosomes, and the alleles they carry, during meiosis.

Building on fundamental nineteenth-century contributions by Charles Darwin and the rediscovery of Mendel's work in 1900, advances in genetics throughout the twentieth century contributed to contemporary evolutionary thought. In particular, the combination of natural selection with Mendel's principles of inheritance and experimental evidence concerning the nature of mutation have all been synthesized into a modern understanding of evolutionary change, appropriately termed the Modern Synthesis. In this, the central contemporary theory of evolution, evolutionary change is seen as a two-stage process. The first stage is the production and redistribution of variation. The second stage is the process whereby natural selection acts on the accumulated genetic variation.

Mutation is crucial to all evolutionary change because it's the only source of completely new genetic material (which increases variation). In addition, the factors of recombination, genetic drift, and gene flow redistribute variation within individuals (recombination), within populations (genetic drift), and between populations (gene flow).

Natural selection is the central determining factor that influences the long-term direction of evolutionary change. How natural selection works can best be explained as differential reproductive success or, how successful individuals are in producing offspring for succeeding generations. To more fully illustrate the mechanics of evolutionary change through natural selection, comprehensive and well-understood examples from other organisms are most helpful. The detailed history of the evolutionary spread of the sickle-cell allele provides the best-documented example of natural selection among recent human populations. It must be remembered that evolution is an integrated process, and this chapter concluded with a discussion of how the various evolutionary factors can be integrated into a single comprehensive view of evolutionary change.

Critical Thinking Questions

1. If two people with blood type A, both with the *AO* genotype, have children, what *proportion* of these children would be expected to have blood type O? Why? Can these two parents have a child with AB blood? Why or why not?

2. After having read this chapter, do you understand evolutionary processes more completely? Carefully explain your answer to this question.

3. What are the causes of sickle-cell anemia and malaria? What do these two diseases have to do with each other?

4. Give some examples of how selection, gene flow, genetic drift, and mutation have acted on populations or species in the past. Try to think of at least one human and one nonhuman example. Why do you think genetic drift might be important today to endangered species?

Media Resources

The Companion Website for *Essentials of Physical Anthropology,* Sixth Edition
http://anthropology.wadsworth.com/jurmain6e_ess

Supplement your review of this chapter by going to this text's companion website to take one of the practice quizzes, use the flash cards to master key terms, and check out the many other resources and study aids.

CD-ROMS IN PHYSICAL ANTHROPOLOGY

Wadsworth Publishing has also developed three CD-ROMs to accompany this text and enhance learning in physical anthropology (for further descriptions of these CD-ROMs, see p. xix):

- Virtual Laboratories for Physical Anthropology CD-ROM, Third Edition

- Basic Genetics for Anthropology CD-ROM: Principles and Applications

- Hominid Fossils CD-ROM: An Interactive Atlas

For this chapter, see especially the Virtual Laboratories for Physical Anthropology CD-ROM, Third Edition, and the Basic Genetics for Anthropology CD-ROM: Principles and Applications.

Readings of Interest

Cummings, Michael R. 2000. *Human Heredity. Principles and Issues.* 5th ed. Pacific Grove, CA: Brooks/Cole.

Little, Peter. 1999. "The Book of Genes." *Nature* 402: 467–468.

Ridley, Matt. 2000. *Genome.* New York: Perennial.

Wake, David B. 2001. "Evolution: Speciation in the Round." *Nature* 409: 299–300.

5 | Macroevolution: Processes of Vertebrate and Mammalian Evolution

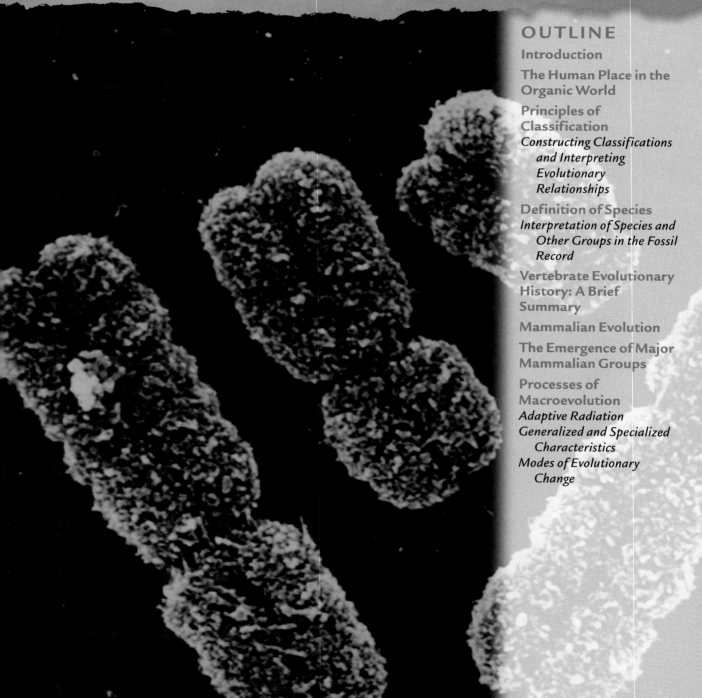

Focus Question

In what ways do humans fit into a biological continuum (as vertebrates and as mammals)?

Introduction

Many people think of paleontology as pretty boring and only interesting to overly serious academics. But have you ever been to a natural history museum—or perhaps to one of the larger, more elaborate toy stores? If so, you may have seen a full-size mock-up of *Tyrannosaurus rex,* one that might even have moved its head and arms and screamed threateningly. These displays are usually encircled by flocks of noisy children who seem anything but bored.

The study of the history of life on earth is full of mystery and adventure. The bits and pieces of fossils are the remains of once living, breathing animals (some of which were extremely large and dangerous). Searching for these fossils in remote corners of the globe is not a task for the faint of heart. Piecing together the tiny clues and ultimately reconstructing what *Tyrannosaurus* (or, for that matter, a small, 50-million-year-old primate) looked like and how it might have behaved are really much like detective work. Sure, it can be serious; but it's also a lot of fun.

In this chapter, we review the evolution of vertebrates and, more specifically, of mammals. It's important to understand these more general aspects of evolutionary history to place our species in its proper biological context. *Homo sapiens* is only one of millions of species that have evolved. Moreover, humans have been around for just an instant in the vast expanse of time that life has existed, and we want to know where we fit in this long and complex story of life on earth. To discover this, we also discuss some contemporary issues relating to evolutionary theory. In particular, we emphasize concepts that relate to large-scale evolutionary processes, that is, *macroevolution* (in contrast to the microevolutionary focus of Chapter 4). The fundamental perspectives reviewed here concern geological history, principles of classification, and modes of evolutionary change, and they serve as a basis for topics covered throughout much of the remainder of this book.

The Human Place in the Organic World

There are millions of species living today; if we were to include microorganisms, the total would likely exceed tens of millions. And if we added in the multitudes of species that are now extinct, the total would be staggering—perhaps hundreds of millions!

How do we deal scientifically with all this diversity? Biologists, being human, approach complexity by simplifying it. One way to do this is to develop a system of **classification** that organizes diversity into categories and, at the same time, indicates evolutionary relationships.

Organisms that move about and ingest food (but don't photosynthesize, as do plants) are called animals. More precisely, the multicelled animals are placed within the group called the **Metazoa** (Fig. 5-1). Within the Metazoa

Click

Go to the following CD-ROM for interactive activities and exercises on topics covered in this chapter:

Virtual Laboratories for Physical Anthropology CD-ROM, Third Edition

classification In biology, the ordering of organisms into categories, such as orders, families, and genera, to show evolutionary relationships.

Metazoa Multicellular animals; a major division of the animal kingdom.

FIGURE 5-1 Classification chart, modified from Linnaeus. All animals are placed in certain categories based on structural similarities. Not all members of categories are shown. For example, there are up to 20 orders of placental mammals (8 are depicted). A more comprehensive classification of the primate order is presented in Chapter 6.

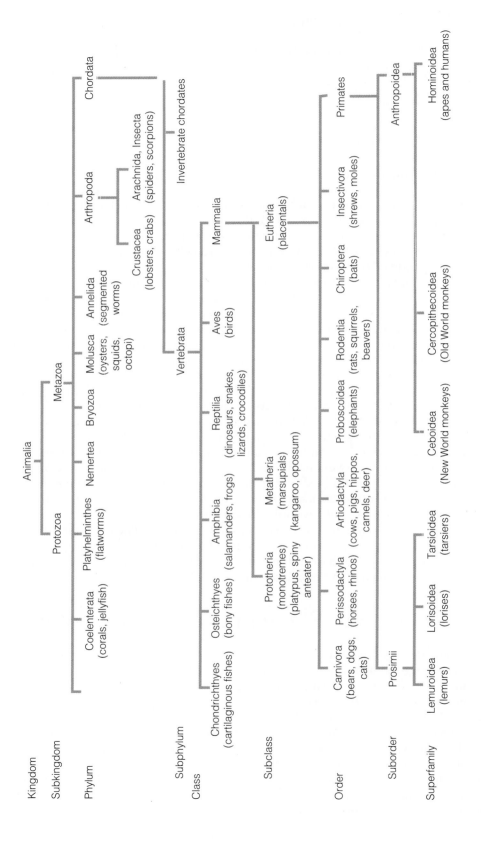

there are more than 20 major groups termed *phyla* (*sing.,* phylum). One of these phyla is the **Chordata,** animals with a nerve cord, gill slits (at some stage of development), and a supporting cord along the back. In turn, most chordates are called **vertebrates,** because they have a vertebral column. Vertebrates also have a developed brain and paired sensory structures for sight, smell, and balance.

The vertebrates themselves are subdivided into six classes: bony fishes, cartilaginous fishes, amphibians, reptiles, birds, and mammals. We will discuss mammalian classification later in this chapter.

By putting organisms into increasingly narrow groupings, this hierarchical arrangement organizes diversity into categories. It also makes statements about evolutionary and genetic relationships between species and groups of species. Further dividing mammals into orders makes the statement that, for example, all carnivores (Carnivora) are more closely related to each other than they are to any species placed in another order. Consequently, bears, dogs, and cats are more closely related to each other than they are to cattle, pigs, or deer (Artiodactyla). At each succeeding level (suborder, superfamily, family, subfamily, genus, and species), finer distinctions are made between categories until, at the species level, only those animals that can interbreed and produce viable offspring are included.

Chordata The phylum of the animal kingdom that includes vertebrates.

vertebrates Animals with segmented bony spinal columns; includes fishes, amphibians, reptiles, birds, and mammals.

Principles of Classification

Before we go any further, we need to discuss the basis of animal classification. The field that specializes in establishing the rules of classification is called *taxonomy.* Organisms are classified first, and most traditionally, on the basis of physical similarities. Such was the basis of the first systematic classification devised by Linnaeus in the eighteenth century (see Chapter 2).

Today, basic physical similarities are still considered a good starting point, but in order for them to be useful, they *must* reflect evolutionary descent. For example, the bones of the forelimb of all terrestrial air-breathing vertebrates are so similar in number and form (Fig. 5-2) that the obvious explanation for the striking resemblance is that all four kinds of air-breathing vertebrates ultimately derived their forelimb structure from a common ancestor.

The way such seemingly major evolutionary modifications in structure could occur likely begins with only relatively minor genetic changes. For example, recent research shows that forelimb development in all vertebrates is directed by just a few regulatory genes, what are called *Hox* genes (see p. 52) (Shublin et al., 1997; Riddle and Tabin, 1999). A few mutations among early vertebrates in certain *Hox* genes led to the basic limb structure seen in all subsequent vertebrates. Additional small mutations in these genes could produce the varied structures that make up the wing of a chicken, the flipper of a porpoise, or the upper limb of a human. You should recognize that *basic* genetic regulatory mechanisms are highly conserved in animals; that is, they've been maintained relatively unchanged for hundreds of millions of years. Like a musical score with a basic theme, small variations on the pattern can produce the different "tunes" that distinguish one organism from another. This is the essential genetic foundation for most macroevolutionary change, and therefore, large anatomical modifications don't always require major genetic alterations.

FIGURE 5-2 Homologies. The similarities in the forelimb bones of these animals can be most easily explained by descent from a common ancestor.

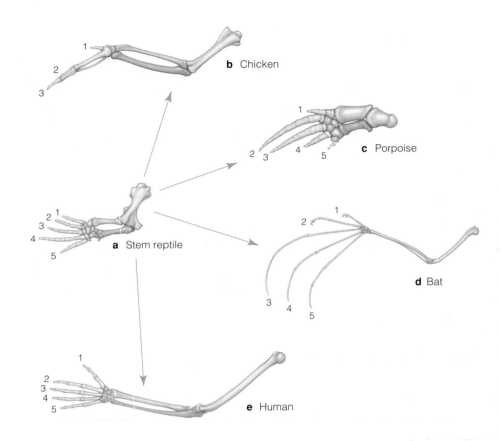

homologies Similarities between organisms based on descent from a common ancestor.

analogies Similarities between organisms based strictly on common function, with no assumed common evolutionary descent.

homoplasy (*homo,* meaning "same," and *plasy,* meaning "growth") The separate evolutionary development of similar characteristics in different groups of organisms.

Structures that are shared by species on the basis of descent from a common ancestor are called **homologies.** Homologies alone are reliable indicators of evolutionary relationship. But we have to be careful not to draw hasty conclusions from superficial similarities. For example, both birds and butterflies have wings, but they shouldn't be grouped together on the basis of this single characteristic; butterflies (as insects) differ dramatically from birds in a number of other, even more fundamental ways. (For example, birds have an internal skeleton, central nervous system, and four limbs. Insects don't.)

What has happened in evolutionary history is that from quite distant ancestors, both butterflies and birds have developed wings *independently.* Thus, their (superficial) similarities are a product of separate evolutionary response to roughly similar functional demands. These kinds of similarities, based on independent functional adaptation and not on shared evolutionary descent, are called **analogies.** The process that leads to the development of analogies (also called analogous structures) such as wings in birds and butterflies is termed **homoplasy.** In the case of butterflies and birds, the homoplasy has occurred in evolutionary lines that share only very remote ancestry. Here, homoplasy has produced analogous structures that are in no way homologous. In some cases, however, homoplasy can occur in lineages that are more closely related and therefore share considerable homology as well. Examples of homoplasy in closely related lineages are evident among the primates (e.g., among New and Old World monkeys and also among the great apes; see Chapter 6).

CONSTRUCTING CLASSIFICATIONS AND INTERPRETING EVOLUTIONARY RELATIONSHIPS

There are two major approaches used by evolutionary biologists to interpret evolutionary relationships and produce classifications. The first of these, called **evolutionary systematics,** is a more traditional approach, whereas the second approach, called **cladistics** (favored by most anthropologists) has emerged primarily in the last 20 years.

Before we discuss the differences between these two approaches, it is first helpful to note the features that they share. First, both trace evolutionary relationships and construct classifications that reflect these relationships. Second, they both recognize that organisms must be compared for specific features (called *characters*) and that some of these characters are more informative than others. Third (and deriving directly from the previous two points), both approaches focus exclusively on homologies.

However, there are also significant differences between these approaches in terms of how characters are chosen, which groups are compared, and how the results are interpreted and eventually incorporated into evolutionary schemes and classifications. The primary difference is that cladistics more rigorously defines the kinds of homologies that provide the most useful information. For example, at a very basic level, all life forms (except for some viruses) share DNA as the molecule that underlies all biological processes. However, beyond implying that all life most likely derives from a single origin (a most intriguing point), the presence of DNA tells us nothing further regarding more specific relationships among different kinds of life forms. To draw further conclusions, we need to look at particular characters that are shared by certain groups as the result of more recent ancestry.

This perspective emphasizes an important point: Some homologous characters are much more informative than others. We saw earlier that all terrestrial vertebrates share homologies in the number and basic arrangement of bones in the forelimb. While these similarities are broadly useful in showing that these large evolutionary groups (reptiles, birds, and mammals) are all related through a distant ancestor, they don't provide any usable information that lets us distinguish one from another (a reptile from a mammal, for example). Such characters (also called traits) that are shared through a very remote ancestry are said to be **primitive,** or **ancestral.** We prefer the term *ancestral* because it doesn't have a negative connotation regarding the evolutionary value of the character in question. So, in physical anthropology, the term *primitive* or *ancestral* simply means that a character seen in two organisms is inherited in both of them from a distant ancestor.

In most circumstances, analysis of ancestral characters does not provide enough information to make accurate evolutionary interpretations regarding relationships between different groups. In fact, misinterpretation of ancestral characters can easily lead to quite inaccurate evolutionary conclusions! The traits that cladistics focuses on, and which are far more informative, are those that distinguish particular evolutionary lineages. Such characters are said to be **derived,** or **modified.** Thus, while the general ancestral bony pattern of the forelimb in land animals with backbones doesn't allow us to distinguish among them, the further modification in certain groups (as hooves, flippers, or wings, for instance) does.

evolutionary systematics A traditional approach to classification (and evolutionary interpretation) in which presumed ancestors and descendants are traced in time by analysis of homologous characters.

cladistics An approach to classification that attempts to make rigorous evolutionary interpretations based solely on analysis of certain types of homologous characters (those considered to be derived characters).

ancestral (primitive) Referring to characters inherited by a group of organisms from a remote ancestor and thus not diagnostic of groups (lineages) that diverged after the character first appeared.

derived (modified) Referring to characters that are modified from the ancestral condition and thus *are* diagnostic of particular evolutionary lineages.

shared derived Relating to specific character states shared in common between two forms and considered the most useful for making evolutionary interpretations.

phylogenetic tree A chart showing evolutionary relationships as determined by evolutionary systematics. It contains a time component and implies ancestor-descendant relationships.

cladogram A chart showing evolutionary relationships as determined by cladistic analysis. It is based solely on interpretation of shared derived characters. No time component is indicated, and ancestor-descendant relationships are *not* implied.

Among vertebrates, *only* birds have feathers and *only* mammals have fur. In comparing mammals with other vertebrates, presence of fur is a *derived* characteristic. Similarly, in describing birds, feathers are derived only in this group.

So how do we know which kind of characteristics to use? That depends on which group we are describing and what we're comparing it to. For the most part, it's best to use characteristics that reflect more specific evolutionary adaptations; in other words, derived characteristics are the most useful. Moreover, we should group two forms together (say, a bat with a mouse, both as mammals) only when they show **shared derived** characteristics (here, both possessing fur). (See Figs. 5-1 and 6-8 for examples of classifications of animals.)

One last point needs to be mentioned. Traditional evolutionary systematics illustrates the hypothesized evolutionary relationships using a *phylogeny*, more properly called a **phylogenetic tree.** Strict cladistic analysis, however, shows relationships in a **cladogram.** A phylogenetic tree incorporates the dimension of time. (Numerous examples can be found in this and subsequent chapters.) But a cladogram doesn't indicate time, because all forms (fossil and modern) are indicated along one dimension. Phylogenetic trees usually attempt to make hypotheses regarding ancestor-descendant relationships. Cladistic analysis (through cladograms) makes no attempt whatsoever to discern ancestor-descendant relationships. In fact, strict cladists are quite skeptical that the evidence really permits such specific evolutionary hypotheses to be scientifically confirmed, since there are many more extinct species than living ones.

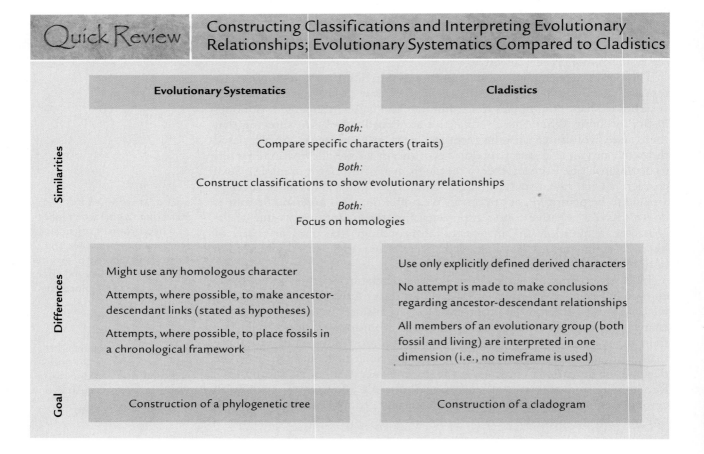

Quick Review — Constructing Classifications and Interpreting Evolutionary Relationships; Evolutionary Systematics Compared to Cladistics

	Evolutionary Systematics	Cladistics
Similarities	*Both:* Compare specific characters (traits)	
	Both: Construct classifications to show evolutionary relationships	
	Both: Focus on homologies	
Differences	Might use any homologous character	Use only explicitly defined derived characters
	Attempts, where possible, to make ancestor-descendant links (stated as hypotheses)	No attempt is made to make conclusions regarding ancestor-descendant relationships
	Attempts, where possible, to place fossils in a chronological framework	All members of an evolutionary group (both fossil and living) are interpreted in one dimension (i.e., no timeframe is used)
Goal	Construction of a phylogenetic tree	Construction of a cladogram

In practice, most physical anthropologists (and other evolutionary biologists) use cladistic analysis to identify and assess the utility of traits and to make testable hypotheses regarding the relationships between groups of organisms. Moreover, they frequently extend this basic cladistic methodology to further hypothesize likely ancestor-descendant relationships shown relative to a time scale (i.e., in a phylogenetic tree). In this way, aspects of both traditional evolutionary systematics and cladistic analyses are combined to produce a more complete picture of evolutionary history.

Definition of Species

Whether biologists are doing a cladistic or more traditional phylogenetic analysis, they're comparing groups of organisms—that is, different species, genera*, families, orders, and so forth. Fundamental to all these levels of classification is the most basic, the species.

It's appropriate, then, to ask just how biologists define species. We addressed this issue briefly in Chapter 1, where we applied the most common definition, which emphasizes interbreeding and reproductive isolation. While not the only definition of species (others will be discussed shortly), this view, called the **biological species concept** (Mayr, 1970), is the one preferred by most zoologists.

The best way to understand what species are is to consider how they come about in the first place—what Darwin called "origin of species." Today, this most fundamental of macroevolutionary processes is called **speciation.** According to the biological species concept, the way new species are first produced involves some form of isolation. Picture a single species (baboons, for example) composed of several populations distributed over a wide geographical area. But if a geographical barrier, such as a river, mountain range, or even just a large distance, effectively separates these populations, then gene exchange between them (gene flow) will be limited. This extremely important form of isolating mechanism is called *geographical isolation.*

If one baboon population (A) is separated from another baboon population (B) by a mountain range, members of population A won't mate with members of B (Fig. 5-3). As time passes (several generations), genetic differences will

biological species concept A depiction of species as groups of individuals capable of fertile interbreeding, but reproductively isolated from other such groups.

speciation The process by which a new species evolves from a prior species. Speciation is the most basic process in macroevolution.

FIGURE 5-3 A speciation model. This model of speciation is called branching evolution, or cladogenesis.

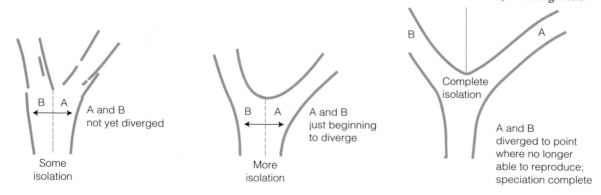

* genera (*pl.* of genus)

accumulate in both populations. And if group sizes are small, genetic drift may cause allele frequencies to change in both populations. Moreover, since drift is *random* in nature, we wouldn't expect the effects to be the same. Consequently, the two populations will begin to diverge.

As long as gene exchange is limited, the populations can only become more genetically different with time. Moreover, further difference can be expected if the baboon groups live in slightly different habitats. In other words, additional genetic differences will come about through natural selection. Certain individuals in population A would be most reproductively fit in their own environment, but would show less reproductive success in the environment occupied by population B. Thus, over time, allele frequencies will shift further, resulting in additional genetic differences between the two groups.

With the cumulative effects of genetic drift and natural selection acting over many generations, the result will be two populations that, even if they were to come back into geographical contact, could no longer interbreed. And at this point, more than just geographical isolation might come into play. For instance, there may be behavioral differences that interfere with courtship. This is an example of what we call *behavioral isolation*. Using our *biological* definition of species, we now would recognize two distinct species where initially only one existed.

While the biological species concept is accepted today by most biologists as the most workable definition of species (see, for example, Wilson, 2002), there still isn't complete agreement on the best approach for defining species. Some biologists have thus proposed alternative definitions, two of which are most relevant to our discussion. One of these definitions emphasizes mate recognition and breeding, while the other is based on ecological separation. It should be emphasized, however, that these varied approaches to defining species are not mutually exclusive. Indeed, aspects of all three concepts could potentially interact in the formation of new species. For example, some species isolation could *begin* the process of speciation and then be further reinforced by selective breeding (i.e., mate recognition) as well as ecological separation.

INTERPRETATION OF SPECIES AND OTHER GROUPS IN THE FOSSIL RECORD

Throughout much of this text, we will be using a number of taxonomic terms for fossil primates, including fossil hominids; consequently, you will be introduced to such terms as *Proconsul, Sivapithecus, Australopithecus,* and *Homo.* Of course, *Homo* is still a living primate. But it's especially difficult to make these types of designations from remains of animals that are long dead (and only partially preserved as skeletal remains). So, what do such names mean in evolutionary terms when we apply them to extinct species?

Our goal when applying species, genus, or other taxonomic labels to groups of organisms is to make meaningful biological statements about the variation that is present. When looking at populations of living or long-extinct animals, we certainly will see some variation. The situation is true of *any* sexually reproducing organism. For example, as a result of recombination (see Chapter 3), each individual organism is a unique combination of genetic material, and the uniqueness is usually reflected to some extent in the phenotype.

In addition to such *individual variation,* there are other kinds of variation in all biological populations. *Age changes* alter overall body size as well as shape in many mammals. One pertinent example for studies of fossil hominids and our closest primate relatives is the change in number, size, and shape of teeth from deciduous (milk) teeth (only 20 present) to the permanent dentition (32 present). It would be an obvious error to differentiate fossil forms solely on the basis of such age-dependent criteria. If one individual were represented just by milk teeth and another (seemingly very different) individual were represented just by adult teeth, they could simply be different-aged individuals from the *same* population. Variation due to sex also plays an important role in influencing differences among individuals. Differences in physical characteristics between males and females of the same species are called **sexual dimorphism** (see p. 132), and these can result in marked variation in body size and proportions in adults of the same species.

Recognition of Fossil Species Keeping in mind all the types of variation present within interbreeding groups of organisms, the minimum biological category we would like to define in fossil primate samples is the *species.* As already defined (according to the biological species concept), a species is a group of interbreeding or potentially interbreeding organisms that is reproductively isolated from other such groups. In modern organisms, this concept is theoretically testable by observations of reproductive behavior. In animals long extinct, such observations are obviously impossible. Therefore, to get a handle on the variation we see in fossil groups, we have to refer to living animals.

We know without doubt that variation is present. The question is, What is its biological significance? Two immediate answers come to mind. Either the variation is accounted for by individual, age, and sex differences seen within every biological species (i.e., it is **intraspecific**) or the variation represents differences between reproductively isolated groups (it is **interspecific**). How do we decide which answer is correct? To do this, we have to look at contemporary species.

If the amount of morphological variation observed in fossil samples is comparable to that seen today *within species of closely related forms,* then we shouldn't "split" our sample into more than one species. We must, however, be careful in choosing modern analogues, because rates of morphological evolution vary among different groups of mammals. So, for example, when studying extinct primates, we need to compare them with well-known species of modern primates.

Nevertheless, studies of living groups have shown that defining exactly where species boundaries begin and end is often difficult. In dealing with extinct species, the uncertainties are even greater. In addition to the overlapping patterns of variation over space, variation also occurs *through time.* In other words, even more variation will be seen in **paleospecies,** since individuals may be separated by thousands or even millions of years. Applying strict Linnaean taxonomy to such a situation presents an unavoidable dilemma. Standard Linnaean classification, designed to take account of variation present at any given time, describes a static situation. However, when we deal with paleospecies, the time frame is expanded, and the situation can be dynamic (i.e., later forms might be different from earlier ones). In such a dynamic situation, taxonomic decisions (where to draw species boundaries) are ultimately going to be somewhat arbitrary.

sexual dimorphism Differences in physical characteristics between males and females of the same species. For example, humans are slightly sexually dimorphic for body size, with males being taller, on average, than females of the same population.

intraspecific Within species; refers to variation seen within the same species.

interspecific Between species; refers to variation beyond that seen within the same species to include additional aspects seen between two different species.

paleospecies Species defined from fossil evidence, often covering a long time span.

Because the task of interpreting paleospecies is so difficult, paleoanthropologists have sought various solutions. Most researchers today define species using clusters of derived traits (identified cladistically). However, owing to the ambiguity of how many derived characters are required to identify a fully distinct species (as opposed to a subspecies), the frequent mixing of characters into novel combinations, and the always difficult problem of homoplasy, there continues to be disagreement. A good deal of the dispute is driven by philosophical orientation. Exactly how much diversity should one expect among fossil primates, including especially among fossil hominids?

Some researchers, called "splitters," claim that speciation occurred frequently during hominid evolution, and they often identify numerous fossil hominid species in a sample being studied. Others, called "lumpers," assume that speciation was less common and see much variation as being intraspecific; consequently, fewer hominid species are identified, named, and eventually plugged into evolutionary schemes. As you will see in succeeding chapters, debates of this sort pervade paleoanthropology, perhaps more than in any other branch of evolutionary biology.

genus A group of closely related species.

Recognition of Fossil Genera   The next, and broader, level of taxonomic classification, the **genus,** presents another problem. To have more than one genus, we obviously must have at least two species (reproductively isolated groups), and the species of one genus must differ in a basic way from the species of another genus. A genus is therefore defined as a group of species composed of members more closely related to each other than they are to species from any other genus.

Grouping species together into genera can be quite subjective and is often much debated by biologists. One possible test for contemporary animals is to check for results of hybridization between individuals of different species—rare in nature but quite common in captivity. If members of two normally separate species interbreed and produce live, though not necessarily fertile, offspring, the two parental species probably are not too different genetically and should therefore be grouped together in the same genus. A well-known example of such a cross is horses with donkeys (*Equus caballus* × *Equus asinus*), which normally produces live but sterile offspring (mules).

As previously mentioned, we cannot perform breeding experiments with extinct animals, but another definition of genus becomes highly relevant. Species that are members of the same genus share the same broad adaptive zone. What this represents is a general ecological lifestyle more basic than the narrower ecological niches characteristic of individual species. This ecological definition of genus can be an immense aid in interpreting fossil primates. Teeth are the most frequently preserved parts, and they often can provide excellent general ecological inferences. Moreover, cladistic analysis also provides assistance in making judgments about evolutionary relationships. That is, members of the same genus should all share derived characters not seen in members of other genera.

As a final comment, we should emphasize that classification by genus is not always a straightforward decision. For instance, many current researchers (Wildman et al., 2003), pointing to the very close genetic similarities between humans (*Homo sapiens*) and chimpanzees (*Pan troglodytes*), place both in the same genus (*Homo sapiens, Homo troglodytes*). When it gets this close to home, it frequently becomes difficult to remain objective!

Vertebrate Evolutionary History: A Brief Summary

In addition to the staggering array of living and extinct life forms, biologists must also contend with the vast amount of time that life has been evolving on earth. Again, scientists have devised simplified schemes—but in this case to organize *time,* not biological diversity.

Geologists have formulated the **geological time scale** (Fig. 5-4), in which very large time spans are organized into eras and periods. Periods, in turn, can be broken down into epochs. For the time span encompassing vertebrate evolution, there are three eras: the Paleozoic, the Mesozoic, and the Cenozoic. The first vertebrates are present in the fossil record dating to early in the Paleozoic 500 m.y.a. and probably go back considerably further. It is

geological time scale The organization of earth history into eras, periods, and epochs; commonly used by geologists and paleoanthropologists.

ERA	PERIOD	(Began m.y.a.)	EPOCH	(Began m.y.a.)
CENOZOIC	Quaternary	1.8	Holocene Pleistocene	0.01 1.8
	Tertiary	65	Pliocene Miocene Oligocene Eocene Paleocene	5 23 34 55 65
MESOZOIC	Cretaceous	136		
	Jurassic	190		
	Triassic	225		
PALEOZOIC	Permian	280		
	Carboniferous	345		
	Devonian	395		
	Silurian	430		
	Ordovician	500		
	Cambrian	570		
PRE-CAMBRIAN				

FIGURE 5-4 Geological time scale.

the vertebrate capacity to form bone that accounts for their more complete fossil record *after* 500 m.y.a.

During the Paleozoic, several varieties of fishes (including the ancestors of modern sharks and bony fishes), amphibians, and reptiles appeared. In addition, at the end of the Paleozoic, close to 250 m.y.a., several varieties of mammal-like reptiles were also diversifying. It's generally thought that some of these forms ultimately gave rise to the mammals.

The evolutionary history of vertebrates and other organisms during the Paleozoic and Mesozoic was profoundly influenced by geographical events. We know that the positions of the earth's continents have dramatically shifted during the last several hundred million years. This process, called **continental drift,** is explained by the geological theory of *plate tectonics,* which states that the earth's crust is a series of gigantic moving and colliding plates. Such massive geological movements can induce volcanic activity (as, for example, all around the Pacific rim), mountain building (e.g., the Himalayas), and earthquakes. Living on the juncture of the Pacific and North American plates, residents of the Pacific coast of the United States are acutely aware of some of these consequences, as illustrated by the explosive volcanic eruption of Mt. St. Helens and the frequent earthquakes in Alaska and California.

While reconstructing the earth's physical history, geologists have established the prior much altered positions of major continental landmasses. During the late Paleozoic, the continents came together to form a single colossal landmass called *Pangea.* (In actuality, the continents had been drifting on plates, coming together and separating, long before the end of the Paleozoic around 225 m.y.a.) During the early Mesozoic, the southern continents (South America, Africa, Antarctica, Australia, and India) began to split off from Pangea, forming a large southern continent called *Gondwanaland* (Fig. 5-5a). Similarly, the northern continents (North America, Greenland, Europe, and Asia) were consolidated into a northern landmass called *Laurasia.* During the Mesozoic, Gondwanaland and Laurasia continued to drift apart and to break up into smaller segments. By the end of the Mesozoic

continental drift The movement of continents on sliding plates of the earth's surface. As a result, the positions of large landmasses have shifted drastically during the earth's history.

FIGURE 5-5 Continental drift. Changes in positions of the continental plates from late Paleozoic to the early Cenozoic. (a) The positions of the continents during the Mesozoic (c. 125 m.y.a.). Pangea is breaking up into a northern landmass (Laurasia) and a southern landmass (Gondwanaland). (b) The positions of the continents at the beginning of the Cenozoic (c. 65 m.y.a.).

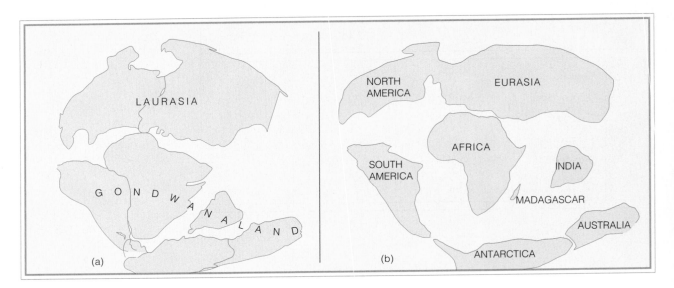

PALEOZOIC							MESOZOIC		
Cambrian	Ordovician	Silurian	Devonian	Carbon-iferous	Permian		Triassic	Jurassic	Cretaceous
Trilobites abundant; also brachiopods, jellyfish, worms, and other invertebrates	First fishes; trilobites still abundant; graptolites and corals become plentiful; possible land plants	Jawed fishes appear; first air-breathing animals; definite land plants	Age of Fish; first amphibians; first forests	First reptiles; radiation of amphibians; modern insects diversify	Reptile radiation; mammal-like reptiles	Major extinction event	Reptiles further radiate; first dinosaurs; egg-laying mammals	Great Age of Dinosaurs; flying and swimming dinosaurs; first toothed birds	Placental and marsupial mammals appear; first modern birds

570 m.y.a.   500 m.y.a.   430 m.y.a.   395 m.y.a.   345 m.y.a.   280 m.y.a.   225 m.y.a.   190 m.y.a.   136 m.y.a.   65 m.y.a.

FIGURE 5-6 Time line of major events in early vertebrate evolution.

(circa 65 m.y.a.), the continents were beginning to assume their current positions (Fig. 5-5b).

The evolutionary ramifications of this long-term continental drift were profound. Groups of land animals became effectively isolated from each other by oceans, and the distribution of reptiles and mammals was significantly influenced by continental movements. These movements continued in the Cenozoic and indeed are still happening, although without such dramatic results.

During most of the Mesozoic, reptiles were the dominant land vertebrates, and they exhibited a broad expansion into a variety of **ecological niches,** which included aerial and marine habitats. The most famous of these highly successful Mesozoic reptiles were the dinosaurs, which themselves evolved into a wide array of sizes and species and adapted to a variety of lifestyles. Dinosaur paleontology, never a boring field, has advanced several startling notions in recent years: that many dinosaurs were "warm-blooded" (see p. 103); that some varieties were quite social and probably also engaged in considerable parental care; that many forms became extinct as the result of major climatic changes to the earth's atmosphere from collisions with comets or asteroids; and finally, that not all dinosaurs became entirely extinct, with many descendants still living today (i.e., all modern birds). (See Fig. 5-6 for a summary of major events in early vertebrate evolutionary history.)

The earliest mammals are known from traces of fossils from early in the Mesozoic, but the first **placental** mammals can't be positively identified until quite late in the Mesozoic, approximately 70 m.y.a. This means that the highly successful mammalian diversifiction, portions of which we still see today, took place almost entirely within the most recent era of geological history, the Cenozoic.

The Cenozoic is divided into two periods, the Tertiary (about 63 million years duration) and the Quaternary, from about 1.8 m.y.a. up to and including the present. Paleontologists often refer to the next, more precise level of subdivision within the Cenozoic, the **epochs.** There are seven epochs within the Cenozoic: the Paleocene, Eocene, Oligocene, Miocene, Pliocene, Pleistocene, and Holocene, the last often referred to as the Recent.

ecological niches The positions of species within their physical and biological environments, together making up the *ecosystem*. A species' ecological niche is defined by such components as diet, terrain, vegetation, type of predators, relationships with other species, and activity patterns, and each niche is unique to a given species.

placental A type (subclass) of mammal. During the Cenozoic, placentals became the most widespread and numerous mammals and today are represented by upwards of 20 orders, including the primates.

epochs Categories of the geological time scale; subdivisions of periods. In the Cenozoic, epochs include the Paleocene, Eocene, Oligocene, Miocene, and Pliocene (from the Tertiary) and the Pleistocene and Holocene (from the Quaternary).

Mammalian Evolution

Following the extinction of the dinosaurs and many other Mesozoic forms (at the end of the Mesozoic), a wide array of ecological niches became available, and this allowed the rapid expansion and diversification of mammals. The Cenozoic was an opportunistic time for mammals, and it is known as the Age of Mammals. Mesozoic mammals were small animals, about the size of mice, which they resembled superficially. The wide diversification of mammals in the Cenozoic saw the rise of the major lineages of all modern mammals. Indeed, mammals, along with birds, replaced reptiles as the dominant terrestrial vertebrates.

How do we account for the rapid success of the mammals? Several characteristics relating to learning and general flexibility of behavior are of prime importance. To process more information, mammals were selected for larger brains than those typically found in reptiles. In particular, the cerebrum became generally enlarged, especially the outer covering, the neocortex, which controls higher brain functions (Fig. 5-7). In some mammals, the cerebrum expanded so much that it came to comprise the majority of brain volume; moreover, the number of surface convolutions increased, creating more surface area and thus providing space for even more nerve cells (neurons). As we will see shortly (in Chapter 6), this is a trend even further emphasized among the primates.

For such a large and complex organ as the mammalian brain to develop, a longer, more intense period of growth is required. Slower development can occur internally (*in utero*) as well as after birth. While internal fertilization and internal development are not unique to mammals, the latter is a major innovation among terrestrial vertebrates. Other forms (birds, most fishes, and reptiles) incubate their young externally by laying eggs, while mammals, with very few exceptions, give birth to live young. Even among mammals, however, there is considerable variation among the major groups in how mature the young are at birth. As you will see, it is in mammals like ourselves, the *placental* forms, where *in utero* development goes farthest.

FIGURE 5-7 Lateral view of the brain. The illustration shows the increase in the cerebral cortex of the brain. The cerebral cortex integrates sensory information and selects responses.

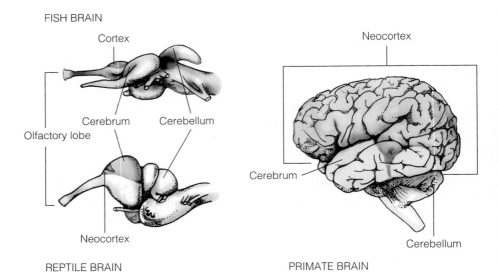

FISH BRAIN

Cortex

Cerebrum   Cerebellum

Olfactory lobe

Neocortex

REPTILE BRAIN

Neocortex

Cerebrum

Cerebellum

PRIMATE BRAIN

Another distinctive feature of mammals is seen in the dentition. While living reptiles consistently have similarly shaped teeth (called a *homodont* dentition), mammals have differently shaped teeth (Fig. 5-8). This varied pattern, termed a **heterodont** dentition, is reflected in the primitive (ancestral) mammalian array of dental elements, which includes 3 incisors, 1 canine, 4 premolars, and 3 molars in each quarter of the mouth. Since the upper and lower jaws are usually the same and are symmetrical for both sides, the "dental formula" is conventionally illustrated by dental quarter (see p. 117 for a more complete discussion of dental patterns as they apply to primates). Thus, with 11 teeth in each quarter of the mouth, the primitive (i.e., ancestral) mammalian dental complement includes a total of 44 teeth. Such a heterodont arrangement allows mammals to process a wide variety of foods. Incisors can be used for cutting, canines for grasping and piercing, and premolars and molars for crushing and grinding.

A final point regarding teeth relates to their disproportionate representation in the fossil record. As the hardest, most durable portion of a vertebrate skeleton, teeth have the greatest likelihood of becoming fossilized (i.e., mineralized). As a result, the vast majority of the available fossil data for most vertebrates, including primates, consists of teeth.

Another major adaptive complex that distinguishes contemporary mammals from reptiles is the maintenance of a constant internal body temperature. Also colloquially (and incorrectly) called "warm-bloodedness," this crucial physiological adaptation is also seen in contemporary birds (and was also perhaps characteristic of many dinosaurs as well). In fact, many contemporary reptiles are able to approximate a constant internal body temperature through behavioral means (especially by regulating activity and exposing the body to the sun). In this sense, reptiles (along with birds and mammals) could be said to be *homeothermic*. So a more useful distinction is to see how the energy to maintain body temperature is produced and channeled. In reptiles, it's obtained directly from exposure to the sun; reptiles are thus said to be *ectothermic*. In mammals and birds, however, the energy is generated *internally* through metabolic activity (by processing food or by muscle action); mammals and birds are hence referred to as **endothermic.**

The Emergence of Major Mammalian Groups

There are three major subgroups of living mammals: the egg-laying mammals, or monotremes (Fig. 5-9), the pouched mammals, or marsupials (Fig. 5-10), and the placental mammals. The monotremes are extremely primitive and are considered more distinct from marsupials or placentals than these latter are from each other.

The most notable difference between marsupials and placentals concerns fetal development. In marsupials, the young are born extremely immature and must complete development in an external pouch. But placental mammals develop over a longer period of time inside the mother, and this is made possible by the evolutionary development of a specialized tissue (the placenta) that provides for fetal nourishment.

REPTILIAN (alligator): homodont

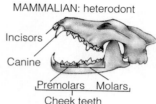

MAMMALIAN: heterodont

Incisors
Canine
Premolars   Molars
Cheek teeth

FIGURE 5-8 Reptilian and mammalian teeth.

heterodont Having different kinds of teeth; characteristic of mammals, whose teeth consist of incisors, canines, premolars, and molars.

endothermic (*endo*, meaning "within" or "internal") Able to maintain internal body temperature through the production of energy by means of metabolic processes within cells; characteristic of mammals, birds, and perhaps some dinosaurs.

FIGURE 5-9 The spiny anteater (a monotreme).

FIGURE 5-10 A wallaby with an infant in the pouch (marsupials).

With a longer gestation period, the central nervous system develops more completely in the fetus. Moreover, after birth, the "bond of milk" between mother and young also allows more time for complex neural structures to form. It should also be emphasized that from a *biosocial* perspective, this dependency period not only allows for adequate physiological development, but also provides for a wider range of learning stimuli. That is, the young mammalian brain receives a vast amount of information channeled to it through observation of the mother's behavior and through play with age-mates. It's not sufficient to have evolved a brain capable of learning. Collateral evolution of mammalian social systems has ensured that young mammal brains are provided with ample learning opportunities and are thus put to good use.

Processes of Macroevolution

As noted earlier, evolution operates at both microevolutionary and macro-evolutionary levels. We discussed evolution primarily from a microevolution-ary perspective in Chapter 4; in this chapter, our focus is on macroevolution. Macroevolutionary mechanisms operate more on the whole species than on individuals or populations and take much longer than microevolutionary processes to have a noticeable impact.

ADAPTIVE RADIATION

As mentioned in Chapter 2, the potential capacity of a group of organisms to multiply is practically unlimited, but its ability to increase its numbers is regu-lated largely by the availability of resources (food, water, shelter, and space).

As population size increases, access to resources decreases, and the environment will ultimately prove inadequate. Depleted resources induce some members of a population to seek an environment in which competition is reduced and the opportunities for survival and reproductive success are increased. This evolutionary tendency to exploit unoccupied habitats may eventually produce an abundance of diverse species.

This story has been played out countless times during the history of life, and some groups have expanded extremely rapidly. Known as **adaptive radiation,** this evolutionary process can be seen in the divergence of the stem reptiles into the profusion of different forms of the late Paleozoic and especially those of the Mesozoic. It's a process that takes place when a life form rapidly takes advantage, so to speak, of the many newly available ecological niches.

The principle of evolution illustrated by adaptive radiation is fairly simple, but important. It may be stated thus: *A species, or group of species, will diverge into as many variations as two factors allow: (1) its adaptive potential and (2) the adaptive opportunities of the available niches.*

In the case of reptiles, there was little divergence in the very early stages of evolution, when the ancestral form was little more than one among a variety of amphibian water dwellers. In reptiles, a more efficient egg than that of amphibians had developed (one that could incubate out of water). This new egg, with a hard, water-tight shell, had great adaptive potential, but initially there were few zones to invade. However, once reptiles became fully terrestrial, a wide array of ecological niches became accessible to them. Once freed from their attachment to water, reptiles were able to exploit landmasses with no serious competition from any other animal. They moved into the many different ecological niches on land (and to some extent in the air and sea), and as they adapted to these areas, they diversified into a large number of species. This spectacular radiation burst forth with such evolutionary speed that it may well be termed an adaptive explosion.

Of course, the rapid expansion of placental mammals at the beginning of the Cenozoic is another excellent example of adaptive radiation.

GENERALIZED AND SPECIALIZED CHARACTERISTICS

Another aspect of evolution closely related to adaptive radiation involves the transition from generalized characteristics to specialized characteristics. These two terms refer to the adaptive potential of a particular trait. A trait that's adapted for many functions is said to be generalized, while one that is limited to a narrow set of functions is said to be specialized.

For example, a generalized mammalian limb has five fairly flexible digits adapted for many possible functions (grasping, weight support, digging). In this respect, human hands are still quite generalized. On the other hand (or foot), there have been many structural modifications in our feet suited for the specialized function of stable weight support in an upright posture.

The terms *generalized* and *specialized* are also sometimes used when speaking of the adaptive potential of whole organisms. Consider, for example, the aye-aye of Madagascar, an unusual primate species. The aye-aye is a highly specialized animal, structurally adapted to a narrow rodent/woodpecker-like econiche—digging holes with prominent incisors and removing insect larvae with an elongated bony finger.

adaptive radiation The relatively rapid expansion and diversification of life forms into new ecological niches.

It's important to note that only a generalized ancestor can provide the flexible evolutionary basis for rapid diversification. Only a generalized species with potential for adaptation to varied ecological niches can lead to all the later diversification and specialization of forms into particular ecological niches.

An issue that we have already raised also bears on this discussion: the relationship of ancestral and derived characters. While not always the case, ancestral characters *usually* tend to be more generalized. And specialized characteristics are almost always also derived ones.

MODES OF EVOLUTIONARY CHANGE

Until fairly recently, the general consensus among evolutionary biologists was that microevolutionary mechanisms could be translated directly into the larger-scale macroevolutionary changes, especially the most central of all macroevolutionary processes, speciation. In the last two decades, this view has been seriously challenged. Many scientists now believe that macroevolution can't be explained solely in terms of accumulated microevolutionary changes. Consequently, these researchers are convinced that macroevolution is only partly understandable through microevolutionary models.

Gradualism vs. Punctuated Equilibrium   The traditional view of evolution has emphasized that change accumulates gradually in evolving lineages, an idea called phyletic gradualism. Accordingly, the complete fossil record of an evolving group (if it could be recovered) would display a series of forms with finely graded transitional differences between each ancestor and its descendant. The fact that such transitional forms are only rarely found is attributed to the incompleteness of the fossil record, or, as Darwin called it, "a history of the world, imperfectly kept, and written in changing dialect."

For more than a century, this perspective dominated evolutionary biology, but in the last 25 years, some biologists have called it into question. The evolutionary mechanisms operating on species over the long run aren't always gradual. In some cases, species persist for thousands of generations basically unchanged. Then, rather suddenly, at least in evolutionary terms, a "spurt" of speciation occurs. This uneven, nongradual process of long stasis and quick spurts has been termed **punctuated equilibrium** (Gould and Eldredge, 1977).

punctuated equilibrium The concept that evolutionary change proceeds through long periods of stasis punctuated by rapid periods of change.

What the advocates of punctuated equilibrium are disputing are the tempo (rate) and mode (manner) of evolutionary change as commonly understood since Darwin's time. Rather than a slow, steady tempo, this alternate view postulates long periods of no change (i.e., equilibrium) punctuated only occasionally by sudden bursts. From this observation, many researchers concluded that the mode of evolution, too, must be different from that suggested by classical Darwinists. Rather than gradual accumulation of small changes in a single lineage, advocates of punctuated equilibrium believe that an additional evolutionary mechanism is required to push the process along. They thus postulate *speciation* as the major influence in bringing about rapid evolutionary change.

How well does the paleontological record agree with the predictions of punctuated equilibrium? Considerable fossil data do, in fact, show long periods of stasis punctuated by occasional quite rapid changes (taking from about 10,000 to 50,000 years). The best supporting evidence for punctuated equilibrium has come from marine invertebrate fossils. Intermediate forms are rare, not so much because the fossil record is poor, but because the speciation events and longevity of these transitional species were so short that we shouldn't expect to find them very often.

And while some of the fossil evidence of other animals, including primates (Gingerich, 1985; Brown and Rose, 1987; Rose, 1991), doesn't fit the expectations of punctuated equilibrium, it would be a fallacy to assume that evolutionary change in these groups must therefore be of a completely gradual tempo. In all lineages, the pace assuredly speeds up and slows down as a result of factors that influence the size and relative isolation of populations. In addition, environmental changes that influence the pace and direction of natural selection must also be considered. Nevertheless, in general accordance with the Modern Synthesis, microevolution and macroevolution need not be "decoupled," as some evolutionary biologists have suggested.

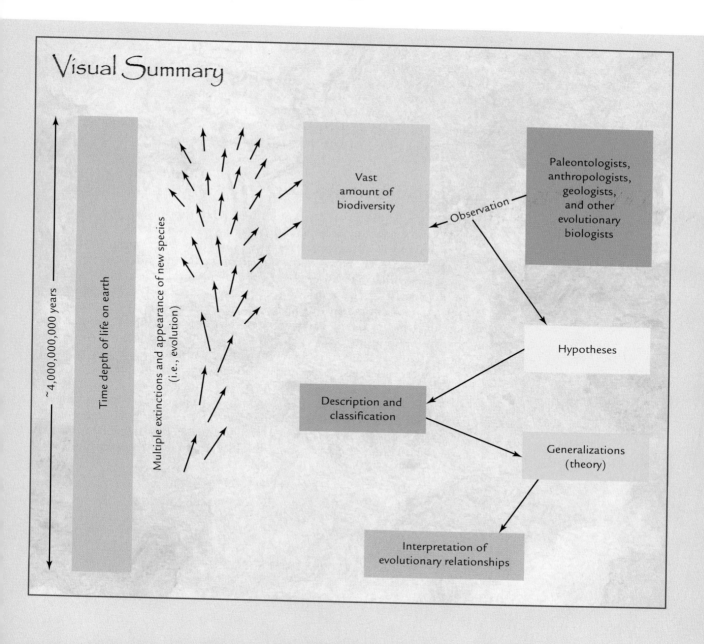

Summary

This chapter has surveyed the basics of vertebrate and mammalian evolution, emphasizing a macroevolutionary perspective. Given the huge amount of organic diversity displayed, as well as the vast amount of time involved, two major organizing perspectives prove indispensable: schemes of formal classification to organize organic diversity and the geological time scale to organize geological time. The principles of classification were reviewed in some detail, contrasting two differing approaches: evolutionary systematics and cladistics. Because primates are vertebrates and, more specifically, mammals, these broader organic groups were briefly reviewed, emphasizing major evolutionary trends.

Theoretical perspectives relating to contemporary understanding of macroevolutionary processes (especially the concepts of species and speciation) are crucial to any interpretation of long-term aspects of evolutionary history, be it vertebrate, mammalian, or primate. As genus and species designation is the common form of reference for both living and extinct organisms (and will be used frequently throughout the text), its biological significance was discussed in depth. From a more general theoretical perspective, evolutionary biologists have postulated two different modes of evolutionary change: gradualism and punctuated equilibrium. At present, the available fossil record does not conform entirely to the predictions of punctuated equilibrium, but one should not conclude that evolutionary tempo was necessarily strictly gradual (which it certainly was not).

Critical Thinking Questions

1. What are the two goals of classification? What happens when meeting both goals simultaneously becomes difficult or even impossible?

2. Remains of a fossil mammal have been found on your campus. If you adopt a cladistic approach, how would you determine (a) that it is a mammal rather than some other kind of vertebrate (discuss specific characters), (b) what kind of mammal it is (again, discuss specific characters), and (c) how it *might* be related to one or more living mammals (again, discuss specific characters)?

3. For the same fossil find (and your interpretation) in question 2, draw an interpretive figure using cladistic analysis (i.e., draw a cladogram). Next, using more traditional evolutionary systematics, construct a phylogeny. Lastly, explain the differences between the cladogram and the phylogeny (be sure to emphasize the fundamental ways the two schemes differ).

4. a. Humans are fairly generalized mammals. What do we mean by this, and what specific features (characters) would you select to illustrate this statement?

   b. More precisely, humans are *placental* mammals. How do humans, and generally all other placental mammals, differ from the other two major groups of mammals?

Introduction

Chimpanzees aren't monkeys. Gorillas and orangutans aren't either. They're apes, and there are many differences between monkeys and apes. Yet, how many times have you seen a greeting card or advertisement with a picture of a chimpanzee and a phrase that goes something like, "Don't monkey around" or "No more monkey business"? Or maybe you've noticed how people at zoos find captive primates especially funny, particularly when they tease them. While these issues may seem trivial, they aren't, because they illustrate how ill informed most people are about their closest relatives. This is extremely unfortunate, because by better understanding these relatives, not only can we better know ourselves, but we can also try to preserve the many primate species that are critically endangered.

One way to better understand any organism, is to compare its anatomy and behavior to other, closely related species. This comparative approach helps us explain how and why both physiological and behavioral systems evolved as adaptive responses. This statement applies to *Homo sapiens* just as it does to any other species, and if we want to identify the components that have shaped the evolution of our species, a good starting point is a comparison between humans and our closest living relatives, the approximately 230 species of nonhuman primates (**prosimians,** monkeys, and apes). (Groves, 2001b, suggests that there may be as many as 350 primate species.)

This chapter describes the physical characteristics that define the order Primates; gives a brief overview of the major groups of living primates; and introduces some methods of comparing living primates through genetic data. (For a comparison of human and nonhuman skeletons, see Appendix A.) But before we go any further, we again want to call attention to a few common misunderstandings about evolutionary processes.

Evolution is *not* a goal-directed process; thus, the fact that prosimians evolved before **anthropoids** doesn't mean that prosimians "progressed," or "advanced," to become anthropoids. Living primate species aren't "superior" to their predecessors or to one another. Each lineage or species has come to possess unique qualities that make it better suited to a particular habitat and lifestyle. Given that all contemporary organisms are "successful" results of the evolutionary process, it's best to avoid altogether the use of such loaded terms as "superior" and "inferior." Finally, you shouldn't make the mistake of thinking that contemporary primates (including humans) necessarily represent the final stage or apex of a lineage. Actually, the only species that represent final evolutionary stages of particular lineages are the ones that become extinct.

Click

Go to the following CD-ROM for interactive activities and exercises on topics covered in this chapter:

Virtual Laboratories for Physical Anthropology CD-ROM, Third Edition

prosimians Members of a suborder of Primates, the *Prosimii* (pronounced "pro-sim´-ee-eye"). Traditionally, the suborder includes lemurs, lorises, and tarsiers.

anthropoids Members of a suborder of Primates, the *Anthropoidea* (pronounced "ann-throw-poid´-ee-uh"). Traditionally, the suborder includes monkeys, apes, and humans.

Characteristics of Primates

All primates possess numerous characteristics they share in common with other placental mammals (see Chapter 5). Some of these traits are body hair; a relatively long gestation period followed by live birth; mammary glands (thus the term *mammal*); different types of teeth (incisors, canines, premolars, and molars); the ability to maintain a constant internal body temperature through physiological means, or *endothermy;* increased brain size; and a considerable capacity for learning and behavioral flexibility. Therefore, to differentiate primates, as a group, from other mammals, we need to describe those characteristics that, taken together, set primates apart from other mammalian groups.

Identifying single traits that define the primate order isn't easy, because compared to many mammals, primates have remained quite *generalized*. That is, primates have retained many ancestral, or **primitive,** mammalian traits that some other mammals have lost over time. In response to particular selective pressures, many mammalian groups have become increasingly **specialized.** For example, through the course of evolution, horses and cattle have undergone a reduction of the number of digits (fingers and toes) from the ancestral pattern of five to one and two, respectively. Moreover, these species have developed hard, protective coverings over their feet in the form of hooves (Fig. 6-1a). While this type of structure is adaptive in prey species, whose survival depends on speed and stability, it restricts the animal to only one type of locomotion. Moreover, limb function is limited entirely to support and movement, while the ability to manipulate objects is completely lost.

Primates can't be simply defined by one or even two traits they share in common precisely because they *aren't* so specialized. As a result, anthropologists have pointed to a group of characteristics that, taken together, more or less characterize the entire order. But you should keep in mind that these are a set of *general* tendencies and aren't all equally expressed in all primates. The following list is meant to give an overall structural and behavioral picture of the animals we call "primates," focusing on those characteristics that tend to set primates apart from other mammals. Concentrating on certain retained (ancestral) mammalian traits along with more specific derived ones has been the traditional approach of **primatologists** and it's an approach still used today. In their limbs and locomotion, teeth and diet, senses, brain, and behaviors, primates reflect a common evolutionary history with adaptations to similar environmental challenges.

A. *Limbs and Locomotion*
   1. *A tendency toward erect posture (especially in the upper body).* Present to some degree in all primates, this tendency is variously associated with sitting, leaping, standing, and, occasionally, bipedal walking.
   2. *A flexible, generalized limb structure, which allows most primates to practice a number of locomotor behaviors.* Primates have retained some bones (e.g., the clavicle, or collarbone) and certain abilities, (e.g., rotation of the forearm) that have been lost in some more specialized mammals. Various aspects of hip and shoulder **morphology** also provide primates with a wide range of limb movement and function. Thus, by maintaining a generalized locomotor anatomy, primates aren't restricted to one form of movement

primitive Referring to a trait or combination of traits present in an ancestral form.

specialized Evolved for a particular function; usually refers to a specific trait (e.g., incisor teeth), but may also refer to the entire way of life of an organism.

primatologists Scientists who study the evolution, anatomy, and behavior of nonhuman primates. Those who study behavior in noncaptive animals are usually trained as physical anthropologists.

morphology The form (shape, size) of anatomical structures; can also refer to the entire organism.

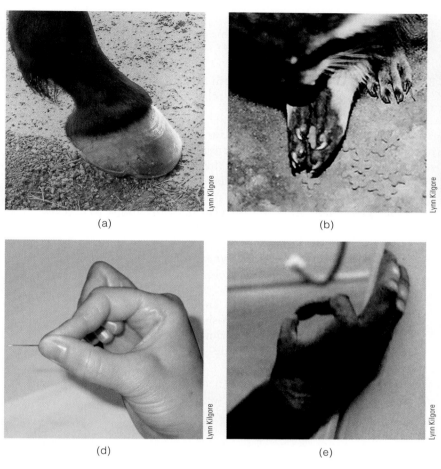

(a)   (b)   (c)

(d)   (e)

FIGURE 6-1 (a) A horse's front foot, homologous with a human hand, has undergone reduction from five digits to one. (b) While raccoons are capable of considerable manual dexterity and can readily pick up small objects with one hand, they have no opposable thumb. (c) Many monkeys are able to grasp objects with an opposable thumb, while others have very reduced thumbs. (d) Humans are capable of a "precision grip." (e) Chimpanzees, with their reduced thumbs, are also capable of a precision grip, but they frequently use a modified form.

(unlike many other mammals). Primate limbs are also used for activities other than locomotion.

3. *Hands and feet with a high degree of __prehensility (grasping ability)__.* Many species can manipulate objects but not as skillfully as primates (Fig. 6-1b). All primates use their hands, and frequently their feet, to grasp and manipulate objects (Fig. 6-1c through e). This is variably expressed and is enhanced by a number of characteristics, including:

   a. *Retention of five digits on hands and feet.* This trait varies somewhat throughout the order, and some species show marked reduction of the thumb or second digit (first finger).

   b. *An opposable thumb and, in most species, a divergent and partially opposable big toe.* Most primates are capable of moving the thumb so that it comes in contact (in some fashion) with the second digit or the palm of the hand (see Fig. 6-1c through e).

   c. *Nails instead of claws.* This characteristic is seen in all primates except some New World monkeys. All prosimians also have a claw on one digit.

   d. *Tactile pads enriched with sensory nerve fibers at the ends of digits.* This enhances the sense of touch.

prehensility Grasping, as by the hands and feet of primates.

omnivorous Having a diet consisting of many kinds of foods, such as plant materials (seeds, fruits, leaves), meat, and insects.

diurnal Active during the day.

nocturnal Active during the night.

stereoscopic vision The condition whereby visual images are, to varying degrees, superimposed on one another. This provides for depth perception, or the perception of the external environment in three dimensions. Stereoscopic vision is partly a function of structures in the brain.

binocular vision Vision characterized by overlapping visual fields provided for by forward-facing eyes. Binocular vision is essential to depth perception.

hemispheres Two halves of the cerebrum that are connected by a dense mass of fibers. (The cerebrum is the large rounded outer portion of the brain.)

B. *Diet and Teeth*
   1. *Lack of dietary specialization.* This is typical of most primates, who tend to eat a wide assortment of food items. In general, primates are **omnivorous.**
   2. *A generalized dentition.* The teeth aren't specialized for processing only one type of food, a pattern related to the lack of dietary specialization.

C. *The senses and the brain.* Primates (**diurnal** ones in particular) rely heavily on the visual sense and less on the sense of smell. This emphasis is reflected in evolutionary changes in the skull, eyes, and brain.
   1. *Color vision.* This is a charactereistic of all diurnal primates. **Nocturnal** primates don't have color vision.
   2. *Depth perception.* **Stereoscopic vision,** or the ability to perceive objects in three dimensions, is made possible through a variety of mechanisms, including:
      a. *Eyes positioned toward the front of the face (not to the sides).* This provides for overlapping visual fields, or **binocular vision** (Fig. 6-2).
      b. *Visual information from each eye transmitted to visual centers in both **hemispheres** of the brain.* In nonprimate mammals, most optic nerve fibers cross to the opposite hemisphere through a structure at the base of the brain. In primates, about 40 percent of the fibers remain on the same side (see Fig. 6-2).

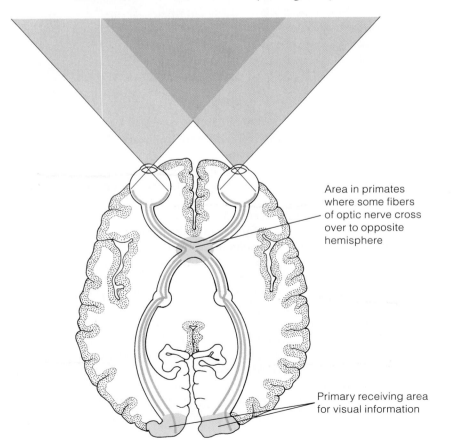

Area in primates where some fibers of optic nerve cross over to opposite hemisphere

Primary receiving area for visual information

FIGURE 6-2 Simplified diagram showing overlapping visual fields that permit binocular vision in primates and many predators with eyes positioned at the front of the face. (The green shaded area represents the area of overlap.) Stereoscopic vision (three-dimensional vision) is provided in part by binocular vision and in part by the transmission of visual stimuli from each eye to *both* hemispheres of the brain. (In nonprimate mammals, most, if not all, visual information crosses over to the hemisphere opposite the eye in which it was initially received.)

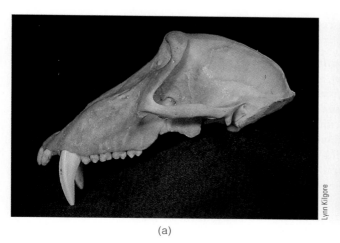

(a)

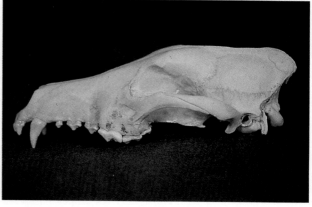

(b)

c. *Visual information organized into three-dimensional images by specialized structures in the brain itself.* The capacity for stereoscopic vision is dependent on each hemisphere of the brain receiving visual information from both eyes and from overlapping visual fields.

3. *Decreased reliance on the sense of smell (olfaction).* This trend is seen in an overall reduction in the size of olfactory structures in the brain. Corresponding reduction of the entire olfactory apparatus has also resulted in decreased size of the snout. In some species, such as baboons, the large muzzle isn't related to olfaction, but to the presence of large teeth, especially the canines (Fig. 6-3).

4. *Expansion and increased complexity of the brain.* This is a general trend among placental mammals, but it's especially true of primates (Fig. 6-4). In primates, this expansion is most evident in the visual and association areas of the neocortex (portions of the brain where information from different **sensory modalities** is integrated). Significant

FIGURE 6-3 The skull of a male baboon (a) compared with that of a red wolf (b). Note the forward-facing eyes positioned above the snout in the baboon, compared with the lateral position of the eyes at the sides of the wolf's face. Also, the baboon's large muzzle doesn't reflect a heavy reliance on the sense of smell. Rather, it supports the roots of the large canine teeth, which curve back through the bone for as much as 1½ inches.

sensory modalities
Different forms of sensation (e.g., touch, pain, pressure, heat, cold, vision, taste, hearing, and smell).

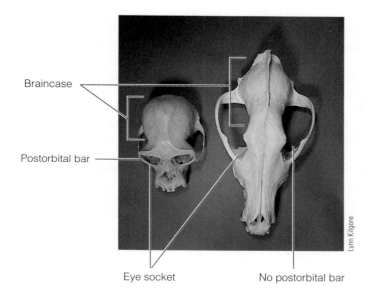

Braincase

Postorbital bar

Eye socket   No postorbital bar

FIGURE 6-4 The skull of a gibbon (left) compared with that of a red wolf (right). Note that the absolute size of the braincase in the gibbon is slightly larger than that of the wolf, even though the wolf (at about 80 to 100 pounds) is six times the size of the gibbon (about 15 pounds).

expansion in regions involved with the hand (both sensory and motor) is seen in many species, particularly humans.

D. *Maturation, learning, and behavior*
1. *A more efficient means of fetal nourishment, longer periods of gestation, reduced numbers of offspring (with single births the norm), delayed maturation, and extension of the entire life span.*
2. *A greater dependence on flexible, learned behavior.* This trend is correlated with delayed maturation and consequently longer periods of infant and child dependency on the parent. As a result of both these trends, parental investment in each offspring is increased, so that although fewer offspring are born, they receive more intense and efficient rearing.
3. *The tendency to live in social groups and the permanent association of adult males with the group.* Except for some nocturnal species, primates tend to associate with other individuals. The permanent association of adult males with the group is uncommon in many mammals but widespread in primates.
4. *The tendency to diurnal activity patterns.* This is seen in most primates; only one monkey species and some prosimians are nocturnal.

Primate Adaptations

EVOLUTIONARY FACTORS

arboreal Tree-living; adapted to life in the trees.

adaptive niche The entire way of life of an organism: where it lives, what it eats, how it gets food, how it avoids predators, etc.

Traditionally, the suite of characteristics shared by primates has been explained as the result of adaptation to **arboreal** living. While other placental mammals were adapting to various ground-dwelling lifestyles and even marine environments, the primates found their **adaptive niche** in the trees. Some other mammals were also adapting to arboreal living, but while many nested in trees, they continued to come to the ground to find food. But throughout the course of evolution, primates increasingly exploited foods (leaves, seeds, fruits, nuts, insects, and small mammals) in the branches themselves. Over time, this dietary shift enhanced the general trend toward increased *omnivory* and, along with this diet, the evolution of the primate generalized dentition.

This adaptive process is also reflected in how primates rely on vision. In a complex, three-dimensional environment with uncertain footholds, acute color vision with depth perception is, to say the least, extremely beneficial. Grasping hands and feet also reflect an adaptation to living in the trees. Obviously, animals like squirrels and raccoons can climb by digging in with claws. But primates adopted a technique of grasping branches with prehensile hands and feet, and grasping abilities were further enhanced with the appearance of flattened nails instead of claws.

arboreal hypothesis The traditional view that primate characteristics can be explained as a consequence of primate diversification into arboreal habitats.

An alternative to this traditional **arboreal hypothesis,** called the *visual predation hypothesis* (Cartmill, 1972, 1992), emphasizes that predators such as cats and owls also have forward-facing eyes. Furthermore, forward-facing eyes, grasping hands and feet, and the presence of nails instead of claws didn't necessarily come about in a purely arboreal environment. Thus, primates may first have adapted to shrubby forest undergrowth and the lowest tiers of the forest canopy, where they hunted insects and other small prey primarily through stealth.

In a third scenario, Sussman (1991) suggests that the basic primate traits developed in conjunction with another major evolutionary occurrence, the appearance of flowering plants. Flowering plants provide numerous resources, including nectar, seeds, and fruits, and their diversification was accompanied by the emergence of ancestral forms of major groups of modern birds and mammals.

These hypotheses aren't mutually exclusive. The complex of primate characteristics might well have begun in nonarboreal settings and certainly may have been stimulated by the new econiches provided by evolving flowering plants. But at some point, the primates did take to the trees, and that's where the majority of them still live today.

GEOGRAPHICAL DISTRIBUTION AND HABITATS

With just a couple of exceptions, primates are found in tropical or semitropical areas of the New and Old Worlds. In the New World, these areas include southern Mexico, Central America, and parts of South America. Old World primates are found in Africa, India, Southeast Asia (including numerous islands), and Japan (see Fig. 6-6, next page).

While the majority of primates are mostly arboreal and live in forest or woodland habitats, some Old World monkeys (e.g., baboons) have adapted to life on the ground in places where trees are sparsely distributed. Moreover, the African apes (gorillas, chimpanzees, and bonobos) spend a considerable amount of time on the ground in forested and wooded habitats. Nevertheless, no nonhuman primate is adapted to a fully terrestrial lifestyle, and they all spend some time in the trees.

DIET AND TEETH

Omnivory is one example of the overall lack of specialization in primates. Although the majority of primate species tend to emphasize some food items over others, most eat a combination of fruit, nuts, seeds, leaves, other plant materials, and insects. Many also get animal protein from birds and amphibians, and some occasionally kill and eat small mammals, including other primates. Others, such as African colobus monkeys and the leaf-eating monkeys (langurs) of India and Southeast Asia, have become more specialized and mostly eat leaves. Such a wide array of choices is highly adaptive, even in fairly predictable environments.

Like the majority of other mammals, most primates have four kinds of teeth: incisors and canines for biting and cutting, and premolars and molars for chewing. Biologists use a *dental formula* to describe the number of each type of tooth that typifies a species. A dental formula indicates the number of each tooth type in each quarter of the mouth (Fig. 6-5). For example, all Old World *anthropoids* have two incisors, one canine, two premolars, and three molars on each side of the **midline** in both the upper and lower jaws, or a total of 32 teeth. This is represented as a dental formula of

$$\frac{2.1.2.3}{2.1.2.3} \text{ (upper)} \\ \text{ (lower)}$$

midline An anatomical term referring to a hypothetical line that divides the body into right and left halves.

FIGURE 6-5 Dental formulae. The number of each kind of tooth is given for one-quarter of the mouth.

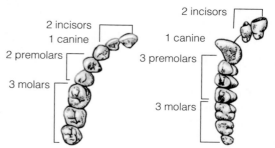

2 incisors
1 canine
2 premolars

3 molars

2 incisors
1 canine
3 premolars

3 molars

(a) Human: 2.1.2.3.
    2.1.2.3.

(b) Most New World monkeys: 2.1.3.3.
    2.1.3.3.

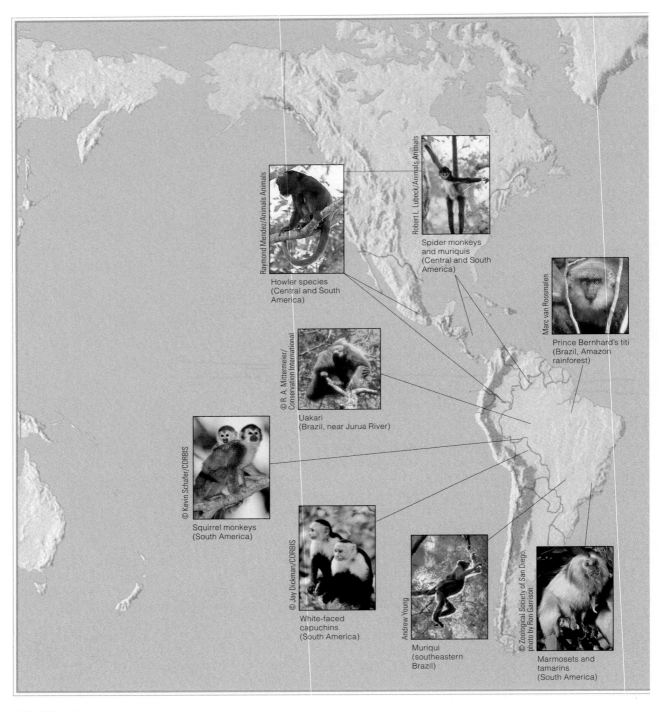

FIGURE 6-6 Geographical distribution of living nonhuman primates. Much original habitat is now very fragmented.

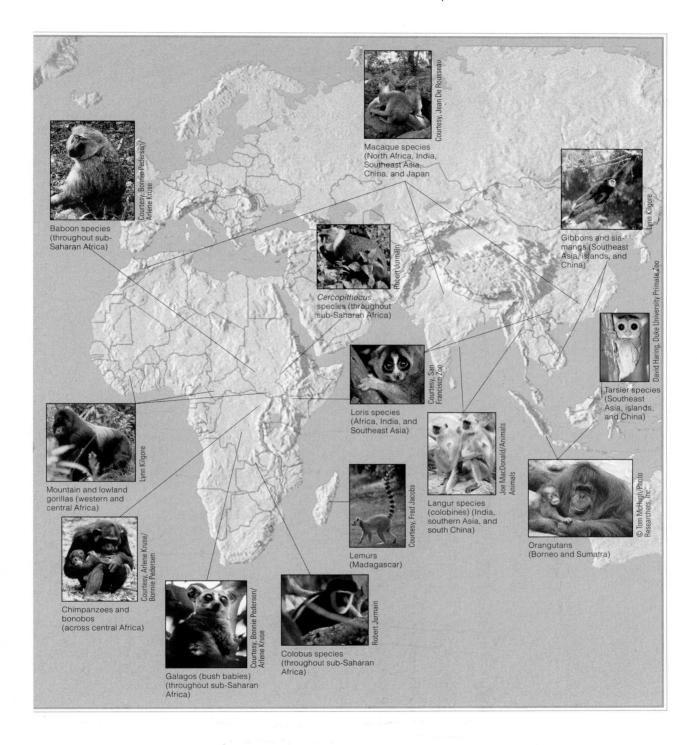

Macaque species (North Africa, India, Southeast Asia, China, and Japan

Courtesy, Jean De Rousseau

Baboon species (throughout sub-Saharan Africa)

Courtesy, Bonnie Pedersen/ Arlene Kruse

Gibbons and siamangs (Southeast Asia, islands, and China)

Lynn Kilgore

Cercopithecus species (throughout sub-Saharan Africa)

Robert Jurmain

Tarsier species (Southeast Asia, islands, and China)

David Haring, Duke University Primate Zoo

Loris species (Africa, India, and Southeast Asia)

Courtesy, San Francisco Zoo

Mountain and lowland gorillas (western and central Africa)

Lynn Kilgore

Langur species (colobines) (India, southern Asia, and south China)

Joe MacDonald/Animals Animals

Orangutans (Borneo and Sumatra)

© Tom McHugh/Photo Researchers, Inc.

Chimpanzees and bonobos (across central Africa)

Courtesy, Arlene Kruse/ Bonnie Pedersen

Lemurs (Madagascar)

Courtesy, Fred Jacobs

Galagos (bush babies) (throughout sub-Saharan Africa)

Courtesy, Bonnie Pedersen/ Arlene Kruse

Colobus species (throughout sub-Saharan Africa)

Robert Jurmain

The dental formula for a generalized placental mammal is 3.1.4.3. (three incisors, one canine, four premolars, and three molars). Primates have fewer teeth than this ancestral pattern because there has been a general evolutionary trend toward reduction of the number of teeth in many mammal groups. Consequently, the number of each type of tooth varies between lineages. For example, in the majority of New World monkeys, the dental formula is 2.1.3.3. (two incisors, one canine, three premolars, and three molars). Humans, apes, and all Old World monkeys have the same dental formula: 2.1.2.3., that is, there is one less premolar than in New World monkeys.

The overall lack of dietary specialization in primates is also correlated with minimal specialization in the size and shape of the teeth. This is because tooth form is directly related to diet. For example, carnivores typically have premolars and molars with high pointed **cusps** adapted for tearing meat, while the premolars of herbivores, such as cattle and horses, have broad, flat surfaces suited to chewing tough grasses and other plant materials. Most primates have premolars and molars with low, rounded cusps, which allows them to process most types of foods. Thus, throughout their evolutionary history, the primates have developed a dentition adapted to a varied diet, and the capacity to exploit many foods has contributed to their overall success during the last 50 million years.

LOCOMOTION

Almost all primates are, at least to some degree, **quadrupedal,** meaning they use all four limbs to support the body during locomotion. However, most primates use more than one form of locomotion, and they're able to do this because of their generalized anatomy.

Although the majority of quadrupedal primates are arboreal, terrestrial quadrupedalism is fairly common and is typical of some lemurs, baboons, and **macaques.** Typically, the limbs of terrestrial quadrupeds are approximately the same length, (Fig. 6-7a). In arboreal quadrupeds, forelimbs are somewhat shorter (Fig. 6-7b).

Quadrupeds also have a relatively long and flexible *lumbar spine* (lower back). This flexibility allows an animal to bend the body while running in order to position the hind limbs well forward under the body and propel forward. (Watch for this the next time you see slow-motion footage of cheetahs or lions on television.)

Vertical clinging and leaping, another form of locomotion, is characteristic of many prosimians and tarsiers. As the term implies, vertical clingers and leapers support themselves vertically by grasping onto trunks of trees while their knees and ankles are tightly flexed (Fig. 6-7c). Forceful extension of their long hind limbs allows them to spring powerfully away in either a forward or backward direction.

Brachiation, or arm swinging, is a type of locomotion where the body is alternatively supported under either forelimb. Because of anatomical modifications at the shoulder joint, apes and humans are capable of true brachiation. However, only the small gibbons and siamangs of Southeast Asia brachiate almost exclusively (Fig. 6-7d).

---

cusps The elevated portions (bumps) on the chewing surfaces of premolar and molar teeth.

quadrupedal Using all four limbs to support the body during locomotion; the basic mammalian (and primate) form of locomotion.

macaques (muh-kaks´) Group of Old World monkeys comprising several species, including rhesus monkeys. Most macaque species live in India, other parts of Asia, and nearby islands.

brachiation A form of locomotion in which the body is suspended beneath the hands and support is alternated from one forelimb to the other; arm swinging.

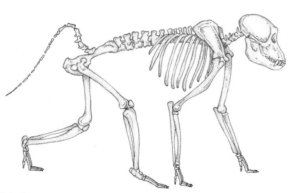

(a) Skeleton of a terrestrial quadruped (savanna baboon).

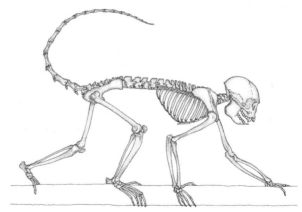

(b) Skeleton of an arboreal New World monkey (bearded saki).

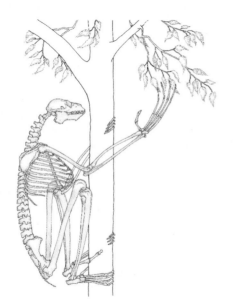

(c) Skeleton of a vertical clinger and leaper (indri).

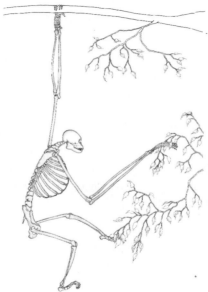

(d) Skeleton of a brachiator (gibbon).

FIGURE 6-7 Differences in skeletal anatomy and limb proportions reflect differences in locomotor patterns. (Redrawn from original art by Stephen Nash in John G. Fleagle, *Primate Adaptation and Evolution,* 2nd ed., 1999. Reprinted by permission of publisher and Stephen Nash.)

Species that brachiate tend to have arms that are longer than legs, a short stable lower back, long curved fingers, and reduced thumbs. Because these are traits seen in all the apes, it's believed that, although none of the great apes (orangutans, gorillas, bonobos, and chimpanzees) habitually brachiates today, they most likely inherited these characteristics from brachiating or perhaps climbing ancestors.

Some New World monkeys (e.g. muriquis and spider monkeys) are called *semibrachiators,* as they practice a combination of leaping with some arm swinging. And in some New World species, arm swinging and other suspensory behaviors are enhanced by use of a *prehensile tail,* which in effect serves as a grasping fifth "hand." Prehensile tails are restricted to New World monkeys and aren't present in any Old World primate species.

Primate Classification

The living primates are commonly categorized into their respective subgroups as shown in Figure 6-8. This taxonomy is based on the system originally established by Linnaeus. (Remember that the primate order, which includes a diverse array of approximately 230 species, belongs to a larger group, the class *Mammalia*.)

As you learned in Chapter 5, in any taxonomic system, animals are organized into increasingly specific categories. For example, the order *Primates* includes *all* primates. However, at the next level down—the *suborder*—the primates have conventionally been divided into two large categories, Prosimii (all the prosimians: lemurs, lorises, and, customarily, the tarsiers) and Anthropoidea (all the monkeys, apes, and humans). Therefore, the suborder distinction is more specific and narrower than the order.

At the level of the suborder, the prosimians are distinct as a group from all the other primates, and this classification makes the biological and evolutionary statement that all the prosimian species are more closely related to one another than they are to any of the anthropoids. Likewise, all anthropoid species are more closely related to each other than they are to the prosimians.

The taxonomy shown in Figure 6-8 is the traditional one, and it's based on physical similarities between species and lineages. However, this approach isn't foolproof. For example, two species that resemble each other anatomically (e.g., some New and Old World monkeys) may in fact not be closely related at all. By looking only at physical characteristics it's possible to overlook the unknown effects of separate evolutionary history (see our discussion of homoplasy on p. 92). But genetic evidence avoids this problem and indeed shows that Old and New World monkeys are evolutionarily quite distinct.

Primate classification is currently in a state of transition, mainly because of genetic evidence that certain relationships, especially between humans and chimpanzees, are even closer than previously thought. Beginning in the 1970s, scientists began to apply genetic analysis to help identify biological and phylogenetic relationships between species.

Direct comparisons of the amino acid sequences of various proteins (products of DNA) are excellent indicators of shared evolutionary history. If two species are similar with regard to protein structure, we know that their DNA sequences are also similar. And if two species share similar DNA, it's highly probable that both inherited their blueprint from a common ancestor.

Another technique, called DNA hybridization, matches DNA strands from two species to determine what percentage of bases match. The higher the percentage, the more closely the two are related.

However, as useful as these techniques have been, they're still only *indirect* methods of comparing DNA sequences between species. But now, the techniques of DNA sequencing used in the Human Genome Project make it possible to make direct between-species comparisons of DNA sequences. This approach is called *comparative genomics*.

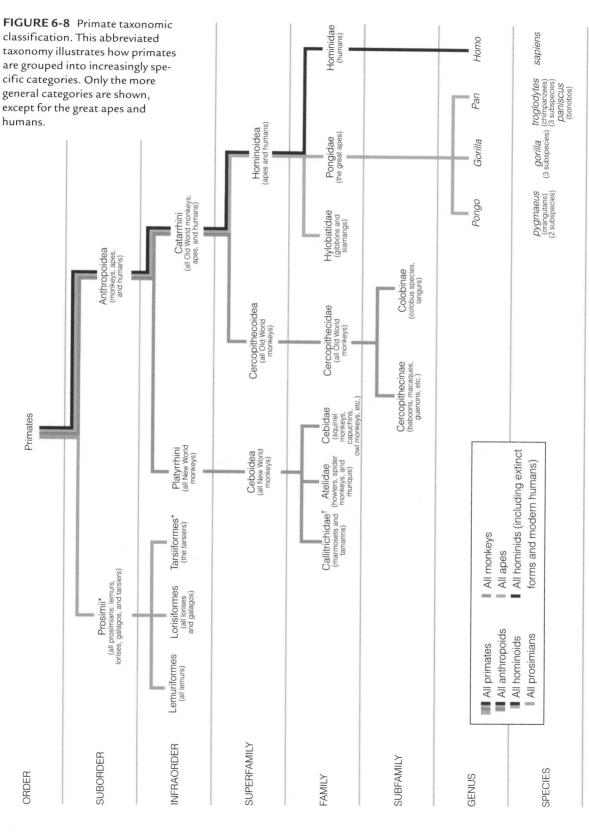

FIGURE 6-8 Primate taxonomic classification. This abbreviated taxonomy illustrates how primates are grouped into increasingly specific categories. Only the more general categories are shown, except for the great apes and humans.

A draft sequence of the chimpanzee genome was completed in 2003—a major advance in human comparative genomics. But even before this, molecular anthropologists had already compared the sequences of several chimpanzee and human genes or groups of genes. For example, Wildman et al. (2003) compared 97 human genes with their chimpanzee, gorilla, and orangutan counterparts and determined that humans are most closely related to chimpanzees and that their DNA sequences are between 98.4 and 99.4 percent identical. They also calculated that humans and chimpanzees last shared a common ancestor with gorillas around 6–7 m.y.a. and that the chimpanzee and human lineages diverged between 5 and 6 m.y.a. These results are consistent with the findings of several other studies, and together they've caused many primatologists to consider changing how they classify the hominoids (Goodman et al., 1998; Wildman et al., 2003). Although there's no formal acceptance of suggested changes, there's a lot of support for placing all great apes in the family Hominidae along with humans. (We'll return to this topic in Chapter 8.)

Another area where changes have been suggested concerns tarsiers (see p. 127). Tarsiers are highly specialized animals that display several unique physical characteristics. Because they possess a number of prosimian traits, they've traditionally been classified as prosimians (with lemurs and lorises). But they also have certain anthropoid features, and they're more similar to the anthropoids biochemically (Dene et al., 1976).

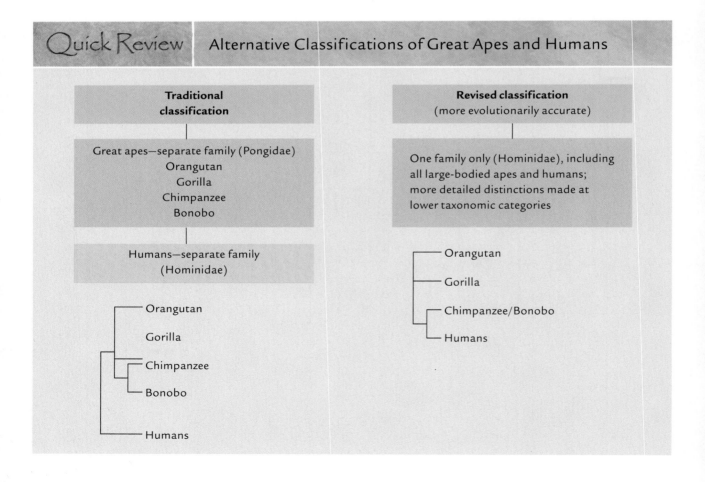

Quick Review   Alternative Classifications of Great Apes and Humans

Traditional classification

Great apes—separate family (Pongidae)
Orangutan
Gorilla
Chimpanzee
Bonobo

Humans—separate family (Hominidae)

Orangutan
Gorilla
Chimpanzee
Bonobo
Humans

Revised classification
(more evolutionarily accurate)

One family only (Hominidae), including all large-bodied apes and humans; more detailed distinctions made at lower taxonomic categories

Orangutan
Gorilla
Chimpanzee/Bonobo
Humans

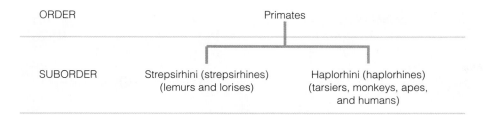

ORDER	Primates	
SUBORDER	Strepsirhini (strepsirhines) (lemurs and lorises)	Haplorhini (haplorhines) (tarsiers, monkeys, apes, and humans)

FIGURE 6-9 Revised partial classification of the primates. In this system, the terms *Prosimii* and *Anthropoidea* have been replaced by *Strepsirhini* and *Haplorhini*, respectively. Tarsiers are included in the same suborder with monkeys, apes, and humans to reflect a closer relationship with these species than with lemurs and lorises. (Compare with Fig. 6-8.)

Today, most primatologists consider tarsiers to be more closely related to anthropoids than to prosimians. But instead of simply moving them into the suborder Anthropoidea, one scheme places lemurs and lorises in a different suborder, Strepsirhini (instead of Prosimii), while tarsiers are included with monkeys, apes, and humans in another suborder, Haplorhini (Szalay and Delson, 1979) (Fig. 6-9). In this classification, the conventionally named suborders Prosimii and Anthropoidea are replaced by Strepsirhini and Haplorhini, respectively. While this designation hasn't been universally accepted, the terminology is now common, especially in technical publications. So if you see the term *strepsirhine*, you know the author is referring specifically to lemurs and lorises.

We've presented the traditional system of primate classification in this chapter, even though we acknowledge the need for change. Until the new designations are formally adopted, we think it's appropriate to use the standard taxonomy along with discussion of some proposed changes. We also want to point out that while specific details and names haven't yet been worked out, the vast majority of experts do accept the evolutionary implications of the revised groupings.

rhinarium (rine-air´-ee-um) The moist, hairless pad at the end of the nose seen in most mammalian species. The rhinarium enhances an animal's ability to smell.

A Survey of the Living Primates

PROSIMIANS (LEMURS AND LORISES)

The most primitive primates are the lemurs and lorises (we don't include tarsiers here.) Remember that by "primitive" we mean that prosimians are more anatomically similar to their earlier mammalian ancestors than are the other primates (monkeys, apes, and humans). Therefore, they tend to exhibit certain more ancestral characteristics, such as a more pronounced reliance on *olfaction* (sense of smell). Their greater olfactory capabilities (compared to other primates) are reflected in the presence of a moist, fleshy pad, or **rhinarium,** at the end of the nose and in a relatively long snout. Moreover, prosimians actively mark territories with scent, something not seen in most other primates.

There are many other characteristics that distinguish lemurs and lorises from the anthropoids, including eyes placed more to the side of the face, differences in reproductive physiology, and shorter gestation and maturation periods. Lemurs and lorises also have a unique trait called a "dental comb" (Fig. 6-10). The dental comb is formed by forward-projecting lower incisors and canines, and together these modified teeth are used in grooming and feeding. Another characteristic that sets lemurs and lorises apart from anthropoids is the retention of a claw on the second toe.

Lemurs Lemurs are found only on the island of Madagascar and nearby islands off the east coast of Africa (Fig. 6-11). As the only nonhuman primates on Madagascar, lemurs diversified into numerous and varied ecological niches with-

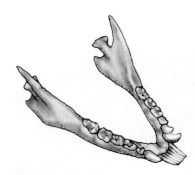

FIGURE 6-10 Prosimian dental comb, formed by forward-projecting incisors and canines.

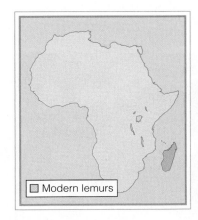

Modern lemurs

FIGURE 6-11 Geographical distribution of modern lemurs.

FIGURE 6-12 Ring-tailed lemur.

FIGURE 6-13 Sifakas in Madagascar.

Courtesy, Fred Jacobs

FIGURE 6-14 Slow loris.

Courtesy, San Francisco Zoo

FIGURE 6-15 Galago, or "bush baby."

Courtesy, Bonnie Pedersen/Arlene Kruse

out competition from monkeys and apes. Thus, the approximately 60 surviving lemur species represent an evolutionary pattern that has vanished elsewhere.

Lemurs range in size from the small mouse lemur, with a body length (head and trunk) of only 5 inches, to the indri, with a body length of 2 to 3 feet (Nowak, 1999). While the larger lemurs are diurnal and exploit a wide variety of dietary items, such as leaves, fruit, buds, bark, and shoots, the smaller species (mouse and dwarf lemurs) are nocturnal and insectivorous.

Lemurs display considerable variation regarding numerous other aspects of behavior. Some are mostly arboreal, but others, such as the ring-tailed lemur (Fig. 6-12), are more terrestrial. Some arboreal species are quadrupeds, and others (sifakas and indris) are vertical clingers and leapers (Fig. 6-13). Socially, several species (e.g., ring-tailed lemurs and sifakas) are gregarious and live in groups of 10 to 25 animals composed of males and females of all ages. Others (the indris) live in family units composed of a mated pair and their offspring. And several nocturnal forms are mostly solitary.

Lorises Lorises (Fig. 6-14), which resemble lemurs, were able to survive in mainland areas by adopting a nocturnal activity pattern at a time when most other prosimians became extinct. In this way, they were (and are) able to avoid competition with more recently evolved primates (the diurnal monkeys).

There are at least eight loris species, all of which are found in tropical forest and woodland habitats of India, Sri Lanka, Southeast Asia, and Africa. Also included in the same general category are six to nine (Bearder, 1987; Nowak, 1999) galago species (Fig. 6-15), which are widely distributed throughout most of the forested and woodland savanna areas of sub-Saharan Africa.

Locomotion in lorises is a slow, cautious, climbing form of quadrupedalism. All galagos, however, are highly agile vertical clingers and leapers. Some lorises and galagos are almost entirely insectivorous; others supplement their diet with fruits, leaves, gums, and slugs. Lorises and galagos frequently forage for food alone (females leave infants behind in nests until they are older). However, ranges overlap, and two or more females occasionally forage together or share the same sleeping nest.

TARSIERS

There are five recognized tarsier species (Nowak, 1999) (Fig. 6-16), all restricted to island areas in Southeast Asia (Fig. 6-17), where they inhabit a wide range of forest types, from tropical forest to backyard gardens. Tarsiers are nocturnal insectivores that leap onto prey (which may also include small vertebrates) from lower branches and shrubs. They appear to form stable pair bonds, and the basic tarsier social unit is a mated pair and their young offspring (MacKinnon and MacKinnon, 1980).

As we've already mentioned, tarsiers present a complex blend of characteristics not seen in other primates. Moreover, they're unique in that their enormous eyes, which dominate much of the face, are immobile within their sockets. To compensate for the inability to move the eyes, tarsiers, like owls, are able to rotate their heads 180°.

FIGURE 6-16 Tarsier.

ANTHROPOIDS (MONKEYS, APES, AND HUMANS)

Although there is much variation among anthropoids, there are certain features that, when taken together, distinguish them as a group from prosimians (and most other placental mammals). Here's a partial list of these traits:

1. Generally larger body size
2. Larger brain (in absolute terms and relative to body weight)
3. Reduced reliance on the sense of smell, indicated by absence of rhinarium and other structures
4. Increased reliance on vision, with forward-facing eyes at the front of the face
5. Greater degree of color vision
6. Back of eye socket formed by a bony plate
7. Blood supply to brain different from that of prosimians
8. Fusion of the two sides of the mandible at the midline to form one bone (in prosimians and tarsiers they are joined by fibrous tissue)
9. Less specialized dentition, as seen in absence of dental comb and some other features
10. Differences with regard to female internal reproductive anatomy
11. Longer gestation and maturation periods
12. Increased parental care
13. More mutual grooming

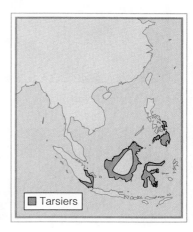

FIGURE 6-17 Geographical distribution of tarsiers.

Approximately 85 percent of all primates are monkeys (about 195 species). It's impossible to give precise numbers of species because the taxonomic status of some primates remains in doubt, and primatologists are still making new discoveries. Monkeys are divided into two groups separated by geographical area (New World and Old World), as well as by several million years of separate evolutionary history.

New World Monkeys The New World monkeys exhibit a wide range of size, diet, and ecological adaptation (Fig. 6-18). In size, they vary from the tiny marmosets and tamarins (about 12 ounces) to the 20-pound howler monkeys (Figs. 6-19 and 6-20). New World monkeys are almost exclusively arboreal, and some never come to the ground. They can be found in a wide range of arboreal environments throughout most forested areas in southern Mexico

FIGURE 6-18 New World monkeys.

Female muriqui with infant

White-faced capuchins

Squirrel monkeys

Prince Bernhard's titi monkey (discovered in 2002)

Male uakari

FIGURE 6-19 A pair of golden lion tamarins.

FIGURE 6-20 Howler monkeys.

and Central and South America (Fig. 6-21). Like Old World monkeys, all except one species (the owl monkey) are diurnal.

New World monkeys have traditionally been divided into two families: **Callitrichidae** (marmosets and tamarins) and **Cebidae** (all others). But molecular data along with recently reported fossil evidence indicate that a major regrouping of New World monkeys is in order (Fleagle, 1999).*

Of the roughly 70 New World monkey species, marmosets and tamarins are the smallest. They have claws instead of nails and usually give birth to twins instead of one infant as in other primates. They are mostly insectivorous, although marmosets eat gums from trees, and tamarins eat fruits. Locomotion is quadrupedal and, like squirrels, they use their claws for climbing. Moreover, some tamarins use vertical clinging and leaping as a form of travel. Socially, these small monkeys live in family groups composed usually of a mated pair, or a female and two adult males, and their offspring. In fact, marmosets and tamarins are among the few primate species in which males are extensively involved in infant care.

Cebids range in size from the squirrel monkey (body length 12 inches) to the howler (body length 24 inches). Diet varies, with most relying on a combination of fruits and leaves supplemented with insects. Most are quadrupedal but some, for example, muriquis and spider monkeys (Fig. 6-22), are semibrachiators. Muriquis, howlers, and spider monkeys also have powerful prehensile tails that are used not only in locomotion but also for suspension under branches while feeding. Socially, most cebids are found in groups of both sexes and all age categories. Some (e.g., titis) form monogamous pairs and live with their subadult offspring.

FIGURE 6-21 Geographical distribution of modern New World monkeys.

Callitrichidae
(kal-eh-trick'-eh-dee)

Cebidae (see'-bid-ee)

---

*One possibility is to include spider monkeys, howler monkeys, and muriquis (woolly spider monkeys) in a third family, Atelidae (see Fig. 6-9). Another is to eliminate the family Callitrichidae altogether and include marmosets and tamarins as a subfamily within the family Cebidae.

FIGURE 6-22 Spider monkey. Note the prehensile tail.

ischial callosities Patches of tough, hard skin on the buttocks of Old World monkeys and chimpanzees.

Cercopithecidae
(serk-oh-pith´-eh-sid-ee)

cercopithecines
(serk-oh-pith´-eh-seens) The subfamily of Old World monkeys that includes baboons, macaques, and guenons.

colobines (kole´-uh-beans) The subfamily of Old World monkeys that includes the African colobus monkeys and Asian langurs.

Old World Monkeys Except for humans, Old World monkeys are the most widely distributed of all living primates. They are found throughout sub-Saharan Africa and southern Asia, ranging from tropical jungle habitats to semiarid desert and even to seasonally snow-covered areas in northern Japan (Fig. 6-23).

Most Old World monkeys are quadrupedal and primarily arboreal, but some (e.g., baboons) are also adapted to life on the ground. In general, they spend a good deal of time sleeping, feeding, and grooming while sitting with their upper bodies erect. They also have areas of hardened skin on the buttocks (**ischial callosities**) that serve as sitting pads. All Old World monkeys are placed in one taxonomic family: **Cercopithecidae.** In turn, this family is divided into two subfamilies: the **cercopithecines** and **colobines.**

The cercopithecines are the more generalized of the two groups, with a more omnivorous dietary adaptation and cheek pouches for storing food. As a group, the cercopithecines eat almost anything, including fruits, seeds, leaves, grasses, tubers, roots, nuts, insects, birds' eggs, amphibians, small reptiles, and small mammals (the last seen in baboons).

The majority of cercopithecine species, such as the mostly arboreal guenons (Fig. 6-24) and the more terrestrial savanna (Fig. 6-25) and hamadryas baboons, are found in Africa. However, the several macaque species, which include the well-known rhesus monkey, are widely distributed in southern Asia and India.

Colobine species have a narrower range of food preferences and mainly eat mature leaves, which is why they're also called "leaf-eating monkeys." The colobines are found mainly in Asia, but both the red colobus and the black-and-white colobus are exclusively African (Fig. 6-26). Other colobines include several Asian langur species and the proboscis monkey of Borneo.

Locomotor behavior among Old World monkeys includes arboreal quadrupedalism in guenons, macaques, and langurs; terrestrial quadrupedalism in baboons, patas, and macaques; and semibrachiation and acrobatic leaping in colobus monkeys.

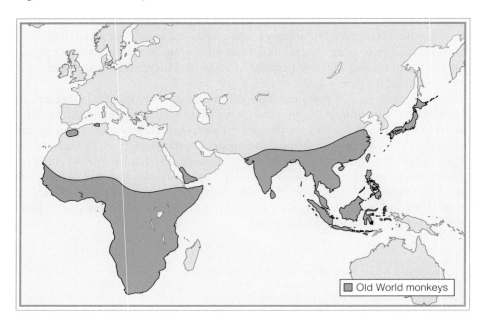

Old World monkeys

FIGURE 6-23 Geographical distribution of modern Old World monkeys.

FIGURE 6-24 Adult male Sykes monkey, one of several guenon species.

Robert Jurmain

(a)

Courtesy, Bonnie Pedersen/Arlene Kruse

(b)

Courtesy, Bonnie Pedersen/Arlene Kruse

FIGURE 6-25 Savanna baboons. (a) Male. (b) Female.

Lynn Kilgore

FIGURE 6-26 Black-and-white colobus monkey.

sexual dimorphism
Differences in physical characteristics between males and females of the same species. For example, humans are slightly sexually dimorphic for body size, with males being taller, on average, than females of the same population.

estrus (ess´-truss) Period of sexual receptivity in female mammals (except humans), correlated with ovulation. When used as an adjective, the word is spelled "estrous."

Marked differences in body size or shape between the sexes, referred to as **sexual dimorphism,** are typical of some terrestrial species and are particularly pronounced in baboons and patas. In these species, male body weight (up to 80 pounds in baboons) may be twice that of females.

In several species (especially baboons and some macaques), females have pronounced cyclical changes of the external genitalia. These changes, including swelling and redness, are associated with **estrus,** a hormonally initiated period of sexual receptivity in female nonhuman mammals correlated with ovulation.

Old World monkeys live in a few different kinds of social groups, and there are uncertainties among primatologists regarding some species. In general, colobines tend to live in small groups, with only one or two adult males. Savanna baboons and most macaque species are found in large social units comprising several adults of both sexes and offspring of all ages. Monogamous pairing isn't common in Old World monkeys, but is seen in a few langurs and possibly one or two guenon species.

HOMINOIDS (APES AND HUMANS)

Hominoidea The formal designation for the superfamily of anthropoids that includes apes and humans.

Hylobatidae (high-lo-baht´-id-ee) The family designation of gibbons and siamangs.

Pongidae (ponj´-id-ee) The traditional family designation of the great apes (orangutans, chimpanzees, bonobos, and gorillas).

The other large grouping of anthropoids (the hominoids) includes apes and humans. The superfamily **Hominoidea** includes the so-called "lesser" apes in the family **Hylobatidae** (gibbons and siamangs); the great apes in the family **Pongidae** (orangutans, gorillas, bonobos, and chimpanzees); and humans in the family Hominidae.* Apes and humans differ from monkeys in numerous ways:

1. Generally larger body size, except for gibbons and siamangs
2. Absence of a tail
3. Shortened trunk (lumbar area shorter and more stable)
4. Differences in position and musculature of the shoulder joint (adapted for suspensory locomotion)
5. More complex behavior
6. More complex brain and enhanced cognitive abilities
7. Increased period of infant development and dependency

Gibbons and Siamangs The eight gibbon species and the closely related siamang are today found in the southeastern tropical areas of Asia (Fig. 6-27). These are the smallest of the apes, with a long, slender body weighing 13 pounds in gibbons (Fig. 6-28) and 25 pounds in siamang.

The most distinctive structural features of gibbons and siamangs are adaptations for brachiation. They have extremely long arms, long, permanently curved fingers, short thumbs, and powerful shoulder muscles. These highly specialized locomotor adaptations may be related to feeding behavior while hanging beneath branches. The diet of these species is largely composed of fruits, although they also eat a variety of leaves, flowers, and insects.

The basic social unit of gibbons and siamangs comprises an adult male and female with dependent offspring. Although they've been described as monogamous, in reality they sometimes do mate with other individuals. As in marmosets and tamarins, male gibbons and siamangs are very much involved in

FIGURE 6-27 Geographical distribution of modern Asian apes.

*Note that this classification is currently being significantly revised. (See pp. 124 and 179 for further discussion.)

FIGURE 6-28 White-handed gibbon.

rearing their young. Both males and females are highly territorial and protect their territories with loud whoops and siren-like "songs."

Orangutans Orangutans (*Pongo pygmaeus*) (Fig. 6-29) are represented by two subspecies found today only in heavily forested areas on the Indonesian islands of Borneo and Sumatra (see Fig. 6-27). Due to poaching by humans and continuing habitat loss on both islands, orangutans are severely threatened by extinction in the wild.

Orangutans are slow, cautious climbers whose locomotor behavior can best be described as "four-handed," since they tend to use all four limbs for grasping and support. Although they're almost completely arboreal, orangutans sometimes travel quadrupedally on the ground. Orangutans are also very large

FIGURE 6-29 Female orangutan.

(a)

(b)

FIGURE 6-33 Chimpanzees.
(a) Male. (b) Female.

more time in the trees. Moreover, whereas gorillas are typically placid and quiet, chimpanzees are highly excitable, active, and noisy.

Chimpanzees are smaller than orangutans and gorillas, and although they are sexually dimorphic, sex differences aren't as pronounced. While male chimpanzees may weigh over 100 pounds, females can weigh at least 80.

In addition to quadrupedal knuckle walking, chimpanzees (particularly youngsters) may brachiate while in the trees. When on the ground, they frequently walk bipedally for short distances when carrying food or other objects.

Chimpanzees eat a huge variety of foods, including fruits, leaves, insects, nuts, birds' eggs, berries, caterpillars, and small mammals. Moreover, both males and females occasionally take part in group hunting efforts to kill small mammals such as red colobus, young baboons, bushpigs, and antelope. When hunts are successful, the prey is shared by the group members.

Chimpanzees live in large, fluid communities of as many as 50 individuals or more. At the core of a chimpanzee community is a group of bonded males. Although relationships between them aren't always peaceful, these males nevertheless act as a group to defend their territory, and they're highly intolerant of unfamiliar chimpanzees, especially nongroup males.

Even though chimpanzees are said to live in communities, it's rare for all members to be together at the same time. Rather, they tend to come and go, so that the individuals they encounter vary from day to day. Adult females usually forage alone or in the company of their offspring, a grouping that might include several individuals, since females with infants sometimes accompany their own mothers and their younger siblings. A female may also leave her group, either permanently to join another community or temporarily while she's in estrus. This may reduce the risk of mating with close male relatives, because males apparently never leave the group in which they were born.

Chimpanzee social behavior is complex, and individuals form lifelong attachments with friends and relatives. Indeed, the bond between mothers and infants can remain strong until one or the other dies. This may be a considerable period, because many wild chimpanzees live into their mid-30s and a few into their 40s.

Bonobos Bonobos (*Pan paniscus*) are found only in an area south of the Zaire River in the DRC (see Fig. 6-34). Not officially recognized by European scientists until the 1920s, they remain among the least studied of the great apes. Although ongoing field studies have produced much information (Susman, 1984; Kano, 1992), research has been hampered by civil war. There are no accurate counts of bonobos, but their numbers are believed to be between 10,000 and 20,000 (IUCN, 1996), but they're highly threatened by human hunting, warfare, and habitat loss.

Bonobos bear a strong resemblance to chimpanzees but are somewhat smaller, earning them the name "pygmy chimpanzees." However, they aren't a great deal smaller. The main anatomical differences between bonobos and chimpanzees are that bonobos have a more linear body build, longer legs relative to arms, a relatively smaller head, a dark face from birth, and tufts of hair at the sides of the face (Fig. 6-34).

Bonobos are more arboreal and less excitable than chimpanzees. While aggression isn't unknown, it appears that physical violence both within and

FIGURE 6-34 Female bonobos with young.

Courtesy, Ellen Ingmanson

between groups is uncommon. Like chimpanzees, bonobos live in geographically based, fluid communities, and they eat many of the same foods, including occasional meat derived from small mammals (Badrian and Malinky, 1984). But bonobo communities aren't centered around a group of closely bonded males. Instead, male-female bonding is more important than in chimpanzees (and most other nonhuman primates), and females aren't peripheral to the group (Badrian and Badrian, 1984). This may be related to bonobo sexuality, which differs from that of other nonhuman primates in that copulation is very frequent and occurs throughout a female's estrous cycle.

HUMANS

Humans are the only living representatives of the habitually bipedal hominids (genus *Homo*, species *sapiens*). Our primate heritage is evident in our overall anatomy and genetic makeup and in many aspects of human behavior. With the exception of reduced canine size, human teeth are typical primate (especially ape) teeth. The human dependence on vision and decreased reliance on olfaction, as well as flexible limbs and grasping hands, are rooted in our primate, arboreal past. Humans can even brachiate, and playgrounds often accommodate this ability in children.

Humans in general are omnivorous, although all societies observe certain culturally based dietary restrictions. Nevertheless, as a species with a rather generalized digestive system, we are physiologically adapted to digest an extremely wide assortment of foods. Perhaps to our detriment, given how humans tend to go to extremes, we also share with our relatives a fondness for sweets that originates from the importance of high-energy fruits in the diets of many nonhuman primates.

But quite obviously, humans are unique among primates and indeed among all animals. For example, no member of any other species has the ability to write or think about issues such as how they differ from other life forms. This ability is rooted in the fact that human evolution, during the last 800,000 years or so, has been characterized by dramatic increases in brain size and other neurological changes.

Humans are also completely dependent on culture. Without cultural innovation, it would never have been possible for us to leave the tropics. As it is, humans inhabit every corner of the planet with the exception of Antarctica, and we've even established outposts there. And lest we forget, a fortunate few have even walked on the moon. None of the technologies (indeed, none of the other aspects of culture) that humans have developed over the last several thousand years would have been possible without the highly developed cognitive abilities we alone possess. Nevertheless, the neurological basis for intelligence is rooted in our evolutionary past, and it's something we share with other primates. Indeed, research has demonstrated that several nonhuman primate species (most notably chimpanzees, bonobos, and gorillas)display a level of problem solving ability and insight that most people would have considered impossible 25 years ago (see Chapter 7).

Aside from cognitive abilities, the one other trait that sets humans apart from other primates is our unique (among mammals) form of *habitual* bipedal locomotion. This particular trait appeared early in the evolution of our lineage, and over time, we have become more efficient at it because of related changes in the musculoskeletal anatomy of the pelvis, leg, and foot (see Chapter 8). Still, while it's certainly true that human beings are unique intellectually and in some ways anatomically, we are still primates. In fact, fundamentally, humans are somewhat exaggerated African apes.

Endangered Primates

In September 2000, scientists announced that a subspecies of red colobus, named Miss Waldron's red colobus, had officially been declared extinct. This announcement came after a six-year search for the 20-pound monkey that had not been seen for 20 years (Oates et al., 2000). Thus, this species, indigenous to the West African countries of Ghana and the Ivory Coast, has the distinction of being the first nonhuman primate to be declared extinct in the twenty-first century. But it won't be the last. In fact, as of this writing, over half of all nonhuman primate species are now in jeopardy, and some face almost immediate extinction in the wild.

There are three basic reasons for the worldwide depletion of nonhuman primates: habitat destruction, hunting for food, and live capture for export or local trade. Underlying these three causes is one major factor: unprecedented human population growth, which is occurring at a faster rate in developing countries than in the developed world. The developing nations of Africa, Asia, and Central and South America are home to over 90 percent of all nonhuman primate species, and these countries, aided in no small part by the industrialized countries of Europe and the United States, are cutting their forests at a rate of about 30 million acres per year. Unbelievably, in the year 2002, deforestation of the Amazon increased by 40 percent over that of 2001. This increase, in large part, was due to land clearing for the cultivation of soybeans. In Brazil, the Atlantic rain forest originally covered some 385,000 square miles. Today, an estimated 7 percent is all that remains of what was once home to countless New World monkeys and thousands of other species.

Much of the motivation behind the destruction of the rain forests is, of course, economic: the short-term gains from clearing forests to create immediately available (but poor) farmland or ranchland; the use of trees for lumber and paper products; and large-scale mining operations (with their necessary roads, digging, etc., all of which cause habitat destruction). And, of course, the demand for tropical hardwoods (e.g., mahogany, teak, and rosewood) in the United States, Europe, and Japan continues unabated, creating an enormously profitable market for rain forest products.

In many areas, habitat loss has been, and continues to be, the single greatest cause of declining numbers of nonhuman primates. But increasingly, human hunting poses an even greater threat (Fig. 6-35). During the 1990s, primatologists and conservationists became aware of a rapidly developing trade in *bushmeat,* or meat from wild animals in western and central Africa. The current slaughter, which now accounts for the loss of thousands of nonhuman primates and other species annually, has been compared to the near extinction of the American bison in the nineteenth century.

FIGURE 6-35 Red-eared guenons (with red tails) and Preuss' guenons for sale in bushmeat market, Malabo, Equatorial Guinea.

Primates have traditionally been a source of food for people; but in the past, subsistence hunters weren't usually a serious threat to nonhuman primate populations, and certainly not to entire species. But now, hunters armed with shotguns and automatic rifles can wipe out an entire group of monkeys or gorillas in minutes.

One major factor in the development of the bushmeat trade has been logging. The construction of logging roads, mainly by French, German, and Belgian lumbar companies, has opened up vast tracts of forest that were previously inaccessible to local hunters. Once the roads are cut, hunters hitch rides on logging trucks (for a fee paid from the proceeds of bushmeat sales). What has emerged is a profitable trade in bushmeat, a trade in which logging company employees and local government officials participate with hunters, villagers, market vendors, and smugglers who cater to growing overseas markets. In other words, the hunting of wild animals for food, particularly in Africa, has quickly shifted from a subsistence activity to a commercial enterprise of international scope.

It's impossible to know how many animals are slaughtered each year. But estimates for monkeys and apes are in the thousands. In addition, hundreds of infants are orphaned and sold in markets as pets. Although a few of these traumatized orphans make it to sanctuaries, most die within days or weeks of capture (Fig. 6-36). Although the slaughter may be most extreme in Africa, it's by no means limited to that continent. In South America, for example, hunting nonhuman primates for food is common. And one report documents that in less than two years, one family of Brazilian rubber tappers killed almost 500 members of various large-bodied species, including spider monkeys, woolly monkeys, and howler monkeys (Peres, 1990). Moreover, live capture and (illegal) trade in endangered primate species continue unabated in China and Southeast Asia, where nonhuman primates are not only eaten

FIGURE 6-36 These orphaned chimpanzee infants are being bottle-fed at a sanctuary near Pointe Noir, Congo. They will probably never be returned to the wild, and they face a very uncertain future.

but also funneled into the exotic pet trade. But perhaps most important is the fact that primate body parts also figure prominently in traditional medicines, and with increasing human population size, the enormous demand for these products (and products from other, nonprimate species, such as tigers) has placed many species in extreme jeopardy.

Fortunately, steps are being taken to ensure the survival of some species. Many developing countries, such as Costa Rica and the Malagasy Republic (Madagascar), are designating national parks and other reserves for the protection of natural resources, including primates. There are also several private international efforts aimed at curbing the bushmeat trade. It's only through such practices and through educational programs that many primate species have a chance of escaping extinction, at least in the immediate future.

Perhaps most encouraging is the establishment of the Great Ape Survival Project (GRASP) in 2000 by the United Nations Environmental Program. GRASP is an alliance of many of the world's major great ape conservation and research organizations. In 2003, GRASP appealed for $25 million to be used in protecting the great apes from extinction. The money (a paltry sum) would be used to enforce laws that regulate hunting and illegal logging. It goes without saying that GRASP and other organizations must succeed if the great apes are to survive in the wild for even 20 more years!

If you are in your 20s or 30s, you will most certainly live to hear of the extinction of some of our marvelously unique cousins. Many more will undoubtedly slip away unnoticed. Tragically, this will occur, in most cases, before we've even gotten to know them. Each species on earth is the current result of a unique set of evolutionary events that, over millions of years, has produced a finely adapted component of a diverse ecosystem. When it becomes extinct, that adaptation and that part of biodiversity is lost forever. What a tragedy it will be if, through our own mismanagement and greed, we awaken to a world without chimpanzees, mountain gorillas, or the tiny, exquisite lion tamarin. When this day comes, we truly will have lost a part of ourselves, and we will certainly be the poorer for it.

Visual Summary

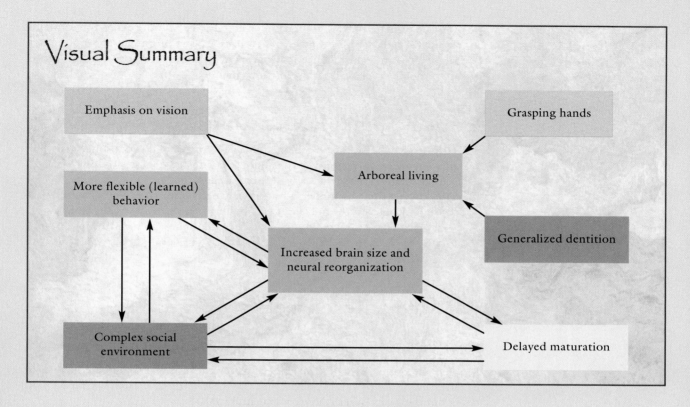

Summary

In this chapter, we introduced you to the primates, the mammalian order that includes prosimians, monkeys, apes, and humans. We discussed how primates, including humans, have retained a number of ancestral characteristics that have permitted them, as a group, to be generalized in terms of diet and locomotor patterns. You also were presented with a general outline of traits that differentiate primates from other mammals.

We also discussed primate classification and how primatologists are redefining relationships between some lineages. In particular, we mentioned the removal of tarsiers from the suborder Prosimii, placing them with the anthropoids in a grouping called the haplorhines. The lemurs and lorises would be kept together under the suborder distinction of strepsirhine. Also, chimpanzees, gorillas, and orangutans would be placed with humans in the family Hominidae. These changes reflect increasing knowledge of the genetic relationships between primate lineages and, particularly in the case of tarsiers, reconsideration of various anatomical characteristics.

You also became acquainted with the major groups of nonhuman primates, especially with regard to their basic social structure, diet, and locomotor patterns. Most primates are diurnal and live in social groups. The only nocturnal primates are lorises, some lemurs, tarsiers, and owl monkeys. Nocturnal species tend to forage for food alone or with offspring and one or two other animals. Diurnal primates live in a variety of social groupings, including monogamous pairs, and groups consisting of one male with several females and offspring or those composed of several males and females and offspring.

Finally, we talked about the precarious existence of most nonhuman primates today as they face hunting, capture, and habitat loss. These threats are all imposed by only one primate species, one that arrived fairly late on the evolutionary stage. In the next chapter, where we discuss various aspects of human and nonhuman primate behavior, you will become better acquainted with this fairly recently evolved primate species, of which you are a member.

Critical Thinking Questions

1. How does a classification scheme reflect biological and evolutionary changes in a lineage? Can you give an example of suggested changes to how primates are classified? What is the basis of these suggestions?
2. How do you think continued advances in genetic research will influence how we look at our species' relationship with nonhuman primates 10 years from now?
3. What factors are threatening the existence of nonhuman primates in the wild? What can you do to help in the efforts to save nonhuman primates from extinction?

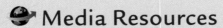 Media Resources

The Companion Website for *Essentials of Physical Anthropology,* Sixth Edition
http://anthropology.wadsworth.com/jurmain6e_ess

Supplement your review of this chapter by going to this text's companion website to take one of the practice quizzes, use the flash cards to master key terms, and check out the many other resources and study aids.

CD-ROMs in Physical Anthropology

Wadsworth Publishing has also developed three CD-ROMs to accompany this text and enhance learning in physical anthropology (for further descriptions of these CD-ROMs, see p. xix):

Virtual Laboratories for Physical Anthropology CD-ROM, Third Edition

Basic Genetics for Anthropology CD-ROM: Principles and Applications

Hominid Fossils CD-ROM: An Interactive Atlas

For this chapter, see especially the Virtual Laboratories for Physical Anthropology CD-ROM, Third Edition.

Readings of Interest

Fleagle, John. 1999. *Primate Adaptation and Evolution.* New York: Academic Press.
Nowak, Ronald M. 1999. *Walker's Primates of the World.* Baltimore: The Johns Hopkins University Press.
Rowe, Noel. 1996. *The Pictorial Guide to the Living Primates.* Charlestown, RI: Pogonias Press.

7 | Primate Behavior

Focus Question

How can behavior be a product of evolutionary processes, and what is one example of a behavior that has been influenced by evolution?

Introduction

behavior Anything organisms do that involves action in response to internal or external stimuli. The response of an individual, group, or species to its environment. Such responses may or may not be deliberate and they aren't necessarily the results of conscious decision making.

Do you think cats are cruel when they play with mice before killing them? Or have you ever been tossed off a horse, when she leaped for no apparent reason? If so, did you think she threw you deliberately just to be obnoxious? These are commonly held views about cats and horses, and they show how little most people really know about nonhuman animal **behavior.**

Behavior, has been shaped over evolutionary time by interactions between genetic and environmental processes and for this reason it's extremely complex. But most people don't give this much thought, and even those who do don't necessarily accept this basic premise. For example, while most social scientists agree that genetic factors influence nonhuman behavior, many object to the suggestion that they might also affect human behavior. This is because of concerns over implications that genetically influenced behaviors are fixed and can't be modified by experience (i.e., learning).

Furthermore, most people assume that there is a fundamental division between humans and all other animals. But at the same time, they often judge other species as if their motives were entirely human. Of course, this isn't a valid thing to do simply because they aren't human. For example, cats do sometimes play with mice before they kill them because that's how, as kittens, they learn to hunt. Cruelty doesn't enter into it, since the cat has no concept of cruelty and no idea of what it's like to be the mouse. Likewise, the horse doesn't necessarily throw you off deliberately when she hears leaves rattling in a shrub. In fact, at that moment, you may be the farthest thing from her mind. Her behavior has been shaped by thousands of generations of horse ancestors who jumped first and asked questions later. Horses evolved as prey animals, and their evolutionary history is littered with animals that didn't jump at a sound in a shrub. In many cases, they learned, too late, that the sound wasn't caused by a breeze at all. This is a mistake that prey animals don't usually survive, and those that don't leap first don't leave many descendants.

Of course, this chapter isn't about cats and horses. It's about what we know and hypothesize about the individual and social behaviors of nonhuman primates. But we begin with the familiar examples of cats and horses because we want to point out that many basic behaviors have been shaped by the evolutionary histories of species. And the same factors that have influenced many behaviors in nonprimate animals also apply to primates. Consequently, if we want to discover the underlying principles of behavioral evolution, including that of humans, we first need to identify the interactions between a number of environmental and physiological variables.

The Evolution of Behavior

Scientists study behavior in free-ranging primates from an **ecological** and evolutionary perspective, meaning that they focus on the relationship between behaviors, the natural environment, and various biological traits of the species in question. This approach is called **behavioral ecology,** and it's based on the underlying assumption that all of the biological components of ecological systems (animals, plants, and even microorganisms) evolved together. Therefore, behaviors are adaptations to environmental circumstances that existed in the past as well as in the present.

Briefly, the cornerstone of this perspective is that since some behaviors are influenced by genes, they're subject to natural selection in the same way physical characteristics are. (Remember that within a specific environmental context, natural selection favors traits that provide a reproductive advantage to the individuals who possess them.) Therefore, behavior constitutes a phenotype, and individuals whose behavioral phenotypes increase reproductive fitness will pass on their genes at a faster rate than others. But this doesn't mean that primatologists think that genes code for specific behaviors, such as a gene for aggression, another for cooperation, and so on. Studying complex behaviors from an evolutionary viewpoint doesn't imply a one gene–one behavior relationship, nor does it suggest that behaviors that are influenced by genes can't be modified through learning.

Much of the behavior of insects and other invertebrates is largely under genetic control. In other words, most of their behaviors aren't learned; they're innate. However, in many vertebrates, especially birds and mammals, the proportion of behavior that is due to learning is substantially increased, while the proportion under genetic control is reduced. This is especially true of primates. And in humans, who are so much a product of culture, most behavior is learned. But at the same time, we also know that in higher organisms, some behaviors are at least partly influenced by certain gene products such as hormones. For example, you're probably aware that elevated levels of testosterone increase aggression in many species. And you may also know that conditions like depression, schizophrenia, and bipolar disorder are caused by abnormal levels of certain chemicals produced by brain cells.

Behavior is a complex trait and is a product of *interactions between genetic and environmental factors*. Among species, there is considerable variation in the limits and potentials for learning and for behavioral **plasticity,** or flexibility. In some species, such as primates, the potentials for learning are extremely broad while, in others, they aren't. Ultimately, those limits and potentials are set by genetic factors that have been favored throughout the evolutionary history of every species. That history, in turn, has been shaped by the ecological setting not only of living species, *but also of their ancestors.*

One of the major goals of primatology is to determine how behaviors influence reproductive fitness and how ecological factors have shaped the evolution of these behaviors. While the actual mechanics of behavioral evolution aren't yet fully understood, new technologies and methodologies are beginning to answer numerous questions. For example, genetic analysis has recently been used to establish paternity in a few primate groups, and this has helped support hypotheses about some behaviors (see p. 158). But in general, an

ecological Pertaining to the relationships between organisms and all aspects of their environment (temperature, predators, nonpredators, vegetation, availability of food and water, types of food, disease organisms, parasites, etc.).

behavioral ecology The study of the evolution of behavior, emphasizing the role of ecological factors as agents of natural selection. Behaviors and behavioral patterns have been favored because they increase the reproductive fitness of individuals (i.e., they are adaptive) in specific environmental contexts.

plasticity The capacity to change. In a behavioral context, the ability of animals to modify actions in response to differing circumstances.

evolutionary approach to the study of behavior doesn't yield definitive answers to many research questions. Rather, it provides a valuable framework within which primatologists analyze data to generate and test hypotheses concerning behavioral patterns.

Because primates are among the most social of animals, social behavior is one of the major topics in primate research. This is a broad subject that includes *all* aspects of behavior that occur in social groupings, even some you may not think of as social behaviors, like feeding or mating. To understand the function of one behavioral element, it's necessary to determine how it's influenced by numerous interrelated factors. As an example, we'll discuss some of the more important variables that influence **social structure.**

social structure The composition, size, and sex ratio of a group of animals. Social structures, in part, are the results of natural selection in specific habitats, and they guide individual interactions and social relationships.

SOME FACTORS THAT INFLUENCE SOCIAL STRUCTURE

Body Size As a general rule, larger animals require fewer calories per unit of weight than smaller animals because they have a smaller ratio of surface area to mass than do smaller animals. Since body heat is lost at the surface, larger animals are better able to retain heat and their overall energy requirements are less than for smaller animals. (This may sound strange but, for unit of body weight, a mouse has greater nutritional needs than an elephant.)

metabolism The chemical processes within cells that break down nutrients and release energy for the body to use. (When nutrients are broken down into their component parts, such as amino acids, energy is released and made available for the cell to use.)

Basal Metabolic Rate (BMR) and Diet Metabolism is the rate at which the body uses energy to maintain all functions while in a resting state. BMR is closely correlated with body size, so in general, smaller animals have a higher BMR than larger ones (Fig. 7-1). Consequently, smaller primates like galagos, tarsiers, marmosets, and tamarins require an energy-rich diet high in protein (insects), fats (nuts and seeds), and carbohydrates (fruits and seeds). Some larger primates, which tend to have a lower BMR, can do well with less energy-rich foods, such as leaves. For example, gorillas eat huge quantities of leaves, pith from bamboo stems, and other types of vegetation (Fig.7-2).

Distribution of Resources Different kinds of foods are distributed in various ways. Leaves can be abundant and dense and will therefore support large groups of animals. Other foods, such as insects, may be widely scattered, and animals that rely on them usually feed alone or perhaps with one or two others.

Fruits and nuts, widely dispersed in trees and shrubs, occur in clumps. These can most efficiently be exploited by smaller groups of animals, so large groups frequently break up into smaller subunits while feeding. Some species that rely on foods distributed in small clumps tend to be protective of resources, especially if their feeding area is small enough to be defended. Some of these species live in very small groups composed of male-female pairs (siamangs) or a female with one or two males (marmosets and tamarins), and dependent offspring.

FIGURE 7-1 This tiny dwarf lemur has a high BMR and requires an energy-rich diet of insects and other forms of animal protein.

Predation Primates are vulnerable to many types of predators, including snakes, birds of prey, leopards, wild dogs, lions, and even other primates. Typically, where predation pressure is high, large communities are advantageous. These may be multimale-multifemale groups or congregations of one-male groups.

Relationships with Other, Nonpredatory Species
Many primate species associate with other primate and nonprimate species for various reasons, including predator avoidance. When they do share habitats with other species, they exploit somewhat different resources.

Dispersal Dispersal is another factor that influences social structure and relationships within groups. As is true of most mammals (and indeed, most vertebrates), members of one sex leave the group in which they were born (their *natal group*) about the time they become sexually mature. Male dispersal is the most common pattern in primates (e.g., ring-tailed lemurs, vervets, and macaques, to name a few). Female dispersal is seen in some colobus species, hamadryas baboons, chimpanzees, and mountain gorillas. Those individuals who leave usually find mates outside their natal group and so dispersal is generally believed to decrease the likelihood of close inbreeding. Another consequence of dispersal is that individuals of either sex who remain in their natal group enjoy certain advantages because they're able to establish long-term bonds with relatives and other animals.

FIGURE 7-2 This large male mountain gorilla does well on a diet of less energy-rich leaves and other plant materials.

Life Histories **Life history traits** are characteristics or developmental stages that typify members of a given species and influence potential reproductive rates. Examples include: length of gestation, length of time between pregnancies (interbirth interval), period of infant dependency and age at weaning, age at sexual maturity, and life expectancy.

Life history traits have important consequences for many aspects of social life and social structure. Shorter life histories are advantageous to species that live in marginal or unpredictable habitats (Strier, 2003). Since these species mature early and have short interbirth intervals, reproduction can occur at a relatively fast rate. Conversely, species with extended life histories, such as gorillas, are well suited to stable environmental conditions.

life history traits Also called life history strategies; characteristics and developmental stages that influence rates of reproduction.

Distribution and Types of Sleeping Sites Gorillas are the only nonhuman primates that sleep on the ground. Primate sleeping sites can be in trees or on cliff faces, and their spacing can be related to social structure, predator avoidance, and how many sleeping sites are available.

Activity Patterns Most primates are diurnal, but several small-bodied prosimians and one New World monkey (the owl monkey) are nocturnal. Nocturnal species tend to forage for food alone or in groups of two or three and many use concealment to avoid predators.

Human Activities Virtually all nonhuman primate populations are now impacted by human hunting and forest clearing. These activities severely disrupt and isolate groups, reduce numbers, reduce resource availability, and eventually can cause extinction.

Why Be Social?

Group living exposes animals to competition with other group members for resources, so why don't they live alone? After all, competition can lead to injury or even death, and it's costly in terms of energy expenditure. One widely accepted answer to this question is that the costs of competition are offset by the benefits of predator defense provided by associating with others. Groups composed of several adult males and females (multimale-multifemale groups) are advantageous in areas where predation pressure is high, particularly in mixed woodlands and on open savannas. Leopards are the most significant predator of terrestrial primates (Fig. 7-3) but they also take a substantial number of arboreal monkeys. Where members of prey species occur in larger groups, the chances of early predator detection (and thus avoidance) are increased simply because there are more pairs of eyes looking about. Savanna baboons have long been used as an example of these principles. They're found in semiarid grassland and broken woodland habitats throughout sub-Saharan Africa. To avoid nocturnal predators, savanna baboons sleep in trees, but during the day, they spend much of their time on the ground foraging for food. If a nonhuman predator appears, baboons flee back into the trees, but if they're some distance from safety, adult males (and sometimes females) may join forces to chase the intruder. The effectiveness of male baboons in this regard shouldn't be underestimated, since they've been known to kill domestic dogs and even to attack leopards and lions.

There is probably no single answer to the question of why primates live in groups. More than likely, predator avoidance is a major factor but not the only one. Group living evolved as an adaptive response to a number of ecological variables, and it has served primates well for a very long time.

FIGURE 7-3 When a baboon strays too far from its troop, as this one has done, it's more likely to fall prey to predators. Leopards are the most serious nonhuman threat to terrestrial primates.

Time Life Pictures/Getty Images

Primate Social Behavior

Because primates solve their major adaptive problems in a social context, we should expect there to be several behaviors that reinforce the integrity of the group. The better known of these are described in the sections that follow. Remember, all these behaviors have evolved as adaptive responses during more than 50 million years of primate evolution.

DOMINANCE

dominance hierarchies
Systems of social organization wherein individuals within a group are ranked relative to one another. Higher-ranking animals have greater access to preferred food items and mating partners than lower-ranking individuals. Dominance hierarchies are sometimes called "pecking orders."

Many primate societies are organized into **dominance hierarchies,** which impose a certain degree of order by establishing parameters of individual behavior. Although aggression is frequently a means of increasing one's status, dominance usually serves to reduce the amount of actual physical violence.

Not only are lower-ranking animals unlikely to attack or even threaten a higher-ranking one, but dominant animals are also frequently able to exert control simply by making a threatening gesture.

Individual rank or status can be measured by access to resources, including food items and mating partners. Dominant animals are given priority by others, and they usually don't give way in confrontations.

A number of primatologists think that the primary benefit of dominance is the increased reproductive success of high-ranking animals. This may be true in general, but there's good evidence that lower-ranking males of some species also successfully mate. High-ranking females have greater access to food than subordinate females, and since they obtain more energy for the production and care of offspring (Fedigan, 1983), they presumably have higher reproductive success.

Pusey et al. (1997) demonstrated that the offspring of high-ranking female chimpanzees at Gombe National Park in Tanzania had significantly higher rates of infant survival. Moreover, daughters of these females matured faster, which meant they had shorter interbirth intervals and consequently produced more offspring.

An individual's social rank isn't permanent and changes throughout life. It's influenced by many factors, including sex, age, level of aggression, amount of time spent in the group, intelligence, perhaps motivation, and sometimes the mother's social position (particularly true of macaques).

In species organized into groups containing a number of females associated with one or several adult males, the males are generally dominant to females. Within such groups, males and females have separate hierarchies, although very high ranking females can dominate the lowest-ranking males (particularly young males). But there are exceptions to this pattern of male dominance. In many lemur species, females are the dominant sex. Moreover, in species that form monogamous pairs (e.g., indris, gibbons), males and females are codominant.

All primates *learn* their position in the hierarchy. From birth, an infant is carried by its mother, and it observes how she responds to every member of the group. Dominance and subordination are indicated by gestures and behaviors, some of which are universal throughout the primate order (including humans), and this gestural repertoire is part of every youngster's learning experience.

Young primates also acquire social rank through play with age peers, and as they spend more time with play groups, their social interactions widen. Competition and rough-and-tumble play allow them to learn the strengths and weaknesses of peers, and they carry this knowledge with them throughout their lives. Thus, young primates *learn* to negotiate their way through the complex web of social interactions that make up their daily lives.

COMMUNICATION

Communication is universal among animals and includes scents and unintentional, **autonomic** responses and behaviors that convey meaning. Such attributes as body posture convey information about an animal's emotional state. For example, a purposeful striding gait implies confidence. Moreover, autonomic responses to threatening or novel stimuli, such as raised body hair (most species) or enhanced body odor (gorillas), indicate excitement.

communication Any act that conveys information, in the form of a message, to another individual. Frequently, the result of communication is a change in the behavior of the recipient. Communication may not be deliberate but may instead be the result of involuntary processes or a secondary consequence of an intentional action.

autonomic Pertaining to physiological responses not under voluntary control. An example in chimpanzees would be the erection of body hair during excitement. Blushing is a human example. Both convey information regarding emotional states, but neither is deliberate, and communication isn't intended.

FIGURE 7-4 An adolescent male savanna baboon threatens the photographer with a characteristic "yawn" that shows the canine teeth. Note also that the eyes are closed briefly to expose light, cream-colored eyelids. This has been called the "eyelid flash."

FIGURE 7-5 One young male savanna baboon mounts another as an expression of dominance.

FIGURE 7-6 Adolescent savanna baboons holding hands.

Many intentional behaviors also serve as communication. In primates, these include a wide variety of gestures, facial expressions, and vocalizations, some of which we humans share. Among many primates, a mild threat is indicated by an intense stare, and indeed, we humans find prolonged eye contact with strangers very uncomfortable. (For this reason, people should avoid eye contact with captive primates.) Other threat gestures are a quick yawn to expose canine teeth (baboons, macaques) (Fig. 7-4); bobbing back and forth in a crouched position (patas monkeys); and branch shaking (many monkey species). High-ranking baboons *mount* the hindquarters of subordinates to express dominance (Fig. 7-5). Mounting may also serve to defuse potentially tense situations by indicating something like, "It's okay, I accept your apology."

Other behaviors indicate submission, reassurance, or amicable intentions. Submission is indicated by crouching (most primates) or presenting the hindquarters (baboons). Reassurance takes the form of touching, patting, hugging, and holding hands (Fig. 7-6). Grooming also serves in a number of situations to indicate submission or reassurance.

A wide variety of facial expressions indicating emotional state is seen in chimpanzees and, especially, in bonobos (Fig. 7-7). These include the well-known play face (also seen in several other primate and nonprimate species), associated with play behavior, and the fear grin (seen in *all* primates) to indicate fear and submission.

Primates also use a wide array of vocalizations for communication. Some, such as the bark of a baboon that has just spotted a leopard, are unintentional startled reactions. Others, such as the chimpanzee food grunt, are heard only in specific contexts. Nevertheless, both serve the same function: They inform

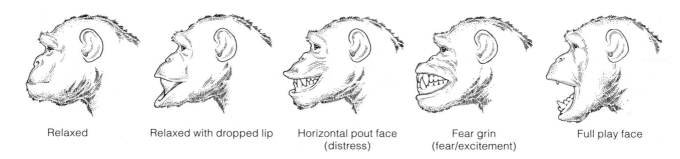

Relaxed   Relaxed with dropped lip   Horizontal pout face (distress)   Fear grin (fear/excitement)   Full play face

FIGURE 7-7 Chimpanzee facial expressions.

others, although not necessarily deliberately, of the possible presence of predators or food.

Primates (and other animals) also communicate through **displays,** which are more complicated, frequently elaborate combinations of behaviors. For example, the exaggerated courtship dances of many male birds, often enhanced by colorful plumage, are displays. Chest slapping and tearing vegetation are common gorilla threat displays.

All nonhuman animals use various vocalizations, body postures, and, to some degree, facial expressions that transmit information. But the array of communicative devices is much richer among nonhuman primates, even though they don't use language the way humans do. Communication is important, for it truly is what makes social living possible. Through submissive gestures, aggression is reduced and physical violence is less likely. Likewise, friendly intentions and relationships are reinforced through physical contact and grooming. Indeed, we humans can see ourselves in other primate species most clearly in their familiar uses of nonverbal communication.

displays Sequences of repetitious behaviors that serve to communicate emotional states. Nonhuman primate displays are most frequently associated with reproductive or agonistic behavior.

AGGRESSIVE INTERACTIONS

Within primate societies, there is an interplay between **affiliative** behaviors, which promote group cohesion, and aggressive behaviors, which can lead to group disruption. Conflict within a group frequently develops out of competition for resources, including mating partners and food items. Instead of actual attacks or fighting, most intragroup aggression occurs in the form of various signals and displays, frequently within the context of a dominance hierarchy. Therefore, the majority of tense situations are resolved through various submissive and appeasement behaviors.

Of course, conflict isn't always resolved peacefully, and it can have serious consequences. For example, high-ranking female macaques frequently intimidate, harass, and even attack lower ranking females to keep them away from food. Dominant females consistently chase subordinates away from food and have even been observed to take food from their mouths. Eventually, these actions can cause weight loss and poor nutrition in low-ranking females, which in turn can reduce their reproductive success.

Competition between males for mates frequently results in injury and even death. In species that have a distinct breeding season (e.g., squirrel monkeys), conflict between males is most common during that time. Male squirrel monkeys form coalitions to compete with other males, and when outright fighting occurs, injuries can be severe. In species not restricted to a mating season, competition between males can be an ongoing process.

affiliative Pertaining to amicable associations between individuals. Affiliative behaviors, such as grooming, reinforce social bonds and promote group cohesion.

territories Portions of an individual's or group's home range that are actively defended against intrusion, especially by members of the same species.

core area The portion of a home range containing the highest concentration and most reliable supplies of food and water. The core area is defended.

Between groups, aggression is used to protect resources or **territories.** Primate groups are associated with a *home range* where they remain permanently. (Although individuals may leave their home range and join another community, the group itself remains in a particular area.) Within the home range is a portion called the **core area,** which contains the highest concentration of predictable resources, and it's where the group is most frequently found. Although parts of the home range may overlap the home ranges of other groups, core areas of adjacent groups don't overlap. The core area can also be said to be a group's territory, and it's the portion of the home range defended against intrusion. However, in some species, other areas of the home range may also be defended. Whatever area is defended is termed the *territory.*

Not all primates are territorial. In general, territoriality is associated with species whose ranges are small enough to be patrolled and protected (e.g., gibbons and vervets). And you already know that in many species, group encounters are frequently nonaggressive.

But male chimpanzees are highly intolerant of unfamiliar chimpanzees, especially other males, and they fiercely defend their territories and resources. Therefore, interactions between different chimpanzee groups are almost always characterized by aggressive displays, chasing, and actual fighting.

Beginning in 1974, Jane Goodall and her colleagues witnessed at least five unprovoked and extremely brutal attacks by groups of chimpanzees on other chimpanzees. To explain these attacks, it's necessary to provide a little background information. Goodall had begun studying chimpanzees at what is now Gombe National Park in Tanzania in 1960. By 1973, the original community had divided into two distinct groups, one located in the north and the other in the south of what had once been the original group's home range. In effect, the smaller offshoot group had denied the others access to part of their former home range.

By 1977, all seven males and one female of the splinter group were either known or suspected to have been killed. All observed incidents involved several animals, usually adult males, who brutally attacked lone individuals. Although it isn't possible to know exactly what motivated the attackers, it was clear that they intended to incapacitate their victims (Goodall, 1986).

A similar situation was also reported for a chimpanzee group in the Mahale Mountains south of Gombe. Over a 17-year period, all the males of a small community disappeared. Although no attacks were actually observed, there was circumstantial evidence that most of these males met the same fate as the Gombe attack victims (Nishida et al., 1985, 1990).

Even though the precise motivation of chimpanzee intergroup aggression may never be fully explained, it appears that acquiring and protecting resources (including females) are involved (Nishida et al., 1985, 1990; Goodall, 1986; Manson and Wrangham, 1991; Nishida, 1991).

Through examination of shared aspects of human and chimpanzee social life, we can develop hypotheses regarding how intergroup conflict may have arisen in our own lineage. Early hominids and chimpanzees may have inherited from a common ancestor the predispositions that lead to similar patterns of strife between populations. It's not appropriate or even possible to draw direct comparisons between chimpanzee conflict and human warfare owing to human cultural elaborations, the use of symbols (e.g., national flags), and language. But it's still important to speculate on the fundamental issues that may have led to the development of similar patterns in both species.

AFFILIATION AND ALTRUISM

As you've just seen, even though it can be destructive, a certain amount of aggression helps to maintain order within groups and to protect either individual or group resources. Fortunately, to minimize actual violence and to defuse potentially dangerous situations, there are many behaviors that reinforce bonds between individuals and enhance group stability.

Common affiliative behaviors include reconciliation, consolation, and simple amicable interactions between friends and relatives. These involve various forms of physical contact; in fact, physical contact is one of the most important factors in primate development and is crucial in promoting peaceful relationships in many primate social groups.

Grooming is one of the most important affiliative behaviors in many primate species, so much so that primatologist Alison Jolly (1985) called it the "social cement" of primate societies. Although grooming occurs in other animal species, social grooming is mostly a primate activity, and it plays an important role in day-to-day life (Fig. 7-8). Because grooming involves using the fingers to pick through the fur of another individual (or one's own) to remove

grooming Picking through fur to remove dirt, parasites, and other materials that may be present. Social grooming is common among primates and reinforces social relationships.

FIGURE 7-8 Grooming primates. (a) Patas monkeys; female grooming male. (b) Longtail macaques. (c) Savanna baboons. (d) Chimpanzees.

(a)

(b)

(c)

(d)

insects, dirt, and other materials, it serves hygienic functions. But it's also an immensely pleasurable activity that members of some species (especially chimpanzees) engage in for long periods of time.

Grooming occurs in a variety of contexts. Mothers groom infants. Males groom sexually receptive females. Subordinate animals groom dominant ones, sometimes to gain favor. Friends groom friends. In general, grooming is comforting. It restores peaceful relationships between animals who have quarreled and provides reassurance during tense situations. In short, grooming reinforces social bonds and consequently helps to maintain and strengthen the structure of the group.

Conflict resolution through reconciliation is another important aspect of primate social behavior. Following a conflict, chimpanzee opponents frequently move, within minutes, to reconcile (de Waal, 1982). Reconciliation takes many forms, including hugging, kissing, and grooming. Even uninvolved individuals may take part, either grooming one or both participants or forming their own grooming parties. In addition, bonobos are unique in their use of sex to promote group cohesion, restore peace after conflicts, and relieve tension within the group (de Waal, 1987, 1989).

Social relationships are crucial to nonhuman primates, and the bonds between individuals can last a lifetime. These relationships serve a variety of functions. Individuals of many species form alliances in which one member supports another against others. Alliances, or coalitions, as they are also called, can be used to enhance the status of members. For example, at Gombe, the male chimpanzee Figan achieved alpha status because of support from his brother (Goodall, 1986, p. 424). In fact, chimpanzees rely so heavily on coalitions and are so skillful politically that an entire book, appropriately titled *Chimpanzee Politics* (de Waal, 1982), is devoted to the topic.

altruism Behavior that benefits another individual but at some potential risk or cost to oneself.

Altruism, behavior that benefits another while involving some risk or sacrifice to the performer, is common in many primate species, and altruistic acts sometimes contain elements of what might be interpreted as compassion and cooperation. (However, to use the term "compassion" to describe any nonhuman behavior is a bit risky because we can't know the animal's true motivation.) The most fundamental of altruistic behaviors, the protection of dependent offspring, is ubiquitous among mammals and birds, and in the majority of species, altruistic acts are confined to this context. However, among primates, recipients of altruistic acts may include individuals who aren't offspring and who may not even be closely related to the performer. Stelzner and Strier (1981) once watched a female baboon chase a hyena that was in pursuit of a young adult male baboon. This female's unsuccessful rescue attempt was intriguing because not only was she too small to engage the hyena, but she was also unrelated to the victim. Chimpanzees routinely come to the aid of relatives and friends; female langurs join forces to protect infants from infanticidal males; and male baboons protect infants and cooperate to chase predators. In fact, the primate literature abounds with examples of altruistic acts, whereby individuals place themselves at some risk to protect others from attacks by conspecifics or predators.

Adoption of orphans is a form of altruism that has been reported for macaques and baboons, and it's common in chimpanzees. When chimpanzee youngsters are orphaned, they are almost always adopted, usually by older siblings who are solicitous and highly protective. Adoption is crucial to the survival of orphans, who would certainly not survive on their own. In fact, it's extremely rare for a chimpanzee orphan less than three years of age to survive, even if it is adopted.

Reproduction and Reproductive Behaviors

In most primate species, sexual behavior is tied to the female's reproductive cycle, with females being receptive to males only when they're in estrus. Estrus is characterized by behavioral changes that indicate that a female is receptive. In Old World monkeys and apes that live in multimale groups, estrus is also accompanied by swelling and changes in color of the skin around the genital area. These changes serve as visual cues of a female's readiness to mate (Fig 7-9).

Permanent bonding between males and females isn't common among non-human primates. However, male and female savanna baboons sometimes form mating *consortships*. These temporary relationships last while the female is in estrus, and the two spend most of their time together, mating frequently. Moreover, lower-ranking baboon males often form "friendships" (Smuts, 1985) with females and occasionally may mate with them, although they may be driven away by high-ranking males when the female is most receptive.

Mating consortships are also sometimes seen in chimpanzees and are particularly common in bonobos. In fact, a male and female bonobo may spend several weeks primarily in each other's company. During this time, they mate often, even when the female isn't in estrus. But these relationships of longer duration aren't typical of chimpanzee (*Pan troglodytes*) males and females.

Such a male-female bond may result in increased reproductive success for both sexes. For the male, there is the increased likelihood that he will be the

FIGURE 7-9 Estrous swelling of genital tissues in a female chimpanzee.

Lynn Kilgore

father of any infant the female conceives. At the same time, the female potentially gains protection from predators or others of her group and perhaps assistance in caring for offspring she may already have.

FEMALE AND MALE REPRODUCTIVE STRATEGIES

Reproductive **strategies,** and especially how they differ between the sexes, have been a primary focus of primate research. The goal of these strategies is to produce and successfully rear to adulthood as many offspring as possible.

Primates are among the most **K-selected** of mammals. By this we mean that individuals produce only a few young, in whom they invest a tremendous amount of parental care. Contrast this pattern with **r-selected** species, where individuals produce large numbers of offspring but invest little or no energy in parental care. Good examples of r-selected species include insects, most fishes, and, among mammals, mice and rabbits. (Note that r-selected species tend to be near the bottom of the food chain and thus species survival depends on short generation spans and the production of numerous, quickly maturing offspring.)

When we consider the degree of care required by young, dependent primate offspring, it's clear that enormous investment by at least one parent is necessary. And in a majority of species, the mother carries most of the burden both before and after birth. Primates are totally helpless at birth. They develop slowly and are thus exposed to expanded learning opportunities within a *social* environment. This trend has been elaborated most dramatically in great apes and humans, especially in the latter. Thus, what we see in ourselves and our close primate kin (and presumably in our more recent ancestors as well) is a strategy wherein a few "high-quality," slowly maturing offspring are produced through extraordinary investment by at least one parent, usually the mother.

Finding food and mates, avoiding predators, and caring for and protecting dependent young are difficult challenges for nonhuman primates. Moreover, in most species, males and females use different strategies to meet these challenges.

Female primates spend almost all their adult lives either pregnant, lactating, and/or caring for offspring, and the resulting metabolic demands are enormous. A pregnant or lactating female, although perhaps only half the size of her male counterpart, may require about the same number of calories per day. Even if these demands are met, her physical resources may be drained. For example, analysis of chimpanzee skeletons from Gombe showed significant loss of bone and bone mineral in older females (Sumner et al., 1989).

Given these physiological costs and the fact that her reproductive potential is limited by lengthy intervals between births, a female's best strategy is to maximize the amount of resources available to her and her offspring. Indeed, as we just discussed, females of many primate species (gibbons, marmosets, and macaques, to name a few) are viciously competitive with other females and aggressively protect resources and territories. In some species, as we have seen, females distance themselves from others to avoid competition. Males, however, face a separate set of challenges. Having little investment in the rearing of offspring and the continuous production of sperm, it's to the male's advantage to secure as many mates and produce as many offspring as possible. And to achieve this goal, males must compete with each other for females.

strategies Behaviors or behavioral complexes that have been favored by natural selection to increase individual reproductive success. The behaviors need not be deliberate, and they often vary considerably between males and females.

K-selected Pertaining to an adaptive strategy whereby individuals produce relatively few offspring, in whom they invest increased parental care. Although only a few infants are born, chances of survival are increased for each one because of parental investments in time and energy. Examples of K-selected nonprimate species are birds and canids (e.g., wolves, coyotes, and dogs).

r-selected An adaptive strategy that emphasizes relatively large numbers of offspring and reduced parental care (compared to K-selected species). *K-selection* and *r-selection* are relative terms; e.g., mice are r-selected compared to primates but K-selected compared to fish.

SEXUAL SELECTION

One outcome of different mating strategies is **sexual selection,** a phenomenon first described by Charles Darwin. Sexual selection is a type of natural selection that operates on only one sex, usually males, whereby the selective agent is male competition for mates and, in some species, mate choice in females. The long-term effect of sexual selection is to increase the frequency of those traits that lead to greater success in acquiring mates.

Sexual selection in primates is most common in species in which mating is polygynous and male competition for females is prominent. In these species, sexual selection produces dimorphism with regard to a number of traits, most noticeably body size. As you have seen, the males of many primate species are considerably larger than females, and males also sometimes have larger canine teeth. Males of multimale-multifemale societies also have relatively larger testes than males of other types of groups, presumably because of the potential need to produce greater numbers of sperm. And producing lots of sperm is advantageous to individual males, since their sperm may ultimately compete with the sperm of other males when females mate with more than one partner.

Conversely, in species that live in pairs (e.g., gibbons) or where male competition is reduced, sexual dimorphism in canine teeth and body size is either reduced or nonexistent, and relative testis size is smaller. For these reasons, the presence or absence of sexually dimorphic traits in a species can be a reasonably good indicator of mating structure.

sexual selection A type of natural selection that operates on only one sex within a species. It's the result of competition for mates, and it can lead to sexual dimorphism with regard to one or more traits.

INFANTICIDE AS A REPRODUCTIVE STRATEGY?

One way males *may* increase their chances of reproducing is by killing infants fathered by other males. This explanation was first offered in an early study of Hanuman langurs in India (Hrdy, 1977). Hanuman langurs (Fig. 7-10) typically live in groups composed of one adult male, several females, and their offspring. Other males without mates form "bachelor" groups that frequently forage within sight of the one-male associations. These peripheral males occasionally attack and defeat a reproductive male and drive him from his group. After such takeovers, some or all of the group's infants (fathered by the previous male) are sometimes killed by the new male.

Such behavior would appear to be counterproductive, especially for a species as a whole. However, individuals act to maximize their *own* reproductive success, no matter what the effect may be on the population or ultimately the species. And that's what the male langur may be doing, albeit unknowingly. While a female is producing milk and nursing an infant, she doesn't come into estrus, and therefore she isn't sexually available. But when an infant dies, its mother resumes cycling and becomes sexually receptive. Consequently, an infanticidal new male avoids waiting two to three years for the infants to be weaned before he can mate with their mothers. Moreover, he doesn't expend energy and put himself at risk defending infants who don't carry his genes.

Hanuman langurs aren't the only primates that practice infanticide. Infanticide has been observed (or surmised) in many species, such as redtail monkeys, red colobus, blue monkeys, savanna baboons, howlers, orangutans, gorillas, chimpanzees (Struhsaker and Leyland, 1987), and humans. (It should also be noted that infanticide occurs in numerous nonprimate species, including rodents, cats, and horses.) In the majority of reported

Joe MacDonald/Animals Animals

FIGURE 7-10 Hanuman langurs.

nonhuman primate examples, infanticide coincides with the transfer of a new male into a group or, as in chimpanzees, an encounter with an unfamiliar female and infant.

Numerous objections to this explanation of infanticide have been raised. Alternative explanations have included competition for resources (Rudran, 1973), aberrant behaviors related to human-induced overcrowding (Curtin and Dohlinow, 1978), and inadvertent killing during aggressive episodes, where it wasn't clear that the infant was actually the target animal (Bartlett et al., 1993). Sussman and colleagues (1995), as well as others, have questioned the actual prevalence of infanticide, arguing that although it does occur, it's not particularly common. These authors have also suggested that if indeed male reproductive fitness is increased through the killing of infants, such increases are negligible. Yet others (Struhsaker and Leyland, 1987; Hrdy, 1995) maintain that the incidence and patterning of infanticide by males are not only significant, but consistent with the assumptions established by theories of behavioral evolution.

Henzi and Barrett (2003) report that when chacma baboon males migrate into a new group, they "deliberately single out females with young infants and hunt them down." This evidence strongly supports the infanticide hypothesis, but it doesn't actually prove it. In order to do this, primatologists must demonstrate two crucial facts:

1. Infanticidal males *don't* kill their own offspring.
2. Once a male has killed an infant, he subsequently fathers another infant with the victim's mother.

Borries et al. (1999) collected DNA samples from the feces of infanticidal males and their victims in several groups of free-ranging Hanuman langurs specifically to determine if these males killed their own offspring. Their results showed that in all 16 cases where infant and male DNA was available, the males were not related to the infants they either attacked or killed. Moreover, DNA analysis also showed that in four out of five cases where the victim's mother subsequently gave birth, the new infants were fathered by the infanticidal male. Although still more evidence is needed, this DNA evidence strongly suggests that infanticide may indeed give males an increased chance of fathering offspring.

Mothers, Fathers, and Infants

polyandry A mating system wherein a female continuously associates with more than one male (usually two or three) with whom she mates. Among nonhuman primates, polyandry is seen only in marmosets and tamarins. It also occurs in a few human societies.

The basic social unit among all primates is the female and her infants (Fig. 7-11). Except in those species in which monogamy or **polyandry** occurs, males usually don't directly participate in the rearing of offspring. The mother-infant bond begins at birth. Although the exact nature of the bonding process isn't fully known, there appear to be predisposing factors that strongly attract the female to her infant, so long as she herself has had a sufficiently normal experience with her own mother. This doesn't mean that primate mothers possess innate knowledge of how to care for an infant and, in fact, they don't. Monkeys and apes raised in captivity without contact with their own mothers not only don't know how to care for a newborn infant, but may fear it and attack or even kill it. Thus, learning is critically important in the establishment of a mother's attraction to her infant.

FIGURE 7-11 Primate mothers with young. (a) Mongoose lemur. (b) Chimpanzee. (c) Patas monkey. (d) Orangutan. (e) Sykes monkey.

The role of bonding between primate mothers and infants was clearly demonstrated by psychologist Harry Harlow (1959), who raised infant monkeys with surrogate mothers made of wire or a combination of wire and cloth. Other monkeys were raised with no mother at all. In one experiment, infants retained an attachment to their cloth-covered surrogate mother (Fig. 7-12). But those raised with no mother were incapable of forming lasting affectional ties. These deprived monkeys sat passively in their cages and stared vacantly into space. None of the motherless males ever successfully copulated, and those females who were (somewhat artificially) impregnated either paid little attention to their infants or were aggressive toward them (Harlow and Harlow, 1961). The point is that monkeys reared in isolation were denied opportunities to *learn* the rules of social and maternal behavior. Moreover, and just as essential, they were denied the all-important physical contact so necessary for normal primate psychological and emotional development.

FIGURE 7-12 Infant macaque clinging to cloth mother.

FIGURE 7-13 This male savanna baboon with a youngster on his back is exhibiting infant care, but he may not be the father.

The importance of a normal relationship with the mother is demonstrated by field studies as well. From birth, infant primates are able to cling to their mother's fur, and they're in more or less constant physical contact with her for several months. During this critical period, infants develop a closeness with mothers that doesn't always end with weaning. It may even be maintained throughout life (especially among some Old World monkeys). And it's reflected in grooming behavior that continues between mother and offspring even after the young reach adulthood and have infants of their own.

In some species, presumed fathers also participate in infant care (Fig. 7-13). Male siamangs are actively involved, and marmoset and tamarin infants are usually carried on the father's back and transferred to their mother only for nursing.

Primate Cultural Behavior

One important trait that makes primates, and especially chimpanzees and bonobos, attractive as models for behavior in early hominids may be called *cultural behavior.* Although many cultural anthropologists and others prefer to use the term *culture* to refer specifically to human activities, most biological anthropologists consider it appropriate to use the term in reference to nonhuman primates too (McGrew, 1992, 1998; de Waal, 1999; Whiten et al., 1999). In fact, the term *cultural primatology* is now being used more frequently.

Undeniably, most aspects of culture are uniquely human, and one must be cautious when interpreting nonhuman animal behavior. But again, since humans are products of the same evolutionary forces that have produced other species, they can be expected to exhibit some of the same *behavioral patterns,* particularly of other primates. However, because of increased brain size and learning capacities, humans express many characteristics to a greater degree. We would argue that the *aptitude for culture* as a means of adapting to the natural environment is one such characteristic.

Among other things, cultural behavior is *learned;* it's passed from generation to generation not biologically, but through learning. Whereas humans deliberately teach their young, free-ranging nonhuman primates (with the exception of a few reports) don't appear to do so. But at the same time, like young nonhuman primates, human children also acquire a tremendous amount of knowledge through observation rather than instruction (Fig. 7-14a). Nonhuman primate infants, through observing their mothers and others, learn about food items, appropriate behaviors, and how to use and modify objects to achieve certain ends (Fig. 7-14b). In turn, their own offspring will observe their activities. What emerges is a *cultural tradition* that may eventually come to typify an entire group or even a species.

The earliest reported example of cultural behavior concerned a study group of Japanese macaques on Koshima Island. In 1952, Japanese researchers began provisioning the 22-member troop with sweet potatoes. The following year, a young female named Imo began washing her potatoes in a freshwater stream prior to eating them. Within three years, several monkeys had adopted the practice, but they had switched from using the stream to taking their potatoes to the ocean nearby. Maybe they just liked the taste of salt.

The researchers pointed out that dietary habits and food preferences are learned and that potato washing was an example of nonhuman culture. Because the practice arose as an innovative solution to a problem (removing dirt) and gradually spread through the troop until it became a tradition, it was seen as containing elements of human culture. A study of orangutans in Borneo and Sumatra) listed 19 behaviors that showed sufficient regional variation to be classed as "very likely cultural variants" (van Schaik et al., 2003). Four of these were differences in how nests were used or built. Other behaviors that varied included the use of branches to swat insects and pressing leaves or hands to the mouth to amplify sounds.

FIGURE 7-14 (a) This little girl is learning the basic skills of computer use by watching her older sister. (b) A chimpanzee learns the art of termiting through intense observation.

Lynn Kilgore

(a)

Manoj Shah/The Image Bank

(b)

Tool use has been an important discovery in nonhuman primates because traditionally, tool use (along with language) was said to set humans apart from other animals. Wild capuchin monkeys use leaves to get water from cavities in trees (Phillips, 1998), and they smash objects against stones (Izawa and Mizuno, 1977W). Their use of stones in captivity (both as hammers and anvils) has also been reported (Visalberghi, 1990). And recently, use of unmodified stones as tools was reported for free-ranging capuchins in an area of Brazil where resources are seasonally available (Moura and Lee, 2004).

Capuchins were observed using stones to dig for tubers, roots and insects and for cracking seeds and nuts. They also used them occasionally to smash small vertebrate prey such as lizards. Moura and Lee point out that this is the only known example of nonhuman primates systematically using stones as digging tools and they speculate that living in a somewhat marginal habitat has encouraged the development of innovative techniques for exploiting resources in these monkeys.

Chimpanzees exhibit even more elaborate examples of *tool use*. They insert twigs and grass blades into termite mounds in a practice called "termite fishing." When termites grab the twig, the chimpanzee withdraws it and eats them. To some extent, chimpanzees even alter objects to a "regular and set pattern" and have been observed preparing objects for later use at an out-of-site location (Goodall, 1986, p. 535). For example, a chimpanzee will carefully choose a piece of vine, bark, twig, or palm frond and modify it by removing leaves, then break off portions until it's the proper length. Chimpanzees have also been seen making these tools even before the termite mound is in sight.

All this preparation has several implications. First, the chimpanzees are involved in an activity that prepares them for a future (not immediate) task at a somewhat distant location, and this implies planning and forethought. Second, attention to the shape and size of the raw material indicates that chimpanzees have a preconceived idea of what the finished product needs to be in order to be useful. To produce even a simple tool based on a concept is an extremely complex behavior. Scientists previously believed that such behavior was the exclusive domain of humans, but now we question this assumption.

Chimpanzees also crumple and chew handfuls of leaves, which they dip into tree hollows where water accumulates. Then they suck the water from their newly made "leaf sponges." Leaves are also used to wipe substances from fur; twigs are sometimes used as toothpicks; stones may be used as weapons; and various objects, such as branches and stones, may be dragged or rolled to enhance displays.

Chimpanzees in several West African study groups use hammerstones along with platform stones to crack nuts and hard-shelled fruits (Boesch et al., 1994) (Fig. 7-15). However, neither the hammerstone nor the platform stone is deliberately manufactured.

Importantly, chimpanzees show regional variation regarding both the types and methods of tool use. Stone hammers and platforms are used only in West African groups. And at central and eastern African sites, chimpanzees "fish" for termites with stems and sticks, but they don't at some West African locations (McGrew, 1992).

Chimpanzees also show regional dietary preferences (Nishida et al., 1983; McGrew, 1992, 1998). For example, oil palm fruits and nuts are eaten at many locations, including Gombe, but even though they're present in the

Mahale Mountains, they aren't eaten by the chimpanzees there. Such regional patterns in tool use and food preferences that aren't related to availability are reminiscent of the cultural variations seen in humans.

Using sticks, twigs, and stones enhances the ability of chimpanzees to exploit resources. They learn these behaviors during infancy and childhood, partly as a result of prolonged contact with the mother. Of course, exposure to other members of a social group provides additional learning opportunities. These statements also apply to early hominids. While sticks and unmodified stones don't remain to tell tales, our early ancestors surely used these same objects as tools in much the same way chimpanzees do today.

While chimpanzees in the wild haven't been observed modifying the stones they use, a male bonobo named Kanzi (see also p. 167) learned to strike two stones together to produce sharp-edged flakes. In a study conducted by Sue Savage-Rumbaugh and archaeologist Nicholas Toth, Kanzi was allowed to watch as Toth produced stone flakes, which were then used to open a transparent plastic food container (Savage-Rumbaugh and Lewin, 1994). Although bonobos don't appear to use objects as tools in the wild, Kanzi readily appreciated the usefulness of the flakes in obtaining food. Moreover, he was able to master the basic technique of producing flakes without having been taught the various components of the process, although initially his progress was slow. Finally, Kanzi realized that if he threw the stone onto a hard floor, it would shatter and he would have an abundance of cutting tools. Although his solution wasn't the one that Savage-Rumbaugh and Toth expected, it was perhaps even more significant because it provided an excellent example of bonobo insight and problem-solving ability. Moreover, Kanzi did eventually learn to produce flakes by striking two stones together, and these flakes were then used to get food. Not only is this behavior an example of tool manufacture and tool use, albeit in a captive situation, it's also a very sophisticated goal-directed activity.

Human culture has become the environment in which modern *Homo sapiens* lives. Quite clearly, the use of sticks in termite fishing and hammerstones to crack nuts is hardly comparable to modern human technology. However, modern human technology had its beginnings in these very types of behaviors. But this doesn't mean that nonhuman primates are "on their way" to becoming human. Remember, evolution isn't goal directed, and such a conclusion has no validity in discussions of evolutionary processes.

FIGURE 7-15 Chimpanzees in Bossou, Guinea, West Africa, use a pair of stones as hammer and anvil to crack oil-palm nuts.

Language

One of the most significant events in human evolution was the development of language. We've already described several behaviors and autonomic responses that convey information in primates. But although we emphasized the importance of communication to nonhuman primate social life, we also said that nonhuman primates don't use language in the way that humans do.

The view traditionally held by most linguists and behavioral psychologists has been that nonhuman communication consists of mostly involuntary vocalizations and actions that convey information solely about the emotional state of the animal (anger, fear, etc.). Nonhuman animals haven't been considered capable of communicating about external events, objects, or other animals, either in close proximity or removed in space or time. For example, when a startled baboon barks, other group members know only that it's startled. They don't know what prompted the bark, and this they can only ascertain by looking around. In general, then, it has been assumed that nonhuman animals, including primates, use a *closed system* of communication, where the use of vocalizations and other modalities doesn't include references to specific external phenomena.

But for several years, these views have been challenged (Steklis, 1985; King, 1994). For example, vervet monkeys (Fig. 7-16) use specific vocalizations to refer to particular categories of predators, such as snakes, birds of prey, and leopards (Struhsaker, 1967; Seyfarth, Cheney, and Marler, 1980a, 1980b). When researchers made tape recordings of various vervet alarm calls and played them back within hearing distance of free-ranging vervets, they saw different responses to various calls. When they heard leopard-alarm calls, the monkeys climbed trees; eagle-alarm calls caused them to look up; and they responded to snake-alarm calls by looking at the ground.

These results demonstrate that vervets use distinct vocalizations to refer to specific components of the external environment. These calls aren't involuntary, and they don't refer solely to the emotional state (alarm) of the individual. While these findings dispel certain long-held misconceptions about nonhuman communication (at least for some species), they also indicate certain limitations. Vervet communication is restricted to the present; as far as we know, no vervet can communicate about a predator it saw yesterday or one it might see in the future.

Other studies have shown that numerous nonhuman primates, including cottontop tamarins (Cleveland and Snowdon, 1982), Goeldi's monkeys (Masataka, 1983), red colobus (Struhsaker, 1975), and gibbons (Tenaza and

FIGURE 7-16 Group of free-ranging vervets.

Tilson, 1977), produce distinct calls that have specific references. There's also growing evidence that many birds and some nonprimate mammals use specific predator alarm calls (Seyfarth, 1987).

In contrast, humans use *language*, a set of written and/or spoken symbols that refer to concepts, other people, objects, and so on. This set of symbols is said to be *arbitrary* in that the symbol itself has no inherent relationship with whatever it stands for. For example, the English word *flower*, when written or spoken, neither looks, sounds, nor smells like the thing it represents. Moreover, humans can recombine their linguistic symbols in an infinite number of ways to create new meanings, and we can use language to refer to events, places, objects, and people far removed in both space and time. For these reasons, language has been described as an *open system* of communication, based on the human ability to think symbolically.

Language, as distinct from other forms of communication, has always been considered a uniquely human achievement. But work with captive apes has raised doubts about certain aspects of this notion. Reports from psychologists, especially those who work with chimpanzees, leave little doubt that apes can learn to interpret visual signs and use them in communication. The fact that apes can't speak has less to do with lack of intelligence than to differences in the anatomy of the vocal tract and *language-related structures in the brain.*

Because of unsuccessful attempts by others to teach young chimpanzees to speak, psychologists Beatrice and Allen Gardner designed a study to test language capabilities in chimpanzees by teaching an infant female named Washoe to use ASL (American Sign Language for the deaf). The project began in 1966, and in three years, Washoe acquired at least 132 signs. "She asked for goods and services, and she also asked questions about the world of objects and events around her" (Gardner et al., 1989, p. 6).

Years later, an infant chimpanzee named Loulis was placed in Washoe's care. Psychologist Roger Fouts and colleagues wanted to know if Loulis would acquire signing skills from Washoe and other chimpanzees in the study group. Within just eight days, Loulis began to imitate the signs of others. Moreover, Washoe deliberately *taught* Loulis some signs.

There have been other chimpanzee language experiments. A chimpanzee called Sara was taught by David Premack to recognize plastic chips as symbols for various objects. Importantly, the chips didn't resemble the objects they represented. For example, the chip that represented an apple was neither round nor red. Sara's ability to associate chips with concepts and objects to which they bore no similarity implies some degree of symbolic thought.

Dr. Francine Patterson, who taught ASL to Koko, a female lowland gorilla, reports that Koko uses more than 500 signs. Furthermore, Michael, an adult male gorilla who was also involved in the study until his death in 2000, had a considerable sign vocabulary, and the two gorillas regularly signed to each other.

In the late 1970s at the Yerkes Regional Primate Center, a two-year-old male orangutan named Chantek began to use signs after one month of training. Eventually, he acquired approximately 140 signs, which were sometimes used to refer to objects and people that weren't present. Chantek also invented signs and recombined them in novel ways, and he appeared to understand that his signs were *representations* of items, actions, and people (Miles, 1990).

Questions have been raised about this type of experimental work. Do the apes really understand the signs they learn, or are they merely imitating their trainers? Do they learn that a symbol is a name for an object or simply that using it will produce that object? Partly in an effort to address some of these questions and criticisms, psychologist Sue Savage-Rumbaugh taught the two chimpanzees Sherman and Austin to use symbols to categorize *classes* of objects, such as "food" or "tool." This was done in recognition of the fact that in previous studies, apes had been taught symbols for *specific* items. Savage-Rumbaugh recognized that using a symbol as a label isn't the same thing as understanding the *representational value* of the symbol. But if the chimpanzees could classify things into groups, it would indicate that they can use symbols referentially.

Sherman and Austin were taught to recognize familiar food items, for which they routinely used symbols, as belonging to a broader category referred to by yet another symbol, "food." Then they were introduced to unfamiliar food items, for which they had no symbols, to see if they would put them in the food category. The fact that they both had perfect or nearly perfect scores further substantiated that they could categorize unfamiliar objects. More importantly, it was clear that they were capable of assigning symbols to unfamiliar objects to indicate membership in a broad category. This ability was a strong indication that the chimpanzees understood that the symbols were being used referentially.

However, subsequent work with Lana, who had different language experiences, wasn't as successful. Although Lana was able to sort actual objects into categories, she was unable to assign generic symbols to novel items (Savage-Rumbaugh and Lewin, 1994). Thus, it became apparent that the manner in which chimpanzees are introduced to language influences their ability to understand the representational value of symbols.

A major assumption, throughout the relatively brief history of ape language studies, has been that young chimpanzees must be *taught* to use symbols, in contrast to the ability of human children to learn language through exposure, without being taught. Therefore, it was significant when Savage-

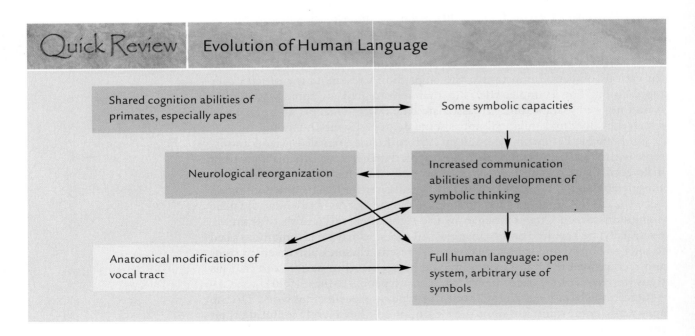

Quick Review Evolution of Human Language

Shared cognition abilities of primates, especially apes → Some symbolic capacities

Increased communication abilities and development of symbolic thinking

Neurological reorganization

Anatomical modifications of vocal tract

Full human language: open system, arbitrary use of symbols

8 | Hominid Origins

Focus Questions

Who are the oldest members of the human family, and how do these early hominids compare with modern humans? With modern apes? How do they fit within a biological continuum?

Introduction

Click

Go to the following CD-ROMs for interactive activities and exercises on topics covered in this chapter:

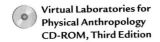

Virtual Laboratories for Physical Anthropology CD-ROM, Third Edition

Hominid Fossils CD-ROM: An Interactive Atlas

biocultural Pertaining to the concept that biology makes culture possible and that culture influences biology.

Plio-Pleistocene Pertaining to the Pliocene and first half of the Pleistocene, a time range of 5–1 m.y.a. For this time period, numerous fossil hominids have been found in Africa.

Our species today dominates our planet, as we use our brains and cultural inventions to invade every corner of the earth. Yet, 5 million years ago, our ancestors were little more than bipedal apes, confined to a few regions in Africa. What were these creatures like? When and how did they begin their evolutionary journey?

In the last two chapters, we have seen how and why humans are grouped as primates, both structurally and behaviorally, and how our evolutionary history coincides with that of other primates. However, we are a unique kind of primate, and our ancestors have been adapted to a particular kind of lifestyle for several million years. Some primitive hominoid may have begun this process more than 10 m.y.a., but fossil evidence indicates a much more definite hominid presence beginning perhaps 5 m.y.a. The hominid nature of these remains is revealed by more than the morphological structure of teeth and bones; in many cases, we know that these animals are hominids also because of the way they behaved—emphasizing once again the **biocultural** nature of human evolution.

In this chapter, we turn first to the physical evidence of earlier primates and then to the hominid fossils themselves. The earliest fossils identifiable as hominids are all from Africa. During the early Pliocene (by 4 m.y.a.), the fossil discoveries become fairly abundant and are considered by paleoanthropologists as unambiguously members of the hominid family. Indeed, the fossil evidence becomes more complete over the next several million years, encompassing the Pliocene and the first half of the Pleistocene epochs. Together, this time period is usually referred to as the **Plio-Pleistocene.**

Hominids, of course, evolved from earlier primates (dating from the Eocene to late Miocene), and we will briefly review this prehominid fossil record to provide a better context for understanding the subsequent evolution of the human family. From new discoveries, the earliest hominids are now thought to date as far back as the end of the Miocene (7–5 m.y.a.). This fossil material is extremely exciting, extending, as it does, the evidence of the human family back 2 million years into prehistory. Moreover, these discoveries have all been made very recently—just in the last five years. As a result, detailed evaluations are still in process, and conclusions must remain tentative.

One thing is certain, however. The earliest members of the human family were confined to Africa. Only much later do their descendants disperse from the African continent to other areas of the Old World. (This "out of Africa" saga will be the topic of the next chapter.)

Early Primate Evolution

Long before bipedal hominids first evolved in Africa, more primitive primates had diverged from even more distant mammalian ancestors. The roots of the primate order go back to the beginnings of the placental mammal radiation circa 65 m.y.a. Thus, the earliest primates were diverging from quite early primitive placental mammals. We have seen (in Chapter 6) that strictly defining living primates using clear-cut derived features is not an easy task. The further back we go in the fossil record, the more primitive and, in many cases, the more generalized the fossil primates become. Such a situation makes classifying them all the more difficult.

In fact, we only have scarce traces of the earliest primates. Some anthropologists have suggested that recently discovered bits and pieces from North Africa *may* be those of a very small primitive primate. But until more evidence is found, we will just have to wait and see.

Fortunately, a vast number of fossil primates from the Eocene (55–34 m.y.a.) have been discovered and now total more than 200 recognized species (see Fig. 5–4, p. 99, for a geological chart). Unlike the available Paleocene forms, those from the Eocene display distinctive primate features. Indeed, primatologist Elwyn Simons (1972, p. 124) called them "the first primates of modern aspect." These animals have been found primarily in sites in North America and Europe (which were then still connected). It is important to recall that the landmasses that connect continents, as well as the water boundaries that separate them, have obvious impact on the geographical distribution of such terrestrially bound animals as primates (see p. 100).

Some interesting late Eocene forms have also been found in Asia, which was joined to Europe by the end of the Eocene epoch. Looking at the whole array of Eocene primates, it is certain that they were (1) primates, (2) widely distributed, and (3) mostly extinct by the end of the Eocene. What is less certain is how any of them might be related to the living primates. Some of these forms are probably ancestors of the *prosimians*—the lemurs and lorises.* Others are probably related to the tarsier. New evidence of Eocene *anthropoid* origins has also recently been discovered in several sites from North Africa, the Persian Gulf, and China. These newly discovered fossils demonstrate that anthropoid origins were well established by 35 m.y.a.

Some new discoveries of very small primates from China are particularly interesting. Dating from the early Eocene (55–45 m.y.a.), some of these Chinese fossils are among the earliest definite primates yet known. They show three particularly interesting and somewhat surprising features. First, because of certain characteristics such as forward rotation of the eyes, they are thought to be on the evolutionary lineage leading to tarsiers and anthropoids (i.e., haplorhines; see p. 125) and thus already distinct from the lemur-loris lineage (i.e., strepsirhines). Second, a newly discovered cranium shows small eye sockets, suggesting that early primates may have been diurnal (Ni et al., 2004). (*Note:* It had previously been assumed that the earliest primates were nocturnal.) And third, these ancient Chinese haplorhine primates were all apparently extremely small, weighing less than 1 ounce (Gebo et al., 2000).

---

*In strict classification terms, especially from a cladistic point of view, lemurs and lorises should
  be referred to as strepsirhines (see p. 125).

FIGURE 8-1 Location of the Fayum, an Oligocene primate site in Egypt.

The Oligocene (34–23 m.y.a.) has yielded numerous additional fossil remains of several different species of early anthropoids. Most of these forms are *Old World anthropoids,* all discovered at a single locality in Egypt, the Fayum (Fig. 8-1). In addition, from North and South America, there are a few known bits that relate only to the ancestry of New World monkeys. By the early Oligocene, continental drift had separated the New World (i.e., the Americas) from the Old World (Africa and Eurasia). Some of the earliest Fayum forms, nevertheless, *may* potentially be close to the ancestry of both Old and New World anthropoids. It has been suggested that late in the Eocene or very early in the Oligocene, the first anthropoids (primitive "monkeys") arose in Africa and later reached South America by "rafting" over the water separation on drifting chunks of vegetation. What we call "monkey," then, may have a common Old World origin, but the ancestry of New and Old World varieties remains separate after about 35 m.y.a. The closest evolutionary affinities humans have after this time are with other Old World anthropoids, that is, with Old World monkeys and apes.

The possible roots of anthropoid evolution are illustrated by different forms from the Fayum; one is the genus *Apidium.* Well known at the Fayum, *Apidium* is represented by several dozen jaws or partial dentitions and more than 100 specimens from the limb and trunk skeleton. Because of its primitive dental arrangement, some paleontologists have suggested that *Apidium* may lie near or even before the evolutionary divergence of Old and New World anthropoids. As so much fossil material of teeth and limb bones of *Apidium* has been found, some informed speculation regarding diet and locomotor behavior is possible. It is thought that this small, squirrel-sized primate ate mostly fruits and some seeds and was most likely an arboreal quadruped, adept at leaping and springing (Table 8-1).

The other genus of importance from the Fayum is *Aegyptopithecus.* This genus, also well known, is represented by several well-preserved crania and abundant jaws and teeth. The largest of the Fayum anthropoids, *Aegyptopithecus* is roughly the size of a modern howler monkey (13 to 20 pounds) (Fleagle, 1983) and is thought to have been a short-limbed, slow-moving arboreal quadruped (see Table 8-1). *Aegyptopithecus* is important because, better than any other known form, it bridges the gap between the Eocene fossils and the succeeding Miocene hominoids.

Nevertheless, *Aegyptopithecus* is a very primitive Old World anthropoid, with a small brain and long snout and not showing any derived features of either Old World monkeys or hominoids. Thus, it may be close to the ancestry of *both* major groups of living Old World anthropoids. Found in geological beds dating to 35–33 m.y.a., *Aegyptopithecus* further suggests that the crucial evolutionary divergence of hominoids from other Old World anthropoids occurred *after* this time (Fig. 8-2).

TABLE 8-1 | Inferred General Paleobiological Aspects of Oligocene Primates

	Weight Range	Substratum	Locomotion	Diet
Apidium	750–1,600 g (2–3 lb)	Arboreal	Quadruped	Fruit, seeds
Aegyptopithecus	6,700 g (15 lb)	Arboreal	Quadruped	Fruit, some leaves?

Source: After Fleagle, 1999.

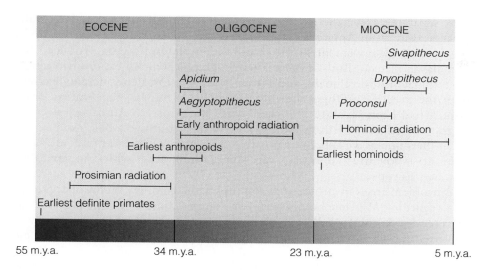

FIGURE 8-2 Major events in early primate evolution.

Miocene Fossil Hominoids

During the approximately 18 million years of the Miocene (23–5 m.y.a.), a great deal of evolutionary activity took place. In Africa, Asia, and Europe, a diverse and highly successful group of hominoids emerged (Fig. 8-3). Indeed, there were many more forms of hominoids from the Miocene than are found today (now represented by the highly restricted groups of apes and one species of humans). In fact, the Miocene could be called "the golden age of hominoids." Many thousands of fossils have been found from dozens of sites scattered in East Africa, southwest Africa, southwest Asia, into western and southern Europe, and extending into southern Asia and China.

During the Miocene, significant transformations relating to climate and repositioning of landmasses took place. By 23 m.y.a., *major* continental locations approximated those of today (except that North and South America

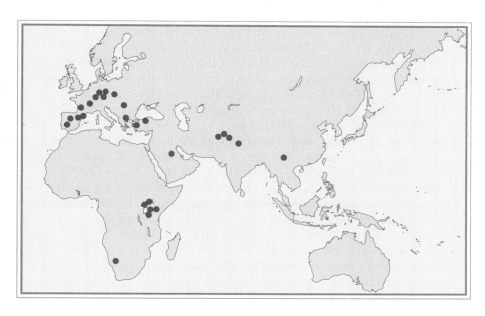

FIGURE 8-3 Miocene hominoid distribution, from fossils thus far discovered.

were separate). Nevertheless, the movements of South America and Australia further away from Antarctica significantly altered ocean currents. Likewise, the continued movement of the South Asian plate into Asia produced the Himalayan Plateau. Both of these paleogeographical modifications had significant impact on the climate, and the early Miocene was considerably warmer than the preceding Oligocene. Moreover, by 16 m.y.a., the Arabian Plate (which had been separate) "docked" with northeastern Africa. As a result, migrations of animals from Africa directly into southwest Asia (and in the other direction as well) became possible. Among the earliest transcontinental migrants (soon after 16 m.y.a.) were African hominoids who colonized Asia and later Europe.

A problem arises in any attempt to simplify the complex evolutionary situation regarding Miocene hominoids. For example, for many years paleontologists tended to think of these fossil forms as either "apelike" or "humanlike" and used modern examples as models. But as we have just noted, very few hominoids remain. Therefore, we should not hastily generalize from the living forms to the much more diverse fossil forms; otherwise, we obscure the evolutionary uniqueness of these animals. In addition, we should not expect all fossil forms to be directly or even particularly closely related to living species. Indeed, we should expect the opposite; that is, most lines vanish without descendants.

Over the last three decades, the Miocene hominoid assemblage has been interpreted and reinterpreted. As more fossils are found, the evolutionary picture grows more complicated. The vast array of fossil forms has not yet been completely studied, so conclusions remain tenuous. Given this uncertainty, it is probably best, for the present, to group Miocene hominoids geographically:

FIGURE 8-4 *Proconsul africanus* skull (from early Miocene deposits on Rusinga Island, Kenya).

1. *African forms (23–14 m.y.a.)* Known especially from western Kenya, these include quite generalized, and in many ways primitive, hominoids. The best-known genus is *Proconsul* (Fig. 8-4). In addition to the well-known East African early Miocene hominoids, a more recent discovery (in 1992) from Namibia has further extended by over 1,800 miles the known range of African Miocene hominoids (Conroy et al., 1992).

2. *European forms (16–11 m.y.a.)* Known from widely scattered localities in France, Spain, Italy, Greece, Austria, Germany, and Hungary, most of these forms are quite derived. However, this is a varied and not well understood group. The best known of the forms are placed in the genus *Dryopithecus;* the Hungarian and Greek fossils are usually assigned to other genera. The Greek fossils are called *Ouranopithecus,* and remains date to sites 9 to 10 million years of age. Evolutionary relationships are uncertain, but several researchers have suggested a link with the African ape/hominid group. New discoveries in 1999 and 2003 from sites in Germany and Turkey of yet another hominoid genus (called *Griphopithecus*) have helped bolster this hypothesis (Begun, 2003).

3. *Asian forms (16–7 m.y.a.)* The largest and most varied group from the Miocene fossil hominoid assemblage, geographically dispersed from Turkey through India/Pakistan and east to the highly prolific site Lufeng, in southern China, most of these forms are *highly* derived. The best-known genus is *Sivapithecus* (known from Turkey and Pakistan). The Lufeng material (now totaling more than 1,000 specimens) is usually placed in a separate genus from *Sivapithecus* (and is referred to as *Lufengpithecus*).

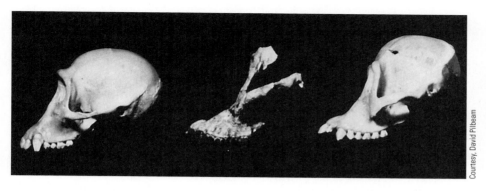

Courtesy, David Pilbeam

FIGURE 8-5 Comparison of *Sivapithecus* cranium (center) with that of modern chimpanzee (left) and orangutan (right). The *Sivapithecus* fossil is specimen GSP 15000, from the Potwar Plateau, Pakistan, c. 8 m.y.a.

Four general points are certain concerning Miocene hominoid fossils: They are widespread geographically; they are numerous; they span a considerable portion of the Miocene, with *known* remains dated between 23 and 6 m.y.a.; and at present, they are poorly understood. However, we can reasonably draw the following conclusions:

1. These are hominoids—more closely related to the ape-human lineage than to Old World monkeys.
2. They are mostly **large-bodied hominoids,** that is, more akin to the lineages of orangutans, gorillas, chimpanzees, and humans than to smaller-bodied apes (i.e., gibbons).
3. Most of the Miocene forms thus far discovered are so derived that they are probably not ancestral to *any* living form.
4. One lineage that appears well established relates to *Sivapithecus* from Turkey and Pakistan. This form shows some highly derived facial features similar to the modern orangutan, suggesting a fairly close evolutionary link (Fig. 8-5).
5. Evidence of *definite* **hominids** from the Miocene has not yet been indisputably confirmed. However, exciting new (and not fully studied) finds from Kenya, Ethiopia, and Chad (the latter dating as far back as 7 m.y.a.) strongly suggest that hominids diverged sometime in the latter Miocene (see pp. 190–192 for further discussion). As we shall see shortly, the most fundamental feature of the early hominids is the adaptation to bipedal locomotion.

large-bodied hominoids Those hominoids including the great apes (orangutans, chimpanzees, gorillas) and hominids, as well as all ancestral forms back to the time of divergence from small-bodied hominoids (i.e., the gibbon lineage).

hominids Colloquial term for members of the family Hominidae, which includes all bipedal hominoids back to the divergence from African great apes.

Definition of Hominid

Dating to the end of the Miocene, the earliest hominid traces that have thus far been found include primarily dental and cranial pieces. Indeed, what has been preserved of the numerous hominoid fossils from throughout the Miocene are primarily teeth and jaws. But dental features alone do not describe the special features of hominids and are certainly not the most distinctive of the later stages of human evolution. Modern humans, as well as our most immediate hominid ancestors, are distinguished from the great apes by more obvious features than tooth and jaw dimensions. For example, various scientists have pointed to such distinctive hominid characteristics as bipedal locomotion, large brain size, and toolmaking behavior as being significant (at some stage) in defining what makes a hominid a hominid.

mosaic evolution A pattern of evolution in which the rate of evolution in one functional system varies from that in other systems. For example, in hominid evolution, the dental system, locomotor system, and neurological system (especially the brain) all evolved at markedly different rates.

FIGURE 8-6 Mosaic evolution of hominid characteristics: a postulated time line.

It must be emphasized that not all these characteristics developed simultaneously or at the same pace. Indeed, over the last several million years of hominid evolution, quite a different pattern has been evident, in which each of the components (dentition, locomotion, brain size, and toolmaking) have developed at quite different rates. Such a pattern, where physiological/behavioral systems evolve at different rates, is called **mosaic evolution.** As we first pointed out in Chapter 1 and will emphasize in this chapter, the single most important defining characteristic for the full course of hominid evolution is **bipedal locomotion.** In the earliest stages of hominid emergence, skeletal evidence indicating bipedal locomotion is the only truly reliable indicator that these fossils were indeed hominids. However, in later stages of hominid evolution, other features, especially those relating to brain development and behavior, become highly significant (Fig. 8-6).

	Locomotion	Brain	Dentition	Toolmaking Behavior
(Modern *Homo sapiens*) 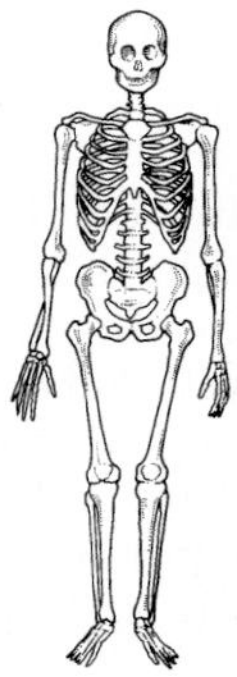	Bipedal: shortened pelvis; body size larger; legs longer; fingers and toes not as long	Greatly increased brain size—highly encephalized	Small incisors; canines further reduced; molar tooth enamel caps thick	Stone tools found after 2.5 m.y.a.; increasing trend of cultural dependency apparent in later hominids
(Early hominid) 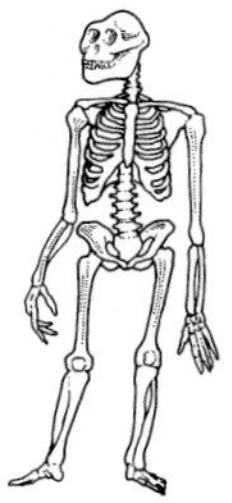	Bipedal: shortened pelvis; some differences from later hominids, showing smaller body size and long arms relative to legs; long fingers and toes; probably capable of considerable climbing	Larger than Miocene forms, but still only moderately encephalized; prior to 6 m.y.a., no more encephalized than chimpanzees	Moderately large front teeth (incisors); canines somewhat reduced; molar tooth enamel caps very thick	In earliest stages unknown; no stone tool use prior to 2.5 m.y.a.; probably somewhat more oriented toward tool manufacture and use than chimpanzees
(Miocene, generalized hominoid) 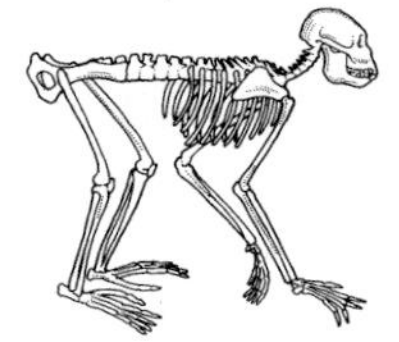	Quadrupedal: long pelvis; some forms capable of considerable arm swinging, suspensory locomotion	Small compared to hominids, but large compared to other primates; a fair degree of encephalization	Large front teeth (including canines); molar teeth variable, depending on species; some have thin enamel caps, others thick enamel caps	Unknown—no stone tools; probably had capabilities similar to chimpanzees

Time line markers: 0.5 m.y.a., 1 m.y.a., 2 m.y.a., 3 m.y.a., 4 m.y.a., 20 m.y.a.

WHAT'S IN A NAME?

Throughout this book, we refer to members of the human family as hominids (technical name for the family is Hominidae). This terminology has been widely used for decades, and the inherent evolutionary relationships it reflects are shown in Fig. 8-7a. However, as we mentioned in Chapter 6, there are a number of problems with this classification, since it fails to recognize several basic evolutionary relationships among the great apes (most importantly, that chimpanzees and bonobos are more closely related to us and our bipedal predecessors than are other great apes).

As a result of the inadequacies of the traditional classification, a revised one has been proposed (e.g., by Wood and Richmond, 2000). In this scheme (Fig. 8-7b), two further levels of classification have been added (subfamily and tribe) to allow finer-tuned and evolutionarily more accurate distinctions. Here, the term *hominid* refers to *all* great apes as well as to the human line ("us"). When referring to the human line ("us") exclusively, the term now used is *hominin*, a distinction made at the taxonomic level of tribe.

This terminology may seem highly confusing; unfortunately, it is—so much so, in fact, that the revised classification has not yet been very widely accepted.* Nevertheless, it is important to recognize that the evolutionary relationships depicted (i.e., Fig. 8-7b) are more accurate and *are* widely accepted by evolu-

bipedal locomotion
Walking on two feet. Walking habitually on two legs is the single most distinctive feature of the family Hominidae.

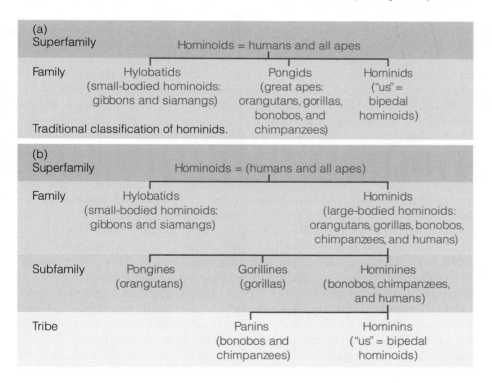

FIGURE 8-7 (a) Traditional classification of hominoids. (b) Revised classification of hominoids. Note that two additional levels of classification are added (subfamily and tribe) to show more precisely and more accurately evolutionary relationships among the apes and humans. In this classification, "hominin" is synonymous with the use of "hominid" in 8-7a.

*For example, at the major meetings of the world's largest professional association of physical anthropologists (The American Association of Physical Anthropologists) in 2003 and 2004, all the sessions dealing with human evolution were listed using the traditional classification (i.e., *hominid*). In 2003, however, 50 percent of specific titles of presentations within these sessions used the revised term, *hominin*, while the other half used *hominid*. In 2004, the majority of presentations reverted to the terminology using *hominid*.

tionary biologists. What to label the various levels remains a decision still in flux. For purposes of clarity in this book, we will continue to use the term *hominid* to refer to the lineage of bipedal hominoids since its divergence from our closest cousins (chimpanzees/bonobos). (If you should see the term *hominin* elsewhere, it is being used synonymously with our usage of *hominid*.)

The Bipedal Adaptation

As we mentioned in Chapter 6, there is a general tendency in all primates for erect body posture. However, of all living primates, efficient bipedalism as the primary form of locomotion is seen *only* in hominids. Functionally, the human mode of locomotion is most clearly shown in our striding gait, where weight is alternately placed on a single fully extended hind limb. This specialized form of locomotion has developed to a point where energy levels are used to near peak efficiency. Such is not the case in nonhuman primates, who move bipedally with hips and knees bent and maintain balance in a clumsy and inefficient manner.

From a survey of our close primate relatives, it is apparent that while still in the trees, our ancestors were adapted to a fair amount of upper-body erectness. Prosimians, monkeys, and apes all spend considerable time sitting erect while feeding, grooming, or sleeping. Presumably, our early ancestors also displayed similar behavior. What caused these forms to come to the ground and embark on the unique way of life that would eventually lead to humans is still a mystery. Perhaps natural selection favored some Miocene hominoids coming occasionally to the ground to forage for food on the forest floor and forest fringe. In any case, once they were on the ground and away from the immediate safety offered by trees, bipedal locomotion could become a tremendous advantage.

First of all, bipedal locomotion freed the hands for carrying objects and for making and using tools. Such early cultural developments had an even more positive effect on speeding the development of yet more efficient bipedalism— once again emphasizing the dual role of biocultural evolution. In addition, in the bipedal stance, animals have a wider view of the surrounding countryside, and in open terrain, early spotting of predators (particularly the large cats, such as lions, leopards, and saber-tooths) would be of critical importance. We know that modern ground-living primates, such as savanna baboons and vervets, occasionally adopt this posture to "look around" when out in open country. It has also been hypothesized that a bipedal stance would more effectively have aided in cooling early hominids while out in the open. In bipeds, less of the body is exposed directly to the sun than in quadrupeds. Moreover, a greater portion of the body is farther from the ground and thus more removed from heat radiating from the ground surface. It would perhaps have been most adaptive to favor such cooling mechanisms if early hominids had adopted activity patterns exposing them in the open during midday. This last supposition is not really possible to test, but if hominids had ranged more freely at midday, they would have avoided competition from more nocturnal predators and scavengers (such as large cats and hyenas).

Moreover, bipedal walking is an efficient means of covering long distances, and when large game hunting came into play (several million years after the initial adaptation to ground living), further refinements in the locomotor complex may have been favored. Exactly what initiated the process is difficult to say, but all these factors probably played a role in the adaptation of hominids to their special niche through a special form of locomotion.

Our mode of locomotion is indeed extraordinary, involving, as it does, a unique kind of activity in which "the body, step by step, teeters on the edge of catastrophe" (Napier, 1967, p. 56). The problem is to maintain balance on the "stance" leg while the "swing" leg is off the ground. In fact, during normal walking, both feet are simultaneously on the ground only about 25 percent of the time, and as speed of locomotion increases, this figure becomes even smaller.

Maintaining a stable center of balance in this complex form of locomotion necessitates many drastic structural and functional changes in the basic primate quadrupedal pattern. Functionally, the foot must be altered to act as a stable support instead of a grasping limb. When we walk, our foot is used like a prop, landing on the heel and pushing off on the toes, particularly the big toe. In addition, the leg has become elongated to increase the length of the stride. An efficient bipedal adaptation required further remodeling of the lower limb to allow full extension of the knee and to keep the legs close together during walking, in this way maintaining the center of support directly under the body. Finally, significant changes are seen in the pelvis that permit stable weight transmission from the upper body to the legs and that help further maintain balance.

These major structural changes that are essential for bipedalism are all seen in the earliest hominids from East and South Africa. (To date, no early hominid postcranial bones have been found in central Africa.) In the pelvis, the ilium (the upper bone of the pelvis, shaped like a blade) is shortened top to bottom, which permits more stable weight support in the erect position by lowering the center of gravity (see Figs. 8-8 and 8-9). In addition, the ilium is bent backward and downward, thus altering the position of the muscles that attach along the bone. Most important, these muscles increase in size and act to stabilize the hip. One of these muscles (the *gluteus maximus*) also becomes important as an extensor, pulling the thigh back during running, jumping, and climbing.

Other structural changes shown by even the earliest definitively hominid postcranial evidence further confirm the morphological pattern seen in the pelvis. For example, the vertebral column, known from beautifully preserved specimens from South and East Africa, shows the same forward curvature as in modern hominids, bringing the center of support forward. In addition, the lower limb is

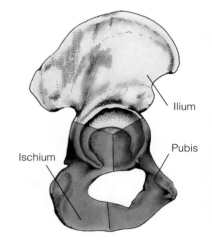

FIGURE 8-8 The human os coxae, composed of three bones (right side shown).

elongated and is apparently proportionately about as long as in modern humans. Fossil evidence of a knee fragment from South Africa and pieces from East Africa also shows that full extension of this joint was possible, thus allowing the leg to be completely straightened, as when a field goal kicker follows through.

Fossil evidence of early hominid foot structure has come from two sites in South Africa, and especially important are some recently announced new fossils coming from the same individual as the mostly complete skeleton currently being excavated (see p. 203) (Clarke and Tobias, 1995). These foot specimens, consisting of four articulating elements from the ankle and big toe, indicate that the heel and longitudinal arch were both well adapted for a

FIGURE 8-9 Ossa coxae. (a) *Homo sapiens*. (b) Early hominid (*Australopithecus*) from South Africa. (c) Great ape. Note especially the length and breadth of the iliac blade (boxed) and the line of weight transmission (shown in red).

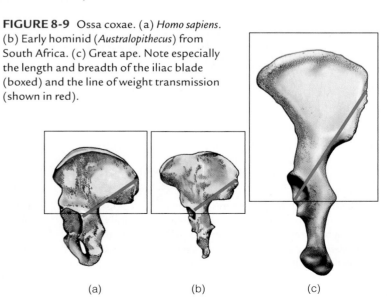

(a)   (b)   (c)

obligate bipedalism
Bipedalism as the *only* form of hominid terrestrial locomotion. Since major anatomical changes in the spine, pelvis, and lower limb are required for bipedal locomotion, once hominids adapted this mode of locomotion, other forms of locomotion on the ground became impossible.

bipedal gait. However, paleoanthropologists Ron Clarke and Phillip Tobias also suggest that the large toe was *divergent* and thus unlike the hominid pattern. If the large toe really did possess this (abducted) anatomical position, it most likely would have aided the foot in grasping. In turn, this grasping ability (as in other primates) would have enabled early hominids to more effectively exploit arboreal habitats. Finally, since anatomical remodeling is always constrained by a set of complex functional compromises, a foot highly capable of grasping and climbing is less capable as a stable platform during bipedal locomotion. Some researchers therefore see early hominids as perhaps not quite as fully committed to bipedal locomotion as are later hominids.

Further evidence for evolutionary changes in the foot comes from two sites in East Africa where numerous fossilized elements have been recovered.

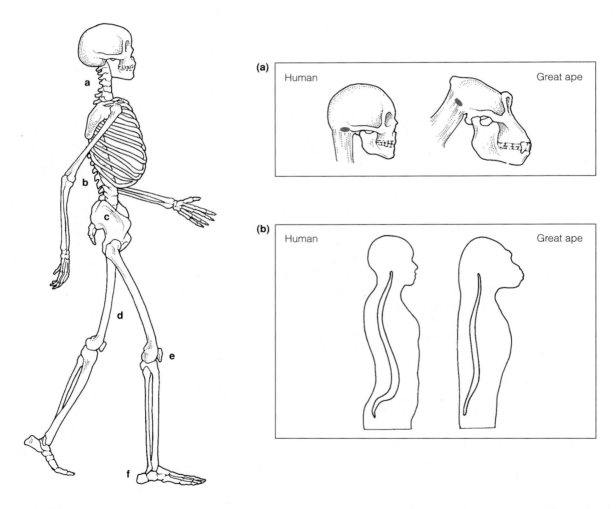

FIGURE 8-10 Major features of hominid bipedalism. During hominid evolution, several major structural features throughout the body have been reorganized (from that seen in other primates) to facilitate efficient bipedal locomotion. These are illustrated here, beginning with the head and progressing to the foot: (a) The *foramen magnum* (shown in red) is repositioned farther underneath the skull, so that the head is more or less balanced on the spine (and thus requires less robust neck muscles to hold the head upright). (b) The spine has two distinctive curves—a backward (thoracic) one and a forward (lumbar) one—that keep the trunk (and weight) centered above the pelvis. (c) The pelvis is

As in the remains from South Africa, the East African fossils suggest a well-adapted bipedal gait. The arches are developed, but some differences in the ankle also imply that considerable flexibility was possible (again, perhaps indicating some continued adaptation to climbing). From this evidence, some researchers have recently concluded that many forms of early hominids spent considerable time in the trees. Nevertheless, to this point, *all* the early hominids that have been identified from Africa are thought by most investigators to have been quite well-adapted bipeds (notwithstanding the new evidence from South Africa, which will require further study), and most, if not all, early hominids probably displayed both **obligate bipedalism** and **habitual bipedalism.** For a review of the anatomical features associated with bipedal locomotion, see Figure 8-10.

habitual bipedalism Bipedal locomotion as the form of locomotion shown by hominids most of the time.

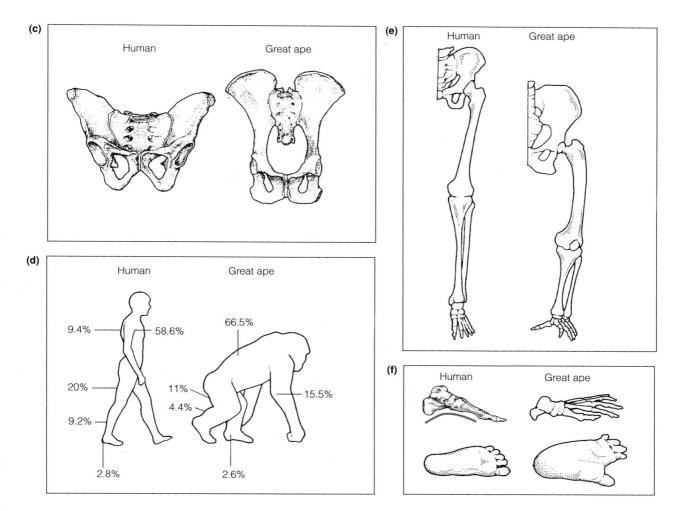

shaped more in the form of a basin to support internal organs; moreover, the ossa coxae (specifically, iliac blades) are shorter and broader, thus stabilizing weight transmission. (d) Lower limbs are elongated, as shown by the proportional lengths of various body segments (e.g., in humans the thigh comprises 20 percent of body height, while in gorillas it comprises only 11 percent). (e) The femur is angled inward, keeping the legs more directly under the body; modified knee anatomy also permits full extension of this joint. (f) The big toe is enlarged and brought in line with the other toes; in addition, a distinctive longitudinal arch forms, helping absorb shock and adding propulsive spring.

Biocultural Evolution: The Human Capacity for Culture

One of the most distinctive behavioral features of humans is our species' extraordinary elaboration of and dependence on culture. Certainly, other primates, and many other animals, for that matter, modify their environments. As we saw in Chapter 7, chimpanzees especially are known for such behaviors as using termite sticks, and some even transport rocks to crush nuts. Given such observations, it becomes tenuous to draw sharp lines between early hominid toolmaking behavior and that exhibited by other animals.

Another point to remember is that human culture, at least as it is defined in contemporary contexts, involves much more than toolmaking capacity. For humans, culture integrates an entire adaptive strategy involving cognitive, political, social, and economic components. The *material culture,* the tools humans use, is but a small portion of this cultural complex.

Nevertheless, when examining the archaeological record of earlier hominids, what is available for study is almost exclusively certain remains of material culture, especially residues of stone tool manufacture. Thus, it is extremely difficult to learn anything about the earliest stages of hominid cultural development prior to the regular manufacture of stone tools. As you will see, this most crucial cultural development has been traced to approximately 2.5 m.y.a. (Semaw et al., 1997). Yet, hominids were undoubtedly using other kinds of tools (made of perishable materials) and displaying a whole array of other cultural behaviors long before this time. However, without any "hard" evidence preserved in the archaeological record, our understanding of the early development of these nonmaterial cultural components remains elusive.

The fundamental basis for human cultural success relates directly to cognitive abilities. Again, we are not dealing with an absolute distinction, but a relative one. As you have already learned, other primates, as documented in chimpanzees and bonobos, possess some of the language capabilities exhibited by humans. Nevertheless, modern humans display these abilities in a complexity several orders of magnitude beyond that of any other animal. Moreover, only humans are so completely dependent on symbolic communication and its cultural by-products that contemporary *Homo sapiens* could not survive without them.

When did the unique combination of cognitive, social, and material cultural adaptations become prominent in human evolution? We must be careful to recognize the manifold nature of culture and not expect it always to contain the same elements across species (as when compared to nonhuman primates) or through time (when trying to reconstruct ancient hominid behavior). Richard Potts (1993) has critiqued such overly simplistic perspectives and suggests instead a more dynamic approach, one that incorporates many subcomponents (including aspects of behavior, cognition, and social interaction).

We know that the earliest hominids almost certainly did *not* regularly manufacture stone tools (at least, none that have been found!). These earliest members of the hominid lineage, dating back to approximately 7–5 m.y.a., could be referred to as **protohominids**. These protohominids may have carried objects such as naturally sharp stones or stone flakes, parts of carcasses, and pieces of wood around their home ranges. At minimum, we would expect them to have displayed these behaviors to at least the same degree as living chimpanzees.

protohominids The earliest members of the hominid lineage, as yet only poorly represented in the fossil record; thus, their structure and behavior are reconstructed mostly hypothetically.

Moreover, as you will see, by at least 5 m.y.a. and perhaps even 7 m.y.a., hominids had developed one crucial advantage: They were bipedal and could therefore much more easily carry all manner of objects from place to place. Ultimately, the efficient exploitation of resources widely distributed in time and space would most likely have led to using "central" locations where key components, especially stone objects, were cached (Potts, 1991).

What is certain is that over a period of several million years, during the formative stages of hominid emergence, numerous components interacted, but not all developed simultaneously. As cognitive abilities developed, more efficient means of communication and learning resulted. Largely as a result of consequent neurological reorganization, more elaborate tools and social relationships also emerged. These, in turn, selected for greater intelligence, which in turn selected for further neural elaboration. Quite clearly, then, these mutual dynamics are at the very heart of what we call hominid *biocultural* evolution.

Paleoanthropology as a Multidisciplinary Science

To understand human biocultural evolution adequately, we need a broad base of information. The task of recovering and interpreting all the clues left by early hominids is the work of paleoanthropologists. Paleoanthropology is defined as the study of early humans. As such, it is a diverse **multidisciplinary** pursuit seeking to reconstruct every bit of information possible concerning the dating, anatomy, behavior, and ecology of our hominid ancestors. In just the last few years, the study of early hominids has marshaled the specialized skills of many diverse scientific disciplines. Included primarily in this growing and exciting adventure are geologists, archaeologists, physical anthropologists, and paleoecologists (Table 8-2).

multidisciplinary Pertaining to research that involves mutual contributions and cooperation of several different experts from various scientific fields (i.e., disciplines).

TABLE 8-2 | Components of Paleoanthropology

Physical Sciences	Biological Sciences	Social Sciences

Geology
    Stratigraphy
    Petrology (rocks, minerals)
    Pedology (soils)
 	
Geomorphology
 	
Geophysics
 	
Chemistry
 	
Taphonomy*
	Physical anthropology
	
	Ecology
	    Paleontology (fossil animals)
	    Palynology (fossil pollen)
	
	Primatology
		Archaeology
		
		Ethnoarchaeology
		
		Cultural anthropology
		    Ethnography
		
		Psychology

*Taphonomy (*taphos* meaning "dead") is the study of how bones and other materials come to be buried in the earth and preserved as fossils. A taphonomist studies such phenomena as sedimentation, the action of streams, preservation properties of bone, and carnivore disturbance factors.

FIGURE 8-11 Excavations in progress at Olduvai. This site, more than 1 million years old, was located when a hominid ulna (arm bone) was found eroding out of the side of the gorge.

Robert Jurmain

sites Locations of discoveries. In paleontology and archaeology, a site may refer to a region where a number of discoveries have been made.

faunal Referring to animal remains; in archaeology, specifically refers to the fossil (or skeletonized) remains of animals.

chronometric (*chronos,* meaning "time," and *metric,* meaning "measure") A dating technique that gives an estimate in actual numbers of years.

artifacts Objects or materials made or modified for use by hominids. The earliest artifacts tend to be tools made of stone or, occasionally, bone.

Geologists, usually working with anthropologists (often archaeologists), do the initial survey to locate potential early hominid **sites.** Many sophisticated techniques can contribute to this search, including aerial and satellite photography. Paleontologists may also be involved in this early search, for they can help find geological beds containing **faunal** remains. (Where conditions are favorable for the preservation of such specimens as ancient pigs or baboons, conditions may also be favorable for the preservation of hominid fossils.) In addition, paleontologists can—through comparison with faunal sequences elsewhere—give quick estimates of the approximate age of sites without having to wait for the expensive and time-consuming **chronometric** analyses. In this way, fossil beds of the "right" geological ages (i.e., where hominid finds are most likely) can be identified.

Once potential early hominid localities have been identified, much more extensive surveying begins. At this point, the archaeologists take over the search for hominid traces (Fig. 8-11). We do not necessarily have to find the fossilized remains of early hominids (which will always be rare) to know that hominids consistently occupied an ancient land surface. Behavioral clues, or **artifacts,** also inform us directly and unambiguously about early hominid occupation. Modifying rocks according to a consistent plan or simply carrying them over fairly long distances is a behavior exhibited by no other animal but a hominid. Therefore, when we see such behavioral evidence at a site, we know that hominids were once present there.

Dating Methods

One of the essentials of paleoanthropology is placing sites and fossils into a chronological framework. In other words, we want to know how old they are. How, then, do we date sites—or, more precisely, how do we date the geological settings in which sites are found? The question is important, so let us examine some of the dating techniques used by paleontologists, geologists, and paleoanthropologists.

Scientists use two basic types of dating for this purpose: *relative dating* and *chronometric dating* (also known as *absolute dating*). Relative dating methods tell you that something is older or younger than something else, but not by how much. If, for example, a fossil cranium is found at a depth of 50 feet and another cranium at 70 feet at the same site, we usually assume that the cranium at 70 feet is older. We may not know the date (in years) of either one, but we would be able to infer a *relative* sequence. This method of dating is based on **stratigraphy** and is called *stratigraphic dating.* This was one of the first techniques used by scholars working with the vast expanses of geological time. Stratigraphic dating is based on the law of superposition, which states that a lower **stratum** (layer) is older than a higher stratum. Given the fact that much of the earth's crust has been laid down by layer after layer of sedimentary rock, stratigraphic relationships have provided a valuable tool in reconstructing the history of the earth and of life upon it.

Stratigraphic dating does, however, have a number of potential problems. Earth disturbances, such as volcanic activity, river action, and faulting, may shift the strata or materials in them, and the chronology may thus be difficult or impossible to reconstruct. Furthermore, given the widely different rates of accumulation, the elapsed time of any stratum cannot be determined with much accuracy.

Another method of relative dating is *fluorine analysis,* which applies only to bone. Bones in the earth are exposed to the seepage of groundwater, which usually contains some fluorine. The longer a bone lies buried, the more fluorine it incorporates during fossilization. Therefore, bones deposited at the same time in the same location should contain the same amount of fluorine.

The use of this technique by Professor Oakley of the British Museum in the early 1950s exposed the famous Piltdown hoax by demonstrating that the human skull was considerably older than the jaw ostensibly found with it (Weiner, 1955). Lying in the same location, the jaw and skull should have absorbed approximately the same quantity of fluorine. But the skull contained significantly more, meaning that if it came from the same site, it had been deposited considerably earlier. The discrepancy of fluorine content led Oakley and others to a much closer examination of the bones, and they found that the jaw was not that of a hominid at all, but one of a juvenile orangutan! Clearly, then, someone had planted it at Piltdown, but who was the devious forger? For decades there were no firm clues, but more recently discovered evidence has perhaps pointed the blame at Martin Hinton, a British zoologist (Gee, 1996).

Unfortunately, fluorine is useful only for dating bones from the same location. Because of the differing concentrations in groundwater, accumulation rates will vary from place to place. Also, some groundwater may not contain any fluorine. For these reasons, comparing fossils from different localities using fluorine analysis is not feasible.

Two other relative dating techniques, *biostratigraphy* and *paleomagnetism,* have also proved quite useful in calibrating the ages of early hominid sites. Biostratigraphy is a relative technique based on fairly regular changes seen in the dentition and other anatomical structures in such groups as pigs, rodents, and baboons. Dating of sites is based on the presence of certain fossil species that also occur elsewhere in deposits whose dates have been determined. This technique has proved helpful in cross-correlating the ages of various sites in southern, central, and eastern Africa. A final type of relative dating, paleomagnetism, is based on the shifting nature of the earth's geomagnetic pole.

stratigraphy Study of the sequential layering of deposits.

stratum (*pl.,* strata) Geological layer.

Although now oriented northward, the geomagnetic pole is known to have shifted several times in the past and at times was oriented to the south. By examining magnetically charged particles encased in rock, geologists can determine the orientation of these ancient "compasses." One cannot derive a date in years from this particular technique, but it is used to double-check other techniques.

In all these relative dating techniques, the age of geological layers or objects within them is impossible to calibrate. To determine age as precisely as possible, scientists have developed a variety of chronometric techniques, many based on the phenomenon of radioactive decay. The theory is quite simple: Certain radioactive isotopes of elements are unstable, decay, and form an isotopic variant of another element. Since the rate of decay follows a predictable mathematical pattern, the radioactive material serves as an accurate geological clock. By measuring the amount of decay in a particular sample, scientists have devised techniques for dating the immense age of the earth (and moon rocks) as well as material only a few hundred years old. Several techniques have been employed for a number of years and are now quite well known.

An important chronometric technique used in paleoanthropological research involves potassium-40 (^{40}K), which has a half-life of 1.25 billion years and produces argon-40 (^{40}Ar). That is, half the ^{40}K isotope changes to ^{40}Ar in 1.25 billion years. In another 1.25 billion years, half the remaining ^{40}K would be converted (i.e., only one-quarter of the original amount would still be present). Known as the K/Ar, or potassium-argon, method, this procedure has been extensively used in dating materials in the 5–1 m.y.a. range, especially in East Africa. Organic material, such as bone, cannot be measured, but the rock matrix in which the fossilized bone is found can be.

Strata that provide the best samples for K/Ar dating are those that have been heated to an extremely high temperature, such as that generated by volcanic activity. Heating drives off previously accumulated argon gas, thus "resetting" the clock to zero. As the material cools and solidifies, ^{40}K continues to break down to ^{40}Ar, but now the gas is physically trapped inside the cooling material. To date the geological material, it is reheated, and the escaping gas is then measured. Potassium-argon dating has been used to date very old events—such as the age of the earth—as well as those less than 2,000 years old.

Another well-known chronometric technique popular with archaeologists involves carbon-14 (^{14}C), with a half-life of 5,730 years. This method has been used to date material as recent as a few hundred years old and can be extended as far back as 75,000 years, although the probability of error rises rapidly after 40,000 years. The physical basis of this technique is also *radiometric;* that is, it is tied to the measurement of radioactive decay of an isotope (^{14}C) into another, more stable form. Radiocarbon dating has proved especially relevant for calibrating the latter stages of human evolution, including the Neandertals and the appearance of modern *Homo sapiens* (see Chapter 11).

Other methods have also proved useful in dating early hominid sites. For example, *fission-track dating* is a chronometric technique that works on the basis of the regular fissioning of uranium atoms. When certain types of crystalline rocks are observed microscopically, the "tracks" left by the fission events can be counted and an approximate age thus calibrated. (Other techniques applicable to dating the later stages of human evolution are discussed briefly in Chapter 11; see Table 11-1.)

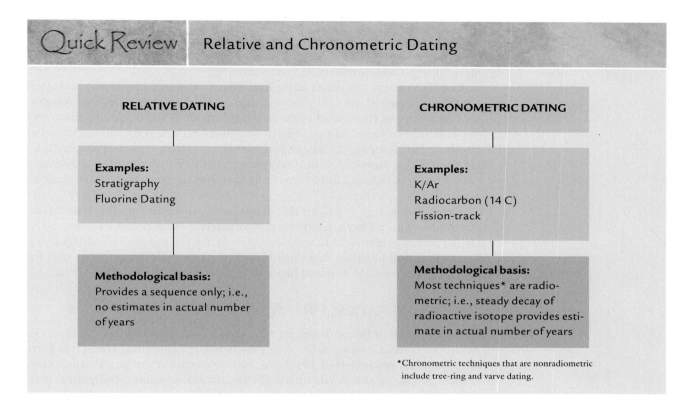

$\mathcal{Q}$uick $\mathcal{R}$eview Relative and Chronometric Dating

RELATIVE DATING

Examples:
Stratigraphy
Fluorine Dating

Methodological basis:
Provides a sequence only; i.e., no estimates in actual number of years

CHRONOMETRIC DATING

Examples:
K/Ar
Radiocarbon (14 C)
Fission-track

Methodological basis:
Most techniques* are radiometric; i.e., steady decay of radioactive isotope provides estimate in actual number of years

*Chronometric techniques that are nonradiometric include tree-ring and varve dating.

Many of the techniques just discussed are used together to provide *independent* checks for dating important early hominid sites. Each technique has a degree of error, and only by *cross-correlating* the results can paleoanthropologists feel confident regarding chronological placement of the fossil and archaeological remains they discover. This point is of the utmost importance, for a firm chronology forms the basis for making sound evolutionary interpretations (as discussed later in the chapter).

Early Hominids from Africa

Over the last 80 years, a tremendous number of hominid fossils have been discovered in Africa. The first finds came from South Africa, but by the 1970s, East Africa (particularly along the Rift Valley in Ethiopia, Kenya, and Tanzania) had taken preeminence. This shift in the focus and significance of discovery came about as a result of many factors. The geological circumstances found in East Africa produce a clearer stratigraphic picture and better association of hominids with archaeological artifacts, and equally important, these materials are much more easily datable (using chronometric methods). Moreover, fossils are generally easier to find in East Africa, although it is never easy anywhere to find hominid fossils! Erosion from wind, rain, and gravity expose fossils on the ground surface, where they can simply be picked up—assuming, of course, one knows exactly *where* to look. In South Africa, by contrast, the fossils are embedded in rock matrix, making precise archaeological recovery extraordinarily difficult. Nevertheless, excavations have continued at several South African sites. From this ongoing work, some new and highly productive locales have been explored, and as of this writing, perhaps the most intact early hominid skeleton ever discovered is being excavated at Sterkfontein Cave, just outside Johannesburg.

The saga of new and more intriguing African hominid discoveries is not yet completed—indeed, not even slowed. Just in 2002, perhaps the most remarkable discovery in the last 75 years was announced. What made this discovery (from Chad) so surprising was (1) its location (in central Africa, *not* in either South or East Africa), (2) its age (estimated at close to 7 m.y.a., making it by far the earliest hominid found anywhere), and (3) its physical appearance (quite unexpected and unlike anything discovered previously; more on this presently).

Thus, if we accept the latest discoveries and provisional dating as accurate, hominid origins go back in Africa approximately 7 million years. Hominids, as far as current evidence indicates, stayed in Africa for the next 5 million years, first emigrating to other Old World locales 2 m.y.a. Thus, it appears that for the first 70 percent of hominid history, our family was restricted to Africa.

EARLIEST TRACES: PRE-*AUSTRALOPITHECUS* FINDS

The distinction of being designated "the earliest hominid" is one that draws worldwide media coverage, but it is a notoriously fickle title. When this textbook was first published in 1992, the earliest hominid was dated at between 3 and 4 m.y.a. By the third edition (1998), based on some Ethiopian fossils, this had been pushed back to 4.4 m.y.a. By 2000 (based on Kenyan material), the date was further extended to close to 6 m.y.a. And in 2002, the startling find from Chad suggested that the current bearer of the "earliest" title is 7 million years old.

This brief history is not intended to force unsuspecting students to memorize exactly what was found when. Our point is to illustrate how rapidly discoveries have taken place; in just the last 12 years, the known span of hominid existence has almost doubled!

Central Africa The most stunning of these new finds is also the oldest. The fossil, a nearly complete cranium, was discovered in 2001 at a site called Toros-Menalla in northern Chad (Brunet et al., 2002). Provisional dating using faunal correlation (biostratigraphy; see p. 187) suggests a date nearly 7 m.y.a. (Vignaud et al., 2002). Surprisingly, the very early suggested age of this fossil places it at almost 1 million years earlier than *any* of the other proposed early hominids (and close to 3 million years earlier than the oldest well-established hominid discoveries).

The morphology of the fossil is unusual, with a combination of characteristics unlike that found in other early hominids. The braincase is small, estimated at no larger than a modern chimpanzee's (preliminary estimate in the range of 320 to 380 cm^3), but it is massively built, with huge browridges in front, a crest on top, and large muscle attachments in the rear (Fig. 8-12). Yet, combined with these apelike features is a smallish vertical face containing front teeth very unlike an ape's. In fact, the lower face, being more tucked in under the brain vault (and not protruding, as in most other early hominids), is more of a *derived* feature more commonly expressed in much later hominids (especially members of genus *Homo*). Moreover, unlike the dentition seen in apes

© Mission Paléoanthropologique Franco-Tchadienne

FIGURE 8-12 A nearly complete cranium of *Sahelanthropus* from Chad, dating to 7 m.y.a.

(and some early hominids), the upper canine is reduced and is worn down from the tip (rather than shearing along its side against the first lower premolar).

In recognition of this unique combination of characteristics, the lead researcher, Michel Brunet (of the University of Poiters, in France), has placed the Toros-Menalla remains into a new genus and species of hominid, *Sahelanthropus tchadensis* (Sahel being the region of the southern Sahara in North Africa).

These new finds from Chad have forced an immediate and significant reassessment of early hominid evolution. Two cautionary comments, however, are in order. First, the dating is only approximate, based, as it is, on biostratigraphic correlation with sites in Kenya (1,500 miles to the east). The faunal sequences, nevertheless, seem to be clearly bracketed by two very well-dated sequences in Kenya. Second, and perhaps more serious, is the hominid status of the Chad fossil. Given the facial structure and dentition, it is difficult to see how *Sahelanthropus* could be anything but a hominid. However, some researchers (Wolpoff et al., 2002) have raised questions regarding the evolutionary interpretation of *Sahelanthropus,* suggesting that this fossil may represent an ape rather than a hominid. As we have previously said, the best-defining anatomical characteristics of hominids relate to bipedal locomotion. Unfortunately, no **postcranial** elements have been recovered from Chad—at least not yet. Consequently, we do not yet know the locomotor behavior of *Sahelanthropus*—and this raises even more fundamental questions: What if further finds show this form not to be bipedal? Should we still consider it a hominid? What, then, are the defining characteristics of our family?

postcranial (*post,* meaning "after") In a quadruped, referring to that portion of the body behind the head; in a biped, referring to all parts of the body *beneath* the head (i.e., the neck down).

East Africa   Two areas in East Africa, one in the Tugen Hills area near Lake Baringo in central Kenya and the other from the Middle Awash area of northeastern Ethiopia, have also quite recently yielded very early hominid remains. The earlier of these finds (dated provisionally by radiometric methods to about 6 m.y.a.) come from four localities in the Tugen Hills and include mostly dental remains, but also some quite complete lower limb bones (the latter interpreted as clearly indicating bipedal locomotion) (Pickford and Senut, 2001; Senut et al., 2001; Galik et al., 2004). Following preliminary analysis of the fossils, the primary researchers (Brigitte Senut and Martin Pickford) have suggested placing these early hominids in a separate genus—*Orrorin.*

The last group of fossil hominids thought to date to the late Miocene comes from five localities in the Middle Awash in the Afar Triangle of Ethiopia. Radiometric dating places the age of these fossils in the very late Miocene, 5.8–5.2 m.y.a. The fossil remains themselves are very fragmentary. Some of the dental remains resemble some later fossils from the Middle Awash (discussed shortly), and Yohannes Hailie-Selassie, the researcher who first found and described these earlier materials, has provisionally assigned them to a new species of the genus *Ardipithecus* (Haile-Selassie et al, 2004) (see Quick Review). In addition, some postcranial elements have been preserved, most informatively a toe bone, a phalanx from the middle of the foot (see Appendix A, Fig. A–8). From clues in this bone, Hailie-Selassie concludes that this primate was a well-adapted biped (once again, the best-supporting evidence of hominid status).

From later in the geological record in the Middle Awash region, along the banks of the Awash River, a very large and significant assemblage of fossil hominids has been discovered at the **Aramis** site. Radiometric calibration firmly dates this site at about 4.4 m.y.a.

Aramis (air'-ah-miss)

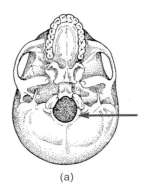

(a)

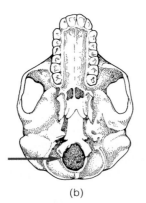

(b)

FIGURE 8-13 Position of the *foramen magnum* in (a) a human and (b) a chimpanzee. Note the more forward position in the human cranium.

Australopithecus An early hominid genus, known from the Plio-Pleistocene of Africa, characterized by bipedal loco-motion, a relatively small brain, and large back teeth.

Fossil remains from Aramis were excavated between 1992 and 1995 and include up to 50 different individuals (Wolpoff, 1999). This crucial and quite large fossil assortment includes several dental specimens as well as an upper arm bone (humerus) and some fragmentary cranial remains. Most exciting of all, in 1995, 40 percent of a skeleton was discovered; there are also reports of other partial skeletons from Aramis. However, in all cases, the bones are encased in limestone matrix, thus requiring a long and tedious process to remove the fossils intact from the cementlike material surrounding them. In fact, as of this writing, the Aramis remains (including the skeletons) have not yet been fully described. Nevertheless, details from initial reports are highly suggestive that these remains are, in fact, very early hominids.

First of all, in an Aramis partial cranium, the *foramen magnum* is positioned farther forward in the base of the skull than is the case in quadrupeds (Fig. 8-13). Second, features of the humerus also differ from those seen in quadrupeds, indicating that the Aramis humerus did not function in locomotion to support weight. From these two features, Tim White, of the University of California, Berkeley, and his colleagues conclude that the Aramis individuals were *bipedal*. Moreover, initial interpretation of the partial skeleton (while not yet fully cleaned and reported) also suggests obligate bipedalism (Wolpoff, 1999).

Nevertheless, these were clearly primitive hominids, displaying an array of characteristics quite distinct from other members of our family. These primitive characteristics include flattening of the cranial base and relatively thin enamel caps on the molar teeth. From measurements of the humerus head, Wolpoff (1999) estimates a body weight of 42 kg (93 pounds); if this humerus comes from a male individual, this weight estimate is very similar to that hypothesized for other Plio-Pleistocene hominids (see Table 8-4).

Thus, current conclusions (which will be either unambiguously confirmed or falsified as the skeleton is fully cleaned and studied) interpret the Aramis remains as among the earliest hominids yet known. These individuals, while very primitive hominids, were apparently bipedal, although not necessarily in the same way that later hominids were.

Tim White and colleagues have argued (White et al., 1995) that the fossil hominids from Aramis are so primitive and so different from other early hominids that they should be assigned to a new genus (and, necessarily, a new species as well): *Ardipithecus ramidus*. Most especially, the thin enamel caps on the molars are in dramatic contrast to all other confirmed early hominids, who show quite thick enamel. These other early hominid forms (all somewhat later than *Ardipithecus*) are placed in the genus *Australopithecus*. Moreover, White and his associates have further suggested that, as the earliest and most primitive hominid yet discovered, *Ardipithecus* may possibly be the root species for all later hominids. This view does not take into account the recently discovered Tugen Hills finds, which are provisionally assigned to the new genus *Orrorin*. However, this interpretation does encompass the earlier remains from the Middle Awash—which, for the moment, are also included within *Ardipithecus*.

Another intriguing aspect of all these late Miocene/early Pliocene locales (i.e., Tugen Hills, early Middle Awash sites, and Aramis) relates to the ancient environments associated with the suggested earliest of hominids. Rather than the more open grassland savanna habitats so characteristic of most later hominid sites, the environments at these early locales is more heavily forested. Perhaps we are seeing at Aramis and these other ancient sites the very beginnings of hominid divergence, very soon after the division from the African apes!

Quick Review	In Summary: Key Very Early Fossil Hominid Discoveries (pre-*Australopithecus;* (prior to 4 m.y.a.)		
	Site	**Dates (m.y.a.)**	**Hominids**
East Africa	Middle Awash (Ethiopia; five localities)	5.8–5.2	*Ardipithecus*
	Aramis (Ethiopia)	4.4	*Ardipithecus ramidus*
	Tugen Hills	~6.0	*Orrorin tugenensis*
Central Africa	Toros-Menalla	~7.0	*Sahelanthropus tchadensis*

Australopithecus from East Africa

The best-known, most widely distributed, and most diverse of the early African hominids are placed in the genus *Australopithecus*. Moreover, these hominids have an established time range of over 3 million years, stretching back as early as 4.2 m.y.a. and not becoming extinct until apparently close to 1 m.y.a.—making them the longest-enduring hominid yet documented. In addition, these hominids have been found in all the major geographical areas of Africa that have, to date, produced early hominid finds, namely South Africa, central Africa (Chad), and East Africa. From all these areas combined, there appears to have been considerable complexity in terms of evolutionary diversity; in fact, as many as eight species are recognized by many (but not all) authorities (see Appendix B for a complete listing and more discussion of early hominid fossil finds).

Before discussing this pivotal group of early hominids, we should make one further point. Many researchers prefer to divide what we are including in one genus (*Australopithecus*) into two different genera (*Australopithecus* and **Paranthropus**). There is, in fact, a good evolutionary justification to split these diverse hominids into two genera. However, for the sake of simplicity (and following close to 50 years of general consensus), we will group all these forms together in the single genus *Australopithecus*. In any case, all these hominids share many features in common:

Paranthropus (par´-an-throw´-puss) A genus of hominid characterized by very large back teeth and jaws. Frequently, this genus is combined into *Australopithecus*.

1. They are all clearly bipedal (although not necessarily identical to *Homo* in this regard).
2. They all have relatively small brains (i.e., at least compared to *Homo*).
3. They all have large teeth, particularly the back teeth, with thick to very thick enamel on the molars.

In short, then, all these species of *Australopithecus* are relatively small-brained, big-toothed bipeds.

The earliest finds of *Australopithecus* have been located at two sites in northern Kenya, dating to about 4.2–3.9 m.y.a. Like many of the other finds discussed in this chapter, these hominids were discovered quite recently (mostly in the mid-1990s). Among the fossils of these earliest **australopithecines** thus far discovered, a few postcranial pieces clearly indicate that locomotion was *bipedal*. There are, however, a few primitive

australopithecine (os-tra-loh-pith´-e-seen) The colloquial name for members of the genus *Australopithecus*. The term was first used as a subfamily designation, but it is now most commonly used informally.

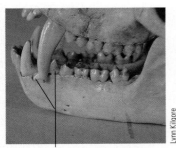

Sectorial lower first premolar

FIGURE 8-14 Left lateral view of the teeth of a male patas monkey. Note how the large upper canine shears against the elongated surface of the sectorial lower first premolar.

sectorial Adapted for cutting or shearing; among primates, refers to the compressed (side-to-side) first lower premolar, which functions as a shearing surface with the upper canine.

features in the dentition, including a large canine and a **sectorial** lower first premolar (Fig. 8-14).

Since these particular fossils have initially been interpreted as more primitive than all the later members of the genus, Meave Leakey and associates have provisionally assigned them to a separate species of *Australopithecus* (see Appendix B). Further study and (with some luck) additional more complete remains will help decide whether such a distinction is warranted.

Slightly later and much more complete remains of *Australopithecus* have come from the sites of Hadar (in Ethiopia) and Laetoli (in Tanzania). Much of this material has been known for some time (since the mid-1970s), and the fossils have been very well studied; indeed, in certain instances, they are quite famous. For example, the Lucy skeleton was discovered at Hadar in 1974, and the Laetoli footprints were first found in 1978.

Literally thousands of footprints have been found at Laetoli, representing more than 20 different kinds of animals (Pliocene elephants, horses, pigs, giraffes, antelopes, hyenas, and an abundance of hares). Several hominid footprints have also been found, including a trail more than 75 feet long made by at least two—and perhaps three—individuals (Leakey and Hay, 1979) (Fig. 8-15). Such discoveries of well-preserved hominid footprints are extremely important in furthering our understanding of human evolution. For the first time, we can make *definite* statements regarding the locomotor pattern and stature of early hominids. Analyses of these Pliocene footprints suggest a stature of about 4 feet 9 inches for the larger individual and 4 feet 1 inch for the smaller individual.

Studies of these impression patterns clearly show that the mode of locomotion of these hominids was bipedal (Day and Wickens, 1980). As we have emphasized, the development of bipedal locomotion is the most important defining characteristic of early hominid evolution. Some researchers, however, have concluded that these early hominids were not bipedal in quite the same way that modern humans are. From detailed comparisons with modern humans, estimates of stride length, cadence, and speed of walking have been

FIGURE 8-15 Hominid footprint from Laetoli, Tanzania. Note the deep impression of the heel and the large toe (arrow) in line (adducted) with the other toes.

ascertained, indicating that the Laetoli hominids moved in a slow-moving ("strolling") fashion with a rather short stride (Chateris et al., 1981).

One extraordinary discovery at Hadar is the Lucy skeleton (Fig. 8-16), found by Don Johanson eroding out of a hillside. This fossil is scientifically designated as Afar Locality (AL) 288-1, but is usually just called Lucy (after the Beatles song "Lucy in the Sky with Diamonds"). Representing almost 40 percent of a skeleton, this is one of the three most complete individuals from anywhere in the world for the entire period before about 100,000 years ago.*

Because the Laetoli area was covered periodically by ashfalls from nearby volcanic eruptions, accurate dating is possible and has provided dates of 3.7–3.5 m.y.a. Dating from the Hadar region has not proved as straightforward; however, more complete dating calibration using a variety of techniques has determined a range of 3.9–3.0 m.y.a. for the hominid discoveries from this area.

AUSTRALOPITHECUS AFARENSIS FROM LAETOLI AND HADAR

Several hundred specimens, representing a minimum of 60 individuals (and perhaps as many as 100), have been removed from Laetoli and Hadar. At present, these materials represent the largest *well-studied* collection of early hominids and as such are among the most significant of the hominids discussed in this chapter. Moreover, it has been suggested that fragmentary specimens from other locales in East Africa are remains of the same species as that found at Laetoli and Hadar. Most scholars refer to this species as *Australopithecus afarensis*.

Without question, *A. afarensis* is more primitive than any of the other later australopithecine fossils from South or East Africa (to be discussed below). By "primitive" we mean that *A. afarensis* is less evolved in any particular direction than are later-occurring hominid species. That is, *A. afarensis* shares more primitive features with other early homin*oids* and with living great apes than do later hominids, who display more derived characteristics.

For example, the teeth of *A. afarensis* are quite primitive. The canines are often large, pointed teeth. Moreover, the lower first premolar is semisectorial (i.e., it provides a shearing surface for the upper canine), and the tooth rows are parallel, even converging somewhat toward the back of the mouth (Fig. 8-17).

The cranial portions that are preserved also display several primitive hominoid characteristics, including a crest in the back as well as several primitive features of the cranial base. Cranial capacity estimates for *A. afarensis* show a mixed pattern when compared to later hominids. A provisional estimate for the one partially complete cranium—apparently a large individual—gives a figure of 500 cm³, but another, even more fragmentary cranium is apparently quite a bit smaller and has been estimated at about 375 cm³ (Holloway, 1983). Thus, for some individuals (males?), *A. afarensis* is well within the range of other australopithecine species (Table 8-3), but others (females?) may have a significantly smaller cranial capacity. However, a detailed

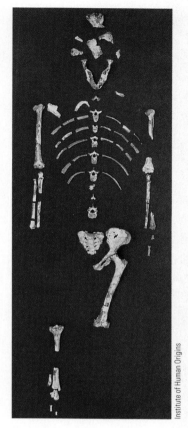

FIGURE 8-16 "Lucy," a partial hominid skeleton, discovered at Hadar in 1974. This individual is assigned to *Australopithecus afarensis*.

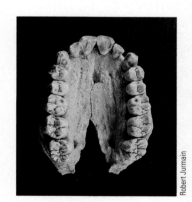

FIGURE 8-17 Jaw of *Australopithecus afarensis*. Maxilla, AL 200-1a, from Hadar, Ethiopia. (Note the parallel tooth rows and large canines.) (photograph of cast)

---

*The others are a specimen from Sterkfontein, in South Africa (see p. 203), and a *Homo erectus* skeleton from west of Lake Turkana, Kenya (p. 231). Also note that the crushed and embedded skeleton from Aramis may be nearly as complete as Lucy.

TABLE 8-3 | Estimated Cranial Capacities in Early Hominids with Comparable Data for Modern Great Apes and Humans

	Cranial Capacity	
Hominid	Range (cm³)	Average(s) (cm³)
Early Hominids		
Sahelanthropus		~350
Ardipithecus	Not presently known	Not presently known
Australopithecus afarensis		420
Later australopithecines		410–530
Early members of genus *Homo*		631
Contemporary Hominoids		
Human	1150–1750	1330
Chimpanzee	285–500	395
Gorilla	340–752	506
Orangutan	276-540	411
Bonobo	–	350

depiction of cranial size for *A. afarensis* is not possible at this time; this part of the skeleton is unfortunately too poorly represented. One thing is clear: *A. afarensis* had a small brain, probably averaging for the whole species not much over 420 cm³.

On the other hand, a large assortment of postcranial pieces has been found at Hadar. Initial impressions suggest that relative to lower limbs, the upper limbs are longer than in modern humans (also a primitive hominoid condition). (This statement does not mean that the arms of *A. afarensis* were longer than the legs.) In addition, the wrist, hand, and foot bones show several differences from modern humans (Susman et al., 1985). From such excellent postcranial evidence, stature can now be confidently estimated: *A. afarensis* was a short hominid. From her partial skeleton, Lucy is estimated to be only 3¹/₂ to 4 feet tall. However, Lucy—as demonstrated by her pelvis—was probably a female, and at Hadar and Laetoli, there is evidence of larger individuals as well. The most economical hypothesis explaining this variation is that *A. afarensis* was quite sexually dimorphic: The larger individuals are male and the smaller ones, such as Lucy, are female. Estimates of male stature can be approximated from the larger footprints at Laetoli, inferring a height of not quite 5 feet. If we accept this interpretation, *A. afarensis* was a very sexually dimorphic form indeed. In fact, for overall body size, this species may have been as dimorphic as *any* living primate (i.e., as much as gorillas, orangutans, or baboons). A controversial recent study has suggested quite a different view, suggesting that *A. afarensis* was not very sexually dimorphic (Reno et al.,

2003). However, this interpretation runs counter to most other paleoanthropological interpretations of early hominids and has not gained wide support (Ruff and McHenry, 2004).

In a majority of dental and cranial features, *A. afarensis* is clearly more primitive than later hominids. In fact, from the neck up, *A. afarensis* is so primitive that without any evidence from the limbs, one would be hard-pressed to call it a hominid at all (although the back teeth are large and heavily enameled, unlike pongids, and the position of the foramen magnum indicates an upright posture).

What, then, makes *A. afarensis* a hominid? The answer is revealed by its manner of locomotion. From the abundant limb bones recovered from Hadar and those beautiful footprints from Laetoli, we know unequivocally that *A. afarensis* walked bipedally when on the ground. (At present, we do not have nearly such good evidence concerning locomotion for *any* of the earlier hominid finds.) Whether Lucy and her contemporaries still spent considerable time in the trees and just how efficiently they walked have become topics of some controversy. Most researchers, however, agree that *A. afarensis* was an efficient habitual biped while on the ground. These hominids were also clearly *obligate* bipeds, which would have hampered their climbing abilities but would not necessarily have precluded arboreal behavior altogether. As one physical anthropologist has surmised: "One could imagine these diminutive early hominids making maximum use of *both* terrestrial and arboreal resources in spite of their commitment to exclusive bipedalism when on the ground. The contention of a mixed arboreal and terrestrial behavioral repertoire would make adaptive sense of the Hadar australopithecine forelimb, hand, and foot morphology without contradicting the evidence of the pelvis" (Wolpoff, 1983b, p. 451).

A CONTEMPORANEOUS NON-AUSTRALOPITHECINE FIND?

The pace of hominid discoveries in East Africa has dramatically intensified in recent years, and many of these new discoveries have revealed a different combination of anatomical features from those recognized in remains discovered previously. Among the most distinctive and intriguing of these newer finds is a cranium unearthed in 1999 on the west side of Lake Turkana in northern Kenya (Leakey et al., 2001).

Dated to 3.5 m.y.a., this fossil hominid is thus contemporaneous with *Australopithecus afarensis*. Yet, it shows a quite distinctive combination of facial and dental features (most especially, a flat lower face and fairly small molar teeth). In these respects, this newly discovered Kenyan hominid is different from *A. afarensis* and, in fact, from *all* known australopithecines. Because the skull has been severely distorted, cranial capacity is difficult to establish clearly. However, the best estimates suggest that the cranial capacity is similar to that of *Australopithecus* (i.e., in the range of 400–500 cm^3).

Because of its unusual anatomical features, Meave Leakey and her colleagues have proposed an entirely new hominid genus for this cranium. Whether this designation will be substantiated by further, more detailed analysis remains to be seen. At minimum, this and all the other discoveries from recent years are forcing a major reassessment of the early stages of hominid evolution (see Appendix B).

LATER EAST AFRICAN AUSTRALOPITHECINE FINDS

An assortment of fossil hominids, including many specimens of later members of the genus *Australopithecus,* has been recovered from geological contexts with dates after 3 m.y.a. at several localities in East Africa. Up to 10 different such sites are now known (in the time range of 3–1 m.y.a.), but here we will concentrate on the three most significant ones: East Lake Turkana, West Lake Turkana (both in northern Kenya), and Olduvai Gorge (in northern Tanzania).

Koobi Fora (East Lake Turkana) Under the direction of Richard Leakey and, for several years, the late Glynn Isaac, research in this vast arid area in northern Kenya has yielded the richest assemblage of Plio-Pleistocene hominids from the African continent. Current archaeological fieldwork is under the supervision of Offer Bar Yosef, of Harvard University. The current total exceeds 150, probably representing at least 100 individuals, with most of these fossils dated to about 1.8 m.y.a. Among this fine sample are several complete skulls, many jaws, and an assortment of postcranial bones. Moreover, with the exception of Olduvai Gorge(discussed shortly), sites on the east side of Lake **Turkana** have produced the most information concerning the behavior of early hominids.

West Turkana Across the lake from the fossil beds discussed above are other deposits that have yielded very exciting discoveries. In 1984, on the west side of Lake Turkana, a nearly complete skeleton of a 1.6-million-year-old *Homo erectus* adolescent was found (see Chapter 9), and the following year, a well-preserved 2.4-million-year-old skull was also found. This latter find—"the black skull"—is a most important discovery and has caused a major reevaluation of Plio-Pleistocene hominid evolution (Fig. 8-18).

Olduvai Gorge Located in the Serengeti Plain of northern Tanzania, **Olduvai** is a steep-sided valley resembling a miniature version of the Grand Canyon (Fig. 8-19). (Indeed, the geological processes that formed the gorge are similar to what happened in the formation of the Grand Canyon.) Following millions of years of accumulation of several hundred feet of geological strata, faulting occurred about 70,000 years ago to the east of Olduvai. As a result, a gradient was established, and a rapidly flowing river proceeded to cut the gorge.

Olduvai today is thus a deep ravine cut into the almost mile-high grassland plateau of East Africa, and it extends more than 25 miles in total length—potentially including hundreds of early hominid localities. Climatically, the semiarid pattern with scrub vegetation observable today is thought to approximate conditions over most of the last 2 million years.

Since the 1930s, when they first worked there, Olduvai came to be identified with Louis and Mary Leakey, two of the key founders of modern paleoanthropology. Louis, thanks to *National Geographic* and television, became more famous than any other paleoanthropologist of his generation. Although occupied with lecture tours, Leakey continued to make periodic trips to Olduvai up until his death in 1972. Mary Leakey, for over 40 years, was responsible for directing archaeological excavations at Olduvai (and later, Laetoli) and was instrumental in many of the most exciting discoveries. She retired from active fieldwork in 1983 and continued her writing and research until her death in 1996.

FIGURE 8-18 The "black skull," WT 17000, discovered at West Lake Turkana in 1985. This specimen is provisionally assigned to *Australopithecus aethiopicus.* It is called the "black skull" owing to the dark color from the fossilization (mineralization) process.

Reproduced with permission of the National Museums of Kenya, copyright reserved, courtesy of Alan Walker

Turkana (tur-kahn´-ah)

Olduvai (ohl´-doo-vye)

Robert Jurmain

FIGURE 8-19 View of the main gorge at Olduvai. Note the clear sequence of geological beds. The discontinuity to the right is a major fault line.

The greatest contribution that Olduvai has made to paleoanthropological research is the establishment of an extremely well-documented and correlated *sequence* of geological, paleontological, archaeological, and hominid remains over the last 2 million years. At the very foundation of all paleoanthropological research is a well-established geological picture, and at Olduvai, owing to four decades of work, this picture is understood in minute detail. Paleontological evidence of fossilized animal bones also has been retrieved in great abundance. More than 150 species of extinct animals have been recognized, and careful analysis of these remains has given us much detailed information about the environments in which early hominids lived.

The archaeological sequence at Olduvai is also extremely well documented. Due to Mary Leakey's meticulous excavations and analyses, a more complete picture of the behavior of early hominids has emerged from Olduvai than from any other locality.

Finally, fossilized remains of several hominids have been found at Olduvai, ranging in time from the earliest occupation levels (circa 1.85 m.y.a.) to fairly recent *Homo sapiens*. Of the more than 40 individuals represented, many are quite fragmentary, but a few (including four skulls and a nearly complete foot) are excellently preserved (see Quick Review). While the center of hominid discoveries has now shifted to other areas of East Africa, it was the initial discovery by Mary Leakey in 1959 of the "Zinj" (a robust australopithecine) cranium that focused the world's attention on this remarkably rich area. This famous discovery provides an excellent example of how financial ramifications directly result from well-publicized hominid discoveries. Prior to 1959, the Leakeys had worked sporadically at Olduvai for almost three decades on a financial shoestring. During this time, they made marvelous paleontological and archaeological discoveries, but there was little support for much-needed large-scale excavation. However, following the discovery of Zinj, the National Geographic Society funded the research, and within the next year, more earth was moved than in the previous 30 years. Ongoing work at Olduvai has yielded yet further hominid finds, with a partial skeleton found in 1987 by researchers from the Institute of Human Origins.

Early *Homo*

In addition to the australopithecine remains in East Africa, there's another largely contemporaneous hominid that is quite distinctive. In fact, as best documented by fossil discoveries from Olduvai and Koobi Fora, these materials have been assigned to the genus *Homo*—and thus are different from all species assigned to *Australopithecus*.

The earliest appearance of genus *Homo* in East Africa may be as ancient as that of the robust australopithecines. (As we have discussed, the black skull from West Turkana has been dated to approximately 2.5 m.y.a.) Discoveries in the 1990s from central Kenya and from the Hadar area of Ethiopia suggest that early *Homo* was present in East Africa by 2.4–2.3 m.y.a.

The presence of a Plio-Pleistocene hominid with a significantly larger brain than seen in *Australopithecus* was first suggested by Louis Leakey in the early 1960s on the basis of fragmentary remains found at Olduvai Gorge. Leakey and his colleagues gave a new species designation to these fossil remains, naming them **Homo habilis.**

The *Homo habilis* material at Olduvai ranges in time from 1.85 m.y.a. for the earliest to about 1.6 m.y.a. for the latest. Due to the fragmentary nature of the fossil remains, interpretations have been difficult and much disputed. The most immediately obvious feature distinguishing the *H. habilis* material from the australopithecines is cranial size. For all the measurable *H. habilis* skulls, the estimated average cranial capacity is 631 cm^3, compared to 520 cm^3 for all measurable robust australopithecines and 442 cm^3 for the less robust species (McHenry, 1988) (see Table 8-3). *Homo habilis*, therefore, shows an increase in cranial size of about 20 percent over the larger of the australopithecines and an even greater increase over some of the smaller-brained forms (from South Africa, discussed shortly). In their initial description of *H. habilis*, Leakey and his associates also pointed to differences from australopithecines in cranial shape and in tooth proportions (larger front teeth relative to back teeth and narrower premolars).

The naming of this fossil material as *Homo habilis* ("handy man") was meaningful from two perspectives. First of all, Leakey argued that members of this group were the early Olduvai toolmakers. Second, and most significantly, by calling this group *Homo*, Leakey was arguing for at least *two separate branches* of hominid evolution in the Plio-Pleistocene. Clearly, only one could be on the main branch eventually leading to *Homo sapiens*. By labeling this new group *Homo* rather than *Australopithecus*, Leakey was guessing that he had found our ancestors.

Because the initial evidence was so fragmentary, most paleoanthropologists were reluctant to accept *H. habilis* as a valid species distinct from *all* australopithecines. Later discoveries, especially those from Lake Turkana, of better-preserved fossils have shed further light on early *Homo* in the Plio-Pleistocene. The most important of this additional material is a nearly complete cranium discovered at Koobi Fora (Fig. 8-20). With a cranial capacity of 775 cm^3, this individual is well outside the known range for australopithecines and actually overlaps the lower boundary for *Homo erectus*. In addition, the shape of the skull vault is in many respects unlike that of australopithecines. However, the face is still quite robust (Walker, 1976), and the fragments of tooth crowns that are preserved indicate that the back teeth in this individual were quite

Homo habilis (hab´-ih-liss) A species of early *Homo*, well known from East Africa but perhaps also found in other regions.

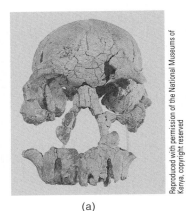

(a)

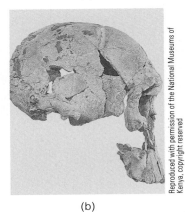

(b)

FIGURE 8-20 A nearly complete early *Homo* cranium from East Lake Turkana (ER 1470), one of the most important single fossil hominid discoveries from East Africa. (a) Frontal view (b) Lateral view.

large.* Dating of the Koobi Fora early *Homo* material places it contemporaneous with the Olduvai remains—that is, about 1.8–1.6 m.y.a.

On the basis of evidence from Olduvai and Koobi Fora, we can reasonably postulate that one or more species of early *Homo* were present in East Africa probably by 2.4 m.y.a., developing in parallel with at least one line of australopithecines. These two hominid lines lived contemporaneously for a minimum of 1 million years, after which the australopithecine lineage apparently disappeared forever. At the same time, probably the early *Homo* line was evolving into one or more species of later *Homo*.

South African Hominids

EARLIEST DISCOVERIES

The first quarter of the twentieth century saw the discipline of paleoanthropology in its scientific infancy. Informed opinions considered the likely origins of the human family to be in Asia, where fossil forms of a primitive kind of *Homo* had been found in Indonesia in the 1890s. Europe was also considered a center of hominid evolution, for spectacular discoveries there of premodern humans (including the famous Neandertals) and millions of stone tools had come to light, particularly in the early 1900s.

Few scholars would have given much credence to Darwin's prediction:

> In each region of the world the living mammals are closely related to the extinct species of the same region. It is, therefore, probable that Africa was formally inhabited by extinct apes closely allied to the gorilla and chimpanzee, and as these two species are now man's nearest allies, it is somewhat more probable that our early progenitors lived on the African continent than elsewhere. (Darwin, *The Descent of Man*, 1871)

Moreover, it would be many more decades before the East African discoveries would come to light. It was in such an atmosphere of preconceived biases that the discoveries of a young Australian-born anatomist were to jolt the foundations of the scientific community in the 1920s. Raymond Dart (Fig. 8-21) arrived in South Africa in 1923 at the age of 30 to take up a teaching position in Johannesburg. Fresh from his evolution-oriented training in England, Dart had developed a keen interest in human evolution. Consequently, he was well prepared when startling new evidence began to appear at his very doorstep.

The first clue came in 1924, when Dart received a shipment of fossils from the commercial limeworks quarry at Taung (200 miles southwest of Johannesburg). He immediately recognized something that was quite unusual, a natural **endocast** of a higher primate. The endocast fit into another limestone block containing the fossilized front portion of the skull, face, and lower jaw (Fig. 8-22). However, these were difficult to see clearly, for the bone was hardened into a cemented limestone matrix. Dart patiently chiseled away for weeks, later describing the task:

> No diamond cutter ever worked more lovingly or with such care on a precious jewel—nor, I am sure, with such inadequate tools. But on the seventy-third day,

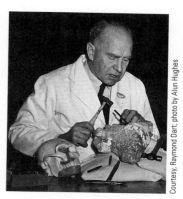

FIGURE 8-21 Raymond Dart, shown working in his laboratory.

Courtesy, Raymond Dart; photo by Alun Hughes

endocast A solid impression of the inside of the skull, often preserving details relating to the size and surface features of the brain.

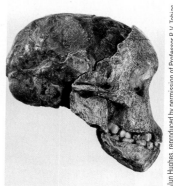

FIGURE 8-22 The Taung child, discovered in 1924. The endocast is in back, with the fossilized bone mandible and face in front.

Alun Hughes, reproduced by permission of Professor P. V. Tobias

---

*In fact, some researchers have suggested that all these "early *Homo*" fossils are better classified as *Australopithecus* (Wood and Collard, 1999a).

December 23, the rock parted. I could view the face from the front, although the right side was still imbedded. . . . What emerged was a baby's face, an infant with a full set of milk teeth and its permanent molars just in the process of erupting. I doubt if there was any parent prouder of his offspring than I was of my Taung baby on that Christmas. (Dart, 1959, p. 10)

As indicated by the formation and eruption of the teeth, the Taung child was probably about three to four years old. Interestingly, the rate of development of this and many other Plio-Pleistocene hominids was more like that of apes than of modern *Homo* (Bromage and Dean, 1985). Dart's initial impression that this form was a hominoid was confirmed when he could observe the face and teeth more clearly. However, as it turned out, it took considerably more effort before the teeth could be seen completely, since Dart worked for four years to separate the upper and lower jaws.

But Dart was convinced long before he had an unimpeded view of the dentition that this discovery was a remarkable one, an early hominoid from South Africa. The question was, What kind of hominoid? Dart realized that it was extremely improbable that this specimen could have been a forest ape, for South Africa has had a relatively dry climate for millions of years.

If not an ape, then what was it? Features of the skull and teeth of this small child held clues that Dart seized on almost immediately. The *foramen magnum* at the base of the skull (see Fig. 8-13) was farther forward in the Taung skull than in modern great apes, though not as much as in modern humans. From this fact Dart concluded that the head was balanced *above* the spine, indicating erect posture. In addition, the forehead did not recede as much as in apes, the milk canines were exceedingly small, and the newly erupted permanent molars were very large, broad teeth. In all these respects, the Taung fossil was more akin to hominids than to apes. There was, however, a disturbing feature that was to confuse many scientists for several years: The brain was quite small. More recent studies have estimated the Taung child's brain size at approximately 405 cm³ (which translates to a full adult estimate of 440 cm³), not very large (for a hominid) when compared to modern great apes (see Table 8-3).

The estimated cranial capacity of the Taung fossil falls within the range of modern great apes, and gorillas actually average about 10 percent greater. It must, however, be remembered that gorillas are very large animals, whereas the Taung specimen derives from a population in which adults may have averaged less than 80 pounds. Since brain size is partially correlated with body size, comparing such differently sized animals is unjustified. A more meaningful comparison would be with the bonobo (*Pan paniscus*), whose body weight is similar. Bonobos have adult cranial capacities averaging 356 cm³ for males and 329 cm³ for females, and thus the Taung child, versus a *comparably sized* ape, displays a 25 percent increase in cranial capacity.

Despite the relatively small size of the brain, Dart saw that the Taung fossil was no ape. Realizing the immense importance of his findings, Dart promptly reported them in the British scientific weekly *Nature* on February 7, 1925—a bold venture, since Dart, only 32, was presumptuously proposing an entirely new view of human evolution. The small-brained Taung child was christened by Dart **Australopithecus africanus** (southern ape of Africa), which he saw as a kind of halfway "missing link" between modern apes and humans. This concept of a single "missing link" was a fallacious one, but Dart correctly emphasized the hominid-like features of the fossil.

Australopithecus africanus
(os-tral-oh-pith´-kus
af-ri-kan´-us)

Not all scientists were ready for such a theory from such an "unlikely" place. Hence, Dart's report was received with indifference, disbelief, and even caustic scorn. Dart realized that more complete remains were needed. The skeptical world would not accept the evidence of one partial immature individual, no matter how suggestive the clues. Most scientists in the 1920s regarded this little Taung child as an interesting aberrant form of ape. Clearly, more fossil evidence was needed, particularly adult crania (since these would show more diagnostic features). Not an experienced fossil hunter himself, Dart sought further assistance in the search for more australopithecines.

FURTHER DISCOVERIES OF SOUTH AFRICAN HOMINIDS

Soon after publication of his controversial theories, Dart found a strong ally in Robert Broom (Fig. 8-23). From two of Dart's students, Broom learned of another commercial limeworks site, called **Sterkfontein,** not far from Johannesburg (and now, counting the more recent discoveries, the most prolific of South African sites). Here, as at Taung, the quarrying involved blasting out large sections with dynamite, leaving piles of debris that often contained fossilized remains. Accordingly, Broom asked the quarry manager to keep his eyes open for fossils, and when Broom returned to the site in August 1936, the manager asked, "Is this what you are looking for?" Indeed it was, for Broom held in his hand the endocast of an adult australopithecine—exactly what he had set out to find! Looking further over the scattered debris, Broom was able to find most of the rest of the skull of the same individual.

Such remarkable success, just a few months after beginning his search, was not the end of Broom's luck, for his magical touch was to continue unabated for several more years. In the 1930s and 1940s, Broom discovered two other hominid sites, including **Swartkrans,** the second most productive of all South African Plio-Pleistocene locales (it has since yielded hundreds of fossils). Numerous extremely important discoveries came from these additional sites, discoveries that would eventually swing the tide of intellectual thought to the views that Dart had expressed back in 1925.

Since the 1970s, more systematic exploration of the South African hominid sites has continued, and many important discoveries have been made. The most spectacular new find was made in 1997 at Sterkfontein, where the remains of a virtually complete australopithecine skeleton were found by Ron Clarke and his associates from the University of Witwatersrand (Fig. 8-24). Most of the remains are still embedded in the surrounding limestone matrix and may require years for removal, cleaning, and reconstruction (Clarke, 1998).

Dating of all the South African Plio-Pleistocene sites has proved most difficult; estimates for the Sterkfontein australopithecine skeleton are between 3.6 and 2.5 m.y.a. Even before the remains have been fully excavated, this is still recognized as an unusual and highly significant find. Because such complete individuals are so rare in the hominid fossil record, this discovery has tremendous potential to shed more light on the precise nature of early hominid locomotion. For example, will the rest of the skeleton confirm what foot bones of the same individual have implied regarding arboreal climbing in this bipedal hominid (see p. 181)? Moreover, relative proportion of brain size to body size, better estimates of overall body size, relative proportions of the limbs, and much more can be more accurately assessed from such a completely preserved skeleton.

FIGURE 8-23 Robert Broom.

Sterkfontein
(sterk´-fon-tane)

Swartkrans (swart´-kranz)

FIGURE 8-24
Australopithecine skeleton embedded in limestone matrix at Sterkfontein. Much of the skeleton still is not visible. Clearly seen are the cranium (with articulated mandible) and part of an upper limb.

REVIEW OF HOMINIDS FROM SOUTH AFRICA

The Plio-Pleistocene hominid discoveries from South Africa are most significant. First, they were the initial hominid discoveries in Africa and helped point the way to later finds in East Africa. Second, morphology of the South African hominids shows broad similarities to the forms in East Africa, but with several distinctive features, which argues for separation at least at the species level. Finally, there is a large assemblage of hominid fossils from South Africa, and exciting discoveries are still being made (Fig. 8-25).

Further discoveries are also coming from entirely new sites. In the 1990s, the site known as Drimolen was found in South Africa, very near to Sterkfontein and Swartkrans (Keyser, 2000). While only provisionally published thus far, we do know that close to 80 specimens have been recovered—including the most complete *Australopithecus* cranium found anywhere in Africa.

A truly remarkable collection of early hominids, the remains from South Africa, coming from nine different caves, exceed 1,000 (counting all isolated teeth as separate items), and the number of individuals is now more than 200. From an evolutionary point of view, the most meaningful remains are those of the pelvis, which now include portions of nine ossa coxae (see p. 181). Remains of the pelvis are so important because, better than any other area of the body, this structure displays the unique requirements of a bipedal animal (as in modern humans *and* in our hominid forebears).

"Robust" Australopithecines In addition to similar discoveries in East Africa, there are also numerous finds of robust australopithecines in South Africa. Like their East African cousins, the South African robust forms also have small cranial capacities. (The only measurable specimen equals 530 cm^3; the Drimolen cranium is smaller and might come from a female, but no cranial measurements have as yet been published.) They also possess large, broad faces and very large premolars and molars (although not as massive as in East Africa). Owing to the differences in dental proportions, as well as important differences in facial architecture (Rak, 1983), most researchers now agree that there is a species-level difference between the later East African robust variety and the South African group.

Despite these differences, all members of the robust lineage appear to be specialized for a diet made up of hard food items, such as seeds and nuts. For many years, paleoanthropologists (e.g., Robinson, 1972) had speculated that robust australopithecines concentrated their diet on heavier vegetable foods than those seen in the diet of other early hominids. Later research that included examining microscopic polishes and scratches on the teeth confirmed this view.

"Gracile" Australopithecines Another variety of australopithecine (also small-brained, but not as large-toothed as the robust varieties) is known from Africa. However, while the robust lineage is represented in both East and South Africa, this other (gracile) australopithecine form is known only from the southern part of the continent. First named *A. africanus* by Dart for the single individual at Taung, this australopithecine is also found at other sites, especially Sterkfontein (Figs. 8-25 and 8-26).

Traditionally, it had been thought that there was a significant variation in body size between the gracile and robust forms. But as mentioned earlier and shown in Table 8–4, there is not much difference in body size among the

FIGURE 8-25 A gracile australopithecine cranium from Sterkfontein (Sts 5). Discovered in 1947, this specimen is the best-preserved gracile skull yet found in South Africa.

Orrorin, and *Ardipithecus*—and are hence each provisionally interpreted as being generically distinct from all the other early hominid forms (listed in sets II and III). Analysis thus far indicates that at least for the later Aramis fossils, these forms were likely bipedal, but with a primitive dentition. Brain size of *A. ramidus* is not yet known, but was almost certainly quite small.

Set II. *Australopithecus*
Subset A. Early primitive forms (4.2–3.0 m.y.a.) This grouping comprises one well-known species, *A. afarensis,* especially well documented at Laetoli and Hadar. Slightly earlier, closely related forms (perhaps representing a distinct second species) come from two other sites and are provisionally called "*Australopithecus anamensis.*" Best known from analysis of the *A. afarensis* material, the hominids in this set are characterized by a small brain, large teeth (front and back), and a bipedal gait (probably still allowing for considerable climbing).

Subset B. Later, more derived *Australopithecus* (2.5–1.4 m.y.a.; possibly as early as 3.5 m.y.a.) This group is composed of numerous species. (Most experts recognize at least three; some subdivide this material into five or more species.) Remains have come from several sites in both South and East Africa. All of these forms have very large back teeth and do not show appreciable brain enlargement (i.e., encephalization) compared to *A. afarensis.*

Set III. Early *Homo* (2.4–1.8 m.y.a.) The best-known specimens are from East Africa (East Turkana and Olduvai), but early remains of *Homo* have also been found in South Africa (Swartkrans and possibly Sterkfontein and Drimolen). This group is composed of possibly just one, but probably more than one, species. Early *Homo* is characterized (compared to *Australopithecus*) by greater encephalization, altered cranial shape, and smaller (especially molars) and narrower (especially premolars) teeth (see Appendix B for more details).

Although hominid fossil evidence has accumulated in great abundance, the fact that so much of the material has been discovered so recently makes any firm judgments concerning the route of human evolution premature. However, paleoanthropologists certainly aren't deterred from making their "best guesses," and diverse hypotheses have abounded in recent years. The vast majority of the hundreds of recently discovered fossils from Africa is still in the descriptive and early analytical stages. At this time, the construction of phylogenies of human evolution is analogous to building a house with only a partial blueprint. We are not even sure how many rooms there are! Until the existing fossil evidence has been adequately studied, to say nothing about possible new finds, speculative hypotheses must be viewed with a critical eye.

Adaptive Patterns of Early African Hominids

As you are by now aware, there are several different African hominid genera and certainly lots of species. This, in itself, is interesting. Speciation was occurring quite frequently among the various lineages of early hominids, more frequently, in fact, than among later hominids. What explains this pattern?

Evidence has been accumulating at a furious pace in the last decade, but is still far from complete. It is clear that we will never have anything approaching a complete record of early hominid evolution—and thus, significant gaps will remain. After all, we are able to discover hominids only in those special environmental contexts where fossilization was likely. All the other potential habitats they might have exploited are now invisible to us.

Nevertheless, patterns are emerging from the fascinating data we do have. First, it appears that early hominid species (pre-*Australopithecus,* australopithecines, and early *Homo*) all had restricted ranges. It is therefore likely that each hominid species exploited a relatively small area and could easily have become separated from other populations of its own species. Consequently, genetic drift (and, to some extent, natural selection as well) could have led to rapid genetic divergence and eventual speciation.

Second, most of these species appear to be at least partially tied to arboreal habitats, although there is disagreement on this point regarding early *Homo* (see Wood and Collard, 1999b; Foley 2002). Moreover, robust australopithecines were probably somewhat less arboreal than *Ardipithecus* or other forms of *Australopithecus.* These highly megadont hominids apparently concentrated on a diet of coarse fibrous plant foods, such as roots. Exploiting such resources may have routinely taken these hominids farther away from the trees than their dentally more gracile—and perhaps more omnivorous—cousins.

Third, with the exception of some early *Homo* individuals, there is very little in the way of an evolutionary trend of increased body size or of markedly greater encephalization. Beginning with *Sahelanthropus,* brain size was no more than that in chimpanzees—although when controlling for body size, this earliest of all known hominids may have had a proportionately larger brain than any living ape. Close to 6 million years later (i.e., the time of the last surviving australopithecine species), relative brain size increased by no more than 10 to 15 percent. Perhaps, tied to this relative stasis in brain capacity, there is no absolute association of any of these hominids with patterned stone tool manufacture.

Although conclusions are becoming increasingly controversial, for the moment, early *Homo* appears to be a partial exception, showing both increased encephalization and numerous occurrences of likely association with stone tools (though at many of the sites, australopithecine fossils were *also* found).

Lastly, all of these early African hominids show an accelerated developmental pattern (similar to that seen in African apes), one quite different from the *delayed* developmental pattern characteristic of *Homo sapiens* (and our immediate precursors). Moreover, this apelike development is also seen in some early *Homo* individuals (Wood and Collard, 1999a). Rates of development can be accurately reconstructed through examination of dental growth markers (Bromage and Dean, 1985), and these data perhaps provide a crucial window into understanding this early stage of hominid evolution.

These African hominid predecessors were rather small, able bipeds, but still closely tied to arboreal/climbing niches. They had fairly small brains and, compared to later *Homo,* matured rapidly. It would take a major evolutionary jump to push one of their descendants in a more human direction. For the next chapter in this more human saga, read on.

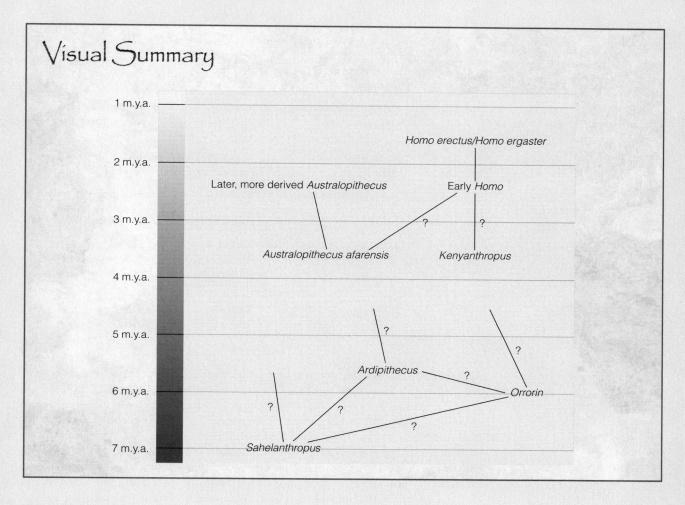

Visual Summary

1 m.y.a.

Homo erectus/Homo ergaster

2 m.y.a.

Later, more derived *Australopithecus*   Early *Homo*

3 m.y.a.   ?   ?

Australopithecus afarensis   *Kenyanthropus*

4 m.y.a.

5 m.y.a.   ?

?

Ardipithecus   ?

6 m.y.a.   ?   *Orrorin*

?   ?

?

7 m.y.a.   *Sahelanthropus*

Summary

The earliest evidence of the evolutionary radiation of the primates dates to the Eocene, approximately 50 m.y.a. These early primates are quite prosimian-like, but during the Oligocene, there was a broad adaptive radiation of early anthropoids. Throughout the Miocene, a wide array of hominoids evolved in the Old World. Most of these are large-bodied forms—that is, they are closely related to great apes and hominids. Although most of these hominoids went extinct by the late Miocene, it is likely that some of the fossils discovered are fairly closely related to ancestors of the great apes and early hominids.

Newly discovered fossils now allow us to trace (at least provisionally) the beginnings of the hominid family to late Miocene locales in central and eastern Africa. Surveying, excavating, and interpreting the fossil remains as well as associated cultural materials (the latter appearing in the archaeological record after 2.5 m.y.a.) is the task of the paleoanthropologists. Paleoanthropology is thus a very broad multidisciplinary approach that allows us to recover data and ultimately better understand the course of human biocultural evolution.

In the Visual Summary, we present a simplified scheme showing tentative relationships among the early African fossil hominids discussed in this chapter.

TABLE 8-5 | Chronological Summary of Most Significant Hominid Fossils Discussed in This Chapter

Epoch	Site	Dates (m.y.a.)	Taxonomic Designation	Comments
Plio-Pleistocene	East Turkana (Koobi Fora) and Olduvai	1.8–1.0	Derived *Australopithecus* and early *Homo*	Highly derived *Australopithecus* and first relatively complete fossils of early *Homo*
	Taung and Sterkfontein	3.3–2.0?	*Australopithecus africanus*	Best-known early hominid from South Africa; many well-preserved fossils
	Hadar and Laetoli	3.7–3.0	*Australopithecus afarensis*	Earliest well-documented group of early hominids; potentially ancestral to later *Australopithecus* and early *Homo*
	Aramis	4.4	*Ardipithecus ramidus*	Earliest large sample of hominid fossils; not yet well described; likely shows very unusual mosaic of characteristics (some highly derived)
Miocene	Toros-Menalla	~7.0	*Sahelanthropus*	Earliest proposed hominid fossils; unusual mosaic of characteristics

Question marks indicate those relationships that are most tentative, particularly obvious for all the earliest material (the pre-*Australopithecus* fossils, dated prior to 4 m.y.a.). Indeed, at present, with all this material so recently discovered and seemingly displaying highly complex patterns of hominid evolution, it is unwise to make anything but the most general of hypotheses.

The picture after 4 m.y.a. is somewhat clearer. It appears, for the moment, that *Australopithecus afarensis* still can be viewed as a good potential common ancestor of most (if not all) later hominids. The relationships among the later, more derived australopithecines are not as clear, nor is it certain which of the earlier Pliocene fossils is most closely related to *Homo*. As a further study aid, Table 8-5 presents the early hominid materials we consider the most significant. For those keen to pursue a more detailed evaluation of the early hominids, see Appendix B.

Science is a journey of discovery, seeking to find as many documented facts as possible. Science is also a search for clarity. The last few years of paleoanthropological research have immensely enriched our record of facts. The search for clarity continues. No doubt, more discoveries are in the offing. We certainly live in interesting times.

Critical Thinking Questions

1. In what ways are the remains of *Sahelanthropus* and *Ardipithecus* primitive? How do we know that these forms are hominids? How sure are we?
2. Assume that you are in the laboratory analyzing the "Lucy" *A. afarensis* skeleton. You also have complete skeletons from a chimpanzee and a modern human. (a) Which parts of the Lucy skeleton are more similar to the chimpanzee? Which are more similar to the human? (b) Which parts of the Lucy skeleton are *most informative*?

3. Discuss the first thing you would do if you found an early hominid fossil and were responsible for its formal description and publication. What would you include in your publication?

4. Discuss two current disputes regarding taxonomic issues concerning early hominids. Try to give support for alternative positions.

5. What is a phylogeny? Construct one for early hominids (7.0–1 m.y.a.). Make sure you can describe what conclusions your scheme makes. Also, try to defend it.

Media Resources

The Companion Website for *Essentials of Physical Anthropology,* Sixth Edition
http://anthropology.wadsworth.com/jurmain6e_ess

Supplement your review of this chapter by going to this text's companion website to take one of the practice quizzes, use the flash cards to master key terms, and check out the many other resources and study aids. Also visit the website to learn about important new discoveries in paleoanthropology by checking the "Latest Dirt" feature authored by Robert Jurmain.

CD-ROMs IN PHYSICAL ANTHROPOLOGY

Wadsworth Publishing has also developed three CD-ROMs to accompany this text and enhance learning in physical anthropology (for further descriptions of these CD-ROMs, see p. xix):

Virtual Laboratories for Physical Anthropology CD-ROM, Third Edition

Basic Genetics for Anthropology CD-ROM: Principles and Applications

Hominid Fossils CD-ROM: An Interactive Atlas

For this chapter, see especially the Virtual Laboratories for Physical Anthropology CD-ROM, Third Edition, and Hominid Fossils CD-ROM: An Interactive Atlas.

Readings of Interest

Begun, David R. 2003. "Planet of the Apes." *Scientific American* 289: 74–83.

Conroy, Glenn C. 1997. *Reconstructing Human Origins. A Modern Synthesis.* New York: Norton.

Tattersall, Ian, and Jeffrey H. Schwartz. 2000. *Extinct Humans.* Boulder, CO: Westview Press.

Wolpoff, Milford H. 1999. *Paleoanthropology.* 2nd ed. Boston: McGraw-Hill.

Wong, Kate. 2003. "An Ancestor to Call Our Own." *Scientific American,* Special Edition 13 (2): 4–13.

9 | The Earliest Dispersal of the Genus *Homo*: *Homo erectus* and Contemporaries

Focus Question

Who were the first members of the human family to disperse out of Africa, and what were they like (behaviorally and anatomically)?

Introduction

Sometime, close to 2 million years ago, something decisive occurred in human evolution. As the title of this chapter suggests, for the first time, hominids expanded widely out of Africa into other areas of the Old World.

All the early hominid fossils have been found *only* in Africa, suggesting that hominids may have been restricted to this continent for perhaps 5 million years. The later, more widely dispersed hominids were quite different both anatomically and behaviorally from their African ancestors. They were much larger, were more committed to a completely terrestrial habitat, used more elaborate stone tools, and perhaps ate meat.

There is some variation among the different geographical groups of these highly successful hominids, and anthropologists still debate how to classify them. Discoveries continue as well. In particular, new finds from Europe are forcing a major reevaluation of exactly which were the first to leave Africa (Fig. 9-1).

Nevertheless, after 2 m.y.a., there's less diversity in these hominids than is apparent in their pre-*Australopithecus* and *Australopithecus* predecessors. Consequently, there is universal agreement that the hominids found outside of Africa are all members of genus *Homo*. Thus, taxonomic debates focus solely on how many species are represented. The species for which there is the most evidence is called *Homo erectus*. Furthermore, this is the one group that almost all paleoanthropologists distinguish. Thus, in this chapter we will concentrate our discussion on *Homo erectus*. We will, however, also discuss alternative interpretations that "split" the fossil sample into more species.

Go to the following CD-ROMs for interactive activities and exercises on topics covered in this chapter:

Virtual Laboratories for Physical Anthropology CD-ROM, Third edition

Hominid Fossils CD-ROM: An Interactive Atlas

A New Kind of Hominid

The discoveries of fossils now referred to as *H. erectus* began in the nineteenth century. Later in this chapter, we will discuss in some detail the historical background of these earliest discoveries in Java and the somewhat later discoveries in China. From this work, as well as presumably related finds in Europe and North Africa, a variety of taxonomic names were suggested. The most significant of these earlier terms were *Pithecanthropus* (for fossils from Java) and *Sinanthropus* (for those from northern China).

It's important to realize that such taxonomic *splitting* (which this terminology reflects) was quite common in the early years of paleoanthropology. More systematic biological thinking came to the fore only after World War II and with the incorporation of the Modern Synthesis into paleontology (see p. 77). Most of the fossils that were given these varied names are now placed in the species *Homo erectus*—or at least they've all been lumped into one genus (*Homo*).

217

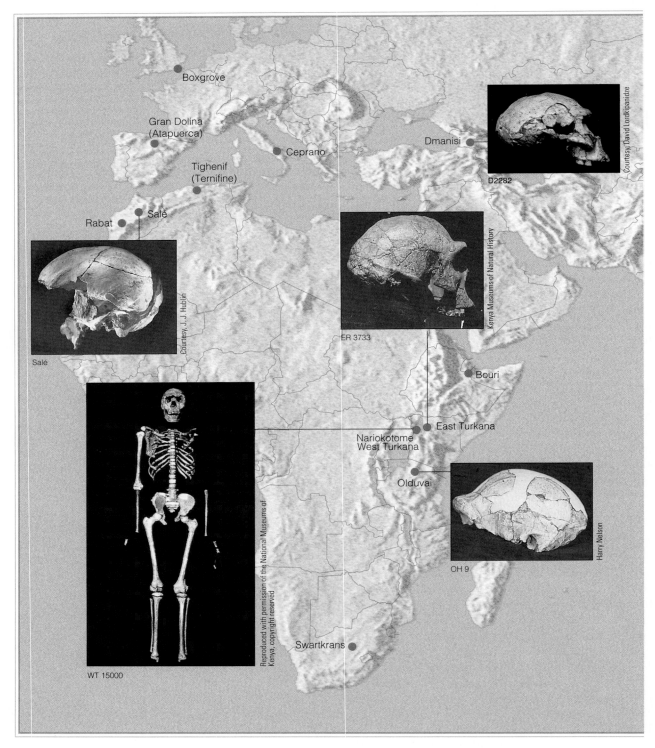

FIGURE 9-1 Major *Homo erectus* sites and localities of other contemporaneous hominids.

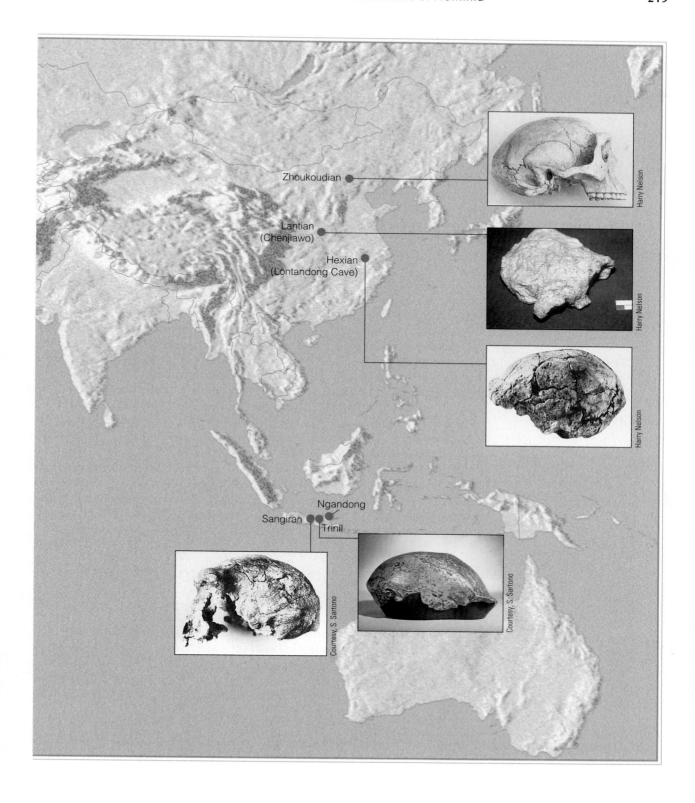

Zhoukoudian

Lantian
(Chenjiawo)

Hexian
(Lontandong Cave)

Ngandong

Sangiran

Trinil

Harry Nelson

Harry Nelson

Harry Nelson

Courtesy, S. Sartono

Courtesy, S. Sartono

In the last few decades, discoveries from East Africa of firmly dated finds have established the clear presence of *Homo erectus* by 1.8 m.y.a. Some researchers see several anatomical differences between these African representatives of an *erectus*-like hominid and their Asian cousins (hominids that almost everybody* refers to as *Homo erectus*). Thus, they place the African fossils into a separate species, one they call *Homo ergaster* (Andrews, 1984; Wood, 1991).

While there are some anatomical differences between the African specimens and those from Asia, they are all clearly *closely* related (either members of one species or of two closely related species). We'll refer to these hominids as either *Homo erectus* (used in the broad sense) or *Homo erectus/ergaster*. When referring to just the Asian fossils (and at least one find from Europe), we will always call them *Homo erectus* (used in the strict sense).

All analyses have shown that *H. erectus/ergaster* represents a **grade** of evolution different from that of their more ancient African predecessors. A grade is an evolutionary grouping of organisms showing a similar adaptive pattern. Increase in body size and robustness, changes in limb proportions, and greater encephalization all indicate that these hominids were more like modern humans in their adaptive pattern than their African ancestors were.[†] We should point out that a grade only implies general adaptive aspects of a group of animals; it implies nothing directly about shared ancestry (organisms that share common ancestry are said to be in the same *clade;* see p. 93). For example, orangutans and African great apes could be said to be in the same grade, but they are not in the same clade (see p. 124).

The hominids discussed in this chapter are not only members of a new and distinct grade of human evolution, they're also closely related to each other. Whether they all belong to the same clade is debatable. Nevertheless, a major adaptive shift had taken place—one setting hominid evolution in a distinctly more human direction.

We mentioned that there is considerable variation in different regional populations of hominids broadly defined as *Homo erectus*. New discoveries are showing even more dramatic variation, suggesting that some of these hominids may not fit closely at all with this general adaptive pattern (more on this presently). For the moment, however, let's review what *most* of these fossils look like.

grade A grouping of organisms sharing a similar adaptive pattern. It is not necessarily based on closeness of evolutionary relationship, but does contrast organisms in a useful way (e.g., *Homo erectus* with *Homo sapiens*).

The Morphology of *Homo erectus*

BRAIN SIZE

Homo erectus differs in several respects from both early *Homo* and *Homo sapiens*. The most obvious feature is cranial size (which, of course, is closely related to brain size). Early *Homo* had cranial capacities ranging from as small as 500 cm^3 to as large as 800 cm^3. *H. erectus,* on the other hand, shows considerable brain enlargement, with a cranial capacity of 750[‡] to 1,250 cm^3 (and

---

*At least one researcher (Wolpoff, 1999) refers to all the hominids discussed in this chapter as *Homo sapiens.*

[†] We did note in Chapter 8 that early *Homo* is a partial exception, being transitional in some respects.

[‡] Considerably smaller cranial capacities have been found in recently discovered fossils from Europe.

a mean of approximately 900 cm³). However, in making such comparisons, we must bear in mind two key questions: What is the comparative sample, and what were the overall body sizes of the species being compared?

In relation to the first question, you should recall that many anthropologists are now convinced that there was more than one species of early *Homo* in East Africa around 2 m.y.a. If so, only one of these could have been ancestral to *H. erectus*. (Indeed, it's possible that neither species gave rise to *H. erectus* and that perhaps we have yet to find direct evidence of the ancestral species.) Taking a more optimistic view that at least one of these fossil groups is a likely ancestor of later hominids, the question still remains—which one? If we choose the smaller-bodied sample of early *Homo* as our presumed ancestral group, then *H. erectus* shows as much as a 40 percent increase in cranial capacity. However, if the comparative sample is the larger-bodied group of early *Homo* (as exemplified by skull 1470, from East Turkana), then *H. erectus* shows a 25 percent increase in cranial capacity.

As we previously discussed, brain size is closely tied to overall body size. We've made a point of the increase in *H. erectus* brain size; however, *H. erectus* was also considerably larger overall than earlier members of the genus *Homo*. In fact, when *H. erectus* is compared with the larger-bodied early *Homo* sample, *relative* brain size is about the same (Walker, 1991). Furthermore, when you compare the relative brain size of *H. erectus* with that of *H. sapiens,* you'll note that *H. erectus* was considerably less encephalized than later members of the genus *Homo*.

BODY SIZE

As we have mentioned, *H. erectus* was larger than earlier hominids, as was conclusively shown by the discovery of a nearly complete skeleton in 1984 from **Nariokotome** (on the west side of Lake Turkana in Kenya). From this specimen and less complete ones, anthropologists estimate that some *Homo erectus* adults weighed well over 100 pounds, with an average adult stature of about 5 feet 6 inches (McHenry, 1992; Ruff and Walker, 1993; Walker and Leakey, 1993). Another point to keep in mind is that *Homo erectus* was quite sexually dimorphic—at least as indicated by the East African specimens. Thus, for male adults, weight and stature in some individuals may have been considerably greater than the average figures just mentioned. In fact, if the Nariokotome boy had survived, he probably would have grown to an adult stature of over 6 feet (Walker, 1993).

Increased height and weight in *H. erectus* is also associated with a dramatic increase in robusticity. In fact, very heavy body build was to dominate hominid evolution not just during *H. erectus* times, but through the long transitional era of premodern forms as well. Only with the appearance of anatomically modern *H. sapiens* did a more gracile skeletal structure emerge, and this is still characteristic of most modern populations.

Nariokotome (nar´-ee-oh-koh´-tow-may)

CRANIAL SHAPE

Homo erectus crania display a highly distinctive shape, partly as a result of increased brain size, but probably more correlated with significant body size (robusticity). The ramifications of this heavily built cranium are reflected in thick cranial bone (most notably in Asian specimens) and large browridges (supraorbital tori) in the front of the skull and a projecting **nuchal torus** at the rear (Fig. 9-2).

nuchal torus (nuke´-ul, pertaining to the neck) A projection of bone in the back of the cranium where neck muscles attach, used to hold up the head.

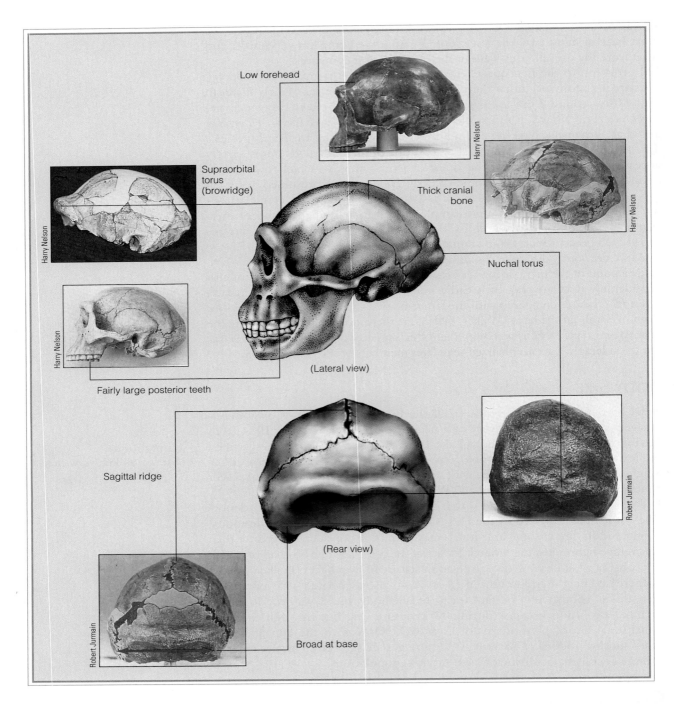

FIGURE 9-2 Morphology and variation in *Homo erectus*.

The brain case is long and low, receding back from the large browridges with little forehead development. Moreover, the cranium is wider at the base compared with earlier or later species of genus *Homo*. The maximum breadth is below the ear opening, giving a pentagonal contour to the cranium (when viewed from behind). In contrast, the skulls of early *Homo* and *H. sapiens* have more vertical sides, and the maximum width is *above* the ear openings.

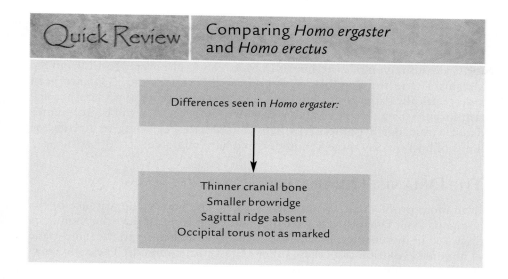

Quick Review

Comparing *Homo ergaster* and *Homo erectus*

Differences seen in *Homo ergaster:*

Thinner cranial bone
Smaller browridge
Sagittal ridge absent
Occipital torus not as marked

DENTITION

The dentition of *Homo erectus* is much like that of *Homo sapiens,* but the earlier species exhibits somewhat larger teeth. However, compared with early *Homo, H. erectus* does show some dental reduction.

Who Were the Earliest African Emigrants?

The fossils from East Africa imply that a new grade of human evolution appeared in Africa not long after 2 m.y.a. Thus, the hominids who migrated to Asia and Europe are generally assumed to be their immediate descendants. This conclusion makes good sense on at least three levels: geography, anatomy, and behavior. Geographically, Africa is where *all* the earlier hominids lived, so *H. erectus/ergaster* would probably have first appeared there (and East Africa especially would have been a likely locality). Moreover, these were now bigger, brainier hominids capable of traveling longer distances. Finally, they also possessed a more advanced tool kit, which allowed them to exploit a wider range of resources.

So, consider the following reasonable hypothesis: *Homo erectus/ergaster* first evolved in East Africa close to 2 m.y.a. and with its new physical/behavioral capacities soon emigrated to other areas of the Old World. This hypothesis helps pull together several aspects of hominid evolution, and much of the fossil evidence after 2 m.y.a. supports it. Nevertheless, there are some difficulties, and recently discovered evidence seriously challenges this tidy view.

First, while 1.8 m.y.a. is a well-established date for the appearance of *H. erectus/ergaster* in East Africa, similar hominids also appear at just about the same time in Indonesia and soon afterward in eastern Europe (see Fig. 9-1). Radiometric dates on sediments on the island of Java have recently placed *H. erectus* (strictly defined) at sites 1.8 and 1.6 million years old. It's possible for our hypothesis to explain these hominids in Asia at this early date

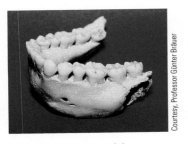

FIGURE 9-3 Dmanisi mandible.

if we assume that *H. erectus* evolved in East Africa by 1.8 m.y.a. (or slightly earlier) and, in just a few thousand years, expanded rapidly to other regions.

Moreover, at an almost equally early date, hominids were also present in the Caucasus region of easternmost Europe. Newly discovered fossils from the Dmanisi site in the Republic of Georgia (see Figs. 9-1 and 9-3) have been radiometrically dated to 1.75 m.y.a. Could this occurrence at yet another distant locality from the presumptive East African homeland still be accommodated within our hypothesis? Perhaps, but we are beginning to stretch the limits of how quickly these hominids could have migrated.

THE DMANISI HOMINIDS

Even more problematic for our hypothesis is the physical appearance of the hominids from Dmanisi. They are quite different from all the other hominids discussed in this chapter. In fact, they may not even belong to the same grade of hominid evolution as all these other (*H. erectus*) hominids. These discoveries thus have dramatic implications.

The discovery of the Dmanisi materials is quite recent, beginning in the early 1990s. The most informative specimens are four well-preserved crania, with one recently discovered (in 2001) being almost complete (Fig. 9-4). These remains are important because they're the best-preserved hominids of this age found anywhere *outside* of Africa. Moreover, they show a mixed pattern of characteristics, some quite unexpected (Vekua et al., 2002).

In some respects, the Dmanisi crania are similar to *H. erectus* (e.g., the long, low braincase, wide base, and thickening along the sagittal midline; see especially Fig. 9-4b and compare with Fig. 9-2). In other characteristics, however, the Dmanisi individuals are different from other hominid finds outside of Africa. In particular, the most complete specimen (specimen 2700; see Fig. 9-4c) has a less robust and thinner browridge, a projecting lower face, and a large upper canine. Thus, at least from the front, this skull is more reminiscent of the smaller early *Homo* specimens from East Africa than of *Homo erectus*. Moreover, cranial capacity in this individual is very small (estimated at only 600 cm³, well within the range of early *Homo*). In fact, all three Dmanisi crania have small cranial capacities (the other two estimated at 650 cm³ and 780 cm³).

A number of stone tools have also been recovered at Dmanisi. The tools are similar to early ones from Africa and are quite different from the ostensibly more advanced technology of the Acheulian (the latter broadly associated with *H. erectus* in much of the Old World).

FIGURE 9-4 Dmanisi crania discovered in 1999 and 2001 and dated to 1.8–1.7 m.y.a.
(a) Specimen 2282.
(b) Specimen 2280.
(c) Specimen 2700.

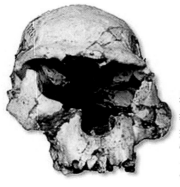

(a)

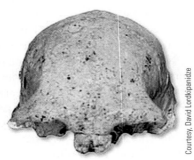

(b)

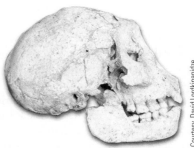

(c)

From these recent, startling revelations from Dmanisi, several questions can be raised:

1. Was *Homo erectus* the first hominid to leave Africa—or was it an earlier form of *Homo?*
2. Did hominids require a large brain and sophisticated stone tool culture to disperse out of Africa?
3. Was the large, robust body build of *H. erectus* a necessary adaptation for the initial occupation of Eurasia?

Of course, since the Dmanisi discoveries are very new, any conclusions must be seen as highly tentative. Nevertheless, the recent evidence raises important and exciting possibilities. It now seems likely that the first transcontinental hominid migrants were a form of early *Homo* (similar to the smaller East African species, *Homo habilis;* see p. 200). At best, and as exemplified at Dmanisi, the first hominids to leave Africa were a very early form of *H. erectus,* apparently one much more primitive than any of the other specimens from Africa, Asia, or Europe discussed in this chapter. Certainly the smaller individuals from Dmanisi didn't have large brains (by *H. erectus* standards), nor did they have an advanced stone tool culture (possessing instead tools very similar to the earliest ones from East and South Africa).

Thus far, only a few isolated postcranial remains have been found at Dmanisi, so we don't yet know the body structure of the earliest hominids to leave Africa. It's possible, however, that the overall body proportions resemble *Homo habilis* more than they do *H. erectus.* Thus, these first pioneers to leave Africa may have been, in the words of Phillip Rightmire, "little people." That is, they may have been very different from the big-bodied, long-legged *H. erectus* body plan. Given these startling and still provisional observations, it appears that the Dmanisi hominids don't meet any of the criteria used to define the more human evolutionary grade of all the other *Homo erectus/ergaster* individuals. At minimum, we have to admit that our hypothesis isn't looking nearly as tidy as we might have hoped!

Accordingly, major reappraisals regarding the status of early *Homo* as well as what constitutes membership in the genus *Homo* itself will be required. Moreover, the core of our hypothesis, explaining those factors that initially "propelled" hominids out of Africa, may well be largely falsified. Note, however, that the hypothesis might still hold for a *second* migration, one that perhaps occurred shortly after the time of the Dmanisi inhabitants. All this evidence is so new, however, that it's premature even to predict what further revisions may be required.

Historical Overview of *Homo erectus* Discoveries

Homo erectus (broadly defined) is found widely distributed across three continents. However, it's difficult to organize these materials in a clear chronological order (as we did for African hominids in Chapter 8). First, we have the problem of complexity. As already noted, the earliest members of the group all appear nearly simultaneously, around 1.8 m.y.a., in Africa, Asia, and Europe. And second, since for most of the later fossils radiometric dating is not possible, our knowledge of the chronological placement of many specimens is still highly tenuous.

The best way to proceed is to discuss these fossil hominids from a historical perspective—that is, in the order in which they were discovered. We believe that this approach is useful, as the discoveries cover a broad range of time—indeed, almost the entire history of paleoanthropology. Given this relatively long history of scientific discovery, the later finds were assessed in the light of earlier ones (and thus can still be best understood within a historical context).

JAVA

Dutch anatomist Eugene Dubois (1858–1940) (Fig. 9-5) was the first scientist to deliberately design a research plan that would take him from his anatomy lab to where fossil bones might be buried. Up until this time, embryology and comparative anatomy were considered the proper methods of studying humans and their ancestry, and the research was done in the laboratory. Dubois changed all this. The publication of Darwin's *On the Origin of Species* in 1859 had ushered in a period of intellectual excitement. This stimulating intellectual climate surrounded the youthful Dubois when he left Holland for Sumatra in 1887 to search for, as he phrased it, "the missing link."

FIGURE 9-5 Eugene Dubois, discoverer of the first *H. erectus* fossil to be found.

In October 1891, along the Solo River, near the town of Trinil, his field crew unearthed a skullcap that was to become internationally famous. The following year, a human femur was recovered about 15 yards upstream in what Dubois claimed was the same level as the skullcap, and he assumed that the skullcap (with a cranial capacity of slightly over 900 cm³) and the femur belonged to the same individual.

After studying these discoveries for a few years, Dubois startled the world in 1894 with a paper titled "*Pithecanthropus erectus*, A Manlike Species of Transitional Anthropoid from Java." Dubois' views were harshly criticized, but eventually, there was general acceptance that he had been correct in identifying the skull as representing a previously undescribed species; that his estimates of cranial capacity were reasonably accurate; that *Pithecanthropus erectus*, or *H. erectus* as we call it today, is a close relative and perhaps an ancestor of *H. sapiens;* and that bipedalism preceded enlargement of the brain.

By 1930, the controversy had faded, especially in light of important new discoveries near Peking (Beijing), China, in the late 1920s (discussed shortly). Similarities between the Beijing skulls and Dubois' *Pithecanthropus* were obvious, and scientists pointed out that the Java form was not an "apeman," as Dubois contended, but instead was closely related to modern *Homo sapiens*. One might expect that Dubois would welcome the finds from China and the support they provided for the human status of *Pithecanthropus*, but he didn't. In fact, he refused to recognize any connection between the Beijing and Java materials.

HOMO ERECTUS FROM JAVA

Six sites in eastern Java have yielded all the *H. erectus* fossil remains found to date on that island. The dating of these fossils has been hampered by the complex nature of Javanese geology, but it's been generally accepted that most of the fossils belong to the Middle **Pleistocene** and are less than 800,000 years old. However, as we noted earlier, more precise chronometric dating estimates

Pleistocene The epoch of the Cenozoic from 1.8 m.y.a. until 10,000 y.a. Frequently referred to as the Ice Age, this epoch is associated with continental glaciations in northern latitudes.

have suggested one find to be close to 1.8 million years old and another fossil from a site called Sangiran may be approximately 1.6 million years old.

At Sangiran, where the remains of at least five individuals have been excavated, cranial capacities range from 813 cm³ to 1,059 cm³. Another site called Ngandong has yielded the remains of another 12 crania (Fig. 9-6), and these finds have surprisingly been dated to the Upper Pleistocene. Two specialized dating techniques (discussed in Chapter 11; see p. 290) have determined that animal bones found at the site (and presumably associated with the hominids) are only about 50,000 to 25,000 years old (Swisher et al., 1996). These dates are controversial, but further confirmation is now establishing a *very* late survival of *Homo erectus* in Java, long after the species had disappeared elsewhere. They would thus be contemporary with *Homo sapiens*—which, by this time, had expanded widely throughout the Old World.

We cannot say much about the *H. erectus* way of life in Java. Very few artifacts have been found, and those have come mainly from river terraces, not from primary sites: "On Java there is still not a single site where artifacts can be associated with *H. erectus*" (Bartstra, 1982, p. 319).

PEKING (BEIJING)

The story of Peking *H. erectus* is another saga filled with excitement, hard work, luck, and misfortune. Europeans had known for a long time that "dragon bones," used by the Chinese as medicine and aphrodisiacs, were actually ancient mammal bones. Scientists eventually located one of the sources of these bones near Beijing at a site called **Zhoukoudian.** Serious excavations were begun there in the 1920s under the direction of a young Chinese geologist named Pei Wenshong. In 1929, a fossil skull was discovered, and Pei brought the specimen to anatomist Davidson Black (Fig. 9-7). The result was worth the labor. The skull turned out to be that of a juvenile, and although it was thick, low, and relatively small, in Black's mind there was no doubt that it belonged to an early hominid. The response to this discovery, quite unlike that which greeted Dubois almost 40 years earlier, was enthusiastically favorable.

Franz Weidenreich (Fig. 9-8), a distinguished anatomist well known for his work on European fossil hominids, succeeded Black. After Japan invaded China in 1933, Weidenreich decided to move the fossils. He left China in 1941, taking plaster casts, photographs, and drawings of the material with him. After he left, the bones were packed, and arrangements were made for the U.S. Marine Corps in Beijing to take them to the United States. However, the bones never reached the United States, and they've never been found. To this day, no one knows what happened to them, and their location remains a mystery.

ZHOUKOUDIAN *HOMO ERECTUS*

The fossil remains of *H. erectus* discovered in the 1920s and 1930s as well as some more recent excavations at Zhoukoudian (Fig. 9-9) constitute by far the largest collection of *H. erectus* material found anywhere. Included in this excellent sample are 14 skullcaps (Fig. 9-10), other cranial pieces, and more than 100 isolated teeth, but only a scattering of postcranial elements (Jia and Huang, 1990). Various interpretations to account for this unusual pattern of preservation have been offered, ranging from ritualistic treatment or cannibalism by the

FIGURE 9-6 Rear view of a Ngandong skull. Note that the cranial walls slope downward and outward (or upward and inward), with the widest breadth low on the cranium, giving it a pentagonal form.

FIGURE 9-7 Davidson Black, responsible for the first study of the Zhoukoudian fossils.

Zhoukoudian
(Zhoh´-koh-dee´-en)

FIGURE 9-8 Franz Weidenreich.

FIGURE 9-9 Zhoukoudian Cave. The grid on the wall was drawn for purposes of excavation. The entrance to the cave can be seen near the grid.

Special Collections, American Museum of Natural History

Robert Jurmain

FIGURE 9-10 *H. erectus* (cast of specimen from Zhoukoudian). From this view, the supraorbital torus, low vault of the skull, and nuchal torus can clearly be seen.

FIGURE 9–11 Chinese tools from Middle Pleistocene sites. (Adapted from Wu and Olsen, 1985.)

hominids themselves to the more mundane suggestion that the *H. erectus* remains are simply the leftovers of the meals of giant hyenas (discussed shortly).

Nevertheless, the hominid remains belong to upward of 40 adults and children and together provide much evidence. Because of meticulous work by Weidenreich, the Zhoukoudian fossils have led to a good overall picture of Chinese *H. erectus*. Like the materials from Java, they possess typical *H. erectus* features, including a supraorbital torus in front and a nuchal torus behind. Also, the skull has thick bones, a sagittal ridge, and a protruding face and, like the Javanese forms, is broadest near the bottom.

Cultural Remains   More than 100,000 artifacts have been recovered from this vast site, which was occupied intermittently for many thousands of years. Early on, tools are generally crude and shapeless but become more refined over time. Common tools at the site are choppers and chopping tools, but retouched flakes were fashioned into scrapers, points, burins, and awls (Fig. 9-11).

The way of life at Zhoukoudian has traditionally been described as that of hunter-gatherers who killed deer, horses, and other animals and gathered fruits, berries, and ostrich eggs. Fragments of charred ostrich eggshells and abundant deposits of hackberry seeds unearthed in the cave suggest that meat was supplemented by the gathering of herbs, wild fruits, tubers, and eggs. Layers of what

Quartzite chopper

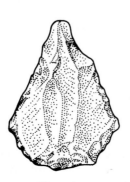

Flint point

Flint awl

Graver, or burin

has long been thought to be ash in the cave (over 18 feet deep at one point) have been interpreted as indicating the use of fire by *H. erectus;* however, as we'll see, whether Beijing hominids could actually make fire is unknown.

More recently, several researchers have challenged this picture of Zhoukoudian life. Lewis Binford and colleagues (Binford and Ho, 1985; Binford and Stone, 1986a, 1986b) reject the description of Beijing *H. erectus* as hunters and argue that the evidence clearly points more accurately to scavenging. Using advanced archaeological techniques of analysis, Noel Boaz and colleagues have even questioned whether the *H. erectus* remains at Zhoukoudian represent evidence of hominid habitation of the cave. By comparing the types of bones as well as the damage to the bones with that seen in contemporary carnivore dens, Boaz and Ciochon(2001) have suggested that much of the material in the cave likely accumulated through the activities of a giant extinct hyena. Indeed, they hypothesize that most of the *H. erectus* remains, too, are the food refuse of hyena meals!

Boaz and his colleagues do recognize that the tools in the cave, and possibly the cut marks on some of the animal bones, do provide evidence of hominid activities at Zhoukoudian. They also recognize that more detailed analysis is required to test their hypotheses and to "determine the nature and scope" of the *H. erectus* presence at Zhoukoudian.

Probably the most intriguing archaeological aspect of the presumed hominid behavior at Zhoukoudian has been the long-held assumption that *H. erectus* deliberately used fire inside the cave. The control of fire was one of the major cultural breakthroughs of all prehistory. By providing warmth, a means of cooking, an aid to further modify tools, and so forth, controlled fire would have been a giant technological innovation. While some potential early African sites have evidence that to some have suggested hominid control of fire, it has long been concluded that the first *definite* evidence of hominid fire use comes from Zhoukoudian.

Recent evidence has radically altered this assumption. Much more detailed excavations at Zhoukoudian were carried out in 1996 and 1997 by biologist Steve Weiner and colleagues. These researchers also carefully analyzed soil samples for distinctive chemical signatures (which would show whether fire had occurred in the cave) (Weiner et al., 1998). They found that burnt bone was only rarely found in association with tools. And in most cases, the burning appeared to have taken place *after* fossilization (i.e., the bones were not cooked). Moreover, the "ash" layers mentioned earlier aren't actually ash, but rather naturally accumulated organic sediment. This last conclusion was derived from chemical testing that showed no sign whatsoever of wood having been burnt inside the cave. Finally, the "hearths" that have figured so prominently in archaeological reconstructions of presumed fire control at this site are apparently not hearths at all. They are simply round depressions formed in the past by water.

Indeed, another provisional interpretation of the cave's geology suggests that the cave wasn't open to the outside like a habitation site, but had access only through a vertical shaft. This has led archaeologist Alison Brooks to remark, "It wouldn't have been a shelter, it would have been a trap" (quoted in Wuethrich, 1998). These serious doubts regarding control of fire, coupled with the suggestive evidence of bone accumulation by carnivores, have led anthropologists Noel Boaz and Russell Ciochon to conclude, "Zhoukoudian cave was neither hearth nor home" (Boaz and Ciochon, 2001).

OTHER CHINESE SITES

More work has been done at Zhoukoudian than at any other Chinese site. Nevertheless, there are other hominid sites worth mentioning. Three of the more important ones, besides Zhoukoudian, are two in Lantian County (often simply referred to as Lantian) and another in Hexian County (usually referred to as the Hexian find).

At Lantian, an almost complete mandible containing several teeth was found in 1963. It's quite similar to those from Zhoukoudian but has been given an earlier date of about 650,000 y.a. The following year, a partial cranium was discovered at a nearby Hexian locality. Provisionally dated to as much as 1.15 m.y.a. (Etler and Tianyuan, 1994), this may be the oldest Chinese *Homo erectus* fossil yet known.

Perhaps the most significant find was the 1980 Hexian discovery, where remains of several individuals were recovered. One of the specimens is a well-preserved cranium (with a cranial capacity of about 1,025 cm^3) lacking much of its base. Dated roughly at 250,000 y.a., it's not surprising that it displays several more derived features. The cranial constriction, for example, is not as pronounced as in earlier forms, and certain temporal and occipital characteristics are "best compared with the later forms of *H. erectus* at Zhoukoudian" (Wu and Dong, 1985, p. 87).

In 1993, Li Tianyuan and Dennis Etler reported that two relatively complete skulls were discovered in 1989 at a site in Yunxian County dated to approximately 350,000 y.a. (Fig. 9-12). The crania are both considerably larger and more robust than those from Zhoukoudian. Unfortunately, both skulls are still covered with a hard matrix, and until they're cleaned and reconstructed, it's too early to make accurate assessments. In any case, these Yunxian crania will ultimately provide considerable data to help clarify hominid evolution in China and perhaps elsewhere in the Old World as well.

The Asian crania from both Java and China share many similar features, which may be explained by *H. erectus* migration from Java to China perhaps around 1 million years ago. African *H. erectus* forms are generally older than most Asian forms and differ from them in several ways.

FIGURE 9-12 (a) EV 9002 (Yunxian, China). The skull is in better shape than its companion, and its lateral view clearly displays features characteristic of *H. erectus:* flattened vault, receding forehead (frontal bone), angulated occiput, and supraorbital torus. (b) EV 9001 (Yunxian). Unfortunately, the skull was crushed, but it preserves some lateral facial structures absent in EV 9002.

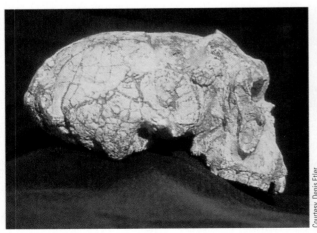

(a)

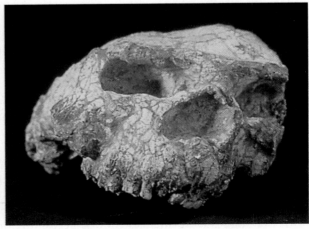

(b)

EAST AFRICA

Olduvai Back in 1960, Louis Leakey unearthed a fossil skull at Olduvai (OH 9) that he identified as *H. erectus*. Skull OH 9 from Upper Bed II is dated at 1.4 m.y.a. and preserves a massive cranium but is faceless except for a bit of nose below the supraorbital torus. Estimated at 1,067 cm^3, the cranial capacity of OH 9 is the largest of all the African *Homo erectus* specimens (defined in the broad sense; these specimens are also referred to as *H. ergaster*). The browridge is huge, the largest known for any hominid, but the walls of the braincase are thin. This latter characteristic is seen in most East African *H. erectus* specimens, and in this respect they differ from Asian *H. erectus* (in which cranial bones are thick). This and other differences have led some researchers to place East African specimens in a separate species.

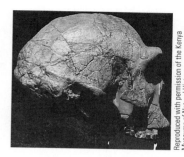

FIGURE 9–13 ER 3733, the most complete East Turkana *H. erectus* cranium.

East Turkana Some 400 miles north of Olduvai Gorge, on the northern boundary of Kenya, is Lake Turkana. Explored by Richard Leakey and colleagues since 1969, the eastern shore of the lake has been a virtual gold mine for australopithecine, early *Homo,* and *H. erectus* fossil remains.

The most significant *H. erectus/ergaster* discovery from East Turkana is a nearly complete skull (Fig. 9-13) dated at 1.8 m.y.a. (i.e., as early as the earliest *H. erectus* from Java). The cranial capacity is estimated at 848 cm^3, at the lower end of the range for *H. erectus,* but this isn't surprising considering its early date. It generally resembles Asian *H. erectus* in many features (but with some important differences, discussed shortly). Not many tools have been found at *H. erectus* sites in East Turkana. Oldowan flakes, cobbles, and core tools have been found, and the introduction of **Acheulian** tools about 1.4 m.y.a. replaced the Oldowan tradition.

Acheulian (ash´-oo-lay-en) Pertaining to a stone tool industry from the Lower and Middle Pleistocene characterized by a large proportion of bifacial tools (flaked on both sides). Acheulian tool kits are very common in Africa, Southwest Asia, and western Europe, but are thought to be less common elsewhere. (Also spelled "Acheulean.")

West Turkana In August 1984, Kamoya Kimeu, a member of Richard Leakey's team, enhanced his reputation as an outstanding fossil hunter when he discovered a small piece of skull on the west side of Lake Turkana. Leakey and his colleague, Alan Walker of Pennsylvania State University, excavated the site known as Nariokotome in the 1980s.

The dig was a resounding success and produced the most complete *H. erectus* skeleton ever found (Fig. 9-14). Known properly as WT 15000, the all but complete skeleton includes facial bones and most of the postcranial bones, a very unusual discovery for *H. erectus* (broadly defined), since these elements are scarce at other sites. The Nariokotome skeleton is quite ancient, dated chronometrically to about 1.6 m.y.a. The skeleton is that of a boy about 12 years of age with an estimated height of about 5 feet 3 inches. Had he grown to maturity, it is estimated that his height would have been more than 6 feet, taller than *H. erectus* was previously thought to have been. The postcranial bones appear to be quite similar, though not identical, to those of modern humans. The cranial capacity of WT 15000 is estimated at 880 cm^3; brain growth was nearly complete, and the boy's adult cranial capacity would have been approximately 909 cm^3 (Begun and Walker, 1993).

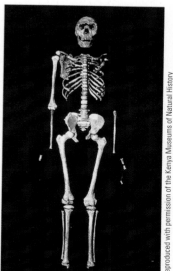

FIGURE 9-14 WT 15000 from Nariokotome, Kenya: the most complete *H. erectus* specimen yet found.

Bouri Two sites from Ethiopia have yielded *H. erectus* fossils, the most significant coming from the Bouri locale in the Middle Awash region (the same area from which numerous remains of earlier hominids have come; see

Chapter 8 and Appendix B). The recent discovery of a mostly complete cranium from Bouri is important because this individual (dated at approximately 1 m.y.a.) is more like Asian *H. erectus* than are most of the earlier East African remains we have discussed (Asfaw et al., 2002). Consequently, the suggestion by several researchers that East African fossils are a different species from (Asian) *Homo erectus* isn't supported by the morphology of the Bouri cranium.

SUMMARY OF EAST AFRICAN *HOMO ERECTUS/ERGASTER*

The *Homo erectus* remains from East Africa show several differences from the Javanese and Chinese fossils. Some African cranial specimens (particularly ER 3733, presumably a female, and WT 15000, presumably a male) aren't as strongly buttressed (by supraorbital or nuchal tori) and don't have such thick cranial bones. As noted, these differences, as well as others in the postcranial skeleton, have so impressed some researchers that they in fact argue for a *separate* species status for the African material (as distinct from the Asian samples). Bernard Wood, the leading proponent of this view, has suggested that the name *Homo ergaster* be used for the African remains and that *H. erectus* be reserved solely for the Asian material (Wood, 1991). In addition, the very early dates now postulated for the dispersal of *H. erectus* into Asia (Java) would argue for a more than 1-million-year separate history for Asian and African populations.

Nevertheless, this species division has not been fully accepted, and the current consensus (and the one we prefer) is to continue to refer to all these hominids as *Homo erectus* (Kramer, 1993; Conroy, 1997; Rightmire, 1998; Asfaw et al., 2002). As with some earlier hominids, we accordingly will have to accommodate a considerable degree of intraspecific variation within this species. Wood has concluded, regarding variation within such a broadly defined *H. erectus* species, "It is a species which manifestly embraces an unusually wide degree of variation in both the cranium and postcranial skeleton" (Wood, 1992a, p. 329).

NORTH AFRICA

North African remains, consisting almost entirely of mandibles (or mandible fragments) and a partial parietal bone, have been found at three sites in Algeria and Morocco. The three Algerian mandibles and the parietal fragment are quite robust and have been dated to about 700,000 y.a. The Moroccan material isn't as robust and may be a bit younger, at 500,000 years. In addition, an interesting cranium was found north of the town of Salé, in Morocco. The walls of the skull vault are thick, and several other features resemble those of *H. erectus*. Some features alternatively suggest that the Salé fossil should be placed in a later species of *Homo,* but an estimated cranial capacity of about 900 cm^3 throws doubt on that interpretation.

EUROPE

As a result of the recent discoveries from Dmanisi (see p. 224), the time frame for the earliest hominid occupation of Europe is being dramatically pushed back. For several decades, it had been assumed that hominids didn't reach Europe until late in the Middle Pleistocene (after 400,000 y.a.) and were already identifiable as a form very similar to *Homo sapiens*. It was thus concluded that *H. erectus* (and contemporaries) never got there. However, as the new discoveries are evaluated, these assumptions are being questioned, and radical revisions concerning hominid evolution in Europe are becoming necessary.

While not as old as the Dmanisi material, fossils from the Gran Dolina site in northern Spain are extending the antiquity of hominids in western Europe. (Gran Dolina is located in the very productive region called Atapuerca, where later hominid fossils have also been found.) The dating of Gran Dolina, based on specialized techniques discussed in Chapter 11 (see p. 290), is approximately 850,000–780,000 y.a. (Parés and Pérez-González, 1995; Falguéres et al., 1999). These early Spanish finds are thus at *least* 250,000 years older than any other hominid yet discovered in western Europe. Because all the remains thus far identified are fragmentary, the taxonomic assignment of these fossils remains somewhat problematic, but initial analysis suggests that these fossils aren't *H. erectus*. The facial remains are especially distinctive, and they look much more modern than does *H. erectus*. Spanish paleoanthropologists who have studied the Gran Dolina fossils have decided to place these hominids into another (separate) species, one they call "*Homo antecessor*" (Bermúdez de Castro et al., 1997; Arsuaga et al., 1999). However, it remains to be seen whether this newly proposed species will prove to be distinct from other species of *Homo* (see p. 237 for further discussion). Another potentially early western European hominid find comes from the 500,000-year-old Boxgrove site in southern England, where a hominid tibia (shinbone) was unearthed in 1994 (the dating here, too, will require further confirmation).

Finally, the southern European discovery of a well-preserved cranium from the Ceprano site in central Italy may be the best evidence yet of *H. erectus* (strictly defined) in Europe (Ascenzi et al., 1996). Provisional dating of a partial cranium from this important site suggests a date between 800,000 and 900,000 y.a. Phillip Rightmire (1998) has concluded that cranial morphology places this specimen quite close to *H. erectus*. Italian researchers have proposed other views. Initially, they agreed with Rightmire's interpretation (Ascenzi et al., 1996), but more recently have suggested that the Ceprano cranium might belong to yet another (and separate) species (Manzi et al., 2001). This degree of "splitting" is quite extreme and isn't likely to be considered favorably by most paleoanthropologists.

After about 400,000 y.a., the European fossil hominid record becomes increasingly abundant. Nevertheless, interpretations relating to the proper taxonomic assessment of many of these remains have been debated, in some cases for decades. In recent years, several of these somewhat later "premodern" specimens have been considered either as early representatives of *Homo sapiens* or as a separate species, one immediately preceding *H. sapiens*. These enigmatic premodern humans are discussed in Chapter 10. A time line for the *H. erectus* discoveries discussed in this chapter, as well as other finds of more uncertain status, is shown in Figure 9-15.

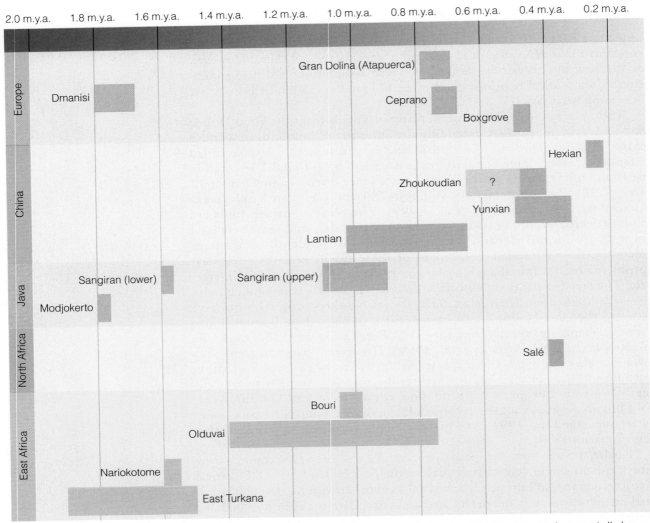

FIGURE 9-15 Time line for *Homo erectus* discoveries and other contemporary hominids. Note that most dates are approximations.

Note: Most dates are only imprecise estimates. However, the dates from East African sites are chronometrically determined and are thus much more secure. In addition, the early dates from Java are also radiometric and are gaining wide acceptance.

Technological and Population Trends in *Homo erectus*

TECHNOLOGICAL TRENDS

Many researchers have noted the remarkable stability of the physical and cultural characteristics of *Homo erectus* populations, which seemed to change so little in the more than 1.5 million years of their existence. There is, however, dispute on this point. Some anthropologists (Rightmire, 1981) see almost no detectable changes in cranial dimensions over more than 1 million years of *H. erectus* evolution.* Others (e.g., Wolpoff, 1984), who use different methodologies to date and subdivide their samples, draw a different conclusion, because they see some significant long-term morphological trends. Accepting a moderate position, we can postulate that there were some changes: The brain of later *H. erectus* was somewhat larger, the nose more protrusive, and the body not as robust as in earlier populations. Moreover, there were modifications in stone tool technology.

Expansion of the brain presumably enabled *H. erectus* to develop a more sophisticated tool kit than seen among earlier hominids. The important change in this kit was a core worked on both sides, called a *biface* (known widely as a hand axe or cleaver; Fig. 9-16). The biface had a flatter core than the roundish earlier Oldowan pebble tool. And, probably even more important, this core tool was obviously a target design, that is, the main goal of the toolmaker. This greater focus and increased control enabled the stoneknapper to produce sharper, straighter edges, resulting in a more efficient implement. This Acheulian stone tool became standardized as the basic *H. erectus* all-purpose tool (with only minor modification) for more than a million years. It served to cut, scrape, pound, and dig. This most useful tool has been found in Africa, parts of Asia, and later in Europe. It should also be noted that Acheulian tool kits also included several types of small tools (Fig. 9-17).

For many years, it was thought that a cultural "divide" separated the Old World, with Acheulian technology found *only* in Africa, southwest Asia, and western Europe, but not elsewhere (i.e., absent in eastern Europe and most of Asia). However, recently reported excavations from more than 20 sites in southern China have forced reevaluation of this hypothesis (Yamei et al., 2000). As noted, the most distinctive tools of the Acheulian are bifaces, and they are the very tools thought lacking throughout most of the Pleistocene in eastern Europe and most of Asia. The new archaeological assemblages from southern China are securely dated at about 800,000 y.a. and contain numerous bifaces, very similar to contemporaneous Acheulian bifaces from Africa (see Figs. 9-16 and 9-18b). It now appears likely that cultural traditions relating to stone tool technology were largely equivalent over the *full* geographical range of *H. erectus* and contemporaries.

While geographical distinctions are not so obvious, temporal changes in tool technology are evident. Early toolmakers employed a stone hammer (simply an ovoid-shaped stone about the size of an egg or a bit larger) to remove flakes from the core, leaving deep scars that produced a sharp edge. Later, they used other materials, such as wood and bone, as soft hammers, and this gave them more control over flaking, ultimately yielding yet sharper edges and a more symmetrical form.

Evidence of butchering is widespread at *H. erectus* sites, and in the past, such evidence has been cited in arguments for consistent hunting. For example, at the Olorgesailie site in Kenya (Fig. 9-18), dated at approximately 800,000 y.a., thousands of Acheulian hand axes have been recovered in association with remains of large animals, including giant, now extinct baboons. However, the assumption of consistent hunting has been challenged, especially by archaeologists who argue that the evidence doesn't prove the hunting

Courtesy, The Museum of Primitive Art and Culture, Peace Dale, RI, photo by William Turnbaugh

FIGURE 9-16 Acheulian biface ("hand axe"), a basic tool of the Acheulian tradition.

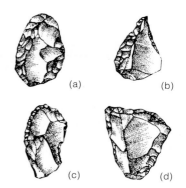

(a)   (b)

(c)   (d)

FIGURE 9-17 Small tools of the Acheulian industry. (a) Side scraper. (b) Point. (c) End scraper. (d) Burin.

---

*This conclusion does not take into account the Dmanisi remains, but refers to more obvious and more derived *H. erectus* specimens.

(a)

(b)

FIGURE 9-18 (a) A Middle Pleistocene butchering site at Olorgesailie, Kenya, excavated by Louis and Mary Leakey, who had the catwalk built for observers. (b) A close-up of the Acheulian tools, mainly hand axes, found at the site.

hypothesis. Instead, they suggest that *H. erectus* was primarily a scavenger, a hypothesis that also has not yet been proved conclusively. We thus discuss *H. erectus* as a potential hunter *and* scavenger. It's crucial to remember, too, that these hominids frequently *gathered* wild plant foods. Indeed, a majority of the calories they consumed probably came from such gathering activities.

Moreover, as we have seen, the mere *presence* of animal bones at archaeological sites doesn't prove that hominids were killing animals or even necessarily eating meat. Indeed, as was the case in the earlier South African sites (discussed in Chapter 8), the hominid remains themselves may have been the meal refuse of large carnivores! Thus, in making interpretations of early hominid sites, we must consider a variety of alternatives. As archaeologist Richard Klein has concluded regarding Middle Pleistocene sites, the interpretations are far from clear: "In sum, the available data do not allow us to isolate the relative roles of humans, carnivores, and factors such as starvation, accidents, and stream action in creating bone assemblages. . . . Certainly, as presently understood, the sites do not tell us how successful or effective *Homo erectus* was at obtaining meat" (1989, p. 221).

POPULATION TRENDS

H. erectus is the first hominid for which we have definite evidence of *wide* geographical dispersion (i.e., across more than one continent). Descendants of early *Homo* ancestors in Africa, the earliest migrants into Eurasia were similar in many ways to their early *Homo* forebears (although they may be seen as a primitive form of *H. erectus*). These initial migrants were possibly succeeded quite quickly by a second migration from Africa into Eurasia. These hominids had by now attained the full physical and cultural capacities of *H. erectus,* and these populations dispersed far and wide in the Old World—far beyond the relatively narrow ranges of earlier hominids.

The life of hunter-scavengers (and, no doubt, *primarily* gatherers) was nomadic, and the woodland and savanna that covered the southern tier of Asia would have been an excellent environment for *H. erectus,* since it was similar to the econiche of their African ancestors. As the population grew, small groups budded off and moved on to find new locations. This process, repeated again and again, led *H. erectus* east, crossing to Java, arriving there, it seems, as early as the most ancient known sites in East Africa itself. At about the same time, another migratory route took hominids to eastern Europe. This migration, however, might have involved a more primitive form of *Homo* and didn't meet with the wide success ultimately attained by *Homo erectus.*

Interpretations of *Homo erectus:* Continuing Uncertainties

There are several aspects of the geographical, physical, and behavioral patterns shown by *H. erectus* (broadly defined) that seem clear. However, new discoveries and more in-depth analyses are making some of our simpler conclusions seem tenuous. The fascinating fossil hominids discovered at Dmanisi are perhaps the most challenging piece of this puzzle.

The approach followed in this chapter and stated in our earlier hypothesis (see p. 223) suggests that *Homo erectus* was able to emigrate from Africa owing to more advanced culture and a more modern anatomy (as compared to earlier African predecessors). Yet, the Dmanisi cranial remains show that these very early Europeans still had small brains, and in one case, the cranium looks more like early *Homo* than like *Homo erectus.* Moreover, these hominids had only a very basic stone tool kit, one apparently no more advanced than very early African ones.

It thus appears that part of our hypothesis is not fully accurate. At least some of the earliest emigrants from Africa didn't yet show the entire suite of *Homo erectus* physical and behavioral traits. How different the Dmanisi hominids are from the full *H. erectus* pattern remains to be determined (discovery of more complete postcranial remains will be most illuminating).

Furthermore, the three crania from Dmanisi thus far published are extremely variable (one of them, in fact, does look more like *Homo erectus*). It would be tempting to conclude that there is more than one type of hominid represented here—but they are all found in the same geological context. The archaeologists who excavated the site are convinced that all the fossils are closely associated with each other. The simplest hypothesis is that they all are members of the *same* species. This degree of apparent intraspecific variation is biologically noteworthy and is influencing how paleoanthropologists interpret all these fossil samples.

This growing awareness of the broad limits of intraspecific variation among some hominids brings us to our second consideration: Is *Homo ergaster* (in Africa) a separate species from *Homo erectus* (as strictly defined in Asia)? While this interpretation has been increasingly popular in the last decade, it now seems to be losing steam. The finds from Dmanisi raise fundamental issues of interpretation. Among these three crania from one locality (see Fig. 9-4), there is more variation than between the African and Asian forms (which many researchers have interpreted as different species). Moreover, the new discovery from Bouri (Ethiopia) of a more *erectus*-looking cranium also further weakens the separate-species interpretation of *Homo ergaster.*

The separate-species status of the early European fossils from Spain (Gran Dolina) is also not yet clearly established. There is not much good fossil evidence yet from this site, but an early date, prior to 750,000 y.a., is well confirmed. Recall also that no other western European hominid fossils are known until at least 250,000 years later, and an ostensibly roughly contemporaneous find from Italy looks like *Homo erectus*. The more modern-looking face of the Gran Dolina hominid might be explained by a fairly early expansion (from Africa into Spain) of more modern-looking humans. Further complicating this intepretation, the best evidence comes from a young individual, estimated to have died at around 12 years of age. Thus, the "modern" facial morphology may be simply a reflection of the immature developmental stage of this adolescent. In any case, whether these hominids ever dispersed elsewhere in Europe remains to be seen. However, later in the Pleistocene, their possible descendants are well established both in Africa and in Europe. These later premodern humans are the topic of the next chapter.

In conclusion, we return again to our hypothesis regarding the initial dispersal of genus *Homo*. It seems that there was more than one such dispersal soon after 2 m.y.a. One, as represented by the Dmanisi fossils, involved a less derived *Homo* than the full-blown *H. erectus* pattern. These hominids, nevertheless, quite remarkably migrated as far as eastern Europe; but current evidence doesn't indicate that this more primitive *Homo* species expanded much beyond this initial foothold.

As we have suggested, perhaps it was a second migration, deriving from early African *H. erectus*, that expanded extremely widely in the Old World. We have evidence of such an expansion of the full *H. erectus* physical and behavioral grade from sites in East Africa, North Africa, southeastern Asia, eastern Asia, and Europe.

When we look back at the evolution of *H. erectus*, we realize how significant this early human's achievements were. It was *H. erectus* who increased in body size with more efficient bipedalism; who embraced culture wholeheartedly as an adaptive strategy; whose brain was reshaped and increased in size to within the range of *H. sapiens;* who became a more efficient scavenger and likely hunter with a greater dependence on meat; and who apparently established more permanent living sites. In short, it was *H. erectus*, committed to a cultural way of life, who transformed hominid evolution to human evolution. As Richard Foley states, "The appearance and expansion of *H. erectus* represented a major change in adaptive strategy that influenced the subsequent process and pattern of human evolution" (1991, p. 425).

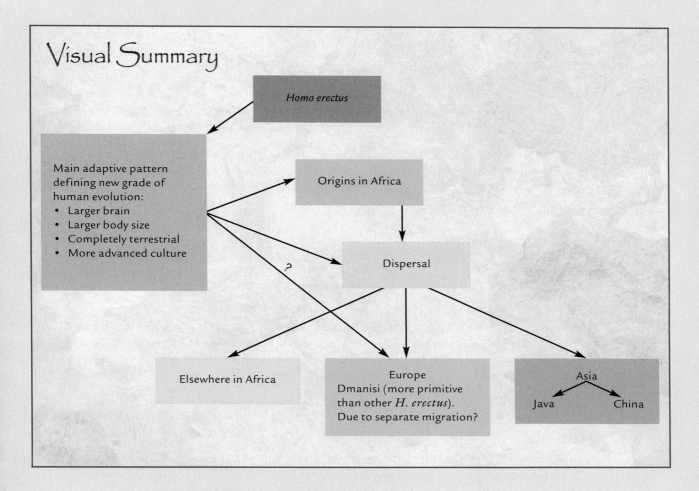

Visual Summary

Homo erectus

Main adaptive pattern defining new grade of human evolution:
- Larger brain
- Larger body size
- Completely terrestrial
- More advanced culture

Origins in Africa

Dispersal

?

Elsewhere in Africa

Europe
Dmanisi (more primitive than other *H. erectus*).
Due to separate migration?

Asia
Java   China

Summary

Homo erectus remains are found in geological contexts dating from about 1.8 million to about 200,000 years ago (and perhaps much later), a period of more than 1.5 million years. While the nature and timing of migrations are uncertain, it is likely that *H. erectus* first appeared in East Africa and later migrated to other areas. This widespread and highly successful hominid defines a new and more modern grade of human evolution, but some more limited dispersal out of Africa by a more primitive species of *Homo* now seems likely.

Historically, the first finds were made by Dubois in Java, and later discoveries came from China and Africa. Differences from early *Homo* are notable in *H. erectus'* larger brain, taller stature, robust build, and changes in facial structure and cranial buttressing.

The long period of *H. erectus* existence was marked by a remarkably uniform technology over space and time. Nevertheless, compared to earlier hominids, *H. erectus* and contemporaries introduced more sophisticated tools and probably ate novel and/or differently processed foods, using these new tools and at later sites perhaps fire as well. They were also able to move into different environments and successfully adapt to new conditions.

TABLE 9-1 | Key Hominid Fossils Discussed in This Chapter

	Site	Dates (y.a.)	Taxonomic Designation	Comments
Asia	Java (6 locales)	1,8000,000–25,000	*Homo erectus*	First *H. erectus* discovery; most finds in disturbed river terrace contexts
	China (6 locales; most significant is Zhoukoudian)	400,000+–200,000?	*Homo erectus*	Up to 40 individuals at Zhoukoudian; also, many artifacts; Zhoukoudian, however, probably not primary living site
Europe	Ceprano	900,000–800,000	*Homo erectus*	One individual; well-preserved cranium; Similar to Asian *H. erectus*
	Gran Dolina (Atapuerca, Spain)	780,000?	Quite likely not *H. erectus*; referred to by discoverers as "*Homo antecessor*"	Remains quite incomplete; oldest W. European fossil hominid discovery
	Dmanisi (Republic of Georgia)	1,800,000–1,700,000	*Homo erectus/Homo ergaster* (very primitive example—or could be classified as early *Homo*)	3 well-preserved crania plus partial mandible; among oldest *H. erectus* found anywhere
Africa	Bouri (Ethiopia)	1,000,000	*Homo erectus*	Well-preserved cranium plus postcranial bones; morphology quite similar to Asian *H. erectus*
	Nariokotome (West Turkana, Kenya)	1,600,000	*Homo erectus*, also frequently referred to as *Homo ergaster*	Nearly complete adolescent skeleton, probably of a male; shows some differences from Asian *H. erectus*
	East Turkana (Kenya)	1,800,000	*Homo erectus*, also frequently referred to as *Homo ergaster*	Well-preserved cranium plus several other postcranial remains likely coming from same group; cranium likely of female; shows several differences from Asian *H. erectus*

It's generally assumed that certain *H. erectus* populations evolved into later premodern humans, some of which, in turn, evolved into *Homo sapiens*. Evidence supporting such a series of transitions is seen in the Ngandong fossils (and others discussed in Chapter 10), which display both *H. erectus* and *H. sapiens* features. There are still many questions about *H. erectus* behavior (e.g., did they hunt? did they control fire?) and about their relationship to later hominids (was the mode of evolution gradual or rapid, and which *H. erectus* populations contributed genes?). The search for answers continues. As a further aid, the most significant hominid fossils discussed in this chapter are summarized in Table 9-1.

Critical Thinking Questions

1. Why is the nearly complete skeleton from Nariokotome so important? What kinds of evidence does it provide?

2. Assume that you are in the laboratory and have the Nariokotome skeleton as well as a skeleton of a modern human. First, given a choice, what age and sex would you choose for the human skeleton, and why? Second, what similarities and differences do the two skeletons show?

3. What fundamental questions of interpretation do the fossil hominids from Dmanisi raise? Does this evidence completely overturn the hypothesis concerning *H. erectus* dispersal from Africa? Explain why or why not.

4. How has the interpretation of fire use by *Homo erectus* at Zhoukoudian been revised in recent years? What kinds of new evidence from this site have been used in this reevaluation, and what does that tell you about modern archaeological techniques and approaches? What kinds of archaeological evidence would convince you that *H. erectus* used fire?

5. You are interpreting the hominid fossils from three sites in East Africa (Nariokotome, Olduvai, and Bouri)—all considered possible members of *H. erectus*. What sorts of evidence would lead you to conclude that there was more than one species? What would convince you that there was just one species? Why do you think some paleoanthropologists (splitters) would tend to see more than one species, while others (lumpers) would generally not? What kind of approach would you have, and why?

Media Resources

The Companion Website for *Essentials of Physical Anthropology,* Sixth Edition
http://anthropology.wadsworth.com/jurmain6e_ess

Supplement your review of this chapter by going to this text's companion website to take one of the practice quizzes, use the flash cards to master key terms, and check out the many other resources and study aids. Also visit the website to learn about important new discoveries in paleoanthropology by checking the "Latest Dirt" feature authored by Robert Jurmain.

CD-ROMs in Physical Anthropology

Wadsworth Publishing has also developed three CD-ROMs to accompany this text and enhance learning in physical anthropology (for further descriptions of these CD-ROMs, see p. xix):

Virtual Laboratories for Physical Anthropology CD-ROM, Third Edition

Basic Genetics for Anthropology CD-ROM: Principles and Applications

Hominid Fossils CD-ROM: An Interactive Atlas

For this chapter, see especially the Virtual Laboratories for Physical Anthropology CD-ROM, Third Edition, and the Hominid Fossils CD-ROM: An Interactive Atlas.

Readings of Interest

Gore, Rick. 2002. "The First Pioneer? A New Find Shakes the Human Family Tree." *National Geographic* 202 (August), Front Supplement (not paginated).

Klein, Richard. 1999. *The Human Career.* 2nd ed. Chicago: University of Chicago Press.

Leonard, William R. 2002. "Food for Thought." *Scientific American* 287(December):106–115.

Shapiro, Harry L. 1980. *Peking Man.* New York: Simon & Schuster.

Wong, Kate. 2003. "Stranger in a New Land." *Scientific American* 299 (November): 74–83.

10 | Premodern Humans

Introduction

Go to the following CD-ROMs for interactive activities and exercises on topics covered in this chapter:

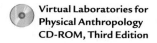

Virtual Laboratories for Physical Anthropology CD-ROM, Third Edition

Hominid Fossils CD-ROM: An Interactive Atlas

What do you think when you hear the term Neandertal? Most people think of imbecilic, bent-over brutes. Yet, Neandertals were quite advanced; they had brains at least as large as ours, and they showed numerous sophisticated cultural capabilities. Moreover, they definitely weren't bent over, but were fully erect (as hominids had been for millions of years previously). Indeed, Neandertals and their immediate predecessors could easily be called "human."

And that brings us to perhaps the most basic of all questions: What does it mean to be "human"? The use of this term is highly varied, encompassing religious, philosophical, and biological considerations. As you know, physical anthropologists primarily concentrate on the biological aspects of the human organism. Living people are all members of one species, all showing a common anatomical pattern and similar behavioral potentials. We call hominids like us "fully modern humans," and the origin of forms essentially identical to living people will be discussed in the next chapter.

When in our evolutionary past can we say that our predecessors were obviously human? Certainly, the further back we go in time, hominids look less like contemporary *Homo sapiens.* This is, of course, exactly what we would expect in an evolutionary sequence. Moreover, the hominid fossil record, which has become increasingly rich in recent years, now provides a detailed picture of this sequence.

We saw in the previous chapter that *Homo erectus* took crucial steps in the human direction and defined a new grade of human evolution. In this chapter, we review those hominids who continued this journey. Both physically and behaviorally, they are much like modern humans; yet, they still show several significant differences. Thus, while most paleoanthropologists are comfortable calling these hominids "human," this recognition is qualified in order to set them apart from fully modern people. And so, we'll refer to these fascinating immediate predecessors as "premodern humans."

When, Where, and What

THE PLEISTOCENE

Middle Pleistocene The portion of the Pleistocene epoch beginning 780,000 y.a. and ending 125,000 y.a.

Upper Pleistocene The portion of the Pleistocene epoch beginning 125,000 y.a. and ending approximately 10,000 y.a.

Most of the hominids discussed in this chapter lived during the **Middle Pleistocene,** a period beginning 780,000 y.a. and ending 125,000 y.a. In addition, some of the later premodern humans, especially the Neandertals, lived well into the **Upper Pleistocene** (125,000–10,000 y.a.).

The Pleistocene has been called the Ice Age because, as had occurred before in geological history, periodic advances and retreats of massive continental glaciations marked this epoch. During the glacial interludes, temperatures were very cold and ice accumulated, since more snow fell each year than melted. We should mention that there were numerous advances and retreats of ice; in fact, during the Pleistocene, at least 15 major and 50 minor glacial advances have been documented in Europe (Tattersall et al., 1988).

Moreover, it must be remembered that these **glaciations,** which enveloped huge swaths of Europe, Asia, and North America (as well as Antarctica), were mostly confined to northern latitudes. As a result, hominids (all still restricted to the Old World) were severely impacted as the climate, flora, and animal life shifted during these Pleistocene oscillations. For the hominids living during this time, the most dramatic of these effects were in Europe and northern Asia —less so in southern Asia and in Africa.

Further south, climates also fluctuated, but in Africa, most notably, the main effects related to changing rainfall patterns. During glacial periods, the climate in Africa became more arid, while during **interglacials,** rainfall increased. The changing availability of food resources certainly affected hominids in Africa, but perhaps even more importantly, migration routes also swung back and forth. In North Africa during glacial periods, the Sahara expanded and blocked migration in and out of sub-Saharan Africa (Lahr and Foley, 1998) (Fig. 10-1).

In Eurasia, as well, glacial advances greatly affected migration routes. As the ice sheets expanded, sea levels dropped, more northern areas became uninhabitable, and some key passages between areas became blocked by glaciers. For example, during glacial peaks, much of western Europe would have been cut off from the rest of Eurasia (Fig. 10-2).

During the warmer (and, in the south, wetter) interglacials, the ice sheets shrank, sea levels rose, and certain migration routes reopened (e.g., from central into western Europe). Clearly, to understand Middle Pleistocene hominids, it is crucial to view them within their shifting Pleistocene world.

glaciations Climatic intervals when continental ice sheets cover much of the northern continents. Glaciations are associated with colder temperatures in northern latitudes and more arid conditions in southern latitudes (most notably in Africa).

interglacials Climatic intervals when continental ice sheets are retreating, eventually becoming much reduced in size. Interglacials in northern latitudes are associated with warmer temperatures, while in southern latitudes the climate becomes wetter.

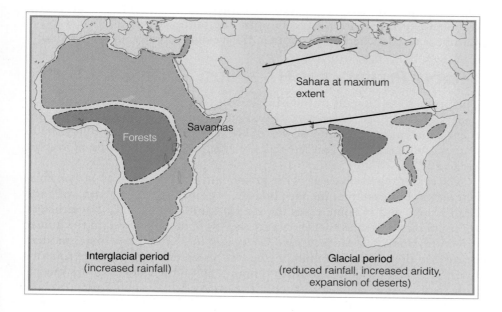

FIGURE 10-1 Changing Pleistocene environments in Africa.

Sahara at maximum extent

Forests

Savannas

Interglacial period (increased rainfall)

Glacial period (reduced rainfall, increased aridity, expansion of deserts)

FIGURE 10-2 Changing Pleistocene environments in Eurasia. Green areas show regions of likely hominid occupation. Blue areas are major glaciers. Arrows indicate likely migration routes

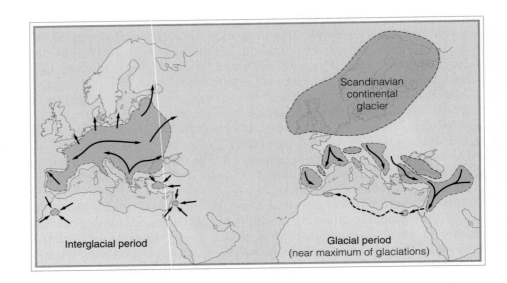

DISPERSAL OF MIDDLE PLEISTOCENE HOMINIDS

Like their *Homo erectus* predecessors, later hominids were widely distributed in the Old World, with discoveries coming from three continents (Africa, Asia, and Europe). For the first time, in fact, it appears that Europe became more permanently and densely occupied (Middle Pleistocene hominids have been discovered widely from England, France, Spain, Germany, Italy, Hungary, and Greece). Africa, as well, probably continued as a central area of hominid occupation, and finds have come from North, East, and South Africa. Finally, Asia has yielded several important finds (most especially from China) (see Fig. 10-4, on pp. 248–249). We should point out, however, that these Middle Pleistocene premodern humans didn't vastly extend the geographical range of *Homo erectus*—but largely replaced the earlier hominids in habitats previously exploited. One exception appears to be the more successful occupation of Europe, a region where earlier hominids have only sporadically been found.

MIDDLE PLEISTOCENE HOMINIDS: TERMINOLOGY

The premodern humans of the Middle Pleistocene (i.e., after 780,000 y.a.) generally succeeded *H. erectus*. However, in some areas, especially in Asia, there apparently was a long period of coexistence, lasting 300,000 years or longer (you'll recall the very late dates for the Javanese Ngandong *H. erectus;* see p. 227).

The earlier representatives of the premoderns retain several *H. erectus* characteristics. For example, the face is large, the brows are projected, the forehead is low, and in some cases the cranial vault is still thick. Nevertheless, there are other features that show that they were more derived (in the human direction) than their predecessors. Compared to *Homo erectus*, more modern features in premodern hominids include increased brain size, a more rounded brain case (i.e., maximum breadth is higher up on the sides), a more vertical nose, and a less angled back of the skull (occipital). We should note that the maximum span of time encompassed by Middle Pleistocene premodern humans is at least 500,000 years. Thus, it is no surprise that certain temporal trends are apparent. The later representatives, for example, show more brain expansion and a less angled occipital than do earlier forms.

So, premodern humans were a diverse group dispersed over three continents. How to classify them has been in dispute for decades, and disagreements still exist. However, a growing consensus has recently emerged. Beginning perhaps as early as 850,000 y.a. and extending up to about 200,000 y.a., the fossils from Africa and Europe are placed within *Homo heidelbergensis* (named after a fossil found in Germany in 1907).

Until recently, many researchers regarded these fossils as early but more primitive members of *Homo sapiens*. In recognition of this somewhat transitional status, they were called "archaic *Homo sapiens*," but most paleoanthropologists find this terminology unsatisfactory. For example, Phillip Rightmire concludes that "simply lumping diverse ancient groups with living populations obscures their differences" (1998, p. 226). In our own discussion, we recognize *H. heidelbergensis* in this transitional period. Keep in mind, however, that this species was probably ancestral to both modern humans and Neandertals. Whether these Middle Pleistocene hominid samples actually represent a fully separate species in the *biological* sense (i.e., following the biological species concept; see p. 95) is debatable. Still, it's useful to give them a separate name to make this important stage of human evolution more easily identifiable. (We'll return to this issue later in the chapter when we discuss the theoretical implications in more detail.)

Premodern Humans of the Middle Pleistocene

AFRICA

In Africa, premodern fossils have been found at several sites (Figs. 10-3 and 10-4). One of the best known is Broken Hill (Kabwe). At this site in Zambia, a complete cranium, together with other cranial and postcranial elements belonging to several individuals, was discovered. In this and other African premodern specimens, a mixture of older and more recent traits can be seen. Dating estimates of Broken Hill and most of the other premodern fossils from Africa have ranged throughout the Middle and Upper Pleistocene, but recent estimates have given dates for most of the localities in the range of 600,000–125,000 y.a.

A total of eight other crania from South and East Africa also show a combination of retained ancestral with more derived (modern) characteristics, and they are all mentioned in the literature as being similar to Broken Hill. The most important of these African finds come from the sites of Florisbad and Elandsfontein in South Africa, Laetoli in Tanzania, and Bodo in Ethiopia (see Fig. 10-4).

Bodo is the most significant of these other African fossils, as it is a nearly complete cranium and is dated to quite early in the Middle Pleistocene (estimated at 600,000 y.a.). The Bodo cranium is also interesting because it shows a distinctive pattern of cut marks, similar to modifications seen in butchered animal bones. Researchers have thus hypothesized that the Bodo individual was

FIGURE 10-3 Broken Hill (Kabwe). Note the very heavy supraorbital torus.

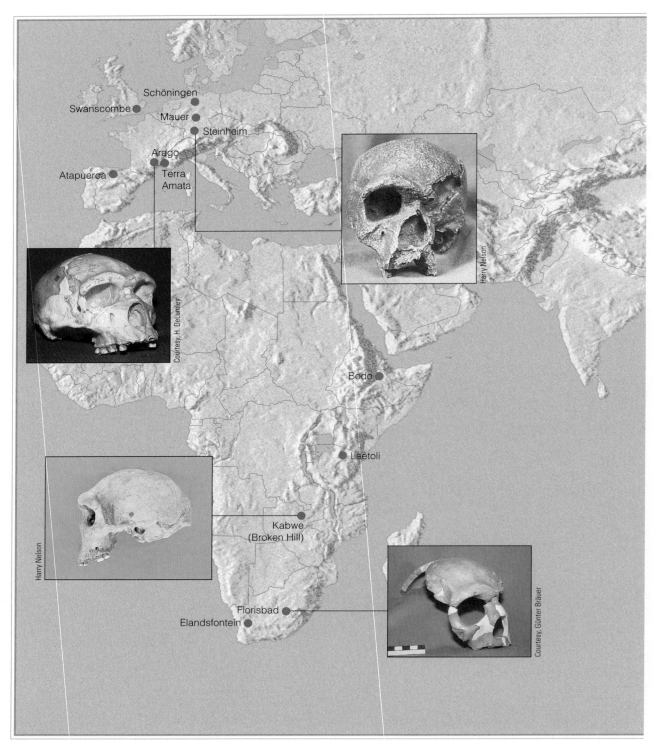

FIGURE 10-4 Fossil discoveries and archaeological localities of Middle Pleistocene premodern hominids.

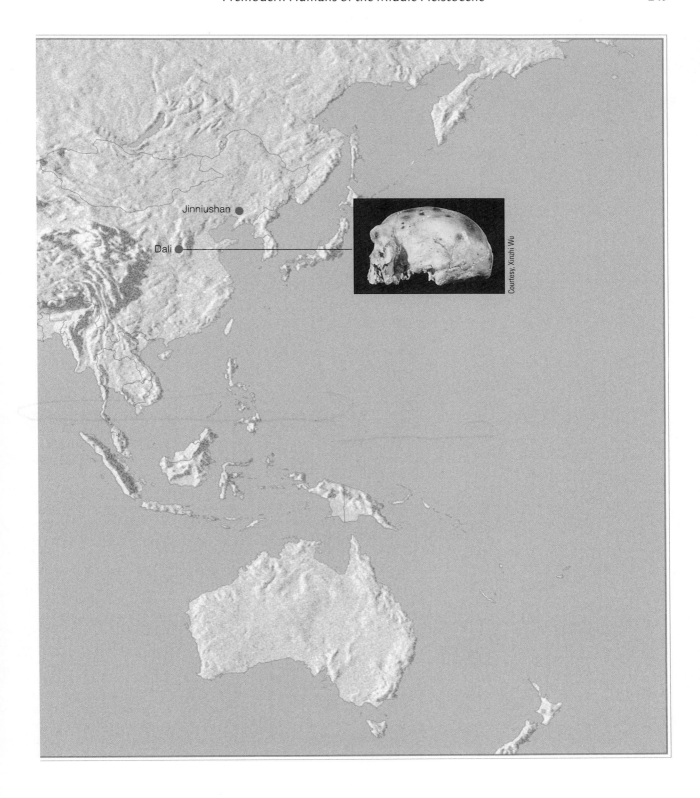

Courtesy, Xinzhi Wu

Quick Review	Key Middle Pleistocene Premodern Human (*H. heidelbergensis*) Fossils from Africa	
Site	**Dates (y.a.)**	**Human Remains** *Homo heidelbergensis*
Bodo (Ethiopia)	Middle Pleistocene (600,000)	Incomplete skull, part of braincase
Broken Hill (Kabwe) (Zambia)	Late Middle Pleistocene; (130,000 or older)	Nearly complete cranium, cranial fragments of second individual, miscellaneous postcranial bones

defleshed by other hominids, but for what purpose is not clear. Perhaps it was cannibalism, perhaps some other purpose. In any case, this is the earliest evidence of deliberate bone processing of hominids by hominids (White, 1986).

The general similarities in all these African premodern fossils indicate a close relationship between them, almost certainly representing a single species (most commonly referred to as *H. heidelbergensis*). Moreover, these African premodern humans are quite similar to those found in Europe.

EUROPE

More fossil hominids of Middle Pleistocene age have been found in Europe than in any other region. Perhaps this is because more archaeologists have been searching longer in Europe than elsewhere. In any case, during the Middle Pleistocene, Europe was more widely and consistently occupied than it was earlier in human evolution.

The time range of European premoderns extends the full length of the Middle Pleistocene and beyond. At the earlier end, the Gran Dolina finds from northern Spain (discussed in Chapter 9; see p. 233) are definitely not *Homo erectus*. As proposed by Spanish researchers, they may be members of yet another hominid species. Conversely, they may represent the same *grade* of hominid discussed in this chapter—that is, a population of premodern humans. As noted in the previous chapter, the Gran Dolina hominids might be representative of the same species (*H. heidelbergensis*) as their later European successors (a view also proposed by Rightmire, 1998). If this interpretation should be further confirmed, Gran Dolina would represent the earliest well-dated occurrence of *H. heidelbergensis* (dating back as early as 850,000 y.a.).

More recent and more completely studied *H. heidelbergensis* fossils have been found throughout much of Europe. Examples of these finds come from Steinheim and Ehringsdorf (Germany), Swanscombe (England), Arago (France), and Atapuerca (Spain). Like their African counterparts, these European premoderns show retention of *H. erectus* traits mixed with more derived ones (e.g., increased cranial capacity, more rounded occiput, parietal expansion, and reduced tooth size) (Fig. 10-5).

The hominids from Atapuerca are especially interesting. These finds come from another cave in the same area as the Gran Dolina discoveries. Dated to approximately 350,000 y.a., a total of at least 28 individuals have been recov-

(b)

(a)

FIGURE 10-5 Cast of an archaic *Homo heidelbergensis* skull from Germany (Steinheim). (a) Frontal view showing damaged skull. (b) Basal view showing how the *foramen magnum* was enlarged, apparently for removal of the brain, perhaps for dietary or ritualistic purposes.

ered from a site called Sima de los Huesos (literally meaning "pile of bones"). In fact, with more than 4,000 fossil fragments recovered, Sima de los Huesos contains more than 80 percent of all the Middle Pleistocene hominid remains from the whole world (Bermudez de Castro et al., 2004)! Excavations continue at this remarkable site, where bones have somehow accumulated within a deep chamber inside a cave. From initial descriptions, the hominid morphology has been interpreted as showing several indications of an early Neandertal-like pattern (arching browridges, projecting midface, and other features) (Rightmire, 1998).

Quick Review	Key Middle Pleistocene Premodern Human (*H. heidelbergensis*) Fossils from Europe	
Site	**Dates (y.a.)**	**Human Remains**
Arago (Tautavel, France)	400,000–300,000; date uncertain	Face; parietal perhaps from same person; many cranial fragments; up to 23 individuals represented
Atapuerca (Sima de los Huesos, northern Spain)	320,000–190,000, probably 300,000	Minimum of 28 individuals, including some nearly complete crania
Steinheim (Germany)	300,000–250,000; date uncertain	Nearly complete skull, lacking mandible
Swanscombe (England)	300,000–250,000; date uncertain	Occipital and parietals

Quick Review	Key Middle Pleistocene Premodern Human (*H. heidelbergensis*) Fossils from Asia	
Site	**Dates (y.a.)**	**Human Remains**
Dali (China)	Late Middle Pleistocene (230,000–180,000)	Nearly complete skull
Jinniushan (China)	Late Middle Pleistocene (200,000)	Partial skeleton, including a cranium

ASIA

China   Like their contemporaries in Europe and Africa, Chinese premodern specimens also display both earlier and later characteristics. Chinese paleoanthropologists suggest that the more ancestral traits, such as a sagittal ridge (see p. 222) and flattened nasal bones, are shared with *H. erectus* fossils from Zhoukoudian. They also point out that some of these features can be found in modern *H. sapiens* in China today, indicating substantial genetic continuity. That is, some Chinese researchers have argued that anatomically modern Chinese did not evolve from *H. sapiens* in either Europe or Africa, evolving instead specifically in China from a separate *H. erectus* lineage. Whether such regional evolution occurred or whether anatomically modern migrants from Africa displaced local populations is the subject of a major ongoing debate in paleoanthropology. This important controversy will be the central focus of the next chapter.

Dali, the most complete skull of the late Middle or early Upper Pleistocene fossils in China, displays *H. erectus* and *H. sapiens* traits, and it also has a relatively small cranial capacity (1,120 cm^3). Like Dali, several other Chinese specimens combine both earlier and later traits. In addition, a partial skeleton from Jinniushan, in northeast China, has been given a provisional date of 200,000 y.a. (Tiemel et al., 1994). The cranial capacity is fairly large (approximately 1,260 cm^3), and the walls of the braincase are thin—both modern features and somewhat unexpected in an individual this ancient (if the dating estimate is indeed correct). How to classify these Chinese Middle Pleistocene hominids has been a subject of debate and controversy. Recently, however, a leading paleoanthropologist has concluded that they are regional variants of *Homo heidelbergensis* (Rightmire, 2004).

A Review of Middle Pleistocene Evolution

The premodern human fossils from Africa and Europe are more similar to each other than they are to the hominids from Asia. The mix of some ancestral characteristics (retained from *Homo erectus* ancestors) with more derived features gives the African and European fossils a distinctive look; they're usually referred to as *H. heidelbergensis*.

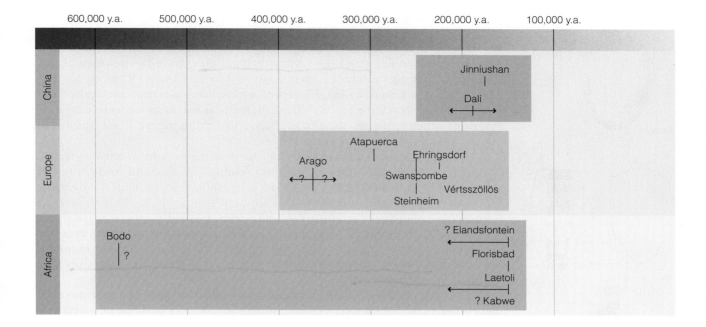

The situation in Asia is less tidy. To some researchers, the remains, especially those from Jinniushan, appear more modern than contemporaries from either Europe or Africa. This observation is why Chinese paleoanthropologists and some American colleagues conclude they're early members of *H. sapiens*. Other researchers (e.g., Rightmire, 1998, 2004) suggest that they represent a regional branch of *H. heidelbergensis*.

The Pleistocene world forced many small populations into geographical isolation. Most of these regional populations no doubt died out. Some, however, did evolve, and their descendants are likely a major part of the later hominid fossil record. In Africa, *H. heidelbergensis* is hypothesized to have evolved into modern *H. sapiens*. In Europe, *H. heidelbergensis* evolved into Neandertals. Meanwhile, the Chinese premodern populations may all have met with extinction. At present, however, there is no consensus regarding the status or the likely fate of these enigmatic Asian Middle Pleistocene hominids (Fig. 10-6).

FIGURE 10-6 Time line of Middle Pleistocene hominids. Note that most dates are approximations. Question marks indicate those estimates that are most tentative.

Middle Pleistocene Culture

The Acheulian technology of *H. erectus* carried over into the Middle Pleistocene with relatively little change until near the end of the period, when it became slightly more sophisticated. Bone, a very useful tool material, was apparently practically unused during this time. Stone flake tools similar to those of the earlier era persisted, perhaps in greater variety. Some of the later premodern humans in Africa and Europe invented a method—the Levallois technique (Fig. 10-7)—for controlling flake size and shape. Requiring several coordinated steps, this was no mean feat and suggests increased cognitive abilities in later premodern populations.

Nodule

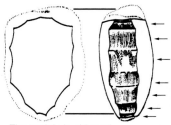

The nodule is chipped
on the perimeter.

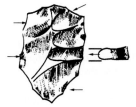

Flakes are radially
removed from top surface.

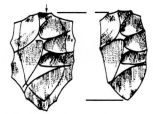

A final blow at one end
removes a large flake.

FIGURE 10-7 The Levallois
technique.

Interpreting the distribution of artifacts during the later Middle Pleistocene has generated considerable discussion among archaeologists. We noted in Chapter 9 that there is a general geographical distribution characteristic of the Lower Pleistocene, with bifaces (mostly hand axes) found quite often at sites in Africa, but only rarely at sites in most of Asia and not at all among the rich assemblage at Zhoukoudian. Moreover, where hand axes proliferate, the stone tool industry is referred to as Acheulian, while at localities without hand axes, various other terms are used (e.g., "chopper/chopping tool"—a misnomer, since most of the tools are actually flakes).

Acheulian assemblages have been found at many African sites as well as numerous European ones (e.g., Swanscombe in England and Arago in France). Even though there are broad geographical patterns in the distribution of what we call Acheulian, this shouldn't blind us to the considerable intraregional diversity in stone tool industries. Clearly, a variety of European sites do show a typical Acheulian complex, rich in bifacial hand axes and cleavers. However, at other contemporaneous sites in Germany and Hungary, a variety of small retouched flake tools and flaked pebbles of various sizes were found, but no hand axes.

It thus appears that different stone tool industries coexisted in some areas for long periods. Various explanations (Villa, 1983) have been offered to account for this apparent diversity: (1) The tool industries were produced by different peoples (i.e., different cultures, perhaps hominids that also differed biologically); (2) the tool industries represent different types of activities carried out at separate locales; (3) the presence (or absence) of specific tool types—bifaces—represents the availability (or unavailability) of appropriate local stone resources.

Premodern human populations continued to live both in caves and in open-air sites, but may have increased their use of caves. Did these hominids control fire? Klein (1989), interpreting archaeological evidence from France, Germany, and Hungary, suggests that they did. Moreover, Chinese archaeologists insist that many Middle Pleistocene sites in China contain evidence of human-controlled fire. However, not everyone is convinced.

That Middle Pleistocene hominids built temporary structures is revealed by concentrations of bones, stones, and artifacts at several sites. There's also evidence that they exploited many different food sources, such as fruits, vegetables, fish, seeds, nuts, and bird eggs, each in its own season. Marine life was also exploited. The most detailed reconstruction of Middle Pleistocene life in Europe comes from Terra Amata, a site in what is now the city of Nice, in southern France (de Lumley and de Lumley, 1973; Villa, 1983). This site provides fascinating evidence relating to short-term, seasonal visits by hominid groups, who built flimsy shelters, gathered plants, exploited marine resources, and possibly hunted medium to large-sized mammals.

The hunting capabilities of premodern humans, as for earlier hominids, remain open to dispute. So far, the evidence doesn't clearly establish widely practiced advanced abilities. In earlier professional discussions (as well as in earlier editions of our texts), archaeological evidence from Terra Amata and Torralba and Ambrona (in Spain) was used to argue for advanced hunting skills. However, reconstruction of these sites by Richard Klein and others has now cast doubt on those conclusions. Once again, we see that application of scientific rigor (which is simply good critical thinking) makes us question previously held assumptions, and sometimes we have to conclude that other less dramatic (and less romantic) explanations fit the evidence as well as or better than those based on initial imaginative scenarios.

A recent and exceptional find is now again challenging some assumptions regarding hunting capabilities of premodern humans in Europe. From the site of Schöningen in Germany, three remarkably well-preserved wooden spears were discovered in 1995 (Thieme, 1997). As we have noted before, fragile organic remains (such as wood) can rarely be preserved more than a few hundred years; yet these beautifully crafted implements are provisionally dated to 400,000–380,000 y.a.! Beyond this surprisingly ancient date, the spears are intriguing on a variety of other counts. Firstly, they are all large (about 6 feet long), very finely made of hard spruce wood, and expertly balanced. Each spear would have required considerable planning, time, and skill to manufacture. Further, the weapons were most likely used as throwing spears, presumably to hunt large animals. Of interest in this context, bones of numerous horses were also recovered at Schöningen. Archaeologist Hartmut Thieme has thus concluded that "the spears strongly suggest that systematic hunting, involving foresight, planning and the use of appropriate technology, was part of the behavioural repertoire of pre-modern hominids" (1997, p. 807). These extraordinary spears from Schöningen thus make a strong case for advanced hunting skills practiced by at least some Middle Pleistocene populations.

As documented by the fossil remains as well as artifactual evidence from archaeological sites, the long period of transitional hominids in Europe was to continue well into the Upper Pleistocene (after 125,000 y.a.). However, here the evolution of premodern humans was to take a unique turn with the appearance and expansion of the Neandertals.

Neandertals: Premodern Humans of the Upper Pleistocene

Since their discovery more than a century ago, the Neandertals have haunted the best-laid theories of paleoanthropologists. They fit into the general scheme of human evolution, and yet they are misfits. Classified either as *H. sapiens* or a sister species, they are like us and yet different. It is not an easy task to put them in their place. Many anthropologists classify Neandertals as *H. sapiens,* but they are included as a subspecies, *Homo sapiens neanderthalensis** (the subspecies for anatomically modern *H. sapiens* is designated as *Homo sapiens sapiens*). However, not all experts agree with this interpretation.

While Neandertal fossil remains have been found at dates approaching 130,000 y.a., in the following discussion of Neandertals, we focus on those populations that lived especially during the last major glaciation, which began about 75,000 y.a. and ended about 10,000 y.a. (Fig. 10-8). We should also note that the evolutionary roots of Neandertals apparently reach quite far back in western Europe, as evidenced by the 300,000-year-old remains from Sima de los Huesos, Atapuerca, in northern Spain. The majority of

---

**Thal,* meaning "valley," is the old spelling, but because of rules of taxonomic naming, this spelling is retained in the formal species designation (note, though, that the "h" was *never* pronounced). The modern spelling is *tal* and is now used this way in Germany; we follow contemporary usage in the text with the spelling "Neandertal."

FIGURE 10-8 Correlation of Pleistocene subdivisions with archaeological industries and hominids. Note that the geological divisions are separate and different from the archaeological stages (e.g., Upper Pleistocene is *not* synonymous with Upper Paleolithic).

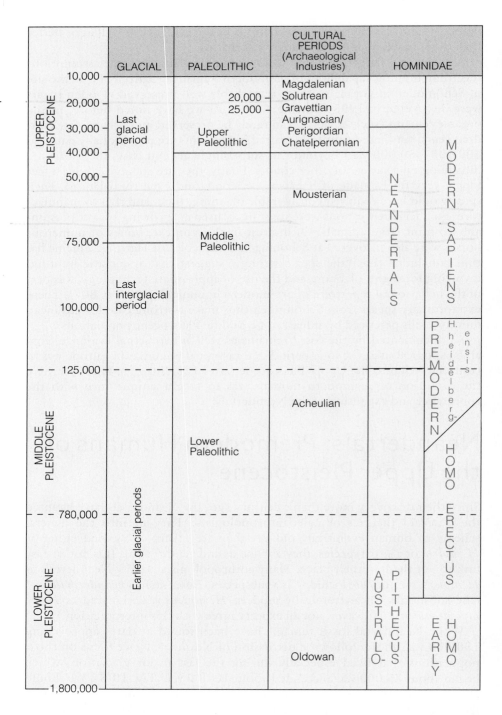

fossils have been found in Europe, where they have been most studied, and our description of Neandertals is based primarily on those specimens from western Europe, who are usually called *classic* Neandertals. Not all Neandertals—including others from eastern Europe and western Asia and those from the interglacial that preceded the last glacial—entirely conform to our description of the classic morphology. They tend to be less robust, perhaps because the climate in which they lived was not as cold as western Europe during the last glaciation.

One striking feature of Neandertals is brain size, which in these hominids actually was larger than that of *H. sapiens* today. The average for contemporary *H. sapiens* is between 1,300 and 1,400 cm³, while for Neandertals it was 1,520 cm³. The larger size may be associated with the metabolic efficiency of a larger brain in cold weather. The Inuit (Eskimo), also living in very cold areas, have a larger average brain size than most other modern human populations. It should also be pointed out that the larger brain size in both premodern and contemporary human populations adapted to *cold* climates is partially correlated with larger body size, which has also evolved among these groups (see Chapter 12).

The classic Neandertal cranium is large, long, low, and bulging at the sides. Viewed from the side, the occipital bone is somewhat bun-shaped, but the marked occipital angle typical of many *H. erectus* crania is absent. The forehead rises more vertically than that of *H. erectus*, and the browridges arch over the orbits instead of forming a straight bar (Fig. 10-9).

Compared with anatomically modern humans, the Neandertal face stands out. It projects almost as if it were pulled forward. This feature can be seen when the distance of the nose and teeth from the eye orbits is compared with that of modern *H. sapiens*. Postcranially, Neandertals were very robust, barrel-chested, and powerfully muscled. This robust skeletal structure, in fact, dominates hominid evolution from *H. erectus* through all premodern forms. Nevertheless, the Neandertals appear particularly robust, with shorter limbs than seen in most modern *H. sapiens* populations. Both the facial anatomy and robust postcranial structure of Neandertals have been interpreted by Erik Trinkaus, of Washington University in St. Louis, as adaptations to rigorous living in a cold climate.

For about 100,000 years, Neandertals lived in Europe and western Asia (see. Fig. 10-12, on pp. 260–261), and their coming and going has raised more questions and controversies than perhaps any other hominid group. As noted, Neandertal forebears date back to the later premodern populations of the Middle Pleistocene. But these were transitional forms, and it's not until the Upper Pleistocene that Neandertals become fully recognizable.

FRANCE AND SPAIN

One of the most important Neandertal discoveries was made in 1908 at La Chapelle-aux-Saints in southwestern France. A nearly complete skeleton was found buried in a shallow grave in a **flexed** position, with several fragments of nonhuman long bones placed over the head, and over them, a bison leg. Around the body were flint tools and broken animal bones.

The skeleton was turned over for study to a well-known French paleontologist, Marcellin Boule, who depicted the La Chapelle Neandertal as a brutish, bent-kneed, not fully erect biped. As a result of this exaggerated interpretation, some scholars, and certainly the general public, concluded that all Neandertals were highly primitive creatures.

Why did Boule draw these conclusions from the La Chapelle skeleton? Apparently, he misconstrued Neandertal posture because of osteoarthritis in

flexed The position of the body in a bent orientation, with arms and legs drawn up to the chest.

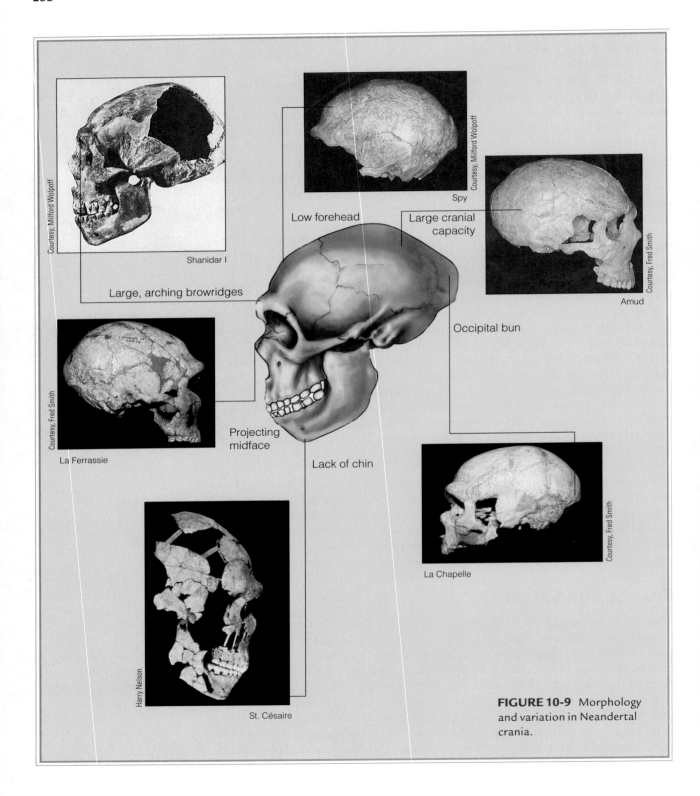

Shanidar I

Spy

Low forehead

Large cranial capacity

Amud

Large, arching browridges

Occipital bun

La Ferrassie

Projecting midface

Lack of chin

La Chapelle

St. Césaire

FIGURE 10-9 Morphology and variation in Neandertal crania.

the spine of this adult male. In addition, and probably more important, Boule and his contemporaries found it difficult to accept fully as a human ancestor an individual who appeared in any way to depart from the modern pattern.

The skull of this male, who was possibly at least 40 years of age when he died, is very large, with a cranial capacity of 1,620 cm³. As is typical for western European "classic" forms, the vault is low and long, the supraorbital ridges are immense, with the typical Neandertal arched shape, the forehead is low and retreating, and the face is long and projecting. The back of the skull is protuberant and bun-shaped (Figs. 10-9 and 10-10).

The La Chapelle skeleton isn't a typical Neandertal, but is an unusually robust male that "evidently represents an extreme in the Neandertal range of variation" (Brace et al., 1979, p. 117). Unfortunately, this skeleton, which Boule claimed didn't even walk completely erect, was widely accepted as "Mr. Neandertal." But not all Neandertal individuals express the suite of "classic Neandertal" traits to the degree seen in this one.

Another Neandertal site excavated recently in southern France has revealed further fascinating details relating to Neandertal behavior. From the 100,000- to 120,000-year-old Moula-Guercy Cave site, Alban Defleur, Tim White, and colleagues have analyzed 78 broken skeletal fragments from probably six individuals (Defleur et al., 1999). The intriguing aspect of these remains concerns *how* they were broken. Detailed analysis of cut marks, pits, scars, and other features clearly suggests that these individuals were *processed*—that is, they "were defleshed and disarticulated. After this, the marrow cavity was exposed by a hammer-on-anvil technique" (Defleur et al., 1999, p. 131). Moreover, the nonhuman bones at this site, especially the deer remains, were processed in an identical fashion. In other words, the Moula-Guercy Neandertals provide the best-documented evidence thus far of Neandertal *cannibalism*.

Some of the most recent of the western European Neandertals come from St. Césaire in southwestern France and are dated at about 35,000 y.a. (Fig. 10-11). The bones were recovered from a bed including discarded chipped blades, hand axes, and other stone tools of an **Upper Paleolithic** tool industry associated with Neandertals. Another late site is located in central Europe, where radiocarbon dating has indicated that the most recent Neandertal remains at Vindija, in Croatia (discussed shortly), are about 28,000 to 29,000 years old (Smith et al., 1999). If this date is further confirmed, then Vindija would gain the distinction of having the most recent Neandertals thus far discovered.

Yet a more recent site in Portugal has recently been interpreted as showing hybridization between Neandertals and modern *Homo sapiens*. (We will discuss this intriguing suggestion in more detail in Chapter 11.)

The St. Césaire and Vindija sites are important for several reasons. Anatomically modern humans were living in central and western Europe by about 35,000 y.a. or a bit earlier. Therefore, it is possible that Neandertals and modern *H. sapiens* were living in close proximity for several thousand years (Fig. 10-13). How did these two groups interact? Evidence from a number of French sites indicates that Neandertals borrowed technological methods and tools (such as blades) from the anatomically modern populations and thereby modified their own tools, creating a new industry, the **Chatelperronian.**

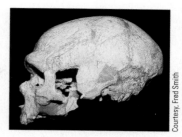

FIGURE 10-10 La Chapelle-aux-Saints. Note the occipital bun, projecting face, and low vault.

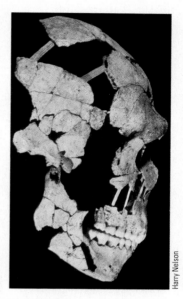

FIGURE 10-11 St. Césaire, among the "last" Neandertals.

Upper Paleolithic A cultural period usually associated with modern humans (but also found with some Neandertals) and distinguished by technological innovation in various stone tool industries. Best known from western Europe, similar industries are also known from central and eastern Europe and Africa.

Chatelperronian Pertaining to an Upper Paleolithic industry found in France and Spain, containing blade tools and associated with Neandertals.

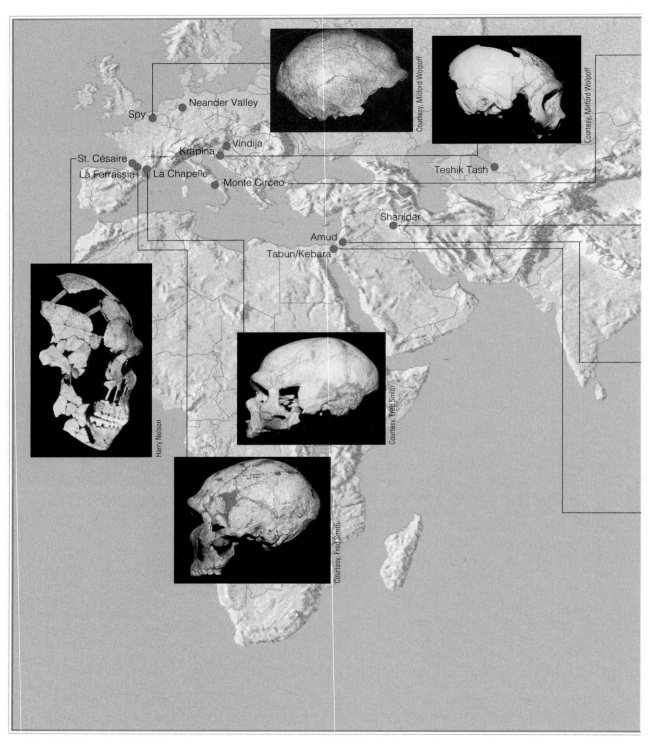

FIGURE 10-12 Fossil discoveries of Neandertals.

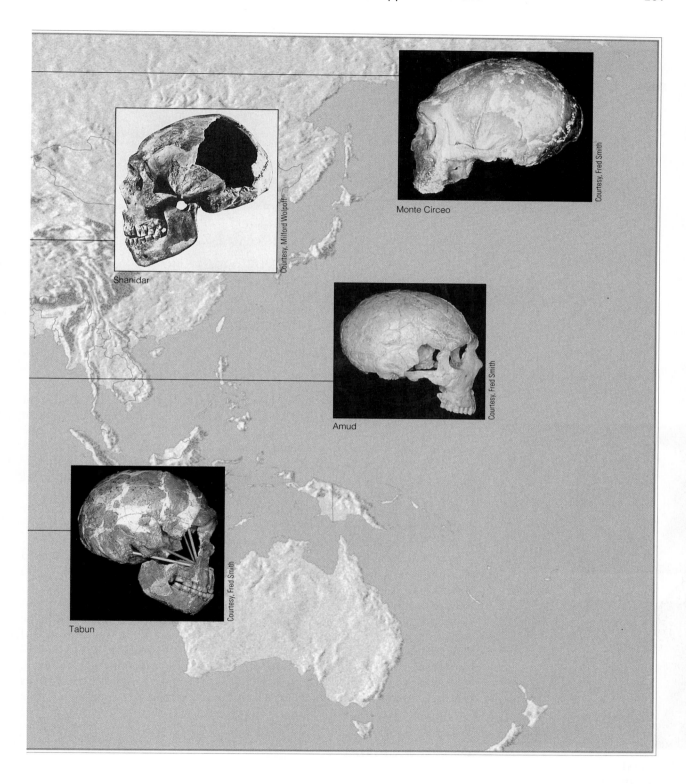

Shanidar

Courtesy, Milford Wolpoff

Monte Circeo

Courtesy, Fred Smith

Amud

Courtesy, Fred Smith

Tabun

Courtesy, Fred Smith

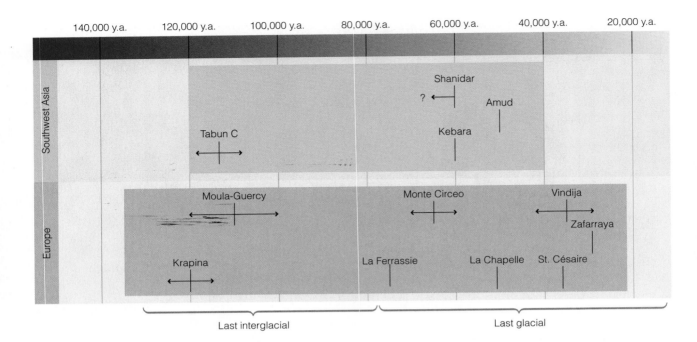

Last interglacial   Last glacial

FIGURE 10-13 Time line for Neandertal fossil discoveries.

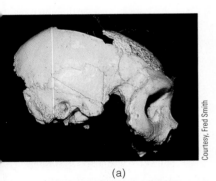

(a)

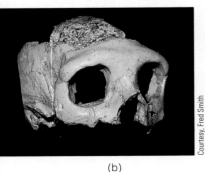

(b)

FIGURE 10-14 Krapina C.
(a) Lateral view showing characteristic Neandertal traits. (b) Three-quarters view.

CENTRAL EUROPE

There are quite a few other European classic Neandertals, including significant finds in central Europe (see Fig. 10-12). At Krapina, Croatia, an abundance of bones (1,000 fragments representing up to 70 individuals) and 1,000 stone tools or flakes have been recovered (Trinkaus and Shipman, 1992). Krapina is an old site, perhaps the earliest showing the full "classic" Neandertal morphology, dating back to the beginning of the Upper Pleistocene (estimated at 130,000–110,000 y.a.). Moreover, despite the relatively early date, the characteristic Neandertal features of the Krapina specimens (although less robust) are similar to the western European finds (Fig. 10-14). Krapina is also important as an intentional burial site, one of the oldest on record.

About 30 miles from Krapina, Neandertal fossils have also been discovered at Vindija. The site is an excellent source of faunal, cultural, and hominid materials stratified in *sequence* throughout much of the Upper Pleistocene. Neandertal fossils consisting of some 35 specimens are dated between about 42,000 and 28,000 y.a. (As already mentioned, the latter date would be among the most recent of all Neandertal discoveries.) Even though some of their features approach the morphology of early modern south-central European *H. sapiens,* the overall pattern is definitely Neandertal. Nevertheless, these modified Neandertal features, such as smaller browridges and slight chin development, have led some researchers to suggest a possible evolutionary trend toward modern *H. sapiens.*

WESTERN ASIA

Israel In addition to European Neandertals, there are numerous important discoveries from southwest Asia. Several specimens from Israel display some modern features and are less robust than the classic Neandertals of Europe, but again, the overall pattern is Neandertal. The best known of these discover-

FIGURE 10-15 Excavation of the Tabun Cave, Mt. Carmel, Israel.

ies is from Tabun (Mugharet-et-Tabun, "Cave of the Oven") at Mt. Carmel, a short drive south from Haifa (Fig. 10-15). Tabun, excavated in the early 1930s, yielded a female skeleton, recently dated by thermoluminescence (TL) at about 120,000–110,000 y.a. If this dating is accurate, Neandertals at Tabun were generally contemporary with early modern *H. sapiens* found in nearby caves. (TL dating is discussed on p. 290.)

A more recent Neandertal burial, a male discovered in 1983, comes from Kebara, a neighboring cave of Tabun at Mt. Carmel. A partial skeleton, dated to 60,000 y.a., contains the most complete Neandertal pelvis so far recovered. Also recovered at Kebara is a hyoid bone, the first from a Neandertal, and this find is especially important from the point of view of reconstructing language capabilities.*

Iraq A most remarkable site is Shanidar, in the Zagros Mountains of northeastern Iraq, where partial skeletons of nine individuals were found, four of them deliberately buried. One of the more interesting individuals is called Shanidar 1. This is a skeleton of a male who lived to be approximately 30 to 45 years old, a considerable age for a prehistoric human (Fig. 10-16). His stature is estimated at 5 feet 7 inches, and his cranial capacity is 1,600 cm^3. This individual shows several fascinating features:

> There had been a crushing blow to the left side of the head, fracturing the eye socket, displacing the left eye, and probably causing blindness on that side. He also sustained a massive blow to the right side of the body that so badly damaged the right arm that it became withered and useless; the bones of the shoulder blade, collar bone, and upper arm are much smaller and thinner than those on the left. The right lower arm and hand are missing, probably not because of poor preservation . . . but because they either atrophied and dropped off or because they were amputated. (Trinkaus and Shipman, 1992, p. 340)

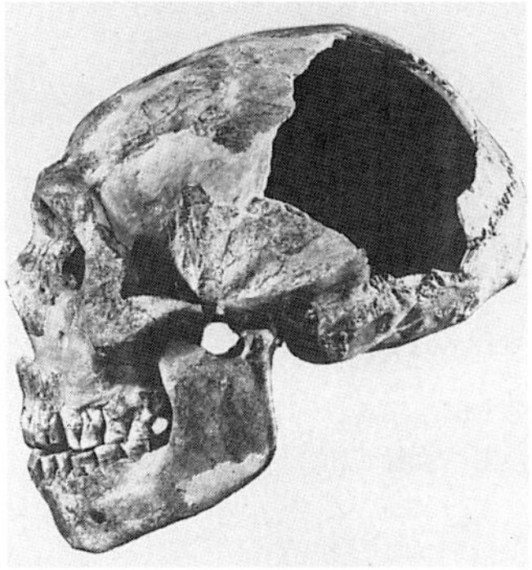

FIGURE 10-16 Shanidar 1. Does he represent Neandertal compassion for the disabled?

---

*The Kebara hyoid is identical to that of modern humans, suggesting that Neandertals did not differ from *H. sapiens sapiens* in this key element.

In addition to these injuries, there was further trauma to both legs, and the man probably limped. How such a person could perform day-to-day activities is difficult to imagine, and both Ralph Solecki, who supervised the work at Shanidar Cave, and Erik Trinkaus, who has studied the Shanidar remains, believe that to survive, he must have been helped by others: "A one-armed, partially blind, crippled man could have made no pretense of hunting or gathering his own food. That he survived for years after his trauma was a testament to Neandertal compassion and humanity" (Trinkaus and Shipman, 1992, p. 341).

CENTRAL ASIA

Uzbekistan About 1,600 miles east of Shanidar in Uzbekistan, in a cave at Teshik-Tash, is the easternmost Neandertal discovery. Actually, new analyses suggest that the Teshik-Tash skeleton may be that of a modern human and thus not a Neandertal (Glantz et al., 2004). The skeleton is that of a nine-year-old boy who appears to have been deliberately buried. It was reported that five pairs of wild goat horns surrounded him, suggesting a burial ritual or perhaps a religious cult, but owing to inadequate published documentation of the excavation, this interpretation has been seriously questioned. The Teshik-Tash individual, like some specimens from Croatia and southwest Asia, also shows a mixture of Neandertal traits (heavy browridges and occipital bun) and modern traits (high vault and definite signs of a chin).

The Teshik-Tash site perhaps represents the easternmost location for Neandertals. Thus, based on the assumed evidence that Teshik-Tash is a Neandertal, geographical distribution of the Neandertals extended from France eastward possibly to central Asia, a distance of about 4,000 miles.

Quick Review	Key Neandertal Fossil Discoveries	
Site	**Dates (y.a.)**	**Human Remains**
Vindija (Croatia)	42,000–28,000	35 specimens; almost entirely cranial fragments
La Chapelle (France)	50,000	Nearly complete adult male skeleton
Shanidar (Iraq)	70,000–60,000	9 individuals (partial skeletons)
Tabun (Israel)	110,000 date uncertain	2 (perhaps 3) individuals, including almost complete skeleton of adult female
Krapina (Croatia)	125,000–120,000	Up to 40 individuals, but very fragmentary

Culture of Neandertals

Neandertals, who lived in the cultural period known as the Middle Paleolithic, are almost always associated with the **Mousterian** industry (although the Mousterian industry is not always associated with Neandertals). In the early part of the last glacial period, Mousterian culture extended across Europe and North Africa into the former Soviet Union, Israel, Iran, and as far east as Uzbekistan and perhaps even China. Moreover, in sub-Saharan Africa, the contemporaneous Middle Stone Age industry is broadly similar to the Mousterian.

TECHNOLOGY

Neandertals improved on previous prepared-core techniques (i.e., the Levallois) by inventing a new variation. They trimmed a flint nodule around the edges to form a disk-shaped core. Each time they struck the edge, they produced a flake, continuing this way until the core became too small and was discarded. Thus, they were able to obtain more flakes per core than their predecessors. They then trimmed (retouched) the flakes into various forms, such as scrapers, points, and knives (Fig. 10-17).

Neandertal craftspeople elaborated and diversified traditional methods, and there is some indication of development in the specialization of tools used in skin and meat preparation, hunting, woodworking, and hafting. There is, however, nearly a complete absence of bone tools, in strong contrast to the succeeding cultural period, the Upper Paleolithic. Nevertheless, Neandertals advanced their technology well beyond that of earlier hominids. It is quite possible that their technological advances helped provide a basis for the remarkable changes of the Upper Paleolithic (discussed in the next chapter).

SUBSISTENCE

Neandertals were successful hunters, as the abundant remains of animal bones at their sites demonstrate. But while it's clear that Neandertals could hunt large mammals, they may not have been as efficient at this task as were Upper Paleolithic hunters. For example, it wasn't until the beginning of the Upper Paleolithic that the spear-thrower, or atlatl, came into use (see p. 294). Shortly thereafter, the bow and arrow greatly increased efficiency (and safety) in hunting large mammals. Lacking such long-distance weaponry, and thus mostly limited to thrusting spears, Neandertals may have been more prone to serious injury—a hypothesis supported by paleoanthropologists Thomas Berger and Erik Trinkaus. Berger and Trinkaus (1995) analyzed the pattern of trauma (particularly fractures) in Neandertals and compared it with that seen in contemporary human samples. Interestingly, the pattern in Neandertals, especially the relatively high proportion of head and neck injuries, was most similar to that seen in contemporary rodeo performers. Berger and Trinkaus thus conclude, "The similarity to the rodeo distribution suggests frequent close encounters with large ungulates unkindly disposed to the humans involved" (Berger and Trinkaus, 1995, p. 841).

Mousterian Pertaining to the stone tool industry associated with Neandertals and some modern *H. sapiens* groups; also called Middle Paleolithic. This industry is characterized by a larger proportion of flake tools than is found in Acheulian tool kits.

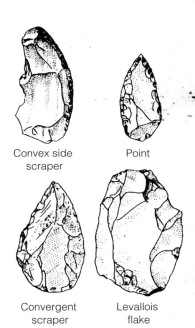

Convex side scraper   Point

Convergent scraper   Levallois flake

FIGURE 10-17 Mousterian tools. (After Bordes.)

We know much more of European Middle Paleolithic culture than of any prior period, as it has been studied longer and by more scholars. In recent years, however, Africa has been a target not only of physical anthropologists, but also of archaeologists, who have added considerably to our knowledge of African Pleistocene hominid history. In many instances, the technology and assumed cultural adaptations in Africa were similar to those in Europe and southwest Asia. We will see in the next chapter that the African technological achievements also kept pace with (or even preceded) those in western Europe.

SYMBOLIC BEHAVIOR

There are a variety of hypotheses concerning the speech capacities of Neandertals, and many of these views are contradictory. Although some researchers argue that Neandertals were incapable of human speech, the prevailing consensus has been that they *were* capable of articulate speech, perhaps even fully competent in the range of sounds produced by modern humans. However, there is new genetic evidence that may require reassessment of just when fully human language first emerged (Enard et al., 2002). As discussed in Chpter 4, in humans today, mutations in a particular gene (locus) are known to produce serious language impairments. From an evolutionary perspective, what's perhaps most significant concerns the greater variability seen in the alleles at this locus in modern humans as compared to other primates. One explanation for this increased variation is intensified selection acting on human populations, perhaps quite recently—and thus potentially after the evolutionary divergence of the Neandertals.

But even if we conclude that Neandertals *could* speak, that doesn't necessarily mean that they had the same language capabilities of modern *Homo sapiens*. Today, paleoanthropologists are highly interested in the apparently sudden expansion of modern *H. sapiens* (discussed in Chapter 11), and they've proposed various explanations for the rapid success of this group. Moreover, as we attempt to explain how and why *H. sapiens sapiens* expanded its geographical range, we're left with the further problem of explaining what happened to the Neandertals. In making these types of interpretations, a growing number of paleoanthropologists suggest that *behavioral* differences are the key. Further corroboration of a recent evolutionary shift resulting from mutation of a crucial gene influencing language capacity will help support this view.

Upper Paleolithic *H. sapiens* is thought to have possessed some significant behavioral advantages that Neandertals (and other premodern humans) lacked. Was it some kind of new and expanded ability to symbolize, communicate, organize social activities, elaborate technology, obtain a wider range of food resources, or care for the sick or injured, or was it some other factor? Were there, compared with *H. sapiens sapiens,* neurological differences that limited the Neandertals and thus contributed to their demise?

The direct anatomical evidence derived from Neandertal fossils isn't especially helpful in answering these questions. Ralph Holloway (1985) has maintained that Neandertal brains (at least as far as the fossil evidence suggests) don't differ significantly from that of modern *H. sapiens*. Moreover, Neandertal vocal tracts and other morphological features, compared with our own, don't appear to have seriously limited them.

Most of the reservations about advanced cognitive abilities in Neandertals have come from archaeological data. Interpretation of Neandertal sites, when

TABLE 10-1	Cultural Contrasts* Between Neandertals and Upper Paleolithic Modern Humans	
Neandertals	**Upper Paleolithic Modern Humans**
Tool Technology Numerous flake tools; few, however, apparently for highly specialized functions; use of bone, antler, or ivory very rare; relatively few tools with more than one or two parts	Many more varieties of stone tools; many apparently for specialized functions; frequent use of bone, antler, and ivory; many more tools comprised of two or more component parts
Hunting Efficiency and Weapons No long-distance hunting weapons; close-proximity weapons used (thus, more likelihood of injury)	Use of spear-thrower and bow and arrow; wider range of social contacts, perhaps permitting larger, more organized hunting parties (including game drives)
Stone Material Transport Stone materials transported only short distances—just "a few kilometers" (Klein, 1989)	Stone tool raw materials transported over much longer distances, implying wider social networks and perhaps trade
Art Artwork uncommon; usually small; probably mostly of a personal nature; some items perhaps misinterpreted as "art"; others may be intrusive from overlying Upper Paleolithic contexts; cave art absent	Artwork much more common, including transportable objects as well as elaborate cave art; well executed, using a variety of materials and techniques; stylistic sophistication
Burial Deliberate burial at several sites; graves unelaborated; graves frequently lack artifacts	Burials much more complex, frequently including both tools and remains of animals

*The contrasts are more apparent in some areas (particularly western Europe) than others (eastern Europe, Near East). Elsewhere (Africa, eastern Asia), where there were no Neandertals, the cultural situation is quite different. Moreover, even in western Europe, the cultural transformations were not necessarily abrupt, but may have developed more gradually from Mousterian to Upper Paleolithic times. For example, Straus (1995) argues that many of the Upper Paleolithic features were not consistently manifested until after 20,000 y.a.

compared with succeeding Upper Paleolithic sites (especially as documented in western Europe), have led to several intriguing contrasts, as shown in Table 10-1.

On the basis of this type of behavioral and anatomical evidence, Neandertals in recent years have increasingly been viewed as an evolutionary dead end. Whether their disappearance and ultimate replacement by anatomically modern Upper Paleolithic peoples (with their presumably "superior" culture) was solely the result of cultural differences or was also influenced by biological variation can't at present be determined.

BURIALS

It's been known for some time that Neandertals deliberately buried their dead. Indeed, the spectacular discoveries at La Chapelle, Shanidar, and elsewhere were the direct results of ancient burial, and this permits much more complete preservation. Such deliberate burial treatment extends back at least 90,000 years at Tabun. Moreover, some form of consistent "disposal" of the dead (but not necessarily below-ground burial) is evidenced at Atapuerca,

Spain, where at least 28 individuals comprising more than 700 fossilized elements were found in a cave at the end of a deep vertical shaft. From the nature of the site and the accumulation of hominid remains, Spanish researchers are convinced that the site demonstrates some form of human activity involving deliberate disposal of the dead (Arsuaga et al., 1997).

The provisional 300,000-year-old age for Atapuerca suggests that Neandertals (more precisely, their immediate precursors) were, by the Middle Pleistocene, handling their dead in special ways, a behavior thought previously to have emerged only much later (in the Upper Pleistocene). And, as far as current data indicate, this practice is seen in western European contexts well before it appears in Africa or in eastern Asia. For example, in the premodern sites at Kabwe and Florisbad (discussed earlier), deliberate disposal of the dead is not documented. Nor is it seen in African early modern sites (e.g., Klasies River Mouth, dated at 120,000–100,000 y.a.; see p. 282).

Yet, in later contexts (after 35,000 y.a.), where anatomically modern *H. sapiens* (*H. sapiens sapiens*) remains are found in clear burial contexts, their treatment is considerably more complex than in Neandertal burials. In these later (Upper Paleolithic) sites, grave goods, including bone and stone tools as well as animal bones, are found more consistently and in greater concentrations. Because many Neandertal sites were excavated in the nineteenth or early twentieth century, before the development of more rigorous archaeological methods, there are questions regarding numerous purported burials. Nevertheless, the evidence seems quite clear that deliberate burial was practiced at La Chapelle, La Ferrassie (eight graves), Tabun, Amud, Kebara, Shanidar, and Teshik-Tash (as well as at several other localities, especially in France). Moreover, in many instances, the *position* of the body was deliberately modified and placed in the grave in a flexed posture (see p. 257). Such a flexed position has been found in 16 of the 20 best-documented Neandertal burial contexts (Klein, 1989).

Finally, the placement of supposed grave goods in burials, including stone tools, animal bones (such as cave bear), and even arrangements of flowers, together with stone slabs on top of the burials, have all been postulated as further evidence of Neandertal symbolic behavior. However, in many instances, again due to poor excavation documentation, these statements are questionable. Placement of stone tools, for example, is occasionally seen, but apparently wasn't done consistently. In those 33 Neandertal burials for which adequate data exist, only 14 show definite association of stone tools and/or animal bones with the deceased (Klein, 1989). It's not until the next cultural period, the Upper Paleolithic, that we see a major behavioral shift, as demonstrated in more elaborate burials and development of art.

Genetic Evidence

As a result of the revolutionary advances in molecular biology (discussed in Chapter 3), fascinating new avenues of research have become possible in the study of earlier hominids. The extraction, amplification, and sequencing of ancient DNA from contexts spanning the last 10,000 years or so are now becoming fairly commonplace (e.g., the analysis of DNA from the 5,000-year-old "Iceman" found in the Italian Alps).

Finding usable DNA in yet more ancient remains is much more difficult because they're mineralized, and organic components, including (usually) the DNA, have been destroyed. Nevertheless, in the past few years, very exciting results have been announced relating to DNA found in eight different Neandertal fossils dated between 29,000 and 50,000 y.a. These fossils come from sites in France (including La Chapelle), Germany (from the original Neander Valley locality), Belgium, Croatia, and Russia (Krings et al., 1997, 2000; Ovchinnikov et al., 2000; Schmitz et al., 2002; Serre et al., 2004).

The technique used in the study of Neandertal fossils involves the extraction of mitochondrial DNA (mtDNA), amplification by PCR (see p. 59), and nucleotide sequencing of portions of the molecule. Results from the eight specimens show that the individuals are genetically more different from contemporary *Homo sapiens* populations than modern human populations are from each other (about three times as much). Consequently, Krings and colleagues (1997) have hypothesized that the Neandertal lineage separated from that of modern *H. sapiens* ancestors between 690,000 and 550,000 y.a.

This intriguing hypothesis, however, hasn't been fully confirmed and is most certainly not accepted by all paleoanthropologists. It's still not clear how rapidly mtDNA evolves, nor is it obvious how genetically different from us we should expect 40,000-year-old relatives to be. In other words, at present, we can't exclude the possibility of evolutionary relationships on the basis of available genetic evidence. Nevertheless, such data probably offer the best hope of ultimately untangling the place of Neandertals in human evolution and perhaps even of understanding something of their fate.

Trends in Human Evolution: Understanding Premodern Humans

As you can see, the Middle Pleistocene hominids are a very diverse group, broadly dispersed through time and space. There is considerable variation among them, and a clear evolutionary picture isn't easily obtained. Given that regional populations were small and frequently isolated, many of these probably died out and left no descendants. To see an "ancestor" in every fossil find is a mistake.

Nevertheless, as a group, these Middle Pleistocene premoderns do reveal some general trends. In many respects, for example, they appear to have been *transitional* between the hominid grades that preceded them (*H. erectus*) and that which followed them (*H. sapiens*). It's not a stretch to say that all the Middle Pleistocene premoderns derived from *H. erectus* forebears and that some of them, in turn, are likely to have been ancestral to the earliest fully modern humans.

Paleoanthropologists are certainly concerned with such broad generalities as these, but they also want to focus on meaningful anatomical, environmental, and behavioral details as well as underlying processes. Thus, regional variability displayed by particular fossil samples is seen as significant—but just *how* significant is debated. Moreover, increasingly sophisticated theoretical approaches are being used to better understand the processes that shaped the evolution of later *Homo,* both at macroevolutionary and microevolutionary levels.

Scientists, like all humans, assign names or labels to phenomena, a point we addressed in discussing classification in Chapter 5. Paleoanthropologists are certainly no exception. Yet, working from a common evolutionary foundation, paleoanthropologists still come to different conclusions regarding the most appropriate way to interpret the Middle/Upper Pleistocene hominids. Consequently, a variety of species names have been proposed in recent years.

At the extreme lumping end of the spectrum, only one species is recognized for all the premodern fossils. They are called *Homo sapiens* and are thus further lumped with modern humans (although partly distinguished by such terminology as "archaic *H. sapiens*") (see Fig. 10-18a).

At the other end of the spectrum, paleontological splitters have identified at least three species, all distinct from *H. sapiens*. Two of these were discussed earlier (*H. heidelbergensis* and *H. neanderthalensis*), and a third species (called *Homo helmei*) has recently been proposed (Foley and Lahr, 1997; Lahr and Foley, 1998). It's been suggested that this last group is a possible African ancestor of *both* modern humans and Neandertals, but one that appears fairly late in the Middle Pleistocene (300,000–250,000 y.a.) and thus coming largely after *H. heidelbergensis*. This more complex evolutionary interpretation is shown in Figure 10-18b.

We addressed similar differences of interpretation in Chapters 8 and 9, and such disparity can be frustrating to students new to paleoanthropology. The proliferation of new names is confusing, and it might seem that experts in the field are endlessly arguing about what to call the fossils.

Fortunately, it's not quite that bad. There's actually more agreement than is initially apparent. No one doubts that all these hominids are closely related to each other as well as to modern humans. Moreover, all agree that only some of the fossil samples represent populations that left descendants. The disagreement centers on which hominids are the most likely to be closely related to later hominids. The grouping of the hominids into evolutionary clusters (clades) and assigning different names to them is a reflection of differing interpretations— and, more fundamentally, of somewhat differing philosophies.

We shouldn't, however, place too much emphasis on such naming/classification debates. Most paleoanthropologists recognize that a large portion of these disagreements result from simple, practical considerations. Even the most enthusiastic of splitters acknowledge that the fossil "species" are not true species as defined by the biological species concept (see p. 95). For example, the scheme shown in Figure 10-18b reflects the views of Robert Foley, who readily admits: "It is unlikely they are all biological species. . . . These are probably a mixture of real biological species and evolving lineages of subspecies. In other words, they could potentially have interbred, but owing to allopatry [i.e., geographical separation] were unlikely to have had the opportunity" (Foley, 2002, p. 33).

Nevertheless, Foley, along with an increasing number of other professionals, distinguishes these different fossil samples with species names to highlight their distinct position in hominid evolution. That is, these hominid groups are more loosely defined as a type of paleospecies (see p. 97) rather than as fully biological species. Giving distinct hominid samples a separate (species) name makes them more easily identifiable to other researchers and makes various cladistic hypotheses more explicit (and, equally important, more directly testable). Eminent paleoanthropologist F. Clark Howell (of the University of California, Berkeley) also recognizes these advantages, but is less emphatic about species designations. Howell recommends the term *paleo-deme* to refer to either a species or subspecies classification (Howell, 1999).

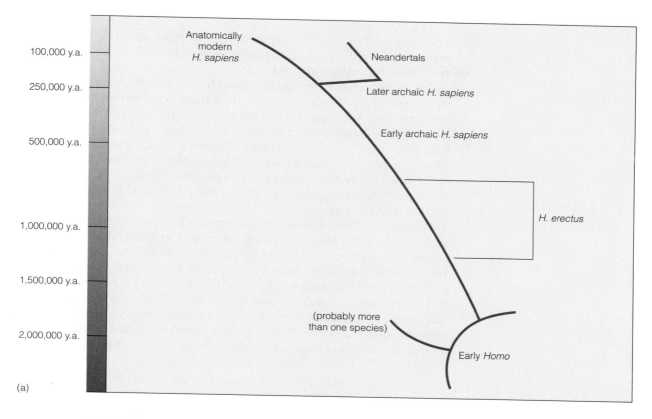

(a)

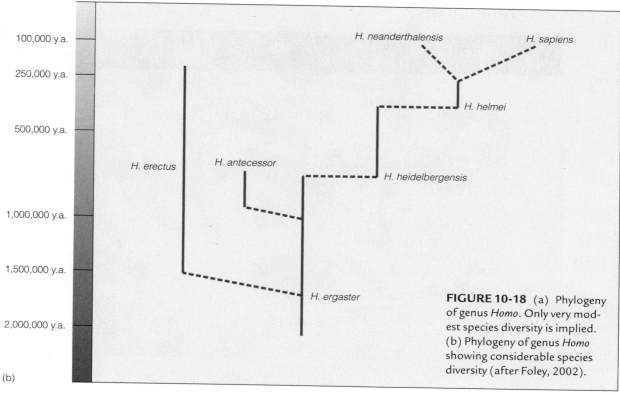

(b)

FIGURE 10-18 (a) Phylogeny of genus *Homo*. Only very modest species diversity is implied. (b) Phylogeny of genus *Homo* showing considerable species diversity (after Foley, 2002).

The hominids that best illustrate these issues are the Neandertals. Fortunately, they are also the best known, represented by dozens of well-preserved individuals. Consequently, many of the differing hypotheses can be systematically tested and evaluated.

Are Neandertals very closely related to modern *H. sapiens*? Certainly. Are they physically and behaviorally distinct from both ancient and fully modern humans? Yes. Are Neandertals, therefore, a fully separate biological species from modern humans—and therefore theoretically incapable of fertily interbreeding with modern people? Probably not. Finally, then, should Neandertals be considered a separate species from, or a subspecies of, *H. sapiens*? For most purposes, it doesn't matter, since the distinction at some point is arbitrary. Speciation is, after all, a *dynamic* process. Fossil groups like the Neandertals represent one point in this process.

We can view Neandertals as a distinctive side branch of later hominid evolution. Similar to the situation among contemporary baboons (savanna compared to hamadryas), we could say that Neandertals were an "incipient species." Given enough time and enough isolation, they likely would have separated completely from their modern human contemporaries. However, as fossil, archaeological, and genetic data are making increasingly clear, Neandertals never got this far. Their fate, in a sense, was decided for them as more successful competitors expanded into Neandertal habitats. These highly successful hominids were fully modern humans, and their story is the focus of the next chapter.

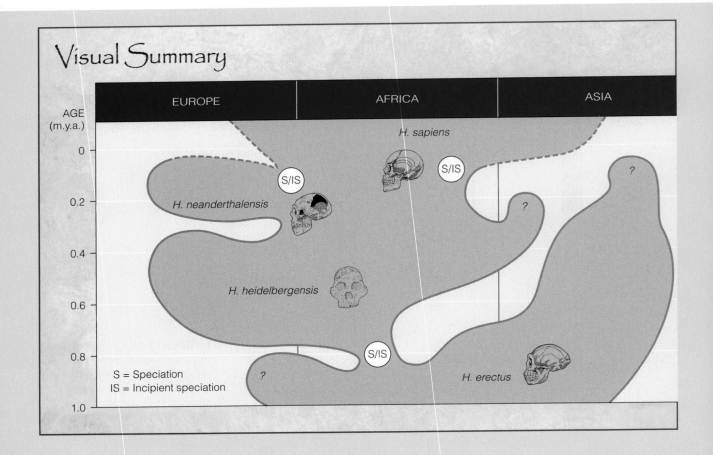

Visual Summary

Summary

The Middle Pleistocene (780,000–125,000 y.a.) was a period of transition in human evolution. Fossil hominids from this period show similarities both with their predecessors (*H. erectus*) and with their successors (*H. sapiens*). Moreover, they've been found in many areas of the Old World, in Africa, Asia, and Europe (in the latter case, representing the first truly successful occupation of that continent). Because these transitional hominids are more derived (and advanced in the human direction) than *H. erectus,* we can refer to them as premodern humans. This terminology also recognizes that these hominids display several significant anatomical and behavioral differences from modern humans.

There is some dispute concerning the best way to formally classify the majority of Middle Pleistocene hominids, but most paleoanthropologists now prefer to refer to them as *H. heidelbergensis*. Similarities between the African and European Middle Pleistocene hominid samples suggest that they all can be reasonably seen as part of this same species. The contemporaneous Asian fossils, however, don't fit as neatly into this model, and conclusions regarding these premodern humans remain more tenuous.

Some of the later *H. heidelbergensis* populations in Europe likely evolved into Neandertals. Abundant Neandertal fossil and archaeological evidence has been collected from the Upper Pleistocene time span of Neandertal existence (circa 130,000–29,000 y.a.). But unlike their Middle Pleistocene (*H. heidelbergensis*) predecessors, Neandertals are more geographically restricted, found only in Europe and southwest Asia. Moreover, various lines of evidence—anatomical, archaeological, and genetic—suggest that they were isolated and distinct from other hominids.

These observations have led to a growing consensus among paleoanthropologists that the Neandertals were largely a side branch of later hominid evolution. Nevertheless, there remain significant differences in theoretical approaches regarding how to best deal with the Neandertals; that is, should they be considered a separate species or as a subspecies of *H. sapiens*? We suggest that the best way to view the Neandertals is within a dynamic process of speciation. Accordingly, Neandertals can be interpreted as an "incipient species," one in the process of splitting from early *H. sapiens* populations.

As a further study aid, the most significant premodern human fossils discussed in this chapter are presented in Table 10-2.

Critical Thinking Questions

1. Why are the Middle Pleistocene hominids called premodern humans? In what ways are they human?
2. What is the general popular conception of Neandertals? Do you agree with this view? (Cite both anatomical and archaeological evidence to support your conclusion.)
3. Compare the skeleton of a Neandertal with that of a modern human. In which ways are they most similar? In which ways are they most different?
4. What evidence suggests that Neandertals deliberately buried their dead? Do you think the fact that they buried their dead is important? Why? How would you interpret this behavior (remembering that Neandertals were not identical to us)?

TABLE 10-2 | Most Significant Premodern Human Fossil Discoveries Discussed in This Chapter

Site	Dates (y.a.)	Taxonomic Designation	Comments
La Chapelle	50,000	Neandertal (*Homo neanderthalensis*, *Homo sapiens neanderthalensis*)	Historically most important site in France in description of Neandertal morphology
Tabun	110,000	Neandertal (*Homo neanderthalensis*, *Homo sapiens neanderthalensis*	Important early Neandertal site; shows clear presence of Neandertals in Near East
Atapuerca (Sima de los Huesos)	320,000–190,000	*Homo heidelbergensis*	Large sample; earliest evidence in Europe of Neandertal morphology; evidence of disposal of the dead
Steinheim	300,000–250,000?	*Homo heidelbergensis*	Transitional-looking fossil
Jinniushan	200,000?	*Homo heidelbergensis* Early *Homo sapiens,* as termed by the Chinese	Possibly oldest example of *H. sapiens* in China, but status uncertain
Kabwe (Broken Hill)	130,000+?	*Homo heidelbergensis*	Transitional-looking fossil; similar to Bodo
Bodo	600,000	*Homo heidelbergensis*	Earliest evidence of *H. heidelbergensis* in Africa and perhaps anywhere

5. How are species defined, both for living animals and for extinct ones? Use the Neandertals to illustrate the problems encountered in distinguishing species among extinct hominids. Contrast specifically the interpretation of Neandertals as a distinct species with the interpretation of Neandertals as a subspecies of *H. sapiens*.

Media Resources

The Companion Website for *Essentials of Physical Anthropology*, Sixth Edition
http://anthropology.wadsworth.com/jurmain6e_ess

Supplement your review of this chapter by going to this text's companion website to take one of the practice quizzes, use the flash cards to master key terms, and check out the many other resources and study aids. Also visit the website to learn about important new discoveries in paleoanthropology by checking the "Latest Dirt" feature authored by Robert Jurmain.

CD-ROMs in Physical Anthropology

Wadsworth Publishing has also developed three CD-ROMs to accompany this text and enhance learning in physical anthropology (for further descriptions of these CD-ROMs, see p. xix):

Virtual Laboratories for Physical Anthropology CD-ROM, Third Edition

Basic Genetics for Anthropology CD-ROM: Principles and Applications

Hominid Fossils CD-ROM: An Interactive Atlas

For this chapter, see especially the Virtual Laboratories for Physical Anthropology CD-ROM, Third Edition, and the Hominid Fossils CD-ROM: An Interactive Atlas.

Readings of Interest

Arsuaga, Jean Louis de. 2002. *The Neanderthal's Necklace: In Search of the First Thinkers*. New York: Four Walls Eight Windows.

Mellars, Paul. 1995. *The Neanderthal Legacy. An Archaeological Perspective from Western Europe*. Princeton, NJ: Princeton University Press.

Tattersall, Ian. 1999. *The Last Neanderthal. The Rise, Success, and Mysterious Extinction of Our Closest Human Relatives*. Boulder, CO: Westview Press.

Trinkaus, Erik, and Pat Shipman. 1993. *The Neandertals: Changing the Image of Mankind*. New York: Knopf.

11 | The Origin and Dispersal of Modern Humans

Focus Question

Is it possible to determine when and where modern people first appeared?

Introduction

Sometime, probably close to 150,000 y.a., the first modern *Homo sapiens* evolved in Africa. Within 100,000 years or so, their descendants dispersed across most of the Old World, even expanding as far as Australia (and somewhat later to the Americas).

Who were they, and why were these early modern people so successful? Furthermore, what was the fate of the other hominids, such as the Neandertals, who were already long established in areas outside Africa? Did they evolve as well, leaving descendants among some living human populations? Or were they completely swept aside and replaced by African emigrants?

In this chapter, we discuss the origin and dispersal of modern *H. sapiens*. All contemporary populations, encompassing the more than 6 billion living humans, are placed in the subspecies *Homo sapiens sapiens*. Most paleoanthropologists agree that several fossil forms, dating back as far as 100,000 y.a., should also be included in the same subspecies.

In addition, some recently discovered fossils from Africa also are clearly *H. sapiens*, but show some (minor) differences from living people and could thus be described as "near-modern." Nevertheless, we can think of these early African humans as well as their somewhat later relatives as "us."

These first modern humans, who evolved by 150,000 y.a., are probably descendants of some of the premodern humans discussed in Chapter 10. Most especially, African populations of *H. heidelbergensis* are the most likely ancestors of the earliest modern *H. sapiens*. This transition of modern humans from more ancient premodern forms and their subsequent wide dispersal throughout most of the Old World were relatively rapid evolutionary events, and they raise several fundamental questions:

1. When (approximately) did modern humans first appear?
2. Where did the transition take place? Did it occur in just one region or in several?
3. What was the pace of evolutionary change? How quickly did the transition occur?
4. How did the dispersal of modern humans to other areas of the Old World (outside that of origin) take place?

These questions concerning the origins and early dispersal of modern *Homo sapiens* continue to fuel much controversy among paleoanthropologists. And it's no wonder, for members of early *Homo sapiens* are our *direct* ancestors and are thus closely related to all contemporary humans. They were much like us skeletally, genetically, and (most likely) behaviorally, too. In fact, it's the various hypotheses relating to the behavioral capacities of our most immediate predecessors that have most fired the imagination of scientists and laypeople alike. In every major respect, these are the first hominids that we can confidently refer to as "fully human."

Click

Go to the following CD-ROMs for interactive activities and exercises on topics covered in this chapter:

 Virtual Laboratories for Physical Anthropology CD-ROM, Third Edition

 Hominid Fossils CD-ROM: An Interactive Atlas

In this chapter, we will also discuss archaeological evidence from the Upper Paleolithic (see p. 259). This evidence will allow us to better understand technological and social developments during the period when modern humans arose and quickly came to dominate the planet.

The evolutionary story of *Homo sapiens sapiens* is really a biological autobiography of all of us. It's a story that still has many unanswered questions; but several theories help us organize the diverse information that is presently available.

Approaches to Understanding Modern Human Origins

There are two major theories that attempt to organize and explain modern human origins: the complete replacement model and the regional continuity model. These two views are quite distinct and in some ways diametrically opposed to each other. Moreover, the popular press has further contributed to a wide and incorrect perception of irreconcilable argument on these points by "opposing" scientists. Indeed, there's a third theory, which we call the partial replacement model, that is a compromise hypothesis incorporating some aspects of the two major theories. Because so much of our contemporary view of modern human origins is driven by the debates linked to these differing theories, let us begin by briefly reviewing each. We will then turn to the fossil evidence itself to see what it can contribute to answer the questions we have posed.

THE COMPLETE REPLACEMENT MODEL (RECENT AFFRICAN EVOLUTION)

The complete replacement model, developed by British paleoanthropologists Christopher Stringer and Peter Andrews (1988), is based on the origin of modern humans in Africa and later replacement of populations in Europe and Asia (Fig. 11-1). This theory proposes that anatomically modern populations arose in Africa within the last 200,000 years, then migrated from Africa, *completely replacing* populations in Europe and Asia. This model does not take into account any transition from premodern forms to modern *H. sapiens* anywhere in the world except Africa. A critical deduction of the Stringer and Andrews theory is that anatomically modern humans appeared as a consequence of a biological speciation event. Thus, in this view there could be no admixture of migrating African modern *H. sapiens* with local non-African populations because the African modern humans were a *biologically* different species. In a taxonomic context, all of the premodern populations outside Africa would, in this view, be classified as belonging to different species of *Homo* (e.g., the Neandertals would be classified as *H. neanderthalensis;* see p. 269 for further discussion). While this speciation explanation fits nicely with, and in fact helps explain, *complete* replacement, Stringer has more recently stated that he isn't dogmatic regarding this issue. But he suggests that while there may have been potential for interbreeding, very little apparently actually took place.

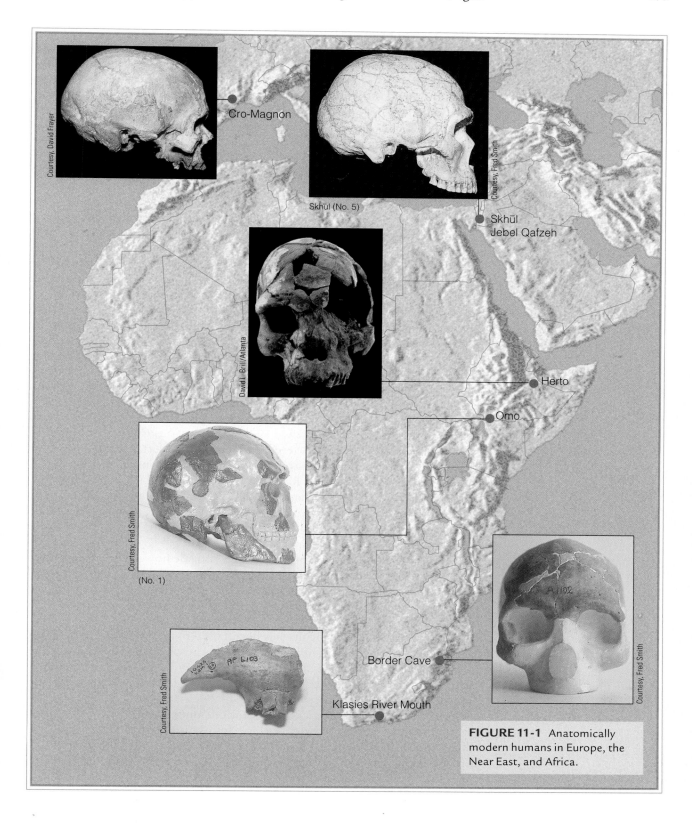

FIGURE 11-1 Anatomically modern humans in Europe, the Near East, and Africa.

Cro-Magnon

Courtesy, David Frayer

Skhūl (No. 5)

Courtesy, Fred Smith

Skhūl
Jebel Qafzeh

David L. Brill/Atlanta

Herto

Omo

Courtesy, Fred Smith

(No. 1)

Border Cave

Courtesy, Fred Smith

Courtesy, Fred Smith

Klasies River Mouth

Interpretations of the latter phases of human evolution have recently been greatly extended by newly available genetic techniques. Advances in molecular biology, which have so revolutionized the biological sciences (including physical anthropology), have been recently applied to the question of modern human origins. Using numerous contemporary human populations as a data source, a wide variety of DNA sequences have been precisely determined and compared. The theoretical basis of this approach assumes that at least some of the genetic patterning seen today can act as a "window" on the past. In particular, the genetic patterns observed today between geographically widely dispersed humans are thought to partly reflect migrations that occurred back in the late Pleistocene. This hypothesis can be further tested as various types of contemporary population genetic patterning are better documented.

In pursuit of such fuller documentation, geneticists have studied both nuclear and mitochondrial DNA (see p. 44). Y chromosome and mitochondrial DNA patterns are considered particularly informative, since neither is significantly recombined during sexual reproduction. As a result, mitochondrial inheritance follows a strictly maternal pattern (inherited through females), while the Y chromosome follows a paternal pattern (transmitted only from father to son).

As these new data have accumulated, consistent relationships have emerged, especially in showing indigenous African populations to have far greater diversity than populations from elsewhere in the world. The consistency of the results is highly significant, because it strongly supports an African origin for modern humans and some mode of replacement elsewhere.

Certainly, most molecular data come from contemporary species, since DNA is not *usually* preserved in long-dead individuals. Nevertheless, exceptions do occur, and these cases provide another genetic window—one that can directly illuminate the past. As discussed in the previous chapter (see p. 269), Neandertal DNA has been recovered from eight Neandertal fossils.

In addition, nine ancient anatomically modern skeletons from sites in Italy, France, Czech Republic, and Russia (Serre et al., 2004) have recently had their mtDNA sequenced (Caramelli et al., 2003; Kulikov et al., 2004). The results show mtDNA sequence patterns very similar to the patterns seen in living humans—and thus significantly different from the mtDNA patterns found in the eight Neandertals thus far analyzed.

If these results are further confirmed, they provide powerful *direct* evidence of a genetic discontinuity between Neandertals (one dating as late as 29,000 y.a.) and these early fully modern humans. In other words, these data suggest that no (or very little) interbreeding took place between Neandertals and anatomically modern humans.

A potentially serious difficulty has been raised regarding these latest DNA results from the early modern skeletons. The mtDNA sequences are so similar to those of modern humans that they could, in fact, be the result of contamination (i.e., the amplified and sequenced DNA could be that of some person who handled the fossil in recent years).

Despite extensive experimental precautions undertaken by the molecular biologists who did this research (which follow standard practices used by other laboratories), there is, at present, no way to rule out such contamination. Nevertheless, the results do fit with an emerging overall consensus regarding likely Neandertal distinctiveness as compared to modern humans.

PARTIAL REPLACEMENT MODELS

Various alternative perspectives also suggest an African origin of modern humans followed by population expansion out of Africa into other areas of the Old World. But unlike the complete replacement hypothesis, these partial replacement models postulate that some interbreeding occurred between emigrating Africans and resident premodern populations elsewhere. Thus, partial replacement assumes that *no* speciation event occurred, and all these hominids should be considered members of *H. sapiens.* Günter Bräuer, of the University of Hamburg, suggests that very little interbreeding occurred—a view supported recently by John Relethford (2001) in what he describes as "mostly out of Africa." Fred Smith, of Loyola University, also favors an African origin of modern humans, but his "assimilation" model hypothesizes that in some regions more interbreeding took place (Smith, 2002).

THE REGIONAL CONTINUITY MODEL (MULTIREGIONAL EVOLUTION)

The regional continuity model is most closely associated with paleoanthropologist Milford Wolpoff, of the University of Michigan, and his associates (Wolpoff et al., 1994, 2001). They suggest that local populations (not all, of course) in Europe, Asia, and Africa continued their indigenous evolutionary development from premodern Middle Pleistocene forms to anatomically modern humans. A question immediately arises: How is it possible for different local populations around the globe to evolve with such similar morphology? In other words, how could anatomically modern humans arise separately in different continents and end up physically (and genetically) so similar? The multiregional model explains this by (1) denying that the earliest modern *H. sapiens* populations originated *exclusively* in Africa, challenging the notion of complete replacement, and (2) asserting that some gene flow (migration) between premodern populations was extremely likely, in which case modern humans cannot be considered a species separate from premodern hominids.

Through gene flow and natural selection, according to the multiregional hypothesis, local populations would *not* have evolved totally independently from one another, and such mixing would have "prevented speciation between the regional lineages and thus maintained human beings as a *single,* although obviously *polytypic* [see p. 308], species throughout the Pleistocene" (Smith et al., 1989).

Advocates of the multiregional model aren't dogmatic regarding the degree of regional continuity. They recognize that a likely strong influence of African migrants existed throughout the world (and is still detectable today). Agreeing with Smith's assimilation model, this modified multiregionalism suggests only perhaps minimal gene continuity in several regions (e.g., western Europe), with most modern genes coming as a result of large African migration(s) and/or more incremental gene flow (Relethford, 2001; Wolpoff et al., 2001).

SEEING THE BIG PICTURE

Looking beyond the arguments concerning modern human origins (which are often overstated and overdramatized by the popular media), most paleoanthropologists now recognize an emerging consensus view. In fact, new evidence from fossils and especially from molecular comparisons is providing more clarity. Data from sequenced ancient DNA, various patterns of contemporary human DNA, and the newest fossil finds from Ethiopia all suggest that a "strong" multiregional model is extremely unlikely. This more extreme form of multiregionalism claims that modern human populations in Asia and Europe evolved *mostly* from local premodern ancestors—with only minor influence coming from African population expansion. Given the breadth and consistency of the latest research, for practical purposes, this strong version of multiregionalism is falsified.

Moreover, as various investigators integrate these new data, views are beginning to converge even further. Several researchers suggest an out-of-Africa model that leads to virtually complete replacement elsewhere. At the moment, this complete replacement rendition can't be falsified. Still, even devoted advocates of this strong replacement version recognize that some interbreeding was possible—although they believe it to have been very minor. In conclusion, then, during the latter Pleistocene, one or more major migrations from Africa fueled the worldwide dispersal of modern humans. However, the African migrants might well have interbred with resident populations outside Africa. In a sense, it is all the same, whether we see this process either as very minimal mulitregional continuity or as not quite complete replacement.

The Earliest Discoveries of Modern Humans

AFRICA

In Africa, several early fossil finds have been interpreted as fully anatomically modern forms (see Fig. 11-1). These specimens come from the Klasies River Mouth on the south coast (which could be the earliest find), Border Cave slightly to the north, and Omo Kibish 1 in southern Ethiopia. With the use of relatively new techniques, all three sites have been dated to about 120,000–80,000 y.a. The original geological context at Border Cave is uncertain, and the fossils may be younger than at the other two sites. For several years, some paleoanthropologists have considered these fossils the earliest known anatomically modern humans. Problems with dating, context, and differing interpretations of the evidence have led other paleoanthropologists to question whether the *earliest* modern forms (Fig. 11-2) really did evolve in Africa. Other modern *H. sapiens* individuals, possibly older than these African fossils, have been found in the Near East.

Herto The announcement in June 2003 of well-preserved and well-dated *H. sapiens* fossils from Ethiopia has now gone a long way toward filling gaps in the later Pleistocene African fossil record, and as a result, they are helping resolve key issues regarding modern human origins. Tim White (of the

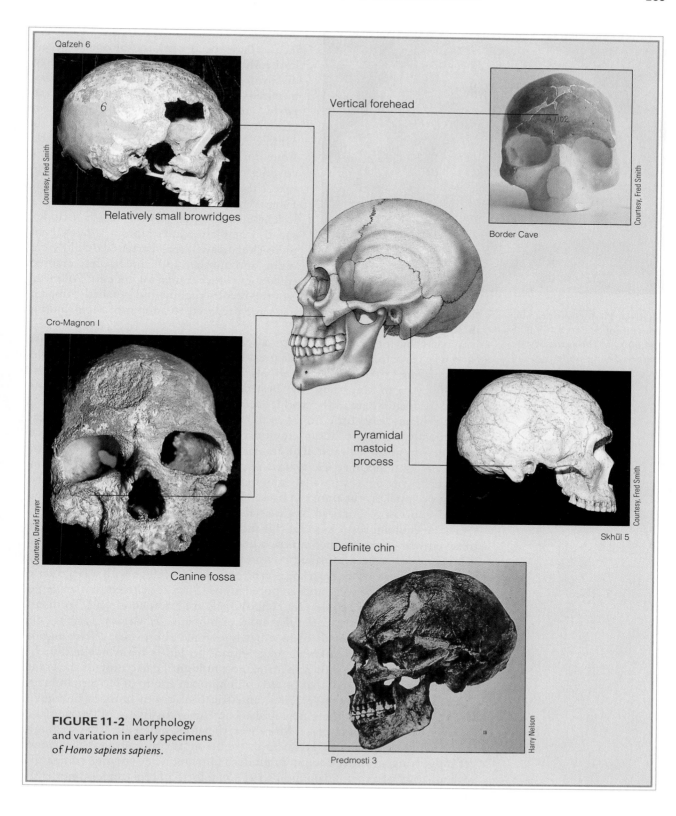

Qafzeh 6

6

Courtesy, Fred Smith

Relatively small browridges

Vertical forehead

Border Cave

Courtesy, Fred Smith

Cro-Magnon I

Courtesy, David Frayer

Canine fossa

Pyramidal
mastoid
process

Skhūl 5

Courtesy, Fred Smith

Definite chin

Predmosti 3

Harry Nelson

FIGURE 11-2 Morphology and variation in early specimens of *Homo sapiens sapiens*.

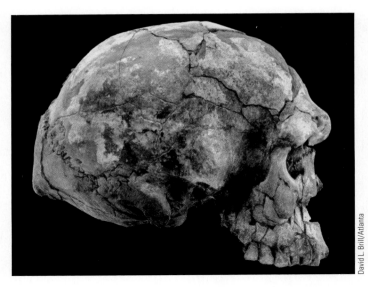

David L. Brill/Atlanta

FIGURE 11-3 Herto cranium from Ethiopia, dated 160,000–154,000 y.a. This is the best-preserved early modern *H. sapiens* cranium yet found.

University of California, Berkeley) and colleagues have been working for over a decade in the Middle Awash area of Ethiopia and have discovered a remarkable array of early fossil hominids (*Ardipithecus* and *Australopithecus garhi*) as well as somewhat later forms (*H. erectus*). From this same area in the Middle Awash (in the Herto member of the Bouri formation), highly significant new discoveries came to light in 1997. For simplicity sake, these new hominids are referred to as the Herto remains.

These exciting new Herto fossils include a mostly complete adult cranium, a fairly complete (but heavily reconstructed) child's cranium, and another adult incomplete cranium (plus a few other cranial fragments). Following lengthy reconstruction and detailed comparative studies, White and colleagues were prepared to announce their findings in 2003.

What they found caused quite a sensation among paleoanthropologists (and was reported in the popular press as well). First, well-controlled radiometric dating (^{40}Ar/^{39}Ar) securely places the remains between 160,000 and 154,000 y.a., making these the best-dated hominid fossils from this time period from anywhere in the world. Second, the preservation and morphology of the remains leave little doubt as to their relationship to modern humans. The mostly complete adult cranium (Fig. 11-3) is very large, with an extremely long cranial vault. The cranial capacity is 1,450 cm^3, well within the range of contemporary *H. sapiens* populations. The skull is also in some respects heavily built, with a large arching browridge in front and a large projecting occipital protuberance in back. Nevertheless, the face is nonprojecting, in stark contrast to Eurasian Neandertals.

The overall impression is that this individual—as well as the child, aged six to seven years, and the incomplete adult cranium—are clearly *Homo sapiens.* White and his team performed comprehensive statistical studies, comparing these fossils with other early *H. sapiens* remains as well as with a large series (over 3,000 crania) from modern populations. They concluded that while not identical to modern people, the Herto fossils are "near-modern." To distinguish these individuals from fully modern humans (*H. sapiens sapiens*), the researchers have placed them in a newly defined subspecies: *Homo sapiens idaltu* (*idaltu,* from the Afar language, means "elder") (White et al., 2003).

Further analysis has shown that the morphological patterning of the crania doesn't specifically match that of *any* contemporary group of modern humans. What can we then conclude? First, an African origin of modern humans is strongly supported by these new finds. The Herto fossils are of the right age and come from the right place. Moreover, they look much like what we might have predicted. These new Herto finds are the most conclusive fossil evidence yet supporting an African origin of modern humans. They are thus compatible with an array of genetic data indicating some form of replacement model for human origins.

Quick Review	Key Early Modern *Homo sapiens* Discoveries from Africa and the Near East	
Site	**Dates (y.a.)**	**Human Remains**
Qafzeh (Israel)	110,000	Minimum of 20 individuals (*H. sapiens sapiens*)
Skhūl (Israel)	115,000	Minimum of 10 individuals (*H. sapiens sapiens*)
Klasies River Mouth (South Africa)	120,000?	Several individuals; highly fragmentary (*H. sapiens sapiens*)
Herto (Ethiopia)	160,000–154,000	Dental and cranial remains of 4 individuals (*H. sapiens idaltu*)

THE NEAR EAST

In Israel, early modern *H. sapiens* fossils (the remains of at least 10 individuals) were found in the Skhūl Cave at Mt. Carmel (Figs. 11-4 and 11-5a), very near the Neandertal site of Tabun. Also from Israel, the Qafzeh Cave has yielded the remains of at least 20 individuals (Fig. 11-5b). Although their overall configuration is definitely modern, some specimens show certain premodern (i.e., Neandertal) features. Skhūl has been dated to about 115,000 y.a., and Qafzeh has been placed around 100,000 y.a. (Bar-Yosef, 1993, 1994) (Fig. 11-6).

Such early dates for modern specimens pose some problems for those advocating local replacement (the multiregional model). How early do premodern *H. sapiens* populations (Neandertals) appear in the Near East? A recent

FIGURE 11-4 Mt. Carmel, studded with caves, was home to *H. sapiens sapiens* at Skhūl (and to Neandertals at Tabun and Kebara).

Courtesy, Harry Nelson

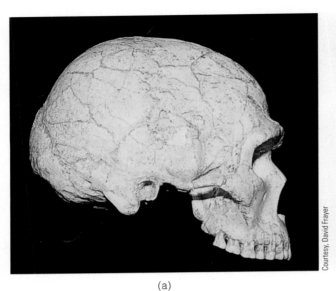

(a)

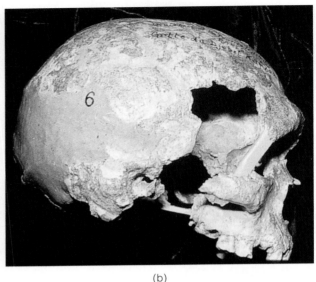

(b)

FIGURE 11-5 (a) Skhūl 5. (b) Qafzeh 6. These specimens from Israel are thought to be representatives of early modern *Homo sapiens*. The vault height, forehead, and lack of facial projection are modern traits.

chronometric calibration for the Tabun Cave suggests a date as early as 120,000 y.a. Neandertals thus may *slightly* precede modern forms in the Near East, but there would appear to be considerable overlap in the timing of occupation by these different humans. And recall, the modern site at Mt. Carmel (Skhūl) is very near the Neandertal site (Tabun). Clearly, the dynamics of *Homo sapiens* evolution in the Near East are highly complex (Shea, 1998), and no simple model may explain later hominid evolution adequately.

CENTRAL EUROPE

Central Europe has been a source of many fossil finds, including numerous fairly early anatomically modern *H. sapiens*. At several sites, it appears that some fossils display both Neandertal and modern features, which supports some form of regional continuity (from Neandertal to modern). Such genetic continuity from earlier (Neandertal) to later (modern *H. sapiens*) populations was perhaps the case at Vindija in Croatia, where typical Neandertals were found in earlier contexts (see p. 259).

Smith (1984) offers another example of local continuity from Mladeč in the Czech Republic. Among the earlier European modern *H. sapiens* fossils, dated to about 33,000 y.a., the Mladeč crania display a great deal of variation, probably in part due to sexual dimorphism. Although each of the crania (except for one of the females) displays a prominent supraorbital torus, it is reduced from the typical Neandertal pattern. Even though there is some suggestion of continuity from Neandertals to modern humans, Smith is confident that, given certain anatomical features, the Mladeč remains are best classified as *H. sapiens sapiens*.

WESTERN EUROPE

This area of the world and its fossils have received the greatest attention for several reasons, one of which is probably serendipity. Over the last century and a half, many of the scholars interested in this kind of research happened to live

anatomically modern material from China, perhaps dating to 50,000 y.a. or more (Etler, personal communication) (see Fig. 11-6).

In addition, the Jinniushan skeleton discussed in Chapter 10 (see p. 252) has been suggested by some researchers (Tiemel et al., 1994) as hinting at modern features in China as early as 200,000 y.a. If this date (as early as that proposed for direct antecedents of modern *H. sapiens* in Africa) should prove accurate, it would cast doubt on the complete replacement model. Indeed, quite opposed to the complete replacement model and more in support of regional continuity, many Chinese paleoanthropologists see a continuous evolution from Chinese *H. erectus* to premodern forms and lastly to anatomically modern humans. This view is supported by Wolpoff, who mentions that materials from Upper Cave at Zhoukoudian "have a number of features that are characteristically regional" and that these features are definitely not African (1989, p. 83).*

In addition to the well-known finds from China, anatomically modern remains have also been discovered in southern Asia. At Batadomba Iena, in southern Sri Lanka, modern *Homo sapiens* finds have been dated to 25,500 y.a. (Kennedy and Deraniyagala, 1989).

AUSTRALIA

During glacial times, the Indonesian islands were joined to the Asian mainland, but Australia was not. It's likely that by 50,000 y.a., Sahul—the area including New Guinea and Australia—was inhabited by modern humans. Bamboo rafts may have been the means of crossing the sea between islands, which would not have been a simple exercise. Just where the future Australians came from is unknown, but Borneo, Java, and New Guinea have all been suggested.

Human occupation of Australia appears to have occurred quite early, with some archaeological sites dating to 55,000 y.a. Dating of the earliest Australian human remains (which are all modern *H. sapiens*), however, is controversial. The earliest finds so far discovered have come from Lake Mungo in southeastern Australia. In agreement with archaeological context and radiocarbon dates, the hominids from this site have been dated at approximately 30,000–25,000 y.a. Newly determined age estimates, using ESR and uranium series dating (Table 11-1), have dramatically extended the suggested time depth to about 60,000 y.a. (Thorne et al., 1999). The lack of correlation of these more ancient age estimates with other data, however, has provoked serious concerns among some researchers (Gillespie and Roberts, 2000).

The recovery and sequencing of mitochondrial DNA from these prehistoric Australians is as intriguing (and controversial) as the early dating estimates (Adcock et al., 2001). While the primary researchers are confident that these samples are authentically ancient, the nagging possibility of contamination can't be entirely ruled out. Indeed, other researchers remain unconvinced that the mtDNA from Lake Mungo is ancient at all (Cooper et al., 2001). Obviously, given the uncertainties, we will need further corroboration for both the dating and DNA findings before passing judgment.

---

*Wolpoff's statement supports his multiregional hypothesis. His reference to Africa is a criticism of the complete replacement hypothesis.

TABLE 11-1 | Additional Techniques for Dating Middle and Upper Pleistocene Sites

Technique	Physical Basis	Examples of Use
Uranium series dating	Radioactive decay of short-lived uranium isotopes	To date limestone formations (e.g., stalagmites) and ancient ostrich eggshells; to estimate age of Jinniushan site in China and Ngandong site in Java, both corroborated by ESR dates
Thermoluminescence (TL) dating	Accumulation of trapped electrons within certain crystals released during heating	To date ancient flint tools (either deliberately or accidentally heated); to provide key dates for the Qafzeh site
Electron spin resonance (ESR) dating	Measurement (counting) of accumulated trapped electrons	To date dental enamel; to corroborate dating of Qafzeh, Skhūl, and Tabun sites in Israel, Ngandong site in Java, Klasies River Mouth and Border Cave in South Africa, and the Lake Mungo site in Australia

Source: Cook et al., 1984; Aiken et al., 1993.

Unlike the more gracile early Australian forms from Lake Mungo are the Kow Swamp people, who are thought to have lived between about 14,000 and 9,000 y.a. (Figs. 11-8 and 11-9). The presence of certain archaic traits, such as receding foreheads, heavy supraorbital tori, and thick bones, are difficult to explain, since these features contrast with the postcranial anatomy, which matches that of recent native Australians.

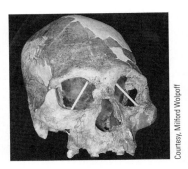

Courtesy, Milford Wolpoff

FIGURE 11-8 Kow Swamp (Australia). Note the considerable robusticity in this relatively late Australian *Homo sapiens sapiens* cranium.

Quick Review — Key Early Modern *Homo sapiens* Discoveries from Europe, Asia, and Australia

Site	Dates (y.a.)	Human Remains*
Abrigo do Lagar Velho (Portugal)	24,500	Four-year-old child's skeleton
Cro-Magnon (France)	30,000	8 individuals
Ordos (Mongolia, China)	50,000	1 individual
Kow Swamp (Australia)	14,000–9,000	Large sample (more than 40 individuals), including adults, juveniles, and infants
Lake Mungo (Australia)	?60,000–30,000	3 individuals, one a cremation

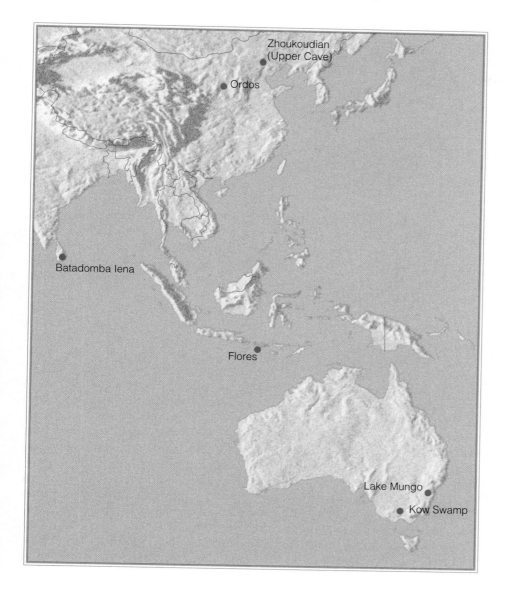

FIGURE 11-9 Anatomically modern *Homo sapiens* and *Homo floresiensis* (Asia and Australia).

Something New and Different

As we have seen, by 25,000 years ago, modern humans had dispersed to all major areas of the Old World, and they would soon journey to the New World as well. But at about the same time, there were still remnant populations of earlier hominids surviving in a few remote and isolated corners. We mentioned in Chapter 9 that populations of *Homo erectus* in Java managed to survive on this island long after their cousins had disappeared from other areas (e.g., China and East Africa). Moreover, even though they persisted well into the Upper Pleistocene, physically these Javanese hominids were still very similar to other *H. erectus* (see p. 227).

However, other populations apparently branched off from some of these remnant Indonesian *H. erectus* groups and either intentionally or accidentally

FIGURE 11-10 Cranium of adult female *Homo floresiensis* from Flores, Indonesia, dated 18,000 y.a.

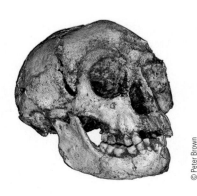

© Peter Brown

found their way to other, smaller islands to the east. Here, under even more extreme isolation pressures, they evolved in an astonishing direction. In late 2004, the world awoke to the startling announcement of an extremely small-bodied and small-brained hominid discovered on the island of Flores, east of Java (see Fig. 11-9). The remains consist of an incomplete skeleton of an adult female and additional pieces from six other individuals. The female skeleton is remarkable in several ways (Fig. 11-10). First, she stood barely 3 feet tall (as short as the smallest australopithecine), and her brain (estimated at a mere 380 cm³) was no larger than that of a chimpanzee (Brown et al., 2004). And perhaps most startling of all, these extraordinary hominids were still living on Flores just 18,000 years ago (Morwood et al., 2004)!

Where did they come from? As we said, their predecessors were probably *H. erectus* populations like those found on Java. How they got to Flores (some 400 miles away, a portion of which is over open ocean) is a mystery. There are several connecting islands, and to get between them, these hominids may have drifted across on rafts; but there's no way to be sure of this. How did they get to be so physically different from all other known hominids? Here we are a little more certain of the answer. Isolated island populations can quite rapidly diverge from their relatives elsewhere—as we noted in Chapter 2 regarding the famous Galápagos finches observed by Darwin. A frequent consequence seen among such isolated animals involves natural selection favoring reduced body size. For example, there are populations of dwarf elephants found on islands in the Mediterranean as well as on some channel islands off the coast of southern California. And perhaps most interesting of all, dwarf elephants *also* evolved on Flores (found in the same beds with the little hominids). The evolutionary mechanism thought to explain such dwarfing in both the elephants and the hominids is an adaptation to a reduced amount of resources, leading through selection to smaller body size.

Other than short stature, what did the Flores hominids look like? In terms of cranial shape, thickness of cranial bone, and dentition, they most resemble *Homo erectus*. Nevertheless, there are derived features that also set them apart from all other hominids. Thus, they have been placed in a separate species, *Homo floresiensis*.

What became of the Flores hominids, and could some still be out there somewhere? They were extremely divergent and probably specialized as well. Not long after 18,000 y.a., modern humans reached Flores, and it seems their arrival spelled the doom for *H. floresiensis*. They seem to have perished quickly, leaving no descendants. It's very unlikely that anything like these strange hominids survived anywhere much after 10,000 years ago. Currently, with more than 6 billion modern humans inhabiting every corner of the planet, devouring resources as we go, the likelihood of finding *any* living "archaic" hominid (Yeti, bigfoot, or an *H. floresiensis* hominid) is extraordinarily slight.

Technology and Art in the Upper Paleolithic

EUROPE

The cultural period known as the Upper Paleolithic began in western Europe approximately 40,000 years ago (Fig. 11-11). Upper Paleolithic cultures are usually divided into five different industries based on stone tool technologies: (1) Chatelperronian, (2) Aurignacian, (3) Gravettian, (4) Solutrean, and (5) Magdalenian. Major environmental shifts were also apparent during this period. During the last glacial period, about 30,000 y.a., a warming trend lasting several thousand years partially melted the glacial ice. The result was that much of Eurasia was covered by tundra and steppe, a vast area of treeless country dotted with lakes and marshes. In many areas in the north, permafrost prevented the growth of trees but permitted the growth, in the short summers, of flowering plants, mosses, and other kinds of vegetation. This vegetation served as an enormous pasture for herbivorous animals, large and small, and carnivorous animals fed off the herbivores. It was a hunter's paradise, with millions of animals dispersed across expanses of tundra and grassland, from Spain through Europe and into the Russian steppes.

Large herds of reindeer roamed the tundra and steppes along with mammoths, bison, horses, and a host of smaller animals that served as a bountiful source of food. In addition, humans exploited fish and fowl systematically for the first time, especially along the southern tier of Europe. It was a time of relative abundance, and ultimately Upper Paleolithic people spread out over Europe, living in caves and open-air camps and building large shelters. Far more elaborate burials are also found, most spectacularly at the 24,000-year-old Sungir site near Moscow, where grave goods included a bed of red ocher, thousands of ivory beads, long spears made of straightened mammoth tusks, ivory engravings, and jewelry (Formicola and Buzhilova, 2004) (Fig. 11-12). During this period, either western Europe or perhaps portions of Africa achieved the highest population density in human history up to that time.

Humans and other animals in the midlatitudes of Eurasia had to cope with shifts in climatic conditions, some of which were quite rapid. For example, at 20,000 y.a. another climatic "pulse" caused the weather to become noticeably colder in Europe and Asia as the continental glaciations reached their maximum extent for this entire glacial period (called the Würm in Eurasia).

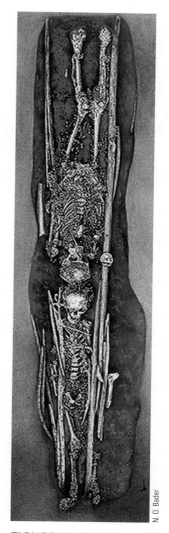

N. O. Bader

GLACIAL	UPPER PALEOLITHIC (beginnings)	CULTURAL PERIODS
W Ü R M	17,000 –	Magdalenian
	21,000 –	Solutrean
	27,000 –	Gravettian
	40,000 –	Aurignacian Chatelperronian
	Middle Paleolithic	Mousterian

FIGURE 11-11 Cultural periods of the European Upper Paleolithic and their approximate beginning dates.

FIGURE 11-12 Skeleton of two teenagers, a male and a female, from Sungir, Russia. Dated 24,000 y.a., this is the richest find of any Upper Paleolithic grave.

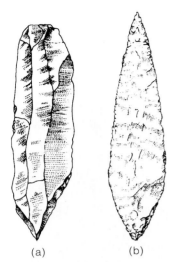

FIGURE 11-13 (a) Burin. A very common Upper Paleolithic tool. (b) Solutrean blade. This is the best-known work of the Solutrean tradition. Solutrean stonework is considered the most highly developed of any Upper Paleolithic industry.

Magdalenian Pertaining to the final phase of the Upper Paleolithic stone tool industry in Europe.

burins Small, chisel-like tools (with a pointed end) thought to have been used to engrave bone, antler, ivory, or wood.

As a variety of organisms attempted to adapt to these changing conditions, *Homo sapiens* had a major advantage: the elaboration of an increasingly sophisticated technology (and probably other components of culture as well). Indeed, probably one of the greatest challenges facing numerous late Pleistocene mammals was the ever more dangerously equipped humans—a trend that has continued to modern times.

The Upper Paleolithic was an age of technological innovation and can be compared to the past few hundred years in our recent history of amazing technological change after centuries of relative inertia. Anatomically modern humans of the Upper Paleolithic not only invented new and specialized tools (Fig. 11-13), but, as we have seen, also greatly increased the use of (and probably experimented with) new materials, such as bone, ivory, and antler.

Solutrean tools are good examples of Upper Paleolithic skill and perhaps aesthetic appreciation as well (see Fig. 11-13b). In this lithic (stone) tradition, stoneknapping developed to the finest degree ever known. Using specialized flaking techniques, the artist/technicians made beautiful parallel-flaked lance heads, expertly flaked on both surfaces, with such delicate points that they can be considered works of art that quite possibly never served, or were intended to serve, a utilitarian purpose.

The last stage of the Upper Paleolithic, known as the **Magdalenian,** saw even more advances in technology. The spear-thrower, or *atlatl* (Fig. 11-14), a wooden or bone hooked rod, acted to extend the hunter's arm, thus enhancing the force and distance of a spear throw. For catching salmon and other fish, the barbed harpoon is a clever example of the craftsperson's skill. There is also evidence that the bow and arrow may have been used for the first time during this period. The introduction of much more efficient manufacturing techniques provided an abundance of standardized stone blades that could be fashioned into **burins** (see Fig. 11-13a) for working wood, bone, and antler; borers for drilling holes in skins, bones, and shells; and knives with serrated or notched edges for scraping wooden shafts into a variety of tools.

The elaboration of many more specialized tools by Upper Paleolithic peoples probably made more resources available to them and may also have had an impact on the biology of these populations. Emphasizing a biocultural interpretation, C. Loring Brace, of the University of Michigan, has suggested that with more efficient tools used for food processing, anatomically modern *H. sapiens* would not have required the large front teeth (incisors) seen in earlier populations.

In addition to their reputation as hunters, western Europeans of the Upper Paleolithic are even better known for their symbolic representation, what has commonly been called "art." Given uncertainties concerning what actually should be called "art," archaeologist Margaret Conkey, of the University of

FIGURE 11-14 Spear-thrower (atlatl). Note the carving.

California, Berkeley, refers to Upper Paleolithic cave paintings, sculptures, engravings, and so forth, as "visual and material imagery" (Conkey, 1987, p. 423). We will continue to use the term *art* to describe many of these prehistoric representations, but you should recognize that we do so mainly as a cultural convention—and perhaps a limiting one.

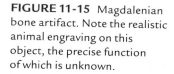

FIGURE 11-15 Magdalenian bone artifact. Note the realistic animal engraving on this object, the precise function of which is unknown.

We must also remember that there is an extremely wide geographical distribution of symbolic images, best known from many parts of Europe, but now also well documented from Siberia, North Africa, South Africa, and Australia. Given a 25,000-year time depth of what we call "Paleolithic art" and its nearly worldwide distribution, there is indeed marked variability in expression.

In addition to cave art, numerous examples of small sculptures have been excavated from sites in western, central, and eastern Europe. Beyond these quite well-known figurines, there are numerous other examples of what is frequently termed "portable art," including elaborate engravings on tools and tool handles (Fig. 11-15). Such symbolism can be found in many parts of Europe and was already well established early in the Aurignacian (by 33,000 y.a.).

Female statuettes, popularly known as "Venus figures," were sculpted not only in western Europe, but in central and eastern Europe and Siberia as well. Some of these figures were realistically carved, and the faces appear to be modeled after actual women (Fig. 11-16). Other figurines may seem grotesque, with sexual characteristics exaggerated, perhaps for fertility or other ritual purposes (Fig. 11-17).

It is, however, during the final phases of the Upper Paleolithic, particularly during the Magdalenian, that European prehistoric art reached its climax.

(a)   (b)

FIGURE 11-16 Venus of Brassempouy. Upper Paleolithic artists were capable of portraying human realism (shown here) as well as symbolism (depicted in Fig. 11-17). (a) Frontal view. (b) Lateral view.

FIGURE 11-17 Venus of Willendorf, Austria. (*Note:* This figure is among the most exaggerated and should be compared with Fig. 11-16.)

Cave art is now known from more than 150 separate sites, the vast majority from southwestern France and northern Spain. Apparently, in other areas the rendering of such images did not take place in deep caves. Peoples in central Europe, China, Africa, and elsewhere certainly may have painted or carved representations on rock faces in the open, but these images long since would have eroded. Thus, it is fortuitous that the people of at least one of the many sophisticated cultures of the Upper Paleolithic chose to journey belowground to create their artwork, preserving it not just for their immediate descendants, but for us as well. The most spectacular and most famous of the cave art sites are Lascaux and Grotte Chauvet (in France) and Altamira (in Spain).

In Lascaux Cave, immense wild bulls dominate what is called the Great Hall of Bulls, and horses, deer, and other animals adorn the walls in black, red, and yellow, drawn with remarkable skill. Equally impressive, at Altamira the walls and ceiling of an immense cave are filled with superb portrayals of bison in red and black, the "artist" taking advantage of bulges to give a sense of relief to the paintings. The cave is a treasure of beautiful art whose meaning has never been satisfactorily explained. It could have been religious or magical, a form of visual communication, or art for the sake of beauty.

Yet another spectacular example of cave art from western Europe was discovered in 1994 at Grotte Chauvet in southeastern France. Preserved inside the cave, unseen for perhaps 30,000 years, are a multitude of images, including dots, stenciled human handprints, and, most dramatically, hundreds of animal representations (Figs. 11-18 and 11-19). Radiocarbon dating has placed the paintings during the Aurignacian (more than 30,000 y.a.), making Grotte Chauvet considerably earlier than the Magdalenian sites of Lascaux and Altamira.

AFRICA

Early accomplishments in rock art, perhaps as early as in Europe, are seen in southern Africa (Namibia), where a site containing such art is dated between 28,000 and 19,000 y.a. In addition, evidence of portable personal adornment is seen as early as 38,000 y.a. in the form of beads fashioned from ostrich eggshells.

In terms of stone tool technology, microliths (thumbnail-sized stone flakes hafted to make knives, saws, etc.) and blades characterize Late Stone Age* African industries. There was also considerable use of bone and antler in central Africa, perhaps some of it quite early. Recent excavations in the Katanda area of the eastern portion of the Democratic Republic of the Congo have shown remarkable development of bone craftwork. In fact, preliminary reports by Alison Brooks of George Washington University and John Yellen of the National Science Foundation have demonstrated that these technological achievements rival those of the more renowned European Upper Paleolithic (Yellen et al., 1995).

The most important artifacts discovered there are a dozen intricately made bone tools excavated from three sites (see Fig. 11-18). These tools, made from the bones of large mammals, apparently were first ground to flatten and sharpen them, and then some were precisely pressure-flaked to produce a row

---

*The Late Stone Age in Africa is equivalent to the Upper Paleolithic in Eurasia.

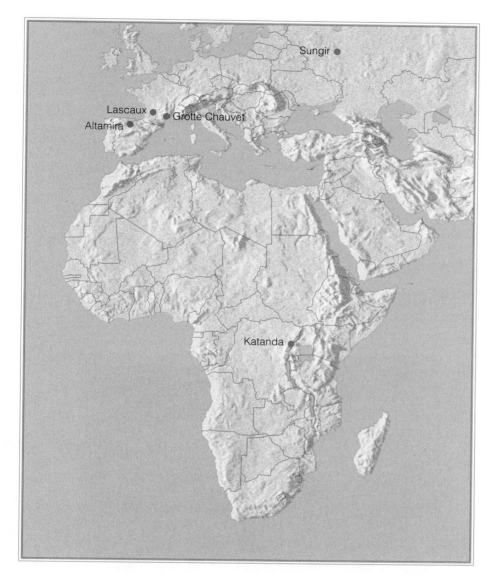

FIGURE 11-18 Upper Paleolithic archaeological sites. (Katanda, in the Democratic Republic of the Congo, may be considerably older than the European sites, perhaps dating to the Middle Stone Age.)

of barbs. In form, these tools are similar to what have been called "harpoons" from the later Upper Paleolithic of Europe (Magdalenian, c. 15,000 y.a.).

The dating of the Katanda sites is crucial for drawing useful comparisons with the European Upper Paleolithic. However, the bone used for the tools was unsuitable for radiocarbon dating (perhaps it was too old and beyond the range of this technique). As a result, the other techniques now used for this time range—thermoluminescence, electron spin resonance, and uranium series dating (see Table 11-1, p. 290)—were all applied. The results proved consistent, indicating dates between 180,000 and 75,000 y.a.*

However, there remain some difficulties in establishing the clear association of the bone implements with the materials that have supplied the

---

*If these dates prove accurate, Katanda would actually be earlier than Late Stone Age (and thus be considered Middle Stone Age).

FIGURE 11-19 Cave art from Grotte Chauvet, France. (a) Bear. (b) Aurochs and rhinoceros.

Jean Clottes/Document elaborated with the support of the French Ministry of Culture and Communication, Regional Direction for Cultural Affairs, Rhône-Alpes, Regional Department of Archaeology.

(a)

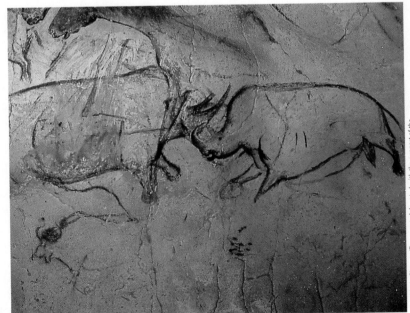

Jean-Marie Chauvet/Document elaborated with the support of the French Ministry of Culture and Communication, Regional Direction for Cultural Affairs, Rhône-Alpes, Regional Department of Archaeology.

(b)

chronometric age estimates. Indeed, Richard Klein, a coauthor of one of the initial reports (Brooks et al., 1995), does not accept the suggested great antiquity for these finds and believes they may be much younger. Nevertheless, if the early age estimates should hold up, we once again will look *first* to Africa as the crucial source area for human origins—not just for biological aspects, but for cultural aspects as well.

Summary of Upper Paleolithic Culture

As we look back at the Upper Paleolithic, we can see it as the culmination of 2 million years of cultural development. Change proceeded incredibly slowly for most of the Pleistocene, but as cultural traditions and materials accumulated and the brain (and, we assume, intelligence) expanded and reorganized, the rate of change quickened.

Cultural evolution continued with the appearance of early premodern humans and moved a bit faster with later premoderns. Neandertals in Eurasia and their contemporaries elsewhere added deliberate burials, technological innovations, and much more.

Building on existing cultures, late Pleistocene populations attained sophisticated cultural and material heights in a seemingly short (by previous standards) burst of exciting activity. In Europe and central Africa particularly, there seem to have been dramatic cultural innovations that saw big game hunting, powerful new weapons (including harpoons, spear-throwers, and possibly the bow and arrow), body ornaments, needles, "tailored" clothing, and burials with elaborate grave goods (the latter perhaps indicating some sort of status hierarchy).

This dynamic age was doomed, or so it appears, by the climatic changes of about 10,000 y.a. As the temperature slowly rose and the glaciers retreated, animal and plant species were seriously impacted, and humans were thus affected, too. As traditional prey animals were depleted or disappeared altogether, other means of obtaining food were sought.

Grinding hard seeds or roots became important, and as familiarity with plant propagation increased, domestication of plants and animals developed. Dependence on domestication became critical, and with it came permanent settlements, new technology, and more complex social organization. The continuing story of human evolution and the ways we study contemporary population diversity will be the topics of the remainder of this text.

Visual Summary

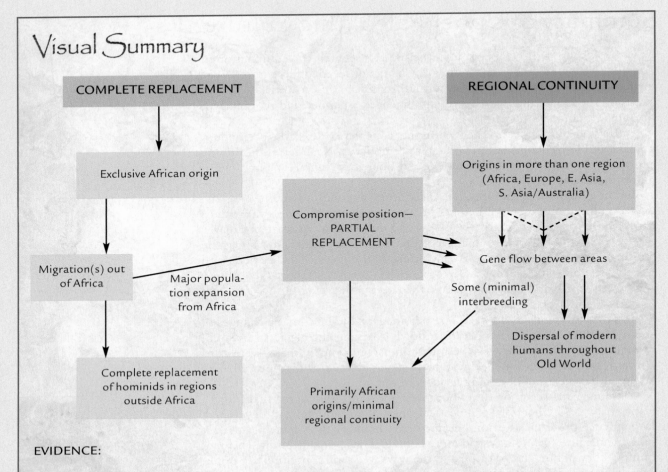

COMPLETE REPLACEMENT

Exclusive African origin

Migration(s) out of Africa

Major population expansion from Africa

Complete replacement of hominids in regions outside Africa

Compromise position—PARTIAL REPLACEMENT

Primarily African origins/minimal regional continuity

REGIONAL CONTINUITY

Origins in more than one region (Africa, Europe, E. Asia, S. Asia/Australia)

Gene flow between areas

Some (minimal) interbreeding

Dispersal of modern humans throughout Old World

EVIDENCE:

Fossils: Herto hominids and other less well-dated and likely later remains

Genetic: Ancient DNA (Neandertal compared with *H. sapiens sapiens*); contemporary human distribution of population variation (derived from mtDNA, automosomal nuclear DNA, Y chromosome, X chromosome)

Archaeological: Rapid replacement in Europe of Mousterian (and Chatelperronian) by Aurignacian; major behavioral innovations correlated with Upper Paleolithic

Fossils: Possible hybridization shown by Abrigo do Lagar Velho

Genetic: Likelihood of larger population size in Africa and migration to other regions with interbreeding; but mostly African genetic ancestry of all living humans

Archaeological: Chatelperronian in Europe, suggesting that tools were imitated or exchanged between Neandertals and modern humans

Fossils: Continuity of some anatomical traits—especially in central and western Europe and Australia

Genetic: Not a prime source of support for regional continuity

Archaeological: Overlap of Mousterian in Near East between Neandertal and modern human sites

Summary

The date and location of the origin of anatomically modern human beings have been the subjects of a fierce debate for the past decade, and the end is not in sight. One hypothesis (complete replacement) claims that anatomically modern forms first evolved in Africa more than 100,000 y.a. and then, migrating out of Africa, completely replaced premodern *H. sapiens* in the rest of the world. Another school (regional continuity) takes a diametrically different view and maintains that in various geographical regions of the world, local groups of premodern *H. sapiens* evolved directly to anatomically modern humans. A third hypothesis (partial replacement) takes a somewhat middle position, suggesting an African origin but also accepting some later hybridization outside of Africa.

Recent research coming from several sources is beginning to provide more clarity concerning the origins of modern humans. Molecular evidence as well as the dramatic new fossil finds from Herto, Ethiopia, suggest that a multiregional origin of modern humans is unlikely. Sometime, soon after 150,000 y.a., perhaps there was complete replacement of all hominids outside Africa as regional populations were displaced by migrating Africans. However, such absolutely *complete* replacement will be very difficult to prove (and is not really what we would expect). More than likely, at least some interbreeding probably did take place. Nevertheless, it is looking more and more like such intermixing was quite minimal.

Archaeological evidence of early modern humans also presents a fascinating picture of our most immediate ancestors. The Upper Paleolithic was an age of extraordinary innovation and achievement in technology and art. Many new and complex tools were introduced, and their production indicates fine skill in working wood, bone, and antler. Cave art in France and Spain displays the masterful ability of Upper Paleolithic painters, and beautiful sculptures have been found at many European sites. Sophisticated symbolic representations have also been found in Africa and elsewhere. Upper Paleolithic *Homo sapiens* displayed amazing development in a relatively short period of time. The culture produced during this period led the way to still newer and more complex cultural techniques and methods.

As a further study aid, the most significant fossil discoveries discussed in this chapter are presented in Table 11-2.

Critical Thinking Questions

1. What anatomical characteristics define "modern" as compared to "premodern" humans? Assume that you are analyzing an incomplete skeleton that may be early modern *H. sapiens*. Which portions of the skeleton would be most informative, and why?

2. Go through the chapter and list all the forms of evidence that you think support the complete replacement model. Now, do the same for the regional continuity model. What evidence do you find most convincing, and why?

3. Why are the fossils recently discovered from Herto so important? How does this evidence influence your conclusions in question 2?

4. What archaeological evidence shows that modern human behavior during the Upper Paleolithic was significantly different from that of earlier hominids? Do you think that early modern *H. sapiens* populations were behaviorally "superior" to the Neandertals? Be careful to define what you mean by "superior."

5. Why do you think some Upper Paleolithic people painted in caves? Why don't we find such evidence of cave painting from a wider geographical area?

TABLE 11-2 | Most Significant Modern *Homo sapiens* and *Homo floresiensis* Discoveries Discussed in This Chapter

Site	Dates (y.a.)	Human Remains	Comments
Flores (Indonesia)	95,000–13,000*	Incomplete skeleton; piecesof 6 other individuals	Dwarfed species (*H. floresiensis*); very divergent, very small body size and brain size; almost certainly an evolutionary dead end
Abrigo do Lagar Velho (Portugal)	24,500	Four-year-old child's skeleton	Possible evidence of hybridization between Neandertals and modern *H. sapiens*
Cro-Magnon (France)	30,000	8 individuals	Famous site of early modern *H. sapiens*, but there are dozens of other sites in Europe and elsewhere
Lake Mungo (Australia)	?60,000–30,000	3 individuals	Early dating estimate is surprising; if confirmed, would be earlier than established evidence in Europe or East Asia
Qafzeh (Israel)	110,000	Minimum of 20 individuals	Quite early site; shows considerable variation
Skhūl (Israel)	115,000	Minimum of 10 individuals	Earliest well-dated modern *H. sapiens* outside of Africa; also perhaps contemporaneous with neighboring Tabun Neandertal site
Herto (Ethiopia)	160,000–154,000	3 individuals and other fragments	Earliest well-dated modern humans; placed in separate subspecies (*H. sapiens idaltu*); location (in Africa) is notable

*The full estimated time range for all seven individuals. The partial skeleton is dated to approximately 18,000 y.a.

🌐 Media Resources

The Companion Website for *Essentials of Physical Anthropology*, Sixth Edition
http://anthropology.wadsworth.com/jurmain6e_ess

Supplement your review of this chapter by going to this text's companion website to take one of the practice quizzes, use the flash cards to master key terms, and check out the many other resources and study aids. Also visit the website to learn about important new discoveries in paleoanthropology by checking the "Latest Dirt" feature authored by Robert Jurmain.

CD-ROMs in Physical Anthropology

Wadsworth Publishing has also developed three CD-ROMs to accompany this text and enhance learning in physical anthropology (for further descriptions of these CD-ROMs, see p. xix):

Virtual Laboratories for Physical Anthropology CD-ROM, Third Edition

Basic Genetics for Anthropology CD-ROM: Principles and Applications

Hominid Fossils CD-ROM: An Interactive Atlas

For this chapter, see especially the Virtual Laboratories for Physical Anthropology CD-ROM, Third Edition, and the Hominid Fossils CD-ROM: An Interactive Atlas.

Readings of Interest

Klein, Richard. 1999. *The Human Career: Human Biological and Cultural Origins.* 2nd ed. Chicago: University of Chicago Press.

Klein, Richard (with Blake Edgar). 2002. *The Dawn of Human Culture.* New York: Wiley

Lewin, Roger. 1998. *The Origin of Modern Humans.* New York: Scientific American Origins.

Relethford, John. 2001. *Genetics and the Search for Modern Human Origins.* New York: Wiley-Liss.

Stringer, Christopher, and Robin McKie. 1997. *African Exodus: The Origins of Modern Humanity.* New York: Holt.

12 | Human Variation and Adaptation

Focus Question

How does the contemporary evolutionary-based approach to understanding human diversity differ from the traditional nineteenth-century approach?

Introduction

At some time or other, you have probably been asked to specify your "race" or "ethnic identity" on an application form or census form. What did you think when you were asked this question? How comfortable were you in answering the question? Usually, there is a variety of racial/ethnic categories to choose from. Was it easy to pick an appropriate category? What about your parents and grandparents? Where would they fit in?

Notions relating to human diversity have for centuries played a large role in human relations, and they still influence political and social perceptions. While it would be comforting to believe that informed views have become almost universal, the gruesome tally of genocidal/ethnic cleansing atrocities in recent years tells us tragically that worldwide, as a species, we have a long way to go before tolerance becomes the norm.

In Chapter 11, we discussed the origin and dispersal of modern humans. That was the last major episode in our lineage of what we have called *macroevolution*. However, our species continues to evolve, and the ongoing process is referred to as *microevolution*. Physical anthropologists study human microevolution from an evolutionary perspective.

As noted, most people don't seem to understand the nature of human diversity, and worse yet, many seem quite unwilling to accept what science has to contribute on the subject. Many of the misconceptions are no doubt rooted in cultural history over the last few centuries, especially regarding how *race* is defined and categorized. Although many cultures have attempted to come to grips with these issues, for better or worse, the most influential of these perspectives developed in the Western world (i.e., Europe and North America). The way many individuals still view themselves and their relationship to other peoples is a legacy of the last four centuries of racial interpretations.

We've also seen (in Chapters 3 and 4) how physical characteristics are influenced by the DNA in our cells. Furthermore, we discussed how individuals inherit genes from parents and how variations in genes (alleles) can produce different expressions of traits. In Chapter 4, we also focused on how the basic principles of inheritance relate to evolutionary change.

In this chapter, we turn once again to topics directly related to genetics—namely, biological diversity in humans and how humans adapt physically to environmental challenges. Following a discussion of historical attempts at explaining human phenotypic diversity and racial classification, we examine contemporary methods of interpreting diversity. In recent years, several new techniques have emerged that permit direct examination of the DNA molecule, revealing differences between individuals even at the level of single nucleotides. But even as discoveries of different levels of diversity emerge, geneticists have also revealed that our species is remarkably uniform genetically, particularly when compared with other species.

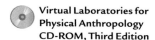

Click

Go to the following CD-ROMs for interactive activities and exercises on topics covered in this chapter:

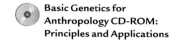

Virtual Laboratories for Physical Anthropology CD-ROM, Third Edition

Basic Genetics for Anthropology CD-ROM: Principles and Applications

Later in the chapter, we consider human phenotypic variation within the context of adaptation to specific environmental contexts. We examine how populations and individuals differ in their adaptive response to such factors as ultraviolet radiation, heat, cold, and high altitude. Finally, we consider the significant role of infectious disease in human evolution and adaptation.

Historical Views of Human Variation

The first step toward understanding natural phenomena is the ordering of variation into categories that can then be named, discussed, and perhaps studied. Historically, when different groups of people came into contact with one another, they offered explanations for the physical differences they saw. Because skin color was so noticeable, it was one of the more frequently explained traits, and most systems of racial classification were based on it.

As early as 1350 B.C., the ancient Egyptians had classified humans on the basis of skin color: red for Egyptian, yellow for people to the east, white for those to the north, and black for Africans south of the Sahara (Gossett, 1963). In the sixteenth century, after the discovery of the New World, Europe embarked on a period of intense exploration and colonization in both the New and Old Worlds. One result of this contact was an increased awareness of human diversity.

Throughout the eighteenth and nineteenth centuries, European and American scientists concentrated primarily on describing and classifying the biological variation in humans as well as in nonhuman species. The first scientific attempt to describe the newly discovered variation between human populations was Linnaeus' taxonomic classification, which placed humans into four separate categories (Linnaeus, 1758). Linnaeus assigned behavioral and intellectual qualities to each group, with the least complimentary descriptions going to black Africans. This ranking was typical of the period and reflected the almost universal European ethnocentric view that Europeans were superior to all other peoples.

Johann Friedrich Blumenbach (1752–1840), a German anatomist, classified humans into five races. Although Blumenbach's categories came to be described simply as white, yellow, red, black, and brown, he also used criteria other than skin color. Moreover, he emphasized that racial categories based on skin color were arbitrary and that many traits, including skin color, weren't discrete phenomena. Blumenbach pointed out that to attempt to classify all humans using such a system would be to omit completely all those who didn't neatly fall into a specific category. Furthermore, it was recognized by Blumenbach and others that traits such as skin color showed overlapping expression between groups.

In 1842, Anders Retzius, a Swedish anatomist, developed the *cephalic index* as a method of describing the shape of the head. The cephalic index, derived by dividing maximum head breadth by maximum length and multiplying by 100, gives the ratio of head breadth to length. (It is important to note that the cephalic index does not measure head size.) The cephalic index is still used to assess head shape in individual skulls, but in the nineteenth century, it was viewed as a precise scientific technique that could be used to categorize groups of people. Furthermore, because people could be quickly categorized by a single number, it provided a superficial but easy method for describing variation. Individuals with an index of less than 75 had long, narrow heads and were labeled "dolichocephalic." "Brachycephalic" individuals, with broad heads, had an index of over 80; and those whose indices were between 75 and 80 were "mesocephalic." Northern Europeans tended to be dolichocephalic, while southern Europeans were brachycephalic. Not surprisingly, these results led to heated and nationalistic debate over whether one group was superior to another.

By the mid-nineteenth century, populations were ranked essentially on a scale based on skin color (along with size and shape of the head), with Africans at the bottom. Moreover, Europeans themselves were ranked so that northern, light-skinned populations were considered superior to their southern, somewhat darker-skinned neighbors.

To many Europeans, the fact that non-Europeans weren't Christian suggested that these "foreigners" were "uncivilized" and implied an even more basic inferiority of character and intellect. This view was rooted in a concept called **biological determinism,** which in part holds that there is an association between physical characteristics and such attributes as intelligence, morals, values, abilities, and even social and economic condition. In other words, cultural variations are *inherited* in the same manner as biological variations. It follows, then, that there are inherent behavioral and cognitive differences between groups and that some groups are *by nature* superior to others. Following this logic, it's a simple matter to justify the persecution and even enslavement of other peoples simply because their appearance differs from what is familiar.

biological determinism The concept that phenomena, including various aspects of behavior (e.g., intelligence, values, morals) are governed by biological (genetic) factors; the inaccurate association of various behavioral attributes with certain biological traits, such as skin color.

After 1850, biological determinism was a constant theme underlying common thinking as well as scientific research in Europe and the United States. Deterministic (and what we today would call racist) views were held to some extent by most people, including such notable figures as Thomas Jefferson, Georges Cuvier, Benjamin Franklin, Charles Lyell, Abraham Lincoln, Charles Darwin, and Oliver Wendell Holmes. Commenting on this usually de-emphasized characteristic of notable historical figures, the late evolutionary biologist Stephen J. Gould (1981, p. 32) remarked that "all American culture heroes embraced racial attitudes that would embarrass public-school mythmakers."

Francis Galton (1822–1911), a cousin of Charles Darwin, shared an increasingly common fear among nineteenth-century Europeans that "civilized society" was being weakened by the failure of natural selection to completely eliminate unfit and inferior members (Greene, 1981, p. 107). Galton wrote and lectured on the necessity of "race improvement" and suggested government regulation of marriage and family size, an approach he called **eugenics.** Although eugenics had its share of critics, its popularity flourished throughout the 1930s, but nowhere was it more attractive than in Germany, where the viewpoint took a horrifying turn. The false idea of pure races was increasingly extolled as a means of reestablishing a strong and prosperous state. Eugenics was seen as scientific justification for purging Germany of its "unfit," and many of Germany's scientists continued to support the policies of racial purity and eugenics during the Nazi period (Proctor, 1988, p. 143), when these policies served as justification for condemning millions of people to death.

eugenics The philosophy of "race improvement" through the forced sterilization of members of some groups and increased reproduction among others; an overly simplified, often racist view that is now discredited.

But at the same time, many scientists were turning away from racial typologies and classification in favor of a more evolutionary approach. No doubt for some, this shift in direction was motivated by their growing concerns over the goals of the eugenics movement. Probably more important, however, was the synthesis of genetics and Darwin's theories of natural selection during the 1930s. As discussed in Chapter 4, this breakthrough influenced all the biological sciences, and some physical anthropologists soon began to apply evolutionary principles to the study of human variation.

The Concept of Race

polytypic Referring to species composed of populations that differ with regard to the expression of one or more traits.

All contemporary humans are members of the same **polytypic** species, *Homo sapiens.* A polytypic species is one composed of local populations that differ with regard to the expression of one or more traits. Moreover, *within* local populations, there's a great deal of genotypic and phenotypic variation between individuals.

In discussions of human variation, people have traditionally clumped together various attributes, such as skin color, shape of the face, shape of the nose, hair color, hair form (curly or straight), and eye color. People possessing particular combinations of these and other traits have been placed together in categories associated with specific geographical localities. Such categories are called *races.*

We all think we know what we mean by the word *race,* but in reality, the term has had a number of meanings since it gained common usage in English in the 1500s. It has been used synonymously with *species,* as in "the human race." Since the 1600s, race has also referred to various culturally defined groups, and this meaning is still common. For example, one hears "the English race" or "the Japanese race," where the reference is actually to nationality. Another often heard phrase is "the Jewish race," where the speaker is really talking about a particular ethnic and religious identity.

Thus, while race is usually a term with biological connotations, it also has enormous social significance. Moreover, there is still a widespread perception that there's an association between certain physical traits (skin color, in particular) and numerous cultural attributes (such as language, occupational preferences, or even morality). Therefore, in many cultural contexts, a person's social identity is strongly influenced by the manner in which he or she expresses those physical traits traditionally used to define "racial groups." Characteristics such as skin color are highly visible, and they facilitate an immediate and superficial designation of individuals into socially defined categories. However, so-called racial traits are not the only phenotypic expressions that contribute to social identity. Sex and age are also critically important. But aside from these two variables, an individual's biological and/or ethnic background is still inevitably a factor that influences how he or she is initially perceived and judged by others.

References to national origin (e.g., African, Asian) as substitutes for racial labels have become more common in recent years, both within and outside anthropology. Within anthropology, the term *ethnicity* was proposed in the early 1950s in order to avoid the more emotionally charged term *race.* Strictly speaking, ethnicity refers to cultural factors, but the fact that the words *ethnicity* and *race* are used interchangeably reflects the social importance of phenotypic expression and demonstrates once again how phenotype is mistakenly associated with culturally defined variables.

In its most common biological usage, the term *race* refers to geographically patterned phenotypic variation within a species. By the seventeenth century, naturalists had begun to describe races in plants and nonhuman animals, because they recognized that when populations of a species occupied different regions, they sometimes differed from one another in the expression of one or more traits. But even today, there are no established criteria by which races of plants and animals, including humans, are assessed.

Prior to World War II, most studies of human variation focused on visible phenotypic variation between large, geographically defined populations, and these studies were largely descriptive. Since World War II, the emphasis has shifted to the examination of differences in allele frequencies within and between populations, as well as the adaptive significance of phenotypic and genotypic variation. This shift in focus occurred partly as a result of the Modern Synthesis in biology and because of advances in genetics.

Hence, the application of evolutionary principles to the study of modern human variation has replaced the superficial nineteenth-century view of race *based solely on observed phenotype*. Additionally, the genetic emphasis has dispelled previously held misconceptions that races are fixed biological entities that don't change over time and that are composed of individuals who all conform to a particular *type*.

Clearly, there are phenotypic differences between humans, and some of these differences roughly correspond to particular geographical locations. But certain questions must be asked. Is there any adaptive significance attached to observed phenotypic variation? Is genetic drift a factor? What is the degree of underlying genetic variation that influences phenotypic variation? These questions place considerations of human variation within a contemporary evolutionary framework.

Although, in part, physical anthropology has its roots in attempts to explain human diversity, no contemporary scholar subscribes to pre-Darwinian and pre–Modern Synthesis concepts of races (human or nonhuman) as fixed biological entities. Also there is general recognition that race isn't a valid concept, especially from a genetic perspective, because the amount of genetic variation accounted for by differences *between* groups is vastly exceeded by the variation that exists *within* groups. But given these considerations, there are anthropologists who continue to view variation in outwardly expressed phenotype as potentially informative of population adaptation, genetic drift, mutation, and gene flow.

Forensic anthropologists, in particular, find the phenotypic criteria associated with race to have practical applications because they are frequently called on by law enforcement agencies to assist in the identification of human skeletal remains. Inasmuch as unidentified human remains are often those of crime victims, identification must be as accurate as possible. The most important variables in such identification are the individual's sex, age, stature, and ancestry or "racial" and ethnic background. Using metric and nonmetric criteria, forensic anthropologists employ a number of techniques for establishing broad population affinity, and they are generally able to do so with about 80 percent accuracy.

On the other side of the issue, there are numerous physical anthropologists who argue that race is a meaningless concept when applied to humans. Race is seen as an outdated creation of the human mind that attempts to simplify

FIGURE 12-1 Some examples of phenotypic variation among Africans.
(a) San (South African).
(b) Bantu (West African).
(c) Ethiopian.
(d) Ituri (central African).
(e) North African (Tunisia).

(a)   (b)   (c)

(d)   (e)

biological complexity by organizing it into categories. Thus, human races are a product of the human tendency to superimpose order on complex natural phenomena. While classification may have been an acceptable approach some 150 years ago, it's no longer valid given the current state of genetic and evolutionary science.

Objections to racial taxonomies have also been raised because classification schemes are *typological*, meaning that categories are discrete and based on stereotypes or ideals that comprise a specific set of traits. Thus, in general, typologies are inherently misleading, because there are always many individuals in any grouping who don't conform to all aspects of a particular type.

In any so-called racial group, there will be individuals who fall into the normal range of variation for another group with regard to one or several characteristics. For example, two people of different ancestry might vary with regard to skin color, but they could share any number of other traits, such as height, shape of head, hair color, eye color, or ABO blood type. In fact, they could easily share more similarities with each other than they do with many members of their own populations (Fig. 12-1).

Moreover, the characteristics that have traditionally been used to define races are *polygenic*; that is, they are influenced by several genes and therefore exhibit a continuous range of expression. So it's difficult, if not impossible, to draw discrete boundaries between populations with regard to many traits. This limitation becomes clear if you ask yourself, "At what point is hair color no longer dark brown but medium brown, or no longer light brown but blond?"

The scientific controversy over race will diminish as we increase our understanding of the genetic diversity (and uniformity) of our species. Given the rapid changes in genome studies and the fact that very few genes contribute to outward expressions of phenotype, dividing the human species into racial categories isn't a biologically meaningful way to look at human variation. But among the general public, variations on the theme of race will undoubtedly continue to be the most common view of human biological and cultural variation. Given this fact, it falls to anthropologists and biologists to continue to explore the issue so that, to the best of our abilities, accurate information regarding human variation is available to anyone who seeks informed explanations of complex phenomena.

Racism

Racism is based on the previously mentioned false belief that such factors as intellect and various cultural attributes are inherited along with physical characteristics. Such beliefs also commonly rest on the assumption that one's own group is superior to other groups.

Since we've already alluded to certain aspects of racism, such as the eugenics movement and persecution of people based on racial or ethnic misconceptions, we won't belabor the point here. However, it's important to point out that racism is hardly a thing of the past, nor is it restricted to European and American whites. Racism is a cultural, not a biological, phenomenon, and it's found worldwide.

We end this brief discussion of racism with an excerpt from an article, "The Study of Race," by the late Sherwood Washburn, a well-known physical anthropologist who taught at the University of California, Berkeley. Although written some years ago, the statement is as fresh and applicable today as it was when it was written:

> Races are products of the past. They are relics of times and conditions which have long ceased to exist. Racism is equally a relic supported by no phase of modern science. We may not know how to interpret the form of the Mongoloid face, or why Rh is of high incidence in Africa, but we do know the benefits of education and of economic progress. We . . . know that the roots of happiness lie in the biology of the whole species and that the potential of the species can only be realized in a culture, in a social system. It is knowledge and the social system which give life or take it away, and in so doing change the gene frequencies and continue the million-year-old interaction of culture and biology. Human biology finds its realization in a culturally determined way of life, and the infinite variety of genetic combinations can only express themselves efficiently in a free and open society. (Washburn, 1963, p. 531)

Intelligence

As we have shown, belief in the relationship between physical characteristics and specific behavioral attributes is popular even today, but evidence is lacking that personality or any other behavioral trait differs genetically *between* human groups. Most scientists would agree with this last statement, but one question that has produced controversy both inside scientific circles and among laypeople is whether population affinity and **intelligence** are associated.

intelligence Mental capacity; ability to learn, reason, or comprehend and interpret information, facts, relationships, and meanings; the capacity to solve problems, whether through the application of previously acquired knowledge or through insight.

Both genetic and environmental factors contribute to intelligence, although it's not possible to measure accurately the percentage each contributes. What can be said is that IQ scores and intelligence aren't the same thing. IQ scores can change during a person's lifetime, and average IQ scores of different populations overlap. Such differences in average IQ scores that do exist between groups are difficult to interpret, given the problems inherent in the design of the IQ tests. Moreover, complex cognitive abilities, however measured, are influenced by multiple loci and are thus polygenic.

Innate factors set limits and define potentials for behavior and cognitive ability in any species. In humans, the limits are broad and the potentials aren't fully known. Individual abilities result from complex interactions between genetic and environmental factors. One product of this interaction is learning, and the ability to learn is influenced by genetic and other biological components. Undeniably, there are differences between individuals regarding these biological components. However, elucidating what proportion of the variation in test scores is due to biological factors probably isn't possible. Moreover, innate differences in abilities reflect individual variation *within* populations, not inherent differences *between* groups. Comparing populations on the basis of IQ test results is a misuse of testing procedures, and there is no convincing evidence *whatsoever* that populations vary with regard to cognitive abilities, regardless of the assertions in some popular books. Unfortunately, despite the lack of evidence of mental inferiority of some populations and mental superiority of others, and despite the questionable validity of intelligence tests, racist attitudes toward intelligence continue to flourish.

Contemporary Interpretations of Human Variation

Since the physical characteristics (such as skin color and hair form) used to define race are *polygenic,* precisely measuring the genetic influence on them hasn't been possible. So physical anthropologists and other biologists who study modern human variation have largely abandoned the traditional perspective of describing superficial phenotypic characteristics in favor of *measuring* actual *genetic* characteristics.

Beginning in the 1950s, studies of modern human variation focused on the various components of blood as well as other aspects of body chemistry. Such traits as the ABO blood types are *phenotypes,* but they are *direct* products of the genotype. (Recall that functional genes code for proteins, and the antigens on blood cells and many components of blood serum are partly composed of proteins; Fig. 12-2). During the twentieth century, this perspective met with a great deal of success, as eventually dozens of loci were identified and the frequency data of many specific alleles obtained from numerous human populations. Nevertheless, in all these cases, it was the phenotype that was observed, and information about the underlying genotype remained largely unobtainable. Beginning in the 1990s, however, with the development of genomic studies, a drastic shift in techniques has taken place.

As a result of precise DNA sequencing, genotypes can now be ascertained directly. Moreover, while a decade ago only a small portion of the human

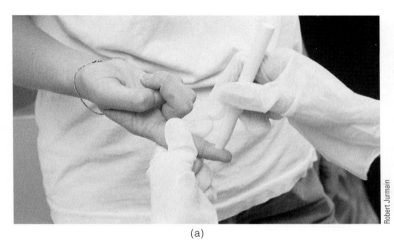

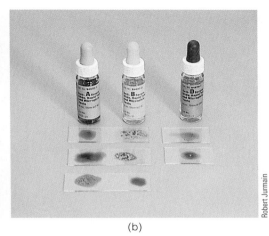

(a)

(b)

FIGURE 12-2 (a) A blood sample is drawn. (b) To determine an individual's blood type, a few drops of blood are treated with specific chemicals. Presence of A and B blood type, as well as Rh, can be detected by using commercially available chemicals. The glass slides below the blue- and yellow-labeled bottles show reactions for the ABO system. The blood on the top slide (at left) is type AB; the middle is type B; and the bottom is type A. The two samples to the right depict Rh-negative blood (top) and Rh-positive blood (bottom).

genome was accessible to physical anthropologists, we are now on the threshold of deciphering the entire genetic blueprint for our species. And as specific differences in DNA within and between human populations are studied, we will dramatically increase our knowledge of human variation.

HUMAN POLYMORPHISMS

As you know, traits such as the ABO blood groups and the various genetic conditions presented in Chapter 4 are Mendelian traits because they can be linked to the action of single, identified loci. Consequently, these simple genetic mechanisms are much more easily studied than are the polygenic characteristics usually associated with traditional racial studies (e.g, skin color, hair form, and shape of face) because the loci that govern these complex traits have not been identified. But new technologies are emerging that will, in the near future, permit the detailed analysis of loci associated with polygenic traits.

The most useful traits to examine in studies of contemporary human variation are those that differ in expression among various populations and between individuals. Such characteristics with different phenotypic expressions are called **polymorphisms.** A genetic trait is *polymorphic* if the locus that governs it has two or more alleles. (Refer back to p. 70 for a discussion of the ABO blood group system governed by three alleles at one locus.)

Understanding polymorphisms requires evolutionary explanations, and geneticists use polymorphisms as a principal tool to understand evolutionary processes in modern populations. Moreover, by using these polymorphisms to compare allele frequencies between different populations, we can begin to reconstruct the evolutionary events that link human populations with one another.

polymorphisms Loci with more than one allele. Polymorphisms can be expressed in the phenotype as the result of gene action (as in ABO), or they can exist solely at the DNA level within noncoding regions.

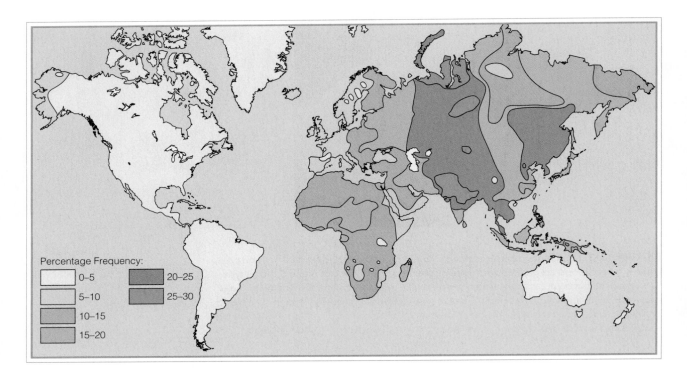

FIGURE 12-3 Distribution of the *B* allele in the indigenous populations of the world. (After Mourant et al., 1976.)

cline A gradual change in the frequency of genotypes and phenotypes from one geographical region to another.

By the 1960s, the study of *clinal distributions* of individual polymorphisms had become a popular alternative to the racial approach to human diversity. A **cline** is a gradual change in the frequency of a trait or allele in populations dispersed over geographical space. In humans, the various expressions of polymorphic traits exhibit a more or less continuous distribution from one region to another. Most of the traits that have been shown to have a clinal distribution are Mendelian. The distribution of the *A* and *B* alleles in the Old World provides a good example of a clinal distribution (Fig. 12-3). Clinal distributions are generally thought to reflect microevolutionary influences of natural selection and/or gene flow. Consequently, clinal distributions are explained in evolutionary terms.

The ABO system is interesting from an anthropological perspective because the frequencies of the *A*, *B*, and *O* alleles vary tremendously among humans. In most groups, *A* and *B* are rarely found in frequencies greater than 50 percent, and usually, their frequencies are much lower. Still, most human groups are polymorphic for all three alleles, but there are exceptions. For example, in native South American Indians, frequencies of the *O* allele reach 100 percent, and this allele is said to be "fixed" in these populations. Exceptionally high frequencies of *O* are also found in northern Australia, and some islands off the Australian coast show frequencies exceeding 90 percent. In these populations, the high frequencies of the *O* allele are probably due to genetic drift (founder effect), although the influence of natural selection can't be entirely ruled out.

Examining single traits can be informative regarding potential influences of natural selection or gene flow. This approach, however, is limited when we try to sort out population relationships, since the study of single traits, by themselves, can lead to confusing interpretations regarding likely population relationships. A more meaningful approach is to study several traits simultaneously.

POLYMORPHISMS AT THE DNA LEVEL

The *Human Genome Project* has facilitated the direct study of both mitochondrial DNA and chromosomal (nuclear) DNA. As a result, considerable insight has recently been gained regarding human variation *directly at the DNA level.* Using these new molecular technologies, molecular biologists have recently uncovered DNA variability in various regions of the genome. Scattered throughout the human genome are hundreds of sites where DNA segments are repeated—in some cases, just a few times, in other cases, many hundreds of times. These areas of nucleotide repetitions are called *microsatellites,* and they vary tremendously from person to person. In fact, each person has their own unique arrangement that defines their distinctive "DNA fingerprint." Forensic scientists can now use PCR (see p. 59) to make copies of DNA contained in, for example, a drop of blood, a hair, or a semen stain and then study the "DNA fingerprints" in order to identify individual persons. As a result, forensic identification of individual human remains at sites of mass disasters (such as the World Trade Center) or from traces left by suspects at crime scenes can be done with great accuracy.

Finally, using these molecular tools, researchers are now rapidly mapping patterns of variation at individual nucleotide sites. Of course, it's been recognized for some time that changes of individual DNA bases can occur within functional loci, producing what are called "point mutations." The sickle-cell allele at the hemoglobin beta locus is the best-known example of such a mutation in humans.

What has only been recently appreciated, however, is that point mutations also frequently occur in *noncoding* portions of DNA, and these sites, together with those in coding regions of DNA, are all referred to as *single nucleotide polymorphisms (SNPs).* Already, more than a million such sites have been recognized dispersed throughout the human genome (96 percent of which are in noncoding DNA), and these single nucleotide polymorphisms are extraordinarily variable (the International SNP Map Working Group, 2001). Thus, at the beginning of the twenty-first century, geneticists have gained access to a vast biological "library," documenting the population patterning and genetic history of our species.

Another fruitful area of recent research holds great promise for future advances. Our specific genetic knowledge of polygenic traits has been woefully inadequate. However, by identifying specific loci at the DNA level (or using these highly variable regions as "markers" for sequencing ever-smaller areas of specific chromosomes), geneticists will soon be able to isolate particular gene variants contributing to skin color, stature, hypertension, and a host of other previously enigmatic human phenotypic traits.

As you can see, the recently developed tools now used by geneticists permit the study of human genetic variation at a level never before conceived. Such research will have a profound influence on our changing views of human diversity in the coming years. Moreover, through the use of these new techniques, the broader history of *Homo sapiens* is coming under closer genetic scrutiny.

Human Biocultural Evolution

We've defined culture as the human strategy of adaptation. Humans live in cultural environments that are continually modified by their own activities; thus, evolutionary processes are understandable only within this *cultural* context. You will recall that natural selection pressures operate within specific environmental settings. For humans and many of our hominid ancestors, this means an environment dominated by culture. For example, you learned in Chapter 4 that the altered form of hemoglobin called Hb^S confers resistance to malaria. But the sickle-cell allele has not always been an important genetic factor in human populations. Before the development of agriculture, humans rarely, if ever, lived close to mosquito-breeding areas for long periods of time. But with the spread in Africa of **slash-and-burn agriculture,** perhaps in just the last 2,000 years, penetration and clearing of tropical rain forests occurred. As a result, rain water was left to stand in open, stagnant pools that provided prime mosquito-breeding areas in close proximity to human settlements. DNA analyses have further confirmed such a recent origin and spread of the sickle-cell allele in a population from Senegal, in West Africa. One recent study estimates the origin of the Hb^S mutation in this group at between 1,250 and 2,100 y.a. (Currat et al., 2002). Thus, it appears that, at least in some areas, malaria began to have an impact on human populations only recently. But once it did, it very rapidly became a powerful selective force.

No doubt humans attempted to adjust culturally to these circumstances, and numerous biological adaptations also probably came into play. The sickle-cell trait is one of these biological adaptations. However, there is a definite cost involved with such an adaptation. Carriers have increased resistance to malaria and presumably higher reproductive success, but some of their offspring may be lost through the genetic disease sickle-cell anemia. So there is a counterbalancing of selective forces with an advantage for carriers *only* in malarial environments. The genetic patterns of recessive traits such as sickle-cell anemia are discussed in Chapter 4.

Following World War II, extensive DDT spraying by the World Health Organization began systematically to control mosquito-breeding areas in the tropics. Forty years of DDT spraying killed many mosquitoes, but natural selection, acting on these insect populations, produced several DDT-resistant strains (Fig. 12-4). Accordingly, malaria is again on the rise, with several hundred thousand new cases reported annually in India, Africa, and Central America.

Lactose intolerance, which involves an individual's ability to digest milk, is another example of human biocultural evolution. In all human populations, infants and young children are able to digest milk, an obvious necessity for any young mammal. One ingredient of milk is the sugar *lactose,* which is broken down in humans and other mammals by the enzyme *lactase.* In most mammals, including many humans, the gene that codes for lactase production "switches off" in adolescence. Once this happens, the lactose ferments in the large intestine, leading to diarrhea and severe gastrointestinal upset. Among many African and Asian populations (a majority of humankind today) most adults are lactose intolerant (Table 12-1).

Why do we see variation in lactose tolerance among human populations? Throughout most of hominid evolution, milk was unavailable after weaning. Perhaps, in such circumstances, the continued action of an unnecessary enzyme might inhibit digestion of other foods. Therefore, there *may* be a selective advan-

slash-and-burn agriculture A traditional land-clearing practice whereby trees and vegetation are cut and burned. In many areas, fields are abandoned after a few years and clearing occurs elsewhere.

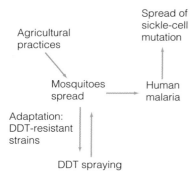

FIGURE 12-4 Evolutionary interactions affecting the frequency of the sickle-cell allele.

tage for the gene coding for lactase production to switch off. So why can some adults (the majority in some populations) tolerate milk? The distribution of lactose-tolerant populations may provide an answer to this question, and it suggests a likely powerful cultural influence on this trait.

Europeans, who are generally lactose-tolerant, are partially descended from Middle Eastern populations. Often economically dependent on pastoralism, these groups raised cows and/or goats and probably drank considerable quantities of milk. In such a cultural environment, strong selection pressures would favor lactose tolerance, and modern European descendants of these populations apparently retain this ancient ability. Very interesting genetic evidence from northern Europe has recently supported this interpretation. In fact, analyses of both cattle *and* human DNA suggest both species have co-evolved, leading to cattle that produce high quality milk and humans with the genetic capacity to digest it (Beja-Pereira et al., 2003).

But perhaps just as informative is the distribution of lactose tolerance in Africa, where the majority of people are lactose-intolerant. But, groups such as the Fulani and Tutsi, who have been pastoralists perhaps for thousands of years, have much higher rates of lactose tolerance than nonpastoralists. Presumably, like their European counterparts, they've retained the ability to produce lactase because of the continued consumption of fresh milk. Within Africa, the population pattern has become somewhat complicated, however, perhaps as a result of recent gene flow (Powell et al., 2003).

As we've seen, the geographical distribution of lactose tolerance is related to a history of cultural dependence on fresh milk products. There are, however, some populations that rely on dairying but don't have high rates of lactose tolerance (Fig. 12-5). It has been suggested that such populations traditionally have consumed their milk in the form of cheese and yogurt, in which the lactose has been broken down by bacterial action (Durham, 1981).

TABLE 12-1 | Frequencies of Lactose Intolerance

Population Group	Percent
U.S. whites	2–19
Finnish	18
Swiss	12
Swedish	4
U.S. blacks	70–77
Ibos	99
Bantu	90
Fulani	22
Thais	99
Asian Americans	95–100
Native Americans	85

Source: Lerner and Libby, 1976, p. 327.

© Michael S. Yamashita/CORBIS

FIGURE 12-5 Natives of Mongolia rely heavily on milk products from goats and sheep, but mostly consume these foods in the form of cheese and yogurt.

The interaction of human cultural environments and changes in lactose tolerance among human populations is another example of biocultural evolution. In the last few thousand years, cultural factors have initiated specific evolutionary changes in human groups. Such cultural factors have probably influenced the course of human evolution for at least 3 million years, and today they are of paramount importance.

Population Genetics

population genetics The study of the frequency of alleles, genotypes, and phenotypes in populations from a microevolutionary perspective.

gene pool The total complement of genes shared by the reproductive members of a population.

Physical anthropologists today use the approach of **population genetics** to interpret microevolutionary patterns of human variation. As we defined it in Chapter 4, a *population* is a group of interbreeding individuals. More precisely, a population is the group within which one is most likely to find a mate. As such, a population is marked by a degree of genetic relatedness and shares a common **gene pool.**

In theory, this is a straightforward concept. In every generation, the genes (alleles) are mixed by recombination and rejoined through mating. What emerges in the next generation is a direct product of the genes going into the pool, which in turn is a product of who is mating with whom.

In practice, however, describing human populations is difficult. The largest population of *Homo sapiens* that could be described is the entire species. All members of a species are *potentially* capable of interbreeding, but are incapable of fertile breeding with members of other species. The problem arises not in describing who potentially can interbreed, but in isolating exactly the pattern of those individuals who are doing so.

breeding isolates Populations that are clearly isolated geographically and/or socially from other breeding groups.

Factors that determine mate choice are geographical, ecological, and social. If people are isolated on a remote island in the middle of the Pacific, there isn't much chance they'll find a mate outside the immediate vicinity. Such **breeding isolates** are fairly easily defined and are a favorite target of microevolutionary studies. Geography plays a dominant role in producing these isolates by rather strictly determining the range of available mates. But even within these limits, cultural rules can easily play a deciding role by prescribing who is most appropriate among those who are potentially available.

endogamy Mating with individuals from the same group.

Human population segments within the species are defined as groups with relative degrees of **endogamy** (marrying/mating within the group). These are, however, not totally closed systems. Gene flow often occurs between groups, and individuals may choose mates from distant localities. With the modern advent of rapid transportation, greatly accelerated rates of **exogamy** (marrying/mating outside the group) have emerged.

exogamy Mating pattern whereby individuals obtain mates from groups other than their own.

Most humans today aren't so clearly defined as members of particular populations as they would be if they belonged to a breeding isolate. Inhabitants of large cities may appear to be members of a single population, but within the city, social, ethnic, and religious boundaries crosscut in a complex fashion to form smaller population segments. In addition to being members of these highly open local population groupings, we are simultaneously members of overlapping gradations of larger populations—the immediate geographical region (a metropolitan area or perhaps a state), a section of the country, a nation, and ultimately, the entire species.

Once specific human populations have been identified, the next step is to ascertain what evolutionary forces, if any, are operating on them. To determine whether evolution is taking place at a given locus, population geneticists measure allele frequencies for specific traits and compare these observed frequencies with a set predicted by a mathematical model called the **Hardy-Weinberg equilibrium** equation. Just how the equation is used is illustrated in Appendix C. The Hardy-Weinberg formula provides a tool to establish whether allele frequencies in a human population are indeed changing. In Chapter 4, we discussed several factors that act to change allele frequencies, including

1. New variation (i.e., *mutation*)
2. Redistributed variation (i.e., *gene flow* or *genetic drift*)
3. Selection of "advantageous" allele combinations that promote reproductive success (i.e., *natural selection*)

The Adaptive Significance of Human Variation

Today, biological anthropologists view human variation as the result of the evolutionary factors we have just listed: mutation, genetic drift/founder effect, gene flow, and natural selection (the latter especially seen in adaptations to environmental conditions, both past and present). As emphasized, cultural adaptations have also played an important role in the evolution of *Homo sapiens,* and although in this discussion we're primarily concerned with biological issues, we must still consider the influence of cultural practices on human adaptive response.

All organisms must maintain the normal functions of internal organs, tissues, and cells in order to survive, and this task must be accomplished within the context of an ever-changing environment. Even during the course of a single, seemingly uneventful day, there are numerous fluctuations in temperature, wind, solar radiation, humidity, and so on. Physical activity also places **stress** on physiological mechanisms. The body must accommodate all these changes by compensating in some manner to maintain internal constancy, or **homeostasis,** and all life forms have evolved physiological mechanisms that, within limits, achieve this goal.

Physiological response to environmental change is, to some degree, influenced by genetic factors. We've already defined adaptation as a functional response to environmental conditions in populations and individuals. In a narrower sense, adaptation refers to *long-term* evolutionary (i.e., genetic) changes that characterize all individuals within a population or species.

Examples of long-term adaptations in *Homo sapiens* include some physiological responses to heat (sweating) and deeply pigmented skin in tropical regions. Such characteristics are the results of evolutionary change in species or populations, and they don't vary as the result of short-term environmental change. For example, the ability to sweat isn't lost in people who spend their entire lives in predominantly cool areas. Likewise, individuals born with deeply pigmented skin won't become pale, even if never exposed to intense sunlight.

Short-term physiological response to environmental change is called **acclimatization.** Tanning, which can occur in almost everyone, is a form of

Hardy-Weinberg equilibrium The mathematical relationship expressing—under ideal conditions—the predicted distribution of alleles in populations; the central theorem of population genetics.

stress In a physiological context, any factor that acts to disrupt homeostasis; more precisely, the body's response to any factor that threatens its ability to maintain homeostasis.

homeostasis A condition of balance, or stability, within a biological system, maintained by the interaction of physiological mechanisms that compensate for changes (both external and internal).

acclimatization Physiological responses to changes in the environment that occur during an individual's lifetime. Such responses may be temporary or permanent, depending on the duration of the environmental change and when in the individual's life it occurs. The *capacity* for acclimatization may typify an entire species or population, and because it is under genetic influence, it is subject to evolutionary factors such as natural selection or genetic drift.

acclimatization. Another example is the very rapid increase in hemoglobin production that occurs when lowland natives travel to higher elevations. This increase provides the body with more oxygen in an environment where oxygen is less available. In both these examples, the physiological change is temporary. Tans fade once exposure to sunlight is reduced; and hemoglobin production drops to original levels following a return to lower altitudes.

In the following discussion, we present some examples of how humans respond to environmental challenges. Some of these examples illustrate adaptations that characterize the entire species. Others illustrate adaptations seen in only some populations. And still others illustrate the more short-term process of acclimatization.

SOLAR RADIATION, VITAMIN D, AND SKIN COLOR

Skin color is often cited as an example of adaptation and natural selection in human populations. In general, prior to European contact, skin color in populations followed a largely predictable geographical distribution, especially in the Old World. Populations with the greatest amount of pigmentation are found in the tropics, while lighter skin color is associated with more northern latitudes, particularly the inhabitants of northwestern Europe.

Skin color is mostly influenced by the pigment *melanin*, a granular substance produced by specialized cells (*melanocytes*) found in the epidermis. All humans appear to have approximately the same number of melanocytes. It's the amount of melanin and the size of the melanin granules that vary.

Melanin has the capacity to absorb potentially dangerous ultraviolet (UV) rays present (although not visible) in sunlight. Therefore, it provides protection from overexposure to ultraviolet radiation, which can cause genetic mutations in skin cells. These mutations may ultimately lead to skin cancer, which, if left untreated, can eventually spread to other organs and result in death.

As we previously mentioned, exposure to sunlight triggers a protective mechanism in the form of tanning, the result of temporarily increased melanin production (acclimatization). This response occurs in all humans except albinos, who carry a genetic mutation that prevents their melanocytes from producing melanin (Fig. 12-6). But even humans who do produce melanin differ in their ability to tan. For instance, many people of northern European descent tend to have very fair skin, blue eyes, and light hair. Their cells obviously produce small amounts of melanin, but when exposed to sunlight, they have little ability to increase production. And in all populations, women tend not to tan as deeply as men.

Natural selection has favored dark skin in areas nearest the equator, where the sun's rays are most direct and thus where exposure to UV light is most intense and constant. In considering the cancer-causing effects of UV radiation from an *evolutionary* perspective, three points must be kept in mind:

1. Early hominids lived in the tropics, where solar radiation is more intense than in temperate areas to the north and south.
2. Unlike modern city dwellers, early hominids spent their days outdoors.
3. Early hominids didn't wear clothing that would have protected them from the sun.

Given these conditions, UV radiation was probably a powerful agent selecting for varied levels of melanin production in early humans, especially as they migrated out of the tropics.

FIGURE 12-6 An African albino.

Norman Lightfoot/Photo Researchers

As hominids migrated out of Africa into Europe and Asia, selective pressures changed. Not only were they moving away from the tropics, where ultraviolet rays were most direct, but they were also moving into areas where it was cold and cloudy during winter. Bear in mind, too, that physiological adaptations weren't sufficient to meet the demands of living in colder climates. Therefore, we must assume that these populations had adopted certain cultural practices, such as wearing animal skins or other types of clothing. Although clothing would have added necessary warmth, it would have also blocked exposure to sunlight. Consequently, the advantages provided by deeply pigmented skin in the tropics were no longer important, and selection for melanin production may have been relaxed (Brace and Montagu, 1977).

However, relaxed selection favoring dark skin may not be adequate to explain the very depigmented skin seen especially in some northern Europeans. Perhaps another factor, the need for adequate amounts of vitamin D, was also critical. The theory concerning the possible role of vitamin D, known as the *vitamin D hypothesis,* offers the following explanation.

Vitamin D is produced in the body partly as a result of the interaction between ultraviolet radiation and a substance similar to cholesterol. It's also available in some foods, including liver, fish oils, egg yolk, butter, and cream. Vitamin D is necessary for normal bone growth and mineralization, and some exposure to ultraviolet radiation is therefore essential. Insufficient amounts of vitamin D during childhood result in *rickets,* which often leads to bowing of the long bones of the legs and deformation of the pelvis (Fig. 12-7). Pelvic deformities are of particular concern for women, for they can lead to a narrowing of the birth canal, which, in the absence of surgical intervention, frequently results in the death of both mother and infant during childbirth.

This example illustrates the potential for rickets as a significant selective factor favoring less pigmented skin in regions where climate and other factors reduce exposure to UV radiation. It's obvious how reduced exposure to sunlight due to climate and increased use of clothing could have been detrimental to dark-skinned individuals in more northern latitudes (Fig. 12-8). In these individuals, melanin would have blocked absorption of the already reduced amounts of available ultraviolet radiation required for vitamin D synthesis. Therefore, selection pressures would have shifted over time to favor individuals with lighter skin. There is substantial evidence, both historically and in contemporary populations, to support this theory.

During the latter decades of the nineteenth century in the United States, African American inhabitants of northern cities suffered a higher incidence of rickets than whites. Northern blacks were also more commonly affected than blacks living in the South, where exposure to sunlight is greater. (The supplementation of milk with vitamin D was initiated to alleviate this problem.) Another example is seen in Britain, where darker-skinned East Indians and Pakistanis show a higher incidence of rickets than people with lighter skin (Molnar, 1983).

Jablonski (1992) and Jablonski and Chaplin (2000) offer an additional explanation for the distribution of skin color, one that focuses on the role of UV radiation in the degradation of folate. Folate is a B vitamin that isn't stored in the body and must be replenished through dietary sources. Folate

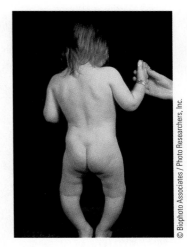

FIGURE 12-7 A child with rickets.

© Biophoto Associates / Photo Researchers, Inc.

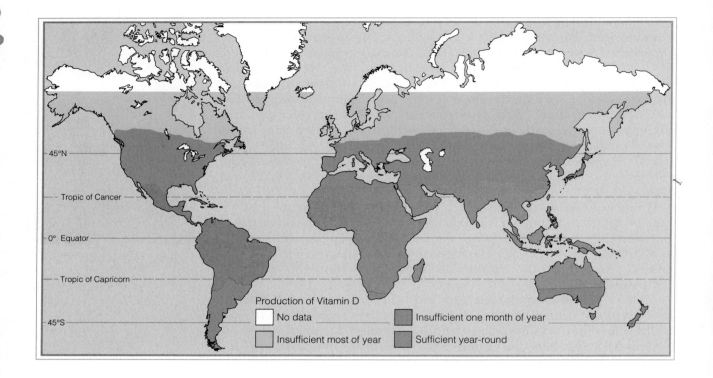

FIGURE 12-8 Populations indigenous to the tropics (blue band) receive sufficient UV radiation for vitamin D synthesis (year-round). The darker brown band represents areas where people with moderately melanized skin do not receive sufficient UV light for vitamin D synthesis for one month of the year. The lighter brown band represents an area where even light skin does not receive enough UV light for vitamin D synthesis on a yearly basis. (Adapted from Jablonski and Chaplin, 2000, 2002.)

neural tube In early embryonic development, the anatomical structure that develops to form the brain and spinal cord.

spina bifida A condition in which the arch of one or more vertebrae fails to fuse and form a protective barrier around the spinal cord.

deficiencies in pregnant women are associated with numerous complications, including maternal death, and in children they can lead to growth retardation and other serious conditions. Folate also plays a crucial role in **neural tube** development very early in embryonic development, and in this context, deficiencies can lead to defects that include various expressions of **spina bifida.** The consequences of severe neural tube defects can include pain, infection, paralysis, and even death. It goes without saying that neural tube defects can dramatically reduce the reproductive success of affected individuals.

A number of studies have shown that UV radiation rapidly depletes folate serum levels both in laboratory experiments and in light-skinned individuals. These findings have implications for pregnant women and children and also for the evolution of dark skin in hominids. Jablonski and Chaplin suggest that the earliest hominids may have had light body skin covered with dark hair, as is seen in chimpanzees and gorillas. (Both have darker skin on exposed body parts.) But as loss of body hair in hominids occurred, dark skin evolved rather quickly as a protective response to the damaging effects of UV radiation on folate.

Perhaps more social importance has been attached to variation in skin color than to any other single human biological trait. But aside from its probable adaptive significance relative to UV radiation, skin color is no more important physiologically than many other biological characteristics. Still, from an evolutionary perspective, it provides a good example of how the forces of natural selection have produced geographically patterned variation as the consequence of at least three selective forces: the need for protection from overexposure to UV radiation, the competing necessity for adequate UV exposure to promote vitamin D synthesis, and protection against folate loss.

THE THERMAL ENVIRONMENT

Mammals and birds have evolved complex mechanisms to maintain a constant internal body temperature. While reptiles must rely on exposure to external heat sources to raise body temperature and energy levels, mammals and birds possess physiological mechanisms that, within certain limits, increase or reduce the loss of body heat. The optimum internal body temperature for normal cellular functions is species-specific, and for humans it's approximately 98.6°F.

Homo sapiens is found in a wide variety of habitats, with temperatures ranging from over 120°F to less than −60°F. In these extremes, human life wouldn't be possible without cultural innovations. But even accounting for the artificial environments in which we live, such external conditions place the human body under enormous stress.

Response to Heat All available evidence suggests that the earliest hominids evolved in the warm-to-hot savannas of East Africa. The fact that humans cope better with heat than they do with cold is testimony to the long-term adaptations to heat that evolved in our ancestors.

In humans, as well as certain other species, such as horses, sweat glands are distributed throughout the skin. This wide distribution of sweat glands makes it possible to lose heat at the body surface through evaporative cooling, a mechanism that has evolved to the greatest degree in humans.

The capacity to dissipate heat by sweating is seen in all humans to an almost equal degree, with the average number of sweat glands per individual (approximately 1.6 million) being fairly constant. However, there is variation in that persons not generally exposed to hot conditions do experience a period of acclimatization that initially involves significantly increased perspiration rates (Frisancho, 1993). An additional factor that enhances the cooling effects of sweating is increased exposure of the skin through reduced amounts of body hair. We don't know when in our evolutionary history loss of body hair began, but it represents a species-wide adaptation. Heat reduction through evaporation can be expensive, and indeed dangerous, in terms of water and sodium loss. Up to 3 liters of water can be lost by a human engaged in heavy work in high heat.

Another mechanism for radiating body heat is **vasodilation,** whereby capillaries near the skin's surface widen to permit increased blood flow to the skin. The visible effect of vasodilation is flushing, or increased redness of the skin, particularly of the face, accompanied by warmth. But the physiological effect is to permit heat, carried by the blood from the interior of the body, to be emitted from the skin's surface to the surrounding air. (Some drugs, including alcohol, also produce vasodilation, which accounts for the increased redness and warmth of the face some people experience after a drink or two.)

Body size and proportions are also important in regulating body temperature. Indeed, there seems to be a general relationship between climate and body size and shape in birds and mammals. In general, within a species, body size (weight) increases as distance from the equator increases. In humans, this relationship holds up fairly well, but there are numerous exceptions.

Two rules that pertain to the relationship between body size, body proportions, and climate are *Bergmann's rule* and *Allen's rule.*

vasodilation Expansion of blood vessels, permitting increased blood flow to the skin. Vasodilation permits warming of the skin and also facilitates radiation of warmth as a means of cooling. Vasodilation is an involuntary response to warm temperatures, various drugs, and even emotional states (blushing).

1. *Bergmann's rule (concerns the relationship of body mass or volume to surface area):* In mammalian species, body size tends to be greater in populations that live in colder climates. This is because as mass increases, the relative amount of surface area decreases proportionately. Because heat is lost at the surface, it follows that increased mass allows for greater heat retention and reduced heat loss.
2. *Allen's rule (concerns shape of the body, especially appendages):* In colder climates, shorter appendages, with increased mass-to-surface ratios, are adaptive because they are more effective at preventing heat loss. Conversely, longer appendages, with increased surface area relative to mass, are more adaptive in warmer climates because they promote heat loss.

According to these rules, the most suitable body shape in hot climates is linear with long arms and legs. In a cold climate, a more suitable body type is stocky with shorter limbs. Considerable data gathered from several human populations generally conform to these principles. In colder climates, body mass tends, on average, to be greater and characterized by a larger trunk relative to arms and legs (Roberts, 1973). People living in the Arctic tend to be short and stocky, while many sub-Saharan Africans, especially East African pastoralists, are, on average, tall and linear (Fig. 12-9). But there's a great deal of variability regarding human body proportions, and not all populations conform so readily to Bergmann's and Allen's rules.

Response to Cold Human physiological responses to cold combine factors that increase heat retention with those that enhance heat production. Of the two, heat retention is more efficient because it requires less energy. This is an important point because energy is derived from dietary sources. Unless food

FIGURE 12-9 (a) This African woman has the linear proportions characteristic of many inhabitants of sub-Saharan Africa. (b) By comparison, the Inuit woman is short and stocky. These two individuals serve as good examples of Bergmann's and Allen's rules.

(a)

(b)

resources are abundant, and in winter they frequently aren't, any factor that conserves energy can have adaptive value.

Short-term responses to cold include increased metabolic rate and shivering, both of which generate body heat, at least for a short time. **Vasoconstriction,** another short-term response, restricts heat loss and conserves energy. In addition, humans possess a subcutaneous (beneath the skin) fat layer that provides an insulative layer throughout the body. Behavioral modifications include increased activity, wearing warmer clothing, increased food consumption, and assuming a curled-up position.

Increases in metabolic rate (the rate at which cells break up nutrients into their components) release energy in the form of heat. Shivering also generates muscle heat, as does voluntary exercise. But these methods of heat production are expensive because they require an increased intake of nutrients to provide energy. (Perhaps this explains why we tend to have a heartier appetite during the winter and why we also tend to increase our intake of fats and carbohydrates, the very sources of energy our body requires.)

In general, people exposed to chronic cold (meaning much or most of the year) maintain higher metabolic rates than those living in warmer climates. The Inuit (Eskimo) people living in the Arctic maintain metabolic rates between 13 and 45 percent higher than observed in non-Inuit control subjects (Frisancho, 1993). Moreover, the highest metabolic rates are seen in inland Inuit, who are exposed to even greater cold stress than coastal populations. Traditionally, the Inuit had the highest animal protein and fat diet of any human population in the world. Such a diet, necessitated by the available resource base, helped maintain the high metabolic rates required by exposure to chronic cold.

Vasoconstriction restricts capillary blood flow to the surface of the skin, thus reducing heat loss at the body surface. Because retaining body heat is more economical than creating it, vasoconstriction is very efficient, provided temperatures don't drop below freezing. However, if temperatures do fall below freezing, continued vasoconstriction can allow the skin temperature to decline to the point of frostbite or worse.

Long-term responses to cold vary among human groups. For example, in the past, desert-dwelling native Australian populations were subjected to wide temperature fluctuations from day to night. As they wore no clothing and didn't build shelters, their only protection from temperatures that hovered only a few degrees above freezing was provided by sleeping fires. They experienced continuous vasoconstriction throughout the night, and this permitted a degree of skin cooling most people would find extremely uncomfortable. But there was no threat of frostbite, and continued vasoconstriction helped to prevent excessive internal heat loss.

By contrast, the Inuit experience intermittent periods of vasoconstriction and vasodilation. This compromise provides periodic warmth to the skin that helps prevent frostbite in below-freezing temperatures. At the same time, because vasodilation is intermittent, energy loss is restricted, with more heat retained at the body's core.

The preceding examples illustrate just two of the many ways human populations adaptively respond to cold. Although all humans respond to cold stress in much the same way, there is variation in how adaptation and acclimatization are manifested.

vasoconstriction Narrowing of blood vessels to reduce blood flow to the skin. Vasoconstriction is an involuntary response to cold and reduces heat loss at the skin's surface.

HIGH ALTITUDE

Studies of high-altitude residents have greatly contributed to our understanding of physiological adaptation. As you would expect, altitude studies have focused on inhabited mountainous regions, particularly in the Himalayas, Andes, and Rocky Mountains. Of these three areas, permanent human habitation probably has the longest history in the Himalayas (Moore et al., 1998). Today, perhaps as many as 25 million people live at altitudes above 10,000 feet. In Tibet, permanent settlements exist above 15,000 feet, and in the Andes, they can be found as high as 17,000 feet (Fig. 12-10).

Because the mechanisms that maintain homeostasis in humans evolved at lower altitudes, they are compromised by the conditions at higher elevations. At high altitudes, many factors produce stress on the human body. These include **hypoxia** (reduced available oxygen), more intense solar radiation, cold, low humidity, wind (which amplifies cold stress), a reduced nutritional base, and rough terrain. Of these, hypoxia exerts the greatest amount of stress on human physiological systems, especially the heart, lungs, and brain.

Hypoxia results from reduced barometric pressure. It's not that there is less oxygen overall in the atmosphere at high altitudes; rather, it's less concentrated. Therefore, to obtain the same amount of oxygen at 9,000 feet as at sea level, people must make certain physiological alterations aimed at increasing the body's ability to transport and efficiently use the oxygen that is available.

At high altitudes, reproduction, in particular, is affected through increased infant mortality rates, miscarriage, low birth weights, and premature birth. An early study (Moore and Regensteiner, 1983) reported that in Colorado, infant deaths are almost twice as common above 8,200 feet (2,500 m) as at lower elevations. One cause of fetal and maternal death is preeclampsia, a severe elevation of blood pressure in pregnant women after the twentieth gestational week.

hypoxia Lack of oxygen. Hypoxia can refer to reduced amounts of available oxygen in the atmosphere (due to lowered barometric pressure) or to insufficient amounts of oxygen in the body.

FIGURE 12-10 (a) La Paz, Bolivia, at just over 12,000 feet above sea level, is home to more than 1 million people. (b) A household in northern Tibet, situated at an elevation of over 15,000 feet above sea level.

Courtesy, William Pratt

(a)

Courtesy, L.G. Moore

(b)

People born at lower altitudes and high-altitude natives differ somewhat in how they adapt to hypoxia. Upon exposure to high altitude people born at low elevation become acclimatized. The responses may be short-term modifications, depending on duration of stay, but they begin within hours of the altitude change. These changes include an increase in respiration rate, heart rate, and production of red blood cells. (Red blood cells contain hemoglobin, the protein responsible for transporting oxygen to organs and tissues.)

A more permanent, developmental acclimatization occurs in high-altitude natives during growth and development. This type of acclimatization is present only in people who grow up in high-altitude areas, not in those who moved there as adults. Compared with populations at lower elevations, life-long residents of high altitudes display slowed growth and maturation. Other differences include larger chest size, associated, in turn, with greater lung volume and larger heart. In addition to greater lung capacity, people born at high altitudes are more efficient than migrants at diffusing oxygen from blood to body tissues. Developmental acclimatization to high-altitude hypoxia serves as a good example of physiological plasticity by illustrating how, within the limits set by genetic factors, development can be influenced by environment.

There is evidence that entire *populations* have also genetically adapted to high altitudes. Indigenous peoples of Tibet who have inhabited regions higher than 12,000 feet for around 25,000 years may have made genetic (i.e., evolutionary) accommodations to hypoxia. Altitude doesn't appear to affect reproduction in these people to the degree it does in other populations. Infants have birth weights as high as those of lowland Tibetan groups and higher than those of recent (20 to 30 years) Chinese immigrants. This fact may be the result of alterations in maternal blood flow to the uterus during pregnancy (Moore et al., 1994, 1999).

Another line of evidence concerns how the body processes glucose (blood sugar). Glucose is critical because it's the only source of energy used by the brain, and it's also used, although not exclusively, by the heart. Both highland Tibetans and the Quechua (inhabitants of high-altitude regions of the Peruvian Andes) burn glucose in a way that permits more efficient use of oxygen. This implies the presence of genetic mutations in the mitochondrial DNA (mtDNA directs how cells use glucose). It also implies that natural selection has acted to increase the frequency of these advantageous mutations in these groups.

As yet, there's no certain evidence that Tibetans and Quechua have made evolutionary changes to accommodate high-altitude hypoxia (since specific genetic mechanisms that underlie these populations' unique abilities have not been identified). But current data strongly suggest that selection has operated to produce evolutionary change in these two groups. If further study supports these findings, we have an excellent example of evolution in action producing long-term adaptation at the population level.

INFECTIOUS DISEASE

Infection, as opposed to other disease categories, such as degenerative or genetic disease, includes those pathological conditions caused by microorganisms (viruses, bacteria, and fungi). Throughout the course of human evolution, infectious disease has exerted enormous selective pressures on populations and consequently has influenced the frequency of certain alleles that affect the immune response. In fact, it would be difficult to overemphasize the importance of infectious disease as an agent of natural selection in human populations. But as important as infectious disease has been, its role in this regard isn't very well documented.

The effects of infectious disease on humans are mediated culturally as well as biologically. Innumerable cultural factors, such as architectural styles, subsistence techniques, exposure to domesticated animals, and even religious practices, all affect how infectious disease develops and persists within and between populations.

Until about 10,000 to 12,000 years ago, all humans lived in small nomadic hunting and gathering groups. And since these groups rarely remained in one location more than a few days at a time, they had minimal contact with refuse heaps that house disease **vectors.** But with the domestication of plants and animals, people became more sedentary and began living in small villages. Gradually, villages became towns, and towns, in turn, developed into densely crowded, unsanitary cities.

As long as humans lived in small bands, there was little opportunity for infectious disease to have much impact on large numbers of people. Even if an entire local group or band were wiped out, the effect on the overall population in a given area would have been negligible. Moreover, for a disease to become **endemic** in a population, sufficient numbers of people must be present. Therefore, small bands of hunter-gatherers weren't faced with continuous exposure to endemic disease.

With the advent of settled living and close proximity to domesticated animals, opportunities for disease greatly increased. As sedentary life permitted larger group size, it became possible for several diseases to become permanently established in some populations. Moreover, exposure to domestic animals, such as cattle and fowl, provided an opportune environment for the spread of several **zoonotic** diseases, such as tuberculosis and SARS (severe acute respiratory disease). Humans had no doubt always contracted diseases occasionally from the animals they hunted; but when they began to live with domesticated animals, they were faced with an entire array of new infectious conditions. Also, the crowded, unsanitary conditions that characterized parts of all cities until the late nineteenth century and that persist in much of the world today further added to the disease burden borne by human inhabitants.

AIDS (acquired immune deficiency syndrome) provides an excellent example of the influence of human infectious disease as a selective agent. In the United States, the first cases of AIDS were reported in 1981. Since that time, perhaps as many as 1.5 million Americans have been infected by HIV (human immunodeficiency virus), the agent that causes AIDS. However, most of the burden of AIDS is borne by developing countries, where 95 percent of all HIV-infected people live. By the end of 2003, an estimated 42 million people worldwide were living with HIV infection, and at least 23 million had died.

HIV is transmitted from person to person through the exchange of bodily fluids, usually blood or semen. It is not spread through casual contact with an infected person. Within six months of infection, most infected people test positive for anti-HIV antibodies, meaning that their immune system has recognized the presence of foreign antigens and has responded by producing antibodies. However, serious HIV-related symptoms may not appear for years. HIV is a "slow virus" that may persist in a person's body for several

vectors Agents that serve to transmit disease from one carrier to another. Mosquitoes are vectors for malaria, just as fleas are vectors for bubonic plague.

endemic Continuously present in a population.

zoonotic (zoh-oh-no´-tic) Pertaining to a zoonosis (*pl.*, zoonoses), a disease that is transmitted to humans through contact with non-human animals.

years before the onset of severe illness. This asymptomatic state is called a "latency period," and the average latency period in the United States is more than 11 years.

Like all viruses, HIV must invade certain types of cells and alter the functions of those cells to produce more virus particles in a process that eventually leads to cell destruction. (The way HIV does this is different from that of many other viruses.) HIV can attack various types of cells, but it especially targets so-called T4 helper cells, which are major components of the immune system. As HIV infection spreads and T4 cells are destroyed, the patient's immune system begins to fail. Consequently, he or she develops symptoms caused by various **pathogens** that are commonly present but usually kept in check by a normal immune response. When an HIV-infected person's T cell count drops to a level indicating that immunity has been suppressed, and when symptoms of "opportunistic" infections appear, the patient is said to have AIDS.

By the early 1990s, scientists were aware of a number of patients who had been HIV positive for 10 to 15 years, but who continued to show few if any symptoms. Awareness of these patients led researchers to suspect that some individuals possess a natural immunity or resistance to HIV infection. This was shown to be true in late 1996 with the publication of two different studies (Dean et al., 1996; Samson et al., 1996) that demonstrated a mechanism for resistance to HIV.

These two reports describe a genetic mutation that involves a major protein "receptor site" on the surface of certain immune cells, including T4 cells. (Receptor sites are protein molecules that enable HIV and other viruses to invade cells.) As a result of the mutation, the receptor site doesn't function properly and HIV is unable to bind to the cell. Current evidence suggests that individuals who are homozygous for a particular (mutant) allele may be completely resistant to many types of HIV infection. In heterozygotes, infection may still occur, but the course of HIV disease is slowed.

Interestingly, and for unknown reasons, the mutant allele occurs mainly in people of European descent, among whom its frequency is about 10 percent. Samson and colleagues (1996) reported that in the Japanese and West African groups they studied, the mutation was absent, but Dean and colleagues (1996) reported an allele frequency of about 2 percent among African Americans. They speculated that the presence of the allele in African Americans may be entirely due to genetic admixture (gene flow) with European Americans. Moreover, they suggest that this polymorphism exists in Europeans as a result of selective pressures favoring an allele that originally occurred as a rare mutation. But we should point out that the original selective agent was *not* HIV. Instead, it was some other, as yet unidentified pathogen that requires the same receptor site as HIV, and some researchers (Lalani et al., 1999) have suggested that it may have been the virus that causes smallpox.

The best-known epidemic in history was that of the Black Death (bubonic plague) in the mid-fourteenth century. Bubonic plague is caused by a bacterium and is transmitted from rodents to humans by fleas. In just a few years, this deadly disease had spread (following trade routes and facilitated by rodent-infested ship cargoes) from the Caspian Sea throughout the Mediterranean area to northern Europe. During the initial exposure to this disease, as many as one-third of the inhabitants of Europe died.

pathogens Any agents, especially microorganisms such as viruses, bacteria, or fungi, that infect a host and cause disease.

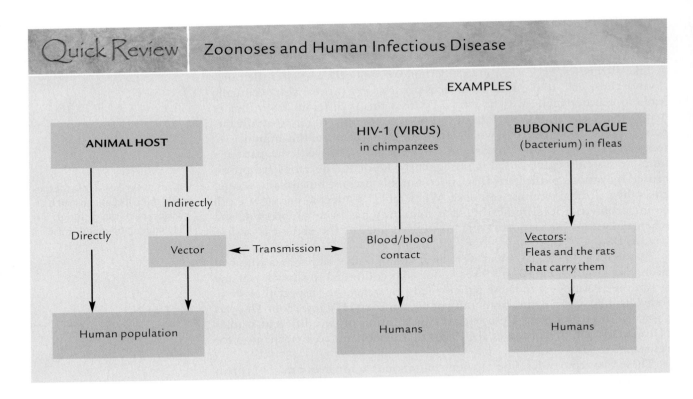

Quick Review Zoonoses and Human Infectious Disease

EXAMPLES

ANIMAL HOST

Indirectly

Directly

Vector ← Transmission →

Human population

HIV-1 (VIRUS)
in chimpanzees

Blood/blood
contact

Humans

BUBONIC PLAGUE
(bacterium) in fleas

Vectors:
Fleas and the rats
that carry them

Humans

pandemic An extensive outbreak of disease affecting
large numbers of individuals
over a wide area; potentially a
worldwide phenomenon.

A lesser-known but even more devastating example was the influenza
pandemic that broke out in 1918 at the end of World War I. This was actually one of a series of influenza outbreaks, but it has remained notable for its
still unexplained virulence and the fact that it accounted for the deaths of
over 21 million people worldwide.

While we have no clear-cut evidence of a selective role for bubonic plague
or influenza, this does not mean that one doesn't exist. The tremendous mortality that these diseases (and others) are capable of causing certainly increases
the likelihood that they influenced the development of human adaptive
responses in ways we haven't yet discovered.

The Continuing Impact of Infectious Disease

It's important to understand that humans and pathogens exert selective pressures on each other, creating a dynamic relationship between disease organisms and their human (and nonhuman) hosts. Just as disease exerts selective
pressures on host populations to adapt, microorganisms also evolve and adapt
to various pressures exerted on them by their hosts.

Evolutionarily speaking, it's to the advantage of any pathogen not to be so
virulent as to kill its host too quickly. If the host dies soon after becoming
infected, the viral or bacterial agent may not have time to reproduce and infect
other hosts (and it will be eliminated along with its host). Thus, selection
sometimes acts to produce resistance in host populations and/or to reduce

the virulence of disease organisms, to the benefit of both. However, members of populations exposed for the first time to a new disease frequently die in huge numbers. This type of exposure was a major factor in the decimation of indigenous New World populations after contact with Europeans introduced smallpox into Native American groups. And this has also been the case with the current worldwide spread of HIV.

Of the known disease-causing organisms, HIV provides the best-documented example of evolution and adaptation in a pathogen. It's also one of several examples of interspecies transfer of infection. HIV is the most mutable and genetically variable virus known. The type of HIV responsible for the AIDS epidemic is HIV-1, which in turn is divided into three major subtypes (Hu et al., 1996; Gao, 1999). Another far less common type is HIV-2, which is present only in populations of West Africa. HIV-2 also exhibits a wide range of genetic diversity, and while some strains cause AIDS, others are far less virulent.

Since the late 1980s, researchers have been comparing the DNA sequences of HIV and a closely related retrovirus called *simian immunodeficiency virus (SIV)*. SIV is found in chimpanzees and several African monkey species. Like HIV, SIV is genetically variable, and each strain appears to be specific to a given species and even subspecies of primate. SIV produces no symptoms in the African monkeys and chimpanzees that are its traditional hosts, but when injected into Asian monkeys, it eventually causes AIDS-like symptoms and death. These findings indicate that the various forms of SIV have shared a long evolutionary history (perhaps several hundred thousand years) with a number of African primate species and that the latter are able to accommodate this virus, which is deadly to their Asian relatives. Moreover, these results substantiate long-held hypotheses that SIV and HIV evolved in Africa.

Comparisons of the DNA sequences of HIV-2 and the form of SIV found in one monkey species (the sooty mangabey) revealed that, genetically, these two viruses are almost identical. These findings led to the generally accepted conclusion that HIV-2 evolved from sooty mangabey SIV. Moreover, sooty mangabeys are hunted for food and also kept as pets in western central Africa, and the transmission of SIV to humans probably occurred through bites and the butchering of monkey carcasses.

But although the likely origin of HIV-2 was established, there was continuing debate over which primate species had been the source of HIV-1. Recently, a group of medical researchers (Gao et al., 1999) compared DNA sequences of HIV-1 and the form of SIV found in chimpanzees indigenous to western central Africa. Their results showed that HIV-1 almost certainly evolved from the strain of chimpanzee SIV that infects the central African subspecies *Pan troglodytes troglodytes*.

Unfortunately for both species, chimpanzees are routinely hunted by humans for food in parts of West Africa (see p. 139). Consequently, the most probable explanation for the transmission of SIV from chimpanzees to humans is, as with sooty mangabeys, the hunting and butchering of chimpanzees (Gao et al., 1999; Weiss and Wrangham, 1999) (Fig. 12-11). Hence, HIV/AIDS is a zoonotic disease. The DNA evidence further suggests that there were at least three separate human exposures to chimpanzee SIV, and at some point the virus was altered to the form we call HIV. When chimpanzee SIV was transmitted to humans is unknown. The oldest evidence of human infection is a frozen HIV-positive blood sample taken from a West African

FIGURE 12-11 These people, selling butchered chimpanzees, may not realize that by handling this meat they could be exposing themselves to HIV or the Ebola virus.

Karl Ammann

patient in 1959. There are also a few documented cases of AIDS infection by the late 1960s and early 1970s. Therefore, although human exposure to SIV/HIV probably occurred many times in the past, the virus didn't become firmly established in humans until the latter half of the twentieth century.

Severe acute respiratory syndrome (SARS) is another contemporary example of zoonotic transmission of disease. In early 2003, an outbreak of SARS in southern China surprised the world health community by quickly spreading through much of Asia, then to North America (especially Canada), South America, and Europe.

When compared to diseases such as HIV/AIDS, tuberculosis, influenza, and malaria, the threat from SARS is relatively minor. Nevertheless, it can be fatal and is especially severe among the elderly. As of July 2003, the total number of SARS-related deaths was 812 out of around 8,500 cases. But there are fears that it may return, and, as of this writing, the development of a SARS vaccine is a long way off.

Scientists don't know the exact mode of SARS transmission in humans, but most believe that it's spread through close contact by means of infected droplets (i.e., when people cough or sneeze). Many health officials believe that it was initially transmitted to humans through contact with either domesticated animals or wild animals, such as civet cats, sold in Asian markets for food. Indeed, many of the influenza strains that frequently originate in China seem to originate in pigs and fowl that live in very close contact with humans (Clarke, 2003).

The fact that SARS spread so quickly around the world, even though it has a fairly low transmission rate, is due to travel. If modern technology didn't exist, this infection would have been confined to one or a few villages, and perhaps a small number of people would have died. But overall, it would have been a fairly unremarkable event, and it certainly wouldn't have become widely known. In fact, this and many other similar scenarios have undoubtedly been repeated countless times throughout the course of human history.

From these SIV/HIV and SARS examples, you can appreciate how, through the adoption of various cultural practices, humans have radically altered patterns of infectious disease. The interaction of cultural and biological factors has influenced microevolutionary change in humans (as in the example of sickle-cell anemia) to accommodate altered relationships with disease organisms.

Until the twentieth century, infectious disease was the number one cause of death in all human populations. Even today, in many developing countries, as much as half of all mortality is due to infectious disease, compared to only about 10 percent in the United States. For example, malaria is a disease of the poor in developing nations. Annually, there are an estimated 1 million deaths due to malaria. That figure computes to one malaria-related death every 30 seconds (Weiss, 2002)! Ninety percent of these deaths occur in sub-Saharan Africa, where 5 percent of children die of malaria before age 5 (Greenwood and Mutabingwa, 2002; Weiss, 2002). In the United States and other developed nations, with better living conditions and sanitation and especially with the widespread use of antibiotics and pesticides beginning in the late 1940s, infectious disease has given way to heart disease and cancer as the leading causes of death.

Optimistic predictions held that infectious disease would be a thing of the past in developed countries and, with the introduction of antibiotics and better living standards, in developing nations too. But between 1980 and 1992, the number of deaths in the United States in which infectious disease was the underlying cause rose from 41 to 65 per 100,000, an increase of 58 percent (Pinner et al., 1996).

Obviously, AIDS contributed substantially to the increase in mortality due to infectious disease in the United States between 1980 and 1992. By 1992, AIDS was the leading cause of death in men aged 25 to 44 years. As of 1998, mortality due to AIDS had decreased significantly; still, even when subtracting the effect of AIDS in mortality rates, there was a 22 percent increase in mortality rates due to infectious disease between 1980 and 1992 (Pinner et al., 1996).

This increase may partly be due to the overuse of antibiotics. It's estimated that half of all antibiotics prescribed in the United States are used to treat viral conditions such as colds and flu. Because antibiotics are completely ineffective against viruses, such therapy not only is useless, but may also have dangerous long-term consequences. There is considerable concern in the biomedical community over the indiscriminate use of antibiotics and pesticides since the 1950s. Antibiotics have exerted selective pressures on bacterial species that have, over time, developed antibiotic-resistant strains (an excellent example of natural selection). Consequently, the past few years have seen the *reemergence* of many bacterial diseases, including influenza, pneumonia, cholera, and tuberculosis, in forms that are less responsive to treatment.

Tuberculosis is now listed as the world's leading killer of adults by the World Health Organization (Colwell, 1996). Of note, the number of tuberculosis cases has risen 28 percent worldwide since the mid-1980s, with an estimated 10 million people infected in the United States alone. Although not all infected persons develop active disease, in the 1990s, an estimated 30 million persons worldwide are believed to have died from TB. One very troubling aspect of the increase in tuberculosis infection is that newly developed strains of *Mycobacterium tuberculosis,* the bacterium that causes TB, are resistant to antibiotics and other treatments.

Various treatments for nonbacterial conditions have also become ineffective. One such example is the appearance of chloroquin-resistant malaria, which has rendered chloroquin (the traditional preventive medication) virtually useless in some parts of Africa. And many insect species have also developed resistance to commonly used pesticides.

In addition to threats posed by resistant strains of pathogens, there are other factors that may contribute to the emergence (or reemergence) of infectious disease. Political leaders (excluding most in the United States) and the overwhelming majority of scientists worldwide are becoming increasingly concerned over the potential for global warming to expand the geographical range of numerous tropical disease vectors, such as mosquitoes. And the destruction of natural environments not only contributes to global warming; it also has the potential of causing disease vectors formerly restricted to local areas to spread to new habitats.

One other factor associated with the rapid spread of disease and directly related to technological change is the mixing of people at an unprecedented rate. Indeed, an estimated 1 million people per day cross national borders by air (Lederberg, 1996)! In addition, new road construction and wider availability of motor-driven vehicles allow more people (armies, refugees, truck drivers, etc.) to travel farther and faster than ever before.

Fundamental to all these factors is human population size (see p. 369), which, as it continues to soar, causes more environmental disturbance and, through additional human activity, adds further to global warming. Moreover, in developing countries, where as much as 50 percent of mortality is due to infectious disease, overcrowding and unsanitary conditions increasingly contribute to increased rates of communicable illness. One could scarcely conceive of a better set of circumstances for the appearance and spread of communicable disease, and it remains to be seen if scientific innovation and medical technology are able to meet the challenge.

It's still unclear what the long-term consequences of recent antibiotic therapy, pesticide-based eradication programs, environmental change, and human population growth will be on disease patterns. But there are many scientists who fear that we may not be able to develop new antibiotics and treatments fast enough to keep pace with the appearance of potentially deadly new bacteria and other pathogens. As we have radically altered the course of evolution in some microbial species, they have, in turn, dramatically influenced our own evolutionary history, and today they continue to do so in an increasingly rapid manner.

Visual Summary

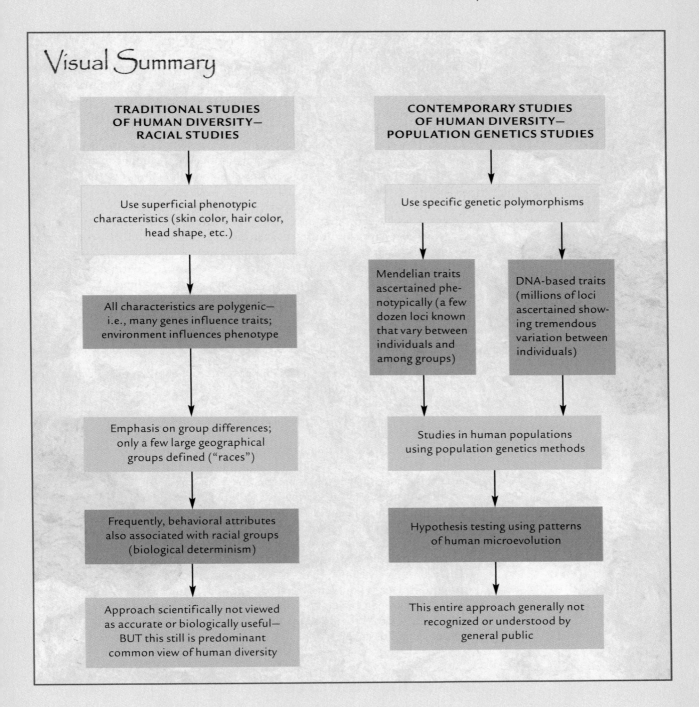

TRADITIONAL STUDIES OF HUMAN DIVERSITY— RACIAL STUDIES

↓

Use superficial phenotypic characteristics (skin color, hair color, head shape, etc.)

↓

All characteristics are polygenic— i.e., many genes influence traits; environment influences phenotype

↓

Emphasis on group differences; only a few large geographical groups defined ("races")

↓

Frequently, behavioral attributes also associated with racial groups (biological determinism)

↓

Approach scientifically not viewed as accurate or biologically useful— BUT this still is predominant common view of human diversity

CONTEMPORARY STUDIES OF HUMAN DIVERSITY— POPULATION GENETICS STUDIES

↓

Use specific genetic polymorphisms

↓

Mendelian traits ascertained phenotypically (a few dozen loci known that vary between individuals and among groups)

DNA-based traits (millions of loci ascertained showing tremendous variation between individuals)

↓

Studies in human populations using population genetics methods

↓

Hypothesis testing using patterns of human microevolution

↓

This entire approach generally not recognized or understood by general public

Summary

In this chapter, we investigated some of the ways in which humans differ from one another, both within and between populations. We first explored how this variation was approached in the past, in terms of racial typologies. We then discussed contemporary approaches that describe simple genetic polymorphisms for which allele frequencies may be calculated, and we emphasized new techniques in which genetic data are obtained from direct analyses of mitochondrial and nuclear DNA. Moreover, we reviewed the theoretical basis of the population genetics approach, the subdiscipline of physical anthropology that seeks to measure genetic diversity among humans. Data on polymorphic traits can be used to understand aspects of human microevolution. For humans, of course, culture also plays a crucial evolutionary role, and the sickle-cell trait and lactose intolerance are thus discussed from a biocultural perspective.

The chapter also considered how populations vary with regard to physiological adaptations to a number of environmental conditions, including solar radiation, heat, cold, and high altitude. We also focused on how infectious disease influences evolutionary processes, and we particularly emphasized AIDS/HIV and the dynamic relationship between pathogens and human hosts.

The topic of human variation is very complicated, and the biological and cultural factors that have contributed to that variation and that continue to influence it are manifold. But from an explicitly evolutionary perspective, it is through the investigation of changes in allele frequencies in response to environmental conditions that we will continue to elucidate the diverse adaptive potential that characterizes our species.

Critical Thinking Questions

1. Imagine you are with a group of three friends discussing human diversity and the number of races. One friend asserts that there are three clearly defined races. A second disagrees, claiming there are five, while the third is positive that there are actually nine races. Would you agree with any of these views? Why or why not?
2. For the same group of friends mentioned in question 1 (none of whom have had a course in biological anthropology), how would you explain how scientific knowledge fits with their preconceived notions about human races?
3. In the twentieth century, how did the scientific study of human diversity change from the more traditional approach?
4. Why can we say that variations in human skin color are the result of natural selection in different environments? Why is less pigmented skin a result of conflicting selective factors?
5. Do you think that infectious disease has played an important role in human evolution? Do you think it plays a *current* role in human adaptation?
6. How have human cultural practices influenced the patterns of infectious disease seen today? Provide as many examples as you can, including some not discussed in this chapter.

🌐 Media Resources

The Companion Website for *Essentials of Physical Anthropology,* Sixth Edition
http://anthropology.wadsworth.com/jurmain6e_ess

Supplement your review of this chapter by going to this text's companion website to take one of the practice quizzes, use the flash cards to master key terms, and check out the many other resources and study aids.

CD-ROMs in Physical Anthropology

Wadsworth Publishing has also developed three CD-ROMs to accompany this text and enhance learning in physical anthropology (for further descriptions of these CD-ROMs, see p. xix):

Virtual Laboratories for Physical Anthropology CD-ROM, Third Edition

Basic Genetics for Anthropology CD-ROM: Principles and Applications

Hominid Fossils CD-ROM: An Interactive Atlas

For this chapter, see especially the Virtual Laboratories for Physical Anthropology CD-ROM, Third Edition, and the Basic Genetics for Anthropology CD-ROM: Principles and Applications.

Readings of Interest

Cavalli-Sforza, C.C. 2000. *Genes, People, and Languages.* New York: North Point Press.

Frisancho, A. Roberto. 1993. *Human Adaptation and Accommodation.* Ann Arbor: University of Michigan Press.

Gould, Stephen Jay. 1981. *The Mismeasure of Man.* New York: Norton.

Nesse, Randolph M., and George C. Williams. 1998. "Evolution and the Origins of Disease." *Scientific American* 279(5): 86–93.

O'Brien, Stephen J., and Michael Dean. 1997. "In Search of AIDS-Resistance Genes." *Scientific American* 277(3): 44–51.

Olson, Steve. 2003. *Mapping Human History: Genes, Race, and Our Common Origins.* Boston: Mariner Books.

Relethford, John. 2003. *Reflections of Our Past. How Human History Is Revealed in Our Genes.* Boulder, CO: Westview Press.

13 | The Anthropological Perspective on the Human Life Course

Focus Question

Given that humans are part of a biological continuum, how does culture make us different from other species?

Introduction

Throughout this book, we have emphasized the importance of the anthropological perspective for understanding human beings through time and space. As defined in the first chapter, anthropology is the study of humankind. Unlike most other fields that have humans as their focus, the anthropological approach to humankind draws on and integrates research about people from all parts of the earth and from both past and contemporary cultures. An anthropological perspective on the life course will serve as a way of further illustrating the breadth of this approach.

Because this is a physical anthropology text, we have placed primary emphasis on human biological evolution and adaptation. We have learned that our biology is the result of millions of years of evolutionary history: 225 million years of mammalian evolution, 65 million years of primate evolution, 7 million years of hominid evolution, 2–2.5 million years of evolution of the genus *Homo*. But are we just another mammal, just another primate? In most ways, of course, we are like other mammals and other primates. But as emphasized throughout the text, modern human beings are the result of *biocultural evolution*. In other words, human biology and behavior today have been shaped by the biological and cultural forces that operated on our ancestors. In fact, it would be fruitless to attempt an understanding of modern human biology and diversity without considering that humans have evolved in the context of culture. It would be like trying to understand the biology of fish without considering that they live in water.

A good place to explore the interaction of biology and culture is the human life course. If we consider how a human develops from an embryo into an adult and examine the forces that operate on that process, then we will have a better perspective of how both biology and culture influence our own lives. Throughout this book, we have focused on the primate order (Chapters 5 and 6), the evolution of the family Hominidae (Chapters 8 through 11), and populations of modern *Homo sapiens* (Chapters 11 and 12). We continue the focus on modern humans in this chapter, but our interest shifts to the life course to understand how past and present evolutionary and cultural forces operate on our own lives.

There is, of course, much variation in the extent to which cultural factors interact with genetically based biological characteristics; these variable interactions influence how characteristics are expressed in individuals. Some genetically based characteristics will be exhibited no matter what the cultural context of growth and development happen to be. If a person inherits two alleles for albinism, for example (see Chapter 4), he or she will be deficient in production of the pigment melanin, resulting in lightly colored skin, hair, and eyes. This phenotype will emerge regardless of the cultural environment in which the person lives.

Click ▲

Go to the following CD-ROMs for interactive activities and exercises on topics covered in this chapter:

 Basic Genetics for Anthropology CD-ROM: Principles and Applications

Other characteristics, such as intelligence, body shape, and growth will reflect the interaction of environment and genes. We know, for example, that each of us is born with a genetic makeup that influences the maximum stature we can achieve in adulthood. But to reach that maximum stature, we must be properly nourished during our growing years and avoid many childhood diseases and other stresses that inhibit growth. What factors determine whether we are well fed and receive good medical care? In the United States, socioeconomic status is probably the primary determinant of nutrition and health. Thus, socioeconomic status is an example of a cultural factor that affects growth.

Fundamentals of Growth and Development

growth Increase in mass or number of cells.

development Differentiation of cells into different types of tissues and their maturation.

The terms *growth* and *development* are often used interchangeably, but they actually refer to different processes. **Growth** refers to an increase in mass or number of cells, whereas **development** refers to the differentiation of cells into different types of tissues and their subsequent maturation. Increase in cell number is referred to as *hyperplasia,* and increase in cell size, or mass, is called *hypertrophy.* Some cells are manufactured only once and are usually not replaced if damaged (e.g., some nerve and muscle cells); some cells are continuously dying and being replaced (skin and red blood cells); and some can be regenerated if damaged (cells in the liver, kidneys, and most glands). (See Chapter 3 for discussions of cell division.)

In humans, growth begins at conception and continues until the late teens or early 20s. Typically, well-nourished humans grow fairly rapidly during the first two trimesters (6 months) of fetal development, but growth slows during the third trimester. After birth, the rate of development increases and remains fairly rapid for about four years, at which time it decreases again to a relatively slow, steady level that is maintained until puberty. At puberty, there is once again a very pronounced increase in growth. During this so-called **adolescent growth spurt,** Western teenagers typically grow 9 to 10 cm per year. Subsequent to the adolescent growth spurt, the rate of development declines again and remains slower until adult stature is achieved by the late teens (Fig. 13-1).

adolescent growth spurt The period during adolescence when well-nourished teens typically increase in stature at greater rates than at other times in the life cycle.

Growth curves for boys and girls are significantly different, with the adolescent growth spurt occurring approximately two years earlier in girls than in boys. At birth, there is slight *sexual dimorphism* in many body measures (e.g., height, weight, head circumference, and body fat), but the major divergence in these characteristics does not occur until puberty.

The head is a relatively large part of the body at birth. The continued growth of the brain after birth occurs at a rate far greater than that of any other part of the body, with the exception of the eyeball. At birth, the human brain is about 25 percent of its adult size. By 6 months of age, the brain has doubled in size, reaching 50 percent of adult size. It reaches 75 percent of adult size at age $2\frac{1}{2}$ years, 90 percent at age 5 years, and 95 percent by age 10 years. There is only a very small spurt at adolescence, making the brain an exception to the growth curves characteristic of most other parts of the body. As we will see later in this chapter, this pattern of brain growth, including the relatively small amount of growth before birth, is unusual among primates and

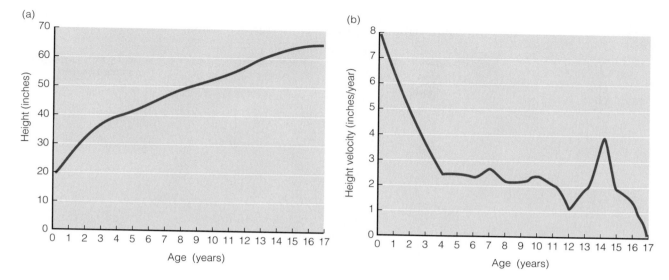

(a)

(b)

FIGURE 13-1 Distance and velocity curves of growth in height for a healthy American girl. (a) The distance curve shows the height attained in a given year. (b) The velocity curve plots the amount gained in a given year.

other mammals. By contrast, the typical picture for most mammalian species is that at least 50 percent of adult brain size has been attained prior to birth. For humans, however, the narrow pelvis necessary for walking bipedally provides limits on the size of the fetal head that can be delivered through it (Rosenberg and Trevathan, 2001). That limitation, in addition to the value of having most brain growth occur in the more stimulating environment outside the womb, has resulted in human infants being born with far less of their total adult brain size than most other mammals.

Nutritional Requirements for Growth

Nutrition has an impact on human growth at every stage of the life cycle. During pregnancy, for example, a woman's diet can have a profound effect on the development of her fetus and the eventual health of the child. Moreover, the effects are transgenerational, because a woman's own supply of eggs is developed while she herself is *in utero* (see Chapter 3). Thus, if a woman is malnourished during pregnancy, the eggs that develop in her female fetus may be damaged in a way that will impact the health of her future grandchildren.

Nutrients needed for growth, development, and body maintenance include proteins, carbohydrates, lipids (fats), vitamins, and minerals. The specific amount that we need of each of these nutrients coevolved with the types of foods that were available to human ancestors throughout our evolutionary history. For example, the specific pattern of amino acids required in human nutrition (the **essential amino acids**) reflects an ancestral diet high in animal protein. Unfortunately for modern humans, these coevolved nutritional requirements are often incompatible with the foods that are available and typically consumed today. To understand this mismatch of our nutritional needs and contemporary diets, we need to examine the impact of agriculture on human evolutionary history.

The preagricultural diet, while perhaps high in animal protein, was low in fats, particularly saturated fats. The diet was also high in complex carbohydrates (including fiber), low in salt, and high in calcium. We do not need to be

essential amino acids The 9 (of 22) amino acids that must be obtained from the food we eat because they are not synthesized in the body in sufficient amounts.

TABLE 13-1	Preagricultural, Contemporary American, and Recently Recommended Dietary Composition		
	Preagricultural Diet	**Contemporary Diet**	**Recent Recommendations**
Total dietary energy (%)			
Protein	33	12	12
Carbohydrate	46	46	58
Fat	21	42	30
Alcohol	~0	(7–10)	—
P:S ratio*	1.41	0.44	1
Cholesterol (mg)	520	300–500	300
Fiber (g)	100–150	19.7	30–60
Sodium (mg)	690	2,300–6,900	1,000–3,300
Calcium (mg)	1,500–2,000	740	800–1,500
Ascorbic acid (mg)	440	90	60

*Polyunsaturated: saturated fat ratio.
Source: Reuse of attached table from p. 84 in *The Paleolithic Prescription* by S. Boyd Eaton, Marjorie Shostack. Copyright © 1988 by S. Boyd, M.D., Marjorie Shostack, and Melvin Konner, M.D., Ph.D. Reprinted by permission of HarperCollins Publishers, Inc.

reminded that the contemporary diet that typifies many industrialized societies has the opposite configuration of the one just described. It is high in saturated fats and salt and low in complex carbohydrates, fiber, and calcium (Table 13-1). There is very good evidence that many of today's diseases in industrialized countries are related to the lack of fit between our diet today and the one with which we evolved (Eaton, Shostak, and Konner, 1988).

Many of our biological and behavioral characteristics evolved because in the past they contributed to adaptation; but today these same characteristics may be maladaptive. An example is our ability to store fat. This capability was an advantage in the past, when food availability often alternated between abundance and scarcity. Those who could store fat during the times of abundance could draw on those stores during times of scarcity and remain healthy, resist disease, and, for women, maintain the ability to reproduce. Today, people with adequate economic resources spend much of their lives with a relative abundance of foods. Considering the number of disorders associated with obesity, the formerly positive ability to store extra fat has now turned into a liability. Our "feast or famine" biology is now incompatible with the constant feast many of us indulge in today.

Perhaps no disorder is as clearly linked with dietary and lifestyle behaviors as the form of diabetes mellitus that typically has its onset in later life, referred to variously as Type II diabetes or NIDDM (non–insulin dependent diabetes mellitus). In 1900, diabetes ranked twenty-seventh among the leading causes of death in the United States; today it ranks seventh. Moreover, the threat to world health from this disease is growing, with projections of an increase in incidence between 2000 and 2010 of 57 percent in Asia, 50 percent in Africa, 44 percent in South America, and 23 percent in North America (Zimmet, Alberti, and Shaw, 2001). Part of this projected increase will be due to decreases in other causes of death (e.g., infectious diseases), but much of it has to do with lifestyle and dietary changes associated with modernization and globalization, especially the decrease in levels of daily activity and increase in dietary intake of fats and refined carbohydrates. In fact, there is some evidence that the genotype that predisposes a person to diabetes may once have been advantageous. This "thrifty genotype" hypothesis states that during times of food abundance, individuals who could readily store excess calories as fat were better able to survive (and, more importantly, continue to reproduce) during times of food scarcity. The negative effects of this genotype were rarely manifested in this "feast or famine" environment, especially when activity levels remained high.

It is clear that both deficiencies and excesses of nutrients can cause health problems and interfere with childhood growth. Certainly, many people in all parts of the world, both industrialized and developing, suffer from inadequate supplies of food of any quality. We read daily of thousands dying from starvation due to drought, warfare, or political instability. The blame must be placed not only on the narrowed food base that resulted from the emergence of agriculture, but also on the increase in human population that occurred when people began to settle in permanent villages and have more children. Today, the crush of billions of humans almost completely dependent on cereal grains means that millions face undernutrition, malnutrition, and even starvation. (See Chapter 14 for a further discussion of world population growth and related problems.)

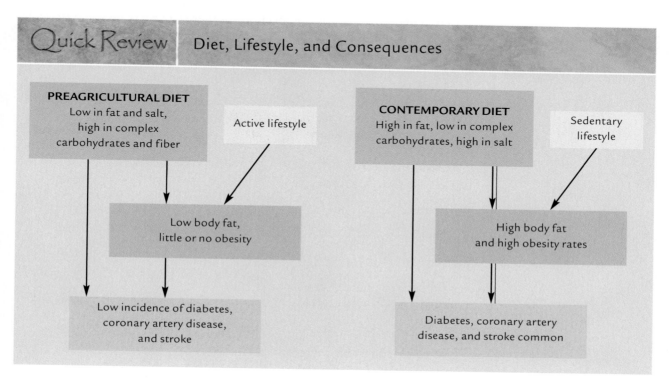

Quick Review — Diet, Lifestyle, and Consequences

PREAGRICULTURAL DIET
Low in fat and salt, high in complex carbohydrates and fiber

Active lifestyle

Low body fat, little or no obesity

Low incidence of diabetes, coronary artery disease, and stroke

CONTEMPORARY DIET
High in fat, low in complex carbohydrates, high in salt

Sedentary lifestyle

High body fat and high obesity rates

Diabetes, coronary artery disease, and stroke common

Other Factors Influencing Growth and Development

GENETICS

Genetic factors set the underlying limitations and potentialities for growth and development, but the life experience and environment of the organism determine how the body grows within those parameters. How do we assess the relative contributions of genes and the environment in their effects on growth? Much of our information comes from studies of monozygotic and dizygotic twins. Monozygotic ("identical") twins come from the union of a single sperm and ovum and share 100 percent of their genes. Dizygotic ("fraternal") twins come from separate ova and sperm and share only 50 percent of their genes, just as any other siblings from the same parents. If monozygotic twins with identical genes but different growth environments are exactly the same in stature at various ages (i.e., show perfect correlation or *concordance* for stature), then we can conclude that genes are the primary, if not the only, determinants of stature. Most studies of twins reveal that under normal circumstances, stature is "highly correlated" for monozygotic twins, leading to the conclusion that stature is under fairly strong genetic control (Table 13-2). Weight, on the other hand, seems to be more strongly influenced by diet, environment, and individual experiences than by genes.

HORMONES

One of the primary ways in which genes have an effect on growth and development is through their effects on hormones. Hormones are substances produced in one cell that have an effect on another cell (see p. 48), and examples include estrogen, testosterone, cortisol, and insulin. Most hormones are pro-

TABLE 13-2	Correlation Coefficients for Height Between Monozygotic (MZ) and Dizygotic (DZ) Twin Pairs from Birth to Age 8			
			DZ	
Age	**Total N**	**MZ**	**Same Sex**	**Different Sex**
Birth	629	0.62	0.79	0.67
3 months	764	0.78	0.72	0.65
6 months	819	0.80	0.67	0.62
12 months	827	0.86	0.66	0.58
24 months	687	0.89	0.54	0.61
3 years	699	0.93	0.56	0.60
5 years	606	0.94	0.51	0.68
8 years	444	0.94	0.49	0.65

Source: From Wilson, 1979, after Bogin, 1988, p. 163.

duced by endocrine glands, such as the pituitary, thyroid, and adrenal glands, in addition to the ovaries and testes. Hormones are transported in the bloodstream, and almost all have an effect on growth. The hypothalamus (located at the base of the forebrain) can be considered the relay station, control center, or central clearinghouse for most hormonal action. This control center receives messages from the brain and other glands and sends out messages that stimulate hormonal action. Most of the hormonal messages transmitted from the hypothalamus result in the inhibition or release of other hormones.

Two hormones that are important in growth include growth hormone and insulin. Growth hormone, secreted by the anterior pituitary, promotes growth and has an effect on just about every cell in the body. Tumors and other disorders can result in excessive or insufficient amounts of growth hormone secretion, which in turn can result in gigantism or dwarfism. One group of people who have notably short stature are African Efe pygmies. Recent research suggests that altered levels of growth hormone and its controlling factors interact with nutritional factors and infectious diseases to produce the relatively short adult stature of these people (Shea and Bailey, 1996), providing another example of the interaction of biological and cultural forces.

ENVIRONMENTAL FACTORS

Environmental factors, such as altitude and climate, have effects on growth and development. Perhaps the primary influence of such external factors comes from their effects on nutrition, but there is evidence of independent effects as well. For example, as noted in Chapter 12, infant birth weight is lower at high altitude, and this is so even when such factors as nutrition, smoking, and socioeconomic status are taken into consideration. In Colorado, for example, birth weight declined an average of 102 g (3.6 ounces) per 1,000 m (3,300 feet) of elevation gain, even when factors such as gestational age, maternal weight gain, smoking, and prenatal care were considered (Jensen and Moore, 1997). In a Bolivian study, the mean birth weight was 3,415 g (7.8 pounds) at low elevations and 3,133 g (7.1 pounds) at high elevations (Haas et al., 1980). Most studies of children have found that those at high elevations are shorter and lighter than those at low elevations.

In general, populations in cold climates tend to be heavier and have longer trunks and shorter extremities than populations in tropical areas. This reflects Bergmann's and Allen's rules, discussed in Chapter 12. Exposure to sunlight also appears to have an effect on growth, most likely through its effects on vitamin D production. Children tend to grow more rapidly in times of high sunlight concentration (i.e., in the summer in temperate regions and in the dry season in monsoonal tropical regions). Vitamin D, necessary for skeletal growth, requires sunlight for its synthesis (see pp. 320–322).

Among the most significant environmental factors having an effect on growth and development is infectious disease, such as malaria, influenza, cholera, and tuberculosis (see pp. 327–334). These diseases have their greatest impact during childhood and can delay growth, particularly when coupled with malnutrition. In fact, the effects of infectious disease and malnutrition are said to be *synergistic;* that is, each worsens the effect of the other so that in combination their effects are potentially more damaging than either is acting alone. Unfortunately, they often occur together because chronic malnutrition lowers resistance to disease organisms that are present in the environment.

The Human Life Cycle

As noted in earlier chapters, primatologists and other physical anthropologists view primate and human growth and development from an evolutionary perspective, with an interest in how natural selection has operated on the life cycle from conception to death, a perspective known as life history theory. Why, for example, do humans have longer periods of infancy and childhood compared with other primates? What accounts for differences seen in the life cycles of such closely related species as humans and chimpanzees? Life history research seeks to answer such questions (see Mace, 2000, for a review).

Life history theory begins with the premise that there is only a certain amount of energy available to an organism for growth, maintenance of life, and reproduction. Energy invested in one of these processes is not available to another. Thus, the entire life course represents a series of trade-offs among life history traits (see p. 147), such as length of gestation, age at weaning, time spent in growth to adulthood, adult body size, and length of life span. For example, life history theory provides the basis for understanding how fast an organism will grow and to what size, how many offspring can be produced, how long gestation will last, and how long an individual will live. Crucial to understanding life history theory is its link to the evolutionary process: It is the action of natural selection that shapes life history traits, determining which ones will succeed or fail in a given environment. Although it isn't clear if life history theory works in contemporary human populations (Strassman and Gillespie, 2002), it serves as a useful guide for examining the various life cycle phases from evolutionary and ecological perspectives.

Not all animals have clearly demarcated phases in their lives; moreover, among mammals, humans have more such phases than do other species (Fig. 13-2). Protozoa, among the simplest of animals, have only one phase; many invertebrates have two: larval and adult. Almost all mammals have at least three phases: prenatal, infancy, and adulthood. Most primates have four phases: prenatal, infancy, juvenile (usually called childhood in humans), and adult. Monkeys, apes, and humans add a phase between the juvenile phase and adulthood that is referred to as the subadult period (adolescence, or teenage, in humans). Finally, for humans there is the addition of a sixth

FIGURE 13-2 Life cycle stages for various animal species.

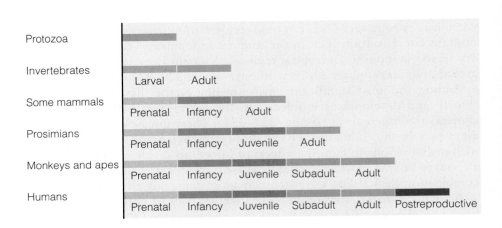

phase in women, the postreproductive years following menopause. One could argue that during the course of primate evolution, more recently evolved forms have longer life spans and more divisions of the life span into phases, or stages.

Most of these life cycle stages are well marked by biological transitions. The prenatal phase begins with conception and ends with birth; infancy is the period of nursing; childhood, or the juvenile phase, is the period from weaning to sexual maturity (puberty in humans); adolescence is the period from puberty to the end of growth; adulthood is marked by the birth of the first child and/or the completion of growth; and menopause is recognized as having occurred one full year after the last menstrual cycle. These biological markers are similar among higher primates, but for humans, there is an added complexity: They occur in cultural contexts that define and characterize them. Puberty, for example, has very different meanings in different cultures. A girl's first menstruation (**menarche**) is often marked with ritual and celebration, and a change in social status typically occurs with this biological transition. Likewise, **menopause** is often associated with a rise in status for women in non-Western societies, whereas it is commonly seen as a negative transition for women in many Western societies. As we shall see, collective and individual attitudes toward these life cycle transitions have an effect on growth, development, and health.

menarche The first menstruation in girls, usually occurring in the early to middle teens.

menopause The end of menstruation in human women, usually occurring at around age 50.

PREGNANCY, BIRTH, AND INFANCY

The biological aspects of conception and gestation can be discussed in a fairly straightforward way, drawing information from what is known about reproductive biology at the present time: A sperm fertilizes an egg; the resulting zygote travels through a uterine (fallopian) tube to become implanted in the uterine lining; and the embryo develops until it is mature enough to survive outside the womb, at which time birth occurs. But this is clearly not all there is to human pregnancy and birth. Female biology may be similar the world over, but cultural rules and practices are the primary determinants of who will get pregnant, as well as when, where, how, and by whom.

Once pregnancy has occurred, there is much variation in how a woman should behave, what she should eat, where she should and should not go, and how she should interact with other people. Almost every culture known, including our own, imposes dietary restrictions on pregnant women. Many of these appear to serve an important biological function, particularly that of keeping the woman from ingesting toxins that would be dangerous for the fetus. (Alcohol is a good example of a potential toxin whose consumption in pregnancy is discouraged in the United States.) The food aversions to coffee, alcohol, and other bitter substances that many women experience during pregnancy may be evolved adaptations to protect the embryo from toxins. The nausea of early pregnancy may also function to limit the intake of foods potentially harmful to the embryo at a critical stage of development (Profet, 1988; Williams and Nesse 1991).

Birth is an event that is celebrated with ritual in almost every culture studied. In fact, the relatively little fanfare associated with childbirth in the United States is unusual by world standards. Because risk of death for both mother and child is so great at birth, it is not surprising that it is surrounded with ritual significance. Perhaps because of the high risk of death, we tend to think

FIGURE 13-3 The relation between the average diameter of the birth canal of adult females and average head length and breadth of newborns of the same species. (After Jolly, 1985.)

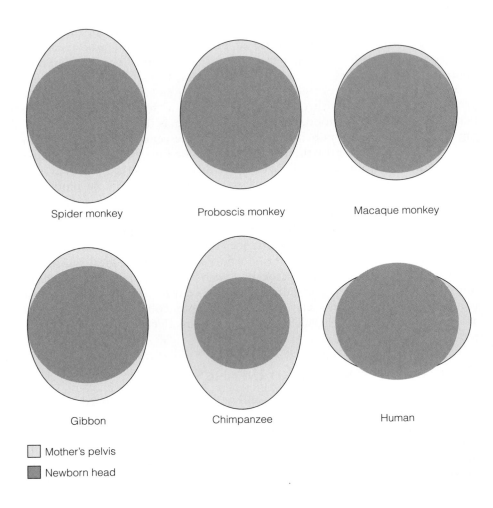

Spider monkey

Proboscis monkey

Macaque monkey

Gibbon

Chimpanzee

Human

☐ Mother's pelvis

■ Newborn head

that birth is far more difficult in humans than it is in other mammals. But since almost all primate infants have large heads relative to body size, birth is challenging to many primates (Fig. 13-3).

An undeveloped brain seems necessary for birth to occur through a narrow pelvis, but it may also be advantageous for other reasons. For a species as dependent on learning as we are for survival, it may be adaptive for most of our brain growth to take place in the presence of environmental stimuli rather than in the relatively unstimulating uterus. This may be particularly true for a species dependent on language. The language centers of the brain develop in the first three years of life, when the brain is undergoing its rapid expansion; these three years are considered a critical period for the development of language in the human child.

Infancy is defined as the period during which nursing takes place, typically lasting about four years in humans. When we consider how unusual it is for a mother to nurse her child for even a year in the United States or Canada, this figure may surprise us. But considering that four or five years of nursing is the norm for chimpanzees, gorillas, and orangutans and for women in foraging societies, most anthropologists conclude that four years was the norm for most humans in the evolutionary past (Eaton, Shostak, and Konner, 1988).

Other lines of evidence confirm this pattern, including the lack of other foods that infants could consume until the origin of agriculture and the domestication of milk-producing animals. In fact, if the mother died during childbirth in preagricultural populations, it is very likely that the child died also, unless there was another woman available who could nurse the child. Jane Goodall has noted that this is also true for chimpanzees: Infants who are orphaned before they are weaned do not usually survive. Even those orphaned after weaning are still emotionally dependent on their mothers and exhibit clinical signs of depression for a few months or years after the mother's death, assuming they survive the trauma (Goodall, 1986).

Human milk, like that of other primates, is extremely low in fats and protein. Such a low nutrient content is typical for species in which mothers are seldom or never separated from their infants and nurse in short, frequent bouts. Not coincidentally, prolonged, frequent nursing suppresses ovulation in marginally nourished women (Konner and Worthman, 1980), especially when coupled with high activity levels and few calorie reserves (Ellison, 2001). Under these circumstances, breast-feeding can help to maintain a four-year birth interval, during which infants have no nutritional competition from siblings. Thus, nursing served as a natural birth control mechanism in the evolutionary past, as it does in some populations today.

Breast milk also provides important antibodies that contribute to infant survival. Throughout the world, breast-fed infants have far greater survival rates than those who are not breast-fed or who are weaned too early. The only exception is in societies where scientifically developed milk substitutes are readily available and appropriately used. The importance of adequate nutrients during this period of rapid brain growth cannot be overestimated. Thus, it is not surprising that there are many cultural practices designed to ensure successful nursing.

CHILDHOOD

Humans have unusually long childhoods, reflecting the importance of learning for our species. Childhood is that time between weaning and puberty when the brain is completing its growth and the acquisition of technical and social skills is taking place. For most other mammals, once weaning has occurred, getting food is left to individual effort. Humans may be unique in the practice of providing food for children or juveniles (Lancaster and Lancaster, 1983). Such sustained care requires much extra effort by parents, but the survival rate of offspring is a great deal higher than in other primates (Table 13-3). During childhood, the roles of fathers and older siblings become very significant. While mothers are highly involved with caring for new infants, the socialization and child care of other children often fall to other family or community members. Clearly, family environment, stress, and other biosocial factors have a major impact on children's health (Flinn, 1999).

ADOLESCENCE

A number of biological events mark the transition to adolescence for both males and females. These include increase in body size, change in body shape, and the development of testes and penes in boys, and breasts in girls. Hormonal changes are the driving forces behind all these physical alterations,

TABLE 13-3	Providing for Juveniles	
	Percent of Those Who Survive	
	Weaning	**Adolescence**
Lion	28	15
Baboon	45	33
Macaque	42	13
Chimpanzee	48	38
Provisioned macaques	82	58
Human Populations		
!Kung*	80	58
Yanomamo †	73	50
Paleoindian ‡	86	50

* A hunting and gathering population of southern Africa.
† Horticultural population of South America.
‡ Preagricultural people of the Americas.
Source: Adapted from Lancaster and Lancaster, 1983.

especially increased testosterone production in boys and increased estrogen production in girls. As already noted, menarche (the first menstruation) is a clear sign of puberty in girls and is usually the marker of this transition in cultures where the event is ritually celebrated.

A number of factors affect the onset of puberty in humans, including genetics, gestational experience, nutrition, disease, activity levels, and stress. In humans and other primates, females reach sexual maturity before males do. An illustration of the effect of diet and other lifestyle factors on puberty is seen in the trend toward a lower age of menarche that has been noted in human populations in the last hundred years (Fig. 13-4), and the tendency for girls who are very active and thin to mature later than those who are heavier and less active. Socioeconomic factors are also implicated in this trend: In less developed nations, girls from higher social classes tend to mature earlier than girls from lower social classes. In general, physical development has accelerated in the past several decades along with worldwide improvements in public health and nutrition (Worthman, 1999).

Adolescence is the time between puberty and the completion of physical growth or the social recognition of adulthood. This social recognition may result from marriage, bearing a child, or a particular accomplishment. In nonhuman primates, the equivalent stage is defined in males as the time from which they are capable of fertilization to the time when physical growth is complete. At this point, they have male-specific features and size and are recognized as adults by other members of the social group. Females begin to engage in sexual behavior, exhibiting signs of sexual receptivity before they are capable of bearing young. These early cycles are usually not ovulatory and define the period of adolescence for them. Adulthood comes with the first pregnancy.

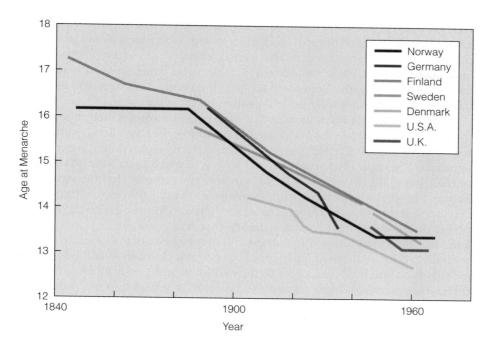

FIGURE 13-4 The secular trend in age at menarche in Europe.
(From Wood, James W., 1994, *Dynamics of Human Reproduction*, New York: Aldine de Gruyter; original redrawn from Eveleth, P. B. and J. M. Tanner, 1976, *Worldwide Variation in Human Growth*, Cambridge: Cambridge University Press.)

ADULTHOOD

Pregnancy and child care occupy much of a woman's adult life in most cultures, as they likely did throughout hominid evolution. For most women, the years from menarche to menopause are marked by monthly menstruation, except when they are pregnant or nursing. A normal menstrual cycle has two phases: the follicular phase, in which the egg is preparing for ovulation, marked by high estrogen production; and the luteal phase, during which the uterus is preparing for implantation, marked by high progesterone production. If the egg is not fertilized, progesterone production drops off and menstruation, the shedding of the uterine lining, occurs. A woman who never becomes pregnant may have as many as 400 cycles between menarche and menopause. Because reliable contraceptives were unavailable in the past, this high number of menstrual cycles is probably a relatively recent phenomenon. It has been suggested, in fact, that highly frequent menstrual cycling may be implicated in several cancers of the female reproductive organs, especially of the breast, uterus, and ovaries (Eaton et al., 1994). During the course of human evolution, females may have had as few as 60 menstrual cycles in their entire lives, unless they were sterile or not sexually active.

At the social level, adulthood for women in the majority of world cultures means, in addition to caring for children, participation in economic activities. Adulthood for men typically includes activities related to subsistence, religion, politics, and family. Women may be equally or less involved in these activities, depending on the culture.

For women, menopause, or the end of menstruation, is a sign of entry into a new phase of the life cycle. Estrogen and progesterone production begin to decline toward the end of the reproductive years until ovulation (and thus menstruation) ceases altogether. This occurs at approximately age 50 in all parts of the world. Throughout human evolution, the majority of females (and males) did not survive to age 50; thus, few women lived much past menopause. But today, this event occurs when women have as much as one-third of their active and healthy lives ahead of them. As already noted, such a long postreproductive period is not found in other primates. Female chimpanzees and monkeys experience decreased fertility in their later years, but most continue to have monthly cycles until their death. Occasional reports of menopause in apes and monkeys have been noted, but it is far from a routine and expected event.

Why do human females have such a long period during which they can no longer reproduce? One theory relates to parenting. Because it takes about 12 to 15 years before a child becomes independent, it has been argued that females are biologically "programmed" to live 12 to 15 years beyond the birth of their last child (Mayer, 1982). This hypothesis assumes that the maximum human life span for preagricultural humans was about 65 years, a figure that corresponds to what is known for contemporary hunter-gatherers and for prehistoric populations. Another theory that has been gaining attention is known as the "grandmother hypothesis." This proposes that women who lived several years beyond the independence of their last children would be freed to provide food and other resources to their children and grandchildren. Because these practices would likely increase the survival of grandchildren, productive postmenopausal years would be favored by natural selection (Hawkes et al., 1997; Lahdenperä et al., 2004). A third theory regarding menopause suggests that it was not itself favored by natural selection; rather it is an artifact of the extension of the human life span that has occurred in the last several centuries.

AGING

Postreproductive years are physiologically somewhat well defined for women, but "old age" is a very ambiguous concept. In the United States, we tend to associate old age with physical ailments and decreased activity. Thus, a person who is vigorous and active at age 70 might not be regarded as "old," whereas another who is frail and debilitated at age 55 may be considered old.

One reason we are concerned with this definition is that old age is generally regarded negatively and is typically unwelcome in the United States, a culture noted for its emphasis on youth. This attitude is quite different from that of many other societies, where old age brings with it wealth, higher status, and new freedoms, particularly for women. This is because high status is often correlated with knowledge, experience, and wisdom, which are themselves associated with greater age in most societies. Such has been the case throughout most of history, but today, in technologically developed countries, knowledge is changing so rapidly that the old may no longer control the most relevant knowledge.

By and large, people today are living longer than they did in the past because, in part, they are not dying from infectious diseases. Currently, the top five killers in the United States, for example, are heart disease, cancer, stroke, accidents, and chronic obstructive lung disease. Together these account for almost 70 percent of deaths (CDC National Vital Statistics Report, 2000). All these conditions are considered "diseases of civilization" in that most can be accounted for by conditions in the modern environment that were not present in the past. Examples include cigarette smoke, air and water pollution, alcohol, automobiles, high-fat diets, and environmental carcinogens. It should be noted, however, that the high incidence of these diseases is also a result of people living to older ages because of factors such as improved hygiene, regular medical care, and new medical technologies.

HUMAN LONGEVITY

Relative to most other animals, humans have a long life span (Table 13-4). The maximum life span potential, estimated to be about 120 years, has probably not changed in the last several thousand years, although life expectancy at birth (the average length of life) has increased significantly in the last 100 years, probably owing to the decreased influence of infectious diseases, which typically take their toll on the young (Crews and Harper, 1998).

To some extent, aging is something we do throughout our entire lives. But we usually think of aging as **senescence,** the process of physiological decline in all systems of the body that occurs toward the end of the life course. Actually, throughout adulthood, there is a gradual decline in our cells' ability to synthesize proteins, in immune system function, in muscle mass (with a corresponding increase in fat mass) and strength, and in bone mineral density (Lamberts, van den Beld, and van der Lely, 1997). This decline is associated with an increase in risk for the chronic degenerative diseases that are usually listed as the causes of death in industrialized nations.

As you know, most causes of death that have their effects after the reproductive years will not necessarily be subjected to the forces of natural selection. One explanation for why we age and are affected by chronic degenerative diseases like atherosclerosis, cancers, and hypertension is that genes that enhance reproductive success in earlier years (and thus were favored by natural selection) may have detrimental effects in later years. These are referred to as **pleiotropic genes,** meaning that they have multiple effects at different times in the life span or under different conditions (Williams, 1957). For example, genes that enhance the function of the immune system in the early years may also damage tissue so that cancer susceptibility increases in later life (Nesse and Williams, 1994).

Pleiotropy may help us understand evolutionary reasons for aging, but what are the causes of senescence in the individual? Much attention has been focused recently on free radicals, highly reactive molecules that can damage cells. Protection against these by-products of normal metabolism is provided by antioxidants such as vitamins A, C, and E and by a number of enzymes (Kirkwood, 1997). Ultimately, damage to DNA can occur, which in turn contributes to the senescence of cells, the immune system, and other functional systems of the body. Additionally, there is evidence that programmed cell death is also a part of the normal processes of development that can obviously contribute to senescence.

Another hypothesis for senescence related to ultimate cell death is known as the "telomere hypothesis." In this view, the DNA sequence at the end of each chromosome, known as the telomere, is shortened each time a cell divides. Cells that have divided many times throughout the life course have short telomeres, eventually reaching the point at which they can no longer divide, and are unable to maintain healthy tissues and organs. Telomere length changes have also been implicated in cancers. In the laboratory, the enzyme telomerase can lengthen telomeres, making the cell young again. For this reason, the gene for telomerase has been called the "immortalizing gene." Although this research is not likely to lead to a lengthening of the life span, it may contribute to better health throughout an individual's lifetime.

Far more important than genes in the aging process, however, are lifestyle factors, such as smoking, physical activity, diet, and medical care. Interestingly,

TABLE 13-4	Maximum Life Spans for Selected Species	
Organism	Approximate Maximum Life Span (in years)
Bristlecone pine	5,000
Tortoise	170
Rockfish	140
Human	120
Blue whale	80
Indian elephant	70
Gorilla	39
Domestic dog	34
Rabbit	13
Rat	5

Source: Stini, 1991.

senescence The process of physiological decline in body function that occurs with aging.

pleiotropic genes Genes that have more than one effect; genes that have different effects at different times in the life cycle.

FIGURE 13-5 Changes in life expectancy due to AIDS in seven African nations. (From United Nations, 1998.)

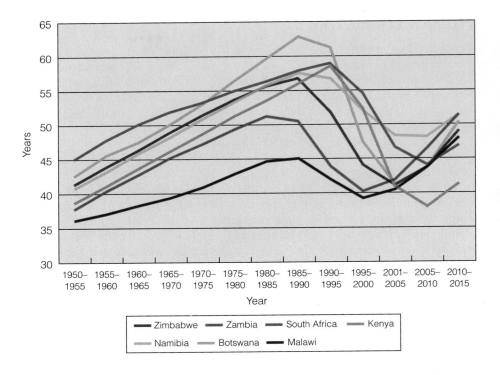

there is evidence that caloric restriction may actually contribute to longer life spans (Kirkwood, 2002). Life expectancy at birth varies considerably from country to country and among socioeconomic classes within a country. Throughout the world, women have higher life expectancies than men.

A Japanese girl born in 2002, for example, can expect to live to age 84, a boy to age 78. Girls and boys born in that same year in the United States have life expectancies of 80 and 73, respectively. In contrast to these children in industrialized nations, girls and boys in Mali have life expectancies of only 48 and 46, respectively. Many African nations have seen life expectancy drop below 40 owing to deaths from AIDS. For example, before the AIDS epidemic, Zimbabweans had a life expectancy of 65 years; today, life expectancy in Zimbabwe is 39 (Fig. 13-5).

Individuals, Society, and Evolution

Throughout this chapter, we have discussed ways in which evolutionary history, genes, and the environment affect the human life course from infancy until death. Humans are social animals, however, and we now turn our attention to the ways in which natural selection has acted on the behaviors of humans imbedded in social contexts. Examining human social behavior in an evolutionary framework is known as *behavioral ecology,* which we discussed in Chapter 6 in the context of primate behavior. Of course, humans are primates, and many biological anthropologists are interested in the extent to which evolution can explain contemporary human behaviors. Behavioral ecologists suggest that humans, like other animals, behave in ways that increase their fitness, or reproductive success. This includes behaviors affecting mating and parenting success. Finding mates and taking care of offspring require time and energy, and as we know all too well, both of these commodities exist in finite amounts. Thus, reproductive efforts require trade-offs in time, energy, and resources invested in mating and parenting. When we read about these concepts as they pertain to monkeys and apes, most of us probably do not find much with which to disagree. But to suggest that evolutionary processes have an impact on human behavior today raises a lot of issues, some of which are not so easily resolved.

For example, this view argues that natural selection is not limited to physical and physiological responses, but has had an effect on the way humans think—in other words, on human cognition, perception, and memory. The argument goes something like this: The ability to remember a dangerous event that may have resulted in loss of life would be favorably selected if it prevented a person from being caught in a similar situation. The ability to distinguish a wildebeest (food) from a lion (danger) would be selectively favored. Likewise, economic behaviors involved in the allocation of resources to increase survival and reproductive success would be favored.

The study of how natural selection has influenced how humans and other primates think is often called *evolutionary psychology*. Among the topics explored by evolutionary psychologists are mate attraction, sexuality, aggression, and violence. As you might guess, all of these are hot topics, and there is no end in sight to the controversy that surrounds them.

Aggression and violence, particularly on the part of males, is the subject of a number of books and papers in evolutionary psychology. Wrangham and Peterson (1996), for example, contrast the behaviors of our two closest living relatives, the chimpanzee and the bonobo. Most striking is that chimpanzee society seems to be based on male-male competition and aggression leading occasionally to violence both within and between troops, whereas bonobo society is described as a female-dominated community based on cooperation and peaceful interaction (Fig. 13-6). To Wrangham and Peterson, these two behavior patterns represent the extremes of human societies and also show potentials for both violence and peace that may be rooted in human evolutionary history. On the other hand, they clearly acknowledge the role of culture and society in fostering aggression and violence in males. Mirroring some of the discussions of terrorism today, chimpanzee communities with abundant resources have far

FIGURE 13-6 (a) These chimpanzees exhibit an aggressive reaction when confronted by others. (b) The bonobos show more relaxed expressions.

(a)

(b)

fewer incidents of violence than communities with limited resources; in general, bonobos live in areas of relative resource abundance. But whatever their roots, it appears to many observers that war, genocide, rape, rioting, and terrorism are unwelcome legacies of human evolutionary history. Unfortunately, because of recent events, such as 9/11 in the United States and the war in Iraq, these arguments resonate more profoundly and convincingly than they did when the last edition of this textbook was written. Perhaps by the next edition, the pendulum of thinking about world events will have swung toward the idea that peaceful cooperation is more fundamental to human behavior.

Are We Still Evolving?

In many ways, culture has enabled us to transcend many of the limitations imposed on us by our biology. But that biology was shaped during millions of years of evolution in environments very different from those in which most of us live today. There is, to a great extent, a lack of fit between our biology and our twenty-first-century cultural environment. Our expectations that scientists can discover a "magic bullet" to enable us to resist any disease that arises have been painfully dashed with death tolls from AIDS reaching catastrophic levels in many parts of the world.

Socioeconomic and political concerns also have powerful effects on our species today. Whether you die of starvation or succumb to disorders associated with overconsumption depends a great deal on where you live, what your socioeconomic status is, and how much control you have over your life, factors not likely to be related to biology. These factors also have an effect on whether or not you are killed in a war or spend most of your life in a safe, comfortable community. Whether or not you are exposed to one of the "new" pathogens, such as HIV, SARS, or tuberculosis, has a lot to do with your lifestyle and other cultural factors, but whether or not you die from a particular disease or fail to reproduce because of it still has a lot to do with your biology. The 4.3 million children dying annually from respiratory infections are primarily those in the developing world, with limited access to adequate medical care, clearly a cultural factor. But in those same areas, lacking that same medical care, are millions of other children who are not getting the infections or are not dying from them. Presumably, among the factors affecting this difference is resistance afforded by genes. By considering this simple example, we can see that human gene frequencies are still changing from one generation to the next in response to selective agents such as disease; thus, our species is still evolving.

Whether we will become a different species or become extinct as a species (remember, that is the fate of almost every species that has ever lived on earth) is not something we can predict. Whether our brains will get larger or our hands will evolve solely to push buttons is the stuff of science fiction, not anthropology. But as long as new pathogens appear or new environments are introduced by technology, there is little doubt that the human species will continue to evolve or will become extinct, just as almost every other species on earth has done.

Culture *has* enabled us to transcend many limits imposed by our biology, and people who never would have been able to do so in the past are today surviving and having children. This in itself means that we are evolving. How many of you would be reading this text if you had been born under the health and economic conditions prevalent 500 years ago?

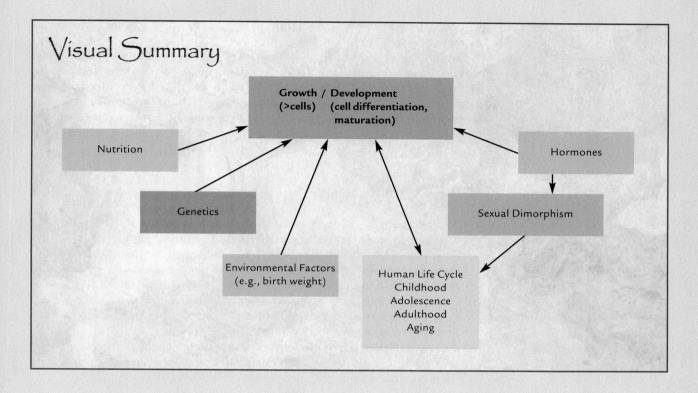

Visual Summary

Growth / Development
(>cells)   (cell differentiation,
maturation)

Nutrition

Genetics

Environmental Factors
(e.g., birth weight)

Hormones

Sexual Dimorphism

Human Life Cycle
Childhood
Adolescence
Adulthood
Aging

Summary

This chapter has reviewed the fundamental concepts of growth and development and how those processes occur within the contexts of both biology and culture. Diet has an important effect on growth, and human nutritional requirements themselves result from biocultural evolution. We reviewed the preagricultural human diet with the suggestion that many of our contemporary ills may result from incompatibilities between our evolved nutritional requirements and the foods that are currently consumed. In particular, the preagricultural diet was probably high in complex carbohydrates and fiber and low in fat and sodium. Diets for many contemporary people are low in complex carbohydrates and fiber and high in fat and sodium. This type of diet has been implicated in many current health problems.

The human life cycle can be divided into six phases: prenatal, infancy, juvenile, subadult, adult, and postreproductive. Each is fairly well defined by biological markers. Pregnancy lasts about nine months in humans, and infants are born with only about 25 percent of their adult brain size. This means that human infants are helpless at birth and therefore dependent on their parents for a long time. Birth is somewhat more challenging for humans than for other mammals because of the very close correspondence between maternal pelvic size (narrow because of bipedalism) and fetal head size (large, even though the brain is relatively undeveloped). Infancy is the period of nursing, approximately four years for most humans and apes. The unusually long period of childhood in humans is important as the time in which social and technological skills are acquired. Sexual maturation is apparent at puberty, but full adult status is not achieved until growth has been completed and childbearing capabilities are reached. The last phase of the human life cycle, the postreproductive period, is marked in women by menopause, the cessation of menstruation and ovulation.

The human legacy from evolutionary history includes thought processes and behaviors that reflect natural selection operating on individuals to increase reproductive success, or fitness. Our review of behavioral ecology summarized the ways in which genes, environment, and culture have interacted to produce complex adaptations to equally complex challenges. A critical review of hypotheses for such human behaviors as aggression, violence, nurturance, and reproduction reveals the complexity of this interrelationship.

Critical Thinking Questions

1. What is meant by the analogy "Water is to fish as culture is to humans"? Do you think that humans could survive without culture?
2. What are some of the major ways in which human health and life course have changed since the origin of agriculture? Do you think that the transition to agriculture has, in general, been good or bad for human health?
3. Consider the following statement: "In the United States, socioeconomic status is the primary determinant of nutrition and health." Do you agree or disagree with this statement? Why or why not?
4. Do you think that natural selection operates on human behaviors such as parenting and aggression? Provide evidence or examples to support your view.
5. What evidence is there that humans are still evolving?

Media Resources

The Companion Website for *Essentials of Physical Anthropology,* Sixth Edition
http://anthropology.wadsworth.com/jurmain6e_ess

Supplement your review of this chapter by going to this text's companion website to take one of the practice quizzes, use the flash cards to master key terms, and check out the many other resources and study aids.

CD-ROMs in Physical Anthropology

Wadsworth Publishing has also developed three CD-ROMs to accompany this text and enhance learning in physical anthropology (for further descriptions of these CD-ROMs, see p. xix):

Virtual Laboratories for Physical Anthropology CD-ROM, Third Edition

Basic Genetics for Anthropology CD-ROM: Principles and Applications

Hominid Fossils CD-ROM: An Interactive Atlas

For this chapter, see especially the Basic Genetics for Anthropology CD-ROM: Principles and Applications.

Readings of Interest

Diamond, Jared. 1992. *The Third Chimpanzee: The Evolution and Future of the Human Animal.* New York: Harper Collins.

Eaton, S. Boyd, Marjorie Shostak, and Melvin Konner. 1988. *The Paleolithic Prescription.* New York: Harper & Row.

Ellison, Peter T. 2001. *On Fertile Ground: A Natural History of Human Reproduction.* Cambridge, MA: Harvard University Press.

Farmer, Paul. 2003. *Pathologies of Power: Health, Human Rights, and the New War on the Poor.* Berkeley: University of California Press.

Hrdy, Sarah Blaffer. 1999. *Mother Nature: A History of Mothers, Infants, and Natural Selection.* New York: Pantheon Books.

14 | Lessons from the Past, Lessons for the Future

Focus Questions

Near the end of this chapter, you will read the statement that culture is "an adaptive strategy gone awry." Why do we say this? Do you agree with this statement? Why or why not?

Introduction

Virtually every day we read or hear something about global climate change, endangered species, environmental degradation, or one of the many other problems facing humanity today. In this chapter, we briefly discuss some of these challenges, challenges that have emerged as a result of our own doing. Although anthropology textbooks don't usually dwell on the topics included here, we feel that it's important to consider them, however brief and simplified our treatment must be. We are living during a critical period in the earth's history. Indeed, the future of much of life as we know it will be decided in the next few decades, and these decisions will be irrevocable. Therefore, it's crucial that we, as individuals, cities, and nations, make wise decisions, and to do this we must be well informed. We also think it's important to consider these problems from an anthropological perspective. This is something not usually done in the media and certainly not by politicians and heads of government. But if we are truly to comprehend the impact that human activities have had on the planet, then such discussions surely must consider our biological and cultural evolution. And we must also emphasize our place in nature and focus on how, since the domestication of plants and animals, we have altered the face of our planet while at the same time shaping the destiny of thousands of species, including our own.

Homo sapiens is one of approximately 1.4 million living species known to science. All of these organisms, including bacteria and plants, ultimately are the results of the same basic evolutionary processes, and all share the same DNA material. But more than any other life form, humans, through cultural innovation and ever-expanding numbers, have come to dominate the planet.

In our discussion of such topics as evolution and adaptation, we've emphasized the importance of culture in the development of our species. The study of human biological and cultural evolution, coupled with an examination of the results of early human activities, can provide some insights from the past that may help us plan for the future. At the very least, we can provide students with an anthropological perspective on the serious problems that face us today.

$Click$

Go to the following CD-ROM for interactive activities and exercises on topics covered in this chapter:

Virtual Laboratories for Physical Anthropology CD-ROM, Third Edition

How Successful Are We?

As we've emphasized, humans are animals and, more specifically, primates. Like all life forms on earth, our very existence is based in the DNA molecule. Since all living forms share this same genetic foundation, it's highly probable that all life evolved from a common ancestor and that human beings are part of a continuum made up of biologically related species. Yet, we humans tend to view ourselves as separate from all other life forms, and we generally regard our species as the masters of the planet. In Western cultures, this view has been reinforced by the conventionally held Old Testament assertion that humans shall have *dominion* over all other species. The teachings of Islam, Judaism, and certain other religions and philosophies have similar interpretations. (Actually, however, the Old Testament, in Genesis, presents two separate versions; the second conveys a quite different meaning: that humans are to have "stewardship" over other animals.) Moreover, there's the prevailing view that nature represents an array of resources that exists primarily to be exploited for the betterment of humankind. This view is as widely held today, unfortunately, as ever before. More than merely being anthropocentric, this perspective reveals a misplaced, unjustified arrogance.

By most standards, we are a successful species. There are currently more than 6 billion human beings living on earth. Each one of these 6,000,000,000 people comprises upwards of 20 trillion cells. Nevertheless, we and all other multicellular organisms contribute only a small fraction of all the cells on the planet, the vast majority of which are bacteria. Thus, if we see life ultimately as a competition among reproducing organisms, bacteria are the winners, hands down.

So, bacteria could actually be viewed as the dominant life form on earth. However, even when only considering multicellular animals, there are additional lessons in evolutionary humility. As mammals, we are members of a group that includes about 4,000 species. It's also a group that's been on the decline for the last several million years. And as primates, we belong to a group that today consists of only about 250 species, far fewer than there were a few million years ago. By contrast, more than 750,000 insect species have been identified, and there may actually be as many as 30 million (Wilson, 1992)! Number of species (as an indicator of biological diversity) is as good a barometer of evolutionary success as any other, and by this standard, humans can hardly be seen as the most successful of species.

Evolutionary success can also be gauged by species longevity. As we have seen, fossil evidence indicates that *Homo sapiens* has been on the scene for at least 200,000 years or even longer. Such time spans, seen through the perspective of a human lifetime, may seem enormous. But consider this: Our immediate predecessor, *Homo erectus,* existed for over 1.5 million years. In other words, we as a species would need to survive more than another million years simply to match *Homo erectus.*

Humans and the Impact of Culture

As you have learned, because humans increasingly came to use culture as a means of adapting to the natural environment, biological anthropologists view culture as an adaptive strategy. Stone tools, temporary shelters, animal products (including skin clothing), and the use of fire all permitted earlier populations to expand from the tropics and exploit resources in regions previously unavailable to them. In fact, it was culture that enabled humans to become increasingly successful as time passed.

For most of human history, technology remained simple, and the rate of culture change was slow. Indeed, humans enjoyed what could be called a "comfortable" relationship with this adaptive strategy. However, as technologies became more complex, and especially when humans began to adopt an agricultural lifestyle, their relationship with culture became more complicated and, over time, less and less comfortable.

From the archaeological record, it appears that around 15,000 years ago, influenced in part by climate change and the extinction of many large-bodied prey species, some human groups began to settle down, abandoning their nomadic lives. Moreover, by about 10,000 years ago (and probably earlier), some people had learned that they could have more abundant and reliable food supplies by keeping domestic animals and growing crops. The domestication of plants and animals is seen as one of the most significant events in human history, one that has had far-reaching consequences for the entire planet.

Keeping domesticated plants and animals requires a settled way of life, and increased sedentism, combined with more reliable food sources, led to increased population growth. Viewed from the perspective of twenty-first-century humans living in industrialized societies, it might seem that adopting a settled lifestyle would lead to better health and nutrition. Yet, scientists believe that health and nutrition among hunter-gatherers was, in fact, quite good compared to that of humans living in early settlements, since, as you learned in Chapter 12, with settled lifestyle comes increased exposure to infectious disease. Thus, it can justifiably be said that increased exposure to infectious disease was one of the earliest changes in the harmonious relationship between humans and cultural innovation.

Early agriculturalists, for whom we have only crude population estimates, probably numbered a few million worldwide. At this level, population density was still low, but human activity was already beginning to have an impact on the natural environment. In truth, it would be inaccurate to assume that human activities have only recently come to have environmental consequences. In fact, human impact on local environments increased dramatically as soon as people began to live in permanent settlements.

Many of the earth's features we think of as natural actually came about as the result of human activities. For example, prior to the **Neolithic,** when people began to live in permanent settlements, much of Britain and continental Europe was blanketed with forests and woodlands. The moorlands and, to some extent, the peat bogs that have provided evocative settings for so many English novels are the result of deforestation that began more than 5,000 years ago (Fig. 14-1). In Britain, local woodland clearing by hunter-gatherers began during the late **Mesolithic,** and it accelerated around 5,000 years ago with the adoption of farming. Late Bronze Age peoples (c. 4,000–3,500 y.a.) continued the process on an even larger scale, so that by 2,500 years

Neolithic The period during which humans began to domesticate plants and animals. The Neolithic is also associated with increased sedentism. Dates for the Neolithic vary from region to region, depending on when domestication occurred.

Mesolithic The period preceding the Neolithic, during which humans increasingly exploited smaller animals (including fish), increased the variety of tools they used, and became somewhat less nomadic.

FIGURE 14-1 The moorland in the foreground is the result of woodland clearing some 2,000 years ago in southwest England.

FIGURE 14-2 Deforestation and erosion in Madagascar.

ago, many of England's forests were disappearing (Bell and Walker, 1992). Today, the majority of European woodlands exist as discontinuous patches, the results of processes that continued until fairly recent times but originated with prehistoric farmers.

Unfortunately, humans began to exploit, and increasingly depend on, non-renewable resources. Forests can be viewed as renewable resources, provided they are given the opportunity for regrowth. However, in many areas, forest clearing was virtually complete and was inevitably followed by soil erosion, frequent overgrazing, and overcultivation, which led to further soil erosion (Fig. 14-2). Therefore, in those areas, trees became a nonrenewable resource, perhaps the first resource to have this distinction.

It wouldn't be inaccurate to say that since the advent of settled life, and to some extent prior to it, humans have virtually waged war on trees. Early European explorers and settlers recorded extensive burning of woodlands and forests by indigenous groups of hunter-gatherers in North America and Australia, presumably to clear undergrowth and drive animals from cover. The effect of such burning was not inconsequential, and as people began to live in agricultural communities and later in towns and cities, the impact on forests became devastating. In fact, as shown in Figure 14–3, only about one-fifth of the earth's original forests remain intact today, and much of the clearing occurred centuries and even millennia ago.

There are many reasons for cutting forests, and the earliest of these were to clear the land for cultivation and grazing and to provide firewood and lumber for construction. As small communities grew into towns and cities, wood came to be used for shipbuilding, fortifications, and even the construction of temples and palaces. In short, the human experience over the last 10,000 to 15,000 years wouldn't have been possible without the exploitation of woodlands and forests.

One of the earliest documented examples of humankind's appetite for lumber is the cutting of the famous cedars of Lebanon. Over 3,000 years ago, the eastern Mediterranean (modern-day Israel, Jordan, Lebanon, and Syria), southern

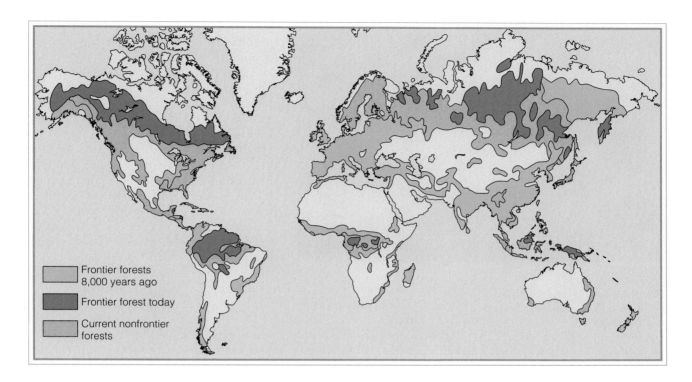

FIGURE 14-3 Map of deforestation.

Turkey, and Mesopotamia (in present-day Iraq) had become major sources of valuable cedar, fir, cypress, and other woods. But by far the most highly prized wood was Lebanese cedar, which was cut and shipped throughout the eastern Mediterranean, where it was used in the construction of buildings and ships (Fig. 14-4). The Old Testament tells us that King Solomon's temple was made of cedar from Lebanon, and numerous other texts, written over several centuries, document the extensive use and desirability of this precious wood. Not surprisingly, the deforestation of the mountains of Lebanon was eventually so complete that the "forest" of today consists of small patches of trees.

Just to prove the old adage "The more things change, the more they stay the same," it's informative to note that classical scholars (most notably Plato and Aristotle) bemoaned the effects of deforestation and other forms of environmental degradation in Greece and other areas of the Mediterranean basin. They warned that the cutting of forests and overuse of land led to soil erosion and agricultural decline, disrupted water supplies, and even caused climate change. Their views, expressed some 2,400 years ago, are verified by combined archaeological and geological data that show sequences of soil accumulation followed by intense human occupation, then soil erosion, and finally abandonment of archaeological sites throughout Greece. Furthermore, this sequence of episodes dates to around 5,000 years ago. But given the relatively small size of human populations, even by the time of the ancient Greeks and Romans, the human impact on ecosystems mostly remained a localized, not global, phenomenon. Nevertheless, these impacts were in some cases significant. The barren (but enchanting) landscape of Greece and much of what is now desert in the Middle East and the Sahara Desert in Africa are the legacies of deforestation, overgrazing, and subsequent erosion over the last few thousand years.

Robert Jurmain

FIGURE 14-4 This eighth-century B.C. Assyrian panel depicts the transport of cedar logs from Lebanon to Assyria.

Destruction of natural resources in the past has also had severe consequences for people living today. In 1990, a typhoon and subsequent flooding killed over 100,000 people in Bangladesh, and the flooding was at least partly due to previous deforestation in parts of the Himalayas of northern India. There is also evidence that continued erosion and flooding in China are partly the results of deforestation that occurred in the past. Lastly, many scientists have long speculated that the collapse of the Maya civilization of southern Mexico around 1,000 years ago was at least somewhat due to climate change, overcultivation, and depletion of nutrient-poor tropical soils.

Archaeologists can provide many examples of what humans have done wrong in the past. But just as importantly, they are also able to provide us with positive examples from earlier cultures, innovative techniques that, for all our modern wisdom, we have yet to match. For example, in the Andean highlands of South America, soil is very poor and subject to erosion. Agricultural peoples living in the region today (in Bolivia and Peru), even with considerable input from modern technology, can barely scrape together a meager existence. Yet, this wasn't always the case. But for centuries the ancestors of these peoples reaped enormous wealth from this same land and built from it one of the largest, best-organized empires in the world. How did they do it?

Archaeologist Clark Erickson (1998) sought an answer. By examining Inka agricultural fields, terracing, and irrigation, he was able to extrapolate the ancient techniques and duplicate many of the same methods. This was no mere academic exercise, however, for the next step was to teach these methods to the modern farmers. As a result, crop yields have greatly improved, with less environmental damage, reduced use of fertilizer, and at less expense than before!

The Loss of Biodiversity

Although the term *biodiversity* is currently a popular one, many people don't really understand what it means. Biodiversity is the totality of all living things, from bacteria and fungi to trees and humans. The term refers not only to species, but to individuals and the various genetic combinations they represent, as well as to entire ecosystems. The fact that we are currently losing biodiversity is indisputable. But we don't know the exact rate of loss or what its impact will be.

The geological record indicates that in the past 570 million years, there have been at least 15 mass extinction events, two of which altered all of the earth's ecosystems (Ward, 1994). The first of these occurred some 250 million years ago and resulted from climatic change following the consolidation of all the earth's landmasses into one supercontinent.

The second event happened around 65 million years ago and ended 150 million years of evolutionary processes that, among other things, had produced the dinosaurs. This mass extinction is believed by many researchers to have resulted from climatic changes following the impact of an asteroid.

A third major extinction event, perhaps of the same magnitude, is occurring now, and according to some scientists, it may have begun in the late Pleistocene or early **Holocene** (Ward, 1994). Unlike all other mass extinctions, this one hasn't been caused by continental drift, climate change (so far), or collisions with asteroids. Rather, it's due to the activities of a single species, our own.

Many scientists, in fact, believe that several large mammalian species were pushed toward extinction by humans, particularly near the end of the Pleistocene, some 10,000 years ago. In North America, at least 57 mammalian species became extinct, including the mammoth, mastodon, giant ground sloth, saber-toothed cat, several large rodents, and numerous grazing animals (Lewin, 1986; Simmons, 1989). There's no dispute that climate change (warming) was a crucial factor in these extinctions, but hunting and other human activities may also have been important. Although we don't know exactly when people first entered North America from Asia, it's certain that they were firmly established by at least 12,000 years ago (and probably much earlier), so they were present when at least some species became extinct.

We have no direct evidence that early American big game hunters contributed to extinctions; but we do have evidence of what can happen to indigenous species when new areas are colonized by humans for the first time. Within just a few centuries of human occupation of New Zealand, the moa, a large flightless bird, was exterminated. Madagascar serves as a similar example. In the last thousand years, after the arrival of permanent human settlement, 14 lemur species and several bird and other mammalian species, have become extinct (Jolly, 1985; Napier and Napier, 1985). One of these was a lemur that weighed an estimated 300 pounds (Fleagle, 1999)! Lastly, scientists have debated for years whether the extinction of all large-bodied animals (some 60 species) in Australia during the late Pleistocene was due to human hunting and other activities or to climate change. Recently, Miller and colleagues (1999), using four different techniques, were able to date the rapid extinction of a large flightless bird, *Genyornis newtoni,* to about 50,000 years ago, a date that roughly coincides with the arrival of humans in Australia. This study suggests that the simultaneous extinction of this species in a number of localities occurred during a period of relative climatic stability and therefore is best explained as a consequence of human activities, especially the widespread burning of large areas and subsequent changes in vegetation. Previous studies have suggested that the incidence of fires increased substantially in Australia after people arrived, and ethnographic reports indicate that the practice was common among indigenous Australians.

Hunter-gatherers, for whom we have some ethnographic evidence, differed in their views regarding conservation of prey species. Some groups believed that overhunting would anger deities. Others (some Great Basin Indians, for example) killed large numbers only every several years, allowing populations of game species, such as antelope, time to replenish. Still others avoided killing pregnant females or were conscientious about using all parts of the body to avoid waste. Nevertheless, there were some groups, such as the Hadza of the Pacific Northwest coast, who appear not to have been especially concerned with conservation.

Moreover, hunting techniques sometimes didn't allow much room for conservation. Prior to the domestication of the horse (or its availability in the New

Holocene The most recent epoch of the Cenozoic. Following the Pleistocene, it is estimated to have begun 10,000 years ago.

World), the only effective way to hunt large herd animals was to organize game drives. In some cases, fire was used to drive stampeding animals into blind canyons or human-made "corrals." Other times, bison were driven over cliffs or into arroyos or deep gullies. As you can imagine, this often led to unavoidable waste, as more animals were killed than could be used. Moreover, there might be so many animals that it was impossible to retrieve those at the bottom of the pile.

The Olsen-Chubbuck site in eastern Colorado is a bison kill site where, in one hunt some 10,000 years ago, 190 bison (*Bison occidentalis*) were driven into an arroyo. (This species, approximately 25 percent larger than the familiar *Bison bison*, is believed to have become extinct approximately 7,000 years ago.) Of the 190 animals killed, 170 (90 percent) were partially or completely butchered (Wheat, 1972). The 20 complete skeletons of those left unbutchered were found at the bottom of the arroyo, where they would have been virtually inaccessible.

The evidence at Olsen-Chubbuck suggests overkill. In addition to the 20 untouched animals, many of those that were partially butchered appear to have remained mostly intact. As the Olsen-Chubbuck scenario was played out thousands of times over the course of many centuries, it's possible that such game drives contributed to the demise of at least some of the large-bodied prey species of the New World.

Since the end of the Pleistocene, human activities have continued to take their toll on nonhuman species. Today, however, species are disappearing at an unprecedented rate. Hunting, which occurs for a number of reasons other than food acquisition, continues to be a major factor. Competition with introduced nonnative species, such as pigs, goats, rats, and snakes, has also contributed to the problem. But in most cases, the single most important cause of extinction is habitat reduction.

Habitat reduction is a direct result of the burgeoning human population and the resulting need for building materials, grazing and agricultural land, and living areas. We're all aware of the risk to such visible species as the elephant, panda, rhinoceros, tiger, and mountain gorilla, to name a few. These risks are real, and within your lifetime some of these animals will certainly become extinct, at least in the wild. But the greatest threat to biodiversity is to the countless unknown species that live in the world's rain forests (Fig. 14-5).

It's estimated that over half of all plants and animals on earth live in rain forests. By 1989, these habitats had been reduced to a little less than half their original size, that is, down to about 3 million square miles. The annual net loss between 1980 and 1995 was almost 67,000 square miles. "The loss is equal to the area of a football field every second. Put another way, in 1989 the surviving rain forests occupied an area about that of the continuous forty-eight states of the United States, and they were being reduced by an amount equivalent to the size of Florida every year" (Wilson, 1992, p. 275). By the year 2022, half the world's remaining rain forests will be gone if destruction continues at its present rate. This will result in a loss of between 10 and 22 percent of all rain forest species, or 5 to 10 percent of all plant and animal species on earth (Wilson, 1992).

Should we care about the loss of biodiversity? If so, why? In fact, it seems that most people don't care, partly because they aren't really aware of the problem. Moreover, reasons as to why we should care are usually stated in terms of the benefits that humans may derive from rain forest species. An example of such a benefit is the chemical taxol (derived from the Pacific yew tree), which may be an effective treatment for ovarian and breast cancer.

Lynn Kilgore

FIGURE 14-5 Stumps of recently felled forest trees are still visible in this newly cleared field in Rwanda. The haze is wood smoke from household fires.

It's undeniable that humans stand to benefit from continued research into potentially useful rain forest products. However, anthropocentric reasons aren't the sole justification for preserving the earth's biodiversity. Each species that is lost is the product of millions of years of evolution, and each one fills a specific econiche. Quite simply, the destruction of so much of life on earth is within our power. But we must ask ourselves if it's within our rights.

The Present Crisis: Our Cultural Heritage?

OVERPOPULATION

If we had to point to one single challenge facing humanity, a problem to which virtually all others are tied, it would have to be population growth. We currently are trapped in a destructive cycle of our own making. Human population size has skyrocketed as we've increased our ability to produce food surpluses. As population size increases, more and more land is converted to crops, pasture, and building sites, providing more opportunities for yet more people. Additionally, through the medical advances of the twentieth century, we have reduced mortality at both ends of the life cycle. Thus, fewer people die in childhood, and having survived to adulthood, they live longer than ever before. Although these medical advances are unquestionably good for individuals (who hasn't benefited from medical technology?), it's also clear that there are significant detrimental consequences to the species and to the planet.

Population size, if left unchecked, increases exponentially, that is, as a function of some percent, like compound interest in a bank account. Currently, human population increases worldwide at an annual rate of about 1.8 percent. Although this figure may not seem too startling at first, it deserves some examination. It's also useful to discuss doubling time, or the amount of time it takes for a population to double in size.

Scientists estimate that around 10,000 years ago, only about 5 million people inhabited the earth (not even half as many as live in Los Angeles County today). By A.D. 1650, there were perhaps 500 million, and by 1800, 1 billion. In other words, between 10,000 years ago and A.D. 1650 (a period of 9,650 years), population size doubled 71 times. On average, then, the doubling time between 10,000 years ago and 1650 was about 1,287 years. But from 1650 to 1800, it doubled again, which means that doubling time had been reduced to 150 years (Ehrlich and Ehrlich, 1990). And in the 37 years between 1950 and 1987, world population doubled from 2 billion to 4 billion.

Dates and associated population estimates up to the present are as follows: mid-1800s, 1 billion; 1930s, 2 billion; mid-1960s, 3 billion; mid-1980s, 4 billion; present, 6 billion (Fig. 14-6). To state this problem in terms we can appreciate, we add 1 billion people to the world's population approximately every 11 years. That comes out to 90 to 95 million every year and roughly a quarter of a million every day!

The rate of growth isn't equally distributed among all nations. Although the world's rate of increase has ranged from 1.7 to 2.1 percent since the 1950s (Ehrlich and Ehrlich, 1990), it's the developing countries that share most of the burden (not to be interpreted as blame). During the 1980s, the population of Kenya grew at a rate of a little over 4 percent per year, while India added a million per month, and 36,000 babies were born every day in Latin America.

Fortunately, by the end of the twentieth century, rates of human population growth began to decline. The average number of children per female worldwide had dropped from 4.3 in 1960 to 2.6 in 2000 (Wilson, 2000). Moreover, by 2000, the replacement rate of 2.1 children per female required for population size to stabilize had been achieved in all western European countries, Thailand, and the nonimmigrant population of the United States (Wilson, 2002). (The extra one-tenth takes into account infant and childhood

FIGURE 14-6 Line graph depicting exponential growth of human population. Note that for almost all of the last 5,000 years, the number of humans increased very slowly. It was not until 1650 that population size was even half a billion (500 million). The rapid increase to 1 billion by about 1850 is, in part, attributable to the Industrial Revolution. Population increase occurs as a function of some percent (in some developing countries, the annual rate is over 3 percent). With advances in food production and medical technologies, humans are now undergoing a population explosion, as this graph illustrates.

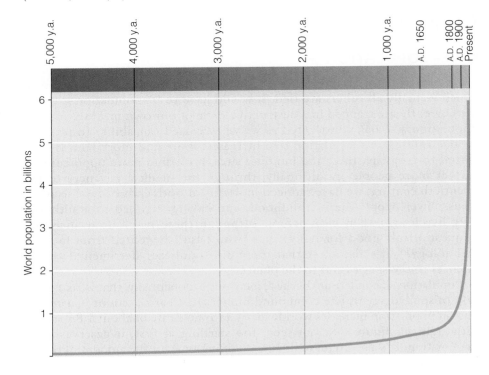

mortality. A rate of 2.0 or less would be ideal.) It must also be mentioned that for the first time in history, the population of South Africa is now declining, but this fact is due primarily to the high incidence of HIV/AIDS (approximately 30 percent of adults are infected).

The decrease in family size worldwide is attributable to several factors, including the shift to a global economy, the migration of rural populations to urban centers with concomitant shifts in employment from agriculture to manufacturing and service sectors, and, at least in some countries, the increasing empowerment of women that has meant better education, increased opportunities in the workplace, and access to family planning.

The most recent United Nations International Conference on Population and Development set as its goal the development of a plan to contain the world's population to about 7.3 billion by the year 2015 and to prevent future growth. Otherwise, by the year 2050, human numbers could approach 10 billion. The United Nations plan emphasizes women's education, health, and rights throughout the world, but has met with stiff resistance from religious groups (primarily in the United States) opposed to abortion and contraception.

The United Nations goal is admirable and ambitious, but achieving it will be a formidable task. Although the average number of live births per woman has declined, it will still be next to impossible to prevent huge population increases in the next century. Bear in mind that *approximately half of all people currently living in the developing world are less than 15 years old*. These young people haven't reproduced yet, but they will.

You might logically ask, Can't we make technological changes sufficient to help feed all these people? This and similar questions are being asked more and more frequently. Certainly, there are methods that would more efficiently use the agricultural lands that are already available, and there are better ways to distribute the food surpluses already produced. But can we continue forever to make technological changes sufficient to feed ever-growing numbers of humans? Is there enough land to support an endless demand for housing, crop cultivation, and grazing? Is there enough water? We probably can develop technologies to meet our species' increasing needs for a while. But can we do so and still meet the requirements of thousands of undomesticated species? The answer for the immediate future is: probably not. For the long term, without major changes in human population growth, the answer is: absolutely not.

THE GREENHOUSE EFFECT AND GLOBAL WARMING

With increases in numbers comes greater consumption of resources. At the same time, activities involved in the production of goods and services produce waste and pollution, all of which leads to further environmental degradation.

Consider for a moment the fact that much of the energy used for human activities is derived from the burning of fossil fuels such as oil and coal. The burning of fossil fuels releases carbon dioxide into the atmosphere, and this, in turn, traps heat. Increased production of carbon dioxide and other "greenhouse gases," such as methane and chlorofluorocarbons (CFCs), is of growing concern to many in the scientific community who anticipate potentially dramatic climate change in the form of global warming.

Deforestation, particularly in the tropics, also contributes to global warming, since we're reducing the number of trees available to absorb carbon dioxide. Moreover, in the tropics, trees are burned as land is cleared, a practice that releases yet more carbon dioxide. In fact, an estimated 20 percent of all carbon dioxide emissions are accounted for by the burning of the Amazon rain forest alone. As a sobering note, Friends of the Earth, an environmental organization, estimated that between 50,000 and 80,000 fires were burning in the forests of Brazil at any given time during October 1991. And in Indonesia, an estimated 370,000 to 740,000 acres of forest were burned in 1997 alone (European Union GIS/Remote Sensing Expert Group, 1997). Most of these fires were caused by land-clearing activities in a region already suffering from severe drought. Because these fires also destroyed peat deposits (layers of ancient, decayed vegetation that serve as storehouses of carbon), an estimated 810 million to 2.6 billion metric tons (2,240 pounds) of carbon were released into the atmosphere. This amounts to between 13 to 40 percent of the world's annual carbon emissions from the burning of fossil fuels (Page et al., 2002).

The scientific community is now in almost complete agreement that we are seeing the effects of global warming. Scientists from numerous fields (including climatology, paleoclimatology, geophysics, and geology) are justifiably concerned, and most agree that the buildup of greenhouse gases results from human activity. A measure of this concern is the number of publications in scientific journals that now concern various aspects of the issue. Take, for example, the prestigious British weekly journal *Nature*. All of the more important scientific discoveries are first published either in this journal or in its American counterpart, *Science*. In the year 2004, both journals averaged close to one article a week devoted to some aspect of climate change!

Unfortunately, the general public and certainly most politicians seem to believe that the obvious warming we are experiencing is part of a "normal" cyclical trend. (In part, this may be wishful thinking, because reversing the trend would be enormously expensive and would require individual sacrifice and huge changes in business and industrial practices.) Certainly, there have been dramatic climatic fluctuations throughout earth's history that had nothing to do with human activity. And many of these fluctuations were sudden and had devastating consequences. But even if the current warming trend (which, incidentally, began during the early years of the industrial revolution and increased use of coal) is part of a general cycle, scientists are concerned that human-produced greenhouse gases could tip the balance toward a catastrophic global climate change.

Uncertainty also surrounds the issue of the myriad ways climate change will be manifested. What is certain is this: Since records began being kept in 1860, the 1990s were the hottest decade, followed closely by the 1980s. The year 2002 had the distinction of being the warmest year on record, with 1998 running a close second. The summer of 2003 was the hottest on record in Europe, and for the first time in recorded history, the temperature reached 100°F in London. An estimated 2,000 people, mainly elderly, died in France of heat-related causes, and many scientists attribute the increased heat to human activities (Houghton, et al., 2001; Stott et al., 2004;). Estimates, based on studies of ice cores, tree ring data and other climate-related phenomena do vary, but according to the United Nations Intergovernmental Panel on Climate Change, the average surface temperature of the earth increased by 0.8 C (1.4°F) between 1961 and 1990. The need for concern cannot be overstated. An increase in the mean annual temperature worldwide of even 0.5–1°C (0.9–1.8°F) could result in some melting of the polar caps with sub-

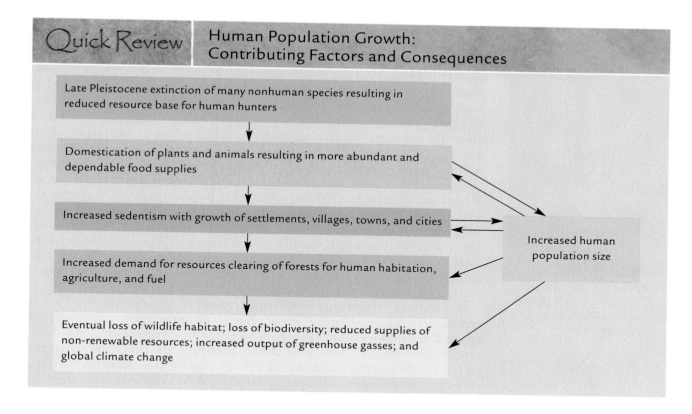

Quick Review — Human Population Growth: Contributing Factors and Consequences

Late Pleistocene extinction of many nonhuman species resulting in reduced resource base for human hunters

↓

Domestication of plants and animals resulting in more abundant and dependable food supplies

↓

Increased sedentism with growth of settlements, villages, towns, and cities

↓

Increased demand for resources clearing of forests for human habitation, agriculture, and fuel

↓

Eventual loss of wildlife habitat; loss of biodiversity; reduced supplies of non-renewable resources; increased output of greenhouse gasses; and global climate change

Increased human population size

sequent flooding of coastal areas. And there is a great deal of concern for Greenland's ice sheet which experts believe will disappear if average temperatures increase 3.0°C (5.4°F). (Schlermeier, 2004; Gregory et al., 2004). The effects of this would be catastrophic and could raise sea levels by as much as 7 meters (23 feet) over the next 1000 years (Gregory, et al., 2004).

Global warming is the result of the interactions of many factors, and the consequences of these interactions aren't possible to predict with accuracy. But the consensus among scientists is that we can anticipate dramatic fluctuations in weather patterns along with alterations in precipitation levels. The results of changing temperatures and rainfall include loss of agricultural lands due to desertification in some regions and flooding in others; increased human hunger; extinction of numerous plant and animal species; and altered patterns of infectious disease. Regarding the latter, health officials are particularly concerned about the spread of mosquito-borne diseases such as malaria, dengue fever, and yellow fever as warmer temperatures increase the geographical range of mosquitoes. And, in addition to altering the geographical distribution of insect and vertebrate disease vectors, changing climate conditions can also increase the range and reproductive rates of the very microbes that are the direct causes of infectious diseases.

LOOKING FOR SOLUTIONS

The massive problems facing our planet reflect an adaptive strategy gone awry. Indeed, it would seem that we no longer enjoy a harmonious relationship with culture. Instead, culture has become the environment in which we live, and every

FIGURE 14-7 Air pollution, increasingly a factor in human respiratory disease, is caused by human activities.

day that environment becomes increasingly hostile. All we need to do is examine the very air we breathe to realize that we have overstepped our limits (Fig. 14-7).

What can be done? Are the problems we've created amenable to human solution? Perhaps, but any objective assessment of the future offers little optimism. The declining quality of the air, depletion of the ozone layer, climate change, reduced amounts of arable land, and accumulation of refuse already seem like catastrophic problems in a world of 6 billion people. How well does the world *now* cope with feeding, housing, and educating its inhabitants? What quality of life do the majority of the world's people enjoy right now? What kind of world have we wrought for the other organisms that share our planet as many are increasingly isolated into fragments of what were once large habitats? If these concerns are not currently overwhelming enough, what kind of world will we see in 30 years, when the world's population numbers perhaps 8 billion?

In recent years, environmental concerns have been more widely discussed. Some world leaders now frequently pay lip service to preserving the environment. All this is well and good, but the real test of any policy will be the willingness of the world's population to sacrifice *now* for rewards that won't become apparent for perhaps several decades.

If there is any real chance of reversing current trends, *everyone* will have to sacrifice. In the developing world, family planning must universally be adopted to halt population expansion. Most cultures are so constructed, however, as to make such behavioral change very difficult. And sacrifice on the part of the developing world alone wouldn't even begin to stem the tide. It's entirely too convenient for someone from North America to point at the people of Bangladesh and demand that they control their rate of reproduction (it runs two to three times that of the United States). But consider this: The average American uses an estimated 400 times the resources consumed by a resident of Bangladesh (Ehrlich and Ehrlich, 1990)! The United States *alone* produces 25 to 30 percent of all carbon dioxide emissions into the atmosphere. In his book *The Future of Life* (2002), evolutionary biologist E. O. Wilson puts it in terms of "ecological footprints" or the average amount of land and sea required for each person to support his or her lifestyle. This includes all resources consumed for energy, housing, transportation, food, water, and waste disposal. In developing nations the ecological footprint per capita is about 2.5 acres, but in the United States it's 24 acres! Wilson goes on to point out that four additional planet earths would be needed for every person on the planet to reach the current levels of consumption in the United States. Clearly, much of the responsibility for the world's problems rests squarely on the shoulders of the industrialized West.

The developed nations (most especially, the United States) must learn to get along with far fewer resources. To accomplish any meaningful reduction in our wasteful habits, major behavioral changes and personal sacrifice will be required. For example, private automobile transportation (especially with only one passenger) and large, single-family dwellings are luxuries many enjoy, but they are luxuries the planet can ill afford. Who is prepared to make the sacrifices that are required, and where will the leadership come from? The planet already faces serious problems, and there is little time left for indecision. Either we, as members of the species *Homo sapiens,* find the courage to make dramatic sacrifices or we are doomed to suffer the consequences of our own folly.

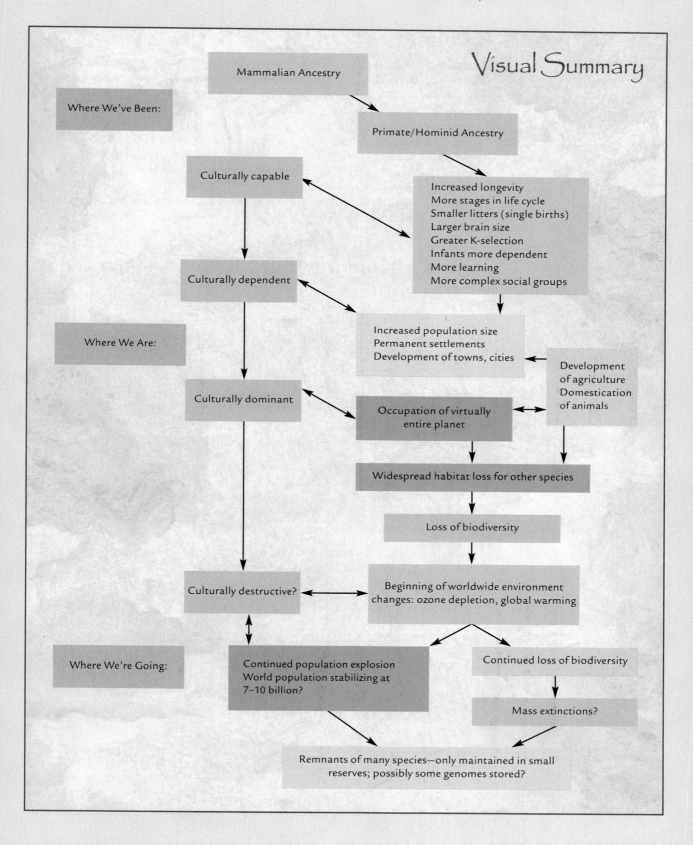

Summary

Studies of human evolution have much to contribute to our understanding of how we, as a single species, came to exert such control over the destiny of our planet. It truly is a phenomenal story of how a small, apelike creature walking on two feet across the African savanna challenged nature by learning to make stone tools. From these humble beginnings came large-brained humans who, instead of stone tools, have telecommunications satellites, computers, and nuclear arsenals at their fingertips. The human story is indeed unique and wonderful. Our two feet have carried us not only across the plains of Africa, but also onto the polar caps, the ocean floor, and even across the surface of the moon! Surely, if we can accomplish so much in so short a time, we can act responsibly to preserve our home and the wondrous creatures who share it with us.

Critical Thinking Questions

1. How is human culture related to environmental degradation and overpopulation?
2. How are loss of biodiversity, environmental degradation, and human population growth related?
3. Why do we say that culture, as an adaptive strategy, has gone awry? Do you agree with this statement? Why or why not?

Media Resources

The Companion Website for *Essentials of Physical Anthropology,* Sixth Edition
http://anthropology.wadsworth.com/jurmain6e_ess

Supplement your review of this chapter by going to this text's companion website to take one of the practice quizzes, use the flash cards to master key terms, and check out the many other resources and study aids.

CD-ROMs IN PHYSICAL ANTHROPOLOGY

Wadsworth Publishing has also developed three CD-ROMs to accompany this text and enhance learning in physical anthropology (for further descriptions of these CD-ROMs, see p. xix):

Virtual Laboratories for Physical Anthropology CD-ROM, Third Edition

Basic Genetics for Anthropology CD-ROM: Principles and Applications

Hominid Fossils CD-ROM: An Interactive Atlas

For this chapter, see especially the Basic Genetics for Anthropology: Principles and Applications CD-ROM.

Readings of Interest

Fagan, Brian. 2000. *The Little Ice Age*. New York: Basic Books.

Karl, Thomas R., Neville Nicholls, and Jonathan Gregory. 1997. "The Coming Climate." *Scientific American* 276(5): 78–83.

Runnels, Curtis N. 1995. "Environmental Degradation in Ancient Greece." *Scientific American* 272(3): 96–99.

Wilson, Edward O. 1992. *The Diversity of Life*. Cambridge, MA: Harvard University Press.

———— 2002. *The Future of Life*. New York: Knopf.

Atlas of Primate Skeletal Anatomy

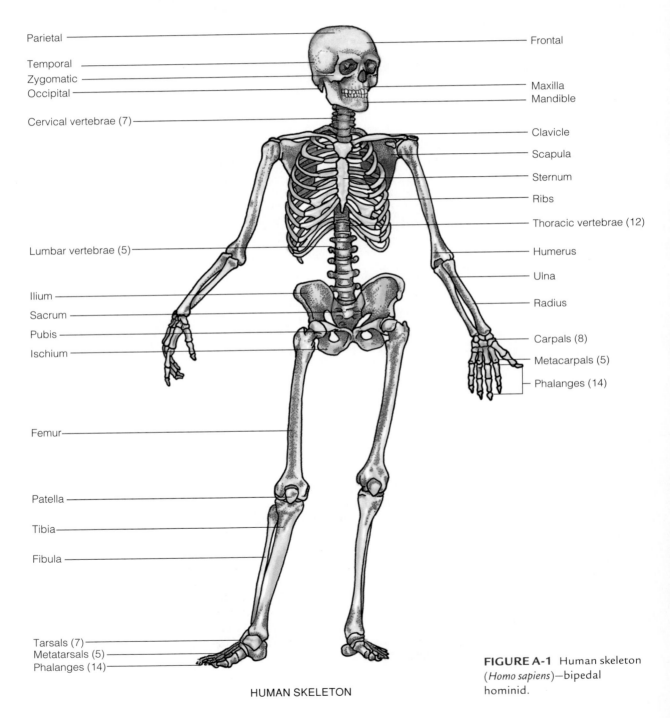

Parietal — Frontal

Temporal —
Zygomatic —
Occipital — Maxilla
— Mandible

Cervical vertebrae (7) —

— Clavicle

— Scapula

— Sternum

— Ribs

— Thoracic vertebrae (12)

Lumbar vertebrae (5) — Humerus

— Ulna

Ilium — Radius

Sacrum —

Pubis —

Ischium — Carpals (8)

— Metacarpals (5)

— Phalanges (14)

Femur —

Patella —

Tibia —

Fibula —

Tarsals (7) —
Metatarsals (5) —
Phalanges (14) —

HUMAN SKELETON

FIGURE A-1 Human skeleton (*Homo sapiens*)—bipedal hominid.

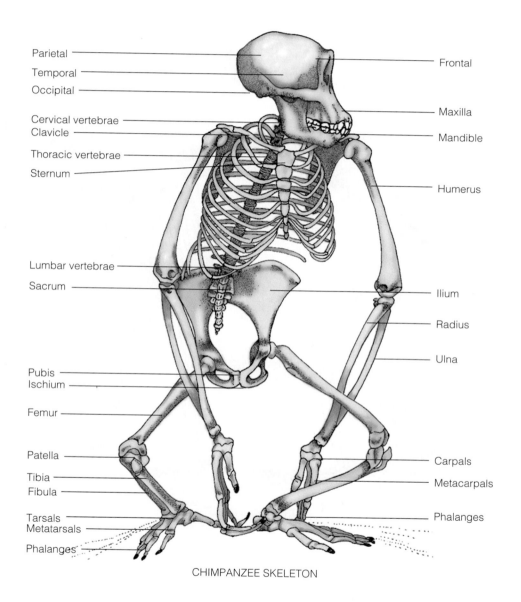

Parietal

Temporal

Occipital

Cervical vertebrae

Clavicle

Thoracic vertebrae

Sternum

Lumbar vertebrae

Sacrum

Pubis

Ischium

Femur

Patella

Tibia

Fibula

Tarsals

Metatarsals

Phalanges

Frontal

Maxilla

Mandible

Humerus

Ilium

Radius

Ulna

Carpals

Metacarpals

Phalanges

CHIMPANZEE SKELETON

FIGURE A-2 Chimpanzee skeleton (*Pan troglodytes*)—knuckle-walking pongid.

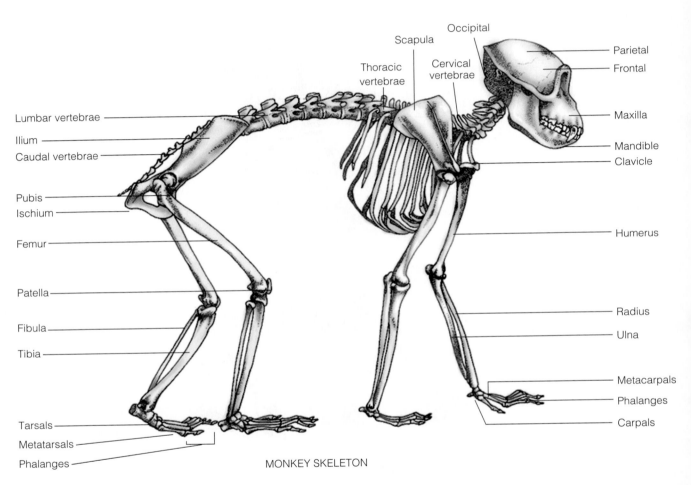

Occipital

Scapula

Parietal

Thoracic
vertebrae

Cervical
vertebrae

Frontal

Lumbar vertebrae

Maxilla

Ilium

Mandible

Caudal vertebrae

Clavicle

Pubis

Ischium

Humerus

Femur

Patella

Radius

Fibula

Ulna

Tibia

Metacarpals

Phalanges

Tarsals

Carpals

Metatarsals

Phalanges

MONKEY SKELETON

FIGURE A-3 Monkey skeleton (rhesus
macaque; *Macaca mulatta*)—a typical
quadrupedal primate.

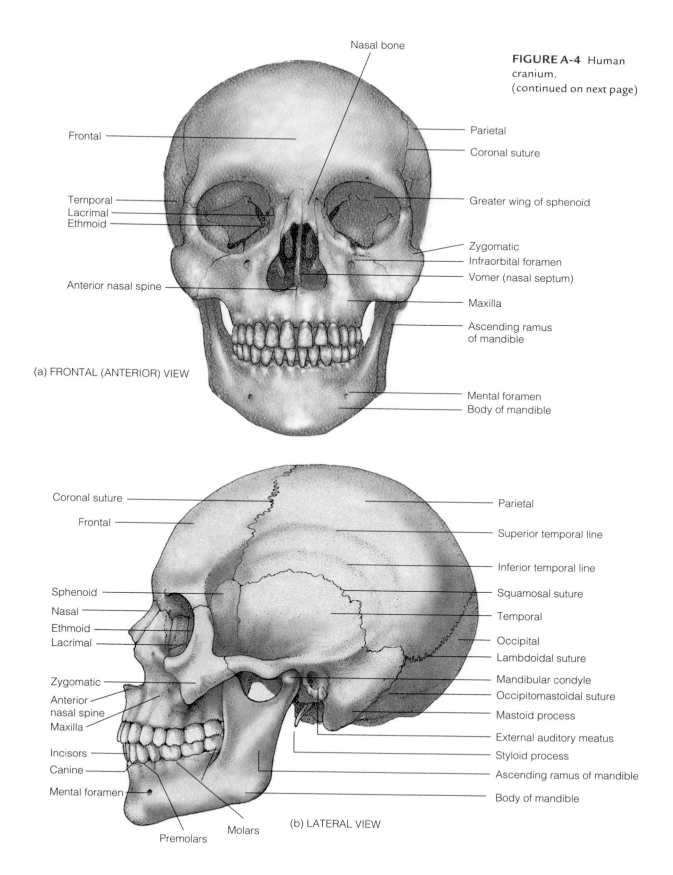

Nasal bone

FIGURE A-4 Human
cranium.
(continued on next page)

Frontal

Parietal

Coronal suture

Temporal
Lacrimal
Ethmoid

Greater wing of sphenoid

Zygomatic
Infraorbital foramen
Vomer (nasal septum)

Anterior nasal spine

Maxilla

Ascending ramus
of mandible

(a) FRONTAL (ANTERIOR) VIEW

Mental foramen
Body of mandible

Coronal suture

Frontal

Parietal

Superior temporal line

Inferior temporal line

Sphenoid

Nasal

Ethmoid

Lacrimal

Squamosal suture

Temporal

Occipital

Lambdoidal suture

Zygomatic

Anterior
nasal spine

Maxilla

Mandibular condyle

Occipitomastoidal suture

Mastoid process

External auditory meatus

Incisors

Canine

Styloid process

Ascending ramus of mandible

Mental foramen

Body of mandible

(b) LATERAL VIEW

Premolars   Molars

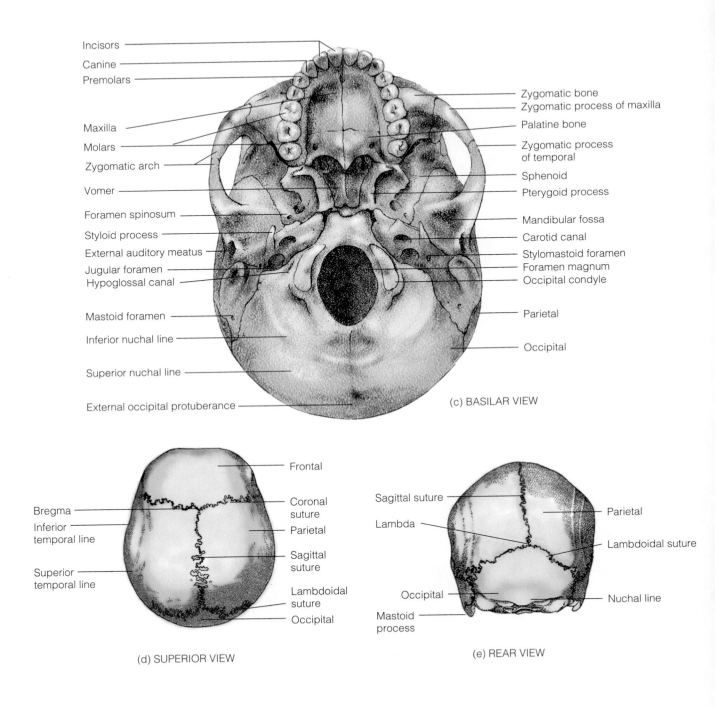

Incisors

Canine

Premolars

Maxilla

Molars

Zygomatic arch

Vomer

Foramen spinosum

Styloid process

External auditory meatus

Jugular foramen

Hypoglossal canal

Mastoid foramen

Inferior nuchal line

Superior nuchal line

External occipital protuberance

Zygomatic bone

Zygomatic process of maxilla

Palatine bone

Zygomatic process of temporal

Sphenoid

Pterygoid process

Mandibular fossa

Carotid canal

Stylomastoid foramen

Foramen magnum

Occipital condyle

Parietal

Occipital

(c) BASILAR VIEW

Frontal

Bregma

Inferior temporal line

Superior temporal line

Coronal suture

Parietal

Sagittal suture

Lambdoidal suture

Occipital

(d) SUPERIOR VIEW

Sagittal suture

Lambda

Occipital

Mastoid process

Parietal

Lambdoidal suture

Nuchal line

(e) REAR VIEW

FIGURE A–4 Human cranium.
(continued)

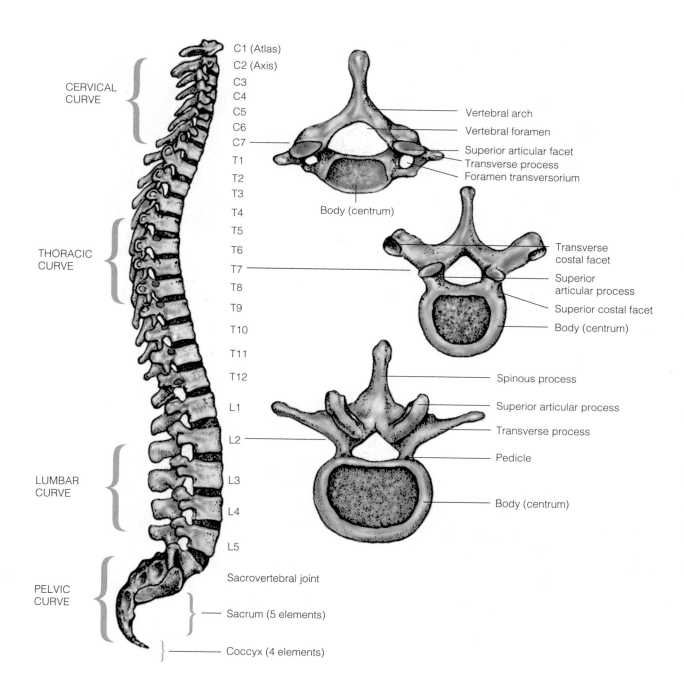

FIGURE A-5 Human vertebral column (lateral view) and representative cervical, thoracic, and lumbar vertebrae (superior views).

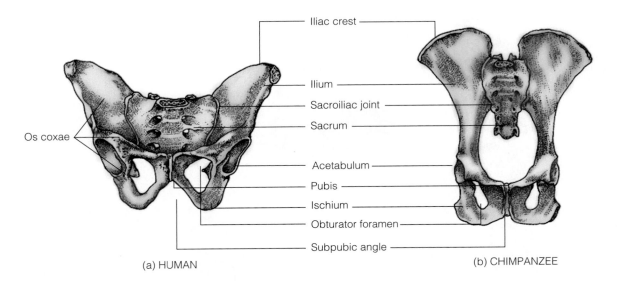

FIGURE A-6 Pelvic girdles.

(a) HUMAN   (b) CHIMPANZEE

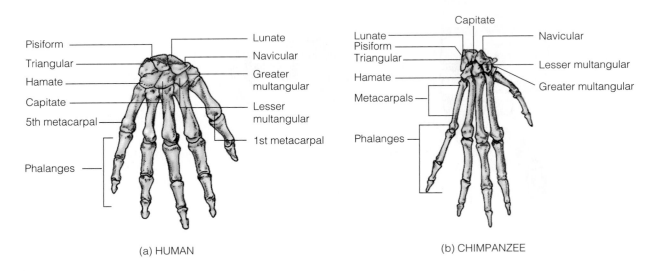

FIGURE A-7 Hand anatomy.

(a) HUMAN   (b) CHIMPANZEE

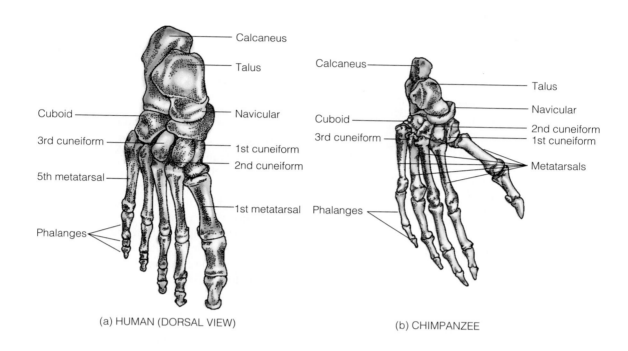

Calcaneus

Talus

Cuboid

Navicular

3rd cuneiform

1st cuneiform

5th metatarsal

2nd cuneiform

1st metatarsal

Phalanges

(a) HUMAN (DORSAL VIEW)

Calcaneus

Talus

Navicular

Cuboid

2nd cuneiform

3rd cuneiform

1st cuneiform

Metatarsals

Phalanges

(b) CHIMPANZEE

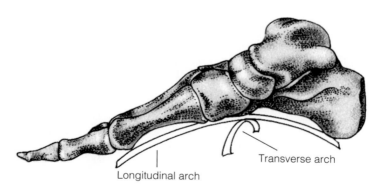

Transverse arch

Longitudinal arch

FIGURE A–8 Foot (pedal) anatomy.

(c) HUMAN (MEDIAL VIEW)

Summary of Early Hominid Fossil Finds from Africa

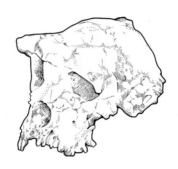

Sahelanthropus
Taxonomic designation: *Sahelanthropus tchadensis*
Year of first discovery: 2001
Dating: ~7 m.y.a.
Fossil material: Nearly complete cranium, 2 jaw fragments, 3 isolated teeth

Location of finds: Toros-Menalla, Chad, central Africa

Ardipithecus
Taxonomic designation: *Ardipithecus ramidus*
Year of first discovery: 1992
Dating: Earlier sites, 5.8–5.6 m.y.a.; Aramis, 4.4 m.y.a.
Fossil material: Earlier materials: 1 jaw fragment, 4 isolated teeth, postcranial remains (foot phalanx, 2 hand phalanges, 2 humerus fragments, ulna). Later sample (Aramis) represented by many fossils, including up to 50 individuals (many postcranial elements, including at least 1 partial skeleton). Considerable fossil material retrieved from Aramis but not yet published; no reasonably complete cranial remains yet published.

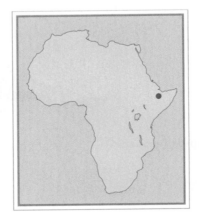

Location of finds: Middle Awash region, including Aramis (as well as earlier localities), Ethiopia, East Africa

Orrorin

Taxonomic designation:
Orrorin tugenensis
Year of first discovery: 2000
Dating: ~6 m.y.a.
Fossil material: 2 jaw fragments, 6 isolated teeth, postcranial remains (femoral pieces, partial humerus, hand phalanx). No reasonably complete cranial remains yet discovered.

Location of finds: Lukeino Formation, Tugen Hills, Baringo District, Kenya, East Africa

Australopithecus anamensis

Taxonomic designation:
Australopithecus anamensis
Year of first discovery: 1965 (but not recognized as separate species at that time); more remains found in 1994 and 1995
Dating: 4.2–3.9 m.y.a.
Fossil material: Total of 22 specimens, including cranial fragments, jaw fragments, and postcranial pieces (humerus, tibia, radius). No reasonably complete cranial remains yet discovered.

Location of finds: Kanapoi, Allia Bay, Kenya, East Africa

Australopithecus afarensis

Taxonomic designation:
Australopithecus afarensis
Year of first discovery: 1973
Dating: 3.7–3.0 m.y.a.
Fossil material: Large sample, with up to 65 individuals represented: 1 partial cranium, numerous cranial pieces and jaws, many teeth, numerous postcranial remains, including partial skeleton. Fossil finds from Laetoli also include dozens of fossilized footprints.

Location of finds: Laetoli (Tanzania), Hadar (Ethiopia), also likely found at East Turkana (Kenya) and Omo (Ethiopia), East Africa

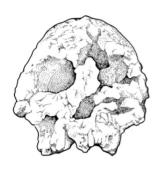

Kenyanthropus

Taxonomic designation:
Kenyanthropus platyops
Year of first discovery: 1999
Dating: 3.5 m.y.a.
Fossil material: Partial cranium, temporal fragment, partial maxilla, 2 partial mandibles

Location of finds: Lomekwi, West Lake Turkana, Kenya, East Africa

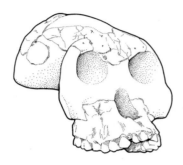

Australopithecus garhi

Taxonomic designation:
Australopithecus garhi
Year of first discovery: 1997
Dating: 2.5 m.y.a.
Fossil material: Partial cranium, numerous limb bones

Location of finds: Bouri, Middle Awash, Ethiopia, East Africa

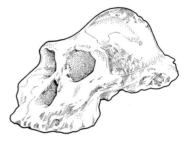

Australopithecus aethiopicus

Taxonomic designation:
Australopithecus aethiopicus (also called *Parantropus aethiopicus*)
Year of first discovery: 1985
Dating: 2.4 m.y.a.
Fossil material: Nearly complete cranium

Location of finds: West Lake Turkana, Kenya

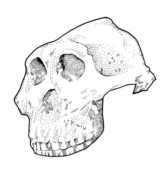

Australopithecus boisei

Taxonomic designation:
  Australopithecus boisei (also called *Paranthropus boisei*)
Year of first discovery: 1959
Dating: 2.4–1.2 m.y.a.
Fossil material: 2 nearly complete crania, several partial crania, many jaw fragments, dozens of teeth. Postcrania less represented, but parts of several long bones recovered.

Location of finds: Olduvai Gorge and Peninj (Tanzania), East Lake Turkana (Koobi Fora), Chesowanja (Kenya), Omo (Ethiopia)

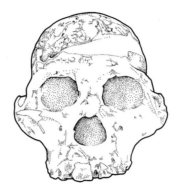

Australopithecus africanus

Taxonomic designation:
  Australopithecus africanus
Year of first discovery: 1924
Dating: ~3.3–1.0 m.y.a.
Fossil material: 1 mostly complete cranium, several partial crania, dozens of jaws/partial jaws, hundreds of teeth, 4 partial skeletons representing significant parts of the postcranium

Location of finds: Taung, Sterkfontein, Makapansgat, Gladysvale (all from South Africa)

Australopithecus robustus

Taxonomic designation:
  Australopithecus robustus (also called *Paranthropus robustus*)
Year of first discovery: 1938
Dating: ~2–1 m.y.a.
Fossil material: 1 complete cranium, several partial crania, many jaw fragments, hundreds of teeth, numerous postcranial elements

Location of finds: Kromdraai, Swartkrans, Drimolen, Cooper's Cave, possibly Gondolin (all from South Africa)

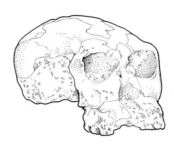

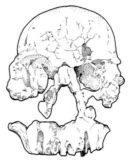

Early *Homo*
Taxonomic designation:
Homo habilis
Year of first discovery:
1959/1960
Dating: 2.4–1.8 m.y.a.
Fossil material: 2 partial crania, other cranial pieces,
jaw fragments, several limb
bones, partial hand, partial
foot, partial skeleton

Early *Homo*
Taxonomic designation:
Homo rudolfensis
Year of first discovery: 1972
Dating: ~1.8 m.y.a.
Fossil material: 4 partial
crania, 1 mostly complete
mandible, other jaw pieces,
numerous teeth, a few
postcranial elements (none
directly associated with
crania)

Location of finds: Olduvai
Gorge (Tanzania), Lake
Baringo (Kenya), Omo
(Ethiopia), Sterkfontein (?)
(South Africa)

Location of finds: East Lake
Turkana (Koobi Fora),
Kenya, East Africa

APPENDIX C
Population Genetics

As noted in Chapter 12, the basic approach in population genetics makes use of a mathematical model called the Hardy-Weinberg equilibrium equation. The Hardy-Weinberg theory of genetic equilibrium postulates a set of conditions in a population where *no* evolution occurs. In other words, none of the forces of evolution are acting, and all genes have an equal chance of recombining in each generation (i.e., there is random mating of individuals). More precisely, the hypothetical conditions that such a population would be *assumed* to meet are as follows:

1. The population is infinitely large. This condition eliminates the possibility of random genetic drift or changes in allele frequencies due to chance.
2. There is no mutation. Thus, no new alleles are being added by molecular changes in gametes.
3. There is no gene flow. There is no exchange of genes with other populations that can alter allele frequencies.
4. Natural selection is not operating. Specific alleles confer no advantage over others that might influence reproductive success.
5. Mating is random. There are no factors that influence who mates with whom. Thus, any female is assumed to have an equal chance of mating with any male.

If all these conditions are satisfied, allele frequencies will not change from one generation to the next (i.e., no evolution will take place), and a permanent equilibrium will be maintained as long as these conditions prevail. An evolutionary "barometer" is thus provided that may be used as a standard against which actual circumstances are compared. Similar to the way a typical barometer is standardized under known temperature and altitude conditions, the Hardy-Weinberg equilibrium is standardized under known evolutionary conditions.

Note that the idealized conditions that define the Hardy-Weinberg equilibrium are just that: an idealized, *hypothetical* state. In the real world, no actual population would fully meet any of these conditions. But do not be confused by this distinction. By explicitly defining the genetic distribution that would be *expected* if *no* evolutionary change were occurring (i.e., in equilibrium), we can compare the *observed* genetic distribution obtained from actual human populations. The evolutionary barometer is thus evaluated through comparison of these observed allele and genotype frequencies with those expected in the predefined equilibrium situation.

If the observed frequencies differ from those of the expected model, then we can say that evolution is taking place at the locus in question. The alternative, of course, is that the observed and expected frequencies do not differ sufficiently to state unambiguously that evolution is occurring at a locus in a population. Indeed, frequently this is the result that is obtained, and in such cases, population geneticists are unable to delineate evolutionary changes at the particular locus under study. Put another way, geneticists are unable to reject what statisticians call the *null hypothesis* (where "null" means nothing, a statistical condition of randomness).

The simplest situation applicable to a microevolutionary study is a genetic trait that follows a simple Mendelian pattern and has only two alleles (*A, a*). As you recall from earlier discussions, there are then only three possible genotypes: *AA, Aa, aa*. Proportions of these genotypes (*AA:Aa:aa*) are a function of the *allele frequencies* themselves (percentage of *A* and percentage of *a*). To provide uniformity for all genetic loci, a standard notation is employed to refer to these frequencies:

Frequency of dominant allele (A) = p
Frequency of recessive allele (a) = q

Since in this case there are only two alleles, their combined total frequency must represent all possibilities. In other words, the sum of their separate frequencies must be 1:

$$p \quad + \quad q \quad = \quad 1$$

p	q	1
(frequency of A alleles)	(frequency of a alleles)	(100% of alleles at that locus)

To ascertain the expected proportions of genotypes, we compute the chances of the alleles combining with one another into all possible combinations. Remember, they all have an equal chance of combining, and no new alleles are being added.

These probabilities are a direct function of the frequency of the two alleles. The chances of all possible combinations occurring randomly can be simply shown as

$$
\begin{array}{r}
p \;+\; q \\
\times\; p \;+\; q \\
\hline
pq \;+\; q^2 \\
p^2 \;+\; pq \\
\hline
p^2 \;+\; 2pq \;+\; q^2
\end{array}
$$

Mathematically, this is known as a binomial expansion and can also be shown as

$$(p + q)(p + q) = p^2 + 2pq + q^2$$

What we have just calculated is simply:

Allele Combination	Genotype Produced	Expected Proportion in Population
Chances of A combining with A	AA	$p \times p = p^2$
Chances of A combining with a;	Aa	$p \times q$
a combining with A	aA	$p \times q$ $= 2\,pq$
Chances of a combining with a	aa	$q \times q = q^2$

Thus, p^2 is the frequency of the *AA* genotype, *2pq* is the frequency of the *Aa* genotype, and q^2 is the frequency of the *aa* genotype, where p is the frequency of the dominant allele and q is the frequency of the recessive allele in a population.

Calculating Allele Frequencies: An Example

How geneticists use the Hardy-Weinberg formula is best demonstrated through an example. Let us assume that a population contains 200 individuals, and we will use the MN blood group locus as the gene to be measured. This gene produces a blood group antigen—similar to ABO—located on red blood cells. Because the *M* and *N* alleles are codominant, we can ascertain everyone's phenotype by taking blood samples and observing reactions with specially prepared antisera. From the phenotypes, we can then directly calculate the *observed* allele frequencies. So let us proceed.

All 200 individuals are tested, and the results are shown in Table C–1. Although the match between observed and expected frequencies is not perfect, it is close enough statistically to satisfy equilibrium conditions. Since our population is not a large one, sampling may easily account for the small observed deviations. Our population is therefore probably in equilibrium (i.e., at this locus, it is not evolving). At the minimum, what we can say scientifically is that we cannot reject the *null hypothesis*.

TABLE C-1 | Calculating Allele Frequencies in a Hypothetical Population

Observed Data

Genotype	Number of Individuals*	Percent	Number of Alleles M	Number of Alleles N
MM	80	40%	160	0
MN	80	40%	80	80
NN	40	20%	0	80
Totals	200	100%	240 +	160 = 400
		Proportion:	.6 +	.4 = 1

*Each individual has two alleles. Thus, a person who is *MM* contributes two *M* alleles to the total gene pool. A person who is *MN* contributes one *M* and one *N*. Two hundred individuals, then, have 400 alleles for the *MN* locus.

Observed Allele Frequencies

M = .6(p)

N = .4(q)   ($p + q$ should equal 1, and they do)

Expected Frequencies

What are the predicted genotypic proportions if genetic equilibrium (no evolution) applies to our population? We simply apply the Hardy-Weinberg formula: $p^2 + 2pq + q^2$.

p^2	=	(.6)(.6)	=	.36
$2pq$	=	2(.6)(.4) = 2(.24)	=	.48
q^2	=	(.4)(.4)	=	.16
Total				1.00

There are only three possible genotypes (*MM:MN:NN*), so the total of the relative proportions should equal 1; as you can see, they do.

Comparing Frequencies

How do the expected frequencies compare with the observed frequencies in our population?

	Expected Frequency	Expected Number of Individuals	Observed Frequency	Actual Number of Individuals with Each Genotype
MM	.36	72	.40	80
MN	.48	96	.40	80
NN	.16	32	.20	40

APPENDIX D
Sexing and Aging the Skeleton

The field of physical anthropology that is directly concerned with the analysis of skeletal remains is called *osteology*. Using an osteological perspective allows researchers to study skeletons of both human and nonhuman primates to understand the ways in which hominids are similar to, and distinct from, other primates. Moreover, paleoanthropologists also use many of the same techniques to analyze the remains of fossil hominids (which mostly consist of teeth and bones). In more recent contexts, encompassing the last few thousand years, skeletal remains of *Homo sapiens* have been investigated by osteologists to learn about the size, nutritional status, and diseases present in prior human populations.

Two very important questions that osteologists ask when analyzing a skeleton are the sex and age of the individual. Such basic demographic variables as sex and age are crucial in any comprehensive osteological analysis, especially of human remains.

Sexing the Skeleton

During infancy and childhood, male and female skeletons do not differ much. Consequently, osteologists usually cannot determine the sex of a skeleton of someone who died before 13 to 15 years of age. However, during development, *sexual dimorphism* is increasingly manifested in the skeleton, making sex determination feasible in adult remains, provided enough of the skeleton is present. We should mention that molecular techniques are sometimes able to detect the presence of the Y chromosome from bone or dental tissue (thus determining that a skeleton is that of a male). While not used widely, molecularly based sexing is becoming more common in osteological analyses.

The differences between male and female skeletons are most clearly expressed in the pelvis (*pl.,* pelves), and this variation is due to the requirements of childbirth in females. In particular, during hominid evolution, the dual influences of bipedal locomotion and relatively large-brained newborns placed adaptive constraints on pelvic anatomy. As a result, in females the pelvis is generally broader and more splayed out than in males. The most useful criteria for sex determination are listed in Table D–1 and illustrated in Figure D–1. While these criteria, taken together, are good indicators of sex, you should be aware that none, taken in isolation, is accurate in all cases. Moreover, this is not a complete listing of all traits used in sexing skeletons, although it does include those most commonly used.

There are also sex differences in cranial dimensions, most especially relating to facial proportions. However, these differences are not as consistent as those in the pelvis. Therefore, it is important to recognize patterns of cranial variation as they are expressed in different populations. The cranial features most commonly used for sex determination are listed in Table D–2 (see also Fig. D–2). These differences reflect the fact that in males, the skeleton is larger

TABLE D-1 | Differences Between the Male and Female Pelvis

Pelvic Characteristic	Female	Male
General	Muscle attachments less robust; overall appearance sometimes less massive	Muscle attachments more robust; overall appearance sometimes more massive
Subpubic angle	Wider (more than 90°)	Narrower (less than 90°)
Greater sciatic notch	Wider—more open (more than 68°)	Narrower—more closed (less than 68°)
Ischiopubic ramus (medial view)	Thinner	Thicker
Ventral arc (elevated ridge on ventral surface of pubis)	Frequently present	Absent
Sacrum	Wider and straighter	Narrower and more curved

FIGURE D-1 Male and female pelves compared.

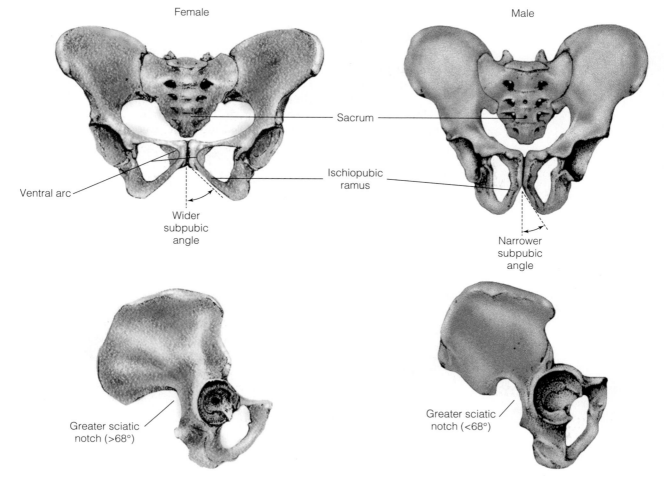

TABLE D-2 | Cranial Variation Between Males and Females

Cranial Feature	Females	Males
Points of muscle attachment (e.g., mastoid process)	Less pronounced	Larger, more pronounced
Supraorbital torus (browridge)	Less pronounced or absent	More pronounced
Supraorbital rim (upper margin of eye orbit)	Sharper	More rounded
Palate	More shallow	Deeper

than in females. The bones are denser, and areas of muscle attachment are frequently more robust. However, such differences are not consistently expressed across various populations, and knowledge of relevant population variation is thus important in drawing reasonable determinations of sex.

Determining Age

During growth, the skeleton and dentition undergo developmental changes that occur within known age ranges. Thus, estimating age in individuals who were younger than 20 when they died is based primarily on the presence of deciduous (baby) and permanent teeth, the appearance of ossification centers of bones, and the fusion of the ends of long bones to bone shafts.

FIGURE D-2 Cranium and mandible.

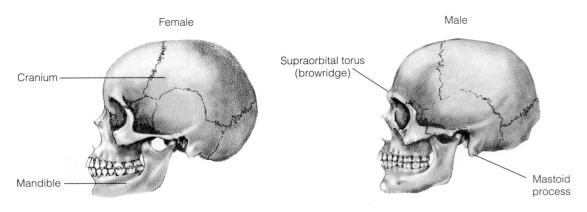

DENTAL ERUPTION

Age estimation based on dental eruption is useful in individuals up to approximately 15 years of age. The third molar (wisdom tooth) erupts after this time, but the age of eruption of this tooth (if it forms at all) is highly variable. Thus, the third molar is not a very reliable indicator of age except that its presence indicates that the individual was at least a young adult (Fig. D–3).

BONE GROWTH

The size of long bones, the development of secondary ossification centers (epiphyses), and the degree of fusion of epiphyses to bone shafts are just as important as dental eruption. Postcranial bones are preceded by a cartilage model that is gradually replaced by bone, both in the diaphyses (shafts) and the secondary centers (the ends of the bones, or epiphyses). In children and adolescents, bones continue to grow until the epiphyses fuse to the diaphyses. Because this fusion occurs within different age ranges in different bones, the age of an individual can be estimated by determining which epiphyses have fused and which have not (Fig. D–4). The characteristic undulating appearance of the unfused surfaces helps differentiate immature elements from the broken end of a mature bone.

FIGURE D–3 Dental development.

Gumline

(a) Birth: The crowns for all the deciduous teeth (shown in color) are present; no roots, however, have yet formed.

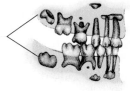

First permanent molar crown

(b) 2 years: All deciduous teeth (shown in color) are erupted; the first permanent molar and permanent incisors have crowns (unerupted) formed, but no roots.

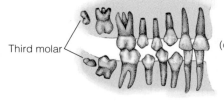

Third molar

(c) 12 years: All permanent teeth are erupted except the third molar (wisdom tooth).

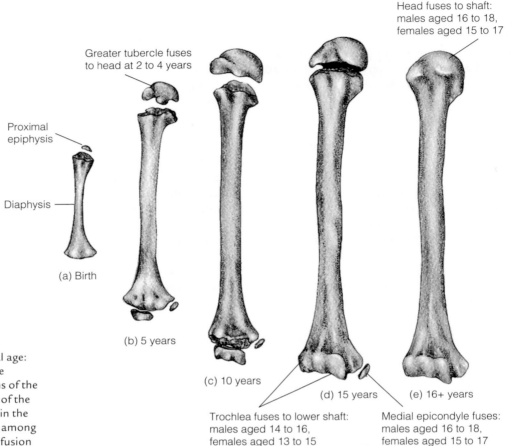

Proximal epiphysis

Diaphysis

(a) Birth

Greater tubercle fuses to head at 2 to 4 years

(b) 5 years

(c) 10 years

Trochlea fuses to lower shaft: males aged 14 to 16, females aged 13 to 15

(d) 15 years

Medial epicondyle fuses: males aged 16 to 18, females aged 15 to 17

(e) 16+ years

Head fuses to shaft: males aged 16 to 18, females aged 15 to 17

FIGURE D-4 Skeletal age: epiphyseal union in the humerus. Some regions of the humerus exhibit some of the earliest fusion centers in the body, while others are among the latest to complete fusion (not until late adolescence).

OTHER SKELETAL CHANGES

Once a person has reached physiological maturity (by the early 20s), determinations of age become more difficult and less precise. Several techniques are used, and these are based on the occurrence of progressive, regular changes in the face of the pubic symphysis (the most common technique), in the sternal ends of the ribs, and in the auricular surface of the ilium (where the ilium articulates with the sacrum). Other indicators are closure of the cranial sutures and cellular changes that are determined by microscopic examination of cross sections of long bones. Degenerative changes, such as arthritis, osteoporosis, and wear of dental enamel, can also aid in the determination of relative age (older versus younger), but they provide imprecise estimates. In fact, it is very difficult to age accurately the skeletons of adults. For example, the presence of severe tooth wear would imply that the individual was not young, but enamel attrition varies between populations and depends on many factors, including diet. Moreover, the appearance of many degenerative changes is influenced by disease, trauma, and the biological makeup of individuals. Thus, at present, osteologists must be content to use broad age ranges when estimating age at death in mature skeletons.

Pubic Symphyseal Face The face of the pubic symphysis in young individuals is characterized by a billowing surface (with ridges and furrows) such as that seen on the surface of an epiphysis (Fig. D–5). The symphyseal face undergoes regular age-related changes from the age of about 18 onward.

The first aging technique based on alterations of the pubic symphysis was developed by T. W. Todd (1920, 1921), utilizing dissection room cadavers. McKern and Stewart (1957) developed a technique by analyzing a sample of American males killed in the Korean War. Both of the samples from which these systems were derived, however, have limitations. The dissection room sample used by Todd contained some individuals of uncertain age, and the Korean War sample was predominantly made up of young white males, with few being older than 35.

More recently, a system has been developed by Judy Suchey and colleagues (Katz and Suchey 1986) based on very well documented autopsy samples of males and females. These samples have proved more representative of the general population than the earlier samples. Because this technique is derived from data collected from a large sample of people of known age at death, it is currently the most accurate method available for estimating age in adult human skeletal remains.

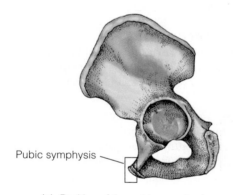

Pubic symphysis

(a) Position of the pubic symphysis.

(b) Age 21. The face of the symphysis shows the typical "billowed" appearance of a young joint; no rim present.

(c) Age mid-50s. The face is mostly flat, with a distinct rim formed around most of the periphery.

FIGURE D-5 Skeletal age: remodeling of the pubic symphysis. This area of the pelvis shows systematic changes progressively throughout adult life. Two of these stages are shown in (b) and (c).

Glossary

acclimatization Physiological responses to changes in the environment that occur during an individual's lifetime. Such responses may be temporary or permanent, depending on the duration of the environmental change and when in the individual's life it occurs. The *capacity* for acclimatization may typify an entire species or population, and because it is under genetic influence, it is subject to evolutionary factors such as natural selection or genetic drift.

Acheulian (ash´-oo-lay-en) Pertaining to a stone tool industry for the Lower and Middle Pleistocene characterized by a large proportion of bifacial tools (flaked on both sides). Acheulian tool kits are very common in Africa, Southwest Asia, and western Europe, but are thought to be less common elsewhere. (Also spelled "Acheulean.")

adaptation Functional response of organisms or populations to the environment. Adaptation results from evolutionary change (specifically, as a result of natural selection).

adaptive niche The entire way of life of an organism: where it lives, what it eats, how it gets food, how it avoids predators, etc.

adaptive radiation The relatively rapid expansion and diversification of life forms into new ecological niches.

adolescent growth spurt The period during adolescence when well-nourished teens typically increase in stature at greater rates than at other times in the life cycle.

affiliative Pertaining to amicable associations between individuals. Affiliative behaviors, such as grooming, reinforce social bonds and promote group cohesion.

allele frequency In a population, the percentage of all the alleles at a locus accounted for by one specific allele.

alleles Alternate forms of a gene. Alleles occur at the same locus on homologous chromosomes and thus govern the same trait. However, because they are slightly different, their action may result in different expressions of that trait. The term is sometimes used synonymously with *gene*.

altruism Behavior that benefits another individual but at some potential risk or cost to oneself.

amino acids Small molecules that are the components of proteins.

analogies Similarities between organisms based strictly on common function, with no assumed common evolutionary descent.

ancestral (primitive) Referring to characters inherited by a group of organisms from a remote ancestor and thus not diagnostic of groups (lineages) that diverged after the character first appeared.

anthropoids Members of a suborder of Primates, the *Anthropoidea* (pronounced "ann-throw-poid´-ee-uh"). Traditionally, the suborder includes monkeys, apes, and humans.

anthropology The field of inquiry that studies human culture and evolutionary aspects of human biology; includes cultural anthropology, archaeology, linguistics, and physical, or biological, anthropology.

anthropometry Measurement of human body parts. When osteologists measure skeletal elements, the term *osteometry* is often used.

arboreal Tree-living; adapted to life in the trees.

arboreal hypothesis The traditional view that primate characteristics can be explained as a consequence of primate diversification into arboreal habitats.

artifacts Objects or materials made or modified for use by hominids (extinct forms and modern humans). The earliest artifacts tend to be tools made of stone or, occasionally, bone.

antigens Large molecules found on the surface of cells. Several different loci govern various antigens on red and white blood cells.

Aurignacian Pertaining to an Upper Paleolithic stone tool industry in Europe beginning at about 40,000 y.a.

australopithecine (os-tra-loh-pith´-e-seen) The colloquial name for members of the genus *Australopithecus*.

The term was first used as a subfamily designation, but it is now most commonly used informally.

Australopithecus An early hominid genus, known from the Plio-Pleistocene of Africa, characterized by bipedal locomotion, a relatively small brain, and large back teeth.

autonomic Pertaining to physiological responses not under voluntary control. An example in chimpanzees would be the erection of body hair during excitement. Blushing is a human example. Both convey information regarding emotional states, but neither is deliberate, and communication isn't intended.

autosomes All chromosomes except the sex chromosomes.

behavior Anything organisms do that involves action in response to internal or external stimuli; the response of an individual, group, or species to its environment. Such responses may or may not be deliberate, and they aren't necessarily the result of conscious decision making.

behavioral ecology The study of the evolution of behavior, emphasizing the role of ecological factors as agents of natural selection. Behaviors and behavioral patterns have been favored because they increase the reproductive fitness of individuals (i.e., they are adaptive) in specific environmental contexts.

binocular vision Vision characterized by overlapping visual fields provided for by forward-facing eyes. Binocular vision is essential to depth perception.

binomial nomenclature (*binomial,* meaning "two names") In taxonomy, the convention established by Carolus Linnaeus whereby genus and species names are used to refer to species. For example, *Homo sapiens* refers to human beings.

biocultural Pertaining to the concept that biology makes culture possible and that culture influences biology.

biocultural evolution The mutual, interactive evolution of human biology and culture; the concept that biology makes culture possible and that developing culture further influences the direction of biological evolution; a basic concept in understanding the unique components of human evolution.

biological continuity Refers to a *biological continuum,* the fact that organisms are related through common ancestry and that behaviors and physical traits present in one species are also seen to varying degrees in others. When expressions of a phenomenon continuously grade into one another so that there are no discrete categories, they exist on a continuum. Color is one such phenomenon, and life forms are another.

biological determinism The concept that phenomena, including various aspects of behavior (e.g., intelligence, values, morals) are governed by biological (genetic) factors; the inaccurate association of various behavioral attributes with certain biological traits, such as skin color.

biological species concept A depiction of species as groups of individuals capable of fertile interbreeding, but reproductively isolated from other such groups.

bipedal locomotion Walking on two feet. Walking habitually on two legs is the single most distinctive feature of the family Hominidae.

brachiation A form of locomotion in which the body is suspended beneath the hands and support is alternated from one forelimb to the other; arm swinging.

breeding isolates Populations that are clearly isolated geographically and/or socially from other breeding groups.

burins Small, chisel-like tools (with a pointed end) thought to have been used to engrave bone, antler, ivory, or wood.

catastrophism The view that the earth's geological landscape is the result of violent cataclysmic events. This view was promoted by Cuvier, especially in opposition to Lamarck.

centromere The constricted portion of a chromosome. After replication, the two strands of a double-stranded chromosome are joined at the centromere.

cercopithecines (serk-oh-pith´-eh-seens) The subfamily of Old World monkeys that includes baboons, macaques, and guenons.

Chatelperronian Pertaining to an Upper Paleolithic industry found in France and Spain, containing blade tools and associated with Neandertals.

Chordata The phylum of the animal kingdom that includes vertebrates.

chromosomes Discrete structures composed of DNA and protein found only in the nuclei of cells. Chromosomes are only visible under magnification during certain phases of cell division.

chronometric (*chronos,* meaning "time," and *metric,* meaning "measure") A dating technique that gives an estimate in actual numbers of years.

cladistics An approach to classification that attempts to make rigorous evolutionary interpretations based solely on analysis of certain types of homologous characters (those considered to be derived characters).

cladogram A chart showing evolutionary relationships as determined by cladistic analysis. It is based solely on interpretation of shared derived characters. No time component is indicated, and ancestor-descendant relationships are *not* implied.

classification In biology, the ordering of organisms into categories, such as orders, families, and genera, to show evolutionary relationships.

cline A gradual change in the frequency of genotypes and phenotypes from one geographical region to another.

clone An organism that is genetically identical to another organism. The term may also be used to refer to genetically identical DNA segments, molecules, and cells.

codominance The expression of two alleles in heterozygotes. In this situation, neither allele is dominant or recessive; thus, both influence the phenotype.

codons Triplets of messenger RNA bases that code for specific amino acids during protein synthesis.

colobines (kole´-uh-beans) The subfamily of Old World monkeys that includes the African colobus monkeys and Asian langurs.

communication Any act that conveys information, in the form of a message, to another individual. Frequently, the result of communication is a change in the behavior of the recipient. Communication may not be deliberate but may instead be the result of involuntary processes or a secondary consequence of an intentional action.

complementary Referring to the fact that DNA bases form base pairs in a precise manner. For example, adenine can bond only to thymine. These two bases are said to be *complementary* because one requires the other to form a complete DNA base pair.

continental drift The movement of continents on sliding plates of the earth's surface. As a result, the positions of large landmasses have shifted drastically during the earth's history.

core area The portion of a home range containing the highest concentration and most reliable supplies of food and water. The core area is defended.

culture All aspects of human adaptation, including technology, traditions, language, religion, marriage patterns, and social roles. Culture is a set of *learned* behaviors; it is transmitted from one generation to the next through learning and not by biological or genetic means.

cusps The elevated portions (bumps) on the chewing surfaces of premolar and molar teeth.

cytoplasm The portion of the cell contained within the cell membrane, excluding the nucleus. The cytoplasm consists of a semifluid material and contains numerous structures involved with cell function.

data (*sing.,* datum) Facts from which conclusions can be drawn; scientific information.

deoxyribonucleic acid (DNA) The double-stranded molecule that contains the genetic code. DNA is a main component of chromosomes.

derived (modified) Referring to characters that are modified from the ancestral condition and thus *are* diagnostic of particular evolutionary lineages.

development Differentiation of cells into different types of tissues and their maturation.

displays Sequences of repetitious behaviors that serve to communicate emotional states. Nonhuman primate displays are most frequently associated with reproductive or agonistic behavior.

diurnal Active during the day.

dominance hierarchies Systems of social organization wherein individuals within a group are ranked relative to one another. Higher-ranking animals have greater access to preferred food items and mating partners than lower-ranking individuals. Dominance hierarchies are sometimes called "pecking orders."

dominant Describing a trait governed by an allele that can be expressed in the presence of another, different allele (i.e., in heterozygotes). Dominant alleles prevent the expression of recessive alleles in heterozygotes. (This is the definition of *complete* dominance.)

ecological Pertaining to the relationships between organisms and all aspects of their environment (temperature, predators, nonpredators, vegetation, availability of food and water, types of food, disease organisms, parasites, etc.).

ecological niches The positions of species within their physical and biological environments, together making up the *ecosystem*. A species' ecological niche is defined by such components as diet, terrain, vegetation, type of predators, relationships with other species, and activity patterns, and each niche is unique to a given species.

empirical Relying on experiment or observation; from the Latin *empiricus,* meaning "experienced."

endemic Continuously present in a population.

endocast A solid impression of the inside of the skull, often preserving details relating to the size and surface features of the brain.

endogamy Mating with individuals from the same group.

endothermic (*endo,* meaning "within" or "internal") Able to maintain internal body temperature through the production of energy by means of metabolic processes within cells; characteristic of mammals, birds, and perhaps some dinosaurs.

enzymes Specialized proteins that initiate and direct chemical reactions in the body.

epochs Categories of the geological time scale; subdivisions of periods. In the Cenozoic, epochs include the Paleocene, Eocene, Oligocene, Miocene, and Pliocene (from the Tertiary) and the Pleistocene and Holocene (from the Quaternary).

essential amino acids The 9 (of 22) amino acids that must be obtained from the food we eat because they are not synthesized in the body in sufficient amounts.

estrus (ess´-truss) Period of sexual receptivity in female mammals (except humans), correlated with ovulation. When used as an adjective, the word is spelled "estrous."

ethnocentric Viewing other cultures from the inherently biased perspective of one's own culture. Ethnocentrism usually results in other cultures being seen as inferior to one's own.

ethnographies Detailed descriptive studies of human societies. In cultural anthropology, an ethnography is traditionally the study of a non-Western society.

eugenics The philosophy of "race improvement" through the forced sterilization of members of some groups and increased reproduction among others; an overly simplified, often racist view that is now discredited.

evolution A change in the genetic structure of a population. The term is also frequently used to refer to the appearance of a new species.

evolution (modern genetic definition) A change in the frequency of alleles from one generation to the next.

evolutionary systematics A traditional approach to classification (and evolutionary interpretation) in which presumed ancestors and descendants are traced in time by analysis of homologous characters.

exogamy Mating pattern whereby individuals obtain mates from groups other than their own.

faunal Referring to animal remains; in archaeology, specifically refers to the fossil (or skeletonized) remains of animals.

fitness Pertaining to natural selection, a measure of *relative* reproductive success of individuals. Fitness can be measured by an individual's genetic contribution to the next generation compared to that of other individu-

als. The terms *genetic fitness, reproductive fitness,* and *differential reproductive success* are also used.

fixity of species The notion that species, once created, can never change; an idea diametrically opposed to theories of biological evolution.

flexed The position of the body in a bent orientation, with arms and legs drawn up to the chest.

forensic anthropology An applied anthropological approach dealing with legal matters. Physical anthropologists work with coroners and others in the identification and analysis of human remains.

founder effect A type of genetic drift in which allele frequencies are altered in small populations that are taken from, or are remnants of, larger populations.

frugivorous (fru-give´-or-us) Having a diet composed primarily of fruits.

gametes Reproductive cells (eggs and sperm in animals) developed from precursor cells in ovaries and testes.

gene A sequence of DNA bases that specifies the order of amino acids in an entire protein, a portion of a protein, or any functional product. A gene may be made up of hundreds or thousands of DNA bases organized into coding and noncoding segments. (Coding sequences produce proteins; noncoding sequences don't.)

gene flow Exchange of genes between populations.

gene pool The total complement of genes shared by the reproductive members of a population.

genetic drift Evolutionary changes—that is, changes in allele frequencies—produced by random factors. Genetic drift is a result of small population size.

genetics The study of gene structure and action and the patterns of inheritance of traits from parent to offspring. Genetic mechanisms are the underlying foundation for evolutionary change.

genome The entire genetic makeup of an individual or species. In humans, it is estimated that each individual possesses approximately 3 billion DNA nucleotides.

genotype The genetic makeup of an individual. Genotype can refer to an organism's entire genetic makeup or to the alleles at a particular locus.

genus A group of closely related species.

geological time scale The organization of earth history into eras, periods, and epochs; commonly used by geologists and paleoanthropologists.

glaciations Climatic intervals when continental ice sheets cover much of the northern continents. Glaciations are associated with colder temperatures in northern latitudes and more arid conditions in southern latitudes (most notably in Africa).

grade A grouping of organisms sharing a similar adaptive pattern. It is not necessarily based on closeness of evolutionary relationship, but does contrast organisms in a useful way (e.g., *Homo erectus* with *Homo sapiens*).

grooming Picking through fur to remove dirt, parasites, and other materials that may be present. Social grooming is common among primates and reinforces social relationships.

growth Increase in mass or number of cells.

habitual bipedalism Bipedal locomotion as the form of locomotion shown by hominids most of the time.

Hardy-Weinberg equilibrium The mathematical relationship expressing—under ideal conditions—the predicted distribution of alleles in populations; the central theorem of population genetics.

hemispheres Two halves of the cerebrum that are connected by a dense mass of fibers. (The cerebrum is the large rounded outer portion of the brain.)

hemoglobin A protein molecule that occurs in red blood cells and binds to oxygen molecules.

heterodont Having different kinds of teeth; characteristic of mammals, whose teeth consist of incisors, canines, premolars, and molars.

heterozygous Having different alleles at the same locus on members of a chromosome pair.

Holocene The most recent epoch of the Cenozoic. Following the Pleistocene, it is estimated to have begun 10,000 years ago.

homeostasis A condition of balance, or stability, within a biological system, maintained by the interaction of physiological mechanisms that compensate for changes (both external and internal).

homeotic genes An evolutionarily ancient family of regulatory genes that directs the development of the overall body plan and the segmentation of body tissues; also called homeobox or *Hox* genes.

Hominidae The taxonomic family to which humans belong; also includes other, now extinct, bipedal relatives.

hominids Colloquial term for members of the family Hominidae, which includes all bipedal hominoids back to the divergence from African great apes.

Hominoidea The formal designation for the superfamily of anthropoids that includes apes and humans.

Homo habilis (hab´-ih-liss) A species of early *Homo*, well known from East Africa but perhaps also found in other regions.

homologies Similarities between organisms based on descent from a common ancestor.

homologous Referring to members of chromosome pairs. Homologous chromosomes carry genes that govern the same traits, and they are alike with regard to size and position of the centromere. During meiosis, homologous chromosomes pair and exchange segments of DNA.

homoplasy (*homo*, meaning "same," and *plasy*, meaning "growth") The separate evolutionary development of similar characteristics in different groups of organisms.

homozygous Having the same allele at the same locus on both members of a chromosome pair.

hormones Substances (usually proteins) that are produced by specialized cells and that travel to other parts of the body, where they influence chemical reactions and regulate various cellular functions.

Human Genome Project An international effort aimed at sequencing and mapping the entire human genome.

hybrids Offspring of individuls that differ with regard to certain traits or certain aspects of genetic makeup; heterozygotes.

Hylobatidae (high-lo-baht´-id-ee) The family designation of gibbons and siamangs.

hypothesis (*pl.*, hypotheses) A provisional explanation of a phenomenon. Hypotheses require verification or falsification through testing.

hypoxia Lack of oxygen. Hypoxia can refer to reduced amounts of available oxygen in the atmosphere (due to lowered barometric pressure) or to insufficient amounts of oxygen in the body.

intelligence Mental capacity; ability to learn, reason, or comprehend and interpret information, facts, relationships, and meanings; the capacity to solve problems, whether through the application of previously acquired knowledge or through insight.

interglacials Climatic intervals when continental ice sheets are retreating, eventually becoming much reduced in size. Interglacials in northern latitudes are associated with warmer temperatures, while in southern latitudes the climate becomes wetter.

interspecific Between species; refers to variation beyond that seen within the same species to include additional aspects seen between two different species.

intraspecific Within species; refers to variation seen within the same species.

ischial callosities Patches of tough, hard skin on the buttocks of Old World monkeys and chimpanzees.

K-selected Pertaining to an adaptive strategy whereby individuals produce relatively few offspring, in whom they invest increased parental care. Although only a few infants are born, chances of survival are increased for each one because of parental investments in time and energy. Examples of K-selected nonprimate species are birds and canids (e.g., wolves, coyotes, and dogs).

knuckle walking A type of terrestrial quadrupedalism seen in African great apes where the weight of the upper body is carried on the backs of the fingers which are bent. This is different from how monkeys carry their upper body weight on the palms of the hands.

large-bodied hominoids Those hominoids including the great apes (orangutans, chimpanzees, gorillas) and hominids, as well as all ancestral forms back to the time of divergence from small-bodied hominoids (i.e., the gibbon lineage).

life history traits Also called life history strategies; characteristics and developmental stages that influence rates of reproduction.

locus (*pl.,* loci) (lo´-kus, lo-sigh´) The position on a chromosome where a given gene occurs. The term is sometimes used interchangeably with *gene,* but this usage is technically incorrect.

macaques (muh-kaks´) Group of Old World monkeys comprising several species, including rhesus monkeys. Most macaque species live in India, other parts of Asia, and nearby islands.

macroevolution Changes that occur only after many generations, such as the appearance of a new species (speciation).

Magdalenian Pertaining to the final phase of the Upper Paleolithic stone tool industry in Europe.

meiosis Cell division in specialized cells in ovaries and testes. Meiosis involves two divisions and results in four daughter cells, each containing only half the original number of chromosomes. These cells can develop into gametes.

menarche The first menstruation in girls, usually occurring in the early to middle teens.

Mendelian traits Characteristics that are influenced by alleles at only one genetic locus. Examples include many blood types, such as ABO. Many genetic disorders, including sickle-cell anemia and Tay-Sachs disease, are also Mendelian traits.

menopause The end of menstruation in human women, usually occurring at around age 50.

Mesolithic The period preceding the Neolithic, during which humans increasingly exploited smaller animals (including fish), increased the variety of tools they used, and became somewhat less nomadic.

messenger RNA (mRNA) A form of RNA that is assembled on a sequence of DNA bases. It carries the DNA code to the ribosome during protein synthesis.

metabolism The chemical processes within cells that break down nutrients and release energy for the body to use. (When nutrients are broken down into their component parts, such as amino acids, energy is released and made available for use by the cell.)

Metazoa Multicellular animals; a major division of the animal kingdom.

microevolution Small changes occurring within species, such as a change in allele frequencies.

Middle Pleistocene The portion of the Pleistocene epoch beginning 780,000 y.a. and ending 125,000 y.a.

midline An anatomical term referring to a hypothetical line that divides the body into right and left halves.

mitochondria (*sing.,* mitochondrion) Structures contained within the cytoplasm of eukaryotic cells that convert energy, derived from nutrients, into a form that is used by the cell.

mitochondrial DNA (mtDNA) DNA found in the mitochondria. Mitochondrial DNA is inherited only from the mother.

mitosis Simple cell division; the process by which somatic cells divide to produce two identical daughter cells.

molecules Structures made up of two or more atoms. Molecules can combine with other molecules to form more complex structures.

mosaic evolution A pattern of evolution in which the rate of evolution in one functional system varies from that in other systems. For example, in hominid evolution, the dental system, locomotor system, and neurological system (especially the brain) all evolved at markedly different rates.

morphology The form (shape, size) of anatomical structures; can also refer to the entire organism.

Mousterian Pertaining to the stone tool industry associated with Neandertals and some modern *H. sapiens* groups; also called Middle Paleolithic. This industry is characterized by a larger proportion of flake tools than is found in Acheulian tool kits.

multidisciplinary Pertaining to research that involves mutual contributions and cooperation of several different experts from various scientific fields (i.e., disciplines).

mutation A change in DNA; can refer to changes in DNA bases (specifically called *point mutations*) and also to changes in chromosome number or structure.

natal group The group in which animals are born and raised. (*Natal* pertains to birth.)

natural selection The mechanism of evolutionary change first articulated by Charles Darwin; refers to genetic change or changes in the frequencies of certain traits in populations due to differential reproductive success between individuals.

Neolithic The period during which humans began to domesticate plants and animals. The Neolithic is also associated with increased sedentism. Dates for the Neolithic vary from region to region, depending on when domestication occurred.

neural tube In early embryonic development, the anatomical structure that develops to form the brain and spinal cord.

nocturnal Active during the night.

nondisjunction The failure of homologous chromosomes or chromosome strands to separate during cell division.

nuchal torus (nuke´-ul, pertaining to the neck) A projection of bone in the back of the cranium where neck muscles attach, used to hold up the head.

nucleotides Basic units of the DNA molecule, composed of a sugar, a phosphate, and one of four DNA bases.

nucleus A structure (organelle) found in all eukaryotic cells. The nucleus contains chromosomes (nuclear DNA).

obligate bipedalism Bipedalism as the *only* form of hominid terrestrial locomotion. Since major anatomical changes in the spine, pelvis, and lower limb are required for bipedal locomotion, once hominids adapted this mode of locomotion, other forms of locomotion on the ground became impossible.

organelles Structures contained within cells, surrounded by a membrane. There are many different types, and each performs specific functions.

omnivorous Having a diet consisting of many kinds of foods, such as plant materials (seeds, fruits, leaves), meat, and insects.

osteology The study of skeletal material. Human osteology focuses on the interpretation of the skeletal remains of past groups. Some of the same techniques are used in paleoanthropology to study early hominids.

paleoanthropology The interdisciplinary approach to the study of earlier hominids—their chronology, physical structure, archaeological remains, habitats, etc.

paleopathology The branch of osteology that studies evidence of disease and injury in human skeletal or, occasionally, mummified remains from archaeological sites.

paleospecies Species defined from fossil evidence, often covering a long time span.

pandemic An extensive outbreak of disease affecting large numbers of individuals over a wide area; potentially a worldwide phenomenon.

Paranthropus (par´-an-throw´-puss) A genus of hominid characterized by very large back teeth and jaws. Frequently, this genus is combined into *Australopithecus.*

pathogens Any agents, especially microorganisms such as viruses, bacteria, or fungi, that infect a host and cause disease.

phenotypes The observable or detectable physical characteristics of an organism; the detectable expressions of genotypes.

phylogenetic tree A chart showing evolutionary relationships as determined by evolutionary systematics. It contains a time component and implies ancestor-descendant relationships.

phylogeny A schematic representation showing ancestor-descendant relationships, usually in a chronological framework.

placental A type (subclass) of mammal. During the Cenozoic, placentals became the most widespread and numerous mammals and today are represented by upwards of 20 orders, including the primates.

plasticity The capacity to change. In a behavioral context, the ability of animals to modify actions in response to differing circumstances.

pleiotropic genes Genes that have more than one effect; genes that have different effects at different times in the life cycle.

Pleistocene The epoch of the Cenozoic from 1.8 m.y.a. until 10,000 y.a. Frequently referred to as the Ice Age, this epoch is associated with continental glaciations in northern latitudes.

Plio-Pleistocene Pertaining to the Pliocene and first half of the Pleistocene, a time range of 5–1 m.y.a. For this time period, numerous fossil hominids have been found in Africa.

polyandry A mating system wherein a female continuously associates with more than one male (usually two or three) with whom she mates. Among nonhuman primates, polyandry is seen only in marmosets and tamarins. It also occurs in a few human societies.

polygenic Referring to traits that are influenced by genes at two or more loci. Examples of such traits are stature, skin color, and eye color. Many polygenic traits are also influenced by environmental factors.

polymerase chain reaction (PCR) A method of producing millions of copies of a DNA segment using the enzyme DNA polymerase.

polymorphisms Loci with more than one allele. Polymorphisms can be expressed in the phenotype as the result of gene action (as in ABO), or they can exist solely at the DNA level within noncoding regions.

polytypic Referring to species composed of populations that differ with regard to the expression of one or more traits.

Pongidae (ponj´-id-ee) The traditional family designation of the great apes (orangutans, chimpanzees, bonobos, and gorillas).

population Within a species, a community of individuals where mates are usually found.

population genetics The study of the frequency of alleles, genotypes, and phenotypes in populations from a microevolutionary perspective.

postcranial (*post*, meaning "after") In a quadruped, referring to that portion of the body behind the head; in a biped, referring to all parts of the body *beneath* the head (i.e., the neck down).

predisposition The capacity or inclination to do something. A situation whereby an organism is susceptible to behavioral or anatomical modification because of preexisting traits.

prehensility Grasping, as by the hands and feet of primates.

primates Members of the order of mammals Primates (pronounced "pry-may´-tees"), which includes prosimians, monkeys, apes, and humans.

primatologists Scientists who study the evolution, anatomy, and behavior of nonhuman primates. Those who study behavior in noncaptive animals are usually trained as physical anthropologists.

primatology The study of the biology and behavior of nonhuman primates (prosimians, monkeys, and apes).

primitive Referring to a trait or combination of traits present in an ancestral form.

principle of independent assortment The distribution of one pair of alleles into gametes does not influence the distribution of another pair. The genes controlling different traits are inherited independently of one another.

principle of segregation Genes (alleles) occur in pairs (because chromosomes occur in pairs). During gamete production, the members of each gene pair separate, so that each gamete contains one member of each pair. During fertilization, the full number of chromosomes is restored, and members of gene or allele pairs are reunited.

prosimians Members of a suborder of Primates, the *Prosimii* (pronounced "pro-sim´-ee-eye"). Traditionally, the suborder includes lemurs, lorises, and tarsiers.

protein synthesis The assembly of chains of amino acids into functional protein molecules. DNA directs the process.

proteins Three-dimensional molecules that serve a wide variety of functions through their ability to bind to other molecules.

protohominids The earliest members of the hominid lineage, as yet only poorly represented in the fossil record; thus, their structure and behavior are reconstructed mostly hypothetically.

punctuated equilibrium The concept that evolutionary change proceeds through long periods of stasis punctuated by rapid periods of change.

quadrupedal Using all four limbs to support the body during locomotion; the basic mammalian (and primate) form of locomotion.

quantitatively In a manner involving measurements of quantity and including such properties as size, number, and capacity. When data are quantified, they are expressed numerically and are capable of being tested statistically.

r-selected An adaptive strategy that emphasizes relatively large numbers of offspring and reduced parental care (compared to K-selected species). *K-selection* and *r-selection* are relative terms; e.g., mice are r-selected compared to primates but K-selected compared to fish.

random assortment The chance distribution of chromosomes to daughter cells during meiosis. There is nothing to dictate which member of a chromosome pair moves to which end of a dividing cell. Along with recombination, a source of variation resulting from meiosis.

recessive Describing a trait that is not expressed in heterozygotes; also refers to the allele that governs the trait. For a recessive allele to be expressed, there must be two copies of the allele (i.e., the individual must be homozygous).

recombinant DNA technology A process in which genes from the cell of one species are transferred to somatic cells or gametes of another species.

recombination The exchange of genetic material between homologous chromosomes during meiosis.

relativistic Pertaining to relativism; viewing entities as they relate to something else. Cultural relativism is the view that cultures have merits within their own historical and environmental contexts and that they shouldn't be judged through comparison with one's own culture.

replicate To duplicate. The DNA molecule is able to make copies of itself.

reproductive success The number of offspring an individual produces and rears to reproductive age; an individual's genetic contribution to the next generation.

rhinarium (rine-air´-ee-um) The moist, hairless pad at the end of the nose seen in most mammalian species. The rhinarium enhances an animal's ability to smell.

ribonucleic acid (RNA) A molecule that is similar in structure to DNA. There are several kinds of RNA, and many are single-stranded. Three forms of single-stranded RNA are essential to protein synthesis. They are messenger RNA (mRNA), transfer RNA (tRNA), and ribosomal RNA (rRNA).

ribosomes Structures composed of a form of RNA called ribosomal RNA (rRNA) and protein. Ribosomes are found in the cell's cytoplasm and are essential to the manufacture of proteins.

savanna (also spelled savannah) A large flat grassland with scattered trees and shrubs. Savannas are found in many regions of the world with warm (or hot) and dry climates.

science A body of knowledge gained through observation and experimentation; from the Latin *scientia,* meaning "knowledge."

scientific method A research method whereby a problem is identified, a hypothesis (or hypothetical explanation) is stated, and that hypothesis is tested through the collection and analysis of data. If the hypothesis is verified, it becomes a theory.

scientific testing The precise repetition of an experiment or expansion of observed data to provide verification; the procedure by which hypotheses and theories are verified, modified, or discarded.

sectorial Adapted for cutting or shearing; among primates, refers to the compressed (side-to-side) first lower premolar, which functions as a shearing surface with the upper canine.

selective pressures Forces in the environment that influence reproductive success in individuals.

senescence The process of physiological decline in body function that occurs with aging.

sensory modalities Different forms of sensation (e.g., touch, pain, pressure, heat, cold, vision, taste, hearing, and smell).

sex chromosomes In mammals, the X and Y chromosomes.

sexual dimorphism Differences in physical characteristics between males and females of the same species. For example, humans are slightly sexually dimorphic for body size, with males being taller, on average, than females of the same population.

sexual selection A type of natural selection that operates on only one sex within a species. It's the result of competition for mates, and it can lead to sexual dimorphism with regard to one or more traits.

shared derived Relating to specific character states shared in common between two forms and considered the most useful for making evolutionary interpretations.

sites Locations of discoveries. In paleontology and archaeology, a site may refer to a region where a number of discoveries have been made.

slash-and-burn agriculture A traditional land-clearing practice whereby trees and vegetation are cut and burned. In many areas, fields are abandoned after a few years and clearing occurs elsewhere.

social structure The composition, size, and sex ratio of a group of animals. Social structures, in part, are the results of natural selection in specific habitats, and they guide individual interactions and social relationships.

somatic cells Basically, all the cells in the body except those involved with reproduction.

specialized Evolved for a particular function; usually refers to a specific trait (e.g., incisor teeth), but may also refer to the entire way of life of an organism.

speciation The process by which a new species evolves from a prior species. Speciation is the most basic process in macroevolution.

species A group of organisms that can interbreed to produce fertile offspring. Members of one species are reproductively isolated from members of all other species (i.e., they can't mate with them to produce fertile offspring).

spina bifida A condition in which the arch of one or more vertebrae fails to fuse and form a protective barrier around the spinal cord.

stereoscopic vision The condition whereby visual images are, to varying degrees, superimposed on one another. This provides for depth perception, or the perception of the external environment in three dimensions. Stereoscopic vision is partly a function of structures in the brain.

strategies Behaviors or behavioral complexes that have been favored by natural selection to increase individual reproductive success. The behaviors need not be deliberate, and they often vary considerably between males and females.

stratigraphy Study of the sequential layering of deposits.

stratum (*pl.*, strata) Geological layer.

stress In a physiological context, any factor that acts to disrupt homeostasis; more precisely, the body's response to any factor that threatens its ability to maintain homeostasis.

taxonomy The branch of science concerned with the rules of classifying organisms on the basis of evolutionary relationships.

territories Portions of an individual's or group's home range that are actively defended against intrusion, especially by members of the same species.

theory A broad statement of scientific relationships or underlying principles that has been at least partially verified through rigorous testing.

transfer RNA (tRNA) The type of RNA that binds to specific amino acids and transports them to the ribosome during protein synthesis.

transmutation The change of one species to another. The term evolution did not assume its current meaning until the late nineteenth century.

uniformitarianism The theory that the earth's features are the result of long-term processes that continue to operate in the present as they did in the past. Elaborated on by Lyell, this theory opposed catastrophism and contributed strongly to the concept of immense geological time.

Upper Paleolithic A cultural period usually associated with modern humans (but also found with some Neandertals) and distinguished by technological innovation in various stone tool industries. Best known from western Europe, similar industries are also known from central and eastern Europe and Africa.

Upper Pleistocene The portion of the Pleistocene epoch beginning 125,000 y.a. and ending approximately 10,000 y.a.

variation (genetic) Inherited differences among individuals; the basis of all evolutionary change.

vasoconstriction Narrowing of blood vessels to reduce blood flow to the skin. Vasoconstriction is an involuntary response to cold and reduces heat loss at the skin's surface.

vasodilation Expansion of blood vessels, permitting increased blood flow to the skin. Vasodilation permits warming of the skin and also facilitates radiation of warmth as a means of cooling. Vasodilation is an involuntary response to warm temperatures, various drugs, and even emotional states (blushing).

vectors Agents that serve to transmit disease from one carrier to another. Mosquitoes are vectors for malaria, just as fleas are vectors for bubonic plague.

vertebrates Animals with segmented bony spinal columns; includes fishes, amphibians, reptiles, birds, and mammals.

world view General cultural orientation or perspective shared by members of a society.

zoonotic (zoh-oh-no´-tic) Pertaining to a zoonosis (*pl.*, zoonoses), a disease that is transmitted to humans through contact with nonhuman animals.

zygote A cell formed by the union of an egg and a sperm cell. It contains the full complement of chromosomes (in humans, 46) and has the potential of developing into an entire organism.

Bibliography

Adcock, Gregory J., Elizabeth S. Snow, Dennis Simon, et al.
  2001 "Mitochondrial DNA Sequences in Ancient Australians: Implications for Modern Human Origins." *Proceedings of the National Academy of Sciences,* 98:537–542.

Aitken, M. J., C. B. Stringer, and P. A. Mellars (eds.)
  1993 *The Origin of Modern Humans and the Impact of Chronometric Dating.* Princeton, NJ: Princeton University Press.

Alexander, R. D.
  1974 "The Evolution of Social Behavior." *Ann. Rev. Ecol. Syst.,* 5:325–383.

Arsuaga, Juan-Luis, et al.
  1993 "Three New Human Skulls from the Sima de los Huesos Middle Pleistocene Site in Sierra de Atapuerca, Spain." *Nature,* 362:534–537.

Arsuaga, Juan-Luis, Carlos Lorenzo, and Ana Garcia
  1999 "The Human Cranial Remains from Gran Dolina Lower Pleistocene Site (Sierra de Atapuerca, Spain)." *Journal of Human Evolution,* 37:431–457.

Arsuaga, J. L., I. Martinez, A. Garcia, et al.
  1997 "Sima de los Huesos (Sierra de Atapuerca, Spain). The Site." *Journal of Human Evolution,* 33:109–127.

Ascenzi, A., I. Bidditu, P. F. Cassoli, et al.
  1996 "A Calvarium of Late *Homo erectus* from Ceprano, Italy." *Journal of Human Evolution,* 31:409–423.

Asfaw, Berhane, W. Henry Gilbert, Yonnas Beyene, et al.
  2002 "Remains of *Homo erectus* from Bouri, Middle Awash, Ethiopia. *Nature,* 416:317–320.

Asfaw, Berhane, Tim White, Owen Lovejoy, et al.
  1999 "*Australopithecus garhi*: A New Species of Early Hominid from Ethiopia." *Science,* 284:629–635.

Badrian, Alison and Noel Badrian
  1984 "Social Organization of *Pan paniscus* in the Lomako Forest, Zaire." *In: The Pygmy Chimpanzee,* Randall L. Susman (ed.), New York: Plenum Press, pp. 325–346.

Badrian, Noel and Richard K. Malenky
  1984 "Feeding Ecology of *Pan paniscus* in the Lomako Forest, Zaire." *In: The Pygmy Chimpanzee,* Randall L. Susman (ed.), New York: Plenum Press, pp. 275–299.

Bartlett, Thad. Q., Robert W. Sussman, and James M. Cheverud
  1993 "Infant Killing in Primates: A Review of Observed Cases with Specific References to the Sexual Selection Hypothesis." *American Anthropologist,* 95(4):958–990.

Bartstra, Gert-Jan
  1982 "*Homo erectus erectus:* The Search for Artifacts." *Current Anthropology,* 23(3):318–320.

Bar-Yosef, O.
  1993 "The Role of Western Asia in Modern Human Origins." *In:* M. J. Aitken, et al. (eds.), q.v., pp. 132–147.

———
  1994 "The Contributions of Southwest Asia to the Study of the Origin of Modern Humans." *In: Origins of Anatomically Modern Humans,* M.H. Nitecki and D. V. Nitecki (eds.), New York: Plenum Press, pp. 23–66.

Bearder, Simon K.
  1987 "Lorises, Bushbabies & Tarsiers: Diverse Societies in Solitary Foragers." *In:* Smuts, et al., q.v., pp. 11–24.

Begun, David R.
  2003 "Planet of the Apes." *Scientific American,* 289:74–83.

Begun, D. and A. Walker
  1993 "The Endocast." *In:* A. Walker and R. E. Leakey (eds), q.v., pp. 326–358.

Beja-Pereira, A., G. Luikart, P. England, et al.
  2003 "Gene-Culture Coevolution between Cattle Milk Protein Genes and Human Lactase Genes." *Nature Genetics,* 35,311–313.

Bell, Martin and Michael J. C. Walker
  1992 *Late Quaternary Environmental Change.* New York: John Wiley and Sons.

Ben Shaul, D. M.
  1962   "The Composition of the Milk of Wild Animals."
          International Zoo Yearbook, 4:333–342.
Berger, Thomas and Erik Trinkaus
  1995   "Patterns of Trauma Among the Neandertals."
          Journal of Archaeological Science, 22:841–852.
Bermudez de Castro, J.M., M. Martinon-Torres, E.
Carbonell, et al.
  2004   "The Atapuerca Sites and their Contribution to
          the Knowledge of Human Evolution in Europe."
          Evolutionary Anthropology, 13:25–41.
Binford, Lewis R.
  1981   *Bones. Ancient Men and Modern Myths.* New
          York: Academic Press.
Binford, Lewis R. and Chuan Kun Ho
  1985   "Taphonomy at a Distance: Zhoukoudian,
          'The Cave Home of Beijing Man'?" *Current
          Anthropology*, 26:413–442.
Binford, Lewis R. and Nancy M. Stone
  1986a   "The Chinese Paleolithic: An Outsider's View."
          AnthroQuest, Fall 1986(1):14–20.

  _____

  1986b   "Zhoukoudian: A Closer Look." *Current
          Anthropology*, 27(5):453–475.
Boaz, N. T. and Russell L. Ciochon
  2001   "The Scavenging of *Homo erectus pekinensis.*"
          Natural History, 110(2):46–51.
Boesch, Christophe and H. Boesch
  1989   "Hunting Behavior of Wild Chimpanzees in the
          Tai National Park." *American Journal of Physical
          Anthropology*, 78:547–573.

  _____

  1990   "Tool Use and Tool Making in Wild
          Chimpanzees." *Folia Primatologica*, 54:86–99.
Boesch, C., P. Marchesi, N. Marchesi, et al.
  1994   "Is Nut Cracking in Wild Chimpanzees a Cultural
          Behaviour?" *Journal of Human Evolution*,
          26:325–338.
Bogin, Barry
  1988   *Patterns of Human Growth.* Cambridge:
          Cambridge University Press.
Borries, C., et al.
  1999   "DNA Analyses Support the Hypothesis that
          Infanticide is Adaptive in Langur Monkeys."
          Proceedings of the Royal Society of London,
          266:901–904.
Brace, C. L. and Ashley Montagu
  1977   *Human Evolution* (2nd Ed.). New York:
          Macmillan.
Brace, C. Loring, H. Nelson, and N. Korn
  1979   *Atlas of Human Evolution* (2nd Ed.). New York:
          Holt, Rinehart & Winston.

Bromage, Timothy G. and Christopher Dean
  1985   "Re-evaluation of the Age at Death of Immature
          Fossil Hominids." *Nature*, 317:525–527.
Brooks, Alison, et al.
  1995   "Dating and Context of Three Middle Stone Age
          Sites with Bone Points in the Upper Semliki
          Valley, Zaire." *Science*, 268:548–553.
Brown, P., T. Sutiikna, M. K. Morwood, et al.
  2004   " A New Small-Bodied Hominin from the Late
          Pleistocene of Flores, Indonesia." *Nature*,
          431:1055–1061.
Brown, T. M. and K. D. Rose
  1987   "Patterns of Dental Evolution in Early Eocene
          Anaptomorphine Primates Comomyidael from
          the Bighorn Basin, Wyoming." *Journal of
          Paleontology*, 61:1–62.
Brunet, Michel, et al.
  1995   "The First Australopithecine 2,500 Kilometers
          West of the Rift Valley (Chad)." *Nature*,
          378:273–274.
Brunet, M., F. Guy, D. Pilbeam, et al.
  2002   "A New Hominid from the Upper Miocene of
          Chad, Central Africa." *Nature*, 418:145–151.

Caramelli, David, Carlos Lalueza-Fox, Cristiano Vernesi, et al.
  2003   "Evidence for Genetic Discontinuity Between
          Neandertals and 24,000-year-old Anatomically
          Modern Humans." *Proceedings of the National
          Academy of Sciences*, 100:6593–6597.
Carbonell, E., et al.
  1995   "Lower Pleistocene Hominids and Artifacts from
          Atapuerca-TDG (Spain)." *Science*, 269:826–830.
Carrol, Robert L.
  1988   *Vertebrate Paleontology and Evolution.* New York:
          W. H. Freeman and Co.
Cartmill, Matt
  1972   "Arboreal Adaptations and the Origin of the
          Order Primates." *In: The Functional and
          Evolutionary Biology of Primates*, R. H. Tuttle
          (ed.), Chicago: Aldine-Atherton, pp. 97–122.

  _____

  1992   "New Views on Primate Origins." *Evolutionary
          Anthropology*, 1:105–111.
Cavalli-Sforza, L. L., A. Piazza, P. Menozzi, and J. Mountain
  1988   "Reconstruction of Human Evolution: Bringing
          Together Genetic, Archaeological, and Linguistic
          Data." *Proceedings of the National Academy of
          Sciences*, 85:6002–6006.
Charteris, J., J. C. Wali, and J. W. Nottrodt
  1981   "Functional Reconstruction of Gait from Pliocene
          Hominid Footprints at Laetoli, Northern
          Tanzania." *Nature*, 290:496–498.

Ciochon, Russell L. and Robert S. Corruccini (eds.)
1983   *New Interpretations of Ape and Human Ancestry.* New York: Plenum Press.

Clark, A. G., S. Glanowski, R. Nielsen, et al.
2003   "Inferring Nonneutral Evolution from Human-Chimp-Mouse Orthologous Gene Trios." *Nature,* 302:1960–1963.

Clark, J. Desmond, Yonas Beyene, Gidoy Wold Gabriel, et al.
2003   "Stratigraphic, Chronological, and Behavioral Contexts of Pleistocene *Homo sapiens* from Middle Awash, Ethiopia." *Nature,* 423:747–752.

Clarke, R. J.
1985   "*Australopithecus* and Early *Homo* in Southern Africa." *In: Ancestors: The Hard Evidence,* E. Delson (ed.), New York: Alan R. Liss, pp. 171–177.

―――― 1998   "First Ever Discovery of a Well-Preserved Skull and Associated Skeleton of an Australopithecine." *South African Journal of Science,* 94:460.

Clarke, Ronald J. and Phillip V. Tobias
1995   "Sterkfontein Member 2 Foot Bones of the Oldest South African Hominid." *Science,* 269:521–524.

Cleveland, J. and C. T. Snowdon
1982   "The Complex Vocal Repertoire of the Adult Cotton-top Tamarin (*Saguinus oedipus oedipus*)." *Zeitschrift Tierpsychologie,* 58:231–270.

Colwell, Rita R.
1996   "Global Climate and Infectious Disease: The Cholera Paradigm." *Science,* 274(5295):2025–2031.

Conkey, M.
1987   "New Approaches in the Search for Meaning? A Review of the Research in 'Paleolithic Art.'" *Journal of Field Archaeology,* 14:413–430.

Conroy, Glenn C.
1997   *Reconstructing Human Origins. A Modern Synthesis.* New York: Norton.

Conroy, G. C., M. Pickford, B. Senut, J. van Couvering, and P. Mein
1992   "*Otavipithecus namibiensis,* First Miocene Hominoid from Southern Africa." *Nature,* 356:144–148.

Cook, J., C. B. Stringer, A. Currant, H. P. Schwarcz, and A. G. Wintle
1982   "A Review of the Chronology of the European Middle Pleistocene Record." *Yearbook of Physical Anthropology,* 25:19–65.

Cooper, Alan, Andrew Rambaut, Vincent Macaulay, et al.
2001   "Human Origins and Ancient DNA." Letter to *Science,* 282:1655–1656.

Corruccini, Robert S.
1994   "Reaganomics and the Fate of the Progressive Neandertals." *In:* R. Corruccini and R. Ciochon (eds.), q.v., pp. 697–708.

Crews, D. E. and G. J. Harper
1998   "Ageing as Part of the Developmental Process." *In: The Cambridge Encyclopedia of Human Growth and Development,* S. J. Ulijaszek, et al. (eds.), Cambridge: Cambridge University Press, pp. 425–427.

Cummings, Michael
2000   *Human Heredity. Principles and Issues* (5th Ed.). St. Paul: Wadsworth/West Publishing Co.

Currat, M., G. Trabuchet, D. Rees, et al.
2002   "Molecular Analysis of the Beta-Globin Gene Cluster in the Niokholo Mandenka Population Reveals a Recent Origin of the Beta S Senegal Mutation." *American Journal of Human Genetics,* 70:207–223.

Curtin, R. and P. Dolhinow
1978   "Primate Social Behavior in a Changing World." *American Scientist,* 66:468–475.

Dart, Raymond
1959   *Adventures with the Missing Link.* New York: Harper & Brothers.

Darwin, Charles
1859   *On the Origin of Species.* A Facsimile of the First Edition, Cambridge, MA: Harvard University Press (1964).

―――― 1871   *The Descent of Man and Selection in Relation to Sex.* Republished, 1981, Princeton: Princeton University Press.

Darwin, Francis (ed.)
1950   *The Life and Letters of Charles Darwin.* New York: Henry Schuman.

Day, M. H. and E. H. Wickens
1980   "Laetoli Pliocene Hominid Footprints and Bipedalism." *Nature,* 286:385–387.

Dean, M., M. Carring, C. Winkler, et al.
1996   "Genetic Restriction of HIV-1 Infection and Progression to AIDS by a Deletion Allele of the CKR5 Structural Gene." *Science,* 273:1856–1862.

Defleur, A, T. White, P. Valensi, et al.
1999   "Neanderthal Cannibalism at Moula-Guercy, Ardèche, France." *Science,* 286:128–131.

de Lumley, Henry and M. de Lumley
1973   "Pre-Neanderthal Human Remains from Arago Cave in Southeastern France." *Yearbook of Physical Anthropology,* 16:162–168.

Dene, H. T., M. Goodman, and W. Prychodko
1976 "Immunodiffusion Evidence on the Phylogeny of the Primates." *In: Molecular Anthropology*, M. Goodman, R. E. Tashian, and J. H. Tashian (eds.), New York: Plenum Press, pp. 171–195.

deReuter, J. R.
1986 "The Influence of Group Size on Predator Scanning and Foraging Behavior of Wedge-Capped Capuchin Monkeys *(Cebus olivaceus).*" *Behaviour*, 98:240–258.

Desmond, Adrian and James Moore
1991 *Darwin*. New York: Warner Books.

Dettwyler, K. A.
1991 "Can Paleopathology Provide Evidence for Compassion?" *American Journal of Physical Anthropology*, 84:375–384.

de Waal, Frans
1982 *Chimpanzee Politics*. London: Jonathan Cape.

———
1989 *Peacemaking among Primates*. Cambridge: Harvard University Press.

———
1999 "Cultural Primatology Comes of Age." *Nature*, 399:635–636.

Doran, D. M. and A. McNeilage
1998 "Gorilla Ecology and Behavior." *Evolutionary Anthropology*, 6(4):120–131.

Dorit, R. L., H. Akashi, and W. Gilbert
1995 "Absence of Polymorphism at the Zfy Locus on the Human Y Chromosome." *Science*, 268:1183–1185.

Duarte, C., J. Mauricio, P. B. Pettitt, et al.
1999 "The Early Upper Paleolithic Human Skeleton from the Abrigo do Lagar Velho (Portugal) and Modern Human Emergence in Iberia." *Proceedings of the National Academy of Sciences*, 96:7604–7609.

Durham, William
1981 Paper presented to the Annual Meeting of the American Anthropological Association, Washington, D.C., Dec. 1980. Reported in *Science*, 211:40.

Eaton, S. Boyd, Marjorie Shostak, and Melvin Konner
1988 *The Paleolithic Prescription*. New York: Harper and Row.

Ehrlich, Paul R. and Anne H. Ehrlich
1990 *The Population Explosion*. New York: Simon & Schuster.

Enard, W., M. Przeworski, S. E. Fisher, et al.,
2002 "Molecular Evolution of FOXP2, a Gene Involved in Speech and Language." *Nature*, 418:869–872.

Erickson, Clark
1998 "Applied Archaeology and Rural Development: Archaeology's Potential Contribution to the Future." *In*: M. Whiteford and S. Whiteford (eds.), *Crossing Currents: Continuity and Change in Latin America*. Upper Saddle, NJ: Prentice-Hall, pp. 34–45.

Etler, Dennis A. and Li-Tianyuan
1994 "New Archaic Human Fossil Discoveries in China and Their Bearing on Hominid Species Definition During the Middle Pleistocene." *In:* R. Corruccini and R. Ciochon (eds.), q.v., pp. 639–675.

Falgeres, Christophe, Jean-Jacques Bahain, Yugi Yokoyama, et al.
1999 "Earliest Humans in Europe: The Age of TD6 Gran Dolina, Atapuerca, Spain. *Journal of Human Evolution*, 37:345–352.

Falk, Dean
1983 "The Taung Endocast: A Reply to Holloway." *American Journal of Physical Anthropology*, 60:479–489.

———
1989 "Comments." *Current Anthropology*, 30:141.

Fedigan, Linda M.
1983 "Dominance and Reproductive Success in Primates." *Yearbook of Physical Anthropology*, 26:91–129.

Fleagle, John
1988/ *Primate Adaptation and Evolution*. New York:
1999 Academic Press. (2nd Ed.), 1999.

———
1994 "Anthropoid Origins." *In:* R. S. Corruccini and R. L. Ciochon (eds.), q.v., pp. 17–35.

Flinn, Mark V.
1999 "Family Environment, Stress, and Health During Childhood." *In*: Panter-Brick, C. and C. M. Worthman (eds.), *Hormones, Health, and Behavior: A Socio-ecological and Lifespan Perspective*. Cambridge: Cambridge University Press, pp. 105–138.

Foley, R. A.
1991 "How Many Species of Hominid Should There Be?" *Journal of Human Evolution*, 30: 413–427.

Foley, R. A. and M. M. Lahr
1997 "Mode 3 Technologies and the Evolution of Modern Humans." *Cambridge Archaeological Journal*: 7:3–36.

Foley, Robert
2002 "Adaptive Radiations and Dispersals in Hominin Evolutionary Ecology." *Evolutionary Anthropology*, 11(Supplement 1):32–37.

Formicola, Vincenzo and Alexandra P. Buzhilova
2004 "Double Child Burial from Sunghir (Russia): Pathology and Inferences for Upper Paleolithic Funerary Practices." *American Journal of Physical Anthropology,* 124:189–198.

Fossey, Dian
1983 *Gorillas in the Mist.* Boston: Houghton Mifflin.

Fouts, Roger S., D. H. Fouts, and T. T. van Cantfort
1989 "The Infant Loulis Learns Signs from Cross-Fostered Chimpanzees." *In:* R. A. Gardner, et al., q.v., pp. 280–292.

Frayer, David
1992 "Evolution at the European Edge: Neanderthal and Upper Paleolithic Relationships." *Préhistoire Européenne,* 2:9–69.

Frazer, K. L., X. Chen, D. A. Hinds, et al.
2003 "Genomic DNA Insertions and Deletions Occur Frequently Between Humans and Nonhuman Primates." *Genome Research,* 3:341–346.

Frisancho, A. Roberto
1978 "Nutritional Influences on Human Growth and Maturation." *Yearbook of Physical Anthropology,* 21:174–191.

———
1993 *Human Adaptation and Accommodation.* Ann Arbor: University of Michigan Press.

Frisch, Rose E.
1988 "Fatness and Fertility." *Scientific American,* 258:88–95.

Gabrunia, Leo, Abesalom Vekua, David Lordkipanidze, et al.
2000 "Earliest Pleistocene Hominid Cranial Remains from Dmanisi, Republic of Georgia: Taxonomy, Geological Setting, and Age." *Science,* 288:1019–1025.

Galik, K., B. Senut, M. Pickford, et al.
2004 "External and Internal Morphology of the Bar1002'00 *Orrorin tugenensis* Femur." *Science,* 305:1450–1453.

Gambier, Dominique
1989 "Fossil Hominids from the Early Upper Palaeolithic (Aurignacian) of France." *In:* P. Mellars and C. Stringer (eds.), q.v., pp. 194–211.

Gamble, C.
1991 "The Social Context for European Palaeolithic Art." *Proceedings of the Prehistoric Society,* 57:3–15.

Gao, Feng, Elizabeth Bailes, David L. Robertson, et al.
1999 "Origin of HIV-1 in the Chimpanzee *Pan troglodytes troglodytes.*" *Nature,* 397:436–441.

Gardner, R. Allen, B. T. Gardner, and T. T. van Cantfort (eds.)
1989 *Teaching Sign Language to Chimpanzees.* Albany: State University of New York Press.

Garner, K. J. and O. A. Ryder
1996 "Mitochondrial DNA Diversity in Gorillas." *Molecular Phylogenetics and Evolution,* 6:39–48.

Gebo, Daniel L., Marian Dagosto, K. Christopher Beard, and Tao Qi
2000 "The Smallest Primates." *Journal of Human Evolution,* 38:585–594.

Gee, Henry
1996 "Box of Bones 'Clinches' Identity of Piltdown Palaeontology Hoaxer." *Nature,* 381:261–262.

Gibbons, Anne
1998 "Ancient Tools Suggest *Homo erectus* was a Seafarer." Research News, *Science,* 279:1635–1637.

Giles, J. and J. Knight
2003 "Dolly's Death Leaves Researchers Woolly on Clone Ageing Issue." *Nature* 421:776.

Gillespie, B. and R. G. Roberts
2000 "On the Reliability of Age Estimate for Human Remains at Lake Mungo." *Journal of Human Evolution,* 38:727–732.

Gingerich, Phillip D.
1985 "Species in the Fossil Record: Concepts, Trends, and Transitions." *Paleobiology,* 11:27–41.

Glantz, M. M. and T. B. Ritzman
2004 "A Re-Analysis of the Neandertal Status of the Teshik-Tash Child." *American Journal of Physical Anthropology,* Supplement 38:100–101 (Abstract).

Goodall, Jane
1986 *The Chimpanzees of Gombe.* Cambridge: Harvard University Press.

Goodman, M., C. A. Porter, J. Czelusniak, et al.
1998 "Toward a Phylogenetic Classification of Primates Based on DNA Evidence Complemented by Fossil Evidence." *Molecular Phylogenetics and Evolution,* 9:585–598.

Gossett, Thomas F.
1963 *Race, the History of an Idea in America.* Dallas: Southern Methodist University Press.

Gould, Stephen Jay
1981 *The Mismeasures of Man.* New York: W. W. Norton.

———
1985 "Darwin at Sea—and the Virtues of Port." *In:* Stephen Jay Gould, *The Flamingo's Smile. Reflections in Natural History.* New York: W. W. Norton, pp. 347–359.

—— 1987 *Time's Arrow, Time's Cycle*. Cambridge: Harvard University Press.

Gould, S. J. and N. Eldredge
1977 "Punctuated Equilibria: The Tempo and Mode of Evolution Reconsidered." *Paleobiology*, 3:115–151.

Gould, S. J. and R. Lewontin
1979 "The Spandrels of San Marco and the Panglossian Paradigm: A Critique of the Adaptionist Programme." *Proceedings of the Royal Society of London*, 205:581–598.

Grant, P. R.
1986 *Ecology and Evolution of Darwin's Finches*. Princeton: Princeton University Press.

Greenwood, B. and T. Mutabingwa
2002 "Malaria in 2000." *Nature*, 415:670–672.

Gregory, J. M., P. Huybrechts, and S. C. B. Raper
2004 "Threatened Loss of the Greenland Ice Sheet." *Nature*, 428:616.

Groves, Colin P.
2001a *Primate Taxonomy*. Washington, DC: Smithsonian Institution Press.

—— 2001b "Why Taxonomic Stability Is a Bad Idea, or Why Are There So Few Species of Primates (or Are There?)." *Evolutionary Anthropology*, 10(6):191–197.

Gursky, Sharon
2002 "The Behavioral Ecology of the Spectral Tarsier, *Tarsius spectrum*." *Evolutionary Anthropology*, 11(6):226–234.

Haas, J. D., E. A. Frongillo, Jr., C. D. Stepick, et al.
1980 "Altitude, Ethnic and Sex Difference in Birth Weight and Length in Bolivia." *Human Biology*, 52:459–477.

Haile-Selassie, Yohannes
2001 "Late Miocene Hominids from the Middle Awash, Ethiopia." *Nature*, 412:178–181.

Haile-Selassie, Yohannes Gen Suwa, and Tim D. White
2004 "Late Miocene Teeth from Middle Awash, Ethiopia, and Early Hominid Dental Evolution." *Science*, 303:1503–1505.

Harlow, Harry F. and Margaret K. Harlow
1961 "A Study of Animal Affection." *Natural History*, 70:48–55.

Harrold, Francis R.
1989 "Mousterian, Chatelperronian and Early Aurignacian in Western Europe: Continuity or Discontinuity." *In: The Human Revolution*, P. Mellars and C. Stringer (eds.), Princeton, NJ: Princeton University Press, pp. 212–231.

Henzi, P. and L. Barrett
2003 "Evolutionary Ecology, Sexual Conflict, and Behavioral Differentiation Among Baboon Populations." *Evolutionary Anthropology*, 12(5):217–230.

Holloway, Ralph L.
1983 "Cerebral Brain Endocast Pattern of *Australopithecus afarensis* Hominid." *Nature*, 303:420–422.

Howell, F. C.
1999 "Paleo-demes, Species, Clades, and Extinctions in the Pleistocene Hominin Record." *Journal of Anthropological Research*, 55:191–243.

Hrdy, Sarah Blaffer
1977 *The Langurs of Abu*. Cambridge, MA.: Harvard University Press.

—— 1999 *Mother Nature: A History of Mothers, Infants, and Natural Selection*. New York: Pantheon Books.

Hrdy, Sarah Blaffer, Charles Janson, and Carel van Schaik
1995 "Infanticide: Let's Not Throw Out the Baby with the Bath Water." *Evolutionary Anthropology*, 3(5):151–154.

Hu, Dale J., Timothy J. Dondero, Mark A. Rayfield, et al.
1996 "The Emerging Genetic Diversity of HIV. The Importance of Global Surveillance for Diagnostics, Research, and Prevention." *Journal of the American Medical Association*, 275(3):210–216.

The International SNP Map Working Group
2001 "A Map of Human Genome Sequence Variation Containing 1.42 Million Single Nucleotide Polymorphisms." *Nature*, 409:928–933.

Isbell, L. A.
1994 "Predation on Primates: Ecological Patterns and Evolutionary Consequences." *Evolutionary Anthropology*, 3(2):61–71.

Isbell, L. A. and T. P. Young
1993 "Social and Ecological Influences on Activity Budgets of Vervet Monkeys and Their Implications for Group Living." *Behavioral Ecology and Sociobiology*, 32:377–385.

Izawa, K. and A. Mizuno
1977 "Palm-Fruit Cracking Behaviour of Wild Black-Capped Capuchin (*Cebus apella*)." *Primates*, 18:773–793.

Jablonski, Nina
1992 "Sun, Skin Colour, and Spina Bifida: An Exploration of the Relationship between Ultraviolet Light and Neural Tube Defects."

Proceedings of the Australian Society of Human Biology, 5:455–462.

Jablonski, Nina G. and George Chaplin
2000 "The Evolution of Skin Coloration." *Journal of Human Evolution,* 39:57–106.

Jensen, G. M. and L. G. Moore
1997 "The Effect of High Altitude and Other Risk Factors on Birthweight: Independent or Interactive Effects?" *American Journal of Public Health,* 87(6):1003–1007.

Jerison, H. J.
1973 *Evolution of the Brain and Behavior.* New York: Academic Press.

Jia, Lan-po
1975 *The Cave Home of Peking Man.* Peking: Foreign Language Press.

Jia, L. and Huang Weiwen
1990 *The Story of Peking Man.* New York: Oxford University Press.

Johanson, Donald and Maitland Edey
1981 *Lucy: The Beginnings of Humankind.* New York: Simon & Schuster.

Johanson, D. C. and T. D. White
1979 "A Systematic Assessment of Early African Hominids." *Science,* 202:321–330.

Jolly, Alison
1985 *The Evolution of Primate Behavior* (2nd Ed.). New York: Macmillan.

Kano, T.
1992 *The Last Ape. Pygmy Chimpanzee Behavior and Ecology.* Stanford: Stanford University Press.

Kay, R., M. Cartmill, and M. Balow
1998 "The Hypoglossal Canal and the Origins of Human Vocal Behavior" (abstract). *American Journal of Physical Anthropology, Supplement,* 26:137.

Kennedy, K. A. R.
1991 "Is the Narmada Hominid an Indian *Homo erectus?*" *American Journal of Physical Anthropology,* 86:475–496.

Kennedy, Kenneth A. R. and S. U. Deraniyagala
1989 "Fossil Remains of 28,000-Year-Old Hominids from Sri Lanka." *Current Anthropology,* 30:397–399.

Keyser, André W.
2000 "New Finds in South Africa." *National Geographic,* (May):76–83.

King, Barbara J.
1994 *The Information Continuum.* Santa Fe: School of American Research.

Kirkwood, T. B. L.
1997 "The Origins of Human Ageing." *Philosophical Transactions of the Royal Society of London B.,* 352:1765–1772.

——— 2002 "Evolution of Ageing." *Mechanisms of Ageing and Development,* 123:737–745.

Klein, R. G.
1989/ *The Human Career. Human Biological and*
1999 *Cultural Origins.* Chicago: University of Chicago Press. (2nd Ed.), 1999.

Konner, Melvin and Carol Worthman
1980 "Nursing Frequency, Gonadal Function, and Birth Spacing among !Kung Hunter-Gatherers." *Science,* 207:788–791.

Kramer, Andrew
1993 "Human Taxonomic Diversity in the Pleistocene: Does *Homo erectus* Represent Multiple Hominid Species?" *American Journal of Physical Anthropology,* 91:161–171.

Krings, Matthias, Cristen Capelli, Frank Tscentscher, et al.
2000 "A View of Neandertal Genetic Diversity." *Nature Genetics,* 26:144–146.

Krings, Matthias, Anne Stone, Ralf W. Schmitz, et al.
1997 "Neandertal DNA Sequences and the origin of Modern Humans." *Cell,* 90:19–30.

Kulikov, Eugene E., Audrey B. Poltaraus, and Irina A. Lebedeva
2004 "DNA Analysis of Sunghir Remains: Problems and Perspectives." Poster Presentation, European Paleopathology Association Meetings, Durham, U.K, August 2004.

Kunzig, Robert
1997 "Atapuerca. The Face of an Ancestral Child." *Discover,* 18:88–101.

Lack, David
1966 *Population Studies of Birds.* Oxford: Clarendon.

Lahdenperä, M., S. Lummaa, S. Helle, et al.
2004 "Fitness Benefits of Prolonged Post-reproductive Lifespan in Women." *Nature,* 428:178–181.

Lahr, Marta Mirazon and Robert Foley
1998 "Towards a Theory of Human Origins: Geography, Demography, and Diversity in Recent Human Evolution." *Yearbook of Physical Anthropology,* 41:137–176.

Lalani, A. S., J. Masters, W. Zeng, et al.
1999 "Use of Chemokine Receptors by Poxviruses." *Science,* 286:1968–71.

Lamberts, S. W. J., A. W. van den Beld, and A. J. van der Lely
1997 "The Endocrinology of Aging." *Science,* 278:419–424.

Lancaster, J. B. and C. S. Lancaster
  1983   "Prenatal Investment: The Hominid Adaptation."
         In: Ortner, D. J. (ed.), *How Humans Adapt: A
         Biocultural Odyssey.* Washington DC: Smithsonian
         Institution Press.
Larick, Roy and Russell L. Ciochon
  1996   "The African Emergence and Early Asian
         Dispersals of the Genus *Homo.*" *American
         Scientist,* 84:538–551.
Leakey, M. D. and R. L. Hay
  1979   "Pliocene Footprints in Laetolil Beds at Laetoli,
         Northern Tanzania." *Nature,* 278:317–323.
Leakey, Meave G., et al.
  1995   "New Four-Million-Year-Old Hominid Species
         from Kanapoi and Allia Bay, Kenya." *Nature,*
         376:565–571.
Leakey, M. G., F. Spoor, F. H. Brown, et al.
  2001   "New Hominin Genus from Eastern Africa Shows
         Diverse Middle Pliocene Lineages." *Nature,*
         410:433–440.
Lederberg, Joshua
  1996   "Infection Emergent." *Journal of the American
         Medical Association,* 275(3):243–245.
Leroi-Gourhan, André
  1986   "The Hands of Gargas." *October* 37:18–34.
Lewin, Roger
  1986   "Damage to Tropical Forests, or Why Were
         There So Many Kinds of Animals?" *Science,*
         234:149–150.
Lewontin, R. C.
  1972   "The Apportionment of Human Diversity." *In:
         Evolutionary Biology* (Vol. 6), T. Dobzhansky, et
         al. (eds.), New York: Plenum, pp. 381–398.
Linnaeus, C.
  1758   *Systema Naturae.*

MacKinnon, J. and K. MacKinnon
  1980   "The Behavior of Wild Spectral Tarsiers."
         International Journal of Primatology, 1:361–379.
Makalowski, W.
  2000   "Genomic Scrap Yard: How Genomes Utilize All
         That Junk." *Gene,* 259(1–2):61–67.
Manzi, G., F. Mallegni, and A. Ascenzi
  2001   "A Cranium for the Earliest Europeans:
         Phylogenetic Position of the Hominid from
         Ceprano, Italy. *Proceedings of the National
         Academy of Sciences,* 98:1011–1016.
Marshack, A.
  1972   *The Roots of Civilization.* New York: McGraw-
         Hill Publishing Co.
Mayer, Peter
  1982   "Evolutionary Advantages of Menopause."
         Human Ecology, 10:477–494.

Mayr, Ernst
  1970   *Population, Species, and Evolution.* Cambridge:
         Harvard University Press.
McConkey, Edwin H. and Ajit Varki
  2000   "A Primate Genome Project Deserves High
         Priority." Letters. *Science,* 289:1295.
McGrew, W. C.
  1992   *Chimpanzee Material Culture. Implications for
         Human Evolution.* Cambridge: Cambridge
         University Press.

  1998   "Culture in Nonhuman Primates?" *Annual
         Review of Anthropology,* 27:301–328.
McHenry, Henry
  1988   "New Estimates of Body Weight in Early
         Hominids and Their Significance to
         Encephalization and Megadontia in 'Robust'
         Australopithecines." *In:* F. E. Grine (ed.), q.v.,
         pp. 133–148.

  1992   "Body Size and Proportions in Early Hominids."
         American Journal of Physical Anthropology,
         87:407–431.
McKusick, V. A. (with S. E. Antonarakis, et al.)
  1998   *Mendelian Inheritance in Man.* (12th Ed.).
         Baltimore: Johns Hopkins University Press.
McRae, M.
  1997   "Road Kill in Cameroon." *Natural History,*
         106(1):36–46.
Miles, H. Lyn Whire
  1990   "The Cognitive Foundations for Reference in a
         Signing Orangutan." *In:* Parker, S. T. and K. R.
         Gibson (eds.) *Language and Intelligence in
         Monkeys and Apes: Comparative Developmental
         Perspectives.* New York: Cambridge University
         Press, pp. 511–539.
Miller, G. H., J. W. Magee, B. J. Johnson, et al.
  1999   "Pleistocene extinction of *Genyornis newtoni:*
         Human Impact on Australian Megafauna."
         Science, 283:205–208.
Mitchell, R. J., S. Howlett, N. G. White, et al.
  1999   "Deletion Polymorphism in the Human
         COL1AZ Gene: Genetic Evidence of a Non-
         African Population Whose Descendants Spread to
         All Continents." *Human Biology,* 71:901–914.
Mittermeir, R. A. and D. Cheney
  1987   "Conservation of Primates in Their Habitats."
         In: B. B. Smuts, et al., q.v., pp. 477–496.
Molnar, Stephen
  1983   *Human Variation. Races, Types, and Ethnic
         Groups* (2nd Ed.). Englewood Cliffs: Prentice-
         Hall.

Moore, Lorna G. and Judith G. Regensteiner
1983 "Adaptation to High Altitude." *Annual Reviews of Anthropology*, 12:285–304.

Moore, Lorna G., et al.
1994 "Genetic Adaptation to High Altitude." *In:* Stephen C. Wood and Robert C. Roach (eds.), *Sports and Exercise Medicine.* New York: Marcel Dekker, Inc., pp. 225–262.

Morwood, M. J., R. P. Suejono, R. G. Roberts, et al.
2004 "Archaeology and Age of a New Hominin from Flores in Eastern Indonesia." *Nature*, 431:1087–1091.

Moura, A. C. de A., and P. C. Lee
2004 "Capuchin Stone Tool Use in Caatinga Dry Forest." *Science*, 306:1909.

Napier, John
1967 "The Antiquity of Human Walking." *Scientific American*, 216:56–66.

Napier, J. R. and P. H. Napier
1967 *A Handbook of Living Primates.* New York: Academic Press.

_____
1985 *The Natural History of the Primates.* London: British Museum (Natural History).

Neese, R. M. and G. C. Williams
1994 *Why We Get Sick.* New York: Times Books.

Nishida, T., M. Hiraiwa-Hasegawa, T. Hasegawa, and Y. Takahata
1985 "Group Extinction and Female Transfer in Wild Chimpanzees in the Mahale National Park, Tanzania." *Zeitschrift Tierpsychologie*, 67:284–301.

Nishida, T., H. Takasaki, and Y. Takahata
1990 "Demography and Reproductive Profiles." *In: The Chimpanzees of the Mahale Mountains*, T. Nishida (ed.), Tokyo: University of Tokyo Press, pp. 63–97.

Nishida, T., R. W. Wrangham, J. Goodall, and S. Uehara
1983 "Local Differences in Plant-feeding Habits of Chimpanzees between the Mahale Mountains and Gombe National Park, Tanzania." *Journal of Human Evolution*, 12:467–480.

Nowak, Ronald M.
1999 *Walker's Primates of the World.* Baltimore: Johns Hopkins University Press.

Oates, John F., Michael Abedi-Lartey, W. Scott McGraw, et al.
2000 "Extinction of a West African Red Colobus Monkey." *Conservation Biology,* 14(5):1526–1532.

O'Brien, S. J., et al.
2002 "The Promise of Comparative Genomics in Mammals." *Science*, 286(5439):458–481.

Olliaro, Piero
1996 "Malaria, the Submerged Disease." *Journal of the American Medical Association*, 275(3):230–233.

O'Rourke, D. H., M. G. Hayes, and S. W. Carlyle
2002 "Spatial and Temporal Stability of mtDNA Haplogroup Frequencies in Native North America." *Human Biology,* 72:15–34.

Ovchinnikov, Igor V., Anders Gotherstrom, Galina P. Romanova, et al.
2000 "Molecular Analysis of Neanderthal DNA from the Northern Caucasus." *Nature*, 404:490–493.

Page, Susan E., et al.
2002 "The Amount of Carbon Released from Peat and Forest Fires in Indonesia During 1997." *Nature*, 420:61–65.

Palumbi, Stephen R.
2001 *The Evolution Explosion: How Humans Cause Rapid Evolutionary Change.* New York: W. W. Norton

Parés, Josef M. and Alfredo Pérez-González
1995 "Paleomagnetic Age for Hominid Fossils at Atapuerca Archaeological Site, Spain." *Science*, 269:830–832.

Pearson, Osbjorn M.
2004 "Has the Combination of Genetic and Fossil Evidence Solved the Riddle of Modern Human Origins?" *Evolutionary Anthropology*, 13:145–159.

Pennisi, Elizabeth
2001 "The Human Genome." *Science,* 291:1177–1180.

Peres, C. A.
1990 "Effects of Hunting on Western Amazonian Primate Communities." *Biological Conservation* 54:47–59.

Phillips, K. A.
1998 "Tool Use in Wild Capuchin Monkeys." *American Journal of Primatology,* 46(3):259–261.

Pickford, Martin and Brigitte Senut
2001 "The Geological and Faunal Context of Late Miocene Hominid Remains from Lukeino, Kenya." *C. R. Acad. Sci. Paris, Sciences de la Terre et des Planètes,* 332:145–152.

Pinner, Robert W., Steven M. Teutsch, Lone Simonson, et al.
1996 "Trends in Infectious Diseases Mortality in the United States." *Journal of the American Medical Association,* 275(3):189–193.

Potts, Richard
1991 "Why the Oldowan? Plio-Pleistocene Toolmaking and the Transport of Resources." *Journal of Anthropological Research,* 47:153–176.

1993 "Archeological Interpretations of Early Hominid Behavior and Ecology." *In:* D. T. Rasmussen (ed.), q.v., pp. 49–74.

Powell, K. B.
2003 "The Evolution or Lactase Persistence in African Populations." *American Journal of Physical Anthropology, Supplement* 36:170 (Abstract).

Proctor, Robert
1988 "From Anthropologie to Rassenkunde." *In: Bones, Bodies, Behavior. History of Anthropology* (Vol. 5), W. Stocking, Jr. (ed.), Madison: University of Wisconsin Press, pp. 138–179.

Profet, M.
1988 "The Evolution of Pregnancy Sickness as a Protection to the Embryo Against Pleistocene Teratogens." *Evolutionary Theory,* 8:177–190.

Pulliam, H. R. and T. Caraco
1984 "Living in Groups: Is There an Optimal Size?" *In: Behavioral Ecology: An Evolutionary Approach* (2nd Ed.), J. R. Krebs and N. B. Davies (eds.), Sunderland, Mass.: Sinauer Associates.

Pusey, A., J. Williams, and J. Goodall
1997 "The Influence of Dominance Rank on the Reproductive Success of Female Chimpanzees." *Science,* 277:828–831.

Rak, Y.
1983 *The Australopithecine Face.* New York: Academic Press.

Rasmussen, D. T. (ed.)
1993 *The Origin and Evolution of Humans and Humanness.* Boston: Jones and Bartlett.

Reddy, B. Mohan, Guangyun Sun, Javier Rodriguez Luis, et al.
2001 "Genomic Diversity of Thirteen Short Tandem Repeat Loci in a Substructured Caste Population, Golla, of Southern Andhra Pradesh, India." *Human Biology,* 73:175–190.

Relethford, John H. and Henry C. Harpending
1994 "Craniometric Variation, Genetic Theory, and Modern Human Origins." *American Journal of Physical Anthropology,* 95:249–270.

Richard, A. F. and S. R. Schulman
1982 "Sociobiology: Primate Field Studies." *Annual Reviews of Anthropology,* 11:231–255.

Ridley, Mark
1993 *Evolution.* Boston: Blackwell Scientific Publications.

Rightmire, G. P.
1981 "Patterns in the Evolution of *Homo erectus.*" *Paleobiology,* 7:241–246.

1990 *The Evolution of* Homo erectus. New York: Cambridge University Press.

1998 "Human Evolution in the Middle Pleistocene: The Role of *Homo heidelbergensis.*" *Evolutionary Anthropology,* 6:218–227.

2004 "Affinities of the Middle Pleistocene Crania from Dali and Jinniushan, China. *American Journal of Physical Anthropology, Supplement* 38:167 (Abstract).

Roberts, D. F.
1973 *Climate and Human Variability.* An Addison-Wesley Module in Anthropology, No. 34. Reading, MA: Addison-Wesley.

Robinson, J. T.
1972 *Early Hominid Posture and Locomotion.* Chicago: University of Chicago Press.

Rose, M. D.
1991 "Species Recognition in Eocene Primates." *American Journal of Physical Anthropology, Supplement* 12, p. 153.

Rosenberg, K. and Wenda Trevathan
2001 "The Evolution of Human Birth." *Scientific American,* 285:72–77.

Roychoudhury, S., S. Roy, A. Basu, et al.
2001 "Genomic Structures and Population Histories of Linguistically Distinct Tribal Groups of India." *Human Genetics,* 109:339–350.

Rudran, R.
1973 "Adult Male Replacement in One-Male Troops of Purple-Faced Langurs (*Presbytis senex senex*) and its Effect on Population Structure." *Folia Primatologica,* 19:166–192.

Ruff, C. B. and H. M. McHenry
2004 "Can Sexual Dimorphism in Skeletal Size Be Used to Assess Sexual Dimorphism in Body Size?" *American Journal of Physical Anthropology, Supplement* 38:171 (Abstract).

Ruff, C. B. and Alan Walker
1993 "The Body Size and Shape of KNM-WT 15000." *In*: A. Walker and R. Leakey (eds.), q.v., pp. 234–265.

Rumbaugh, D. M.
1977 *Language Learning by a Chimpanzee: The Lana Project.* New York: Academic Press.

Ruvolo, M., D. Pan, S. Zehr, T. Goldberg, et al.
1994 "Gene Trees and Hominoid Phylogeny." *Proceedings of the National Academy of Sciences,* 91:8900–8904.

Samson, M., F. Libert, B. J. Doranz, et al.
  1996   "Resistance to HIV-1 Infection in Caucasian
         Individuals Bearing Mutant Alleles of the CCR-5
         Chemokine Receptor Gene." *Nature*
         382(22):722–725.

Savage-Rumbaugh, S.
  1986   *Ape Language: From Conditioned Responses to
         Symbols*. New York: Columbia University Press.

Savage-Rumbaugh, S. and R. Lewin
  1994   *Kanzi. The Ape at the Brink of the Human Mind*.
         New York: John Wiley and Sons.

Savage-Rumbaugh, S., K. McDonald, R. A. Sevic, W. D.
Hopkins, and E. Rupert
  1986   "Spontaneous Symbol Acquisition and
         Communicative Use by Pygmy Chimpanzees
         (*Pan paniscus*)." *Journal of Experimental
         Psychology: General*, 115(3):211–235.

Schaller, George B.
  1963   *The Mountain Gorilla*. Chicago: University of
         Chicago Press.

Schlermeier, Q.
  2004   "A Rising Tide." *Nature*, 428:114–115.

Scott, K.
  1980   "Two Hunting Episodes of Middle Paleolithic
         Age at La Cotte Sainte-Brelade, Jersey (Channel
         Islands)." *World Archaeology*, 12:137–152.

Scriver, Charles R.
  2001   "Human Genetics: Lessons from Quebec
         Populations." *Annual Review of Genomics and
         Human Genetics*, 2:69–101.

Semaw, S., P. Renne, W. K. Harris, et al.
  1997   "2.5-million-year-old Stone Tools from Gona,
         Ethiopia." *Nature*, 385:333–336.

Senut, Brigitte, Martin Pickford, Dominique Grommercy,
et al.
  2001   First Hominid from the Miocene (Lukeino
         Formation, Kenya). *C. R. Acad. Sci. Paris,
         Sciences de la Terre et des Planètes*, 332:137–144.

Serre, David, André Langaney, Marie Chech, et al.
  2004   "No Evidence of Neandertal mtDNA
         Contribution to Early Modern Humans." *PloS
         Biology*, 2:313–317.

Seyfarth, Robert M.
  1987   "Vocal Communication and Its Relation to
         Language." *In:* Smuts, et al., *Primate Societies*.
         Chicago: University of Chicago Press, pp.
         440–451.

Seyfarth, Robert M., Dorothy L. Cheney, and Peter Marler
  1980a "Monkey Responses to Three Different Alarm
         Calls." *Science*, 210:801–803.

———   1980b "Vervet Monkey Alarm Calls." *Animal Behavior*,
         28:1070–1094.

Shea, Brian T. and Robert C. Baily
  1996   "Allometry and Adaptation of Body Proportions
         and Stature in African Pygmies." *American
         Journal of Physical Anthropology*, 100:311–340.

Sibley, Charles and Jon E. Ahlquist
  1984   "The Phylogeny of the Hominoid Primates as
         Indicated by DNA-DNA Hybridization." *Journal
         of Molecular Evolution*, 20:2–15.

Simmons, J. G.
  1989   *Changing the Face of the Earth*. Oxford: Basil
         Blackwell Ltd.

Simons, E. L.
  1972   *Primate Evolution*. New York: Macmillan.

Smith, Fred H.
  1984   "Fossil Hominids from the Upper Pleistocene of
         Central Europe and the Origin of Modern
         Europeans." *In:* F. H. Smith and F. Spencer
         (eds.), *The Origins of Modern Humans*. New
         York: Alan R. Liss, pp. 187–209.

———   2002   "Migrations, Radiations and Continuity: Patterns
         in the Evolution of Late Pleistocene Humans. *In:*
         W. Hartwig (ed.), *The Primate Fossil Record*.
         Cambridge: Cambridge University Press, pp.
         437–456.

Smith, Fred H., A. B. Falsetti, and S. M. Donnelly
  1989   "Modern Human Origins." *Yearbook of Physical
         Anthropology*, 32:35–68.

Smith, Fred H., Erik Trinkaus, Paul B. Pettitt, et al.
  1999   "Direct Radiocarbon Dates for Vindija G_1 and
         Velika Pécina Late Pleistocene Hominid
         Remains." *Proceedings of the National Academy of
         Sciences*, 96:12281–12286.

Smuts, B., et al. (eds.)
  1987   *Primate Societies*. Chicago: University of Chicago
         Press.

Snyder, M. and M. Gerstein
  2003   "Genomics. Defining Genes in the Genomics
         Era." *Science*, 300(5617):258–260.

Soffer, Olga
  1985   *The Upper Paleolithic of the Central Russian
         Plain*. New York: Academic Press.

Stanford, C. B., J. Wallis, H. Matama, and J. Goodall
  1994   "Patterns of Predation by Chimpanzees on Red
         Colobus Monkeys in Gombe National Park."
         American Journal of Physical Anthropology,
         94(2):213–228.

Steklis, Horst D.
  1985   "Primate Communication, Comparative
         Neurology, and the Origin of Language Re-
         examined." *Journal of Human Evolution*,
         14:157–173.

Stelzner, J. and K. Strier
  1981   "Hyena Predation on an Adult Male Baboon."
         Mammalia, 45:106–107.
Stoneking, Mark
  1993   "DNA and Recent Human Evolution."
         Evolutionary Anthropology, 2:60–73.
Stott, P. A., D. A. Stone, and M. R. Allen
  2004   "Human Contribution to the European
         Heatwave of 2003. *Nature*, 432:610–614.
Straus, Lawrence Guy
  1993   "Southwestern Europe at the Last Glacial
         Maximum." *Current Anthropology*, 32:189–199.
Strier, Karen B.
  2003   *Primate Behavioral Ecology.* (2nd Ed.). Boston:
         Allyn and Bacon.
Stringer, C. B.
  1995   "The Evolution and Distribution of Later
         Pleistocene Human Populations." *In:* E. Vrba, et
         al. (eds.), q.v., pp. 524–531.
Stringer, C. B. and P. Andrews
  1988   "Genetic and Fossil Evidence for the Origin of
         Modern Humans." *Science*, 239:1263–1268.
Struhsaker, T. T.
  1967   "Auditory Communication among Vervet
         Monkeys (*Cercopithecus aethiops*)." *In: Social
         Communication Among Primates*, S. A. Altmann
         (ed.), Chicago: University of Chicago Press.

  1975   *The Red Colobus Monkey.* Chicago: University of
         Chicago Press.
Struhsaker, Thomas T. and Lysa Leland
  1979   "Socioecology of Five Sympatric Monkey Species
         in the Kibale Forest, Uganda." *Advances in the
         Study of Behavior*, Vol. 9, New York: Academic
         Press, pp. 159–229.

  1987   "Colobines: Infanticide by Adult Males." *In:* B.
         Smuts, et al. (eds.), q.v., pp. 83–97.
Sugiyama, Y. and J. Koman
  1979   "Tool-using and -making Behavior in Wild
         Chimpanzees at Bossou, Guinea." *Primates*,
         20:513–524.
Sumner, D. R., M. E. Morbeck, and J. Lobick
  1989   "Age-Related Bone Loss in Female Gombe
         Chimpanzees." *American Journal of Physical
         Anthropology*, 72:259.
Susman, Randall L. (ed.)
  1984   *The Pygmy Chimpanzee. Evolutionary Biology and
         Behavior.* New York: Plenum.
Susman, Randall L., Jack T. Stern, and William L. Jungers
  1985   "Locomotor Adaptations in the Hadar
         Hominids." *In: Ancestors: The Hard Evidence*,

E. Delson (ed.), New York: Alan R. Liss, pp.
         184–192.
Sussman, Robert W.
  1991   "Primate Origins and the Evolution of
         Angiosperms." *American Journal of Primatology*,
         23:209–223.
Sussman, Robert W., James M. Cheverud, and Thad Q.
Bartlett
  1995   Infant Killing as an Evolutionary Strategy: Reality
         or Myth?" *Evolutionary Anthropology*,
         3(5):149–151.
Swisher, C. C. III, G. H. Curtis, T. Jacob, et al.
  1994   "Age of the Earliest Known Hominids in Java,
         Indonesia." *Science*, 263:1118–1121.
Swisher, C. C., W. J. Rink, S. C. Anton, et al.
  1996   "Latest *Homo erectus* of Java: Potential
         Contemporaneity with *Homo sapiens* in Southwest
         Java." *Science*, 274:1870–1874.
Szalay, Frederick S. and Eric Delson
  1979   *Evolutionary History of the Primates.* New York:
         Academic Press.

Tattersall, Ian, Eric Delson, and John Van Couvering
  1988   *Encyclopedia of Human Evolution and Prehistory.*
         New York: Garland Publishing.
Templeton, Alan R.
  1996   "Gene Lineages and Human Evolution." *Science*,
         272:1363–1364.
Tenaza, R. and R. Tilson
  1977   "Evolution of Long-Distance Alarm Calls in
         Kloss' Gibbon." *Nature*, 268:233–235.
Teresi, Dick
  2002   *Lost Discoveries. The Ancient Roots of Modern
         Science – from the Babylonians to the Maya.* New
         York: Simon and Schuster.
Thieme, Hartmut
  1997   "Lower Palaeolithic Hunting Spears from
         Germany." *Nature*, 385:807–810.
Thorne, A., R. Grün, G. Mortimer, et al.
  1999   "Australia's Oldest Human Remains: Age of the
         Lake Mungo 3 Skeleton." *Journal of Human
         Evolution*, 36:591–612.
Thorne, A. G. and M. H. Wolpoff
  1992   "The Multiregional Evolution of Humans."
         Scientific American, 266:76–83.
Tiemel, Chen, Yang Quan, and Wu En
  1994   "Antiquity of *Homo sapiens* in China." *Nature*,
         368:55–56.
Tishkoft, S. A., E. Dietzsch, W. Speed, et al.
  1996   "Global Patterns of Linkage Disequilibrium at the
         CD4 Locus and Modern Human Origins."
         Science, 271:1380–1387.

Tobias, Phillip
1971 *The Brain in Hominid Evolution*. New York: Columbia University Press.

_____

1983 "Recent Advances in the Evolution of the Hominids with Especial Reference to Brain and Speech." Pontifical Academy of Sciences, *Scrita Varia*, 50:85–140.

Trinkaus, Erik and Pat Shipman
1992 *The Neandertals*. New York: Alfred A. Knopf.

van Schaik, C.P., M. Ancrenaz, G. Bogen, et al.
2003 "Orangutan Cultures and the Evolution of Material Culture." *Science*, 299:102–105.

Vignaud, P., P. Duringer, H. MacKaye, et al.
2002 "Geology and Palaeontology of the Upper Miocene Toros-Menalla Hominid Locality, Chad. *Nature*, 418:152–155.

Villa, Paola
1983 *Terra Amata and the Middle Pleistocene Archaeological Record of Southern France*. University of California Publications in Anthropology, Vol. 13. Berkeley: University of California Press.

Visalberghi, E.
1990 "Tool Use in Cebus." *Folia Primatologica*, 54:146–154.

Von Koenigswald, G. H. R.
1956 *Meeting Prehistoric Man*. New York: Harper & Brothers.

Walker, A.
1976 "Remains Attributable to *Australopithecus* from East Rudolf." *In: Earliest Man and Environments in the Lake Rudolf Basin*, Y. Coppens, et al. (eds.), Chicago: University of Chicago Press, pp. 484–489.

_____

1991 "The Origin of the Genus *Homo*." *In:* S. Osawa and T. Honjo (eds.), *Evolution of Life*. Tokyo: Springer-Verlag, pp. 379–389.

_____

1993 "The Origin of the Genus *Homo*." *In:* D. T. Rasmussen (ed.), *The Origin and Evolution of Humans and Humanness*. Boston: Jones and Bartlett, pp. 29–47.

Walker, Alan and R. E. Leakey
1993 *The Nariokotome* Homo erectus *Skeleton*. Cambridge: Harvard University Press.

Walsh, P. D., K. A. Abernathy, M. Bermejo, et al.
2003 "Catastrophic Ape Decline in Western Equatorial Africa." *Nature*, 422:611–614.

Ward, Peter
1994 *The End of Evolution*. New York: Bantam.

Washburn, S. L.
1963 "The Study of Race." *American Anthropologist*, 65:521–531.

Waterston, R. H., K. Lindblad-Toh, E. Birney, et al. (Mouse Genome Sequencing Consortium)
2002 "Initial Sequencing and Comparative Analysis of the Mouse Genome." *Nature*, 421:520–562.

Watson, J. B. and F. H. C. Crick
1953a "Genetical Implications of the Structure of the Deoxyribonucleic Acid." *Nature*, 171:964–967.

_____

1953b "A Structure for Deoxyribonucleic Acid." *Nature*, 171:737–738.

Weiner, J. S.
1955 *The Piltdown Forgery*. London: Oxford University Press.

Weiner, Steve, Qinqi Xu, Paul Goldberg, Jinyi Liu, and Ofer Bar-Yosef
1998 "Evidence for the Use of Fire at Zhoukoudian, China. *Science*, 281:251–253.

Weiss, Robin A. and Richard W. Wrangham
1999 "From *Pan* to Pandemic." *Nature*, 397:385–386.

Weiss, U.
2002 "Nature Insight: Malaria." *Nature* 415:669.

Wheat, Joe Ben
1972 "The Olsen-Chubbuck Site; A Paleo-Indian Bison Kill." *American Antiquity*, 37:1–180.

White, Tim D., Gen Suwa, and Berhane Asfaw
1994 "*Australopithecus ramidus*, a New Species of Early Hominid from Aramis, Ethiopia." *Nature*, 371:306–312.

_____

1995 Corrigendum (White, et al., 1994). *Nature*, 375:88.

Whiten, A., J. Goodall, W. C. McGrew, et al.
1999 "Cultures in Chimpanzees." *Nature*, 399:682–685.

Wildman, Derek E., Monica Uddin, Guozhen Liu, et al.
2003 "Implications of Natural Selection in Shaping 99.4% Nonsynonymous DNA Identity Between Humans and Chimpanzees: Enlarging Genus *Homo*." *Proceedings of the National Academy of Sciences*, 100:7181–7188.

Williams, G. C.
1957 "Pleiotopy, Natural Selection, and the Evolution of Senescence." *Evolution*, 11:398–411.

Williams, George C. and Randolph M. Nesse
1991 "The Dawn of Darwinian Medicine." *The Quarterly Review of Biology*, 66:1–22.

Wilmut, I., A. E. Schnieke, et al.
  1997 "Viable Offspring Derived from Fetal and Adult Mammalian Cells." *Nature,* 385:810–813.
Wilson, E. O.
  1992 *The Diversity of Life,* Cambridge, MA: The Belknap Press of Harvard University Press.

  2002 *The Future of Life.* New York: Alfred A. Knopf.
Wolpoff, Milford H.
  1983b "*Ramapithecus* and Human Origins. An Anthropologist's Perspective of Changing Intepretations." *In*: R. L. Ciochon and R. S. Corruccini (eds.), q.v., pp. 651–676.

  1984 "Evolution in *Homo erectus:* The Question of Stasis." *Paleobiology,* 10:389–406.

  1989 "Multiregional Evolution: The Fossil Alternative to Eden." *In:* P. Mellars and C. Stringer, (eds.) q.v., pp. 62–108.

  1999 *Paleoanthropology.* (2nd Ed.). New York: McGraw-Hill.
Wolpoff, M., et al.
  1994 "Multiregional Evolutions: A World-Wide Source for Modern Human Populations." *In:* M. H. Nitecki and D. V. Nitecki (eds.), q.v., pp. 175–199.
Wood, Bernard
  1991 *Koobi Fora Research Project IV: Hominid Cranial Remains from Koobi Fora.* Oxford: Clarendon Press.

  1992 "Origin and Evolution of the Genus *Homo.*" *Nature,* 355:783–790.
Worthman, Carol
  1999 "Evolutionary Perspectives on the Onset of Puberty." *In:* Trevethan, W. R., E. O. Smith, and J. J. McKenna (eds.), *Evolutionary Medicine.* New York: Oxford University Press.

Wrangham, R. W.
  1990 "An Ecological Model of Female-Bonded Primate Groups." *Behaviour,* 75:262–300.
Wrangham, Richard and Dale Peterson
  1996 *Demonic Males: Apes and the Origins of Human Violence.* New York: Houghton Mifflin.
Wu, Rukang and Xingren Dong
  1985 "*Homo erectus* in China." *In: Palaeoanthropology and Palaeolithic Archaeology in the People's Republic of China,* R. Wu and J. W. Olsen (eds.), New York: Academic Press, pp. 79–89.
Wu, Rukang and S. Lin
  1983 "Peking Man." *Scientific American,* 248:(6)86–94.
Wuehrich, Bernice
  1998 "Geological Analysis Damps Ancient Chinese Fires." *Science,* 28:165–166.

Yamei, Hon, Richard Potts, Yaun Baoyin, et al.
  2000 "Mid-Pleistocene Acheulean-like Stone Technology of the Bose Basin, South China." *Science,* 287:1622–1626.
Yellen, John E., et al.
  1995 "A Middle Stone Age Worked Bone Industry from Katanda, Upper Semliki Valley, Zaire." *Science,* 268:553–556.

Zimmet, P., K. G. M. M. Alberti, and Jonathan Shaw
  2001 "Global and Societal Implications of the Diabetes Epidemic." *Nature,* 414:782–787.
Zubrow, Ezra
  1989 "The Demographic Modeling of Neanderthal Extinction." *In:* P. Mellars and C. Stringer (eds.), q.v., pp. 212–231.

Credits

This constitutes an extension of the copyright page. We have made every effort to trace the ownership of all copyrighted material and to secure permission from copyright holders. In the event of any question arising as to the use of any material, we will be pleased to make the necessary corrections in future printings. Thanks are due to the following authors, publishers, and agents for permission to use the material indicated.

1, Chapter opener, © Biophoto Associates/Science Source/ Photo Researchers, Inc.; **2,** Fig. 1-1, Courtesy, Peter Jones; **3,** Fig. 1-2, © Bettmann/CORBIS; **5,** Fig. 1-3a–c, Lynn Kilgore; Fig. 1-3d, Robert Jurmain; **9,** Fig. 1-4, © Kenneth Garrett/NGS Image Collection; Fig. 1-5, Lynn Kilgore; **10,** Fig. 1-6, Courtesy, Judith Regensteiner; Fig. 1-7, Courtesy, Kathleen Galvin; **11,** Fig. 1-8, Robert Jurmain; Fig. 1-9, Courtesy, Bonnie Pedersen/ Arlene Kruse; **12,** Fig. 1-10a and b, Lynn Kilgore; **12,** Fig. 1-11, Courtesy, Lorna Pierce/Judy Suchey; **13,** Fig. 1-12, Courtesy, Linda Levitch; **20,** Chapter opener, © Biophoto Associates/ Science Source/Photo Researchers, Inc.; **24,** Fig. 2-1, Courtesy, Dept. of Library Services, American Museum of Natural History; Fig. 2-2, Courtesy, Dept. of Library Services, American Museum of Natural History; **25,** Fig. 2-3, © Michael Nicholson/CORBIS; Fig. 2-4, © Bettmann/CORBIS; **26,** Fig. 2-6, Courtesy, Dept. of Library Services, American Museum of Natural History ; **27,** Fig. 2-7, Courtesy, Dept. of Library Services, American Museum of Natural History; Fig. 2-8, Courtesy, Dept. of Library Services, American Museum of Natural History; **28,** Fig. 2-9, The Natural History Museum, London; **29,** Fig. 2-10, © Bettmann/CORBIS; **31,** Fig. 2-13, Wolf: John Giustina/Getty Images; Dogs surrounding wolf: Lynn Kilgore and Lin Marshall; **32,** Fig. 2-14, Courtesy of Down House and The Royal College of Surgeons of England; **33,** Fig. 2-15a, Michael Tweedie/Photo Researchers; Fig. 2-16b, Breck P. Kent/Animals Animals; **42,** Chapter opener, © Biophoto Associates/Science Source/Photo Researchers, Inc.; **45,** Fig. 3-2, A. Barrington Brown/Photo Researchers, Inc.; **52,** Fig. 3-8, Biophoto Associates/Science Source/Photo Researchers; **59,** Fig. 3–13, Cellmark Diagnostics, Abingdon, UK; **64,** Chapter opener, © Biophoto Associates/Science Source/Photo Researchers, Inc.; **65,** Fig. 4-1, Raychel Ciemma and Precision Graphics; **75,** Fig. 4-7a, Lynn Kilgore; Fig. 4-7b, Lynn Kilgore; Fig. 4-7c, Corbis; Fig. 4-7d–f; Lynn Kilgore; Fig. 4-7g, Robert Jurmain; **81,** Fig. 4-8a and b, © Dr. Stanley Flegler/Visuals Unlimited; **88,** Chapter opener, © Biophoto Associates/Science Source/Photo Researchers, Inc.; **104,** Fig. 5-9, Hansejudy Beste/Animals Animals; Fig. 5-10, J. C. Stevenson/Animals Animals; **111,** Chapter opener, © Jay Dickman/CORBIS; **113,** Fig. 6-1a–e, Lynn Kilgore; **115,**

Fig. 6-3 a and b, Lynn Kilgore; Fig. 6-4, Lynn Kilgore; **118,** Fig. 6-6 (Howler species), Raymond Mendez/Animals Animals; (Spider and woolly monkeys), Robert L. Lubeck/ Animals Animals; (Prince Bernhard's titi), Marc van Roosmalen; (Marmosets and tamarins), © Zoological Society of San Diego, photo by Ron Garrison; (Muriqui), Andrew Young; (White-faced capuchins), © Jay Dickman/CORBIS; (Squirrel monkeys), © Kevin Schafer/CORBIS; (Uakari), R. A. Mittermeier/ Conservation International; **119,** Fig. 6-6 (Baboon species), Courtesy, Bonnie Pedersen/Arlene Kruse; (Macaque species), Courtesy, Jean De Rousseau; (Gibbons and siamangs), Lynn Kilgore; (Tarsier species), David Haring, Duke University Primate Zoo; (Orangutans), © Tom McHugh/Photo Researchers, Inc.; (Colobus species) Robert Jurmain; (Galagos), Courtesy, Bonnie Pedersen/Arlene Kruse; (Chimpanzees and bonobos), Courtesy, Arlene Kruse/Bonnie Pedersen; (Mountain and lowland gorillas), Lynn Kilgore; (*Cercopithecus* species), Robert Jurmain; (Loris species), Courtesy, San Francisco Zoo; (Langur species), Joe MacDonald/Animals Animals; (Lemurs), Courtesy, Fred Jacobs; **121,** Fig. 6-7a–d, Redrawn from original art by Stephen D. Nash in John G. Fleagle, *Primate Adaptation and Evolution,* 2nd ed., 1999. Reprinted by permission of publisher and Stephen Nash; **126,** Fig. 6-12, Courtesy, Fred Jacobs; Fig. 6-13, Courtesy, Fred Jacobs; **126,** Fig. 6-14, Courtesy, San Francisco Zoo; Fig. 6-15, Courtesy, Bonnie Pedersen/Arlene Kruse; **127,** Fig. 6-16, David Haring, Duke University Primate Zoo; **128,** Fig. 6-18, (Muriqui), Andrew Young; (Squirrel monkeys), © Kevin Schafer/ CORBIS; (Prince Bernhard's titi), Marc van Roosmalen; (Uakari), R. A. Mittermeier/Conservation International; (White-faced capuchins), © Jay Dickman/CORBIS; **129,** Fig. 6-19, © Zoological Society of San Diego, photo by Ron Garrison; Fig. 6-20, Raymond Mendez/Animals Animals; **130,** Fig. 6-22, Robert L. Lubeck/Animals Animals; **131,** Fig. 6-24, Robert Jurmain; Fig. 6-25a and b, Courtesy, Bonnie Pedersen/Arlene Kruse; Fig. 6-26, Lynn Kilgore; **133,** Fig. 6-28, Lynn Kilgore; Fig. 6-29, Robert Jurmain, photo by Jill Matsumoto/Jim Anderson; **134,** Fig. 6-31a, and b, Lynn Kilgore; **135,** Fig. 6-32a and b, Lynn Kilgore; **136,** Fig. 6-33a and b, Robert Jurmain, photo by Jill Matsumoto/Jim Anderson; **137,** Fig. 6-34, Courtesy, Ellen Ingmanson; **139,** Fig. 6-35, Courtesy, John Oates; **140,** Fig. 6-36, Karl Ammann; **143,** Chapter opener, © Jay Dickman/CORBIS; **146,** Fig. 7-1, © Russ Mittermeir; **147,** Fig. 7-2, Lynn Kilgore; **148,** Fig. 7-3, Time Life Pictures/Getty Images; **150,** Fig. 7-4, Lynn Kilgore; Fig. 7-5, Lynn Kilgore; Fig. 7-6, Lynn Kilgore; **153,** Fig. 7-8a, Robert Jurmain; Fig. 7-8b, Courtesy, Meredith Small; Fig. 7-8c and d, Courtesy, Arlene Kruse/Bonnie Pedersen; **155,** Fig. 7-9, Lynn

Kilgore; **157,** Fig. 7-10, Joe MacDonald/Animals Animals; **159,** Fig. 7-11a, Courtesy, David Haring, Duke University Primate Center; Fig. 7-11b, Courtesy, Arlene Kruse/Bonnie Pedersen; Fig. 7-11c, Robert Jurmain; Fig. 7-11d, © Tom McHugh/Photo Researchers, Inc.; Fig. 7-11e, Robert Jurmain; **160,** Fig. 7-12, Harlow Primate Laboratory, University of Wisconsin; Fig. 7-13, Lynn Kilgore; **161,** Fig. 7-14a, Lynn Kilgore; Fig. 7-14b, Manoj Shah/The Image Bank; **163,** Fig. 7-15, Courtesy, Tetsuro Matsuzawa; **164,** Fig. 7-16, Lynn Kilgore; **167,** Fig. 7-17, Rose A. Sevcik, Language Research Center, Georgia State University; photo by Elizabeth Pugh; **168,** Fig. 7-18, Lynn Kilgore; **171,** Chapter opener, Harry Nelson; **176,** Fig. 8-4, Robert Jurmain; **177,** Fig. 8-5, Courtesy, David Pilbeam; **186,** Fig. 8-11, Robert Jurmain; **190,** Fig. 8-12, © Mission Paléoanthropologique Franco-Tchadienne; **194,** Fig. 8-14, Lynn Kilgore; Fig. 8-15, Courtesy Peter Jones; **195,** Fig. 8-16, Institute of Human Origins; Fig. 8-17, Robert Jurmain; **198,** Fig. 8-18, Reproduced with permission of the National Museums of Kenya, copyright reserved, courtesy of Alan Walker; **199,** Fig. 8-19, Robert Jurmain; **200,** Fig. 8-20a and b, Reproduced with permission of the National Museums of Kenya, copyright reserved; **201,** Fig. 8-21, Courtesy, Raymond Dart, photo by Alun Hughes; Fig. 8-22, Photo by Alun Hughes, reproduced by permission of Professor P. V. Tobias; **203,** Fig. 8-23, AP/Wide World Photos; Fig. 8-24, Robert Jurmain; **204,** Fig. 8-25, Transvaal Museum, South Africa; **205,** Fig. 8-26, (Toros-Menalia) © Mission Paléoanthropologique Franco-Tchadienne (WT 17000), Reproduced with permission of the National Museums of Kenya, copyright reserved, courtesy Alan Walker; (Lucy), Robert Jurmain; (SK 48), Transvaal Museum, South Africa; (Sts 5), Transvaal Museum, South Africa; (Taung Child), Courtesy, P. V. Tobias; photo by Alun Hughes; ("Zinj"), Harry Nelson; **207,** Fig. 8-27, (ER 406), Reproduced with permission of the National Museums of Kenya, copyright reserved; (WT 17000), Reproduced with permission of the National Museums of Kenya, copyright reserved, courtesy Alan Walker; (SK 48), Transvaal Museum, South Africa; (ER 729), Reproduced with permission of the National Museums of Kenya, copyright reserved; (ER 732), Reproduced with permission of the National Museums of Kenya, copyright reserved; (OH 5), Harry Nelson; **216,** Chapter opener, Harry Nelson; **218,** Fig. 9-1, (Dmanisi), Courtesy, David Lordkipanidze; (ER 3733), Kenya Museums of Natural History; (OH 9), Harry Nelson; (WT 15000), Reproduced with permission of the National Museums of Kenya, copyright reserved; (Salé), Courtesy, J. J. Hublin; **219,** Fig. 9-1, (Zhoukoudian), Harry Nelson; (Lantian), Harry Nelson; (Hexian), Harry Nelson; (Trinil), Courtesy, S. Sartono; (Sangiran), Courtesy, S. Sartono; **222,** Fig. 9-2, (Low forehead), Harry Nelson; (Thick cranial bone), Harry Nelson; (Nuchal torus), Robert Jurmain; (Sagittal ridge), Robert Jurmain; (Posterior teeth), Harry Nelson; (Supraorbital torus), Harry Nelson; **224,** Fig. 9-3, Courtesy, Professor Günter Bräuer; Fig. 9-4a–c, Courtesy, David Lordkipanidze; **226,** Fig. 9-5, The New York Academy of Medicine Library; **227,** Fig. 9-6, Courtesy, S. Sartono; Fig. 9-7, The New York Academy of Medicine Library; Fig. 9-8, Special Collections, American Museum of Natural History; **228,** Fig. 9-9, Special Collections, American Museum of Natural History; Fig. 9-10, Robert Jurmain; **230,** Fig. 9-12a and b, Courtesy, Denis Etler; **231,** Fig. 9-13, Reproduced with permission of the Kenya Museums of Natural History; Fig. 9-14, Reproduced with permission of the Kenya Museums of Natural History; **235,** Fig. 9-16, Courtesy, The Museum of Primitive Art and Culture, Peace Dale, RI, photo by William Turnbaugh; 236, Fig. 9-18a and b, Robert Jurmain; **243,** Chapter opener, Harry Nelson; **247,** Fig. 10-3, Harry Nelson; **248,** Fig. 10-4, (Steinheim), Harry Nelson; (Florisbad), Courtesy, Günter Bräuer; (Kabwe), Harry Nelson; (Arago), Courtesy, H. DeLumley; **249,** Fig. 10-4, Courtesy, Xinzhi Wu; **251,** Fig. 10-5a and b, Harry Nelson; **258,** Fig. 10-9, (Shanidar I), Courtesy, Milford Wolpoff; (Spy), Courtesy, Milford Wolpoff; (Amud), Courtesy, Fred Smith; (La Chapelle), Courtesy, Fred Smith; (St. Césaire), Harry Nelson; (La Ferrassie), Courtesy, Fred Smith; **259,** Fig. 10-10, Courtesy, Fred Smith; Fig. 10-11, Harry Nelson; **260,** Fig. 10-12, (Spy), Courtesy, Milford Wolpoff; (Krapina), Courtesy, Milford Wolpoff; (La Chapelle), Courtesy, Fred Smith; (La Ferrassie), Courtesy, Fred Smith; (St. Césaire), Harry Nelson; **261,** Fig. 10-12 (Shanidar), Courtesy, Milford Wolpoff; (Monte Circeo), Courtesy, Fred Smith; (Amud), Courtesy, Fred Smith; (Tabun), Courtesy, Fred Smith; **262,** Fig. 10-14a and b, Courtesy, Fred Smith; **263,** Fig. 10-15, Harry Nelson; Fig. 10-16, Courtesy, Milford Wolpoff; **276,** Chapter opener, Harry Nelson; **279,** Fig. 11-1 (Cro-Magnon), Courtesy, David Frayer; (Skhūl [No. 5]), Courtesy, Fred Smith; (Herto), David L. Brill/Atlanta; (Omo), Courtesy, Fred Smith; (Klasies River Mouth), Courtesy, Fred Smith; (Border Cave), Courtesy, Fred Smith; **283,** Fig. 11-2 (Qafzeh 6), Courtesy, Fred Smith; (Border Cave), Courtesy, Fred Smith; (Skhūl 5), Courtesy, Fred Smith; (Predmosti 3), Harry Nelson; (Cro-Magnon I), Courtesy, David Frayer; **284,** Fig. 11-3, David L. Brill/Atlanta; **285,** Fig. 11-4, Harry Nelson; **286,** Fig. 11-5a and b, Courtesy, David Frayer; **288,** Fig. 11-7a and b, Courtesy, David Frayer; **290,** Fig. 11-8, Courtesy, Milford Wolpoff; **292,** Fig. 11-10, © Peter Brown; **293,** Fig. 11-12, Courtesy, N. O. Bader; **296,** Fig. 11-17, Jim Cartier/Photo Researchers; **298,** Fig. 11-19a, Jean Clottes/Document elaborated with the support of the French Ministry of Culture and Communication, Regional Direction for Cultural Affairs, Rhône-Alpes, Regional Department of Archaeology; Fig. 11-19b, Jean-Marie Chauvet/Document elaborated with the support of the French Ministry of Culture and Communication, Regional Direction for Cultural Affairs, Rhône-Alpes, Regional Department of Archaeology; **304,** Chapter opener, Courtesy of Earth Data Analysis Center; **310,** Fig. 12-1a, © Peter Johnson/CORBIS; Fig. 12-1b, © Charles & Josette Lenars/CORBIS; Fig. 12-1c, © Gallo Images/CORBIS; Fig. 12-1d, © Otto Lang/CORBIS; Fig. 12-1e, Lynn Kilgore; **313,** Fig. 12-2a and b, Robert Jurmain; **317,** Fig. 12-5, © Michael S. Yamashita/CORBIS; **320,** Fig. 12-6, Norman Lightfoot/Photo Researchers; **321,** Fig. 12-7, © Biophoto Associates/Photo Researchers, Inc.; **324,** Fig. 12-9a, © Renee Lynn/Photo Researchers; Fig. 12-9b, © George Holton/Photo Researchers; Fig. 12-10a, Courtesy, William Pratt; Fig. 12-10b, Courtesy, L. G. Moore; **332,** Fig. 12-11, Karl Ammann; Chapter opener, Courtesy of Earth Data Analysis Center; **355,** Fig. 13-6a, © Steve Bloom/stevebloom.com; Fig. 13-6b, © Karl Ammann/CORBIS; **360,** Chapter opener, Courtesy of Earth Data Analysis Center; **363,** Fig. 14-1, Lynn Kilgore; **364,** Fig. 14-2, © Russ Mittermeier, Conservation International; **366,** Fig. 14-4, Robert Jurmain; **369,** Fig. 14-5, Lynn Kilgore; **374,** Fig. 14-7, Jerome Wikoff/Visuals Unlimited

Index

Page numbers in *italics* indicate figures or illustrations.
Page numbers in **bold** indicate definitions.

World Political Map

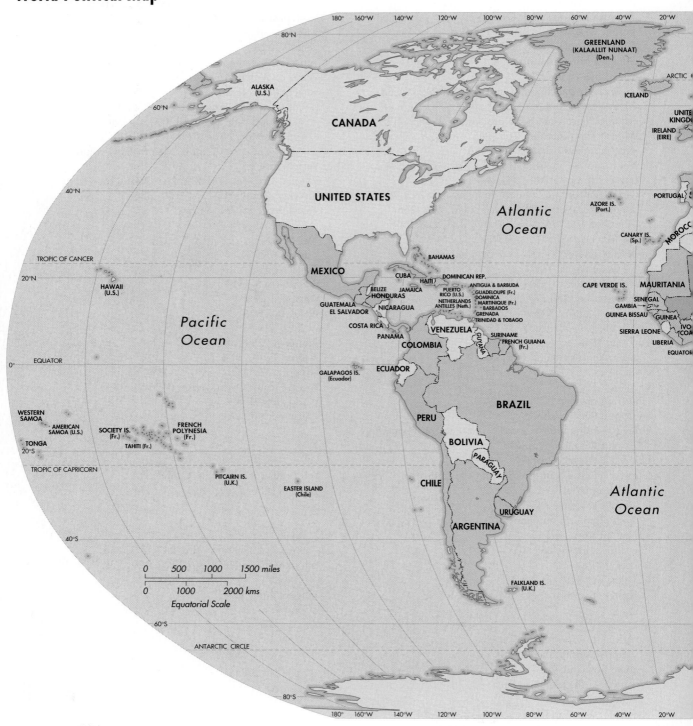

GREENLAND
(KALAALLIT NUNAAT)
(Den.)

ARCTIC

ICELAND

ALASKA
(U.S.)

UNITED
KINGD

IRELAND
(EIRE)

CANADA

PORTUGAL

Atlantic
Ocean

AZORE IS.
(Port.)

UNITED STATES

CANARY IS.
(Sp.)

MOROCC

TROPIC OF CANCER

BAHAMAS

MEXICO

CUBA
HAITI

DOMINICAN REP.

CAPE VERDE IS.

MAURITANIA

HAWAII
(U.S.)

BELIZE
HONDURAS

JAMAICA

ANTIGUA & BARBUDA
GUADELOUPE (Fr.)
DOMINICA
MARTINIQUE (Fr.)
BARBADOS
GRENADA
TRINIDAD & TOBAGO

SENEGAL

GUATEMALA
EL SALVADOR

NICARAGUA

PUERTO
RICO (U.S.)
NETHERLANDS
ANTILLES (Neth.)

GAMBIA
GUINEA BISSAU

GUINEA

Pacific
Ocean

COSTA RICA

PANAMA

VENEZUELA

SIERRA LEONE

IVO
COA

COLOMBIA

SURINAME
FRENCH GUIANA
(Fr.)

LIBERIA

GUYANA

ECUADOR

EQUATOR

GALAPAGOS IS.
(Ecuador)

ECUADOR

EQUATOR

WESTERN
SAMOA

AMERICAN
SAMOA (U.S.)

PERU

BRAZIL

SOCIETY IS.
(Fr.)

FRENCH
POLYNESIA
(Fr.)

BOLIVIA

TONGA

TAHITI (Fr.)

PARAGUAY

20°S

TROPIC OF CAPRICORN

PITCAIRN IS.
(U.K.)

CHILE

Atlantic
Ocean

EASTER ISLAND
(Chile)

URUGUAY

0   500   1000   1500 miles

ARGENTINA

0   1000   2000 kms

Equatorial Scale

FALKLAND IS.
(U.K.)

40°S

60°S

ANTARCTIC CIRCLE

80°S